BLOCH 1/26/77 12-

PERPETUAL DILEMMA

PERPETUAL DILEMMA

Jewish Religion in the Jewish State

S. ZALMAN ABRAMOV

Foreword by W. Gunther Plaut

Rutherford • Madison • Teaneck
Fairleigh Dickinson University Press
London: Associated University Presses

© 1976 by Associated University Presses, Inc.

Associated University Presses, Inc.
Cranbury, New Jersey 08512

Associated University Presses
Magdalen House
136–148 Tooley Street
London SE1 2TT, England

Library of Congress Cataloging in Publication Data

Abramov, Shene' ur Zalman, 1908–
    Perpetual dilemma.

    Bibliography: p.
    Includes index.
    1. Judaism—Israel—History. 2. Judaism and state—Israel—History.
3. Israel—Politics and government. 4. Jews—Identity. I, Title.
BM390.A4   296'.095694   74-5897
ISBN 0-8386-1687-9

To Hadassah,
who is no longer.

Contents

Foreword

"When you enter the land that the Lord your God has given you as a heritage and you occupy it and settle in it . . ."—thus begins a weekly portion in the Book of Deuteronomy. It is one of those passages in which the Torah anticipates what would or should happen once the people occupied the Promised Land and sets forth ethical and social rules for the governance of its society. In these and similar prescriptions the overriding idea of the Torah is that once the people set up their own independent government in the land which was to become the inheritance of Israel, they would organize a theocracy imbued with justice and compassion. It would be a land ruled not by priests (or later, rabbis), kings, or other appointed or self-appointed men, but rather by the invisible God of the Covenant and of the Torah which gives expression to His will.

Such was the hope and the record, but practice proved otherwise. Where the Torah provided that idolaters and idolatries were to be rooted out, the people of Israel instead assimilated the inhabitants and often were assimilated by them. Idolatry continued to play an important role in Jewish history and was for hundreds of years the target of prophetic ire. Contrary to the desires of Samuel, the people forced him to accede to their request for converting the theocracy into a monarchy. Subsequently the priesthood served not only the Temple but also the temporal and political powers. It became allied with government and was controlled by—and sometimes controlled—its uses and abuses. In turn this gave rise to the spiritual opposition of the prophets, who were often suppressed or at other times ignored, and who on the whole were acclaimed only after their death. Their revolution lay frequently in the seeding of ideas rather than in immediate political changes.

In the fifth and fourth centuries, in consequence of the efforts made by Ezra after the return from Babylonian exile, a new attempt was

11

made to establish a theocracy. Here began the development of what to-day we call Halakhah, a body of rules which developed the laws of the Torah in systematic and structural fashion, and here also, through the Great Sanhedrin and the authorities which arose in later times, the idea emerged (though it was not at once accepted) that the orderly growth of Halakhah was a direct continuation of the divine inspiration derived from Sinai. But the progress of these ideas was not at all smooth nor did it follow a direct line. Political and social upheavals, wars and rebellions and foreign oppression combined to alter the course of the Jewish tradition violently from time to time. In the end, toward the latter days of the Second Temple, the religious structure of ancient Israel showed a new dichotomy: there was a priesthood which was generally, although not always, allied with the ruling political powers; and there arose populist reform movements which attempted to chart a different religious course for the people, one that was both more inward and more private. While the priesthood emphasized the Deuteronomic insistence on the centrality of the cult in the sanctuary in Jerusalem, various brotherhoods and Pharisaic parties, while not denying the importance of the Temple cult, aimed to privatize religion significantly. They did this through self-isolation in retreats, or through the development of a new class of religious leaders, rabbis, who functioned outside of the Temple and shifted the basis of authority from the political to the scriptural. It was because of them that, when the Temple was destroyed, law and tradition, Halakhah and Minhag, could become substitutes for the vanished, visible presence of God in the sanctuary. As long as the Temple had stood these populist reformers had been generally supportive of its cult as the manifestation of public religion, but when the sanctuary lay in ashes, the privatism of Judaism gained the upper hand. It was a salvational process with its imperfections built into it from the beginning.

For while the Halakhah had the effect of making Judaism a portable religion and made the continued spiritual viability of the faith possible, it also separated itself by force of circumstance from the original major locus of Judaism, namely, the Land of Israel. To be sure, there always were Jews in the land, and they would remain there in smaller or larger numbers throughout the centuries, but never again, until 1948, would they have complete control of their own political destiny. With statehood denied them, the external government of their society, both in the land of Israel and in the Diaspora, became a function of the sovereign power under whom they lived. In earlier centuries of occupancy in Palestine, they had had to grapple with national, economic, military, and social pressures and to fashion the political organs of their society. They had to take care of their own internal system of security and their external international relations. Now, as a minority in a foreign-ruled Palestine and as well as in the Diaspora, their portable religion became divorced from these considerations. The privatism of Judaism became complete and with it its Diaspora nature. While there were still ancient treatises dealing with sacrifices and ownership in the Holy Land, and pious souls continued to study them in anticipation of the day when Israel would return to the land at the time when the Messiah would come, they had very little relation to life as it was. For the years between 70 and 1948 C.E. Judaism was a Diaspora religion, and remained so essentially even in the years of pre-state settlement after 1880. The law book of Judaism which summarized and codified the centuries of earlier tradition, Joseph Karo's *Shulhan Arukh,* regulated every vestige of personal life, but had not a single chapter on the administration of an army or police force. For both in Safad where Caro wrote and throughout the lands of dispersion, these considerations were not relevant to the Jewish community. Foreign powers administered these areas of public life, and it was no different in 1517 under Turkish rule or 400 years later when the British took on this responsibility.

Nothing demonstrates this gap more clearly than the Shemittah controversy of the 1880s (see below, chap. 1, § E). It had to do with the biblical rule that the land was not to be worked in the sabbatical year, that is, once every seven years. By common consent of the tradition, the law was applicable only to Eretz Yisrael, but now that the settlers had returned, it suddenly became evident that either the ancient rules had to be enforced or adjusted or they would be disregarded altogether. The very process and ultimate resolution of the controversy made it clear that while some groups of immigrants came to the land in the hope that all problems could be met on the basis of a Diaspora-based and developed Halakhah, others arrived with different concepts of how religious precepts were or were not to be realized in Eretz Yisrael.

What ultimately determined the development of this inherent tension were a number of factors which sometimes were related and at other times were not. The primary one was *who* immigrated and *when,* for each new wave of settlers brought along a set of religious and social ideals which on occasion were in sharp contrast with each other. In addition, the political struggle (first against the British and then against the Arabs) determined to a significant degree the external environment in which such developments were taking place.

Important aspects of this constellation were the original settlement (the so-called Old Yishuv), in both its Sephardic and Ashkenazic components; the fact that the New Yishuv was mostly socialist and usually atheistic in conviction, foreshadowing the ultimate conflict or at least continuing tension between the State and the Synagogue; the relatively

late arrival of German Jews with their components of the Liberal religious element; the presence of Holocaust survivors for many of whom
the traditional framework of life had been emptied of meaning; the
large-scale immigration of Oriental and North African Jews who trans-
posed both their religion and culture from medieval context into the
twentieth century; and last but not least, a small but significant aliyah
from countries with a Western industrial background. This mixture is
what modern Israel presents today. The country was not subject to a
slow, organic development of many centuries; it was an instant society
with components both ancient and new, both rigid and flexible, auto-
cratic and democratic. It thus became a nation of great piety and im-
piety, of magnificent social vision on the one hand and crude acquisi-
tional instincts displayed at times on the other.

This book, after a brief Introduction, concerns itself with the way
in which the people of Israel have attempted to deal with the realization of varying and often conflicting religious ideologies, theologies, and
anti-theologies, the tensions between the State and its religious institutions. The latter was frequently expressed in law both legislative and
judicial, and because a large area of public and private life was given
over to official Orthodoxy, the book shows how the traditional approach
to Halakhah has met or failed to meet these challenges. The work puts
into bold relief the important ways in which the conflicts between State
and Synagogue have surfaced, and especially so in the application of
the Law of Return, and the question "Who is a Jew?"

What emerges is a picture of law and history intimately intertwined
in a manner hardly duplicated in any other country or perhaps any
other time, and for this reason alone the book presents a landmark. It
should be of interest not only to the people of Israel or students of
law and politics, but also, and especially so, to the Jews of the Diaspora.
They must be intimately concerned with its subject matter, for the religious and social influence of Israel upon Diaspora Jewry far exceeds
the borders of the land. Every religious divorce granted, every conversion performed outside of Israel must at present stand the scrutiny of
the rabbinate in Israel, and the status of whole families is thereby determined. Every Jew in the Diaspora is a potential settler in Israel and
therefore his own religious or nonreligious convictions as well as his
status may ultimately have a bearing on or be subject to the realities
of Israel. On the other hand, Orthodoxy in Israel itself and its allied
Orthodoxies of the Diaspora must ultimately make their peace with the
existence of vigorous Reform and Conservative movements in the lands
of dispersion, and these in turn will have their influence on the life of
Israel and its emergent dissident religious expressions. One cannot un-

derstand the land and its people as they are today without comprehending the complexity of its religious life.

This book therefore has its particular fascination. It is enhanced by its scholarly grounding and the unique qualifications of the author, who brings to the subject a wide range of information and historical comprehension. Not every aspect of the problem has been covered, but that is the nature of the subject, which in itself is changing from day to day. The ultimate conclusion which the author presents to us more implicitly than explicitly is clear: the future of the land lies not in the reintroduction of a theocratic or semi-theocratic society, however much it is desired by those who support it, but in the openness and mutual respect of varying religious convictions. Such openness does not exist at the present time, but it will have to be achieved if Israel is to have a religious future which is fundamentally different from that of a transplanted ghetto. This book, it is hoped, will contribute to this development.

RABBI W. GUNTHER PLAUT, J.D., D.D.

Preface

Students of political science whose field of interest is in the state-religion relationship have found in the history of modern Israel a fertile ground for research. In the last fifteen years a number of works on this subject have appeared in the United States and in England. This book is an attempt by an Israeli to deal with this subject.

The author's encounter with the problem took place in the Law and Constitution Committee of the Knesset, which, inter alia, deals with bills relating to religion. The initial approach to legislation bearing on this subject was that of an advocate of civil rights who is concerned with asserting the autonomy of the individual vis-à-vis organized society.

On further inquiry, however, it became apparent that this subject cannot be intelligibly discussed in terms of state-religion relationship as understood in the countries of the West, for it is one that is *sui generis*. Nowhere in the Western world are people concerned with the question of "Who is a Frenchman" or "Who is a Swede" or a Russian or an American. In Israel, the problem of "Who is a Jew," that is, the problem of Jewish identity—of the identity of the Jew as an individual and of the Jewish people in its homeland, as a collectivity —is the underlying cause of the religious controversy. The uniqueness of the problem is inherent in the circumstance that the Jews, unlike other nations in the world, are at one and the same time a community of faith, as well as an ethnic-national entity, and that in Judaism, these two components are so intimately interwoven as to be indissoluble. Consequently the confrontation is not between two mutually exclusive schools of thought, that is, between the adherents of religion and its opponents, but rather between those who regard the precepts of Judaism as divinely ordained and therefore immutable, and those who regard Judaism as a product of an evolutionary process, which has ex-

17

erted a significant influence on historical developments, and has likewise been influenced by them. The tension between these schools of thought has been accentuated by the impact of religious pluralism on the monolithic structure of religion in the Jewish state.

The treatment of the subject in terms of West European and American principles, will, therefore, fall short of encompassing the essence and totality of the problems arising out of the state-religion relationship. Neither a separation of the two nor a Kulturkampf is a relevant or viable alternative. This problem, it is suggested, should rather be viewed as an aspect of the confrontation between tradition and change, between preservation and innovation, that has always loomed large in the unfolding panorama of Jewish history, which in this generation has escalated in the State of Israel as a result of the attainment of Jewish sovereignty. The tension between these elements constitutes the perpetual dilemma that has always accompanied the Jewish people and has exercised a fructifying effect on its thought and action.

It is my pleasant duty to express appreciation and gratitude to all those who have been helpful to me. To Mrs. Erika Yeshayahu, Chief Librarian, and to Mr. Yosef Stavi of the staff of the Library of the Knesset, I wish to express thanks for having placed at my disposal the resources of this library, and particularly of its rich and well-organized collection of periodical literature, as well as for having procured for me numerous photostatic copies of source material found in the National and University Library in Jerusalem. I have also benefited from the resources of the Zionist Archives and Library in New York and the Library of Jewish Information of the American Jewish Committee, as well as of the archival material of the Union of American Hebrew Congregations in New York. I am grateful to these institutions and their staffs.

An especial debt of gratitude I owe to the late Dr. Maurice N. Eisendrath of New York, to Dr. Jacob K. Shankman of New Rochelle, N.Y., and to Rabbi Richard G. Hirsch, now of Jerusalem, for their friendly interest, encouragement, and assistance. To Rabbi Alexander M. Schindler of New York I wish to express my sincere gratitude for his constant and untiring cooperation and assistance in the publication of this work.

Dr. Bernard J. Bamberger of New York, Dr. David Polish of Evanston, Ill., and Professor Ezra Zevi Spicehandler of the Hebrew Union College in Jerusalem have read the manuscript. To them I wish to express my thanks for their comments and observations. I am likewise indebted to Professor Raphael Patai for his active interest and assistance.

Dr. W. Gunther Plaut of Toronto has devoted much time and effort to the editing of nearly the entire manuscript, and I wish to express to him my sincere appreciation and gratitude. I am also indebted to Mrs. Mathilde E. Finch, Editor in Chief of Associated University Presses, Inc., for the final editing of the manuscript.

Thanks are due to my secretary, Mrs. Rachel Ginsburg, who typed the entire manuscript, and to Miss Nehamah Golombok, who checked the edited version.

The greatest debt of all I owe to Hadassah, my wife and collaborator. Without her patience, encouragement, and active participation in the preparation of this work, this book would not have been written. It is to her that this book is dedicated in love and gratitude. Alas, she is no longer.

PERPETUAL DILEMMA

1

The Origins and Growth
of the Old Yishuv

A. HISTORICAL BACKGROUND

At the beginning of the Christian Era, the Jewish state in Palestine was nearing its end. In the year A.D. 70 the Romans put down a military insurrection and destroyed the Temple. Large masses of Jews left their homeland or were exiled by the conqueror. The exodus from Palestine assumed even larger proportions in A.D. 135, after the Jewish revolt led by Bar Kokhba against the armies of Emperor Hadrian had been crushed. In order to prevent further uprisings, the Romans razed the city of Jerusalem and ploughed its soil, put to death all who were suspected of participation in the rebellion, and carried large numbers off into slavery. Judea became Palestine, a Roman colony. Thus began the long Diaspora, the period of Jewish homelessness.

It should be noted that this homelessness had to do with the loss of statehood, not with the numbers of Jews who lived in the land. For even prior to the destruction of the state, the majority of the Jewish people dwelt outside Palestine. They lived in every quarter of the Roman Empire of which they were a part. Flourishing communities existed in Egypt, Cyrenaica, Syria, and Mesopotamia, as well as in Italy and other parts of Europe.

Furthermore, the loss of sovereignty in Judea was not followed by the total disappearance of the Jews from Palestine. Although reduced in numbers they were never completely dislodged. A remnant persisted through the four centuries of Roman and later Byzantine rule, the occupation of Palestine by the Persians in the early sixth century, its reoccupation by the emperor Heraclius, and the Moslem conquest of the early seventh century. Indeed, in the early period of Moslem rule, the number of Jewish inhabitants increased. But in the eighth century, when Palestine became involved in the strife between Arab dynasties, the position of the Jewish community deteriorated seriously. All non-Moslem minorities were subjected to discrimination, but until the eleventh century there was an organized Jewish community.

The First Crusade, with its accompanying massacres, dealt a major blow to the Jewish community, which was almost entirely wiped out. A small Jewish community survived the collapse of the Latin Kingdom at the end of the twelfth century, the annexation of Palestine by Egyptian Mamelukes, and the Mongol invasion. In 1211, 300 rabbis from England and France arrived in Palestine, to be followed by other groups.[1]

Rabbi Meshulam ben Menachem of Volterra, who came to Jerusalem in 1481, found there 250 families. By 1488 the Jewish population had declined and Rabbi Obbadia who arrived there from Italy found 70 families only. It was during this period that the Jewish community in Safed began its development.[2]

In the closing years of the fifteenth century and during the sixteenth century, the Jewish community increased in numbers through the arrival of refugees from Spain and Portugal, many of them Marranos who were escaping from the terror of the Inquisition. These were distinguished by their education, scholarship, and business acumen, and they rose to leading positions in the community; they consolidated the Sefardic* community, which constituted the majority of the Yishuv** until the second half of the nineteenth century.[3]

In 1517 began the four-hundred-year period of Turkish rule in Palestine. The principal features of Turkish rule, or rather misrule, were heavy taxation, lack of security to persons and property, arbitrary action of local officials, and neglect of economic development. The Turkish rulers did not object to a numerical expansion of the Jewish community; but despite the general tolerance displayed toward non-Moslems, the Jews were not safe from occasional outbursts of religious

---

* Literally, "Spanish."
** The word *Yishuv* means settlement, or community. In contemporary Hebrew usage, the term applies to the Jewish community of Palestine. The "Old Yishuv" was the Jewish community as it evolved in Palestine from the early centuries of the Christian era, which by the end of the nineteenth century had developed its distinctive characteristics as a community dedicated to the observance of the minutiae of the religious law and to the pursuit of the Orthodox life-style as crystallized in the ghettos of Eastern Europe. Until the First World War, the Old Yishuv constituted the predominant element in Palestine Jewry.

fanaticism, persecutions from local officials, devastating incursions by Bedouins, and the general misrule of the government. During the sixteenth and seventeenth centuries Safed rather than Jerusalem developed into the major Jewish community and center of learning. Here Rabbi Joseph Karo (author of the Shulhan Arukh, code of the religious law) lived, and here the great mystic Rabbi Isaac Luria established a center for the study of the Kabbalah.* By the middle of the eighteenth century, the Jewish population of Safed and that of the adjoining villages reached about 3,000,[4] which constituted the bulk of the Jewish population of Palestine.

At the same time, there was an attempt at an organized Jewish settlement in Tiberias by Don Joseph Nasi, Duke of Naxos, a fugitive from the Inquisition who had become a favorite of the Sultan. He received permission to rebuild the community, and construction actually started in 1570. But the attempt failed of its grand objectives, not only because conditions in Galilee and adjoining Lebanon were too unsettled, but also because the project found Jews generally indifferent. During the seventeenth century the mutinies of the Janissaries against the Turks and the unrest among the Druze population severely reduced the Jewish population in the area.

The material conditions of the small Jewish community in Jerusalem in the sixteenth century were deplorable. Poverty, epidemics, and Turkish misrule made existence most difficult. Early in the seventeenth century, there began a growth in the population.[5] Systematic attempts were made at that time by leading rabbis to raise funds in the Diaspora in order to preserve the community of Jerusalem. Appeals for contributions were made in Italy, Poland, Bohemia, and Hungary. The funds were distributed among the needy, and thus this system of relief, which soon became a dominant feature of the Yishuv, became known as Halukkah (distribution).

Toward the close of the seventeenth century, the Jewish community in Jerusalem numbered about 1,200.[6] In 1700, Judah HaHasid, a mystic who followed the ways of the Sabbatians,** led a large number of Jews from Poland to Palestine. Some 1,300 accompanied him, but some five hundred died on the way. Others were disillusioned with conditions in Jerusalem, and when their leader died three days after arrival, considerable numbers converted to Islam and Christianity and others returned to Europe.

From the middle of the eighteenth century on, organized groups of

---

* The mystical tradition.
** Followers of the pseudo-Messiah Sabbatai Zevi.

Hasidim,* followers of the Baal Shem Tov, arrived from Poland, Russia, and Galicia. One group of some three hundred was headed by two famous rabbis, Mendel of Vitebsk and Abraham of Kalisch. They settled in Safed, and thereby helped in the revival of the Jewish community. The example of the Hasidim was soon followed by their opponents, the Mitnagdim.** In 1770, the number of Jews in Palestine was estimated at about 5,000;[7] the majority were Sefardim, whose affairs were conducted by the officials of the Jewish community in Constantinople. In 1800, the number of Jews was still at the same figure, while the total population of the country was estimated at about 300,000.[8]

The controversy between the Hasidim and their opponents in Eastern Europe, as well as the initiatives of the several Hasidic groupings, had the side effect of increasing the number of immigrants to Palestine early in the nineteenth century. They all sought to establish a foothold for themselves in Palestine. From this time on, the majority of arrivals were Ashkenazim,*** and their flow increased with the opening of a steamship service between Odessa and Jaffa. In 1820 the first Ashkenazic community was set up in Hebron by the followers of Rabbi Shneur Zalman of Ladi, founder of the Habad† school of Hasidim. In 1845 the Jewish population of Palestine was estimated at 12,000,[9] of whom half resided in Jerusalem, constituting about one third of the population of the city. Safed, which had possessed the largest Jewish population in the country, had lost its preeminence following the earthquake in 1837, when only about 2,000 survived the disaster.[10] Of the other two centers, Tiberias in 1857 had a Jewish population of 1,500, mostly Ashkenazim, all except nineteen of whom subsisted on the Halukkah,[11] and Hebron had about 400. Thus by the middle of the nineteenth century, the bulk of Palestinian Jewry, numbering between ten and twelve thousand, was concentrated in the four "Holy Cities" of Jerusalem, Safed, Tiberias, and Hebron. In Haifa there were about one hundred Jews, 400 in Jaffa, and some 300 in other places throughout the country.

---

* "Pious Ones," The name *Hasidim* was given to the followers of Baal Shem Tov, who in the eighteenth century had created a mass movement of deep spiritual appeal.

** Literally, "opponents," i.e., of the Hasidim. (This name was given them by the Hasidim. They themselves preferred to be known as Perushim, or Pharisees, but the former name stuck). The Mitnagdim were rationalists and strongly Talmud oriented; they disapproved of the Hasidic emphasis on feeling and of the cult of Tzaddikim (rabbis said to possess special powers).

*** Literally, "Germans," signifying non-Sefardic Jews from Central and Eastern Europe.

† Habad, so called after the first letters of its three objectives, *Hokhhah* (wisdom), *Binah* (insight), *De'ah* (knowledge).

The modern period of uninterrupted growth of the Jewish population began in the middle of the nineteenth century. The wars of Mohammed Ali with the central government in Constantinople had threatened to dismember the Ottoman Empire and the great powers intervened to preserve the authority of the Sultan. From then on there was a European presence in the Middle East, and this encouraged a measure of reform within the Ottoman Empire. It was for the purpose of accommodating the European powers that Sultan Abdul Majid decreed in 1839 a series of reforms aimed at curbing the arbitrary powers of the local rulers; he introduced laws promoting economic development and removing many of the disabilities imposed on Jews, Christians, and foreigners. The great powers established consulates in Jerusalem that were concerned with the application of the so-called system of capitulation. Under this system foreign nationals were not only protected by their respective consuls but also enjoyed immunity from the Turkish courts, being subject to the jurisdiction of the consular courts only. In order to enlarge their sphere of influence, the consuls offered their protection even to nationals of other countries. Before long the British, who had neither an Anglican religious establishment nor any considerable number of their own nationals living in Palestine, were desirous of obtaining a foothold among the local population. Therefore they instructed their consul in Jerusalem to regard it as part of his duty "to afford protection to Jews generally," and to report upon "the present state of the Jewish population in Palestine."[12] Even the Russian government, while persecuting the Jews in its own dominions, afforded effective protection to its Jewish nationals in Palestine.

The general reforms introduced by the Ottoman government brought about a greater measure of security to life and property, and the protection afforded by the consuls of the great powers under the capitulation system enabled the nationals of these powers to avoid some of the hardships of Turkish rule. As a result of these changed conditions, the Jewish community increased rapidly. Between 1856 and 1880, Jewish immigration, predominantly from Eastern Europe, more than doubled. The bulk of the new arrivals settled in Jerusalem, bringing the Jewish population to about 14,000, more than half the total population in Palestine, which then numbered 25,000. It is worth noting that from 1874 on, the Jews constituted the majority of the population of Jerusalem.[13] By that time, the Ashkenazim formed about 60% of all Jews, now outnumbering the Sefardim, and their proportion continued to grow.

By 1880, the Old Yishuv* had assumed its general contours: it was a community largely devoted to the study of Torah, and its Ashkenazic majority generally subsisted on Halukkah, charitable contributions from

---

* As distinguished from the New Yishuv, i.e., the modern Zionist settlement.

Jews abroad. This majority enjoyed the protection of the foreign consuls, while the Sefardim were chiefly Turkish nationals and, since a number of them were artisans and merchants, were more actively integrated into the economic life of the country. It was the Ashkenazic community which, by its preponderance and economic dependence on Halukkah, developed its unique characteristics and imposed its image on the Old Yishuv.

B. THE HALUKKAH SYSTEM

The most important single factor that made increased Jewish immigration possible under the political and economic conditions prevailing in Palestine by the middle of the nineteenth century was the institution of Halukkah. The immigration itself was motivated by a religious impulse; the immigrants did not leave their homes in Europe for the purpose of improving their material welfare. In any case, the rather primitive and backward state of the economy of Turkish-ruled Palestine held out no promise of material betterment. Many of the newcomers arrived after their prime of life, in order to spend the rest of their days in learning and prayer. Others, fearing the inroads of modernization and the secularizing effect of the Haskalah (enlightenment), which continued to spread in Eastern Europe, sought in Jerusalem a haven where nothing would interfere with a truly religious way of life.

Thus the period following the mid-century saw feverish activity in the promotion of Yeshivot* in the four Holy Cities, but particularly in Jerusalem. This was especially true of the Ashkenazic community, which gradually drifted apart from the Sefardim and adopted a way of life peculiarly its own, a way of life largely isolated from external contacts and immune to worldly pressures, an exclusive universe of its own creation. Thus, these pietists aimed at fulfilling all the 613 Mitzvot; not only to pursue a life devoted to piety, to the study of the Torah, and to the strict observance of all the minutiae of the religious code, but also to live in the Holy Land, in itself a high-ranking rabbinic injunction. The Halukkah system provided the economic base for this unique community, for it relieved its members of the need to earn a livelihood and thereby enabled them to resist external pressures, and by its static nature minimized all internal ferment.

Palestinian Yeshivot had since medieval times been in the habit of receiving support from congregations abroad. In 1257, Rabbi Yechiel transferred his Yeshivah from Paris to Jerusalem; when he found

---

* Yeshivah (plural, *yeshivot*), the traditional seminary for Talmudic study.

himself short of funds, he sent a Meshullah* (emissary) to solicit support for the institution. In 1441 the Jewish community in Jerusalem sent a Meshullah to European countries to beg relief for the group then threatened by famine. Following the influx of refugees from Spain early in the sixteenth century, the appeals for relief were systematized. Till the middle of the eighteenth century, the management of the Halukkah was entirely in the hands of the Sefardim, who then constituted the majority of the Jews in the Holy Land. Meshullahim from Palestine operated in Turkey and Western Europe, and two of them even reached America. In 1759 Rabbi Moses Malki of Safed visited Newport, Rhode Island, and the city was also visited by Isaac Carrigal of Hebron a few years later.[14]

For the purpose of distributing the proceeds from Halukkah, the Palestinian community was classified into various categories: wealthy; dependent on their own relatives; working people; and Yeshivah students. The latter received one-third of all the proceeds, one-third went to the needy, and the remainder was used for the defraying of communal expenses.

With the arrival of the Hasidic groups in the eighteenth century, and of the Mitnagdim in the latter half of that century, conflicts began to arise between the Ashkenazic and Sefardic Jews. The Ashkenazic arrivals, both Hasidim and Mitnagdim, complained that the Sefardim, who were in control of Halukkah funds, discriminated against them in the matter of distribution. The Sefardim, mostly Ottoman subjects, had a central authority. They were officially recognized by the Turkish government, and the Hakham Bashi (Chief Rabbi) of Jerusalem, was the acknowledged head of the community. The Ashkenazim, mostly retaining their European nationalities and split into many groups, had no central organization. Before long various Ashkenazic groups began despatching their own emissaries (Meshullahim), primarily to the countries of Western Europe, to solicit funds for their respective groups. A good deal of criticism was leveled against the Meshullahim, and the contributors complained that their proliferation was wasteful and that they were not subject to public control. In order to do away with the Meshullahim, a new institution was created in 1809 at the initiative of a number of leading Dutch Jews. This was the *Pekidim ve-Amarkalim* (Officials and Overseers), with its center in Amsterdam, to serve as the institution to which contributors to Halukkah would send their donations. Before long, it became the recognized center for the collection of contributions in Western Europe. The institution of Meshullahim was abolished, and the recipients of the funds in Palestine undertook not to engage in any further independent fund-raising activities.

---

* Plural, *Meshullahim.*

As the income grew, the Amsterdam center gained control of the distribution of the funds through its appointees in Palestine. It brooked no interference with its long-distance control. In order to preserve the dominant position of *Pekidim ve-Amarkalim,* the Amsterdam center resisted not only any attempts at making the Yishuv self-supporting, but objected to other charitable institutions that would not be under their control. They maintained audited accounts and distributed the funds between the Sefardim and the Ashkenazim in accordance with a fixed formula, which was revised every ten years. The funds were distributed on the basis of equality, that is, each family received a per-capita allocation, regardless of whether it possessed independent income or was self-supporting.[15]

The high-handed manner in which *Pekidim ve-Amarkalim* administered the Halukkah and the constant complaints of the Ashkenazim, whose numbers were growing, led to the first break in the exclusivity that the Amsterdam center had achieved for itself. In the early thirties of the nineteenth century, a number of Jews in Germany, many of them young and well educated, settled in Palestine and urged reforms. When their request that they, settlers from Western Europe, be entrusted with the administration of Halukkah was rejected, they founded in 1837 a unique institution that set a precedent for many others. They established a Landsmanschaft* known as "Kolel Hod" (Hod being an abbreviation of Holland and Deutschland), with the object of administering funds collected in these countries for the benefit of Jews who arrived in Palestine from those countries. This precedent was followed by Jews from other countries and toward the end of the nineteenth century, there were about 30 Kolelim operating in Palestine. Some of the prominent Kolelim were Kolel Ungarn (Hungary), Kolel Warsaw, Kolel Grodno, Kolel America, and smaller ones, such as Kolel Pinsk. The Sefardim, however, maintained their central organization and had no Kolelim.[16]

The proliferation of Kolelim was encouraged by the desire of arrivals from the richer communities to enjoy a larger income than that afforded by the old Halukkah. There was competition between the Kolelim, leading in several cases to a good deal of jealousy. Thus there was resentment that the relatively small number of members of Kolel America and of Kolel Hod were the recipients of large incomes, while the more numerous members of Kolelim from Eastern Europe had to content themselves with far smaller sums. In order to avoid further tension, all the Ashkenazic Kolelim eventually formed a Va'ad Kelali, a Central Committee, which was to coordinate all fund-raising

---

* An association of people from the same country, region, or town. *Kolel,* plural *Kolelim,* is the Hebrew word for *Landsmanschaft.*

activities, to send emissaries to countries where no fund-raising had previously been attempted, and to provide for joint needs in general. A serious controversy broke out over Halukkah funds raised in the United States. In 1879 the first synagogue of American Jews was established in Jerusalem. Feeling aggrieved at the allocation made to them by the Va'ad Kelali, they determined to establish direct contact with the contributors in America, so as to benefit from a greater revenue for their Kolel. It led to a bitter controversy, in which the American Consulate in Jerusalem was often involved. Finally a settlement was effected between the Va'ad Kelali and Kolel America: the latter was to receive one-third of the funds raised in the U.S.A., while two-thirds were to be allocated to the poorer Kolelim.[17]

The Sefardim also had their Halukkah, which was under the control of the Hakham Bashi of Jerusalem, whose emissaries operated in Italy, North Africa, Turkey, Persia, and India. This complete separation of the Halukkah of the Ashkenazim and of the Sefardim contributed to an estrangement between the two communities.

The Halukkah of the Sefardim was directed primarily to the needy and to Yeshivah students. Replying to the criticism leveled at the Halukkah system by Westerners like the historian Heinrich Graetz, Sefardic leaders enunciated the principle that "there is no Torah like the Torah of Eretz Yisrael, which is the shield and the protector of our brethren in the Diaspora," and for this reason they claimed that their scholars, and those engaged in the study of the Torah, had a right to be maintained by Diaspora Jewry.[18] The Sefardim, settled in the country for centuries and conversant with the Arabic language, were better integrated into the economy and, as noted above, included a considerable proportion of self-supporting families engaged in trade and handicrafts.

In this respect they were distinctly different from the Ashkenazim,[19] among whom fewer were occupied in a gainful manner. The Ashkenazim, being relative newcomers and living segregated in their Kolelim, needed a greater measure of support. Their attitude was that the mere fact of living in Eretz Yisrael was a Mitzvah, and that it was the duty of the Diaspora to support all those who dwelt in the Holy Land and not only those in their midst who devoted all their time to the study of the Torah. Consequently, it was the practice of the Ashkenazic Kolelim to afford Halukkah to all their members, regardless of their material condition, although scholars and Yeshivah students received an extra share.[20] The distribution of the funds was administered by the Gabaim (officers) of the individual Kolelim, and these were appointed by their respective communities in the Diaspora. The powers of these officers and particularly of the principal Gabai of the Kolel were extensive, for they determined the amount to be paid out to each individual member. They enforced communal discipline and laid down the rules for that kind of religious life which would justify the Yishuv's claim to Halukkah in the eyes of their brethren of the Dispersion.

Their regulations prescribed that recipients of extra allocations over and above the general norm must spend the entire day in the Yeshivah or Bet Midrash;* each Friday night they were to study in one of two shifts, either until midnight, or from midnight until sunrise, and to assemble on Sabbaths and Holydays.[21] At times, opposition did develop to the Gabaim, and attempts were made to curb their powers; the attempts, however, met with no success.[22] Altogether, from 85% to 90% of all the Jews in Jerusalem, who themselves constituted two-thirds of the entire Jewish population of Palestine, subsisted on the Halukkah, which at best afforded them a meager living.[23]

The sums raised in the Diaspora for Halukkah in Palestine grew and assumed considerable proportions. Thus, in 1850, the funds raised by the Amsterdam center amounted to some 22,000 gold francs (25 francs per pound sterling) and within a few years they tripled.[24] In 1889 the amount was estimated at 1,500,000 francs, while the American Consul in Jerusalem reported in 1879 that he was informed by the local bankers that the monthly income was between 8,000 and 10,000 pounds sterling (200,000 to 250,000 francs).[25] Mordecai Eliav, the historian of this period, estimates that in the early years of this century the sum was up to 5,000,000 francs, exclusive of remittances from unorganized sources. It was a very substantial amount, whch assured the subsistence of some 60,000 out of 85,000 Jews who were in Palestine on the eve of World War I.

As the system of Halukkah grew and expanded, it was subjected to a good deal of criticism, especially in the Diaspora. The historian Heinrich Graetz in Germany, and the followers of the Haskalah in Eastern Europe, drew attention to the dangers inherent in the very principle of Halukkah. It was pointed out that it promoted mendicancy and pauperism, encouraged idleness, and inculcated an unworldly approach to life; it was creating a rift between Ashkenazim and Sefardim, it afforded Gabaim and rabbis excessive powers over their wards, and altogether it hampered the potential productivity of the Jewish community. It also created a barrier between the Old Yishuv and the incipient New Yishuv and led to their estrangement. In the process it shaped the pattern of the religious life of Palestinian Jewry for the generations to come and left an imprint that continues to be felt in modern-day Israel.

Despite its many negative aspects, Halukkah did promote Jewish immigration to Palestine. The numerous arrivals from Europe could no

---

* House of study.

longer be accommodated in the congested Jewish quarters within the walled city of Jerusalem. In 1860, Sir Moses Montefiore established the first Jewish quarter outside the city walls, directly opposite the Zion Gate, and afforded housing for sixteen families of rabbinical students. Though it was feared that their unprotected position would make them the target of brigands, the students persisted and in 1867 another small settlement for North African Jews was established at Mahaneh Israel, even further removed from the protection of the wall. The first large extramural settlement, to be known as Meah Shearim, was set up in 1874; it provided housing and appropriate communal services for 140 families. The various Kolelim followed suit, and by the close of the nineteenth century, a New City, predominantly Jewish, had come into existence, extending a considerable distance west and south of the Old City. On a smaller scale, a similar urban expansion also took place in Tiberias and Safed. Dr. Arthur Ruppin, one of the founding fathers of Zionist agricultural settlement in Palestine, though himself an opponent of the Old Yishuv way of life, observed that "without Halukkah, Jews would not have constituted a majority of the population of Jerusalem."[26]

Indeed, under the conditions prevailing in Palestine in the nineteenth century, it was Halukkah that made it possible for the Jewish community to grow from 10,000 in 1856 to 25,000 in 1880. As late as 1914, when there were 85,000 Jews in Palestine, 60,000 belonged to the Old Yishuv, that is, were maintained largely by Halukkah.[27] The institution had encouraged the existence and growth of the Jewish population of Palestine, had imparted to the Old Yishuv its particular characteristics, and had given it strength and cohesion.

C. THE INNER LIFE OF THE OLD YISHUV

The Jews of Palestine were treated by the Turkish government on a par with other religious minorities, and consequently enjoyed a wide measure of autonomy. In 1842, in pursuance of a decree of the Sultan reorganizing the administrative districts of Southern Syria, the first Hakham Bashi was installed in Jerusalem.[28] In his capacity as Chief Rabbi (also referred to as Rishon L'Tziyon, First in Zion), he appointed a Rabbinical Council, which was to exercise jurisdiction in matters of personal status, that is, marriages, divorces, and wills, and generally to act as a court of law in civil cases.

The Hakham Bashi was the recognized head of the Jewish community and, since he derived his authority from the Sultan, he was accorded by the Turkish government the honor due to his office. He was not only the spiritual but also the political leader of the community and, in certain respects, an official of the Turkish government. As such, the Hakham Bashi was responsible to the government for the collection of the head tax (haraj) due from the members of the community. While his jurisdiction extended de jure over the entire Jewish community of Palestine, only the Sefardim, whose charitable funds and institutions he administered, acknowledged his authority. The Ashkenazim, taking refuge in the capitulations system, had their own rabbinical courts.

The Ashkenazim had never formed a united community. At first they split into Hasidim and Mitnagdim and later into numerous groups largely based on the Kolelim, each with its own rabbinic court and lay officials. While thus retaining the nationality of their country of origin, they benefited from the capitulations system and the protection of foreign consuls and could keep aloof from the officially recognized community headed by the Hakham Bashi.

Each Ashkenazic rabbinic court (Bet Din) administered justice according to Jewish religious law, and tried not only cases involving family law but civil cases generally. Although these judgments were not enforced by the government (as they were in the Sefardic community), they were generally obeyed by the parties involved, since the rabbis had sufficient moral weight and material power. The mere threat of withholding Halukkah privileges was sufficient to enforce communal discipline and ensured the strict observance of the religious way of life. Members of the Kolel had no voice in the administration of their congregation, nor was any instrumentality provided to enable them to air their grievances. It was a theocratic regime, maintained by the moral power of the rabbis and the economic power invested in the Gabaim as controllers of the Halukkah.[29]

If the exercise of these powers was not sufficient to ensure obedience, the extreme pressure of excommunication (Herem) was applied. The Herem decreed the exclusion of a person from the religious community and prohibited all social intercourse with him. This old rabbinic institution (the Talmud deals with 24 offenses punishable by excommunication)[30] was originally promulgated to preserve the solidarity of national discipline and to strengthen the authority of the synagogue.

The Ashkenazic rabbis imposed the Herem both on members of their own congregations and on outsiders. Thus, in 1872, when Heinrich Graetz visited Palestine, a Herem was pronounced against him because of his criticism of the Halukkah system.[31] Five years later, Israel Dov Frumkin, editor of the Jerusalem periodical *Havazelet,* was excommunicated, also because of his censure of Halukkah practices.[32] In 1878 a Herem was decreed against parents who allowed their children to learn a foreign language. Even the world's best-known Jewish philanthropist, Sir Moses Montefiore, was threatened by a Herem in 1857 when he projected the establishment of a school for girls. The matter did not come to a head because Sir Moses abandoned the plan.

The two educational institutions of the Old Yishuv were the Talmud Torah for young boys and Yeshivah for the older ones. Both were of the strictly traditional type. Learning was confined to the study of the Talmud and the rabbinical commentaries; neither the Bible, nor Hebrew literature, nor Jewish history were taught as such, let alone general subjects such as arithmetic, natural science, or a foreign language. In the Ashkenazic institutions the language of instruction was exclusively Yiddish. The mode of life of the Yishuv, and more particularly that of the Ashkenazim, did not require a school curriculum that would qualify boys and girls for a life based on work and oriented to making a living. For them, there would be Halukkah to meet their material needs. Even the older students who were married and had families could pursue their Yeshivah studies indefinitely, profiting from the premium paid over and above the Halukkah portion to needy students. No schools of any kind were provided for girls.

Leading European Jews who visited Palestine—among them representatives of the House of Rothschild and of the Alliance Israélite Universelle—shared the views of Montefiore and Graetz about the dangers inherent in the Halukkah system. They sought to promote schools that would enable the younger generation to engage in useful occupations. During the third visit of Sir Moses in 1849 the Ashkenazic rabbis heard of his project to establish a modern school and submitted to him a memorandum in which they pleaded with him to abandon his plan. Such a school, they wrote, would be for the young "as a stumbling-block before the House of Israel." It would lead them "to take pleasure in the world and its vanities," and thus close to them the path to eternal life. Such a school, too, would lead to the "evil that befell the Children of Israel in Russia," an obvious reference to the early inroads made by the Haskalah in Eastern Europe. Sir Moses heeded the plea and abandoned his scheme.[33]

In 1856 Jerusalem was visited by the Austrian Jewish writer and poet Ludwig August Fraenkel, who came to found a school for Jewish children. This project generated an acrimonious controversy, which lasted several years.[34] He consulted the heads of the Kolelim and the rabbis, as well as the Hakham Bashi. With the exception of the latter and his Sefardic colleagues, the project was rejected. When it was decided to proceed with the opening of the school—later known as the Laemel School after a Viennese philanthropist, Simon Edel von Laemel —the Ashkenazi leaders, heads of Kolelim, and rabbis were up in arms. Even the intervention of the Austrian consul, whose government took an interest in the school, was of no avail. A Herem was imposed, and Halukkah would be denied to parents who dared send their children to this school. The school was opened in 1857, after the Hakham Bashi approved the program. All the pupils were children of Sefardim.[35]

In 1870, the Alliance Israélite Universelle founded Mikveh Israel, the first agricultural school in Palestine, near Jaffa. Like all schools established by this organization throughout the Middle East and North Africa, in this one religious observances were strictly adhered to. The need for this school was urgent in view of the numerous Christian missionary schools that attracted Jewish boys; it had great difficulty in drawing pupils and in 1872 it had only 17 pupils. But even these pupils were subjected to pressure. In a letter dated May 21, 1872, Charles Netter, the founder of the school, described how the pupils, who during the Passover spent their holiday with their families in Jerusalem, were subjected to persecutions, publicly vilified, and their parents urged to withdraw their children from this school. Why? "Because it is feared that Halukkah funds will be reduced," Netter wrote. He inveighed against the rabbis, who viewed the attendance of Jewish children at Protestant missions with apparent equanimity.[36] A similar fate awaited the opening of the Alliance elementary school in Jerusalem in 1882. A Herem was imposed, but on account of the intervention of the French Consulate, it did not assume an extreme form. When Joshua Yellin, a respected Jerusalemite, the first Ashkenazic Jew to send his son—David, the future professor and Oriental scholar—to this school, refused to obey the Herem, Halukkah was denied to him and his shop was boycotted.[37]

In 1854 the first girls' school, later maintained by the Anglo-Jewish Association and known as the Evelina de Rothschild School, was opened in Jerusalem. It aimed at imparting to the girls, along with a strict religious discipline, an elementary education, domestic arts, and a knowledge of the rudiments of the English language. In 1867 it had fifty pupils, all but two of them Sefardim. Thus the Sefardim took advantage of the schools founded by Jewish organizations in Europe and, unlike their Ashkenazic brethren, acquired a modicum of general knowledge, which enabled them to engage in trade and commerce.

In March 1872, Heinrich Graetz, the leading Jewish historian of the nineteenth century, visited Palestine, where he spent several weeks studying the condition of the Yishuv and exploring the possibility of establishing a Jewish orphanage. The report he submitted to the leaders of the Jewish community in Germany is one of the most valuable documents for understanding the Old Yishuv.

Graetz was struck by the general poverty, lack of education, and the prevailing decadence in the four Holy Cities, particularly in Jerusalem. In spite of the increasing flow of Halukkah funds, poverty was omnipresent. In Jerusalem, wholesale and retail trade was mostly in the hands of Christians. "There are a few craftsmen, but they work in a primitive way and cannot compete with the Christian craftsmen." Jews would refuse productive jobs offered to them. Because of the inequality in the distribution of funds between the richer and poorer Kolelim, there were many instances of most severe poverty.

The root cause of the evil was Halukkah, Graetz wrote. Whereas receipt of charity was everywhere considered undesirable, among the Jews in Palestine it was considered an honor to be the recipient of Halukkah. "Most of the men, meager as their knowledge of the Talmud may be, considered themselves as rabbis and scholars" and therefore as entitled to a larger share of Halukkah. Graetz inveighed against the idleness resulting from the absence of a trade or calling. "They do not know what to do with their free time. They presume to engage in scholarship: in fact only the few devote themselves to the study of Torah. They rather roam about the streets, awaiting news. The result of this idleness is gossiping, insinuation, slandering and the like. . . . This system encourages obscurantism." In contrast, Graetz singled out the small communities that had developed outside the four Holy Cities. In Jaffa, Haifa, and Acre there was no Halukkah; there the Jews were self-supporting and therefore enjoyed the respect of everyone.[38] As was to be expected, Graetz was condemned by the Old Yishuv, which interpreted his attack on Halukkah as an attempt to undermine religious Orthodoxy.

The Ashkenazic majority set the pattern for the entire Yishuv. Piety, strict observance of the minutiae of the religious law, and absorption in the study of the Talmud were the dominant features of the Old Yishuv. It was remote from the great European centers of Jewish life; in fact, most of the new arrivals in the nineteenth century were escaping from these Jewish centers, where the observant Jew found himself confronted by modernizing tendencies. There was nothing in the political and cultural climate of the Ottoman Empire, of which Palestine was then a part, to upset the intellectual calm of traditional Jewish life. It was exposed neither to the challenge of the Haskalah nor to the stimuli of a secular environment. The Old Yishuv had no political aspirations whatsoever, and the capitulations system made it possible to avoid close contact with the state authorities. It was not concerned with its security within the political and legal framework of the Ottoman Empire, for the consuls of the European powers afforded the necessary protection.

It cannot be emphasized sufficiently that the Ashkenazic community of the Old Yishuv was unique in that it did not have to concern itself with the primary object of all societies (apart from closed religious orders), that is, to make a living. This was, of course, directly contrary to the experiences of the Jewish ghettos in Europe. For all their otherworldliness and concentration on religious duty, the Jews of the East European ghettos were constrained to deal with the outside world by reason of economic necessity; the old Yishuv was largely free to ignore that world. It was able to turn its energies entirely to the pursuit of a religious way of life, and this in turn was its justification for living on Halukkah. This shaped the character of the Yishuv's internal organization. The rabbis and the Gabaim who controlled the allocations of funds thereby controlled the community, with hardly any fear of interference. It was in many respects the nearest approximation to a theocracy achieved by any Jewish community in modern times.

This meticulously guarded isolation could not help but breed an attitude of self-righteousness and superiority; the Old Yishuv's general approach to life was anti-intellectual and unworldly, and was characterized by rigidity and obscurantism. Toward the end of the nineteenth century the Ashkenazic majority had created the basic patterns for an ultra-Orthodox Judaism in Palestine, which had built into it exclusiveness, resistance to change, and a tendency toward militancy. If anything, the revolutionary upheavals that shook Jewish life in the Diaspora and in Palestine from the last quarter of the nineteenth century on only served to solidify the Orthodox Yishuv and caused it to draw together and put up its defenses. The first serious challenge to its way of life arose with the bloody Russian pogroms that occurred in 1881 and radically altered the distribution of Jews in the world. Millions left for North America, and Palestine too began to receive its first large-scale modern immigration. Small as this immigration was, it constituted the first wave of a new type of immigrant, who laid the foundations of a modern community.

D. FERMENT IN THE OLD YISHUV

The ultra-Orthodox regime in the four Holy Cities was from time to time subjected to attacks from within. These were directed neither at the religious way of life, at the authority of Jewish law, nor at the dominant positions of the rabbis and Gabaim, but rather at the institution of Halukkah itself. These critics attacked it as demoralizing, and they looked for ways to make the community productive and self-supporting. In this they were encouraged by Jewish organizations and philanthropists in the Diaspora.

The first attempt to introduce productive employment for the Jews in Jerusalem was made in the eighteen-fifties by Sir Moses Montefiore. His plans to interest Jewish families in agriculture failed, however, and the flour mill as well as the weaving plant he had built in Jerusalem closed down. Other philanthropic organizations met similar failures. The Mikveh Israel Agricultural School near Jaffa, established in 1870 by the Alliance Israélite, attracted only a few pupils from Jerusalem. Indifference on the part of the community and open antagonism on the part of the rabbinical and Halukkah authorities rendered these attempts abortive.

In 1878 Rabbi Yehiel Mikhal Pines, an outstanding rabbinical scholar, arrived in Palestine from Russia. Though he was a consistent foe of Haskalah and an uncompromising opponent of any religious reform, he was convinced that a gradual emancipation from Halukkah was essential for the healthy development of the Yishuv. His articles advocating economic productivity of the Yishuv attracted the attention of Sir Moses Montefiore, who proceeded to set up a special fund for this purpose,[39] and on behalf of this "Montefiore Memorial Fund" Rabbi Pines was sent to Jerusalem. He was appalled by the conditions he found. "Wherever I turned, I found poverty and pauperism," he wrote. "Young people are neglected, hungry . . . moving like shadows aimlessly pursuing the wind."[40] To his principals in London he submitted plans for the setting up near Jerusalem of an agricultural settlement that was to be based on strict Torah observance. He further suggested the establishment of workshops and small industries in Jerusalem itself.

Before he could proceed with his plans, however, he incurred the hostility of the rabbis. The project itself would have been suspect, but in addition, Rabbi Pines participated in a controversy surrounding an orphanage that had shortly before been established by the Jewish Berlin-Frankfurt Society. The rabbis had attacked it on the ground that foreign languages were to be taught, and Rabbi Pines had sided with the founders. He was further suspected of aiding in the establishment of the Alliance Israélite school. His denial was of no avail, and he was condemned by the rabbis in pamphlets and public statements.[41] The rabbinic extremists called for a gathering in front of the Wailing Wall and there, to the accompaniment of the Shofar, excommunicated him. The Herem was not endorsed by all the rabbis,[42] and was not effectively enforced, for fear that its repercussions might affect fund-raising for the Halukkah in Russia.

The greatest controversy raged around Rabbi Pines's project to set up a workshop for woodworking. Though it was stated that each workday would open with prayer and be concluded by the study of Talmud, the plan elicited fierce attack from the Halukkah establishment. Unable to attack the rabbi on the merits of the project, his detractors alleged that his writings contained heretical views, and they rejected his appeal to have them examined by learned scholars. A large public assembly was summoned, where Rabbi Pines was denounced as an *Epikoros* (heretic). Another decree of excommunication was issued; some of the apprentices in the workshops were molested, and others were so intimidated that they did not report for work.[43] This controversy was widely publicized in Eastern Europe, and Rabbi Pines, fearing that Halukkah funds might decline and the Yishuv be further impoverished, admonished his supporters in the Diaspora not to diminish their Halukkah contributions. Eventually, under pressure from Europe, the ban imposed on the workshop was lifted,[44] but Rabbi Pines, realizing the futility of operating in Jerusalem, in 1882 shifted his center of activities to Jaffa, where he found scope for his plans in helping to lay the foundations of the New Yishuv.

Similar difficulties and even greater personal animosities awaited the attempts of Eliezer Ben Yehuda, the father of modern Hebrew, to reform the Old Yishuv from within. He settled in Jerusalem, adopted the Orthodox garb, and conformed in all respects to the traditional way of life. He changed his name from Perlman to Ben Yehuda when he took the unprecedented step of becoming a Turkish subject. Together with Rabbi Pines, Ben Yehuda founded the society "Tehiat Yisrael,"* which advocated, *inter alia,* the spread of the Hebrew language in lieu of Yiddish, and making productive the Halukkah-supported population. In 1885 he published the weekly *Hatzvi,* in which he proposed the teaching of crafts to Yeshivah students. His activities led to his first excommunication in 1886,[45] and a second six months later. Subscribers to his weekly drifted away after the Herem, and Ben Yehuda found himself in financial straits. But worse was still to come. When his wife died shortly thereafter, the Ashkenazic rabbis refused to sanction her burial; only when the Sefardim agreed to have her interred in their cemetery did the rabbis relent. The precedent of an Ashkenazi being buried in a Sefardic cemetery was to them more threatening than to bury the wife of an excommunicate.

In 1893, the rabbis took their full revenge on Ben Yehuda. In the Hanukkah issue of his weekly he had extolled the virtues of the Hasmoneans, who had liberated Palestine in the second pre-Christian century. The rabbis denounced him to the Turkish authorities as a potential political rebel, suggesting that Ben Yehuda's article had hinted at the desirability of detaching Palestine from the Ottoman Empire.[46] As a Turkish subject he no longer enjoyed the protection of a foreign consul and he was thrown into jail, where he spent a month. He was

---

* The revival of Israel.

then tried and sentenced to a year's imprisonment and was released only through the intervention of Baron Edmond de Rothschild of Paris. His bitter experience had, however, one beneficial result: in jail Ben Yehuda commenced his work on the dictionary that later developed into the monumental *Complete Dictionary of the Hebrew Language*.[47]

The incident created an uproar throughout the Jewish world, especially when it became known that some of the leading rabbis not only had participated in informing the Turkish authorities, but had falsified the translation of Ben Yehuda's article in order to make it appear seditious. When all these acts were exposed, the culprits attempted to shift the blame on the Hakham Bashi. For a while this agitation brought about a diminution of Halukkah collections.[48]

Thus failed another attempt to reform the way of life of the Old Yishuv from within. The beneficiaries and administrators of Halukkah found it effective to accuse would-be reformers of heresy and thus formed a natural alliance with the Ashkenazic rabbis. The latter were the judicial authority, and while they possessed no official powers of coercion, the threat of withdrawing the privileges of Halukkah usually sufficed. It was a watertight system, unchanging and unchangeable for those who lived under it.

The alienation of the Ashkenazic community from the Sefardim further reinforced the status quo. The latter were gradually beginning to liberate themselves from Halukkah,[49] and while they too were strict traditionalists, their religious leaders were far less rigid and permitted them to send their children to the new schools founded by European Jewish philanthropists. The Ashkenazic majority withstood pressures from without and ferment from within. It proved impervious to reform; a change could therefore only be brought about by the creation of a New Yishuv. The occasion for this arose in the wake of the traumatic events that afflicted the Jewish masses in Eastern Europe in 1881.

E. THE BEGINNINGS OF THE NEW YISHUV

For nearly a century, from the eighteen-fifties and on, Palestinian Jewry drew its strength from the Jews of Eastern and Central Europe, largely from the former. East European Jews were the primary source of immigration and material assistance, and they were the bearers of both tradition and revolutionary ideas. What happened in Eastern Europe, particularly till the early thirties of the twentieth century, exerted a dominant influence on the evolution of the Yishuv in Palestine, so that the Yishuv came to reflect to an ever-increasing degree the powerful political and cultural ferment of East European Jewry. This Jewry was the creator of the New Yishuv, and shaped the destiny of the land for nearly three generations.

In 1880 the total number of Jews in the world was estimated at 7,750,000,[50] of whom 75% lived in Eastern Europe and the Balkans, 8% in Islamic countries, 13.5% in Central and Western Europe, and only 3.5% beyond the ocean, including North America, which then had a Jewish population of about a quarter of a million. Eastern Europe, and particularly the Russian Empire, was the heartland of world Jewry; here lived the masses of the Jewish people who possessed all the attributes of a national entity except that of territorial sovereignty. They existed in the midst of a vast Christian majority, yet lived quite apart from them. They had evolved Yiddish as their national language, had developed a meaningful cultural and social life of their own, and were intensely loyal to the religious way of life. They determined the course of Jewish history far beyond their geographic confines.

As early as the first half of the nineteenth century, the strict traditionalism that dominated the religious way of life had come under attack by the movement known as Haskalah. This special form of Jewish enlightment had originated among the Jews in Germany in the last quarter of the eighteenth century, with the object of spreading modern European culture and secular knowledge. It had sought to emancipate Jewish education from its limitation to the study of the Talmud and had brought about a renaissance of studies in biblical Hebrew and of the poetical, historical, and critical portions of Hebrew literature. This had led to a scientific approach to the study of Jewish culture in general. "The battle between light and darkness," as the proponents of the Haskalah described their movement, spread to Bohemia and Galicia (where a vigorous revival of Hebrew literature first occurred), and later to Russia. There, attempts were made in the second half of the nineteenth century to establish Jewish schools, where, in addition to sacred subjects, instruction was given in Hebrew, modern languages, and the natural sciences. These attempts, however, made little impact on the wider community and met with little success.

Indeed, more often than not, the followers of the Haskalah (known as Maskilim) were estranged from the Jewish community and were occasionally even persecuted, and they met with little or no sympathy or recognition in the outside world, where their efforts were entirely unknown. Similar failures awaited the mild and cautious attempts at religious reform.

The great and lasting achievement of the Haskalah in Russia lay in the creation not of reform institutions but of a new Hebrew literature, and with it a large Hebrew-reading public. The difficulties encountered by young Jews in their efforts to obtain a broader education caused them to turn to Hebrew studies. Here they could read about contemporary problems. Here they met the masters of Hebrew literature, whose works went through many editions. A flourishing Hebrew periodical press came into being and several large publishing houses further stimulated and encouraged the spread of Haskalah in Russia. It was this literature that first questioned the relevance of religious Orthodoxy to contemporary existence, and urged the easing of some of the hardships caused by strict adherence to the details of the Sacred Law.[51]

The liberal regime inaugurated by Czar Alexander II (1855–1881) opened new prospects for Jewish emancipation. In 1863, the Society for the Promotion of Culture among the Jews of Russia was founded. Its leaders adopted the program of Moses Mendelssohn, the German father of Haskalah, to suit Russian conditions. They believed that raising the standards of education among the Jewish masses would facilitate their struggle for civil rights and legal equality; indeed, there was much in the reforms introduced by Alexander II to lead the founders of the Society to believe in the possibility of attaining their goal. These hopes were shattered when the reformer Czar was assassinated in 1881.

Few years in Jewish history form such a clear turning-point as the year 1881. The new reactionary regime of Alexander III let loose an outburst of murderous fury against the Jews of Russia, and this bloody violence, condoned by the government, continued for over a year. It first engulfed the Jewish communities in the Ukraine, including such large cities as Odessa and Kiev, and then spread to Western Russia, culminating in a pogrom in Warsaw that was a large-scale massacre, planned, coordinated, and directed from a central source.[52] Pogroms and repression became the policy of the new regime. The lot of the Jews was to be made so miserable that most of them would be compelled to emigrate. Russian ministers indicated to a British member of Parliament that they expected some three million Jews to leave.[53]

In May 1882, when the grossest violence had spent itself, restrictive laws were enacted to make the existence of the Jewish community permanently unattractive. The infamous "May Laws" barred Jews from living outside the cities of the Pale of Settlement, prohibited the buying of estates, and made their movements from place to place subject to permission. A *numerus clausus* was introduced into schools and universities. Jewish traders (who then generally observed the Sabbath) were forced to close their shops also on Sundays, even in those towns where they constituted a majority. Other rules and regulations restricted Jewish economic and social life. Jews were unwanted in Russia, and millions of them began to plan for a new existence elsewhere.

These developments destroyed the hopes of emancipation that had been cherished by the leaders and followers of the Society for the Promotion of Culture and by the Maskilim generally. Under the impact of those tragic events, the Haskalah changed its orientation. Instead of worshiping at the shrine of European cultures, it placed itself at the service of the national regeneration of the Jewish people. Conspicuous among the leaders was Leo Pinsker, who in 1882 published his revolutionary pamphlet *Auto-Emancipation*. In this he called for the creation of a Jewish nation in a land of its own. Although he did not designate Palestine as the land in which such a Jewish nationality could be re-created, few who heeded his call thought of any other place.

A movement to establish a Jewish settlement in Palestine quickly spread throughout Russia and other countries. Societies of Hovevei Zion (Lovers of Zion) were organized to encourage settlement in Palestine. Young people, many of them university students, chose to become pioneers in Palestine. They adopted the name *Bilu,* a word compounded from the initials of the Hebrew words "House of Jacob, come and let us go" (Isaiah 5:5). The first detachment of the Bilu pioneers reached Jaffa in 1882. While the Hovevei Zion merely advocated emigration to Palestine and the settlement there of Jews as tillers of the soil, the Bilu went further and aimed at creating a political center for the Jewish people.[54]

The new type of immigrant to Palestine had to strike out on a hitherto untrodden path. The way of life pursued in the four Holy Cities was entirely incompatible with the aspirations of this First Aliyah,* a wave of immigration that lasted from 1882 till 1903. From twenty to thirty thousand persons are estimated to have arrived in that period.[55] Since the Old Yishuv could offer neither guidance nor assistance to the new type of immigrant, a totally new approach was adopted. Various groups in Russia and Rumania raised funds for the purchase of land in various parts of Palestine and often did so independently of each other. In the summer of 1882 the village of Rosh Pinah (The Cornerstone) was established on a rocky tract of land in Upper Galilee. The following winter, the village of Zikhron Yaakov (Remembrance of Jacob) was founded in the hills of Samaria; these were followed by Rishon L'Tziyon (First in Zion) south of Jaffa, and by Yesod Hamaalah (Foundation of Ascent) in the eastern part of Upper Galilee. In 1884 Gedera and Ekron were established, near Rishon L'Tziyon; Rehovot in the south and Hedera, south of Haifa, were founded in 1890–91; these were followed by a number of other villages, and by

---

* *Aliyah* is Hebrew for ascent; specifically, immigration to Palestine, the act of coming to the Jewish homeland being regarded as ascent, while emigration from Palestine is termed *yeridah,* descent.

1900 their number was twenty-two and their population approached 5,000.[56]

Ignorant of agriculture, unused to the climate and to hard physical labor, handicapped by lack of water, and exposed to attacks of Bedouins, the pioneers found themselves saddled with tasks of Herculean dimensions. The Turkish authorities were unfriendly, and much time and money had to be spent in securing permits for the construction of houses. Before long the settlers found that the purchase of land and the erection of buildings had exhausted their means, and many of them would have had to abandon their farms had it not been for the loans and facilities extended to them by Baron Edmond de Rothschild of Paris, and by members of the Hovevei Zion of Russia. So the pioneers persisted, and by the early years of the twentieth century they were on the whole self-supporting and had laid the foundations of the New Yishuv.

There were other arrivals who settled in Jaffa and Haifa, where they found small self-supporting communities. They engaged, in commerce and in crafts, and laid the foundation for the urban New Yishuv. In 1903 the Jewish population in these towns had risen to about 5,000 and 2,000 respectively. Altogether, the New Yishuv constituted about one-fifth of the total Jewish population of Palestine at this time.[57]

Of all the Aliyot that preceded the First Aliyah, all motivated by an intense urge to live in the Holy Land in accordance with the precepts of religion, the New Aliyah was the first to be motivated by other powerful considerations, from which the religious urge was not excluded but was subordinate to the ideal of creating in the ancient homeland a productive and self-supporting community, with particular stress on the importance of tilling the soil. While the new arrivals did not articulate their political views, the ideal of Jewish Palestine was implicit in their attitudes and actions, and in the case of the Biluim, it was openly expressed. It was only natural that the Old Yishuv should view these new arrivals with fear and hostility. Their very stress on the importance of being productive and self-supporting was a challenge to the institution of Halukkah and the vested interests built into it. The pursuit of worldly activities was bound to open the gates to secularism. To the Old Yishuv, the new arrivals appeared as "Russian Anarchists," lax in the observance of religious precepts. Occasionally they showed open hostility toward the Bilu, informing against them to the Turkish authorities.[58]

The members of the First Aliyah were mostly traditional Jews, but the pattern of life they evolved set them against the Old Yishuv. In the first instance, they repudiated Halukkah as a parasitic form of existence. They established schools totally at variance with those of the Old Yishuv. They evolved a modern educational system for boys and girls, in which Hebrew replaced Yiddish and secular subjects were also introduced.

In the villages the new settlers developed a form of self-government that stood in marked contrast to the theocratic system of the Old Yishuv. The farmers took charge of all their communal affairs: the administration of the schools, the water supply, the maintenance of watchmen, and other services. The Ottoman regime was totally unconcerned with the provision of any social or other services to the populace, but on the other hand it did not interfere with the internal life of small localities. This meant that the new villages could constitute territorial units that were practically autonomous.

It is indeed remarkable that the first modern attempt at farming was made, in 1878, by three Jews from Jerusalem, one a native of that city and two recent arrivals from Hungary. They acquired a tract of land some nine miles east of Jaffa and there founded the village of Petah Tikvah (Gate of Hope). Because of malaria and general lack of agricultural experience, the settlement made little headway until, some years later, members of the first Aliyah infused it with new blood and capital. Petah Tikvah incurred the wrath of the Jerusalem rabbis from its very inception. In 1880 Rabbi Joshua Diskin inveighed against its proposed school, which he foresaw as driving the children away from religion.[59] In 1881 the rabbis issued a proclamation against the new settlers, "who presume to bring redemption by force,"* and who engage in farming, an occupation "which is not needed in this land."[60]

Gedera also came under attack by the rabbis, who appealed directly to the Hovevei Zion in Russia, who were helping the new settlers, and asked them to discontinue all aid to the village. They accused the settlers of being nihilists, violators of the Sabbath, and of allowing men and women to dance together. The Hovevei Zion were informed that they were aiding and abetting "transgressors who pollute the land"; the rabbis stated that they would have "the land of our fathers become rather the dwelling of jackals than a den of robbers."[61] This appeal aroused a good deal of controversy among the Russian Hovevei Zion, and there were some in fact who withheld their contributions "until the land is purified of children that are corruptors."[62] It was largely due to the efforts of Rabbi Yehiel Mikhal Pines, who was regarded as the religious supervisor of Gedera, that the Hovevei Zion were persuaded to continue their association with the settlement.

---

* Meaning that, unlike the pious traditionalists who wait for God to bring redemption in His own time, they were impatient and with their work tried to force God's hand.

In 1889 a direct confrontation occurred between the new settlers and the Jewish religious law, in connection with the application of the biblical law of Shemittah. According to the Bible, the land is to lie fallow every seventh year, which is reckoned as the year of Shemittah (remission), when the "land shall observe a sabbath of the Lord."[63] Not only must the land lie fallow, but whatever grows on it is to be treated as ownerless property (hefker) so that all may freely partake of it. The regulations of the Sabbatical year include in addition the prohibition to cultivate, dispose of, or trade in the produce of the Shemittah year, and provide for the annulment of all monetary obligations between Israelites, the creditor being legally barred from making any attempt to collect his debt. "And this shall be the nature of the remission: every creditor shall remit the due that he claims from his neighbour; he shall not dun his neighbour or kinsman, for the remission proclaimed is of the Lord's."[64]

According to the rabbis, these laws were to promote the idea of holiness, so that one year in seven might be devoted to the Lord, even as the weekly Sabbath is devoted to rest from labor and to the study of Torah. At first the Shemittah was applied to Palestine only. The rabbis extended the law to Syria in order to discourage Jews from settling there.[65] Later, the application of Shemittah was again confined to Palestine, and Jews living in the lands of the Diaspora were exempted from its application. The law providing for the annulment of debts was abrogated de facto by Hillel the Elder, in the first century B.C.E., by means of a legal fiction known as the Prosbul. Since all debts were canceled at the end of the Shemittah year, it became difficult to obtain loans before the onset of that year, and all commercial activities were seriously affected. Hillel devised the Prosbul to get around the biblical provision. He permitted a declaration by the partners to the transaction that the loan was given to the court for collection. Because the annulment of debts during the Sabbatical year was applied only to individual persons and not to public institutions, the effect of Hillel's move was to make the loan a public matter and hence immune to cancellation.[66]

Now, in the seventh year of the New Yishuv, a problem arose that had never confronted the Old Yishuv. In anticipation of the critical Shemittah year (noted throughout the centuries in the Jewish calendar, however far divorced the Jews might be from agriculture), the question came up for discussion and the suggestion was made that the problem might be solved by a Prosbul similar to that which Hillel had instituted. The proposal was rejected by the rabbis. The matter was brought to the attention of the leaders of Hovevei Zion in Russia. In 1887 three leading rabbis in Russia, Naftali Zvi Yehuda Berlin (Ha-Natziv) of Volozhin, Mordecai Eliasberg of Boysk, and Samuel Mohilever of Bialystock met together in Vilna to consider a question addressed to them by a farmer from Rishon L'Tziyon: Was he allowed to cultivate the land in 1889? Rabbi Berlin's opinion was that the law of Shemittah must be enforced. Rabbi Mohilever admitted that Shemittah posed a serious problem for the new settlement, but he considered that, inasmuch as this was the first opportunity in many centuries to observe the law, the commandment should be carried out on this occasion, and this would attract the Orthodox to the idea of tilling the soil.[67] Rabbi Eliasberg urged that a solution be found and counseled against rigidity in so important a matter, which might endanger the very survival of the New Yishuv.[68] Rabbi Mohilever subsequently changed his mind and searched for rabbinical authority to obviate the application of the Sabbatical law for that year. Meanwhile, the representatives of Baron Edmond de Rothschild of Paris, who had already made substantial investments in the development of agricultural settlements in Palestine, had applied to Rabbi Isaac Elchanan Spector of Kovno, a leading rabbinical scholar, for his advice. Rabbi Spector ruled that the problem could be solved by a temporary sale to a Gentile, that is to say, a modern-day fiction analogous to the Prosbul.[69] This ruling was followed by other rabbis in Russia, who announced that such a measure was necessary "in order to save souls and to save the Yishuv." The sale was to be effected by a proper deed executed before a rabbinical court in Jerusalem. This decision was referred to the rabbis in Jerusalem "out of respect and to avoid controversy."

In Palestine, however, a storm broke out. For the farmers the matter was of utmost material importance to their existence. To save the situation, Baron Edmond de Rothschild sent emissaries to Jerusalem in order to solicit the authority of the rabbis for the removal of the ban. The Hakham Bashi, Rabbi Yaacov Shaul Eliashar, agreed to solve the problem by a quasi-conveyance of the land to a non-Jew, and expressed his readiness to attach the seal of his office to this transaction. In this move he was supported by the other Sefardic rabbis in Jerusalem. Such a deed of conveyance was duly executed in the office of the Hakham Bashi, and the representatives of Baron Rothschild notified the settlers that those farmers who failed to cultivate the land would be denied any assistance. The Baron was also prompted in his action by the Turkish authorities, who expressed concern at the loss of state revenue in case of failure of cultivation.[70] The leading Ashkenazic rabbi in Jerusalem, Rabbi Shmuel Salant, to whom Baron de Rothschild applied, rejected the solution of his Sefardic counterpart and suggested that the Baron maintain the farmers during the Shemittah year. The Ashkenazic rabbis issued, in the autumn of 1888, a proclamation that stated: "As the year 5649 is drawing nigh, we inform our brethren the settlers that, in accordance with our religion, they are not permitted to plough, to sow or to reap, or to allow gentiles to perform these agricultural operations in their fields (apart from such work as may be necessary to keep the trees in a healthy condition, which is legally permitted). Inasmuch as the settlers have hitherto endeavoured to obey God's law, they will, we trust, not violate this biblical command. By order of the Bet Din* of the Ashkenazim in Jerusalem."[71]

Thus it came about that the Ashkenazic rabbinate of the Old Yishuv found itself pitted against the European rabbis, whose scholarly eminence and piety were not questioned, as well as the Sefardic rabbinate in Jerusalem and the new settlers, who were generally traditional Jews. It was ultimately a confrontation between the emerging New Yishuv and the Jerusalem rabbinate, which was totally committed to ideals of the Old Yishuv. The rabbis of Russia, who lived in a community engaged in a struggle to eke out a livelihood, were prepared to adapt the religious law in order to save their brethren from ruination. The Jerusalem rabbis sought to save the situation by issuing an appeal to the Jews of the Diaspora, calling upon them to raise funds to enable the settlers to observe the law of Shemittah,[72] a policy wholly in consonance with the Halukkah outlook.

The struggle produced a profound dilemma for all who were concerned with the Yishuv. Baron Edmond de Rothschild, unwilling to fight the rabbis of Jerusalem, appealed to the settlers whom he aided to discontinue cultivation of the fields. The rabbis in Russia, however, urged the settlers to continue such cultivation. When the settlers of Gedera, Petah Tikvah, and Ekron, under pressure from the Jerusalem rabbinate, agreed to abide by their edict, they were bitterly criticized by their supporters in Russia. In particular, the farmers of Gedera came under severe criticism from their benefactors, the Hovevei Zion, and in the middle of the year they resumed cultivation. In Petah Tikvah and in Ekron the edict was only partially observed. In Zikhron Yaakov, the farmers completely ignored the rabbis and cultivated the fields.[73] The majority of the Jewish farmers in Palestine violated the injunction of the Jerusalem rabbis and tilled the soil. This was the first direct confrontation between the Old and the New Yishuv, in which the latter asserted its position contrary to what was regarded as a religious precept.

In the years of Shemittah that followed 1889, the gulf between the New and the Old Yishuv widened. The law posed a vital problem for the new settlers; it posed an equally important problem for the guardians of the Jewish law. The settlers did cultivate the land in the ensuing years, while the rabbis in Jerusalem adhered to their earlier strict

---

* Rabbinical court of law

interpretation, but, since they lacked coercive power their injunctions were disobeyed. The problem was thus not only not solved in terms of Jewish religious law; to many of the New Yishuv it was a demonstration of the ultimate incompatibility of religious tradition with the requirements of a community that sought to be productive and self-supporting.

F. THE STRUGGLE FOR DEMOCRACY

When the first attempts at settling Jews on the land were about to be made, Rabbi Pines had been the first to consider the way of life the new settlers would adopt and the laws they would apply to it. To him it was obvious that "all the laws of the village shall be in accordance with the Torah; there must be no retreat from its commandments. The great scholars have faithfully promised me that they will endeavour to find mitigations based on the sayings of the Sages, in such matters as *Kilayim,* which could be a stumbling-block before the feet of Jewish farmers."[74] The law of *Kilayim,* as applied to plants, is a biblical prohibition of sowing, grafting, or mixing diverse kinds of seeds or trees that differ in name, appearance, or taste.[75] Rabbi Pines, realizing that this prohibition would hinder the development of farming, apparently consulted the Jerusalem rabbis with a view to securing from them certain mitigations. He also realized that there were provisions of the Torah that it would be difficult to circumvent by such legal fictions. He proposed, therefore, that "every member of the village shall himself till the soil. It is also essential that a Gentile should be taken into the farm, either as tenant or employee. This is for two reasons: (a) the Arabs, too, hire labour to assist them in their work, and (b) it is necessary for the days of Sabbaths, Holydays, and years of Shemittah."[76] It was clear to Rabbi Pines that Jews could not properly engage in farming unless they resorted at certain periods to the services of Gentiles. It was a common practice of the Jews in the Diaspora to do this and to employ non-Jews to perform those labors which are forbidden to Jews at certain times. Rabbi Pines's proposed solution might have worked if the new settlers who were now coming into the land in ever-larger numbers had been willing to work in the context of traditional law and if the Ashkenazic authorities had welcomed them wholeheartedly.

In 1880 the founders of the first agricultural settlement drew up a document entitled "Regulations of the Founders of the settlement Petah Tikvah," a covenant binding for all members.[77] It was a constitution

that regulated the economic, educational, and religious life of the settlers and provided for the administration of the village. For the first
time in many centuries was such an attempt made for Jewish autonomy
in Palestine, where self-government was practiced in a defined territorial unit.

These regulations provided, *inter alia,* that "the rabbi will be invested with authority, with full power to see that the sacred Torah is observed . . . and he who disobeys him will be punished." It was the duty
of every person to assist the rabbi in the enforcement of his orders. He
was to be salaried and be the sole judicial authority, who would adjudicate "matters, small and large, be it damage to property or injury
to persons." The rabbi was to enforce the religious commandments that
deal with the cultivation of the soil. "At appointed periods the rabbi
shall in person tour the gardens, fields and vineyards to see whether
everything is executed in accordance with law . . . including gifts for
the priesthood." He would celebrate marriages and hear divorce cases,
and would further have the power to make additional regulations, as
well as to interpret old ones, provided he would first consult the Ashkenazic rabbinate in Jerusalem in these matters. Detailed provisions
were made by the covenant for synagogue attendance, ritual slaughter,
burial grounds, visitation of the sick, and ritual baths. The chapter
dealing with education provided for the traditional type of Talmudic
learning; no tongue but the Sacred Tongue was to be taught. Provisions
were finally made for the strictest observance of Sabbaths and Holydays.[78]

Here was a blueprint for a theocratic form of self-government
drawn up by the few pioneers from Jerusalem who planned to establish
the first Jewish village in Palestine. It fully reflected the spirit of the
Old Yishuv and was designed to allay the suspicions of the rabbis of
Jerusalem.

But malaria and other hardships reduced the numbers of the original settlers, and it was necessary to attract people from outside Jerusalem. For their sake a new set of regulations was drawn up. While
provisions were made for proper religious observances, the preamble
introduced a new element. It provided for participatory democracy:
"Everything in the community shall be decided by a majority of those
who have a house therein; and the owner of a house, be he poor or be
he rich, shall have one vote." The administration of the village was to
be entrusted to an elected committee, "and the most respected person
amongst them shall be its head, and he will act as a trustee for the
treasury." The term of office of the first committee was limited to one
year, and thereafter to three years.[79] While the second constitution of

Petah Tikvah retained many of its theocratic features, its arrangement for representative communal government represented a significant innovation.

In 1883 a group of Russian Jews founded the settlement of Yesod HaMaalah, on the shores of Lake Huleh in Upper Galilee.* They too drew up a set of regulations, which they entitled "The Book of Regulations for the Pioneers of Yesod HaMaalah in the Holy Land." The committee that drafted the regulations included no one from Jerusalem, a fact reflected both in the simple and unadorned style of the document and in its practical approach to the problems of administering the affairs of a village. The regulations provided that the administrative committee would be elected by the heads of all families, and that the decisions of general meetings would be binding on all the inhabitants. In order to prevent members from appealing from the decisions of the general assembly to some outside body (presumably the rabbinical authorities), it was stated that "none of its decisions shall be subject to appeal; members are to respect them and in no way to make light of them; as otherwise pain would be caused to the public and peace would depart." Here was a clear warning against any intervention in the affairs of the settlement, where all matters were to be run by the members of the village on a democratic basis.[80] While the Book of Regulations made provision for the upkeep of a synagogue, no reference was made to, nor any authority vested in, a rabbi. The document thus constituted a distinct move away from the Old Yishuv.[81]

An even more far-reaching instrument was drawn up by the founders of Rehovot in 1891. Following the first general meeting of all the settlers "called to lay the foundation for the autonomy of the village," a committee was elected to administer its affairs. The general meeting adopted the following resolution: "We, the members assembled, whose names are set out above, hereby authorize the elected committee to enact right and honest laws for the community, both in matters relating to religion, faith and opinions, and those relating to matters of dispute between one member and another. When the committee draws up regulations, we shall examine them at our next general meeting, and until then we shall do what the committee requests us to do, and in no way contest their decision or call it into question. And whatever we shall be requested to contribute for public needs, we shall contribute without questioning the authority of the committee in this matter. Should any one of us disobey these orders, he shall be regarded as a violator of the law and of the covenant, and his rights in the public assets of the village shall be forfeited, and he shall no longer be regarded as a member of the community."[82]

---

* The lake has since been drained and has disappeared from the landscape.

The founders of Rehovot thus assumed direct control over their own religious affairs. The constitution of Rehovot ordained the autonomy of the committee and its elected officers, and its spirit became the guide of the settlements of the First Aliyah. All of them sooner or later adopted the democratic system of government in their local affairs and eliminated all vestiges of theocracy and rabbinical control. To be sure, many of the villages supported rabbis from public funds, but these rabbis were subject to the decisions of the village committee and had no powers vested in them by the village regulations.

The emancipation of the New Yishuv from some of the traditional norms was slow but irreversible. In Rehovot and other new villages, the first schools were patterned on the traditional Heder, where only sacred subjects were taught. But a little later arithmetic was introduced, and still later Hebrew grammar, history, and geography were taught, "and nature studies bearing on the life of a farmer and on agriculture."[83] A controversy arose when some of the farmers "who were under the influence and authority of the rabbis of Jerusalem" requested the elimination of all secular subjects, and the removal of girls from the schools. When the majority of the farmers refused to yield, the dissidents established a traditional Heder, where instruction was given by a teacher appointed by the Jerusalem rabbinate. Moshe Smilansky, the leading man of letters of the First Aliyah and one of the founders of Rehovot, observed: "The influence of the Jerusalem rabbis was considerable, for the wine sold to Jews in the Diaspora required the Kashrut* certificate of the rabbis."[84]

In 1903 a delegation of the Hovevei Zion from Russia arrived. It was headed by Menahem Ussishkin, one of the outstanding leaders of Russian Zionism. The delegation sought to establish an organization that would be the representative body of Palestine Jewry, and "unite all material and spiritual forces of the Jewish population in Palestine in order to foster and accelerate the development of the Jewish element in the country, both in numbers and in quality."[85] After local leaders had been consulted, it was decided to convene a *Kenessiah* (assembly) to work out an organizational framework for Palestinian Jewry. All males who had reached the age of twenty-one, had resided in Palestine for at least one year, and did not subsist on Halukkah would be eligible to vote for the election of representatives to the Kenessiah.

It was obvious that these provisions excluded the bulk of Palestine Jewry, who at that time still lived from the proceeds of Halukkah. Consequently, when the newly elected Kenessiah assembled in Zikhron Yaakov on August 23, 1903, it represented a mere ten percent of the entire Jewish population of Palestine.[86] The ten to twelve thousand

---

* Dietary laws; from *Kasher*, clean.

Jews who constituted the New Yishuv hardly provided an adequate basis for a national organization. The time was not yet ripe.

In sum, Palestinian Jewry evolved after 1881 into two distinct communities, the Old and the New Yishuv, each developing its own distinct characteristics but with little interaction between them. Each repudiated the outlook and way of life of the other; each developed its own sets of values. So long as there was no national framework that could embrace both communities, there was no direct confrontation between the two, and little need for mutual accommodation. Each community went its own way, mindful of its own ideals, and on the whole each acted as if the other were nonexistent.

Yet it was obvious to the Old Yishuv that the settlers of the First Aliyah, with its aspirations and life-style, were bound to undermine its position as the dominant element in Jewish Palestine and to challenge its cherished values. The Shemittah controversy served notice that the New Yishuv would not abide by the Sacred Law when it conflicted with what it considered to be a vital national interest. It was also obvious that the development of autonomous and democratic administrations in the new villages would throw the gates wide open to the inroads of secularism.

2

The Rise of Jewish Nationalism

A. THE EMERGENCE
OF THE JEWISH PROBLEM

Till the closing decades of the nineteenth century, the bulk of the Jewish people, then dwelling in Eastern Europe, were generally committed to the religious ways of traditional Judaism. The Maskilim had failed to reach the large masses who conceived of their sufferings in the Diaspora as a penalty for the sins committed by their ancestors and by themselves; their entire religious discipline was directed toward obtaining Divine forgiveness, which in turn would pave the way for the Messiah. They regarded their sojourn in the lands of the Diaspora as temporary; for them the instrumentalities for ushering in the Messianic era were prayer, and observance and study of Torah as the revealed word of God. Thus, despite all the miseries, their condition posed to them no problem calling for a practical solution; they knew the supernatural cause of their sufferings and they also knew that the means for achieving redemption from their earthly punishment was strictest adherence to the Law. The vast majority never thought of themselves as Russians, Poles, or Lithuanians; to themselves and to others they were Jews and nothing else.

This contrasted sharply with the position of the Jews in Western Europe, who had been enjoying a measure of civic equality for some decades, and who now considered themselves to be primarily Germans, Frenchmen, or other nationals, and adopted their country's garb, speech, and intellectual outlook. They aimed at positions to which their efforts and abilities seemed to entitle them, and in many cases they attained prominence in economic, cultural, and political life. To them,

Diaspora was no longer a punishment for sin; rather, the dispersal of the Jews throughout the world was the divine means whereby the Jewish people could carry out their mission of teaching ethical monotheism to mankind and of offering it an example of righteous living.[1] These Western Jews resembled their Eastern brethren in that they too felt their future to be assured, only it would lie not in Divine fiat but in human progress, and since Jews themselves were the beneficiaries of such progress, it was their duty to participate to the utmost in its promotion. It was not surprising that Western Jews looked down with impatience and disdain on the Ostjuden (Eastern Jews), who shut themselves off into spiritual and cultural ghettos.

A major turning point came with the disasters that befell East European Jewry in 1881–82. Prayer and the observance of religious injunctions appeared suddenly to many as too passive a reaction. Traditional Judaism no longer seemed to offer an adequate explanation for suffering, nor did it solve the urgent and concrete problems of the moment. The Jewish condition, which until then had not constituted a major problem, now appeared as a source of perplexity. Mass immigration to the West and beyond the ocean were merely a geographical redistribution, a palliative and not a solution. The growing awareness of what both Gentiles and Jews began to call the "Jewish problem" (albeit with different meanings) now agitated the younger intellectuals and before long communicated itself to the Jewish masses in Eastern Europe, as well as to many Jews in the West. Once the problem was posed, it was inevitable that some of the basic assumptions underlying Jewish existence would be reappraised and that a radical reexamination of the traditional concepts of Judaism as a religion and of the Jews as a people—which heretofore had been confined to the religious reformers of the West—would be undertaken.

Nor did the awareness of a Jewish problem remain confined to East European Jewry; it made its appearance among the emancipated Jews of Western Europe also. This was brought about by the unexpected emergence of modern anti-Semitism, which appealed to the "civilized" upper classes although it seemed to run counter to the generally accepted view of the law of progress. Anti-Semitism emerged surprisingly from the soil of Germany, where it was endowed with an aura of science and metaphysics and where the teachings of Eugene Duehring, Heinrich von Treitschke, and Houston Stewart Chamberlain found a particularly receptive audience. Their main theme was that nationality was in essence a matter of race, from which it followed that the perfect nation-state had no room for social or religious minorities. German anti-Semitism created its own terminology, such as "blood and soil" and "the authentic German spirit." There was hardly a land in Europe where this ideology—duly adjusted to local needs—did not penetrate. In consequence, the conviction grew among Jews that emancipation had not brought about the dignity and security for which the Western Jews had hoped; the very success they had achieved as Europeans and their contributions to European culture seemed to draw upon them the slings and arrows of the new anti-Semitism. The world they had sought to enter brutally reminded them of their unchangeable origin. The more single-minded the patriotism of the Jew, the more bewildering was the rebuff and the more bitter his disillusionment. If neither emancipation nor a voluntary return to the ghetto was the solution in the sphere of practical politics, what was? Certainly Jews could never again renounce their rightful share in the normal activities of mankind. The time called for new developments. Throughout the centuries of their dispersal the Jews had merely reacted to situations not of their making; now that they realized the existence of their problem, they also looked for solutions. It dawned upon them that they did not necessarily have to remain the pawns of history, but might, as a collective, take part in the shaping of their own destiny.

The forerunner of this revolutionary approach was Peretz Smolenskin (1842–1885), who in 1869 founded the Hebrew periodical *Ha-Shahar* (The Dawn). His Hebrew novels and stories are marked by realistic description of life in Eastern Europe, and are informed by a desire to inculcate a national and secular ideology. In his work *Am Olam* (Eternal People), Smolenskin contended that the Jews are not only a religious group but also constitute a nation, and that they should strive toward achieving full nationality. The Messianic era would be hastened if Jews achieved political and spiritual emancipation. Here was the first intimation of secular nationalism, of a Messianic ideal deprived of its primary theological content and instead conceived in terms of political liberty.

A more original exponent of Jewish nationalism was the historian Simon Dubnow (1860–1941). A Russian Jew who had devoted much of his early research to the study of the history of the Jews in Russia and Poland, Dubnow in time addressed himself to the whole course of Jewish history, and distilled from it his principles of Jewish nationalism. While the Jews had lost their territorial base and their political independence, he said, they nevertheless constituted a distinct national entity in the various lands of the Diaspora. In each period of history there was always one Jewish community that, more than any other, developed and perfected the inner life and thus served as the spiritual center for the entire Diaspora. The first center was Babylonia; later it shifted to Spain, and from there to the Rhineland, and to Central and Eastern Europe. Dubnow conceived of the Jews as a minority dwelling in the midst of a majority, but retaining and developing its cultural autonomy. Since this cultural autonomy was the highest form of nationalism, there was no need for Jews to seek a territory of their own and attain political independence. Dubnow's ideas were in consonance with the prevailing mood at the beginning of the century, when the existence of the Russian and Austro-Hungarian empires encouraged the concept of multinational states where each ethnic group would be entitled to cultural autonomy and certain minority rights. To give practical effect to this philosophy, Dubnow founded in 1906 in Russia the "Jewish People's Party" (the "Volkspartei," generally known as "Folkists"), which advocated the participation of Jews as a national group within the political life of Russia.[2]

Dubnow regarded the Jewish religion as closely integrated with Jewish nationalism and as performing the function of a defense mechanism; that is to say, it no longer held a position of primacy but was one of several elements within Jewish existence. Dubnow himself was an agnostic, but he always remained alive to the significance of religion in the totality of Jewish life. "By aspiring to secularism," he wrote, "by separating the national idea from religion, we are only aiming at negating the supremacy of religion, but not at eliminating it from the storehouse of our national cultural treasures. If we wish to preserve Judaism as a cultural-historical type of nation, we must realize that the religion of Judaism is one of the integral foundations of national culture, and that anyone who seeks to destroy it thereby undermines the very basis of national existence. Between us and the Orthodox Jews there is only this difference: they recognize a traditional Judaism, the forms of which were set from the beginning for all eternity, while we believe in an evolutionary Judaism, in which new and old forms are always being assumed and discarded, and which adjusts itself . . . to new cultural conditions."[3]

Here was a novel attempt at a solution of the Jewish problem and a reevaluation of the role played by religion (which to Dubnow meant Orthodoxy). While mindful of its importance in contemporary Jewish life, his solution envisaged the demotion of religion and in its stead the elevation of nationalism as the dominant and all-embracing principle of Jewish existence.

Because Dubnow's autonomy-nationalism proposed full economic participation by Jews in the lands of Diaspora, it appealed chiefly to middle-class elements who thereby undergirded their potential with a workable philosophy. It was not surprising, therefore, that there would also develop a type of nationalism answering to the needs of the Jewish proletariat. In White Russia, Russian Poland, and Galicia a considerable Jewish working-class had sprung up and was engaged in home industries and small factories. It became the focus of a new revolutionary movement, and before long it adopted the socialist program. At a conference held in Vilna in 1897, several groups founded "The General Federation of Jewish Workers in Lithuania, Poland and Russia"; this was the Jewish "Arbeiterbund"* (generally known simply as the "Bund"), which became affiliated with the Russian Social Democratic Party.

Like good socialists, they played down nationalism and extolled the principle of the class struggle, but because of the peculiar condition of the Jewish social and economic order, they developed their own brand of nationalism. In 1903 the Bund withdrew from the Russian Social Democratic Party, because the latter refused to recognize the Jews as a nationality and the Bund as the representative of the Jewish working class. While believing that with the advent of socialism the Jewish problem would thereby be solved, the Bundists conceived of the solution in terms of a distinct Jewish entity within the new social order. This solution rendered Zionism superfluous, and indeed dangerous to the course of progress. Zionism as a bourgeois movement deflected the people from the class struggle. For the Bund, Zionism was the archenemy.

Since the Bund had to appeal to the working people in their own language, it promoted Yiddish as the national tongue and as the cultural vehicle of the Jewish masses. Before long the Bund developed a Jewish school system with Yiddish as the language of instruction. Unlike the followers of Dubnow, the Bundists rejected the Jewish religion in general, and tried to remake Jewish society along strictly secular lines. They had a considerable following and until the destruction of Jewry in the Second World War exerted a significant influence on organized Jewish life in Eastern Europe. But because of its deliberate break with the sources of the Jewish religious heritage and its rejection of the universality of the Jewish people, the influence of the Bund did not extend beyond Eastern Europe's Jewry, and when that Jewry perished, the Bund as a dynamic factor perished with it. Jewish communists of today's Europe cannot be considered its legitimate successors.[4]

B. THE RISE OF POLITICAL ZIONISM

The founder of political Zionism, Dr. Theodor Herzl, a journalist and playwright, was born in Budapest and trained as a lawyer in Vienna. He matured in an assimilationist milieu and had only a superficial acquaintance with Jewish culture. The movements and writings that preceded him in the cause of the national restoration of his people were

* "Society of Workers."

completely unknown to him. In his case, personal experience took the place of traditional education in quickening his Jewish consciousness. In his capacity as correspondent of a leading Viennese daily, he witnessed the Dreyfus affair in Paris, and the thought that, a whole century after the French Revolution had proclaimed the Rights of Man, the very existence of the Jewish people was still in jeopardy drove him to a radical reappraisal of the Jewish condition. In a pamphlet entitled *Der Judenstaat,* which was published in 1896, Herzl set forth his revolutionary views.

He conceived of Zionism, the movement he proposed to create, as a response to the challenge of anti-Semitism. The Jewish question existed wherever there were Jews in perceptible numbers, and since they naturally moved to places where they were not persecuted, they only succeeded in importing anti-Semitism through their migrations.[5] They might perhaps be able to merge entirely with the nations surrounding them if they could only be left in peace for a few generations; but, Herzl believed, the nations would not leave them in peace. The Jewish problem "is no more a social than a religious one, notwithstanding the fact that it sometimes takes that and other forms. It is a national question . . . we are a people, one people."[6] The solution he proposed was that the Jews be "granted sovereignty over a portion of the globe large enough to satisfy the rightful requirements of a nation."[7] His definition of Jewish nationhood suggested that for him anti-Semitism was the primary problem. "We are one people—our enemies made us one in our despair, as repeatedly happens in history. Distress binds us together, and thus united, we suddenly discover our strength."[8] It was the existence of a common enemy that welded the scattered Jewish people into a nation. This was nationalism pure and simple, in itself devoid of any religious content. In his attempt to give this nationalism a viable form, Herzl sought to provide it with what it most obviously lacked, namely, a Jewish state.

It was a grand vision, and its surprising simplicity gained it considerable popularity. It even appealed to many Western and Westernized Jews; for in their world secular implications of nationalism were in the ascendant. If the Jews were indeed members of a nation, they too could strive for political unity and independence. This was the ideology behind the declaration of the First Zionist Congress, convened in Basle in August 1897, that the aim of Zionism was the creation for the Jewish people of a "home in Palestine secured by public law," and that one of the means for attaining this object was the "strengthening and fostering of Jewish national sentiment and consciousness."

To this Herzlian and essentially Western view, the adherents of East European Zionism opposed their own view of nationalism. They regarded their nationhood not as a mere reaction to the external pressure but as a function of vital forces within themselves. The classical form of this type of nationalism was formulated by Ahad Ha'Am, for whom the primary problem was the development of the "Jewish spirit," by which he understood something larger than the Jewish religion.[9] Like the teachers of Reform Judaism, Ahad Ha'Am saw in the prophets the very essence of the Jewish spirit, but rejected the Reform doctrine that viewed Diaspora as an aspect of the "Mission of Judaism." Ahad Ha'Am deplored the spiritual disintegration of Judaism, which could not be checked in the Diaspora. A full development of Jewish national life could take place only in Palestine, which should provide a home not only for Jewry but also for Judaism. To Ahad Ha'Am, political Zionism could have significance only to the extent that the future Jewish state would become a spiritual center "which will be a new spiritual bond between the scattered sections of the people, and by its spiritual influence will stimulate them all to a new national life."[10]

Even so, Ahad Ha'Am's conception of spiritual Zionism, with its emphasis on Judaism rather than on Jews, was essentially secular and as such was rejected both by Reform Jews in the West and by the Orthodox in the East. He was inspired by the prophetic books of the Bible, which emphasized social justce and righteous living, but he relegated religion to the status of one of the forms of Jewish culture and held that Judaism was something wider than a sum of its parts: it represented the national creative power, which in the past had expressed itself in a primarily religious culture, but in the future might conceivably express itself in a quite different form. He recognized historic Judaism as a national religion, but would not accept the description of Jewish nationalism as a religious nationalism. Reviewing the modest achievements of Jewish settlement as he saw them on his visit in 1912, Ahad Ha'Am wrote: "What has already been accomplished in Palestine entitles me to say with confidence that that country will be a national spiritual centre for Judaism, to which all Jews will turn with affection, and which will bind all Jews together; a centre of study and learning, of language and literature, of bodily labor and spiritual purification, a true miniature of the people of Israel as it ought to be."[11]

Ahad Ha'Am entitled his collection of essays *At The Crossroads,* to indicate that his time was decisive as a crossroads both for the Jewish people and for Judaism. He agreed with Herzl that the Jews were a nation and that Palestine should be their territorial center, but he differed with him in his emphasis on nationalism as the embodiment of the people's spiritual and cultural values. With the Orthodox, Ahad Ha'Am saw the importance of religion in national life, but he parted with their idea of religion as the sum total of national life. Again, he was at one with the Reform Jews in stressing the centrality of the prophets to Judaism and the pursuit of social justice and ethical values as the highest expression of the Jewish tradition, but he parted with them by rejecting their idea of a Jewish mission among the Gentiles as the raison d'être for the existence of the Jews as a minority, and by insisting on the need for the historic homeland as the territorial base for a spiritual center.

Thus the rise of Zionism, far more than the rise of the Bund, or the Folkism of Dubnow, initiated a reinterpretation of the nature of the Jewish people. Zionism spoke in contemporary terms and at the same time tapped vast resources of idealism and devotion; it released pent-up energies and in doing so produced a leadership of vision and stature. It galvanized young and old into efforts of at times heroic dimensions and activated Jewish life beyond anything the founders themselves had imagined. In fact, before it revived an ancient land, Zionism revived the Jewish people.

In the process, ideological differences were sharpened, and especially so when the debate touched on the role of religion. The closer the Zionist idea came to realization, the more acute the debate became. It grew in intensity as it moved from the realm of theoretical disquisition to a discussion of the day-by-day role of traditional observances in national life. It was then, in fact, that the debate, which to this day has remained unfinished, assumed greater significance and, with it, greater intensity.

C. THE REACTION OF THE RABBIS TO ZIONISM

The delegates who journeyed to Basle to attend the first Zionist Congress in 1897 were as heterogeneous a group as the countries of the Diaspora from which they came. They hailed from nearly all the countries of Europe, from North America, North Africa, and Palestine. There were among them bourgeois and radicals, Orthodox, Reform, and agnostics, the younger generation and the older, and the languages they spoke were as diverse as their countries of origin. For the first time in Jewish history, representatives of the Diaspora were gathered at a world congress, which became the parliament of the Jewish people on the march toward national restoration. So at least it was regarded by Herzl and his followers. On reviewing the proceedings in his diary, Herzl wrote: "Were I to sum up the Basle Congress in a word . . . it would be this: at Basle I founded the Jewish state."[12]

With his conception of the World Zionist Organization as a "state in becoming," Herzl took into consideration the manifold aspects of a sovereign state, and this naturally included the position of religion.[13] Taking for granted that there would be complete freedom of belief, he wrote: "Shall we end by having a theocracy? No, indeed. Faith unites us, knowledge gives us freedom. We shall therefore prevent any theocratic tendencies from coming to the fore on the part of our priesthood. We shall keep our priests within the confines of their temples, in the same way as we shall keep our professional army within the confines of their barracks. Army and priesthood shall receive honours as high as their valuable functions deserve, but they must not interfere in the administration of the state which confers distinction upon them, lest they conjure up difficulties without and within."[14]

Reflecting the prevailing mood in Western Europe, at the end of the nineteenth century, Herzl enunciated the principle of the separation of religion and state. To make sure that the law of the land would not be the religious law, Herzl suggested the appointment of a council of jurists to do the preparatory work of legislation. "During the transition period, these must act on the principle that every emigrant Jew is to be judged according to the laws of the country which he has left. But they must try to bring about a unification of these various laws to form a modern system of legislation based on the best portions of the previous systems."[15]

Even before the opening of the first congress, Herzl had to confront the problem in its practical form. The congress was originally scheduled to be held in Munich, but the Jewish community of that city protested against the choice and the congress was moved to Basle. In July 1897, prior to the opening of the sessions, the Orthodox rabbis of Germany published in the leading papers a statement that they felt compelled to issue because "through the call for a Zionist Congress and through the publication of its agenda . . . mistaken notions have been spread about on the whole subject of Zionism." The statement went on to say that "the efforts of the so-called Zionists to found a Jewish national state in Palestine contradict the Messianic promises of Judaism as contained in the Holy Writ and in later religious sources."[16] Dr. Herman Adler, Chief Rabbi of Great Britain, vehemently condemned Zionism, and was followed by Moritz Guedemann, Chief Rabbi of Vienna. In his reply Herzl referred to the concept of a Jewish mission to spread monotheism. "We must not confuse this application of the word with that given to it in speaking of those poor monks who set forth to the wild places of the world in order to carry the Christian gospel to cannibalistic tribes. The Jewish mission is something comfortable, sated and well-to-do. For years now I have been observing the people who retort with

'Israel's Mission' whenever I come to talk to them about the wretchedness of the Jewish poor. These missionaries are excellently situated."[17]

Equally negative was the attitude of the Reform rabbis in America. Rabbi Rudolph Grossman of New York stated the attitude of the Reform movement to Zionism in the following terms: "I see in it a fatal blow to the mission of the Jew in history. The destruction of the Temple and the dispersion of the Jews were not punishments, but rather an act of Divine Providence . . . the Jews have a mission to spread their teachings."[18] Similarly, Rabbi Joseph Silverman said: "The fact is that the greatest blessing in disguise that ever happened to Israel was the overthrow of the Palestinian Kingdom, and the dispersion of Israel throughout the world. It gave Israel a religious mission."[19]

Despite the official attitude of the American Reform movement, Reform rabbis were among the founders and leaders of Zionism. Rabbi Gustav Gottheil of New York was one of the early supporters of Zionism, and it was under his influence that his son Richard, an Orientalist of repute, became in 1898 the head of the Central Bureau of the Federation of Zionist Organizations.[20] Another exponent of Zionism in the Reform camp was Rabbi Bernard Felsenthal of Chicago. He rejected the view that "the mission of Israel was spiritual," and advocated the restoration of the Jews to Palestine. At the first Annual Conference of American Zionists held in 1898, Rabbi Felsenthal was elected Vice-President of the organization.[21] Rabbi Stephen S. Wise, a rising star in the Reform rabbinate, became a confirmed Zionist following his attendance at the Second Zionist Congress in 1898. He said: "I was a Jew by faith up to the day of the Congress in Basle, and little more. At Basle I became a Jew in every sense of that term. . . . If I use the term re-birth, it is not too strong a term to use for the overwhelming experience that befell me at Basle. For the first time in my then youthful life, I got a glimpse of World Jewry."[22] Another early leader in American Zionism was Judah L. Magnes, a graduate of Hebrew Union College and at one time rabbi of America's leading Reform congregation, Temple Emanu-El in New York. There was little in his background to suggest that Magnes would become one of the leaders of the reconstituted Jewish people in Palestine.

Although the Reform rabbinate provided Zionism from the very beginning with some of its most gifted and devoted leaders, these few men did not attempt to organize their followers and form a religious Reform party within the Zionist movement, a policy which, however, was shortly to be adopted by the adherents of Orthodoxy in Eastern Europe.

In Western Europe most Orthodox and Reform rabbis had declared their opposition to Zionism on religious grounds. The Orthodox Chief Rabbi of France, Zadoc Kahn, also opposed the Zionist program, although he maintained friendly contact with Herzl, was helpful to him in many ways, and admired him as a person. But Kahn's arguments were of a special kind. They were practical as well as prophetic. He knew that the application of some traditional laws to agriculture, such as Shemittah, would not work in modern practice. As an Orthodox Jew, he could not conceive of a Jewish state as based on anything but the religious law. Since this was, however, impractical in modern times, he resolved the conflict between the need for the application of religious law in a Jewish state and its manifest inapplicability to modern life by rejecting the very idea of a Jewish state. A theocracy, he held, may be desirable but it is an impossibility; a modern state is a possibility, but it is not admissible in the view of the Jewish religious law. "If the state is theocratic as it once was, what will become of the freedom of thought? And if it is a secular state, how will it be Jewish?"[23] Thus the incompatibility of the immutable divine law with the operation of democracy negated the possibility of establishing a state that deserved to be called Jewish.

The Orthodox in Eastern Europe found Zionism a baffling phenomenon. If the redemption of Israel at the end of the Exile were destined to come about with the advent of the Messiah, as traditionally believed, then surely the way to facilitate that day was by strict observance of the words of God as revealed in the Torah. Yet the leaders and adherents of the new movement seemed to reject in their whole way of life everything that had always been regarded as the condition precedent to national redemption. Here was a movement purporting to revive the Jewish people, led and directed by Western or Westernized Jews, predominantly secular in outlook, who were firing the imagination and enthusiasm of many of the youth.

This enthusiasm and fervor had indeed Messianic elements within it. Writing in the last year of the century, Dubnow, himself an opponent of Zionism, said: "Political Zionism is merely a renewed form of Messianism, transmitted from the enthusiastic minds of the religious idealists to the minds of political communal leaders. In it the ecstasy bound up in the great idea blurs the lines between reality and fantasy. Here too we find the continuing effects of secularization. In the same way that the Jewish national idea in its completeness now divests itself of its religious forms, and takes on a secular form, so does Messianism pass over from the religious to the political sphere."[24] While Dubnow viewed the new movement as secular Messianism, some of the Orthodox rabbis saw it as a false Messianism, a conception that evoked sad associations with, and bitter memories of, the pseudo-Messianic movements that had plagued the Jewish people in the seventeenth and eighteenth centuries.

If most Orthodox Jews viewed Zionism as an attempt to "force the hand of the Almighty,"[25] and expected salvation to come about in God's good time, not all agreed. Rabbi Zvi Hirsch Kalischer, a renowned Talmudic scholar (1795–1874), had already put forth a different viewpoint in his book *Derishat Zion* (Quest for Zion), published in 1861. He argued that the salvation of the Jews as foretold by the prophets could only come about in the natural way, by self-help, and did not need the advent of the Messiah; he therefore advocated immediate reclamation of the Holy Land and proposed the establishment of a "Jewish Society for the Resettlement of Palestine."[26] Under his influence the Alliance Israélite Universelle had in 1870 established Mikveh Israel, the first Jewish agricultural school in Palestine. A generation later Herzl was able to secure the support of the venerable Rabbi Samuel Mohilever (1834–1898) of Bialystock, one of the outstanding Hovevei Zion leaders, who was helpful to him in getting Russian Jewry to participate in the First Zionist Congress. Mohilever himself was too ill to be present in Basle, but his message to the assembled delegates created a deep impression.

Herzl realized how tenuous the support of the Orthodox within the World Zionist Organization was. He therefore bent every effort to attract them. Since the primary activities of the organization concerned diplomatic negotiations with Turkey (with a view to obtaining a charter for Jewish settlement in Palestine), as well as with the creation of the financial institutions of the movement, there was no ground for controversy on the issue of religion. In order to allay the apprehensions of the Orthodox elements, the Second Zionist Congress in 1898 adopted the following resolution: "Zionism aspires not only to a political and economic revival of the Jewish people, but to a spiritual revival as well, based on modern culture and its attainments. Zionism will not undertake anything contrary to the commandments of the Jewish religion."[27] This resolution, however, could only delay and not avoid a controversy with the Orthodox.

At the Third Congress, held in Basle in 1899, a group of young delegates, headed by Chaim Weizmann, Martin Buber, and Leo Motzkin, organized what later became known as the Democratic Faction, and formed a kind of opposition to Herzl. Being disciples of Ahad Ha'Am, they felt that the activities of the Zionist Organization should not be confined to political, diplomatic, and organizational work, but should also include a cultural and educational program. The Orthodox elements at the congress objected to this proposal and supported Herzl's position that the organization should concentrate solely on political and propaganda work. Their objection was based on the principle that any cultural or educational program must arise from a traditional religious approach, and since they suspected the views held by the proponents of the program, the Orthodox preferred the Zionist organization to stay completely out of all educational work.

To Herzl, the paramount consideration was the maintenance of unity within the organization, and in order to achieve the objective he gave his support to the Orthodox. To his critics Herzl replied: "Let us not weaken ourselves by emphasizing our differences at this time, differences which will certainly appear eventually, and will themselves contribute to the useful life of our people; for those differences are not bad in themselves, so long as they are brought out at the right time, and serve as cultural correctives." No resolution on cultural work was adopted at the congress; a similar attempt by the Democratic Faction at the Fourth Congress held in 1900 in London was again side-tracked by Herzl.[28]

The Democratic Faction persisted, however, and proceeded to organize its forces for the forthcoming congress. At a preliminary conference the Faction drafted its program, which contained the following clause: "Cultural work, including in particular the encouragement of the use of Hebrew and the study of Hebrew literature, must be vigorously prosecuted in the Diaspora and also in Palestine. There must be a campaign for the establishment of a Jewish university for both general and Jewish studies."[29] At the Fifth Congress, held in Basle in 1901, there was an acrimonious debate, but eventually a resolution was passed declaring that "this Congress regards as a principal part of the Zionist program the raising of the cultural level by means of educating the Jewish people in the spirit of nationalism."[30] The adoption of this resolution dealt a blow to the Orthodox, some of whom left the Zionist organization; the majority, however, decided to stay within the movement, fight secularist tendencies from within, and organize themselves for that purpose into a party. This controversy brought about the rise of the first political party within the World Zionist Organization, a religio-political party that created a precedent and pattern of far-reaching importance.

D. THE RISE OF THE MIZRAHI

The resolution on the cultural program by the Fifth Congress had no immediate practical result because the World Zionist Organization did not have the means to initiate any such scheme either in the Diaspora or in Palestine. The Orthodox were in a dilemma. They did not want to leave the organization, which already had a mass following; to stay was of value only if they could constitute a force within it. Rabbi Isaac Joseph Reines, the generally acknowledged leader of the Orthodox in the Zionist movement, prompted his followers to call a Zionist Orthodox conference. In 1902 the meeting assembled in Vilna; it was attended by seventy-two delegates from some thirty cities, and included twenty-four rabbis. They founded the Mizrahi,* which gradually evolved into a worldwide organization of Orthodox Jews who were Zionists. The new group adopted the Basle program of 1897, adding to it their specific formula of "the Land of Israel for the People of Israel in accordance with the Torah of Israel."[31]

Following the Vilna conference, the new organization issued a "Proclamation" setting out its ideology as well as replying to its opponents. It was not the distress of the Jewish people nor anti-Semitism that gave rise to Zionism, it stated. These phenomena were permanent features of Diaspora existence. It was the spiritual distress arising out of the attraction of modern culture that led to assimilation that justified the rise of Zionism. "In the lands of the Golah, the soul of our people, the Torah, can no longer exist in its fullness, nor can the observance of the precepts." Consequently, the solution was a return to Zion. In regard to the criticism leveled against the Zionists that many of their leaders were not observant, that men and women attended conferences, that they advocated a modern education that stressed the study of the Hebrew language and of Jewish history, the proclamation asserted that two distinct spheres of activity were to be considered, the material (the profane), and the spiritual. On the material level there could be no objection to participation in such Zionist activities as strengthening the Zionist organization, promoting settlements in Palestine, participating in its financial projects, and assisting the sale of Palestine products. In the field of the spirit, Mizrahi would pursue an independent policy in the spirit of the Torah.[32]

Herzl, anxious to limit the influence of the Democratic Faction, had encouraged the Orthodox to unite and form a strong group within the organization. In order to facilitate its initial steps, he had made a personal contribution, and he later arranged financial assistance for them.[33] The Mizrahi on its part regarded it as its primary task to win adherents

---

* An abbreviation of the two Hebrew words *Merkaz Ruhani* (spiritual center); the full word also has the meaning *Easterner*.

to Zionism from among the Orthodox. Before long Mizrahi was recognized by the Zionist Congress as a world union within the World Zionist Organization, and was officially represented on the latter's governing bodies.

During Herzl's lifetime there was one further encounter between the Orthodox and their opponents. This took place at a well-attended and memorable congress of Russian Zionists held in Minsk in 1902. The proceedings were followed with great interest by the Zionist world. Ahad Ha'Am addressed the conference and suggested that an organization be set up, separately from the World Zionist Organization, that would concern itself with cultural work. Chaim Weizmann and his followers of the Democratic Faction, as well as many others, objected to the creation of a separate body, and advocated instead a cultural program to be undertaken directly by the Zionist organization. Nahum Sokolow urged that the Zionist organization declare Hebrew to be its official language, and that it proceed to found schools with Hebrew as the medium of instruction. Rabbi Reines, on the other hand, urged the conference to adopt no resolution on cultural work, since the rabbis would not agree to any cultural program unless it was implemented by them.[34]

The conference was faced with a serious crisis. A compromise was finally effected, following Ahad Ha'Am's alternative suggestion that the conference set up two distinct cultural commissions, representing the religious and the purely national points of view. Speaking on behalf of the Democratic Faction, Chaim Weizmann contended that his group was not anti-religious, and appealed for coexistence of the two schools of thought and cooperation between them within the framework of one organization.[35] The conference did in fact elect two cultural committees, but neither made any significant contribution to the actual promotion of cultural activities.[36] Still, the decision did have significant results, in that it made coexistence of the Orthodox and the non-Orthodox possible, and laid down the proposition that within the Zionist organization, "the state in becoming," there would be schools representing both views and that both would be the continuing concern and the responsibility of the Zionist movement.

It was now incumbent on Mizrahi to justify Zionism in the eyes of the Orthodox, and in particular their participation in a movement that was largely dominated by non-Orthodox elements. Rabbi Samuel Mohilever, replying to criticism, observed: "How surprising it is that some people great in Torah and in piety oppose the settlement of the Holy Land by the acquisition of lands and vineyards . . . on the ground that the young farmers do not observe the Torah. . . . For we have already written that the Almighty would rather have His sons dwell in His land, although they may not observe the Torah properly, than have them dwell abroad, and there observe the Torah."[37]

To substantiate this proposition, Rabbi Mohilever pointed out that *Yishuv Ha'Aretz* (settling in the Land) was one of the most important commandments of our Torah, and that some of the ancients had said that this commandment outweighs the whole Torah because it was the foundation for the existence of the nation.[38] In his message to the First Zionist Congress, Rabbi Mohilever restated his basic philosophy by saying that "the cornerstone of the love of Zion is the observance of the entire Torah, as inherited by generation after generation, without detracting from it or adding to it." He followed the formulation of this fundamental approach by adding: "I do not intend thereby to reprimand individuals for their behaviour; I wonder, in the words of our sages, if there exists in our generation anyone who has the right to reprimand."[39]

He reiterated this opinion in a letter written shortly before his death: "The foundation for the love of Zion is our holy Torah . . . and therefore it is incumbent upon the leaders of the Zionists, in the pursuit of their national task, to seek to avoid a situation where Zionism may incur slander, as has recently happened, on the ground of Torah violation. It is true that we do not inquire into the personal conduct of any individual who joins us in working on behalf of our people and our land—we are brothers in distress, and brothers shall we be at the time of our revival."[40] In reply to some critics who attacked him violently for his association with nonobservant Jews, Rabbi Mohilever wrote: "Supposing a fire broke out, and there were danger to life and property, would you not accept with love and with pleasure the assistance of someone who, in your opinion, was guilty of non-observance? . . . And now, when we have found brothers in distress, who are stretching their hands out to us to beg us to do whatever is in our power to save our people . . . should we then repulse them?"[41] He went on to reprimand some of his Orthodox colleagues who belittled "the commandment of *Yishuv Eretz Yisrael,* which is a positive commandment that we in the Galut are obligated to fulfill. The argument that many of the settlers are not observant is true, and the Almighty knows how much it pains me to think that it is those who have become alienated from Judaism who are dedicating their lives to the rebuilding of the land, while the observant not only neglect this important commandment but even place obstacles in its way."[42]

The founders of Mizrahi were imbued with a sense of *Kelal Yisrael,* deep concern for the totality of the Jewish people. They preached tolerance toward the nonobservant, the secularists as they termed them, and did not disqualify them from the great venture. Rabbi Reines, one of the founders of Mizrahi, even hinted at an element of holiness that was inherent in the secularists. "There is no greater sacrilege than to allege that Zionism is part and parcel of secularism," he stated, "for the truth is that it is precisely the holiness of the land that induces the secularists to participate in the movement . . . it is in this that we may see the greatness of Zionism, for it has succeeded in uniting people of diverse views, and directing them toward a noble aim—the saving of the people—and this is its glory."[43]

It was such adherence of the Mizrahi to the principle of *Kelal Yisrael,* their consistent rejection of any separatist tendency, and their willingness to cooperate with the secularists that enabled them to secure a solid foothold for themselves within the Zionist movement in the Diaspora and later in Palestine. By propounding the proposition that Jewish nationalism was an aspect of Judaism and of the Jewish religion, the Mizrahi succeeded in harnessing the nationalist sentiments that had by then become prevalent in many Orthodox communities. Mizrahi did not, however, appeal to all Orthodox. The Hasidic rabbis and the masses of their adherents in the Russian part of Poland and in Galicia were at first indifferent and later even became hostile. The Old Yishuv and its rabbis were also unreceptive to Mizrahi, even as they were to political Zionism.

The program adopted at the Mizrahi conference in Pressburg in 1904 conceived of Judaism "as being at once religious and nationalist . . . concerned with the Torah of Israel, aspiring to the revival of both the people and the Torah in Eretz Yisrael. . . . The movement aims at reviving all that was good and useful, sacred and precious, noble and sublime which has been in Israel's possession from time immemorial." This meant to allude not only to the revival of Jewish religious law in general, but also to that of the Hebrew language.[44]

Rabbi Judah L. Fishman,* another of the founders of the Mizrahi, expounded the historical warrant for the supremacy of religious law in the future state. He set forth the theory that generally the state or the political system precedes the law; in fact, law is the creation of an organized state. For instance, the Roman state evolved Roman law in the course of centuries. The case of the Jewish people is, however, quite different, for the Law of the Hebrews preceded the Hebrew state. "The Hebrew state is the product of the Hebrew law. Before Israel had a king, it had laws, and before there was a state, there were already laws for that state which were handed unto Moses on Mount Sinai. . . . It is for this reason that the Hebrew state was not monarchic in the full sense of the word . . . for the King of Israel, absolute ruler as

* He later changed his name to Maimon.

he was, was nevertheless subject to the Law."[45] Consequently, no political authority would be able to change the objectives of the state, for the law, being divine, was the state's foundation and could not be changed.

This was a classical exposition of the nature and character of the future Jewish state as conceived by the Orthodox nationalists. Jewish religious law is not merely the law of ritual and religious observance; it is also civil law, criminal law, and family law—in short, it encompasses the entire legal system. For, says Rabbi Fishman: "We refer not merely to the Written Law . . . we refer, in particular, to the Oral Law."[46]* Just as this law preceded the Hebrew state of old and could not be altered because of its divine origin, so this same law, in all its ritual and legal aspects, would be binding on the future Jewish state. In fact, the very justification for the creation of a renewed sovereign state lay in its duty to accept in advance this whole Jewish corpus juris.

Rabbi Fishman, like other Mizrahi leaders, did not consider whether this law was compatible with the needs and norms of a modern state. Grand Rabbi Zadoc Kahn of Paris did indeed express such apprehension, but no attention was paid to him. There is no evidence in the Mizrahi literature of the time that this problem was even raised, let alone given due consideration. It was assumed axiomatically that the religious law could be made applicable to any future Jewish state. It may very well be that the very remoteness of the prospect of an independent state made any discussion of the problem seem unnecessary. This may also be he explanation for the failure of the secularists to raise the issue of theocracy in the future state. They hardly realized that the Mizrahi program, which called for full acceptance of the religious law, meant ultimately that the future state could not have ordinary powers to legislate, for the Jewish law, embodied in Torah and interpreted by the rabbis, could be neither altered nor modified by any legislative assembly. Being of divine provenance, it lent itself only to interpretation by persons competent to interpret it, namely, the rabbis.

Having been recognized as an autonomous world union within the World Zionist Organization, Mizrahi experienced little difficulty in coexisting with the secularist majority. One point of contention, however, was the foundation of the Herzliah High School in Tel Aviv in 1908. It was the first secondary school where Hebrew was the sole medium of instruction in all subjects, including the sciences. Even Ahad Ha'Am had expressed his doubts about the possibility of employing Hebrew in all subjects of instruction, but the founders persevered. This was not the only claim to fame of Herzliah (the name by which the school is

---

* The Talmud and the entire body of rabbinic jurisprudence, which is in itself the interpretation of both the Torah (the Written Law) and the Talmud.

known to this day). It was also the first Jewish secular and coeducational school in Palestine. No prayers were offered on the premises. The Bible was taught to boys with uncovered heads, and in the more advanced classes Higher Criticism* was employed to explain difficult biblical passages, and a historical rather than dogmatic approach to Judaism was adopted. Although the school was not founded by the Zionist organization itself but by individual Zionists, it was taken amiss by the followers of Mizrahi. As a result, they resolved to create a network of modern religious schools and in 1909 began by taking over the Tachkemoni School in Jaffa. This was to be a school in which general subjects would be taught, with Hebrew as the language of instruction and traditional Judaism as the general framework. The new Tachkemoni became the model for the later religion-oriented school system.[47] Jaffa, the urban center of the New Yishuv, thus became the first foothold established by Mizrahi. The Old Yishuv continued to be hostile both to the Mizrahi and to Zionism in general.

As an organization, Mizrahi was based on democratic rather than theocratic principles. Its leaders on the local, national, and international levels were democratically elected. Periodic conferences were held and reports were rendered. In the organizational realm, rabbis enjoyed no special privileges; the leadership included rabbis and laymen. At first Mizrahi admitted no women to its own organization but it participated in the general Zionist institutions to which women were admitted. The Mizrahists fought stubbornly and consistently for their principles, but however great the provocation, they always stayed within the fold of the World Zionist Organization.

At the Tenth Zionist Congress held in 1911, a resolution was adopted making cultural and educational work obligatory and calling for the establishment of a Hebrew University. This loomed as a far more serious step than the establishment of a high school. Mizrahi summoned a world conference in Berlin to define its attitude to this resolution, which at the time seemed likely to see early realization.** A number of delegates suggested that Mizrahi secede from the Zionist organization. The motion was defeated by a large margin,[48] but a minority, most of them members of the Frankfurt branch, did secede. The majority remained determined "to fight from within with the utmost persistence and vehemence against any educational project which would be devoid of religious and traditional content."[49] They were nevertheless moved to stay because of their longing for "a general national renaissance that

---

* Higher Criticism denies the Mosaic authorship of the Torah and instead suggests a variety of literary sources and authors.
** The University did not, in fact, come into being until 1925.

would embrace all parts of the nation, with all its trends and groups," and thus they would become partners in the upbuilding of the land and the revival of the nation.[50] They undertook the planning of an educational school system in Palestine that would be at once modern and religious, and would include a modern Yeshivah for the training of rabbis.

This decision firmly attached Mizrahi to the Zionist movement, in whose rapid development it shared. The minority who had seceded from the Mizrahi eventually founded Agudat Israel.

E. THE ESTABLISHMENT
OF AGUDAT ISRAEL

The nucleus of Agudat Israel* and its initial driving force came from German neo-Orthodoxy, and from the leadership of the Free Union for the Interests of Orthodox Judaism (Freie Vereinigung fuer die Interessen des orthodoxen Judentums), founded in 1885 at the instance of Rabbi Samson Raphael Hirsch. It took the initiative in organizing anti-Zionist Orthodox Jews on an international basis. In 1909, Rabbi Salomon Breuer of Frankfurt had arranged a meeting, in which Orthodox rabbis from Russia and Hungary also participated, to discuss ways and means of combating the emergence of secularism in Jewish life. The "cultural" controversy at the Tenth Zionist Congress in 1911 and the consequent secession of some of the Mizrahi spurred the drive for a worldwide organization. In 1912 a founding convention was held in Kattowitz (Silesia). With some three hundred delegates present, the World Agudat Israel was officially established. Its program was summed up in its manifesto, which stated: "The Jewish people stands outside the framework of the political peoples of the world, and differs essentially from them: the Sovereign of the Jewish people is the Almighty, the Torah is the Law that governs them, and the Holy Land has been at all times destined for the Jewish people. It is the Torah which determines all the actions of Agudat Israel."[51]

Agudat Israel experienced considerable difficulties in organizing its diverse elements into one body; its members differed in their political and cultural backgrounds and consequently also in their attitudes toward Jewish communal organizations. For instance, the Hungarians and some of the Germans insisted on leaving the general Jewish communities and forming their own separate Orthodox enclaves. This conflict was eventually resolved by allowing each branch of Agudat Israel to define its own policy for the country in which it operated. There were

---

* "Community of Israel."

also marked differences between the adherents of Agudat Israel in Russia, Poland, and Lithuania on the one hand, and those in Germany on the other. The former dissociated themselves completely from Western culture, opposed the teaching of general subjects in the schools, and retained their traditional garb; the latter followed the teachings of Samson Raphael Hirsch and, while meticulously observing the minutiae of the religious law, adapted themselves to Western culture and dress, used the German language rather than Yiddish, and attended German universities. In the early years of Agudat Israel, the influence of the German group with its superior economic, social, and cultural attainments, was predominant. After the defeat of Germany in World War I the center of the movement shifted to Poland where, unlike in Germany, Agudat Israel became a movement of the masses. This was largely due to the direction and guidance of the Hasidic dynasties. The Hasidim of Gur, numbering tens of thousands, became the most significant and powerful single group within the movement.

The ideology of Agudat Israel was also reflected in its organizational pattern. While the internal set-up of Mizrahi was along democratic lines, that of the Agudah assumed a somewhat different form. There was the *Kenessiah Gedolah* (Grand Assembly), consisting of delegates representing local groups. This assembly chose the Central World Council, the Executive Committee, and finally the *Moetzet Gedolei HaTorah* (Council of Sages). It was the function of the latter body of learned rabbis to judge whether any action of Agudat Israel ran counter to the religious law, which was to govern all aspects of Jewish life even as a constitution governs a nation. The Council of Sages acted as a Supreme Court, which had the authority to invalidate all decisions of the elected representatives. Thus the organizational structure of the Agudah contained a theocratic principle, and although at times pressures from below found ways of asserting themselves, the principle of the supremacy of the Council of Sages was never questioned and its rulings were adhered to.

Unlike Mizrahi, Agudat Israel rejected any cooperation with non-Orthodox groups in the Diaspora. It therefore rejected, in many instances, the Zionist organization because it included non-Orthodox elements, even as it rejected its basic ideas because they purposed to force the hand of the Almighty in bringing about the Redemption. Although the Agudah considered living in the Holy Land a divine commandment, it took no practical steps to encourage their followers to settle there. It regarded the Old Yishuv as embodying that religious way of life that should be expected of every Jew in the Holy Land.

Although Mizrahi and Agudah agreed on many points, all attempts at reconciliation, or even at a modus vivendi, met with failure. Indeed,

Mizrahi leaders always stressed that they were at one with the Agudah in stressing the paramount place of Torah in all phases of Jewish life. They vehemently denied even the slightest deviation from Orthodoxy on their part.[52] The divergence between Mizrahi and Agudah was due to their conflicting approaches to the nature of Jewish nationalism. The founders and earlier ideologists of Agudat Israel were German Jews who had absorbed the view then prevalent throughout Germany that Jews were members of a religious group and did not constitute a nation. In this respect they agreed with their bitterest opponents, the Reform Jews. Like the latter, the founding fathers of the Agudah viewed Jews and Jewish groups through the spectacles of religion only. They would not regard a nonobservant Jew as one with whom one could cooperate on any meaningful level. They therefore practiced separation from the non-Orthodox community and, in Germany and Hungary, set up their own religious institutions with their own rabbis. They objected to a revival of the Hebrew language, because nonobservant Jews promoted it and used it for profane purposes. Similarly, the Agudists considered the work of the Palestinian settlers as a profanation of the Holy Land, while the Mizrahists held that the holiness of that Land lent such workers a degree of sanctity.[53] Although religion was both the raison d'être of the nation and the instrument for its preservation, even those who did not share this view retained their membership in the nation.[54] To the Mizrahi the concept of *Kelal Yisrael* embraced the totality of Israel and its role in the land of Israel.

Thus the emergence of the Jewish problem in the closing years of the nineteenth century gave rise to a diversity of ideologies and organizational formations. Religion played a prominent role in the debates and constituted an important ideological factor from the beginning. While the proliferation of ideas and organizations had taken place mostly in the Diaspora, with the Second Aliyah, early in the century, matters changed. The New Yishuv now became the main stage on which the Old World controversies were reenacted with renewed vigor.

F. THE SECOND ALIYAH

The term *Second Aliyah* refers to that wave of immigration to Palestine, predominantly from Czarist Russia, which began with the revolutionary movement and the ensuing pogroms of 1903–1906 and came to an abrupt end with the outbreak of World War I. The total number of immigrants of this period was about forty thousand, but a large number left again because of poor economic opportunities and the severe hardship of the pioneering life. However, those who stayed on and endured transformed the Yishuv more than the First Aliyah had been able to do and laid the foundations of a new social, cultural, and political order. Its impact dominated the life of the Yishuv for the next two generations and contributed a major share to the ideological background of the present state. It was an immigration of young people who were deeply frustrated when the Russian revolution of 1905 collapsed. They were tired of theoretical discussions, and decided to change the unvaried routines of their life. They left their old homes in order to realize in the old-new land those ideas which they had so ardently debated in the Diaspora. The radical approach to problems that characterized so many of the young intellectuals in the Russian realm was now transplanted to backward and Ottoman-ruled Palestine, where it struck deep roots and gave the Yishuv a new image. The new immigrants were part of that generation of Russia's Jews who during the decades preceding World War I made the rapid move from one intellectual world to another; from the old tradition-bound religious life of synagogue, cheder, and yeshivah, to the secular world of Russian radicalism, a transformation as swift as the cataclysmic changes that were convulsing that vast empire. It was a revolutionary generation that accepted few of the old axioms and was ready to experiment with new social ideas and forms of social organization, and to do so with singular dedication and fervor.

The First Aliyah, which had scored pioneering feats in the agricultural settlement of Palestine, had come to a virtual standstill in the closing years of the old century. The hardships its members had encountered, the frustrations inherent in agricultural experimentation, and the limited funds at their disposal had slowed their early élan. They were employing cheap Arab labor in a number of settlements, which began to threaten or even obliterate their Jewish character. There were other problems with which the settlers seemed incapable of coping. Their pioneering drive seemed exhausted so that, even though their economic position was improving somewhat by the turn of the century, they appeared unable to overcome an emotional stagnation. At this difficult juncture the Second Aliyah began. It was a movement of individuals, not organized or directed by the Zionist organization or any other body. The immigrants were predominantly unmarried young men and fewer women, political radicals, many of whom were escaping punishment by the Czarist government for revolutionary activities. Still others were members of self-defense groups formed during the pogroms of 1903–1906 to protect Jewish life and property. To these explosive elements of the Second Aliyah were added middle-class elements of strong nationalist spirit. Some of these had capital and skills and were looking for an opportunity to become productive in a modern Jewish community.

The Second Aliyah thus proceeded along a wide front; it affected not only the agricultural but also the urban basis of the country. It conceived of the Yishuv as a national-political unity, the vanguard of a vast movement that would found a modern Jewish society in Palestine within the framework of national autonomy. It gave rise to a network of secular elementary and secondary schools where the Hebrew language was the sole medium of instruction. It gave further rise to political parties and democratic institutions that had been transplanted from the old countries, and it created the nucleus of a self-defense force by organizing its watchmen into a group known as HaShomer.* Its purpose was to protect the lives and property of the settlers.

The outstanding development in urban pioneering took place in 1909, when Tel Aviv was founded on the sand dunes north of Jaffa, the first new city in Palestine and the first all-Jewish city in the world. By 1914 Tel Aviv had some two thousand inhabitants, and was regarded as the cultural and political center of the New Yishuv. It was a self-contained municipal unit, administered by elected representatives. It was characteristic of its secular spirit that the new city did not employ an official rabbi; later on, Haifa followed the same practice. For a while Jaffa, which was the port of entry for new immigrants, developed faster than the other towns, and by 1914 it had ten thousand Jewish inhabitants. It became he center of the incipient labor movement and thereby of the first resident political parties in Palestine. Poalei Zion (Workers of Zion) was a Marxist party preaching class struggle, while HaPoel HaTzair (Young Workers) was a populist, nondoctrinaire labor movement that stressed the importance of physical toil and attachment to the soil as a precondition for both political and spiritual rehabilitation. From these groups came the impulse for social experimentation and the establishment of the first kevutzah—Deganiah —a communal settlement that was the forerunner of the kibbutz.**

In 1913 the New Yishuv gave open and organized expression to its nationalist spirit. For some time it had viewed with some disfavor the numerous schools maintained by Jewish philanthropic organizations, because they employed foreign languages as the medium of instruction. In the school of the Anglo-Jewish Association in Jerusalem, English was used; French in the schools of the Alliance Israélite Universelle; and German in those of the Hilfsverein der Deutschen Juden. In 1911

---

* The watchman.
** Kibbutz and Kevutzah both come from a root meaning *to gather.*

a number of Russian Zionists initiated a project for the setting up of
an engineering college in Haifa; the Hilfsverein and other German philanthropists associated themselves with the project, and a joint board
was established to administer it. When the building neared completion,
the question of the language of instruction came to the fore. Contrary
to the wishes of the Zionist board members, it was decided to let two
languages be used in the college, Hebrew for general subjects and German for the sciences. The New Yishuv was up in arms, demanding exclusive instruction in Hebrew. There ensued a "war of languages," and
most of the teachers employed by the Hilfsverein, who themselves were
imbued with a nationalist spirit, resigned their posts. The agitation resulted in a spontaneous movement for the establishment, with the aid
of the Zionist organization, of a school network with Hebrew as the
sole language of instruction.[55]

The Second Aliyah gave rise to several Hebrew periodicals and to
a literature reflecting the mood of the New Yishuv. The novelist Chaim
Yosef Brenner rejected Orthodoxy as irrelevant to the new type of Jew.
He was severely criticized by Ahad Ha'Am, who was not prepared to
endorse the total repudiation of the Jewish religion.[56] Other publicists
in *HaPoel HaTzair*, the Labor weekly, also went to great lengths rejecting religion in all its forms. This was the time when the voice of
A. D. Gordon began to be heard. Gordon had been a white-collar employee in Russia, but on his arrival in Palestine he became a farm hand
and later settled in Deganiah, the first cooperative. He endowed the
new secularist mood with spiritual content. In his essays he proclaimed
that the redemption of man, and of the Jew in particular, could come
about only through physical labor on the land. He saw a mystical bond
between the Jew and the soil of Palestine, and in the toil of Jewish
hands he detected therefore an ennobling element. His philosophy, often referred to as the Religion of Labor, infused into Jewish nationalism a spiritual component that expressed the ideals of a pioneering
community whose supreme form of self-fulfillment could be its attachment to and continual physical contact with the land.[57]

The Old Yishuv, too, gained new adherents in the period between
1882–1914, when immigration from Eastern Europe was at its height.
In numbers it was still the majority. On the eve of World War I, the
Old Yishuv counted about sixty thousand souls, and the New Yishuv
about twenty-five thousand, half of whom were settled on the land, with
the remainder in Jaffa, Tel Aviv, and Haifa, and a few in Jerusalem.
Yet, small though the New Yishuv was in numbers, it developed in
miniature the attributes of a modern and forward-looking society, and
in the following decade, outpaced the Old Yishuv numerically, socially, and politically.

G. CONCLUSION

While "the Jewish Problem" was not in itself an innovation in Jewish history, the feeling of its acuteness in the closing decades of the
nineteenth century assumed such dimensions as to call forth a debate
on a variety of solutions, each expressing or implying a distinct concept
of the nature of the Jewish people and its identity. Each of the solutions advanced had to consider the role of religion in modern Jewish
life.

The classical Reform and the Orthodox, although differing in their
interpretation of Judaism, regarded the Jewish people as a community
of believers, a religious community. They differed in their solution, for
while the Reform considered that human progress as conceived by liberal-minded people, would bring about the disappearance of the Jewish
problem, the Orthodox awaited the arrival of the Messianic age. Both
rejected a territorial solution by the restoration of a Jewish commonwealth and eschewed the concept of Jewish nationalism. The Bundists
and the followers of Simon Dubnow, the Folkists, were at one in viewing the Jewish people as a nation and in their rejection of a territorial
solution, but they differed in their attitude to religion: while the former
rejected religion and sought to promote a secular Yiddishist culture,
the latter viewed religion as a significant aspect of the Jewish cultural
heritage, but not the exclusive content of that heritage.

The political-territorial solution advanced by the Zionists, as formulated in the Basle Program of 1897, was before long constrained to
confront the religious issue. Hard as Herzl tried to sidetrack this issue
and to exclude any Zionist activity that might give rise to it, he failed
to achieve this objective. While all those who joined this movement adhered to the concept of Jewish nationhood, differences as to the content
of that concept asserted themselves. Because of the wide appeal of the
Zionist movement, many shades of opinion within this movement made
their appearance. Along with ardent socialists, there were middle-class
liberals. Along with secularists, there were Orthodox, and the confrontation between the latter two came early to the fore.

In his desire to preserve the unity of the World Zionist Organization, Herzl, having failed to avoid the religious issue, encouraged the
Orthodox elements within the movement to organize themselves into
a political party within the Organization. By this act of statesmanship,
Herzl not only assured the unity of the movement, but also made it
possible for the Orthodox to join it and participate in its activities. The
unity of the movement survived the crisis of 1911, when, following the
adoption of a cultural program by the Zionist organization, the Mizrahi
was placed in a critical dilemma when some of their members, in pro-

test against the adoption of this program, withdrew and joined in the establishment of the anti-Zionist Agudat Israel. This period also witnessed the beginning of the evolution of a compromise on the thorny issue of the "cultural program," leading to the emergence of two school systems in Palestine, both under the aegis of the World Zionist Organization, one of which was religious and the other designated "general." This compromise, achieved for the sake of Zionist unity, set a significant precedent of far-reaching importance for the future.

Parallel to the grand debate on the solution for the Jewish problem began the Second Aliyah to Palestine, motivated by the conviction that the need of the hour called for implementing a solution rather than discussing it in the abstract. Unlike the First Aliyah, which was largely traditional and politically inarticulate, the Second Aliyah was of a different character. It was politically minded and, being largely secularist, it offered a direct challenge to Orthodoxy. The Second Aliyah laid the foundation for a vigorous and purposeful modern community, which before long undermined the supremacy of the Old Yishuv.

3

The Problem of Religion
in British-Ruled Palestine
1918-1948

A. WORLD WAR I

World War I changed the course of Jewish history, creating a new reality that no one could possibly have foreseen. The four war years, the social and political cataclysm in Russia which up to then had encompassed the largest community of Jews in the world, and the changes resulting from the peace settlements transformed Jewish existence beyond recognition. The war was the major cause of the decline of Europe as the center of the Jewish people and the concomitant rise to prominence of the Jewish community in the United States, and it was the underlying cause of the emergence of Palestine as a new center of Jewish life and creativity.

What Jewish effort and endurance had laboriously built up in Palestine in the course of the preceding thirty years seemed doomed to destruction when the war broke out. Turkey, which at first maintained neutrality between the warring parties, joined the Central Powers in November 1914. Palestine became a battlefield when the Turco-German forces attempted to capture the Suez Canal and met the British armies moving up from Egypt in prolonged and bloody battles. In the process Palestine was thoroughly impoverished, and especially so its Jewish community, which suffered greatly because of its peculiar political and economic structure. At times the Yishuv seemed on the verge of destruction.

Shortly after the outbreak of war the Turkish government announced the abolition of the capitulations regime, and the majority of the Yishuv who were dependent on the protection of the foreign consuls found themselves suddenly at the mercy of Turkish officials. Jews who were subjects of any of the Allied Powers were offered the alternative of becoming Ottoman subjects (and as such serving in the Turkish army), or of leaving the country. Many accepted naturalization, for which they had to pay a high fee, and then underwent the rigors of military service. Some left the country, and many others were deported. In January 1915, the Turkish Commander-in-Chief in Syria and Palestine issued a manifesto against certain "subversive elements" that were said to aim at the creation of a Jewish government in the Palestinian part of the Ottoman Empire.[1] He proclaimed all Zionist institutions illegal and closed them down, including the Anglo-Palestine Company, the principal Zionist bank. He forbade the use of Hebrew and tried to disarm the Jewish settlers. In 1917 a group of young Jews were discovered to have organized an intelligence service, known as NILI, on behalf of the advancing British armies. Many arrests followed and some were executed.

The economic effects of the war were disastrous, for Palestine quickly found its essential ties with Europe severed. The funds that had sustained the Old Yishuv dried up, for Russian Jewry, which had provided the bulk of Halukkah money, was in no position to transmit funds to enemy aliens. For the Old Yishuv this spelled dire poverty, starvation, disease, and death. The New Yishuv, too, was adversely affected, although on a less drastic scale. War and blockade shut off the overseas markets for its principal export commodities—citrus fruit, almonds, and wines —on which the agricultural communities depended. The year 1915 saw a locust plague of unusual severity, which ravaged the vegetation of the country. To these difficulties were added army requisitions, which often approximated devastation, and the direct effects of battles fought in Southern Palestine.

That the Yishuv managed to survive at all was largely due to the economic assistance afforded by the Jews of America until the spring of 1917, when the United States entered the war on the side of the Allied Powers. Up to then it could still bring political pressure on the Turkish authorities not to apply in Palestine the extreme repressive measures against non-Islamic peoples that had been introduced in the Ottoman Empire during the war years. On August 30, 1914, the Provisional Executive Committee for General Zionist Affairs headed by

Louis D. Brandeis issued a call for an Emergency Fund, and this lead was followed by other Jewish groups in America. The money collected was sent to Henry Morgenthau, the American Ambassador to Turkey, and was transmitted to Palestine. Early in 1915 the American coaler *Vulcan* arrived in Jaffa with a supply of foodstuffs.

Both Henry Morgenthau and Abram J. Elkus, his successor as Ambassador in Constantinople, intervened repeatedly with the central Turkish authorities in behalf of the Jews of Palestine. The situation deteriorated seriously after America entered the war and severed diplomatic relations with Turkey. Thereafter the protection of the Yishuv against the excesses of the Turkish military was left to the German government, which did exert itself on behalf of the Jewish population through its representatives in Constantinople and Palestine. Zionist leaders in both places were given the opportunity of communicating with the Central Zionist Office in Berlin through German diplomatic channels, and Zionist emissaries moving between Berlin and the Turkish capital were protected by German diplomatic passports. Particularly effective was the German intervention when the NILI espionage group was uncovered and the Turkish authorities were about to take extreme measures against the whole Yishuv.[2]

Without American and, later, German friendly intervention, the Yishuv might not have managed to survive the war. Still, the losses it suffered were great. In 1918, the victorious British army found the Jewish population reduced by a third; a total of fifty-six thousand survived in a state of impoverishment and, in the case of the Old Yishuv, of absolute destitution.[3]

The outbreak of the war also interrupted the normal activities of the World Zionist Organization, whose adherents were found both in the countries of the Allied Powers and in those of the Central Powers. The Central Council of the World Zionist Organization met in neutral Copenhagen in December 1914 and decided to observe strict neutrality between the warring camps; they were aware of the importance of avoiding any action that might antagonize Turkey, in whose hands lay the fate of the Yishuv, or of Turkey's ally, Germany.[4]

As the war proceeded, Zionist leaders on both sides realized that in the wake of the great upheaval there would be opportunities for placing the Yishuv on a new political basis. Acting on the assumption that the Ottoman Empire would be dismembered as a result of the war, Chaim Weizmann and Nahum Sokolow in England, and Louis D. Brandeis in America sought to obtain from the Allied Powers a declaration of support for Zionist aspirations in Palestine. A series of well-coordinated diplomatic moves on the part of Zionist leaders in London, Paris, Rome, and Washington resulted in a declaration issued on behalf of the British government on November 2, 1917. This statement, since known as the Balfour Declaration, gave political legitimization to the centuries-old dream of the Jews: "His Majesty's Government view with favour the establishment in Palestine of a national home for the Jewish people, and will use their best endeavours to facilitate the achievement of this object, it being clearly understood that nothing shall be done which may prejudice the civil and religious rights of existing non-Jewish communities in Palestine, or the rights and political status enjoyed by Jews in any other country." It was the first time since the loss of Jewish sovereignty in A.D. 70 that a great power had given official recognition to the Jews as a nation and to their right to a home of their own.

Public opinion in the allied countries received the Declaration with satisfaction as an act of justice due to a long-suffering people. Jews throughout the world, including those in Germany and Austria-Hungary, welcomed it with jubilation. Even the Reform rabbinate in the United States of America could not dissociate themselves from the enthusiasm that greeted the Declaration. Although reiterating the view that "the ideal of the Jew is not the establishment of a Jewish State," the Central Conference of American Rabbis nevertheless noted "with grateful appreciation the declaration of the British government by Mr. Balfour as an evidence of goodwill toward the Jews. We naturally favor the facilitation of immigration to Palestine of Jews who, either because of economic necessity, or political or religious persecution, desire to settle there."[5] So strong was the impact of the Declaration that the Germans and Austrians pressured Talaat Pasha, the Grand Vizier of Turkey, to make a pronouncement in favor of free Jewish immigration into Palestine and of local self-administration.[6] He made the statement in December 1917, but by that time Jerusalem and Southern Palestine were already occupied by the British army, and in September 1918 the whole country was wrested from the Turks, bringing to a close four hundred years of Ottoman rule in Palestine.

While the war was still in progress, Dr. Chaim Weizmann secured the authorization of the British government for the despatch to Palestine of a special commission, which would include Jewish leaders in allied countries and would be "an advisory body to the British authorities in Palestine in all matters relating to Jews, or which may affect the establishment of a National Home for the Jewish people."[7] The most immediate object of the Zionist Commission was to afford relief to the starving and impoverished Yishuv, to assist in the repatriation of the deported and evacuated, and to aid in organizing a united Jewish community that would be able to confront the task of building up a national home. The commission reached Palestine on April 4, 1918, and soon found that one of its more difficult tasks would be to bridge the wide gulf between the Old Yishuv and the New.

B. ATTEMPTS AT UNITING THE YISHUV

The concept of a national home was altogether novel. No definition for it was ready at hand in international law or practice. To the Jewish masses in their enthusiasm, a national home seemed synonymous with a sovereign state; at the very least, it would be a transitional stage to statehood. Anticipation was running high, and a feeling of deliverance was in the air. Palestine had been emancipated from Turkish misrule and was to be placed under the benevolent rule of an enlightened nation, whose government had committed itself to restore the Jews to their ancient land.

The sober minds in the Yishuv recognized the task ahead as Herculean. The country was in a state of devastation, and the Yishuv seriously reduced in numbers. Immigrants had to be attracted and cared for and practically everything had to be rebuilt. The Russian Jewish community, the largest in the world, was in the throes of the Communist revolution, civil war, and the inevitable pogroms. The tiny Yishuv now regarded itself as the nucleus of the newly proclaimed national home and the vanguard of thousands of Jews in search of a home. Its first obstacle was a not-too-friendly British military administration, which ruled the country until the middle of 1920. Even more important, if the Yishuv was to be equal to the tasks awaiting it, it had to be united; the barriers separating the New Yishuv from the Old had to come down. Now that the capitulations system had been abolished and separate Jewish groups could no longer seek protection from consular representatives of foreign powers, it was only with a united front that the Yishuv could hope to assert its rights vis-à-vis the new government. While the New Yishuv, at least, possessed a common nationalist spirit, the Old Yishuv was split into Kolelim, and the Sefardim formed an entity of their own. When the Balfour Declaration was issued and General Allenby's armies invaded Palestine, the old anti-nationalist Yishuv still constituted the majority of the Jewish population. They welcomed the material relief afforded by the Zionist Commission headed by Weizmann; they could not fail to perceive, however, that the new groups of Jewish leaders who were arriving from Europe under the aegis of the British government were decidedly of the type they so much resented in the New Yishuv. Chaim Weizmann himself fully realized the seriousness of the continuing rift and endeavored to conciliate the Old Yishuv and to draw it into the arena of general Jewish activity. It was clear to him and his colleagues that the British colonial administration might otherwise try to play off one group against the other, to the detriment of both.

In order to promote a better relationship with the Old Yishuv, the Zionist commission allocated subventions for the maintenance of the Yeshivot and of Talmudei Torah (traditional Orthodox school for boys), which were in great distress because of the interruption of the flow of Halukkah. Chaim Weizmann went a step further, and meeting the heads of Yeshivot in Jerusalem on May 13, 1918, he offered additional financial assistance if the Yeshivot were to introduce the Hebrew language. Weizmann was conciliatory and stressed the importance of Yeshivot in Palestine, which would have to replace the Yeshivot destroyed by the new regime in Russia, and he urged his listeners to adopt a friendlier attitude to the new Yishuv. He repeated his appeal to a gathering of Jerusalem rabbis held the following month. Great as was their financial distress, the Yeshivot rejected Weizmann's request to introduce Hebrew, which they regarded as a step toward religious reforms. Instead, in order to be independent of the emerging modern Yishuv, they attempted to rejuvenate the Halukkah system, and all of Weizmann's further attempts to bring about a measure of reconciliation between the Old Yishuv and the Zionist organization failed.[8]

If the Yishuv was to become the nucleus of a national home, it needed an organization altogether different from its European and Turkish models. The old system whereby the Hakham Bashi was the ecclesiastical and lay leader of the Jewish community was obsolete. The Millet system of the Ottoman Empire and the "Gemeinde" of Germany and Austria were also based on the religious structure of the community. The New Yishuv found this unacceptable for a potentially sovereign nation. It required a wide range of autonomy formally recognized and legally established by the colonial power. A democratically elected representative assembly of the Jews of Palestine could now come into being. Ideally, such an assembly would enjoy autonomy in matters of education, health, and social welfare, with adequate powers of taxation both nationally and locally, in the predominantly Jewish towns and settlements. If with increased immigration and the internal growth of the Yishuv the Jews were in time to become the majority of the population of Palestine, this national autonomy would eventually expand into full-fledged sovereignty. This was the plan of Zionist leaders and, consequently, the achievement of unity within the ranks of the small Yishuv was deemed essential for the achievement of autonomy in the National Home.

Immediately after the conquest of Palestine by the British, a conference of representatives of Jewish settlements and other communal leaders met in Petah Tikvah on November 19, 1917, for the purpose of convening a fully representative convention.[9] Soon after the conquest of Jerusalem, another more representative assembly was convened in Jaffa, in order to consider the establishment of a general organization of Palestinian Jewry. Since the northern part of Palestine was still under Turkish rule, the meeting elected a provisional committee charged with the task of arranging for the election of delegates to a constituent assembly, which in turn would be empowered to decide on the formation of a permanent organization and constitution. Elections to the constituent assembly were to be direct, equal, and by secret ballot; the question of female suffrage was raised, but no decision on it was taken.

Half a year passed and Northern Palestine was still held by the Turks. A second preparatory assembly, at which representatives of the Jews of Jerusalem also took part, was convened in Jaffa in July 1918. Dr. Chaim Weizmann, Chairman of the Zionist Commission, addressed the assembly. He stressed the importance of unity in facing the challenges and opportunities created by the Balfour Declaration. Again, the delegates resolved to call a constituent assembly, but the debate on the qualification of voters caused dissension. The Orthodox, who on this occasion were more numerous, strongly opposed giving women the right to vote, their opposition being based on religious grounds. After a lengthy debate it was decided that all persons aged twenty-one and over, whether male or female, were entitled to vote; the question of the right of women to be elected was left in abeyance. The bitter nature of the debate, however, weakened the hoped-for spirit of unity.[10]

The elections to the constituent assembly were scheduled to be held at the end of 1918. Before this could take place, the Armistice was declared in November and a peace conference was projected to which Palestinian Jewry expected to send representatives. It was therefore necessary to summon at once a fully representative assembly of the Yishuv, and for that purpose invitations were sent to every party, community, and settlement. The assembly took place in Jaffa on December 18, 1918, and was attended by one hundred and fourteen delegates, including soldiers from the Jewish battalions that were part of the British Expeditionary Force in Palestine. The assembly was designated as *HaMo'etza HaEretzyisraelit* (The Palestinian Council), but was in fact the third preparatory assembly.[11] It discussed the status of Palestine and the demands the Yishuv should make at the Peace Conference. Chaim Weizmann and Nahum Sokolow were elected to go to Paris as representatives of Palestinian Jewry. The question of female suffrage was again raised by the Orthodox, and again the debate caused considerable tension. This time women were granted the right both to vote and to be elected. The Orthodox faction realized that they were coming to be a minority and before long would be numerically overwhelmed by a non-Orthodox majority. In consequence, some Orthodox delegates threatened that they might not participate in the projected general Yishuv organization. They took the position that religious considerations were more important than questions of political unity.

The elections to the constituent assembly were postponed several more times. The leaders of the Old Yishuv in Jerusalem meanwhile resumed their campaign against female suffrage. The leaders of Mizrahi, who represented the Orthodox element in the New Yishuv and participated in Zionist Congresses and other Zionist gatherings at which they sat together with women, tried to persuade the Jerusalem Orthodox to take part in the constituent assembly. In order to appease them it was decided to change the name of the assembly from *constituent* to *elected* (*Asefat HaNivharim*), thus indicating that its decisions, whatever they might be, would not have the force of a constitutional decision, but might be changed by ordinary procedure at any subsequent meeting. The Mizrahi, however, failed to make the Old Yishuv leaders adopt a more conciliatory attitude.

In May 1919 it was announced that the Council of Ten of the Allied Powers assembled at the Paris Peace Conference had appointed a commission to proceed to the Middle East to ascertain the wishes of the peoples of the region regarding the choice of a mandatory power under whose tutelage the territories were to be placed. The Jews actively supported Great Britain's bid for the Palestine Mandate, while France and Italy demanded the internationalization of the Holy Land. In view of the impending visit of the commission (known as the Crane Commission), Palestinian Jewry decided to postpone the elections to the Assembly of the Elected in order to avoid the possibility that the Jewish leaders might be found at loggerheads with each other over the question of the choice of mandatory power. At that particular stage, the future of the Jewish National Home appeared closely tied to the selection of a mandatory power. Great Britain, being committed to the Balfour Declaration, was considered by Zionists as the best choice; internationalization, on the other hand, was regarded as a danger to Jewish aspirations. It appears that at least some of the leaders of the Old Yishuv in Jerusalem, desirous of curbing Zionist ambitions, had established contacts with the agent of the Italian Foreign Office in Jerusalem in order to work with him for internationalization rather than mandating Great Britain.[12]

The Orthodox in Jerusalem began an organized agitation in favor of forming a separate community unless the decision to grant female suffrage were rescinded.[13] Elections were at first postponed, in the hope of finding ways and means for a compromise, and were finally fixed for

October 26, 1919, but at the insistence of Chaim Weizmann were again postponed because dissension within the Yishuv would be harmful while the choice of the mandatory power was still pending. Only after it was clear that Great Britain would be awarded the mandate was it decided to proceed with the elections and a date was set.

The elections to the Asefat HaNivharim (Hebrew: Assembly of the Elected) were held throughout the country on April 19, 1920, except for Jerusalem, where elections were held on May 3. Of the twenty-six thousand registered voters, some twenty-two thousand went to the polls.[14] The Orthodox in Jerusalem arranged their own polls, from which women were excluded. The election rules provided that every eighty voters were entitled to one delegate at the Asefat HaNivharim while the Orthodox claimed a delegate for every forty voters, since women would not vote. As a result of this arrangement, two hundred and sixty-three delegates were elected in the general polls, and fifty-one in the special Orthodox polls; of the two hundred and sixty-three delegates, the Zionist-oriented religious parties (Mizrahi, Young Mizrahi, and Progressive Orthodox) secured thirteen delegates, about five percent of the total votes cast.

The opening of the Asefat HaNivharim took place in Jerusalem on October 7, 1920, and was a solemn occasion. In order to assure unity, the Assembly voted to admit the fifty-one Orthodox delegates elected in the separate polls in Jerusalem as full-fledged members of the Assembly. The latter at once introduced a motion that this Assembly should confine its deliberations to formulating a new election law for another assembly to be convened within six months, "based on the religious spirit and the ancient Jewish tradition."[15] The motion was rejected. The Assembly elected an Executive Committee, the Va'ad Leumi (National Committee), to carry on the affairs of the Yishuv until the next session, which was to be held not later than May 31, 1921. The Va'ad Leumi was directed to draft for submission to the second session a set of rules regulating the elections to the Elected Assembly and to the local communities, and also to draft a general constitution for the internal organization of Palestine Jewry.[16] Since the question of female suffrage had not been finally decided, the Old Yishuv representatives stayed on.

Even at this first session of the Assembly, the aspirations and principles guiding the Yishuv were already clearly enunciated. The Assembly proclaimed itself as the "supreme authority for dealing with the public and national interests of the Jewish people in Palestine," and as its sole representative for internal and external affairs. It proclaimed that it had "laid the foundation for the national autonomy of the Jewish people in Palestine." It charged the Va'ad Leumi with the task of obtaining recognition by the government of Palestine. Conceiving of national autonomy in wide terms, the Assembly requested the Va'ad Leumi "in consultation with rabbis and expert jurists" to draft proposals for the setting up of Jewish courts of law, for the consideration of the second session.[17]

The newly elected Va'ad Leumi submitted these resolutions to Sir Herbert Samuel, the first High Commissioner for Palestine. The delegation that waited upon him urged that the Palestine government grant official recognition to the Elected Assembly and the Va'ad Leumi as its executive organ. In his reply dated October 24, 1920, the High Commissioner indicated that the government of Palestine would be prepared to accord recognition as requested, provided that the Assembly retained its representative character by giving assurance in the future of the support of the bulk of the adult Jewish population, it being clearly understood by the Assembly that it would not be within the scope of its authority "to deal with matters affecting the whole of Palestine, but merely to deal with the internal matters of the Jewish community."[18] Sir Herbert also added a significant proviso that such recognition would not prevent any sect, group, or individual, of any faith, from applying to the government in connection with any matter, nor from lodging any complaint.[19]

The White Paper of 1922, promulgated by the then Colonial Secretary, Winston Churchill, which set out guidelines for British policy in Palestine, confirmed that the term *Jewish National Home* implied a wide measure of self-government. It attempted to describe this term, which was without precedent in international law:

> This community has its own political organs: an elected assembly for the direction of its domestic concerns, elected councils in the towns, and an organization for the control of the schools. It has an elected Chief Rabbinate and a Rabbinical Council for the direction of its religious affairs. Its business is conducted in Hebrew as a vernacular language, and a Hebrew press serves its needs. It has its distinctive intellectual life, and displays considerable economic activity. This community, then, with its town and country population, its political, religious and social organization, its own language, its own life, has in fact "national" characteristics. When it is asked what is meant by the development of a Jewish National Home in Palestine, it may be answered that it is . . . the further development of the existing Jewish community with the assistance of Jews in other parts of the world, in order that it may become a centre in which the Jewish people as a whole may take, on grounds of religion and race, an interest and pride.[20]

Still, it took nearly eight years before official recognition was accorded to the Assembly and the Va'ad Leumi as the official organs of

Jewish self-government in Palestine. When finally granted it was severely circumscribed in scope and consequently limited in its effective-
ness. It was evident that the Churchill White Paper took the term *National Home* to be far broader than a religious community, and the
autonomy to be enjoyed by it was far more comprehensive than the
Turkish Millet system had provided. The Home was "national" in the
sense that it contained most of the attributes of a nation; religion was
merely one of its several facets. The latter aspect, however, gave rise
to tension and barred progress toward unity. This was soon demonstrated in the next issue that called for a solution, the creation of a
chief rabbinate that would enjoy official recognition and exercise statutory powers.

C. THE ESTABLISHMENT
OF THE CHIEF RABBINATE

On April 24, 1920, the Supreme Council of the Peace Conference,
meeting in San Remo, had resolved that the Balfour Declaration be incorporated in the Treaty of Peace with Turkey, and that the Mandate
for Palestine be allotted to Great Britain, subject to the approval of the
League of Nations that was about to come into being. This paved the
way for the termination of military rule in Palestine and its replacement
by a civil administration. Shortly thereafter the British government appointed Sir Herbert Samuel, a prominent Anglo-Jewish statesman, as
High Commissioner for Palestine; he had taken an active part in the
developments that had led to the issuance of the Balfour Declaration.
On July 1, 1920, Sir Herbert Samuel landed in Jaffa to inaugurate the
civil administration and, in accordance with Article 2 of the Mandate
of Palestine, to place the country "under such political, administrative
and economic conditions as will secure the establishment of a Jewish
National Home."

The Jews received the appointment of a Jewish High Commissioner
enthusiastically. They were gratified to hear him read a royal message
in which the Balfour Declaration was reiterated. A few weeks later, on
the Sabbath following the fast of the Ninth Day of Av (which com-
memorates the destruction of the Temple), the High Commissioner attended a service in the Hurvah Synagogue in the Old City of Jerusalem. When he read from chapter 40 of Isaiah, the portion traditionally
chosen for the day—"Comfort ye, comfort ye, my people"—the worshipers were electrified. It was as though the Messianic era had dawned.
Eager anticipation was in the air.

The terms of the British Mandate were set out in an instrument unanimously approved on July 22, 1922, by the League of Nations. Although Palestine was being administered like a colony, and was in fact under the jurisdiction of the Colonial office in London, the Mandate set some limitations on the powers to be exercised by the Mandatory. Among these were several provisions dealing with religion. Article 9 provided: "Respect for the personal status* of the various peoples and communities and for their religious interests shall be guaranteed." The Mandatory Power was enjoined to retain the Turkish system under which religious minority groups—the various Christian denominations and the Jews—had enjoyed a measure of religious and cultural autonomy, primarily through their own religious courts for the adjudication of matters of marriage, divorce, adoption of children, inheritance, and charitable endowments. Palestine was no ordinary country; it was the Holy Land, inhabited by adherents of the three principal monotheistic religions, who jealously safeguarded their rights and vested interests. Under the circumstances it was deemed best to leave the Turkish system undisturbed.

In line with the principle of cultural autonomy, Article 15 of the Mandate stipulated that "the right of each community to maintain its own schools for the education of its members in its own language, while conforming to such educational requirements of a general nature as the Administration may impose, shall not be denied nor impaired." English, Arabic, and Hebrew were declared to be the official languages of Palestine (Article 22). Article 15 also guaranteed "complete freedom of conscience and the free exercise of all forms of worship." Article 23 provided: "The Administration of Palestine shall recognize the Holydays of the respective communities in Palestine as the legal days for the members of such communities."

Thus, the Articles of the Mandate applied the term *community* not to the Arab and Jewish peoples, but to religious communities, that is, to Moslems, Christians, and Jews. These operative clauses seriously altered the concept of Jewish National Home as appearing in the preamble of the Mandate and in Article 2, which clearly implied a nation and a home for that nation.[21] Whether the Jewish community in its national home was a nation or a religious group gave rise to a long-standing controversy within the Yishuv, as well as between the Yishuv and the Palestine Administration.

In the course of Sir Herbert Samuel's High Commissionership a civil administration came into being. The courts of law were modernized, a Western-style judiciary was set up, and many of the Turkish laws were replaced by legislative enactments borrowed from British law and procedure. Since there was no elected legislative body, the country

---

* I.e., family laws.

was governed by the High Commissioner, assisted by an Executive Council consisting of the heads of the government departments. These, as well as all senior civil servants, were British colonial officials, while the middle and lower echelons were recruited from the Arab and Jewish population. The High Commissioner exercised legislative as well as executive powers, subject to instructions issued to him by the Secretary of State for the Colonies, in London, and further subject to the provisions of the Mandate.[22]

In retaining the Turkish system of religious courts for the adjudication of matters of personal status, the civil administration found the Jewish community to present certain difficulties. The Hakham Bashi who had been appointed by the Sultan was recognized by the Sefardim only. The Ashkenazic Jews had no central ecclesiastical authority, and their religious courts (Batei Din) had no official status. When Chaim Weizmann visited Palestine in 1918 and 1920, he tried to persuade the rabbis to create a central rabbinic authority, but to no avail.[23]

In the autumn of 1921, Sir Herbert Samuel appointed a committee of rabbis and laymen, headed by Attorney-General Norman M. Bentwich, to study the problem of creating a central rabbinical authority. The committee recommended the convening of an assembly (two-thirds rabbis and one-third laymen) to elect two Chief Rabbis, one Ashkenazi and one Sefardi, and a Rabbinical Council. A thorny problem arose because the Palestine government insisted that there be established a rabbinical appellate court in addition to district courts as courts of the first instance. The rabbis contended that, in accordance with Jewish religious law, the judgment of a Bet Din is final, and is not subject to appeal. The government, however, refused to give way, insisting that a court of appeal was essential in order to remedy possible mistakes in judgments and thereby give litigants additional confidence, knowing that their cases might receive further consideration. The rabbis of the Old Yishuv also refused to yield on this point, and did not participate in the Assembly. Realizing that the government would not otherwise give recognition to any rabbinical ecclesiastical court, the other rabbis agreed to the setting up of a court of appellate jurisdiction.[24]

This Assembly was a solemn occasion. The High Commissioner addressed it in person. He expressed the hope that the Assembly would be a blessing to the whole Jewish community, and that those who would be elected to high office "would be leaders in the full sense of the word," who would "enjoy the confidence of the community, as well as possess the qualities usual in persons in whom authority is vested." He expressed regret that it was necessary to elect two Chief Rabbis, and hoped that before long the largest possible degree of unity would be achieved. He reminded the assembled rabbis that Palestine and Jerusalem were foremost in the affection of the fourteen million Jews scattered throughout the world. Hinting at the disunity engendered by the Orthodox, he pointed out that "unity and good will on the soil of Israel is the first step for fostering unity and good will among our dispossessed and scattered people."[25]

Norman Bentwich, the Attorney-General, also addressed the conference and presented the report of the Commission, of which he was chairman. He expressed the hope that the Rabbinical Council would "foster peace and fellowship" among Jews. He specifically suggested that when the rabbis would apply "the fundamental principles" of Jewish religious law, they would do so "in accordance with the demands of justice and equality of the present era."[26] Here was an appeal to the rabbis to bear in mind the "present era," and his mention of "equality" was to remind his hearers that in Jewish religious law women were subjected to legal disabilities. The Attorney-General therefore hoped that the rabbis would be guided by "the fundamental principles" of the law, rather than by its details. A Rabbinical Council of eight rabbis was subsequently established; four of them were Sefardim and four were Ashkenazim and from these eight, two Chief Rabbis would be selected. The two Chief Rabbis elected were Yaakov Meir for the Sefardim and Abraham Isaac Kook for the Ashkenazim.

Following the setting up of the rabbinate, the government of Palestine announced that "the appointment of Hakham Bashi no longer exists in Palestine," and that "no person is recognized by the government as a Chief Rabbi in Palestine except the Rabbis elected by the Assembly." Official recognition was accorded to the Rabbinical Council elected at the Assembly: "The Government of Palestine will recognize the Council and any Bet Din (religious court of law) sanctioned by it, as the sole authorities in matters of Jewish law." It would execute through the civil courts judgments given by the Bet Din as a court of first instance and judgments given on appeal.[27]

Thus, by dint of law, the Jewish religion became an established religion for the Jews of Palestine. In an important legal sphere, the religious law became binding on Jews and the Rabbinical Council was made its sole authority. By implication, the Jewish religion was equated with Orthodoxy, and Jewish religious law was to be interpreted by Orthodox rabbis.*

The scope of this jurisdiction was set out in Article 5 of the Palestine Order-in-Council, 1922, as follows:

---

* Similar jurisdiction was accorded to the ecclesiastical courts of the several Christian communities. Wider jurisdiction was bestowed on Moslem religious courts, as was the case in the Ottoman Empire, where Islam was not merely "recognized" (a Millet), but was the established religion.

"The Rabbinical Courts of the Jewish Community shall have:

(a) Exclusive jurisdiction in matters of marriage and divorce, alimony and confirmation of wills of members of this community, other than foreigners as defined in Article 59.

(b) Jurisdiction in any other matters of personal status of such persons, where all the parties to the action consent to their jurisdiction.

(c) Exclusive jurisdiction over any case as to the constitution or internal administration of a Wakf or a religious endowment constituted before the Rabbinical Courts according to Jewish law.[28]

The exclusive jurisdiction conferred on the rabbinical courts in matters of family law and confirmation of wills was limited to Jews who were not nationals of a foreign state. The British government apparently felt that it would not be fair to impose a religious law on residents of Palestine who were not citizens of Palestine. Thousands of Jews living in Palestine had retained foreign nationality, and could thus contract civil marriages before consular officers. Marriages contracted abroad and decrees of divorce issued abroad were recognized as valid by the civil courts of Palestine, which unhesitatingly applied the principles of private international law. Furthermore, the rabbinical courts could assume jurisdiction in all other matters of personal status only with the consent of all parties concerned; otherwise these matters were dealt with by the civil courts. To meet the wishes of those who hoped to see the rabbinical courts developing Jewish law in general, and not merely in the area of personal status, the rabbinical courts were later given the authority to "arbitrate in accordance with the provisions of the Arbitration Ordinance in force from time to time in any dispute arising between Jews, where a written submission of the parties has been obtained."[29]

The rabbinical courts and the Chief Rabbinate were thus the creation of the British authorities in Palestine. The Mizrahi and the New Yishuv in general, as well as the leadership of the Zionist organization, promoted the rabbinical establishment, hoping that it would lead the Old Yishuv to become an integral part of a unified community. This hope failed to materialize. The leaders of the Old Yishuv in Jerusalem, who from the early twenties had regarded themselves as the Palestinian branch of the ultra-Orthodox World Agudat Israel, rejected the Assembly and the Rabbinical Council, refused to accept their authority, and set up their own Bet Din. The Sefardic Jews, on the other hand, did acknowledge the authority of the Rabbinical Council, and in spite of occasional controversies made themselves part of the organs of Jewish self-government.

As it subsequently transpired, the Rabbinical Council, headed by the two Chief Rabbis, played a rather minor role in the development of religious life in Palestine during the thirty years of British rule. The growing secularization of the Yishuv was not conducive to the development of Orthodoxy. The dissension that occasionally developed between the Ashkenazic and Sefardic rabbis did not serve to enhance the standing of the rabbinate. The first Rabbinical Council was elected for three years, but when it became impossible to reach agreement on procedures for the election of a new Rabbinical Council, the same rabbis stayed in office for over twelve years. The Old Yishuv leadership, now identified as Agudat Israel, disowned the official rabbinate as a creation of the Mizrahi, and accused it of association with the secularists; at one time some of their extremists assaulted the widely revered Rabbi Kook.

Mizrahi, on the other hand, consistently supported the Chief Rabbinate, and sought to strengthen its prestige as a means of promoting religious Zionism and combating the separatist activities of the Agudat Israel. The secularists paid little attention to the rabbis, whether official or otherwise. The Chief Rabbis on their part failed to cultivate a meaningful relationship with the Yishuv and its democratically elected institutions.[30] Their occasional utterances on public issues were concerned with violations of ritual observance rather than with moral issues. Thus, lacking widespread public support and isolated within its own milieu, the official rabbinate played a marginal role in the life of the Yishuv.

D. THE FUNCTION OF RELIGIOUS LAW

The failure of the Rabbinical Council to live up to the expectations of its founders and supporters was to a large extent due to circumstances inherent in Jewish religious law. It is worth examining them in some detail.

This law is "religious" in the sense that it is attributed to Divine Revelation, as embodied in the Torah (the first five books of the Bible) and as authoritatively interpreted by the rabbinical authorities from ancient times until today. Until the rise of the Haskalah this *corpus juris* was the national law of the Jewish people. It encompassed not only statutes dealing with moral rules, religious observances, and ritual, but also the entire field of civil and criminal law.

The religious law is generally referred to by its Hebrew term, Halakhah, a term referring to the proper road by which one must walk. The laws that are embodied in the Torah are referred to as the Written Law, whereas later interpretations and regulations were termed the Oral Law.

Together they constituted the Halakhah. The Oral Law was incorporated into the Mishnah, which represents the endeavor of several generations of jurists to apply the ancient principles to their own times, and which was given definite form at the hands of Rabbi Yehuda Ha-Nasi toward the close of the second century C.E. It contains orderly exposition of the Halakhah as taught in the academies. The post-Mishnaic scholars, known as the Amoraim, further expounded the Law, and their teachings in turn served as the basis for the compilation of the Talmud. The Palestinian Talmud was edited at the end of the fifth century, and the Babylonian a century later. From then on, the Talmud was regarded as the authoritative and comprehensive statement of the Halakhah. Since the Talmud was not drawn up in the form of a systematic code, many attempts were made to codify it, to order it (and the rulings based upon it) into a codex. The two greatest codifications were those of Maimonides, which was compiled toward the end of the twelfth century, and of Joseph Karo, in the middle of the sixteenth century. The latter's monumental work, the Shulhan Arukh (The Set Table), became the standard Halakhic code.

The rise of Jewish nationalism in modern times brought about a renewed interest in the application of Halakhah to contemporary issues. This resulted in the creation of scholarly works on the evolution of Jewish law and of Jewish arbitration tribunals to which Jews were urged to refer their disputes. This was encouraged by the Zionist Organization, which tried to promote an institution for the revival of the Jewish law. These courts, known as "courts of peace," to which Jews would resort voluntarily, functioned alongside the Turkish courts and later, for some years, alongside the civil courts of Mandatory Palestine. The rabbinical courts in turn urged the faithful to bring their disputes before them for adjudication.

However, these attempts to revitalize Halakhah as the Jewish national law failed, both in the case of the rabbinical courts and in that of the courts of peace. The latter ceased to function early in the Mandatory period, for the great majority of the Yishuv was content with the British administration of justice. The rabbinical courts, although endowed with governmental authority in Palestine, failed to make themselves a vital part of a growing and creative community. The roots of this failure are to be found in the nature of Halakhah as it was interpreted and applied.[30]

Halakhah had flourished for centuries in the Diaspora and had enjoyed a vigorous development. This was possible because it possessed flexibility and adaptability to changing circumstances. Although deprived of a territorial base, Halakhah developed as the core function of living communities endowed with internal autonomy. The political framework of the corporate medieval state allowed for the Jewish enclave to be in the state but not of the state. The disciplined Jewish community lived largely by its own law, which the rabbis, through their interpretations, applied to concrete situations and changing circumstances. Thus the theory that the Halakhah was divinely instituted and therefore not subject to change by legislation, did not prevent its development, which Menahem Elon has described as follows:

> The source of the Halakhah is Heaven; its place, its life, its development and formation, is not in Heaven, but in the life of man and mankind, in the life of society. The Halakhic scholars saw no inconsistency in all this, since they believed whole-heartedly that in their interpretative work, their amendments, innovations and creativeness, they were merely giving expression to a further part of the revelation at Sinai, a task which had from the very beginning been assigned to each generation for its own requirements. In the words of the Midrash: "Not the prophets alone received the prophecy at Sinai, but each scholar of every generation received his part at Sinai."[31]

The French Revolution and the Emancipation brought about the disintegration of Jewish autonomous life in Europe. The traditionalists fiercely resisted this process, but found it eventually irresistible. "Among the Jews themselves, the communal leadership fought almost to the very end to strengthen the internal autonomous structure of the Jewish community, and their control of it. The price for the equality, the ending of all formal separation on the part of the Jews, was not paid easily and as a matter of course," says a contemporary historian.[32] Emancipation spelled the decline of the judicial autonomy, and this in turn dealt a paralyzing blow to the development of Halakhah. In Western and Central Europe, Jews began to have recourse to the civil courts; rabbinic functions were confined to matters of marriage and divorce, and in countries where separation of Church and State obtained, these remaining functions of the rabbinate declined further.

Even the traditional Jewry of Eastern Europe showed signs of weakening adherence to the Halakhah. Although many still resorted voluntarily to *Din Torah*, that is, litigation and adjudication according to religious law, the "decisions of the rabbinical courts became more and more arbitral awards and compromise settlements, lacking the semblance of judgment under a living and organic law. . . . The destruction of Jewish legal autonomy since the spread of Emancipation brought about a radical change in the character of Jewish law. It ceased to be a living and developing law. Unfortunately, this decisive historical event occurred in the course of the nineteenth century, which also saw a social, economic, and industrial revolution that gave rise to a spate of new legal problems. It is sufficient merely to mention the vast developments in company, commercial, tort and contract law, and the decisive changes in wide areas of public and international law."[33]

Thus circumstances drove Halakhic scholars to concentrate on rules governing ritual observances, such as Kashrut and Sabbath observance, and on family law. Lacking wider scope and working within narrow confines, the Halakhah as a national law became increasingly inflexible; by assuming primarily a ritualistic direction, it became estranged from current demands and became essentially ecclesiastical, something it had not been hitherto.[34]

The establishment of self-government within the framework of a Jewish National Home could have afforded a unique opportunity for resuming the interrupted development of Halakhah; this opportunity, however, was missed. On assuming the office of Ashkenazic Chief Rabbi, Abraham I. Kook indicated that he was aware of the need to adapt the Halakhah to new conditions. "The Jewish legal system," he said, "has two main foundations: law (*dinim*) and rules (*takanot*). In the form of law, we connot make any changes in the prescribed system; but by way of *takanot* there is freedom to initiate and amend what the courts by majority approval find necessary in the interest of public order, and with genuine religious intention. Scholars of every generation have enacted many important takanot. . . . In our renewed national life in Eretz Israel there will at times certainly be high need to make important takanot which, as long as they are consented to by the majority of competent scholars and are then weighed by the community, will carry the force of the law of the Torah."[35]

Rabbi Kook (1865–1935) was an extraordinary personality. He made the effort to understand the idealism of the builders of the National Home and, by attributing to it an aspect of holiness, attempted to interpret it to the Orthodox. In 1904 he had arrived from Lithuania and had become the Rabbi of Jaffa and the surrounding settlements. He spent the years of World War I in Switzerland and England and returned to Palestine in 1919. In 1920 he was elected one of the two Chief Rabbis and shortly thereafter founded a Yeshivah in Jerusalem, which differed from the other Talmudic academies in that the language of instruction was Hebrew and not Yiddish, and also in that Jewish philosophy in addition to the Talmud was studied.[36]

It was Rabbi Kook's teaching that Jewish nationalism and Jewish religion are not distinct and self-sufficient entities. Both together constitute the "unity of the Jewish spirit," and a division of the two "would falsify both the nationalism and the religion, for every element of thought, emotion and idealism that is present in the Jewish people belongs to an indivisible entity, and all together make up its specific character. . . .

Any individual element in the Jewish spirit cannot help but include all the values that the sunderers [i.e., the secularists] hope to forget and to destroy." He did not despair of the secularists, because "the values they attempted to banish were nonetheless present, if only in an attenuated and distorted form, in their theories."[37]

Addressing himself to the Orthodox, Rabbi Kook pointed out that "it is even a greater error to imagine that such a sundering could possibly succeed: it is, therefore, pointless to wage a bitter and ill-conceived war against those who are loyal to only one aspect of the Jewish character. If the only bar to separating the various spiritual elements that are present within the congregation of Israel were that this is prohibited by the law of the Torah, then we would indeed be duty-bound to resist them to the very end. But since such a sundering is an absolute impossibility, we can rest assured that its protagonists can err only in theory, but not in practice. No matter what they think, the particular element of the Jewish spirit that they make their own, being rooted in the total life of our people, must inevitably contain every aspect of its ethos."[38]

To Rabbi Kook, the secularists did not reject Judaism, but merely stressed and preached one aspect of it, namely, nationalism, and he held that this aspect, too, partakes of the divine. "The spirit of Israel is so closely linked to the spirit of God that the Jewish nationalist, no matter how secularist his intention may be, must despite himself, affirm the divine."[39] Addressing himself to the Orthodox diehards, Rabbi Kook warned that "to oppose Jewish nationalism, even in speech, and to denigrate its values, is not permissible, for the spirit of God and the spirit of Israel are identical. What they must do is to work all the harder at the task of uncovering the light and holiness implicit in our national spirit, the divine element which is its core. The secularists will thus be constrained to realize that they are immersed and rooted in the life of God, and bathed in the radiant sanctity that comes from above."[40]

In word and deed Rabbi Kook endeavored to build a bridge to the secularists, and to maintain a dialogue with them. He justified his willingness to discourse with his opponents: "Moderation is not indifference, and does not counteract the struggle for the attainment of victory for one's own truth. It does not mean, however, that if you believe you are in possession of the truth, you are either bound or entitled to eliminate or to do away with him who holds another belief. And if it is true that there is but one truth, it is still worth your while to listen and to pay attention to what all sort of persons may have to say."[41] In reply to some of his followers who complained of the total rejection of ritual observances on the part of the Halutzim, Rabbi Kook replied: "When the Temple existed, no one was admitted to the Holy of Holies, except the High Priest, and even he would not enter, except once a year on Yom Kippur, when he would don priestly garments, white garments. But when the Temple was under construction, any working man could enter in, on any day and at any time and at any hour, in the working clothes of an ordinary working day."[42]

Even though Rabbi Kook enjoyed a wide and devoted following, his hope of making the Halakhah a living force by interpretation and, when necessary, by court legislation, did not come to fruition. There was little support on the part of other rabbis, some of whom feared the displeasure of the Agudat Israel and its single-minded adherents. Even in matters of personal status, which were assigned to their exclusive jurisdiction, the rabbis displayed little initiative and imagination. They found it far easier to dwell on problems of ritual and issue exhortations to the nonobservant. Before long Halakhah, for so long the undisputed Jewish *corpus juris,* appeared in the public mind as being concerned primarily with matters of family law and the minutiae of ritual.

E. THE GROWTH AND CHARACTER OF THE NATIONAL HOME

With the establishment of the Civil Administration, there began an almost uninterrupted period of Jewish immigration into Palestine. During the thirty years of British rule from 1918–1948, a half million Jews entered the land, bringing their population from one-tenth of the total population to one-third. This influx of newcomers transformed the Yishuv into a dynamic society that created a flourishing cultural, economic, and political life. It changed Palestine itself from a backward and primitive country into the most advanced in the Middle East. This immigration altered the character of the Yishuv and endowed it with the characteristics of a closely knit national entity. In the closing years of British rule the Jewish National Home became a state-within-a-state, with the result that, when independence came in 1948, the transition to sovereign statehood was accomplished with relative ease.

The most remarkable development took place in the field of agriculture. Large tracts of malaria-infested land were drained and some two hundred and fifty new settlements were established. The Jewish farming population, which numbered some twelve thousand in 1914, grew more than tenfold by 1948. No less remarkable was the industrial development; the newcomers, the majority of whom hailed from Eastern and Central Europe, brought skills and capital with them, so that when the Middle East was cut off from its sources of supplies during World War II, Palestine became the chief supplier of manufactured goods to the countries of the region. An educational system, kindergarten to University, was now at the disposal of the Yishuv, with Hebrew as the medium of instruction.

With the rise of Nazism, Palestine became the principal refuge for the victims of persecution; from the beginning of 1933 until 1939 Palestine absorbed more than 60,000 refugees from Germany, and their contribution to the cultural and economic development of the National Home was inestimable.[43] Although the Yishuv was predominantly an immigrant community, beset with the daily problems of making a living in a difficult environment, it developed social cohesion and a deep sense of national solidarity, which enabled it to survive attacks from without and to overcome formidable political difficulties.

The Yishuv withstood a nationwide attack by the Arabs in 1929; then came the warlike years of 1936–1939, when the Arabs had the support of Nazi and Fascist agents. The Jews assured their physical survival by gradually evolving a clandestine self-defense organization (called Haganah, from a word meaning "defense"). The Haganah consisted entirely of volunteers and developed in the World War II years into an efficient fighting unit and eventually served as the basis of the Defense Army of Israel.

Of the three principal waves of immigration of the period, the Third Aliyah (1920–1922) consisted chiefly of agricultural pioneers; the Fourth Aliyah (1923–1926) mainly of members of the urban middle-class; and the Fifth Aliyah (1932–1939) largely of refugees from Nazi persecution who went to both the cooperative settlements and the cities. Of these, the Third Aliyah, although a small minority in the total number of immigrants, became a dominant element and shaped the image of the National Home. Its twenty-two thousand immigrants stemmed largely from Russia,[44] and its Halutzim* dominated the Yishuv spiritually as well as politically. They infused the emerging nation with a spirit of dedication and afforded it purpose and drive. The pioneering movement had begun in 1917 in Russia, amid the intense ideological controversies attending the Communist October Revolution. The Jewish youth of the era were radicals; their aspirations knew few limits and their optimism no boundaries. They aimed not only at creating a home for the Jewish people, but also at transforming society itself, providing it with a totally new way of life based on social justice and equality of reward.

Joseph Trumpeldor, the only Jewish officer in the Czarist army and a member of the Second Aliyah, had initiated Halutziut** in Russia. Soon the movement reached some hundred and twenty localities.

---

* Pioneers. From this the term *Halutziut* is derived.
** Pioneering movement.

The Communist government restricted its activities and later persecuted it, and by 1924 had driven it underground. Many of the Halutzim managed to leave Russia, and it was they who constituted the majority of the Third Aliyah. From Russia the movement spread to the border states and especially to Poland. By 1935 it numbered some ninety thousand organized and trained young people, who were committed not only to Aliyah and the performance of physical labor, primarily in agriculture, but also to the acceptance of the authority of the Zionist organization and the study of the Hebrew language. Training camps for Halutzim were established throughout Eastern and Central Europe, where some twenty thousand at a time were being trained in farming as they waited their turn for immigration certificates to Palestine. The Third Aliyah was further distinguished by its large proportion of university students and graduates. These were the men who built the first roads, drained the swamps in the Jezreel Valley, and established the first settlements of the postwar period. From their ranks came many of the Haganah membership. They developed the *kibbutz,* an egalitarian form of society, and the *moshav ovdim,* a smallholders' settlement bound together by extensive cooperation. The Third Aliyah extolled physical labor and considered tilling the soil as man's most praiseworthy pursuit.

In order to redress the social imbalance found in Diaspora Jewry, which was predominantly middle-class, the Halutzim set out to create a Jewish labor class that would eventually transform the Yishuv into a workers' society and would be self-employed in that it would own the means of production. The model of the workers' society was the kibbutz, and it was based on voluntary association. It was this volunteer aspect that characterized not only the great pioneering enterprise of reclaiming the inhospitable soil, but also the formation of the Haganah and other organizations of the Jewish National Home. "Without compulsion, Halutzim have abandoned the psychologically easier road of individualism, and pooled their efforts to create a new society founded on political democracy and economic equality. They have refused to impose the collective way of life on anyone; all are free to come or go. They have refrained from becoming dogmatic about any single form of co-operative or collective. . . . It is not a matter of ethics; it is a matter of faith in the moral potentialities of man, and in the power he possesses to make the most of his life. Nor is it simply humanism, for the faith involves nature as well as man in the pattern of optimism. . . . The burden of Halutziut is the burden of all liberal religious philosophies, namely, that life is worthwhile, worth fighting for and living for, and that man and nature are so constituted as to make possible the achievement of the highest human goals. Halutziut emerges as this-worldly religious philosophy."[45]

The Halutzim were moved by a quasi-religious spirit, and indeed their devotion to the arduous pioneering tasks often had the intensity of religious experience. To the Orthodox, however, they appeared to be irreligious, if not altogether anti-religious. In the new kibbutzim religious observances and kashrut were ignored; the Sabbath was not observed; no synagogues were built, and to the extent that the Festivals were celebrated at all, they were given a distinct national and social bent. Passover became the Spring Festival, and the traditional Haggadah was replaced by new versions, from which references to God were omitted. Shavuot (Pentecost) was celebrated as the Festival of the First Fruits, and Sukkot (Tabernacles) as the Harvest Festival. In the kibbutz schools the Bible was taught as the outstanding literary and ethical expression of the Hebrew spirit, while all references to divinity were explained as ancient mythology. Contacts with the rabbinic authorities were avoided as much as possible, and common-law marriages were the order of the day. Programmed secularism had its base in the kibbutzim and it soon informed the general climate of the Yishuv, where Halutziut became for many a substitute for religion.

The Mizrahi, although well organized and dedicated to the promotion of a network of modern Orthodox schools, was no match for the new mood that was sweeping the Yishuv. The adherents of Agudat Israel regarded these new developments as calamitous to the cause of religion and, finding the trend irreversible, withdrew into their own shell. With Jerusalem as its center, Agudat Israel isolated itself and in fact lived as a small minority, self-ghettoed in the midst of their own brethren.

The Palestine administration enacted no legislation on matters of religion as such. Under the provisions of the Municipal Corporations Ordinance, the Local Council of Tel Aviv in 1926 had enacted a bylaw providing for the closing of shops on Sabbaths and Jewish holidays, while exempting from its provisions the few Christians and Moslems residing within the municipal boundaries. Two years later, the Supreme Court of Palestine invalidated this by-law on the ground of its inconsistency with Article 15 of the Mandate, which provided that "no discrimination of any kind shall be made between the inhabitants of Palestine on the ground of race, religion or language."[46] In 1937, the Municipal Council of Tel Aviv enacted another ordinance providing for the closing of shops on Sabbaths and holidays, but this time without reference to non-Jews. This by-law was upheld by the Supreme Court and was followed by similar enactments in the other Jewish towns. In cities with a mixed Arab-Jewish population, such as Jerusalem, Jaffa, and Haifa, no such regulations were enacted, although the Jewish-owned shops and factories closed on religious holy days. In the all-Jewish city of Tel Aviv the bus service did not function on the Sabbath, while in Haifa, with a mixed population, it remained in operation. In purely Jewish areas post offices and other government departments, except the public utilities, were closed; in places with a mixed population, individual adherents of the three religions stayed away from their offices during their respective days of rest. Thus, in the mixed towns, Jewish members of the police force generally rested (there being others to maintain order), while in Tel Aviv and other Jewish towns they carried on their duties. To the majority of the Yishuv, Sabbath observance had a social rather than a religious significance, while the festivals of Passover, Shavuot, Sukkot, Hanukkah, and Lag B'Omer* assumed the character of national holidays.

F. THE STRUGGLE
FOR NATIONAL AUTONOMY

Communal Structure

The difficulties involved in securing a legal framework for the Yishuv sprang from two sources: the lack of unity within the Jewish community, which was largely the result of differences of opinion between the ultra-Orthodox and the bulk of the Yishuv, and the insistence of the British government on treating the Jewish population of Palestine as a religious rather than as a national entity.

There were several attempts to secure a legal status for Jewish self-government. In a memorandum submitted to the High Commissioner by the Va'ad Leumi on December 7, 1922, it was pointed out that the Yishuv, consisting of Jews from so many different countries, needed an officially recognized autonomous framework. This required the enactment of a law that would recognize a communal organization to which all Jews would belong and would enjoy the rights of a legal person. Its governing bodies should be empowered to levy taxes for the satisfaction of communal needs.[47]

Objections to this project were raised by the Rabbinical Council and by Agudat Israel. The objection of the Rabbinical Council was directed not against the proposed constitution for Jewish autonomy, but against the failure of the proposed draft to deal with the authority of the rabbinate, its budget, and its mode of elections. The Va'ad Leumi maintained that these matters should be left to later decisions by the governing organs of the community. The objection of Agudat Israel

* The 33rd day after Passover, a festive day popular for marriages.

was directed against the very idea of setting up a general organization for the Yishuv that would enjoy statutory powers and would be the sole representative body of Palestine Jewry. It presented its views not only to the High Commissioner and to the Colonial Office in London, but also to the Mandate Commissioner of the League of Nations. The proposed constitution, the Agudah pointed out, would give women the right to vote and would not recognize the formal supremacy of religion; both these points were fundamental to the Agudat Israel. They insisted constantly that the Jews were not a national but a religious group, and reiterated their demand that they, Agudat Israel, be allowed to organize a separate community officially recognized by the government.[48] The Mandate Commission devoted a good deal of attention to these representations, and the Attorney-General of Palestine, Norman Bentwich, assured Agudat Israel leaders that the proposed constitution would not compel all Jews to participate in the community.[49]

Several disagreements developed between the Yishuv and the British administration. The former demanded that it be obligatory for every Jew to be a member of the community. In order to meet objections to this demand, the draft constitution proposed by the Va'ad Leumi made provision for the satisfaction of the religious and cultural requirements of minority groups. It was hoped that this provision would satisfy the British and also meet the needs of Agudat Israel, who would then be enabled to maintain their institutions within the framework of the general organization of Palestinian Jewry. But the Agudah would not agree and the British rejected the principle of the obligatory nature of membership in the community, and could not be moved from this position by the representations of the leaders of the Yishuv or of the Executive of the Zionist Organization.

A further difference of opinion arose from the demand of the Yishuv that it be given the right to impose direct taxes upon the members of the Jewish community. The Va'ad Leumi asserted that it would be impossible to maintain a network of schools and social services for the Jews of Palestine on the basis of voluntary contributions and drew the attention of the British government to its obligation to facilitate the establishment of a national home. Such a home, said the Va'ad Leumi in its memorandum, must aspire to become self-supporting and free the Diaspora from the heavy burden of helping to support the educational, medical, and other services of the community. "Where shall we obtain all these means, unless we possess the basic right—possessed in many countries where the Jews do not enjoy a special status—of imposing taxes by the free will of the community?"[50]

There was finally the question of recognizing the overall organization of the Yishuv as a legal personality, capable of holding property,

of being a party to litigation, and generally enjoying the rights accorded
to a legally established corporate entity. This point was conceded by
the British, while on the other matters lengthy negotiations took place
between the Va'ad Leumi, and the Palestine administration and the
Colonial Office.

At the end of 1923, the Palestine government submitted to the
Va'ad Leumi a draft proposal of a constitution for the Yishuv. Unlike
the draft of the Va'ad Leumi, which conceived of the Yishuv as a national entity in the sense that it would be self-governing and democratic,
with the rabbinate being one of its several institutions, the government
draft treated the Yishuv primarily as a religious community. It granted
the ecclesiastical authority not only prominence but also powers which,
in the opinion of the Yishuv, should belong to an Elected Assembly.
The government draft provided that only those Jews who would voluntarily recognize the constituted community would be subject to its jurisdiction. The right of the community to levy taxes was denied, but it
would be recognized as a legal personality. This draft was rejected by
the Va'ad Leumi.

Female Suffrage

The Orthodox continued to insist that women be not given suffrage,
and the controversy over this issue further hindered all attempts to
present a united front to the British. In October 1923, the leaders of
Mizrahi suggested that the issue be submitted to a referendum, at which
all adult males of the Yishuv would be entitled to vote. This suggestion
gave rise to an acrimonious debate, and Mizrahi threatened that without
such a referendum they would withdraw from the community. Fearing
an irreparable split within the Yishuv, the Va'ad Leumi decided to
hold a referendum in which, however, both men and women would be
entitled to participate. The date for this was fixed for November 8,
1925.[51] Agudat Israel issued a public statement opposing female suffrage
under all circumstances and enjoined their followers to boycott the referendum. Thereupon the Mizrahi leaders declared that such a boycott
would defeat the purpose for which they had suggested the referendum,
namely, to keep all Jews within the framework of the organized community. The referendum, they stated, had now become unnecessary and
the Va'ad Leumi, with the agreement of Mizrahi, therefore decided to
cancel the referendum. This occurrence marked the final break between
the great majority of the Yishuv, including Mizrahi, and Agudat Israel.[52]

Now that the issue of female suffrage was definitely settled, voting
for the Second Elected Assembly was held on December 6, 1925. The
Yishuv had doubled in numbers since 1920, and the number of eligible

voters was now 64,764. Of these, 57% availed themselves of their franchise; the rather low percentage of participants was probably due to the various delays, the unfamiliarity of many women with polling procedures, and to the Agudat Israel boycott. Two hundred and twenty-one deputies were elected; nineteen were Orthodox, including six who belonged to Torah ve'Avodah (the Mizrahi labor wing), which for the first time appeared as a separate group, although it remained part of the World Mizrahi movement.[53]

The Religious Communities Organization Ordinance

The Yishuv was now in a better position to negotiate a final settlement with the government. Three years of further negotiations, as well as Dr. Weizmann's personal intervention with the British Secretary of State for the Colonies, brought about a compromise. The framework for the constitution was incorporated in an Enabling Act promulgated by the High Commissioner on February 15, 1926, under the title of "Religious Communities Organization Ordinance."[54] The ordinance was preceded by a preamble that included the phrase, ". . . each Religious Community recognized by the government shall enjoy autonomy for the internal affairs of this Community, subject to the provisions of any Ordinance or Order issued by the High Commissioner for Palestine." Thus in the sight of the law the Yishuv was conceived of in terms of a religious community, and was recognized as such by the government. Besides the Moslem community, which in accordance with Ottoman Law enjoyed a somewhat privileged status, the religious communities officially recognized by the government of Palestine were the Jewish, the Roman Catholic and the Greek Orthodox, the Gregorian Armenian Community, the Armenian (Catholic), the Syrian (Catholic), the Chaldaean (Uniate), the Greek Catholic Melkite, the Maronite, and the Syrian Orthodox Community. All of these maintained ecclesiastical courts exercising jurisdiction in matters of the personal status of their member.[55] Other communities desirous of organizing themselves for the purpose of governing their internal affairs could make application to the High Commissioner.

None but the Jewish community, through the Va'ad Leumi, made application under section 2(1) of the Religious Communities Organization Ordinance. The Palestine government prepared a draft of regulations that would be applicable to the Jewish community and submitted it to the Va'ad Leumi, to the Rabbinical Council, to the Agudat Israel, and to the Executive of the Zionist Organization. The government considered their comments and decided to give the Rabbinical Council and the local rabbinical authorities priority over the Elected

Assembly and the other democratically elected bodies of the Yishuv. In their final form, "The Jewish Community Rules," promulgated in the Official Gazette of the Government of Palestine on January 1, 1928, established a recognized "Community of the Jews in Palestine," known as "Knesset Yisrael."[56]

Of the several organs of this community, the Rules first dealt with the Rabbinical Council, as the central ecclesiastical authority, and the local ecclesiastical offices. Rather than leaving it to the democratically elected organs of the Knesset Yisrael to determine the scope and authority of the rabbinate, the Rules invested the rabbinate with official power, and made its maintenance obligatory upon and the financial responsibility of the Yishuv. It is worthy of note that while the Rules thus imposed the duty of maintaining an official rabbinate, they did not require Knesset Yisrael to maintain educational or other institutions.

The Rules next provided for an Elected Assembly. Its term of office was fixed for a period of three years; its function was to determine policy, approve a budget, and provide for taxation to cover the budget. The taxes thus imposed were, however, subject to the approval of the Palestine government. The Election Regulations, promulgated on March 1, 1930,[57] provided for a general and direct election by secret ballot. Voters were to be at least twenty years old, but there were no qualifications as to property or sex. Representation was to be proportional, that is, the whole of Palestine was declared one electoral area, and voters would give their votes to party lists. The number of Assembly members was fixed at seventy-one; in 1944 the number was increased to one hundred and seventy-one.

The executive organ of the Knesset Yisrael was the Va'ad Leumi, elected annually by the Assembly. The Va'ad Leumi drew up a budget for submission to the Elected Assembly; after it had been approved by the Assembly it had to be submitted to the High Commissioner for his approval, without which it could not come into operation (Section 13 (6) of the Rules).

Membership in "the Community of the Jews in Palestine" was not obligatory. Section 17 (1) of the Rules provided: "On the coming into force of these rules, the Va'ad Leumi shall forthwith draw up a register of adult Jews who have been resident in Palestine not less than three months, and the relevant portions of the register shall be published in every town and village in which one or more registered persons reside. . . . Any person who desires his name to be struck off the register shall, within one month of the publication of the relevant portion thereof, give notice, either personally or by an agent duly authorized in writing, to the Va'ad Leumi, which shall acknowledge the receipt of the notice, and strike off his name accordingly." It was further provided that persons wishing their names to be added to or struck off the register could do so in the month of Iyar of each year. A person whose name was struck off the list was not liable to pay the communal tax.

Finally, the regulations dealt with local communities. Section 20 provided: "There shall be not more than one local community in each town or village, but any section of such community comprising not less than thirty adults may claim the satisfaction of its religious and cultural needs according to its own principles." In towns or villages, or quarters where the population was Jewish, there was complete identity between the elected local municipal authority and the Community, and since the bulk of the Yishuv dwelt in areas where it constituted a majority of population, the municipal authority discharged the functions of the local community. As a result of this provision, the municipal governments in those places in Palestine where the population was Jewish, maintained the local rabbinate and provided for religious services, such as ritual slaughterhouses, ritual baths (Mikveh), Kashrut certification, et cetera.

The constitution of Knesset Yisrael (The Community of Jews in Palestine) thus represented a compromise between the conflicting interests of three elements: the British administration, the great majority of the Yishuv, and the Agudat Israel. The British were determined to downgrade the nationalist character of the Yishuv and to stress its religious character instead; hence the prominence given to the rabbinate and the duty imposed on the democratically elected organs of the Community to maintain it. The recognition of the official rabbinate as the sole interpreter of Jewish religion implied the recognition of Orthodox Judaism as the established religion of Palestinian Jewry. The Rules could not be altered by the democratically elected organs of the Community, but only by the High Commissioner. In stressing the religious character of the Yishuv, the British went so far as to insist that the term *Va'ad Leumi* be rendered in its English version as "General Committee" and not "National Committee," which is the translation of the words *Va'ad Leumi*. It was after a lengthy controversy that a compromise was reached when it was agreed that in the English version of the Rules the words *Va'ad Leumi* should follow in brackets the words *General Committee*.

The Jewish Community Regulations, although in many respects a disappointment, nevertheless afforded a framework for the development of Jewish autonomy. They did recognize only one community on the national and local level, so that none but the Va'ad Leumi was the officially recognized spokesman for Palestine Jewry. Further, through its powers of taxation, the Elected Assembly was able to develop nationwide activities in several fields. The fact that on the local level the municipal authorities also discharged communal functions tended to strengthen the national-secular aspect of Jewish autonomy.[58]

Agudat Israel succeeded in securing the provision that enabled any Jew to opt out of the community and thus be freed from the payment of communal taxes, an arrangement that greatly weakened the position of Knesset Yisrael. The British hoped that this option would be welcomed not only by Agudat Israel but also by those who would rather not pay communal taxes. But despite this arrangement Agudat Israel repudiated the very concept of Jewish self-government even in the limited form in which it was cast by the Rules.

The date of the promulgation of the Rules was proclaimed by the Agudah as a day of fast, and its members gathered at the Wailing Wall to mourn the event. The ultra-Orthodox elements who were outside Agudat Israel organized themselves into a separate community, the Adat Israel, and the two groups together founded a Committee of Dissidents from the Jewish Community. They urged their followers to opt out of the community and applied to the High Commissioner for recognition as a separate community with powers to tax its members, basing themselves on the provisions of the Religious Communities Organization Ordinance. They also made representations to the Mandates Commission of the League of Nations. The Palestine government, however, rejected their request and denied them recognition.[59]

The Va'ad Leumi proceeded to draw up a register of all adult Jews in Palestine, and in February 1929 a list containing eighty thousand names was published. All persons whose names had been omitted from the list were urged to apply for inclusion, and during the following month some fourteen thousand persons made their application.[60] At the same time, some sixteen thousand requested to have their names struck off the register, but of these some six thousand reregistered. When the register was completed in March 1929, nearly ninety thousand adults were recorded, while the number of dissidents was between five and six thousand. The majority of the Yishuv opted for the autonomous institutions and assumed their obligations. In the month of Iyar of each following year, Agudat Israel urged their adherents to exercise their right of withdrawing from the community, but they failed and the number of the dissidents did not grow. With the rapid growth of immigration their percentage of the total Yishuv declined further.

The withdrawal of Agudat Israel and of the other ultra-Orthodox had several effects. It put an end to the interminable quarrels about female suffrage and it made harmonious cooperation possible between the Va'ad Leumi and the Executive of the World Zionist Organization. After 1929, this applied equally to relations between the Va'ad Leumi and the newly established Jewish Agency, which created a framework for both Zionists and non-Zionists to work on behalf of the Jewish National Home. The Executive of the Jewish Agency was in charge of relations with the British government in London and in Jerusalem; it was responsible for fund-raising activities on behalf of the upbuilding of Palestine, and, through its offices in Jerusalem, was concerned with the promotion of agricultural settlements, urban development, and a variety of economic activities. The political parties represented in the Elected Assembly were also represented in the World Zionist Organization and, through the latter, in the Executive of the Jewish Agency. Mizrahi participated actively both in the World Zionist Organization and in the governing organs of the Community of Jews in Palestine, and the relations between Mizrahi and the secular majority were, on the whole, harmonious. They participated in the elections to the Assembly and usually obtained between seven to ten percent of the votes.

Education

Jewish self-government scored its greatest successes in the field of education and health services. From 1919 until 1933, the Zionist Organization, through its department of education, later taken over by the Jewish Agency, administered the network of Jewish schools in Palestine and was largely responsible for its financing. Thus Palestine had two separate and officially recognized public school systems: one for Arab children, maintained and administered by the Education Department of the Palestine Government, and the other for Jewish children, administered by the Jewish Agency with a limited financial subvention from the Mandatory government. In 1933, the administration of the Jewish schools was transferred from the Jewish Agency to the "Community of Jews in Palestine," and the Va'ad Leumi set up a department of education for that purpose. In 1919 the Zionist organization had provided nearly eighty-nine percent of the education budget; by 1947 its share in the budget was reduced to nine percent, the bulk now being supplied by the Va'ad Leumi and the local communities, with the government of Palestine providing an annual grant-in-aid.

After the First World War, certain trends in the Jewish school system began to develop: a general trend, and a religious trend, the latter promoted by Mizrahi. At the first World Zionist conference after World War I, held in London in 1920, it was decided to maintain these trends in the school system, with the parents having the right to determine for their children the type of school. The proponents of the General Trend held that "the spiritual content and the actual curriculum of a school must be above parties and classes, and above particularist views and aspirations, and must in addition be based on the spiritual values shared by the entire people. . . . It is the function of the school to mold the unity of the nation. . . ."[61] The Religious Trend sponsored by the Mizrahi was defined as follows: "Mizrahi education combines the traditional religious Jewish education prevalent in the advanced countries of Europe and America; thus the children will absorb Jewish religious values as the basis for their world outlook, will observe the religious commandments on the one hand, and on the other will acquire the knowledge and qualifications which a citizen in a modern society requires. . . . All teachers who instruct in the Mizrahi schools in any subject whatsoever must be religious in their views and behaviour."

Thus, within the Jewish school system, two autonomous trends developed, the General and the Religious. In the middle twenties a third system arose and eventually achieved official recognition. This was the Labour Trend, evolved primarily in the kibbutzim and the agricultural settlements, but maintaining a number of urban schools as well. Each trend maintained institutions for the training of its teachers and had a staff of inspectors, and each trend was authorized to engage and dismiss teachers within its system. There was a good deal of competition for pupils, for each trend was anxious to enlarge its own educational network. Outside the officially recognized Jewish public school system, there existed, of course, the school system of Agudat Israel. Numerically it was the smallest; education was restricted to religious subjects and Yiddish was the medium of instruction.

The number of pupils in the public school system arose from about ten thousand in 1919 to some ninety thousand in 1947. Within the General Trend, forty percent of teaching time was devoted to Jewish studies, that is, to Hebrew language and literature and Bible and Jewish history, and sixty percent to general studies, including foreign languages and the sciences. In the Religious Trend the proportion was reversed, with sixty percent of the time being devoted to Jewish studies. In the Labour Trend thirty percent of the time was allotted to Jewish studies, and seventy percent for general studies, including crafts and agriculture.[62] More than half the pupils attended the schools of the General Trend; the Religious Trend had less than a third of the total, while the Labour Trend catered to a small minority. When a decision was taken in 1932 to transfer the Jewish public schools system from the Jewish Agency to the Va'ad Leumi, the latter passed a resolution stating: "With the transfer of the educational system to the Community of the Jews in Palestine, the rights of the three recognized trends to develop their own activities will be preserved. Rules will be laid down that will enable each trend to broaden its educational institutions and to establish new ones in accordance with its growing needs."[63]

The Va'ad Leumi had a political department that was headed by Yitzhak Ben Zvi* and was concerned with the relations of the Yishuv with the Palestine administration. Another department was in charge of health services; the department of social welfare was headed for many years by Henrietta Szold.** There was also the department in charge of budgets. These, together with the departments of the local communities and of education, constituted the network of activities of Jewish self-government, which afforded the Yishuv an invaluable experience in democratic practice and procedure. The Elected Assembly, the Va'ad Leumi, and the local communities were in themselves schools where self-government was learned and democratic precedent established. Since these institutions possessed limited coercive powers and subsisted largely on the voluntary cooperation of the various groups, a large degree of accommodation and moderation was required to make democracy function. On occasion the Va'ad Leumi exceeded the powers accorded to it by the Jewish Community Rules, but its authority was not seriously challenged by any group.

When the independence of the Jewish state was proclaimed on May 14, 1948, the Va'ad Leumi transferred to the Provisional Government of the State of Israel the departments that it had administered and ceased to exist. Thus, the Community of the Jews in Palestine transferred to the Jewish state not only administrative departments, but, more important, it bequeathed a democratic tradition, extensive experience in harmonious cooperation between widely differing groups, and a *modus vivendi* between the nonobservant majority and the moderate Orthodox elements. In addition, it bequeathed to the Jewish state a "religious status qo"[64]: an established religion and a tax-supported rabbinic establishment exercising judicial powers, as well as a religious trend as part of the public school system. Finally, the new state inherited the religious parties from the Community.

G. THE DEVELOPMENT OF THE RELIGIOUS PARTIES

The four Holy Cities, the locale of the Old Yishuv, underwent a considerable decline after World War I. The normal flow of Halukkah funds had been interrupted by the war and the revolutions in Europe and it never recovered from the reverses. The Jewish community in Hebron, which in 1890 had numbered fifteen hundred, was reduced in 1928 to some seven hundred, most of whom were Yeshivah students.

---

* Later the second president of the State of Israel.
** Founder of Youth Aliyah.

In 1929 an Arab mob attacked them and massacred a large number
of the defenseless community; the rest fled and Hebron remained empty of Jews. In Safed the number of Jews was estimated in 1899
at 7,140[65]; this was reduced to 2,986 in 1922, to 2,547 in 1935, and
to 1,800 in 1948, at the beginning of the Jewish state. The picture in
Tiberias was rather different. Five thousand lived there in 1914 and
this number remained constant, but only because the period 1919–1948
saw the town transformed from a typical Old Yishuv stronghold to a
largely New Yishuv community. The population declined during the
war years, but recovered its position through the advent of new immigrants.

Thus the three Holy Cities of Hebron, Safed, and Tiberias ceased
being centers of the Old Yishuv, which during the thirty-year period
of the British Mandate was largely confined to Jerusalem. The ravages
of the war had been felt there also. Of the fifty thousand Jews living
in the city in 1914, many did not survive the rigors of the time. Exact
statistical data are not available, but it appears that only in 1931, after
some ten years of immigration, was the prewar figure attained again.
In that year, fifty-one thousand Jews lived in Jerusalem; they were now
fifty-seven percent of the total population, while in 1912 they had constituted sixty-four percent.[66]

The several waves of immigration in the Mandatory period did not
strengthen the ultra-Orthodox element, except to a limited extent. The
Palestine administration created two categories of immigrants: "Persons
of Independent Means," and immigrants entering on the "Labor Schedule." To the first category belonged persons who could prove to the
satisfaction of the immigration authorities that they possessed at least
£1,000. The Third Aliyah from Poland (like the later large Aliyah of
the Nazi period) brought in many immigrants under this category. It
is probable that the number of ultra-Orthodox Jews among these immigrants was rather limited, and those who came did not expect to
live on Halukkah.

An interesting feature of the Fourth Aliyah (1923–1926) was the
appearance of Hasidim as tillers of the soil. In Poland and Galicia the
Hasidim had constituted a powerful element within Jewish life, both
numerically and politically, but all attempts to draw them closer to the
cause of resettling Palestine had been of no avail. In 1924, however,
the heads of two Hasidic dynasties, the Rabbi of Yablona and the Rabbi of Kozenitz, urged their followers to go to Palestine and engage in
farming. They founded two societies, Nahlat Yaakov and Avodat Yisrael, and acquired a tract of land east of Haifa Bay, on which they
established the village of Kfar Hasidim. In the same year a group of

Orthodox Jews from Poland set up an agricultural settlement east of Tel Aviv, on the site of the ancient town of Bnei Brak, which before long became an urban center. These were the only organized attempts on the part of Orthodox immigrants to engage in practical work in Palestine, and to do so outside the framework of the Zionist organization.

The immigration policy of the Palestine administration was based on the country's economic capacity to absorb labor, and therefore semi-annual estimates of the demand for additional labor were made. Once the figure of the labor schedule was fixed, the government would issue a corresponding number of immigration certificates for persons without means. These certificates were to be distributed by the Executive of the Zionist Organization and later by the Jewish Agency. The number of certificates was small and met only a fraction of the great demand; they were consequently used primarily to assure the immigration of Halutzim who had been undergoing special training in Europe. The number of certificates was not sufficient even for this category and, after Hitler came to power in 1933, the struggle to obtain a certificate to Palestine became intense. As a rule the Jewish Agency would withhold such certificates from members of Agudat Israel, but when the latter made representations to the government of Palestine, the Agency was forced to set aside a small number of certificates for the Agudah. Of the ninety-four thousand immigrants admitted to Palestine between 1922 and 1931, fifty-two percent entered under the Labor schedule and twenty-five percent as Persons of Independent Means, the rest being relatives or dependents of Palestine citizens, students, experts, and so on.[67] During the period of the Fifth Aliyah (1933–1939) many immigrants of independent means arrived from Germany, including a number of adherents of Agudat Israel.

Throughout the Mandatory period secularism represented the prevailing mood of the Yishuv. Mizrahi reacted by concentrating on education and directed their energies to the promotion of the religious trend within the Jewish public school system. In order to afford material assistance to their adherents, and especially to the new immigrants among them, they established economic institutions, aid societies, and a bank of their own. Since they were represented on the governing bodies of the Zionist organization and of the Jewish Agency, they succeeded in obtaining their share of immigration certificates for their followers in Eastern and Central Europe. After 1933 they also benefited from the immigration of their German adherents, among whom were persons prominent in the professions, sciences, education, and public life. Among them were also distinguished rabbis who had occupied positions of prominence in German Orthodoxy, but the rabbinate viewed them with suspicion, for they possessed a general academic background in addition to their Talmudic training.

The leadership of Mizrahi had realized that, in order to combat secularism effectively, it was essential to develop a following also among the working people, especially in view of the fact that organized labor was gradually assuming a dominant position in the life of the Yishuv. As early as 1919 Rabbi Yehudah L. Maimon had pointed out: "Before long the influence of the working people will be dominant in Palestine, both materially and spiritually, and if it is our wish that traditional Judaism . . . be not weakened, we must from now on endeavour to organize the religious working people, so that they remain loyal to us."[68]

Samuel Haim Landau (1892–1926) of Poland gave this idea theoretical as well as practical grounding. In 1921 a group of young followers of Mizrahi met in Warsaw and organized the movement of Tze'irei (Young) Mizrahi. At this conference Landau developed his views of a synthesis of religion and labor. The Orthodox had to overcome the downgrading of physical labor that had characterized the Diaspora. He pointed out that the Torah enjoined not only the observance of the Sabbath but also commanded: "Six days you shall labour and do all your work." A return to Zion implied a return to labor and to working the soil. While in the Diaspora Torah might be seen as detached from life; in Zion *Torah ve Avodah* (Torah and Labor) were the integral components of a full religious life. Landau rejected socialism and contended that the principles of social justice proclaimed by the prophets should serve as a basis for a new religion-oriented Jewish society in Palestine.[69]

In 1922 HaPoel HaMizrahi (The Mizrahi Worker) was founded in Palestine in the spirit of Torah veAvodah, as taught by Landau. At first there was considerable antagonism between the new group and the Histadrut, the General Federation of Jewish Labor, but in the early thirties an agreement between the two was reached and HaPoel Ha-Mizrahi agreed to follow a united trade union policy.

HaPoel HaMizrahi was in many ways a striking innovation in the Orthodox community. The students in the Yeshivot did not engage in bodily toil and cultivated a sense of aloofness from mundane affairs; the new movement elevated physical labor to the level of a religious duty and was ready to merge with the totality of the Jewish community in its pioneering drive toward a new society. The stress on labor and pioneering projected a new image of Orthodoxy, especially when it succeeded in establishing progressive agricultural settlements. In 1927 they founded Sde Yaakov, a smallholders' settlement in the eastern part of the Jezreel valley, and some ten years later a number of kibbutzim and moshavim in the Beisan valley and other parts of the country. At the same time institutions for Orthodox workers were created in the cities: cooperatives, housing projects, credit banks, and various welfare services. Their members participated in the Haganah, where they gave a good account of themselves. They were strengthened by the arrival of members of religious pioneering groups from Eastern and Central Europe, and later by an important Western-educated group from Germany.

In contrast, the development of Agudat Israel took a different course. In the years following World War I it greatly strengthened its position in Poland, where it had a mass following and was represented in the Polish parliament; it also increased its following in the other countries of Eastern and Central Europe. There were small groups of adherents in the United States and in England, where the Agudah had a political office that maintained contact with the Colonial Office. At its World Assembly (Knessio Gedolo) held in Vienna in the summer of 1923, two viewpoints clashed; one was represented by Rabbi Jacob Rosenheim, who called for a Torah-dominated organization of Jews without any reference to Palestine; and the other, represented by Dr. Jacob Breuer of Frankfurt, who urged a Palestinian orientation. The latter moved that the aim of Agudat Israel should be the "preparation of the People of God and of the Land of God, with a view to re-uniting them in the State [*medinah*] of God under the rule of the Divine law." Dr. Breuer's view was rejected and a compromise formula adopted: "The aim of Agudat Israel is to solve in the spirit of the Torah all the problems that will arise in the life of the Jewish people." There was no specific reference to Palestine. During this period the Agudah was primarily concerned with the demands of some of its constituent organizations, particularly those in Hungary and in Palestine, to separate from the established Jewish communities, and form separatist enclaves of their own.

In Palestine, Agudat Israel continued to identify itself with the Old Yishuv, and before long became its spokesman. Its principal centers were in the pre-1914 neighborhoods of Jerusalem, particularly Meah Shearim and Batei Ungarn (Hungarian Houses), as well as the Jewish quarter of the Old City. Agudat Israel failed to promote immigration to Palestine, as all other groups did, and its energies were primarily directed toward opposing the Yishuv's struggle for Jewish self-government. It carried on a propaganda campaign against Zionism, but its most intense opposition was directed against the Mizrahi and the official rabbinate.

In the early twenties the Agudah established contact with Arab leaders as well as with British politicians who were opposed to the policy of the Jewish National Home. Dr. Jacob De Hahn, a lawyer and journalist of Dutch origin, became the political secretary of the organization. In his despatches to European journals he described the new settlers of Palestine as Bolsheviks bent on imposing their will on the Orthodox. He established contact with the British press magnate, Lord Northcliffe, and assisted the latter in his anti-Zionist campaign. He also arranged for a delegation headed by Rabbi Joseph Haim Sonnenfeld to call on King Hussein of Arabia, who was then visiting his son, the Emir Abdallah of Transjordan, and acquaint them with the opposition of the Agudah to the Jewish National Home. Before long De Hahn proceeded to organize, together with the anti-Jewish Arab Executive, a joint front to combat Zionism. His vigorous anti-Yishuv activities aroused bitter resentment, and on June 30, 1924, he was shot and killed in Jerusalem. Although the police failed to apprehend the culprits, it was generally believed at the time that the assassination had been carried out by Jews, and indeed, this was admitted by the Haganah some forty years later.[70] The act was viewed with satisfaction by many of the Yishuv, while other voices were raised in revulsion against political murder.[71] The Agudah leadership vehemently protested the killing and requested the government to apprehend the murderers. After the death of De Hahn, the Agudah desisted from further cooperation with Arab leaders and anti-Zionist Britishers, and confined its political activity to the promotion of separatist interests.

The attitude of Agudat Israel began to change in the early thirties, particularly after the rise of Nazism, when some of their followers from Poland and Germany arrived in Palestine. They were mostly members of the middle class and some had considerable means. They established themselves outside the quarters of the Old Yishuv and settled wherever economic opportunities presented themselves. The arrivals from Germany, in particular, were anxious to introduce their program of combining Talmudic studies with the secular subjects they had learned in the West. In 1934 a delegation from the Central Office of the Agudah arrived in Palestine, and assumed control of the Palestine Agudah, which up to then had been in the hands of the Old Yishuv. Following this reorganization of the Palestine office, a number of ultra-Orthodox withdrew from Agudat Israel and founded their own group, Neturei Karta, "Guardians of the City."

The growing danger to European Jewry resulting from the rise of Nazism and the political developments in Palestine itself created a new situation that Agudat Israel could not ignore. In 1936, new Arab riots occurred, which at first were directed against the Jews but before long developed into an uprising against the British. On August 7, 1936, the British government appointed a Royal Commission under the chairmanship of Lord Peel to "ascertain the underlying causes of the disturbances . . . to inquire into the manner in which the Mandate for Palestine is being implemented in relation to our obligations as Mandatory toward the Arabs and the Jews respectively, and to ascertain whether, upon a proper construction of the terms of the Mandate, either the Arabs or the Jews have any legitimate grievance on account of the way in which the Mandate has been and is being implemented."[72]

The report produced by the Royal Commission in 1937 was of far-reaching consequences and altered the course of the history of Palestine. The Commission recommended that the mandate for Palestine should terminate, that the territory of Palestine be divided, and "two sovereign independent States be established, the one an Arab State, consisting of Transjordan united with that part of Palestine which lies East and South" of a suggested frontier, and the other a "Jewish State consisting of that part of Palestine which lies North and West of the frontier. Jerusalem and Bethlehem would belong to neither State, but would form an enclave, which should be placed under a new Mandate."[73]

The Royal Commission realized that the small area allocated to the Jewish state, some five thousand square kilometres, was bound to disappoint the Jews. It therefore stressed the advantages of the plan: "Partition enables the Jews in the fullest sense to call their National Home their own: for it converts it into a Jewish State. Its citizens will be able to admit as many Jews into it as they themselves believe can be absorbed."[74] At a time when the flood of refugees from Nazi atrocities was continually mounting, the reference to a Jewish state able to admit refugees had indeed an enormous attraction, despite the small size of the projected state.

The report came like a bombshell. The Zionist leaders, in their representations to the British government, had never gone beyond asking for an honest implementation of the terms of the mandate. Quite unexpectedly they had been offered a state. But against the alluring prospect of sovereignty stood the miniature size of the proposed area. The condition to give up about eighty percent of Palestine, including Jerusalem with its Jewish majority, weighed heavily against accepting the idea of partition. The Yishuv was deeply divided on the issue, and so were both Zionists and non-Zionists in the Diaspora. In the summer of 1937 the whole Jewish world was involved in a heart-searching debate on the subject, and the matter was not laid to rest when the Zionist Congress of that year accepted in principle the proposal for partition.

The partition controversy also engulfed Agudat Israel in a protracted debate, which came to a head at the World Agudah Conference held in Marienbad in August 1937. The Conference itself was preceded by a session of the Council of Sages, who were asked to render a decision on the "legality" of a Jewish state from the Halakhic point of view.

The opponents were of two categories: those who rejected a Jewish state as being contrary to the divine scheme of Messianic redemption, and those who contended that giving up the larger part of the Holy Land was contrary to the Halakhah. There were, however, other Talmudic luminaries who, leaving Halakhic consideration aside, drew attention to the impending calamity in Europe and to the need of rescuing as many Jews as possible from the Nazi menace. The majority of the rabbis from Poland, Rumania, and the Baltic States favored a Jewish state; the majority of the rabbis from Germany, Hungary, Czechoslovakia, and England opposed it. The Council of Sages was divided and finally an ambiguous ruling was handed down to the plenary session of the conference.[75]

The Conference, being itself not competent to render a decision, which was within the exclusive competence of the Council of Sages, could only try to interpret the ruling of the Council of the Sages. The division of opinions was largely according to the countries that the delegates represented. Those from Eastern Europe drew attention to the dangers of Nazism, and interpreted the decision of the Council of Sages to mean that the Conference should support the partition plan, while their opponents advanced Halakhic counterarguments. The debate was prolonged, and at times it was impossible to maintain order between the two factions. The final session took place on August 23, 1937, on which occasion it appeared as if there would be a split in the Agudah.[76] Ultimately the Conference decided in favor of a Jewish state.

If Agudat Israel had done in the years preceding 1937 what it now proceeded to do, namely, urged its followers to settle in Palestine, many of the Jews of Eastern Europe might have survived the Holocaust. The resolution reluctantly adopted in 1937, under the shadow of imminent calamity, came too late. The British government, encountering opposition from the Arabs, who were supported by Nazi Germany and Fascist Italy, abandoned the partition plan and, in order to appease the Arabs, proceeded to restrict Jewish immigration. World War II broke out, bringing in its wake the destruction of nearly the whole of European Jewry and, with it, of the great reservoir of Orthodoxy. At the end of the war, Agudat Israel found itself deprived of its mass following.

Throughout the period of British rule in Palestine, the Agudah and its followers had isolated themselves from the expanding and dynamic Yishuv. They maintained their own traditional Talmud Torahs and Yeshivot; their young men did not join the Haganah. They were content to be left alone, without seeking contact with the larger community. By opting out of "the Community of the Jews in Palestine," they had placed themselves outside the democratic life of the Yishuv, and their political contacts, made with a view to protecting their particularist interests, had been directly with the British administration. In those years they were a world apart, and by their self-isolation they facilitated the relatively harmonious cooperation between the secularists and the Zionist-oriented religious elements within the framework of the National Home.

The Balfour Declaration and the new political order that emerged in Palestine dealt a major blow to the Old Yishuv. Under the Ottoman rule the Old Yishuv had outnumbered the new; it enjoyed financial security by the ever-growing flow of Halukkah funds. Politically it was protected by the consular representatives of the European powers and the United States. It could thus ignore the slow-growing new Yishuv. The First World War shattered the Halukkah system, which failed to recover its preeminence after the arrival of peace. The abolition of the capitulations systems and the recognition of Zionist aspirations by Great Britain assured the political supremacy of the new Yishuv. By failing to promote the settlement of Palestine and to encourage Aliyah, Agudat Israel also assured the numerical supremacy of the new Yishuv. The early period of British rule witnessed bitter opposition to Zionism on the part of the Old Yishuv. The latter withdrew from all organs of the legally recognized organs of Jewish autonomy. It was, in fact, a withdrawal from the Jewish body politic. Only in 1937, under the impact of the Nazi menace, did Agudat Israel adopt a more conciliatory attitude. The delay resulted in a distinct weakening of the ultra-Orthodox elements.

Mizrahi, on the other hand, by reason of its intimate involvement with the Zionist movement, achieved notable results. By encouraging Aliyah, it increased the number of its adherents in Palestine. By actively participating in land settlement and other constructive efforts, it secured a firm foothold in the political, educational, and economic life of the National Home. Through its effort, the Chief Rabbinate was recognized as the sole religious authority in the Yishuv, as was the right to develop a religious school system maintained by the organs of Jewish autonomy. The relation between Mizrahi and the other political parties was on the whole amicable. There were no Halakhic controversies, since the Jewish community possessed no legal powers and could not legislate on matters of Halakhah. Thus, the observance of religious precepts was a matter of persuasion rather than the subject of political controversy and party politics.

In one significant respect Mizrahi did, however, fail. The Chief

Rabbinate, contrary to expectations, did not make a significant religious impact. It was an institution rather than a spiritual force. The great opportunity for the renewal of the religious law within the autonomous framework of the national home was missed, and no serious thought was devoted to making Halakhah compatible with the needs of a modern society.[77]

4

Legal and Constitutional Problems

A. THE ESTABLISHMENT
OF A JEWISH STATE

The outbreak of World War II found the Yishuv in the throes of a conflict with Great Britain, a consequence of the policy of appeasement pursued by the government headed by Neville Chamberlain. At a time when the need to rescue Jews from the peril of Nazism was at its greatest, the White Paper promulgated on May 17, 1939, threatened to restrict immigration drastically and to reduce the Yishuv to the status of permanent minority in their National Home. In this desperate situation the Yishuv resorted to the promotion of illegal immigration, even in violation of the White Paper policy, and, if necessary, to offering physical resistance to the British authorities.

The outbreak of the war and the need to fight a common enemy made it necessary to postpone the resolution of the Anglo-Jewish conflict. Immediately after the beginning of hostilities, the leaders of the Yishuv proclaimed their readiness to support the war effort against Nazi Germany. The Va'ad Leumi appealed to the Jews of Palestine to volunteer for service in the British army and about one-fourth of the total Jewish population, men and women, responded to the appeal. The British authorities, however, were reluctant to avail themselves of so large a number of volunteers, and admitted to military service only as many Jews as would equal the number of Arab volunteers, and since the latter were very few, the formation of Palestinian units was a very slow process. Only after France fell and pro-German regimes were installed in Syria and in Lebanon, and after German troops began to appear on the North African coast intent on capturing and crossing the

Suez Canal, did the British drop the principle of Arab-Jewish parity and proceed to form Jewish Palestinian battalions within the British army. Finally a Jewish brigade was permitted to be formed, which saw active service on the Italian front. Altogether some thirty thousand Palestinian Jewish men and women served in various units in the British army during World War II.

In 1943, with the arrival of the news of the mass massacres of Jews in Nazi-dominated Europe, attempts were made to mount a rescue operation. Clandestine emissaries were despatched to Europe from Palestine, but even the limited possibilities that existed came to naught because of the unwillingness of the British and American governments to take any affirmative action. At last, in January 1944, under the pressure of Jewish organizations in America, President Roosevelt set up a War Refugee Board, which came too late and achieved still less. With the German collapse in May 1945, the full extent of the tragedy became apparent. To the great majority of the Yishuv it was a tragedy in a most personal way, for there were few victims of the Holocaust who had no relatives in Palestine. Rescue of the hundreds of thousands of survivors in the displaced persons camps in liberated Europe now became the immediate objective of the Yishuv.

Prime Minister Churchill gave a promise that with the end of the war the policy of the White Paper would be modified. In the summer of 1945, however, the Labor government under Clement Attlee came to power and therewith the hopes of the Zionists and their friends were dashed. The new Foreign Minister, Ernest Bevin, was determined to enforce the policy of the White Paper of 1939, and at his instigation an Anglo-American Commission was set up late in 1945 to enquire into the Palestine problem. This commission, consisting of six American and six British members, submitted its report on April 20, 1946. To Bevin's surprise they recommended the abrogation of the White Paper and called for the immediate admission of a hundred thousand refugees. The subsequent refusal of the British government to act on these recommendations gave rise to armed Jewish resistance to the British authorities in Palestine, and to an intensification of "illegal" immigration. The resistance, equipped with clandestinely acquired arms, was countered by some hundred thousand British troops deployed in Palestine. The severe measures adopted by them against the Yishuv, including the arrest of the members of the Executive of the Jewish Agency, failed to quell the revolt; military installations, airports, and army camps were continually attacked, and both Jews and British suffered casualties.

Realizing that they were unable to restore order in Palestine, the British announced on April 2, 1947, that they intended to refer the whole Palestine problem to the United Nations. The General Assembly of the United Nations appointed a United Nations Special Committee on Palestine (UNSCOP), which submitted a report on August 31, 1947, and recommended the partition of Palestine into two independent states, Jewish and Arab.

As the prospects of a Jewish state became tangible, the Executive of the Jewish Agency made an effort to secure unity among the various groups of the Yishuv. Discussions were held with Agudat Israel, with a view to securing their full cooperation. The agreement arrived at was formulated in a letter addressed by the Executive of the Jewish Agency to the Agudah dated June 19, 1947, assuring them that the Jewish Agency would use its best endeavors to see to it that in the future Jewish state matters of personal status would be regulated by religious law, that the Sabbath would be the official day of rest, that Kashrut would be observed in all state-maintained kitchens intended for Jews, and that religious education would be provided if the parents desired it.[1] Agudat Israel were content with this statement of policy, and lent their support to the diplomatic efforts of the Jewish Agency. Appearing before UNSCOP in Jerusalem, Rabbi Isaac Meir Levin, one of the few surviving leaders of Agudat Israel of Poland, rejected any suggestion of the displaced persons returning to their former places of residence in Europe, and insisted upon the establishment of a Jewish state.[2]

On November 29, 1947, the Assembly of the United Nations approved the recommendations of UNSCOP by a two-thirds majority. At this Assembly the representatives of the Arabs announced that they would resist the implementation of the United Nations resolution by force of arms, and this they immediately proceeded to do. The following half-year was a period of guerrilla attacks by the Arabs on the Yishuv. The British government announced that they would withdraw their forces from Palestine on May 15, 1948. In accordance therewith, the leaders of the Yishuv proclaimed, on Friday, May 14, 1948, the establishment of a Jewish state, to be known as Medinat Israel (the State of Israel).

The Declaration of the Independence of the State of Israel proclaimed that the state "would be based on freedom, justice and peace as envisaged by the prophets of Israel; it would ensure complete equality of social and political rights to all its inhabitants irrespective of religion, race or sex; it would guarantee freedom of religion, conscience, language, education and culture." A provisional government was set up, consisting of thirteen ministers and headed by David Ben-Gurion; it included Rabbi I. M. Levin, representing Agudat Israel, and two ministers representing Mizrahi. On this occasion complete unity was achieved: for the first time Agudat Israel participated in an all-Jewish united effort with the secularists. A Jewish state, that bone of contention that had divided the ultra-Orthodox from the Mizrahi and from the secularists for nearly two generations, proved to be the very cement that promoted the integration of diverse groups into one nation.

In the drafting committee of the Declaration of Independence, a controversy had arisen when the representatives of the religious parties insisted that the name of God be included in the text of the Declaration. There was opposition to this demand, especially on the part of the left-wing parties. To avoid an open split, a compromise was reached and the concluding paragraph of the Declaration was drafted as follows: "Placing our trust in the Rock Of Israel, we affix our signatures to this Proclamation." The word *Rock* was acceptable to both Orthodox and secularists, each lending it his own interpretation.[3]

B. HALAKHAH AND LAW
IN THE JEWISH STATE

Although committed to the principle that the Halakhah is to be the law governing a Jewish state, Orthodox rabbis and scholars have failed to evolve guidelines for the application of the traditional Jewish law to a concrete and viable state, let alone prepare a blueprint for a Halakhah-based constitution. Agudat Israel neither desired nor expected a Jewish state, and consequently devoted little thought to the place of the Halakhah in the legal and constitutional system of the future state. But neither did Mizrahi, attached though they were to the idea of a Jewish state. The official rabbinate likewise ignored this problem. They all reiterated the maxim of "the Land of Israel for the People of Israel in accordance with the Torah of Israel," but failed to propound the principles for the implementation of this maxim into a legal and constitutional system that would meet the requirements of a modern state.[4]

In the closing months of British rule, urgent plans for the setting up of an administration of the future state were made. Equally urgent was the task of creating a defense force to resist the imminent invasion of the armies of the neighboring Arab states. There was also another problem that brooked no delay, namely, the decision on the constitutional framework and the legal system that would be applied on the morrow of the proclamation of independence of the new state. A special commission was appointed to deal with this problem, but before it could complete its task, the proclamation of independence had to be proceeded with.

On basic issues confronting the organization of a state, the Halakhah offered little guidance. Should a Jewish state be a monarchy or a republic? If a republic, should it be a presidential democracy, as in the United States, or a parliamentary democracy, as in England? Should it be based on the principle of separation of powers, or should it be an authoritarian state? And what should be the foreign policy of this state—neutralist or oriented toward one of the great powers? Who, in accordance with the Halakhah, would be the legislative body—elected representatives or a group of rabbinic scholars? Or should the Jewish state be a theocracy, where all legislative and judicial powers would be vested in a body of Halakhic experts?

On these and other questions of constitutional importance, the leaders of Orthodoxy offered no guidance. Not that it would be easy to do; on the contrary. Halakhah had, over a period of nearly two thousand years, evolved out of and in response to a reality based on the denial of political sovereignty to the Jewish people. The Halakhah had to confine its scope to matters affecting a minority group dwelling in a Gentile world, where all matters of state policy were determined by the non-Jewish majority. The rich rabbinic literature that developed over the centuries was focused on the relationship of the Jew to his Creator and to his fellow man but, with few exceptions, was not concerned with the relationship of the Jew to the body politic. Over the ages, the Halakhah had become detached from matters over which the Jew could exercise no control.

It was not surprising therefore that, while all shades of Orthodoxy proclaimed that Halakkah ought to encompass every aspect of life, they fought shy of evoking whatever guidance it might have to offer on matters of state policy. Such guidance would in fact have become embarrassing. The application of Halakhic rules would curtail the basic principles of a democratic order, and would discriminate between Jew and Jew, and between Jew and non-Jew. A nonobservant Jew might not be eligible to hold public office in a Jewish state. Did not Maimonides say:

> It is forbidden to appoint as king one who is from an assembly of strangers, even one several generations removed in origin . . . as it is said, "You may not place over yourself a foreigner who is not your brother." And not only as regards the monarch, but as regards all positions of authority in Israel, whether it be a general in the army, a captain of fifty, or a captain of ten, even one appointed to take care of a well which is used for irrigation. And it goes without saying that a judge or a Nasi [President of a Sanhedrin] must be a Jew, as it says, "From the midst of your brethren shall you place over you a king." All appointments which you make must be from your own group.[5]

Isaac H. Herzog, Ashkenazic Chief Rabbi of Palestine (and later, of Israel), advocated that the constitution of the Jewish state be based *in principle* on Torah. In an article written in 1948 on this subject, Rabbi Herzog attempted to deal with the problem.[6] He realized that the democratic character of the state must be taken into account, for "the state was granted by a resolution of the United Nations calling for a democratic structure." Further, since a substantial and important minority of the citizens would be non-Jews, who would probably not be prepared to live under the laws of Torah, Rabbi Herzog suggested that special courts for non-Jews be set up, where matters would be adjudicated in accordance with their own laws.* The same would apply to criminal matters, where two separate legal systems would obtain. Rabbi Herzog admitted "that difficulties might arise in mixed places," including instances where legislation involved both Jews and non-Jews. "This calls for further consideration," he wrote, but failed to indicate how the problem might be solved. The jurisdiction of the rabbinical courts, which during the period of the Mandate was confined to matters of personal status, would now include all matters. Only persons "who are fit from a religious, moral and scholarly point of view shall be qualified as judges." Realizing, however, that this demand would not be acceptable, he suggested that further consideration be given to the problem of admitting nonobservant Jews to positions in the judiciary.

Rabbi Herzog insisted that matters of family law be regulated in accordance with Halakhah. In this field of law, he pointed out, there was no possibility of creating new Takanot (ordinances) that would in any wise change the existing law. "In matters of civil law," he continued, "we have the possibility of making Takanot . . . resulting from changes in the economic, commercial and industrial order." He realized that difficulties were involved in disqualifying women and nonobservant Jews from giving evidence in court, but advanced no solution.[7] He concluded by pronouncing that the Jewish state "within the framework of the Torah, and with due regard to reality, will not be entirely theocratic, nor entirely democratic in the modern sense."[8] He failed to indicate, however, how the governing bodies of the future state would be organized—whether they would be elected, and if so, what the qualifications of the voters would be. In dealing with the two systems of law courts, he also avoided any discussion of a Supreme Court. Would the Jewish system of courts and the non-Jewish system each have its own Supreme Court? In that case, what would happen if a judgment of one Supreme Court on a certain matter conflicted with a judgment of the other Supreme Court? Nor did Rabbi Herzog deal with the laws that would apply to the non-Jewish courts. If these were indeed religious laws, would it not be necessary to set up separate courts

---

* Rabbi Herzog apparently referred here to religious laws.

for Moslems, Catholics, Greek Orthodox, and others? In the case that the non-Jewish minority rejected a multiplicity of courts, would they be allowed to decide for themselves what system of law they wished?

Another distinguished leader of Mizrahi, Rabbi Meir Berlin, went so far as to admit the inadequacy of Halakhah for much of modern life, and suggested that this be remedied by enacting Takanot in many fields of law. Only thus could the law of Torah be made applicable to the citizens of Israel, irrespective of religion. Such developments would obviate the need to set up two systems of law courts. He failed, however, to indicate which reforms he wished to introduce in order to make Halakhah applicable to non-Jews as well as to Jews, observant and nonobservant.[9]

A different and more realistic approach was adopted by Rabbi Judah Leib Maimon, himself one of the founders of Mizrahi. He was an outstanding Talmudic scholar and became the first Minister for Religious Affairs in Israel. He realized that Halakhah in its present form could not serve as the law of the new state. While he pointed out to the secularists that "the State of Israel cannot exist without the Torah of Israel," he also addressed himself to the Orthodox, stressing that "it is impossible for the Torah of Israel to exist fully without a State of Israel."[10] He further pointed out that a modern state raised serious Halakhic problems that must be considered and solved. "There are problems arising out of new inventions, some of which tend to aggravate the situation, while others tend to mitigate; these must be fully considered and not hurriedly forbidden or permitted, for the future of the nation is at stake." To integrate state and religion was a challenge with which the rabbis had not been confronted for many generations, and it was incumbent upon them now "to rise to a height which they have not attained for many centuries."[11] This task could not be accomplished by any rabbi or group of rabbis, but rather by a supreme and authoritative Halakhic institution. The time for a revival of a Sanhedrin had therefore arrived, he concluded.

This was indeed a revolutionary suggestion, made in order to cope with the equally revolutionary emergence of the Jewish state. To allay possible apprehensions, Rabbi Maimon reiterated the traditional principle that Halakhah cannot be legislated, but he insisted on the need for "a revival and a broadening of the Torah law. . . . This cannot be achieved by a Ministry for Religious Affairs, nor by a religious-political party in the Knesset, nor by the Chief Rabbinate as presently constituted."[12] For this purpose, he said, an authoritative institution was required, consisting of persons "who are not only great in Torah . . . but also scholars whose entire life is that of great personalities, whose way of life can be seen as an example and source of inspiration. Their hearts must be full of love for every Jew, for the State of Israel . . . they must also be distinguished by their courage and firmness."[13] Such leaders would be able to establish a renewed Sanhedrin.

The Sanhedrin had functioned in the latter part of the Second Commonwealth. A Great Sanhedrin in Jerusalem had consisted of seventy-one members, and Small Sanhedrins in each city or region had twenty-three members. The Great Sanhedrin was a legislative body as well as a court of appeal. After the destruction of Jewish independence in 70 C.E., the term *Sanhedrin* was applied to assemblies of rabbinical scholars in Palestine who performed the function of a legislative institution in religious matters until the end of the fourth century when it ceased to function. In the sixteenth century an attempt was made in Safed to prepare the ground for renewing the Sanhedrin, but the project failed to materialize.

Rabbi Maimon enquired into rabbinic literature in order to deal with the contention that the Sanhedrin could not be reconvened until after the advent of the Messiah. Basing himself on an authentic manuscript of Maimonides, he quoted the great master as saying that a Sanhedrin could be reestablished even before the coming of the Messiah; such a Sanhedrin would be competent to adjudicate all matters of civil law, but not criminal matters, "for these may not be dealt with until the Temple is rebuilt."[14] According to Maimonides, only rabbis residing in Palestine might establish a Sanhedrin, and even if all of them did not wish to do so, a half of them might. In addition to interpreting the Torah, the Sanhedrin would issue Gzerot (edicts) and enact new Takanot. "Now that we have lived to see the day when the State of Israel has been revived, there is no room for doubt as to our duty to revive the Sanhedrin," Rabbi Maimon wrote. He repeated that the Sanhedrin would not be called to reform Judaism. "I stress: it will enact Takanot, not Reforms." To those of his opponents who suggested that this generation was unworthy of the great task, Rabbi Maimon replied: "If this generation has been worthy to re-establish a Jewish state, its rabbis are worthy to re-establish the supreme Torah institution."[15] He envisaged the renewed Sanhedrin not merely as a court of law and as a legislator of Takanot, but as a major educational institution that would assert its influence not by means of coercion or sanction, but by study and learning, "by revealing the sublime and making known the social justice . . . inherent in the Written and the Oral Law." He concluded by saying: "What we need is to possess the conviction that the star of Torah Judaism must and can rise—but only by reviving the Sanhedrin."

Rabbi Maimon's project had in it all the ingredients of a statesman's approach to the great challenge that would inevitably confront a renewed Jewish state. To give effect to this project, he invited the rabbis in Israel to hold a conference in Tiberias. He chose Tiberias for the venue because in that city the last Sanhedrin had held its sessions, and also because there the grave of Maimonides was located. Many rabbis accepted the invitation to the conference, at which Rabbi Maimon expounded his plan. "It seems to me that my lecture was listened to with great attention, but when I ended, the rabbis were stricken by silence . . . and did not enter into deliberations on the subject." He felt that this reaction could be interpreted either as a complete endorsement of the plan, or that they had felt it unworthy of consideration. "But I shall allow myself to state that there probably existed a different reason for the silence: cowardice. To our great regret, many of the rabbis fear not only God, but also mortals."[16] Rabbi Maimon was obliquely referring to the ultra-Orthodox who, claiming to be the sole authentic exponents of Torah Judaism, would condemn rabbis like Rabbi Maimon and his followers as unfaithful to true religion and suspect of Reform. Not only did the attending individual rabbis maintain their silence, but so did the Chief Rabbis. Subsequent attempts by Rabbi Maimon to arouse interest in the project also met with no success. Thus passed the opportunity to renew Halakhah through a revival of the Sanhedrin, not so much because the majority of rabbis in Israel objected to the idea on its merits, but because they stood in fear of the ultra-traditionalists.

Another approach to the laws of the future state was made by Dr. Moshe Silberg, an eminent jurist and Talmudic scholar, and later a member of the Supreme Court. In an article published on the eve of the establishment of the state, he assessed the possibilities available. He objected to the retention of the Palestine law as lacking organic unity, composed as it was of remnants of Turkish and British-based statutes, and English Common Law as the general guiding principle. He likewise opposed the introduction of another country's complete legal system, such as the Swiss Code, as had been done by Mustapha Kemal Pasha in Turkey, who had abolished the old Turkish law by a single edict and had replaced it by a borrowed modern code. Such a procedure might be possible in a nation that could not boast of a rich legal tradition and heritage, but would be unthinkable in the case of the Jewish people.

The law of the Jewish state, Silberg averred, must therefore be "a new code, an original or an almost original code." It must be a Jewish law "in the sense that it must be based on the ideas of Jewish law, the national law that accompanied us for two thousand years . . . based on the ideas of Jewish law, but not identical with it; it is not suggested that the Shulhan Arukh be proclaimed in toto as the law of the land. Even if we had the possibility of doing so, we would not possess the moral right to do it, in view of the non-Jewish population of the State of Israel."[17] Silberg emphasized that he aimed at an original Israeli code of law that would be secular yet essentially Jewish. It would as far as possible absorb the basic principles of Jewish law, but would reject such of its provisions as appeared to be unsuitable to this age. "This is a task for many years, perhaps for a whole generation, but the result would be a modern law that would at the same time retrieve the basic principles of the traditional law, and also constitute a historical continuity of the ancient legal tradition."[18]

The plan advocated by Moshe Silberg was favorably received in many quarters, but as it called for many years of legislative endeavor, it was regarded as a guideline for the future rather than as an immediate project. The suggestion made by some for the adoption of a modern European code, such as the Swiss, was never seriously pursued. Because the day of independence was approaching rapidly, there was no alternative but to retain the law of Palestine. On May 14, 1948, the Provisional Council of State issued a proclamation in which it declared itself to be the legislative authority. Article 3 of the Proclamation provided: "So long as no laws have been enacted by or on behalf of the Provisional Council of State, the law which existed in Palestine on Iyar 5, 5708 (May 14, 1948), shall continue in force in the State of Israel, insofar as such continuance in force is consistent with the contents of the Proclamation, with the future laws, and with the changes arising from the establishment of the state and its authorities."[19]

The first law enacted by the Provisional Council of State was the Law and Administration Ordinance of May 19, 1948, which was made to apply retroactively as from May 14.[20] Section 11 provided: "The law which existed in Palestine on Iyar 5, 5708 (May 14, 1948), shall remain in force, insofar as there is nothing therein repugnant to this Ordinance, or to the other laws that may be enacted by or on behalf of the Provisional Council of State, and subject to such modification as may result from the establishment of the State and its authorities." Although essentially a repetition of Article 3 of the Proclamation, it was necessary to repeat this provision in the Law and Administration Ordinance because the former, being a mere proclamation, did not have the force of law.

The Ordinance explicitly repealed the provisions of the Chamberlain White Paper of 1939, which had restricted Jewish immigration and land sale to Jews. Section 14 (a) provided: "Any power vested under the law (i.e., the law of Palestine) in the King of England or in any of his Secretaries of State, and any power vested under the law in the High Commissioner, the High Commissioner in Council, or in the Government of Palestine, shall henceforth vest in the Provisional Government." Section 15 (a) of the Ordinance provided: " 'Palestine,' whenever appearing in the law, shall henceforth be read as 'Israel.' "

These provisions assured that no legal vacuum would result from the termination of the mandate and the establishment of the state, and that the laws of Palestine, unless and until changed, should apply in the new state. By replacing the word "Palestine" by the word "Israel," legal continuity was assured. In order to ensure not only the continuity of the law, but of the law courts as well, Section 17 provided: "So long as no new law concerning law courts has been enacted, the law courts existing in the territory of the state shall continue to function within the scope of the powers conferred on them by law." Thus the State of Israel retained the law of Palestine and courts of law of Palestine "with the powers conferred upon them." As a result of this enactment, Israel inherited the ecclesiastical courts and the ecclesiastical law applied by them; in the case of the Jews, it also inherited the official rabbinate and the religious services maintained by the taxpayer, as well as municipal by-laws regulating Sabbath observance. This "religious status quo," which included the rights of parents to give their children a religious education in state-supported public schools of the religious trend, was consolidated and broadened by subsequent legislation.

C. THE CONSTITUTIONAL DEBATE

The Provisional Government and the Provisional Council of State were preoccupied with defending the state against the invasion of the regular armies of Lebanon, Syria, Iraq, Jordan and Egypt, an invasion that commenced a few hours after the Declaration of Independence on May 14, 1948. The war continued, with some interruptions, until the signing of an armistice agreement with Syria on July 20, 1949.

The Provisional Government had to create an army and the organs of administration. The legislative program of the Provisional Council of State was concerned primarily with emergency measures. It found time, however, to deal with two subjects of religious import. On June 3, 1948, the Provisional Council enacted the "Days of Rest Ordinance," of which the operative clause was as follows: "The Sabbath and the Jewish festivals, namely, the two days of New Year, the Day of Atonement, the First Day of the Feast of Tabernacles, the Eighth Day of Solemn Assembly, the First and Seventh Days of the Feast of Passover shall be prescribed Days of Rest in the State of Israel. Non-Jews shall have the right to observe their own Sabbaths and festivals as Days of Rest."[21] Unlike Article 23 of the mandate, which enjoined the Palestine govern-

ment to recognize the Holydays "of the respective communities in Palestine as days of rest for the members of such communities," the new
law made the Jewish Holydays "the prescribed days of rest in the State
of Israel," and not merely for the Jewish community. This law reflected
the fact that the State of Israel was in fact a Jewish state.

The other law enacted by the Provisional Council of State was the
Kasher Food for Soldiers Ordinance, of November 25, 1949. It became
necessary to solve a problem that had arisen out of the Defense Army
of Israel Ordinance enacted on May 26, 1948, which provided for compulsory military service.[22] In some quarters it was urged that special units
be formed for the thousands of Orthodox young men, so that they could
pursue a religious way of life in their own military environment. David
Ben-Gurion, who was both prime minister and minister of defense, resisted this demand and insisted on mixed units. Since it was manifestly
impossible to provide facilities for both kasher and for nonkasher food
within the same army unit, the Kasher Food for Soldiers Ordinance was
enacted, which provided: "The supply of kasher food shall be ensured
to all Jewish soldiers of the Defense Army of Israel." It was the only
practical solution to a delicate problem, and as a result of this law only
kasher food was made available in military camps to Jewish as well as
non-Jewish soldiers.

The Declaration of Independence had proclaimed that the Provisional
Government would function "until the establishment of elected, regular authorities of the state in accordance with the Constitution which
shall be adopted by the Elected Constituent Assembly not later than
October 1, 1948." Because of the war it proved impossible to proceed
with elections to a Constituent Assembly, and not until November 18,
1948, did the Provisional Council of State enact its Constituent Assembly Elections Ordinance, in pursuance of which elections were duly held
on January 25, 1949.[23] By way of preparation for the first national elections, a population census was held on November 8, which revealed that
on that day there were seven hundred and eighty-two thousand persons
living in Israel, of whom seven hundred and thirteen thousand were
Jews.[24]

The provisions of the Constituent Assembly Elections Ordinance,
which purported to lay down rules for governing the elections to a Constituent Assembly only, provided in actual fact the basic principles for
elections in the future. "The elections shall be based on universal and
equal suffrage, and shall be direct and by secret ballot; seats shall be allocated on the principle of proportional representation. Voting shall be
for lists of candidates" (Section 3). The number of persons to be elected would be one hundred and twenty (Section 8). "For purposes of
counting the votes and the calculation of the results, the entire area of

elections shall be deemed to be a single district" (2b). Thus the proportional system of representation bequeathed by the Zionist Congresses and the Va'ad Leumi to the new state was perpetuated.

To ensure a smooth transition of authority from the Provisional Government to the permanent authorities to be set up by the Constituent Assembly, the Constituent Assembly (Transition) Ordinance was enacted on January 13, 1949.[25] Section 1 provided: "The Provisional Council of State shall continue in office until the convening of the Constituent Assembly of the State of Israel. . . ." Section 4 provided: "The Provisional Government shall continue in office until the establishment of a new Government by the Constituent Assembly." Finally, Section 4 laid down: "The Constituent Assembly shall, as long as it does not itself otherwise decide, have all the powers vested by law in the Provisional Assembly of State." This provision reflected the anticipation that the Constituent Assembly would in fact become a parliament engaged in legislation, rather than a body engaged in the drafting of a written constitution.

Two days after first convening on February 14, 1949, instead of proceeding with the drafting of a constitution, the Constituent Assembly enacted "the Transition Law," commonly referred to as the "small constitution." This in effect negated the very nature of the Constituent Assembly and converted it into a legislative body. This radical change was accomplished by general acquiescence.

Section 1 of the Transitional Law 5709–1949[26] provided that "the legislative body of the State of Israel shall be called the Knesset. The Constituent Assembly shall be called: the First Knesset." Section 2 provided that "an enactment of the Knesset shall be called a Law." Section 3 provided for the President of the State, who would be elected by the Knesset. The powers of the President resembled those of a constitutional monarch, and his principal constitutional function was "after consultations with representatives of the party groups in the Knesset," to entrust "a member of the Knesset with the task of forming a government" (Section 9). The government was to be responsible to the Knesset "and shall hold office as long as it enjoys the confidence of the Knesset. The government which receives a vote of non-confidence from the Knesset . . . shall immediately tender its resignation to the President of the State" (Section 11).

These were the principal features of the "small constitution" that made Israel a parliamentary democracy, with a unicameral parliament whose legislative powers were not limited by any constitutional provisions. In deference to the wishes of the religious parties, the Transition Law of 1949 provided that on assuming office the President of the State and the members of the government would, instead of taking an oath (which though not prohibited in the Torah is not customarily taken by the Orthodox) sign a declaration pledging "to be loyal to the State of Israel and to its laws." Although the Transition Law was often amended and later replaced by another law, its principal features were retained. It is within the framework of a parliamentary democracy, patterned as nearly as possible on the British model, that the political system of Israel has evolved. It differed from the British system in one important aspect: whereas the system of elections in England was based on election by constituencies, which encouraged a two-party system, in Israel it was based on proportional representation, the entire country being one constituency. As a result, a proliferation of political parties was inescapable, a development that has had far-reaching effects on Israeli politics in general, and on the impact of religion on politics in particular.

The Provisional Council of State had appointed a Constitutional Committee "to assemble, study and catalogue pertinent recommendations and material, and to prepare a draft constitution, which, together with minority opinions in the Committee, shall be submitted to the Constituent Assembly for its consideration."[27] However, there was a growing feeling against a written constitution. The various views on this subject found their full expression in the course of a parliamentary debate that lasted for nine sittings, between February 1 and June 13, 1950.

The proponents of a written constitution urged that the United Nations resolution of November 29, 1947, had imposed on the two states that were to be created on the territory of Palestine the duty of adopting a constitutional instrument that would provide, *inter alia,* safeguards for religious freedom and for minority rights. Furthermore, the Declaration of Independence of the State of Israel had announced that a constitution would be adopted.[28] It was urged that the principle of the separation of powers could be safeguarded only within the framework of a written constitution.[29] Furthermore, it was held, such a document had distinct educational value for training in good citizenship. While England with her long democratic tradition and generally respected precedents could get along without a constitution, a new state that was expected to receive immigrants from countries without a democratic tradition could not afford to dispense with it. Finally, in a period of ingathering of exiles, a constitution would be a unifying factor, and would unequivocally establish the rule of law.[30]

The leading opponent of a written constitution, Prime Minister David Ben-Gurion, pointed out that great as was the occasion of the Proclamation of Independence, it was not "the Redemption," but merely the beginning of a long process. In the meantime, only a small minority of the Jewish people were dwelling in the state, and it would not be proper for them alone to enact a constitution.[31] A debate on constitutional problems would create acrimonious controversies on social, economic, and religious issues.

At first, the Mizrahi was in favor of a constitution. Mizrahi leader Zerah Wahrhaftig was chairman of the Constitutional Committee appointed by the Provisional Council of State,[32] and he urged the adoption of a constitution. But under pressure of Agudat Israel, Mizrahi eventually joined the latter in vehemently opposing what they had at first favored. It was Wahrhaftig himself who spoke in the Knesset on behalf of his party, detailing their opposition to a constitution.[33] He urged delay and, in the meantime, the enactment of "fundamental laws" that would deal with specific subjects and that could, if necessary, be altered without the restrictive procedures imposed by a constitution. "Even the Torah was not given in one instance. The Torah was given, chapter by chapter, over a period of forty years; forty years passed until the Torah was given by the Almighty."[34] He added: "A constitution is not enacted; a constitution is granted; it is granted by the Almighty."[35]

Speaking on behalf of the Agudah, Meir David Levinstein rejected a constitution under all circumstances. "There is no need in Israel for a man-made constitution; if it contradicts the Torah of Israel, it is a revolt against the Almighty; if it is identical with the Torah, it is superfluous. A constitution will lead to an uncompromising fight . . . a Kulturkampf. * There will be neither compromises nor mutual concessions, for one cannot make concessions in matters of faith. Let us not endanger constructive work for a matter which is a luxury. We shall regard the imposition of a secular constitution as an attempt to give a bill of divorcement to our sacred Torah. It must be understood that a secular constitution will be boycotted by Torah-true Jews, not only in our state, but throughout the lands of the Diaspora."[36]

Here was a clear warning that a constitution would unleash a bitter Kulturkampf. Coming as it did at a time when the infant state was confronted with external and internal difficulties threatening its very survival, the warning fell on receptive ears and was reflected in the speeches of some of the secularists who were also opponents of a constitution.

The most forceful argument of the Orthodox was presented by Rabbi I. M. Levin, the Agudat Israel leader, who propounded the view of "loyal Judaism." He defined the issue as involving one's view of the Torah. "Our Torah is eternal, even as its Giver is eternal. The Torah must not be adapted to life, it is rather for life to adapt itself to the Torah. This truth can only be attained through faith. The Torah will not change; it must not be changed. . . . Any attempt at reform will result in failure."[37] He also issued a warning: "If you wish to impose

---

* This German word meaning "culture struggle" was coined when Chancellor Bismarck in 1872 tried to deprive the German Catholic Church of certain privileges.

upon us a constitution that will be contrary to the laws of the Torah, we shall not tolerate it. In the course of our exile, we have passed through every stage of suffering, and no force and no inquisition could subdue us. Do you think that what our enemies have failed to do, what blood and fire have failed to do, you will be able to achieve by means of the power of the state? . . . It may be that the cup of suffering is not yet full, and that we still have to endure another period of Galut—a Galut in the midst of Jews, after the Galut we have known in the midst of gentiles. I must emphasize—this attempt will split the nation into two, and I do not think this will benefit the infant state. I am convinced that it will be a disaster for the state."[38]

On the surface it appeared as if Rabbi Levin might be replying to the proponents of a constitution that would impair religious freedom, interfere with the free exercise of religious worship, or prevent the pursuit of a religious way of life. In fact, all the speakers who supported the project of a written constitution, professed atheists included, stressed that such a constitution would afford a constitutional guarantee to the free exercise of religion. Some were of the opinion that the interest of religion would be best served by the separation of religion from state, while others felt that the constitution should provide for a state-supported religion. Still others suggested that the constitution should not at all be concerned with the question of state and religion; this, they thought, should be left to ordinary legislation, as had previously been the case. However divergent the views expressed were, they had one common denominator—respect for religion and the safeguards of its freedom, as well as readiness to lend state support for the maintenance of religious institutions.

What the Orthodox were objecting to was a man-made constitution for a Jewish state. They did not, however, object to man-made laws enacted by the parliament of a Jewish state. In fact, Rabbi Levin pointed out: "We prefer there to be ordinary legislation, and I emphasize that those laws that are not permeated with the spirit of the Torah will be regarded by Orthodox Jewry as temporary: but in any case they are preferable to a constitution."[39] Thus Rabbi Levin did not deny the right of the Knesset to make laws, even laws "not permeated with the spirit of the Torah." Neither did any of the Orthodox speakers suggest the adoption of a constitution that would be based on the Torah. Such a constitution would be a mere restatement of the Torah and therefore superfluous. This attitude relieved the spokesmen for Orthodoxy from stating what laws should, in accordance with the Torah, be adopted for the governance of the state and for all matters relating to the maintenance of law and order and the operation of public services.

Rabbi Levin emphasized that in the long run Orthodoxy aspired to having the laws of the Torah alone apply to all levels of state life, but he realized that such a time had not yet been reached. He saw, however, the possibility of coexistence until that ideal time should come. "We have presented you with a minimum program that would satisfy the principal demands of Orthodoxy. If these demands are satisfied, we can envisage the possibility of our co-operation with the institutions of the state."[40] This minimum program, on which both the Agudah and the Mizrahi were united, became the basis of the *Hakikah Datit* (Religious Legislation) that has engaged the attention of the Knesset and of public opinion ever since.

In retrospect one must come to the conclusion that this was one of the most momentous debates ever held in the parliament of Israel. It was highlighted by Ben-Gurion who spoke on behalf of the government and as the leader of the Israel Labor Party—Mapai, the largest party in the Knesset. He joined the religious parties in opposing the drafting of a written constitution, but his reasons were entirely different from theirs. He preferred the flexible British system of constitutional precedents over a rigid system that would not lend itself to alteration except by a special procedure. The dynamic development of Israel would not benefit from a written and static constitution; he considered such a document indispensable only in federal states that needed an instrument to define the powers of the central and local governments. A unitary state could manage without it, and it would be better to gain parliamentary experience and build up a democratic tradition before a constitution was crystallized.

Nevertheless Ben-Gurion took the Orthodox to task for some of their arguments. Spokesmen for the religious parties had claimed the Written and Oral Torah to be sovereign authority in the life of Israel, which made it clear that they were advocating a theocratic regime.[41] Ben-Gurion reminded them that the Agudat Israel had publicly announced, prior to the establishment of the state, that they did not propose the establishment of a theocracy. But if the Torah were to be the sovereign authority in Israel, then the rabbis alone would be both the legislative and the executive authorities of the state. Ben-Gurion went on to challenge the Orthodox conception of the sovereignty of divinely given law as against the secular character of man-made law. "Since when is a man-made creation unsuitable for Israel?" he asked. The major activities in which the state is engaged are secular by their very nature: public works, farming, housing, communications, road building—all these are secular matters. The sovereignty of the people expressed itself in the making of laws. "Do you," Ben-Gurion asked, "respect the principle of the sovereignty of the people?"[42] None of the Orthodox speakers took up Ben-Gurion's challenge.

Ben-Gurion proceeded to assail the very conception of the "secular character of man-made laws"; he adduced from the Bible the principle of the validity of man-made laws and of the people's sovereignty. He related the story of Moses and Jethro, his father-in-law.* Moses had complained of the hardships involved in being the sole judge of the people, and of the hardship involved in trying cases "from morning until the evening." Jethro replied: "The thing you are doing is not good; you will surely wear yourself out, and these people as well. For the task is too heavy for you." Jethro then suggested that Moses appoint "capable men who fear God . . . and place them as chiefs of thousands, hundreds, fifties, and tens, and let them judge the people at all times." Ben-Gurion concluded from this: "Jethro was not a Jew, but Moses accepted the constitutional advice tendered to him, and set up a judicial administration, as he was advised to do by a person who had had administrative experience, and although he was a Gentile, it was not considered as contrary to the law of Moses."[43] The second biblical instance quoted by Ben-Gurion was the controversy over the institution of a monarchy in the time of Samuel.** The story tells of the elders of Israel who came to Samuel and said: "Behold you are old, and your sons do not walk in your ways; give us a king to judge us." Samuel was displeased, for he regarded this as a rejection of God, and he proceeded to enumerate the hardships and calamities likely to befall the people at the hands of a king. But the elders insisted on having a king, "that we may also be like all the nations, and that our kings may judge us . . . and fight our battles." Finally God Himself intervened and advised Samuel: "Hearken unto their voice, and make them a king." Here the will of the people, a truly secular act, prevailed, and was given divine approval to boot.

While thus opposing the Orthodox downgrading of man-made legislation and their ambivalent attitude toward the principle of the people's sovereignty, Ben-Gurion remained for all practical purposes at one with the Orthodox wing on the principle of rejecting a constitution. Their arguments differed widely, but they voted alike.

On June 13, 1950, three motions were put to the vote in the Knesset. The motion of the religious parties read: "The foundations of the government and the separation of powers shall be set out in basic laws." This motion, which negated a constitution, received fourteen votes. A motion was supported by the General Zionist, Herut, and Mapam parties that would impose upon the Knesset Committee on Law, Justice and Constitution the task of preparing the draft of a constitution. This motion received thirty-nine votes.[44] The Mapai and Progressive parties

* Exodus 18:13ff.
** 1 Samuel 8:1ff.

sponsored a resolution that was submitted by Izhar Harari. It read: "The Knesset resolves to impose upon the Committee on Law, Justice and Constitution the task of preparing a draft of a constitution for the state. The constitution will be built up chapter by chapter in such a way that each chapter will by itself constitute a fundamental law. The chapters will be submitted to the Knesset to the extent to which the Committee completes the work, and the chapter will be incorporated in the constitution of the state."[45] This motion received fifty votes, and was passed. Thus a constitution was approved in principle, but its enactment was postponed for the foreseeable future.

It took eight years before even the first fruits of this resolution made their appearance. In 1958, the Knesset enacted a basic law dealing with the Knesset. It restated in detail the principles of a parliamentary democracy, with power vested in a unicameral chamber of one hundred and twenty members elected once in four years.[46] In 1960, the Basic Law *Israel Lands* was adopted, dealing with public ownership of lands.[47] Further basic laws dealt with the executive branch of the government and the President. On June 16, 1969, the Knesset enacted Basic Law *The President of the State,* and on August 13, 1968, Basic Law *The Government* was enacted.[48]

The basic laws, dealing as they do with the setting up of the organs of government and with the delineation of their powers, are not concerned with problems of religion. It was only in Basic Law *Israel Lands*, that is, the law regulating state-owned lands, that, at the instance of the Orthodox, the following provision was enacted as Article 3; "the Basic Law shall not affect acts designed solely to enable the observance of the commandment concerning the Sabbatical year." This provision was essential for the Orthodox, to enable them to execute a quasi-conveyance of lands cultivated by them to a non-Jew for the duration of the Sabbatical year. Under this provision the Orthodox farmers could resort to the legal fiction of a conveyance to a non-Jew, and continue cultivating their farms without violating the law of Shemittah.

These basic laws as well as those to be enacted in the future are in no way different from other laws, except for their different designation. Like all other laws, they may be amended—as, in fact, they occasionally have been—through the ordinary processes of legislation. The word *basic* attaching to the title of each of these special laws merely denotes that they deal with matters of constitutional import and in the future may serve as elements for a written constitution. In the two decades since the debate of 1950, no further attempts have been made in the Knesset to frame a constitution.

Neither the religious parties nor the rabbinate have made any effort to suggest to the Knesset that specific laws should be enacted based on the Halakhah. The Orthodox were not ready, and their unwillingness to summon a Sanhedrin put an end to any legislative initiative on their part. In fact, when non-Orthodox legislators sought to introduce principles of the Torah into legislative enactments, resentment and even opposition were displayed by the Orthodox. From an Orthodox viewpoint, the legislative program of the parliament of the Jewish state was regarded as temporary, to be replaced in the future by the Halakhah—not by Halakhic legislation, but by the Halakhah as interpreted by qualified scholars. Except for a minority, the Orthodox rejected the very process of legislation as a means for enacting Halakhah-based laws, on the ground that legislation was man-made law, while the Halakhah, being divine, did not require ratification by a human agency. By treating man-made law as temporary, that is, as valid for an unspecified duration only, the Orthodox were able to recognize the validity of those laws and to consider themselves bound by them.

There have been instances when the government has refrained from enforcing the law because of likely opposition from the Orthodox. Thus, the Minister of Defense has desisted from drafting Yeshivah students into the army, as the law[49] required him to do, and has in effect exempted them from military service by an extra-legal arrangement, despite the protests of a large segment of the public. The government also overlooked certain violations of the Independence Day Law of April 12, 1949,[50] which provides that "Independence Day shall be a day of rest." On this day many of the Yeshivot, especially in Jerusalem and Bnei-Brak, have continued their normal programs and have not allowed their students to participate in the celebrations—this even in Yeshivot, which obtain subventions from the Ministry of Religions. The government has likewise refrained from fully enforcing the National Service Law of 1953, which imposed upon unmarried women who had exempted themselves from military service on the permissible ground of religion, the duty of performing a "public service," such service consisting of aiding and teaching immigrants in religious educational institutions or on agricultural settlements, and in general of engaging in social work.

Ben-Gurion, however, resisted the demand that separate battalions should be formed in the army that would consist solely of Orthodox Jews. Both Agudat Israel and Mizrahi made this request. Rabbi Kalman Kahana, speaking for the Labor wing of the Agudah, said: "If we wish to create a type of soldier healthy in body and mind, we must create a spiritual climate for him which accords with his education, upbringing and views. If another way of life is imposed on him, he will deteriorate. We must, therefore, insist on battalions of religious soldiers within the framework of the national army. Observance of Kashrut and of Sabbath

are not sufficient to assure a religious way of life. . . . There must be
an environment suitable for him in the army, that will develop his spiritual treasures acquired by him during his youth."[51] Rabbi Kahana was
supported by Moshe Unna of HaPoel HaMizrahi, a leader of the Orthodox kibbutz movement, who pleaded to save Orthodox boys "from the
negative effects of being stationed . . . among a non-religious majority,
and under the command of non-religious officers."[52] Ben-Gurion held
that separate battalions would not only adversely affect the morale of
the whole army and give rise to complaints of discrimination, but would
also make it impossible to use the limited manpower of the nation in
the most effective manner; even more seriously, such an arrangement
would divide the nation. Ben-Gurion's view prevailed.

The Orthodox did not fail to display a keen interest in both the
legislative and executive branches of the government. They participated
in coalition governments and their pivotal position in the Knesset enabled
them to implement and extend the religious status quo. Although the
declared objective of the religious parties was to preserve the status quo
as established under British rule, they have, in fact, succeeded in extending it. This they were able to achieve largely because of the proportional system of representation, where in the absence of a party enjoying a parliamentary majority, government by a coalition of parties
became inevitable. This system afforded even minor constituents of the
coalition to exercise a measure of influence far exceeding their electoral
strength.

The months of anxiety preceding and following the establishment
of the State of Israel, were, in many respects, the most critical in the
history of the Yishuv. To meet the political and the military emergency,
every effort had to be made to achieve political unity. The first step in
this direction was the co-option of Agudat Israel. To preserve the unity
of the army, kasher food was provided for all army units, and to allay
the apprehensions of all Orthodox groups, the jurisdiction of the rabbinical courts in matters of personal status was confirmed, a law for
the observance of the Sabbath was enacted, and state-supported religious schools were by law established. What might have developed into
an acute conflict, the adoption of a written constitution, was averted by
the readiness of the non-Orthodox to shelve this issue, or at least to
postpone it for a long period.

The creation of the State of Israel revealed the ambivalence in the
attitude of the Orthodox to it. Welcoming, as most of them did, the establishment of a Jewish state, they were also aware that it was not
achieved within the framework of the Messianic scheme, and that the

majority of the Jewish people were alienated from the observance of the precepts of the Torah. At the same time, they realized that the newly born state was Jewish, that it afforded refuge to the survivors of the Holocaust and to the oppressed Jews in the Islamic countries, and that it provided scope, encouragement, and assistance for the development and maintenance of religious schools and institutions.

The total unpreparedness of the Orthodox to offer a viable Halakhic alternative to a legal and constitutional system and their failure to reestablish a Sanhedrin, made it extremely difficult for them to press for the incorporation of the Halakhah into the law of the land. The Orthodox reconciled themselves to man-made laws and justified their compliance with such laws by regarding them as provisional, to be replaced in God's own time by the Halakhah. There being no written constitution, the road for the eventual reign of the Torah as the supreme law of the land was left open. In the long period of time that will elapse until the ripening of a Torah-bound state, it was incumbent upon the Orthodox to avail themselves of the opportunities afforded by a democratic society, in order to advance the cause of traditional Judaism.

5

Religion and Party Politics

A. GOVERNMENT BY COALITION

The day following the Proclamation of Independence, the gates of the new state were thrown wide open for the "ingathering of the exiles." And indeed there were exiles clamoring for a safe refuge, first from the concentration and displaced persons camps in Nazi-devastated Europe, and later from Arab states, which had made the lives of the Jewish minority in their midst unbearable. From 1948 until 1951 the Jewish population in the state of Israel doubled. From some 650,000 in 1948, it reached over 1,800,000 in 1958 and exceeded 2,900,000 in 1975—an increase of some 400% within 25 years, largely due to the process of "the ingathering of exiles."

In many respects it was in fact an "ingathering of exiles," and in some respects it was also the "end of exile." Thus nearly the entire Jewish community of Bulgaria moved to Israel, as did the old established communities of Yemen, Iraq, and Libya, and the vast majority of those who had survived in Poland, Hungary, Czechoslovakia, and Rumania. Tens of thousands came from Morocco, Tunis, Turkey, Persia, and India. Thousands came also from North and South America and from Western Europe and South Africa, but their percentage of the total immigration remained small.

Until 1948 the predominant majority of the Yishuv had consisted of persons of European origin; now, the post-1948 period saw the arrival of many Sefardic and Oriental Jews who had lived in Moslem lands. In the period from 1948 to 1962 the number of these immigrants was 54 percent, compared to 46 percent from Europe and America. After 1962 the percentage of the Euro-American group rose again, but the total net result of the immigration has been that Jews of European origin on the one hand, and those of Oriental and Sefardic origin on the other are equally balanced. The rate of marriage between the two groups has been constantly on the increase, reaching twenty percent of all the marriages celebrated in 1967.

No data are available detailing the number of Orthodox Jews who have come to Israel since 1948. Among the arrivals from Europe, and especially from Eastern and Central Europe, were a large number of observant Jews, including many adherents of Hasidic rabbis, some of whom migrated with their followers and succeeded in reestablishing "courts" in Israel. In Jerusalem, Natanya, and Beersheba, the Orthodox erected quarters inhabited almost exclusively by religious Jews. Bnei Brak attracted thousands of them, and before long became the site of many Yeshivot and a center of Talmudic learning. There, the Orthodox control the City Council, which has an Orthodox mayor to preside over it. The city's by-laws prohibit all traffic, private as well as public, on the Sabbath and on festivals; chains are stretched across the main roads of the township to enforce these rules, with special arrangements made for first aid and police vehicles.

The Oriental Jews, whether from Asia or from Africa, are traditionally observant, but on the whole are more tolerant than Ashkenazic Orthodoxy. In some ways they have found it easier to fit into a rapidly developing modern society than have the Orthodox Ashkenazim, many of whom prefer a degree of self-imposed isolation reminiscent of the Old Yishuv.

Israeli democracy has developed dynamically, and the intensity of its political life shows how seriously it is taken. The proportional system of representation has enabled nearly every shade of opinion to be represented in the parliament; it has resulted in a multiplicity of parties reminiscent of the French Fourth Republic. In the elections to the First Knesset in January 1949, as many as seventeen lists succeeded in securing representation, with Mapai (Hebrew initials of Mifleget Po'alei Eretz Israel, Israel Labor Party) gaining forty-six seats, the largest number, and WIZO, the Women's International Zionist Organization, gaining one. In the elections held in 1951, sixteen lists gained representation; in the elections to the Third Knesset in 1955, the number of lists dropped to twelve, and remained the same for the next two elections in 1959 and 1961; in the elections to the Sixth Knesset held in 1965, the number of lists rose to thirteen.[1] Twelve parties were represented in the Knesset elected in 1965 and ten in the Knesset elected in 1973. All of this reflected a checkered history of parties splitting, amalgamating, and then splitting again, and was characterized by two conflicting tendencies: a desire for larger political formations and a passion for asserting every possible view. Yet, the most remarkable feature of Israeli democratic life has been that in spite of the proliferation of parties, the country has enjoyed political stability and scarcely any large-scale change in the relative size of the major parties. This governmental stability was primarily the product of the proportional system, which made a landslide practically impossible. The absence of outright majorities at the polls, as well as the need for unity, has produced a tradition of coalition governments, and each coalition government, with a few brief exceptions, has included the religious parties.

Still, fragmentation of political groupings might well have endangered the political stability of the nascent state, had it not been for a large, disciplined, and ably-led party which, although unable to win an outright majority at the polls, was yet strong enough to constitute a firm base for a coalition government. This party was Mapai, a moderate social-democratic party. At the elections to the first Knesset it received 35.7% of the total vote and was represented by 46 deputies. In the second Knesset elected in July 1951 it was represented by 45 deputies; its representation dropped to 40 deputies in the third Knesset, elected in 1955, raised its representation to 47 deputies in the elections of 1959, and dropped to 42 deputies in the premature elections held in 1961. In the elections of 1965, it joined hands with a smaller left-wing labor group, Ahdut HaAvodah and obtained 45 seats in the sixth Knesset. In the elections of 1969 it co-opted the leftist Mapam party within the framework of a "labor alignment," which obtained 56 seats in the seventh Knesset, and 51 seats in the elections to the eighth Knesset, which were held in December 1973. Whether on its own or having been joined by Ahdut HaAvodah and since named "Mifleget HaAvodah" (the Labor Party), the historic Mapai has remained the central and guiding element in Israeli politics. Its empirical approach and its capacity to adjust its policies to the rapid economic and social changes have enabled it to survive external crises and internal tensions. Outside the Labor Party, there were left in the Knesset numerous formations, but none was able to constitute a focus around which others might group to create an alternative government. The latter were so split on a variety of issues that there was no common denominator to unite them.

The General Zionists never succeeded in securing more than sixteen percent of the vote; when they merged with the Progressives to form the Liberal Party they secured 13.7 percent. The religious parties combined secured an average of about 14 percent; their highwater point was in 1961 when they received 15.4 percent. The two leftist parties, Mapam (United Labor Party) and Ahdut HaAvodah (Unity of Labor) averaged together about 14 percent, reaching their highest mark in 1955, when they received 15.5 percent together.[2] Inasmuch as the two nonsocialist parties, Herut and the General Zionists (later known as the Liberals), could not form a coalition with the two leftist parties for ideological reasons, Mapai became the basis of all the coalition governments from the beginning of the state onwards.

Mapai had come into being in 1930 as a merger of the Socialist Ahdut HaAvodah and the populist HaPoel HaTzair, with the former as the dominant element; it was dedicated both to socialism and to the upbuilding of Palestine as a Jewish homeland. It inherited the radical traditions of the Second Aliyah, and during the period of the Jewish National Home it identified itself with the spirit of the pioneers who settled desolate lands with meager means. Before long Mapai became the dominant force in the Histadrut (General Federation of Labor), and from 1933 also in the World Zionist Organization. Relying on cadres of politically educated and devoted members, and controlling the network of economic and social institutions of the Histadrut and of the Jewish Agency, it had no difficulty in establishing itself as the major party in the Jewish state. Its policy was based on economic development through government planning and spending rather than through the traditional market mechanisms; on strict supervision of economic activity; on toleration and encouragement of monopolies and preference for special sectors; and above all on securing the preeminence of the Histadrut, both as a trade union and as the largest single entepreneur in many branches of the economy. The socialist policy of Mapai was generally opposed by the General Zionists and by Herut, who objected to rigid governmental controls and called rather for conditions where individual initiative could develop. They resented what they regarded as the preferential treatment accorded by the government to the Histadrut economic and business enterprises.

Mapai could form a coalition by inviting either the General Zionists (Liberals) or Herut to join it; but in order to secure the cooperation of both or either of these parties, Mapai would have been obliged to make considerable concessions in the realm of economic policy. This Mapai was unwilling to do. As a result, except for a brief period from 1952 to 1954, the nonsocialist parties were kept out of the government coalition until the Six Days War in 1967, when a Government of National Unity was formed that possessed a common policy in matters of defense and foreign policy, but not in matters of economic policy, and which held office till August 1970.

Nor could Mapai turn to the Left for its coalition partners, for until the middle of the fifties the two leftist parties were committed to a far-reaching pro-Soviet orientation and vehemently opposed the pro-Western policy of the government of Israel. Therefore Mapai had no alternative but to seek its coalition partners in the camp of the Orthodox, and the latter became its constant and loyal associates. From 1948 until the formation of the National Unity government in May 1967, Israel was thus ruled by a Socialist-Religious coalition. From the religious parties Mapai secured support both for its socialist-economic policies and for its pro-Western orientation in foreign policy. The religious, on their part, found no difficulty in affording support to Mapai in the fields of economics and foreign policy, since the Halakhah was neutral in these secular concerns. In return Mapai was willing to satisfy the specific interests of its coalition partners. The Socialist-Religious coalition evolved a pattern that, with the passage of time, became more and more embedded in political traditions and administrative practices.[3]

In the coalition government formed following the elections to the First Knesset in January 1949, the Religious Front (including Agudat Israel) was represented by three cabinet ministers. Following the withdrawal of Agudat Israel from the government, the National Religious Party (known as Madfal, Hebrew initials for: Miflagah Datit Leumit, it included the Mizrahi and the Poalei Mizrahi after their merger in 1956) was represented by two cabinet ministers in the Second, Third, and Fourth Knessets. Although in the elections to the Fifth Knesset in 1961 Mafdal did not obtain a larger number of seats, they nevertheless were represented by three cabinet ministers; this increase was due to the weaker position in which Mapai found itself in that parliament, a circumstance that Mafdal exploited to the full. For the same reason Mafdal retained its three cabinet seats in the Sixth and Seventh Knessets, although it had actually lost one seat. In general, Mafdal representation in the national government—as in the municipalities—was dependent on the strength of Mapai: the weaker it was, the greater its dependence on Mafdal.

Except for a brief interruption, the portfolio of the Ministry for Religious Affairs was always held by a member of Mafdal. Thus Mafdal received wide control over the rabbinic establishment and over the administration of religious affairs in general, through the direct and indirect power of the Ministry to determine or influence rabbinic appointments, to grant subsidies to Yeshivot and for the construction of synagogues, and to make appointments to the 186 local religious councils.[4]

The other portfolio usually allocated to Mafdal has been the Ministry of the Interior, which through the control of the finances of the municipal and local councils has exerted considerable influence, especially regarding budgetary provisions for the maintenance of the local religious councils. The Ministry of the Interior is in charge of the Bureau of the Registration of Inhabitants, which registers personal particulars, including nationality, religion, and marital status. This control has enabled the ministry to make sure that no person is registered as a

Jew unless he is Halakhically qualified to be so registered.

The pattern evolved on the national level is repeated in the munici-palities and the local councils. In these organs of local government, too, the proportional system of representation persists, with the result that in the great majority of towns no one party manages to obtain a ma-jority. Thus on the local as on the national level, Mapai-Mafdal coali-tions have usually been formed in order to secure a majority of coun-cillors to vote for the election of a mayor and for the management of the town. Mafdal's cooperation has been obtained by satisfying "religious demands," which usually include the election of a religious deputy may-or, and indeed at least one religious deputy mayor holds office in the majority of townships.[5]

Other demands are usually that members of religious parties be em-ployed in the local civil services, that a substantial subvention for the maintenance of the local religious council be voted from the municipal budget, that by-laws be enacted regarding public transport and perfor-mances in places of amusement on Sabbaths and holidays, and that the sale of pork products in restaurants and shops be forbidden. In most cases, these demands of the religious parties have been met, except in Haifa, where the municipal council has had a large labor majority, and has allowed the functioning of public transport on the Sabbath.

It is worthy of note that in those localities where Mapai is not the stronger party, Mafdal has not hesitated to form a municipal coalition with the anti-Mapai parties. Thus, Mafdal joined the coalition in Ramat Gan headed by a mayor who is a member of the Liberal Party. In 1962–63 and in 1965 in Beersheba, and in Givat Shmuel since 1962, it formed a municipal coalition with Marxist-oriented Mapam. Consid-erations of economic and social policies of a municipal government are of secondary importance to Mafdal, so long as it is able to obtain its own religious objectives within any kind of political combination.

Mapai, and its successor the Labor Party, does contain elements that would like to see religion and state separated. Its membership is predominantly nonobservant, but it is not in any way anti-religious or atheistically oriented. Its attitude to religion can be described as one of benevolent neutrality. It is determined, however, to avoid a confronta-tion with the Orthodox, and being mindful of the importance of national unity, it is prepared to put up with the religious status quo as evolved in the course of years.

Although this pragmatic approach has made a coalition with Mafdal necessary, it has nevertheless created strains and stresses within the Labor Party. On occasions when public opinion was agitated by instances

---

* *Mamzerut* is the status of a child born of a union within the biblically forbidden degrees of propinquity, or a child born of its mother's adultery.

of denial of marriage to a cohen or to persons tainted with mamzerut*
or when the issue of "Who is a Jew" came to prominence, an outcry
for reform or for the introduction of civil marriage would be sounded.
The party, however, has always been able to pacify its critics, and as
the issue that gave rise to the controversy was either solved or shelved,
the agitation would subside. True to its pragmatic policy, the Labor Party tried to attract to its fold observant Jews, but its success was limited.
At the same time, there were some observant Jews who at Knesset election voted for the Labor Party.[6]

While the Labor Party appears reconciled to the religious status
quo, Mapam, a leftist group dominated by the HaShomer HaTzair Kibbutz Federation and, since 1969, federated with the Labor Party within
the framework of the Labor Alignment, has consistently stood for the
separation of religion and state. It advocates the introduction of civil
marriage, while retaining religious marriage for those who opt for it, but
is in favor of maintaining the rabbinic establishment and the local religious councils at the expense of the taxpayer. It is rather an inconsistent position, for it aims at retaining some links between religion and
state while in theory advocating separation.

The Liberal Party, represented by 13 deputies elected to the Eighth
Knesset in 1973, and the Independent Liberal Party, represented by 4
deputies, advocate a more limited program than Mapam. To avoid a
major clash with the Orthodox, they are prepared to put up with the
religious status quo, with the reservation that civil marriage be introduced
for those couples who are Halakhically disqualified for marriage, such
as a cohen and a divorcée, or a cohen and a proselyte, or when one of the
parties is a Mamzer. Both parties are in favor of granting recognition to
Conservative and Reform rabbis, and of treating their synagogues on an
equal footing with Orthodox synagogues.

Herut, although containing significant non-Orthodox and secularist
elements, many of whom are still loyal to the secularist tradition of
Zeev Jabotinsky, has largely followed its Orthodox-oriented leadership
and generally supported Mafdal, and has even at times voted for legislation introduced by Agudat Israel.

The coexistence of Mapai and Mafdal has necessarily been an uneasy
one, on the level of both national and local government. Occasionally
there have been crises that have threatened the stability of the coalition
government. The relationship between the government and the Chief
Rabbinate has also given rise to tension, with Mafdal trying to mediate
between the two. Mapai, in its turn, has usually been subjected to strong
internal pressures whenever it was constrained to yield to Mafdal. The
latter could always afford to wait for the opportunity when the Labor
Party was at its weakest in order to press its demands. From the point
of view of Mafdal, every concession obtained was a permanent gain,

for it became part of the religious status quo. Thus there has been a slow but steady enlargement of the religious status quo, and although the pace has varied, the progress has been steady.

Neither the Labor Party nor the two Liberal Parties, are in any way anti-religious, and the attitude of all can be described as benevolent, unlike Mapam which, professing to be a Marxist party, is anti-religious, although its militance has lost a good deal of its vigor. All of these parties would like to curb the encroachments of the creeping religious status quo, but it is the Labor Party, as the pillar of any government coalition, that has to bear the brunt of Orthodox pressure on the one hand, and the blame for giving in to it on the other.

B. NETUREI KARTA

Of the varied trends in Orthodoxy, only Neturei Karta has maintained total consistency and ideological integrity. Those who call themselves Neturei Karta—Guardians of the City[7]—assert that the Halakhah, as at present codified, cannot be made to apply to a modern state. From this they draw the conclusion, not that the Halakhah needs to be reformed, but rather that a Jewish state is presently impossible and is, in fact, illegitimate. The very inadequacy of the Halakhah is in itself conclusive proof that the creation of the Jewish state is neither divinely ordained, nor part of the Messianic scheme, nor—as some Orthodox hold—a "beginning of redemption." It is not Halakhah that has to conform to the world, but the world that has to be so transformed as to fit the Halakhah; this will come about in God's own time, when the advent of the Messiah will create a new physical and spiritual reality adapted to the Halakhah. Until that distant time, the State of Israel is a betrayal of the divinely ordained "Israel." The very idea of statehood is pseudo-Messianic, and must consequently be anathema to a God-fearing Jew. This modern state is a product of the profound secular malaise that has afflicted the Jewish people. The Jewish state is a "heresy to our faith—for it implies that the existence of our people is not dependent on the observance of religion, but on human activity. It also implies a denial of the reward for observances and good deeds, and of the punishment for violations of the Torah. The Jewish state also implies a repudiation of the original conception of the Exile and of Redemption, that is, a repudiation of the principle that the Exile is a penalty for sin, and that the Redemption is dependent on repentance. The State of Israel is a denial of all the Laws of Sinai . . . a total heresy."[8]

By considering the Jewish state as religiously invalid—and, in fact, denying its Jewishness altogether—Neturei Karta do not have to be concerned with the Halakhic problems that an authentic Jewish state would present. For in their own eyes, Neturei Karta are still in Galut, although physically domiciled in the Holy Land. They would be content, indeed would prefer, to live under foreign rule, as they are commanded to do until the coming of the Messiah. This would be in conformity with the Halakhah, which does not deal with a possible sovereign Jewish state, but relates always to a Jewish community constituting a minority within a non-Jewish state, with the latter performing all the functions with which the Halakhah is not concerned. If the State of Israel did not call itself a Jewish state, they would have no quarrel with it; but because of its very claim to be *the* Jewish state, they are in a position of constant warfare against it. They do not participate in its political life; they do not vote nor seek to be elected to public office—in fact, at election time they conduct vigorous propaganda against entering the polling booths; their sons and daughters do not serve in the army; they do not employ the Hebrew language in everyday life in order not to profane the holy tongue with secular matters; they do not observe the Day of Independence and treat it as a day of mourning.[9] Their children do not attend state schools, or even state-supported schools, and they do not resort to the courts of law. They maintain their own facilities for shehitah (ritual slaughtering), for they do not recognize the state-supported rabbinate as entitled to supervise shehitah and other matters of Kashrut. Neturei Karta are few in number—a few thousand at most—yet by virtue of their ideological consistency, they exercise a powerful influence on Orthodoxy in general, and on the official rabbinate, in particular. The latter are put on the defensive in that they feel constrained to apologize for their very association with, and dependence on, the secular authorities.

The resistance of Neturei Karta to the state is not merely passive but has often assumed militant and violent proportions. For weeks on end in 1964, they stoned cars passing on the Sabbath through the Mandelbaum Gate (at that time the crossing-place between Israeli and Jordanian Jerusalem) when non-Jewish tourists, in order to reach Israel from Jordan, used a road that bordered on the Orthodox Meah Shearim quarter. From time to time Neturei Karta ventured forth beyond their own neighborhood in order to attack Sabbath violators in the modern quarters, and thus found themselves involved in pitched battles with the police. In 1965 they arranged for a public burning of the national flag on the Day of Independence.[10] On several occasions they even lodged complaints with the United Nations against the government of Israel. It was Neturei Karta also who organized the kidnaping of young Yossele Shuhmacher, ostensibly to prevent him from receiving a secular education. They kept him hidden for months, first in Europe and then in America, until Israeli detectives revealed his whereabouts.

The spiritual leader of the group is the Satmarer rabbi of Williamsburg, New York. In 1967 he published a summary of his sermons delivered on the subject of the Six Days War, in which he called for the liquidation of the Jewish state and its subjection to foreign rule.[11] On April 7, 1969, some fourscore students of Neturei Karta Yeshivot broke into the house of Dr. David Mayer, recently appointed as director of the Shaarei Zedek Hospital in Jerusalem, and wrecked his apartment. Dr. Mayer, though himself an observant Jew, was suspected of tolerating the performance of autopsies.

Unlike other ideological groups or parties, Neturei Karta have no periodical publications, nor do they produce literature to explain their point of view. From time to time they have issued proclamations of protest exposing the evil-doing of their opponents. Their vehemence is directed against Agudat Israel and Mafdal no less than against the secularists.

They denounced Rabbi I. M. Levin of Agudat Israel, who had expressed satisfaction at the government's support of the Agudah schools: "The great luminaries in the Holy Land used to do everything in their power to avoid help proffered by an alien authority, and indeed experienced indescribable hardships in maintaining their independence from the secular authority. If they had wished to submit to government or other alien influences, there would have been no need to form a separate community with its rabbis and separate ritual slaughter facilities, thus saving themselves suffering, insults and toil. Instead, they too, could have occupied a respectable position, like all the political parties, rather than become an object of hatred."[12]

This was a sideswipe at Agudat Israel, suggesting that after forty years of unabated hostility to Zionism, they had now succumbed to the temptations of power and profit that accrue to those who cooperate with the authorities. It was a challenge that has remained essentially unanswered and has proved to be a thorn in the flesh of the Agudah, a permanent embarrassment to their leaders and followers.

Neturei Karta have held neither conventions nor conferences, nor have they debated the issues in any organizational forum or framework. While their numbers have been small, they have managed to arouse the attention of many Israelis and often the sympathies not only of their own adherents, but also of thousands of adherents of Agudat Israel and even of Mafdal. When they staged the Sabbath riots in Jerusalem and wounded scores of policemen who were trying to maintain law and order, they had the obvious support of many Orthodox who were not among their regular followers, and neither Agudat Israel nor Mafdal had ever come out in open condemnation of the acts of violence. Many of the latter parties were glad that there existed militants who dared to take the law into their own hands, and particularly relished the fact that in a number of cases the authorities had yielded to Neturei Karta. Neturei Karta have consistently reminded the religious parties of their cardinal "sin"—of associating themselves with and obtaining benefits from heretics who repudiated the tenets of the Sacred Law. This repeated confrontation has paved the way for the widening influence of the extremists who, in the words of Professor S. N. Eisenstadt, "enjoy full religious legitimation. . . . In the debate between tradition and modernization, tradition is in general becoming increasingly militant and intolerant, and the potentially radical and innovative religious groups and the movement of the religious kibbutzim . . . have lost much of their importance in the last decade."[13]

Thus Neturei Karta enjoy a position of complete legitimacy unequaled by any other religious group; they have the power and authority to challenge the standing and conduct of the other religious groups and parties, including the rabbinate, which derives its legal power and financial support from a sovereign state that in itself is anathema. Neturei Karta, in contrast to the other Orthodox groups, are never on the defensive; therefore they cannot be ignored and frequently have to be taken seriously into account. Because of their uncompromising ideological consistency, their self-imposed refusal to accept any possible material benefit that might accrue to them from the state, their total dedication in the midst of abject poverty and deprivation, they cast a long shadow over the Orthodox parties and the rabbinate itself. Their small numbers, their lack of organization, and their shortage of means have been more than compensated for by fanatical adherence to their belief and by their courage in outfacing opponents who are not always entirely sure of their own position.

C. AGUDAT ISRAEL

Agudat Israel, in common with Neturei Karta, do not view the State of Israel as part of a Messianic scheme; in fact, they have made a specific declaration that the emergence of the state must not be regarded as the "beginning of redemption." Nevertheless, they do not repudiate the state; they are not only in it, but they are of it also, and consider it to be a Jewish state capable of developing along religious lines. They are not primarily concerned with promoting legislation aimed at enforcing religious observances; they are, rather, concerned with preventing legislation that might be prejudicial to the interests of religion, or that runs counter to the Halakhah. They actively participate in the political life of the state, on the national as well as on the local level, and are eager to derive support for their institutions from the state and the local authorities.

While the members and sympathizers of Agudat Israel are scattered throughout the country, their largest concentrations are in Jerusalem and in Bnei Brak. Like Neturei Karta, they are nearly all Ashkenazim; their manner of life and thought has never appealed to the Sefardim or to the Oriental Jews. Their majority are of the middle class, although a considerable number of working men belong to their labor formation, Poalei Agudat Israel (Pagi). The relations between Poalei Agudat Israel and the parent organization have not always been harmonious. When the Agudat labor group was founded in Poland in 1922, it accepted the spiritual guidance of the parent Agudah, but when in 1944 the Poalei Agudah established Kibbutz Hafetz Haim and accepted the aid of the Zionist organization in doing so, relations between them and Agudat Israel were aggravated. In 1960 Poalei Agudah declared that they no longer accepted the authority of the Council of Sages; from then on until 1973 they became a separate political party, independent of the parent body. While Agudat Israel are primarily concerned with the maintenance of their separate elementary school system and the promotion of Yeshivot, Poalei Agudah have emphasized land settlement and the establishment of agricultural and trade schools. They have also looked after the material interests of their members.

When the State of Israel was proclaimed, Agudat Israel joined the Provisional Council of State and were represented by three members out of a total of thirty-seven. They also joined the Provisional Government, where they were represented by Rabbi I. M. Levin, who obtained the portfolio of Social Welfare. In the elections to the First Knesset, in January 1949, Agudat Israel did not put up a separate list of candidates, but formed part of a United Religious Front, which then included Mizrahi, Poalei Mizrahi, Agudat Israel, and Poalei Agudat Israel. This list received 12.2 percent of the total vote, and fourteen seats in the Knesset. It was the only time, however, that the Orthodox presented a united list; in the 1951 elections to the Knesset, the two Agudah formations received 3.6 percent, and five seats in the Knesset, as compared to 8.2 percent obtained by the two Mizrahi groups. In the 1955 and 1959 elections, the two Agudah groups, with their joint list, obtained 4.7 percent of the total, with six seats. In 1961 the two Agudah lists together had 5.6 percent of the total, with Agudat Israel having four seats and Poalei Agudah two, and they gained the same number in 1965. In the elections held in 1973, the groups joined forces and obtained five seats. Mass immigration had not altered the relative strength of the Agudah within Israel. Its loyal following has not fluctuated, neither has the party benefited from a floating vote.

The party was a member of the Coalition Government during the period of the First Knesset and for the first year of the Second Knesset. Then a crucial issue arose, in consequence of which they withdrew from the government on November 3, 1952. At stake was compulsory army service for girls. The government had decided to draft girls into the army for a period of twelve months, so that they might perform various administrative and technical tasks and thus free considerable numbers of men for combat service. In order to meet vehement opposition on the part of the religious, the law, as passed in its final form on September 15, 1949, exempted from service married women, mothers, and pregnant women, as well as any girl "who has declared that reasons of conscience or religious conviction prevent her from serving."[14]

The attitude of the Agudah to this bill was determined by Halakhic considerations. The proposed law was seen as contrary to traditional law, which provides that women must devote themselves to family duties. Rabbi I. M. Levin, speaking in the Knesset for the Agudah, stated that this was the kind of law an observant Jew was duty-bound to resist, and that one should be prepared to die in order to avoid such a transgression.[15] According to the rabbi, the exemption accorded to religious girls in no way altered the position of shirkers; the former were no less devoted to their people than others, but felt obliged to obey a religious in preference to a human commandment.

The ensuing controversy agitated public opinion for a considerable time, with the Agudah and the rabbinate resisting not only this bill but also a later one that drafted religious girls for work in immigrant camps, educational or welfare institutions, and agriculture.[16] The Agudah was at odds with the majority in the government on the issue of compulsory service for girls and withdrew from the coalition, never since to rejoin it. Mafdal, on the other hand, while protesting strongly on the issue, remained within the coalition. A considerable number of religious girls, chiefly those associated with the Bnei Akiva youth movement, have always chosen to serve with the forces rather than take advantage of their exemption.

As a party, Agudat Israel has played the role of loyal opposition in matters where no Halakhic issues were involved. At times, Agudah deputies have supported bills dealing with fiscal and administrative matters, and always lent their support when major issues of defense and foreign policy came up for consideration. They have displayed considerable parliamentary initiative by raising issues of public interest, and by introducing private members' bills. The principal object of their parliamentary endeavors, however, was to embarrass Mafdal by demonstrating to the faithful that the "National Religious Party" continues to participate in coalition governments that are guilty of acts that any observant Jew should condemn. On occasion Agudah placed Mafdal in embarrassing predicaments and served as an effective brake on any liberalizing tendencies that the latter might have adopted. Mafdal always found itself looking over its shoulder at the Agudah before taking any action or any decision, even as Agudah looked back at Neturei Karta.

A typical instance of such harassment of Mafdal by the Agudah occurred on February 9, 1960, in the Knesset. In the debate on Sabbath work permits issued by the Ministry of Labor, Rabbi Menahem Porush introduced a motion on behalf of the Agudah. Section 12 of the Hours of Work and Rest Law of 1951[17] provides that the Minister of Labor may permit employees to work if he is satisfied that otherwise the defense of the state, the security of persons or property, or the economy itself would be seriously prejudiced, or that the services in question are essential to the public. The Agudist deputy complained that the number of Sabbath work permits had increased very greatly and that they were not confined either to defense work or to vital services. The Minister of Labor explained in considerable detail that the permits were issued in strict accordance with the law, and were confined to the most essential works. The number of such permits was not on the increase, and there was no instance where an Orthodox workingman had been requested to work on the Sabbath. The Minister moved that the motion be rejected. The Speaker then put the motion to a vote and it was defeated, with Mafdal abstaining. In accordance with the rules of the House, a party that abstains may make a statement explaining the reason for its abstention. Isaac Rafael, rising to make such a statement on behalf of Mafdal, deplored the large number of Sabbath work permits, and regretted that the Ministry of Labor was the sole authority for deciding whether or not any work is essential. At this point, Rafael was interrupted by Agudah deputy Shlomo Lorenz who shouted: "Why then did you abstain?" When Rafael continued to castigate the government for the indiscriminate issuance of permits, Lorenz heckled him again, exclaiming: "You are bound by the principle of collective responsibility;* please explain how you can hold yourself responsible for such acts? When you stand on this platform, integrity is expected of you—this is pure hypocrisy!"[18] He was followed by Rabbi Porush, who called out: "Is this what you promised your electors? Why don't you read your pre-election platform, and what you promised there?"

Isaac Rafael appeared unable to extricate himself from this predicament and made the following significant reply: "If I saw that my vote

---

* Members of a coalition government are bound to support a government decision even though they may disagree with it.

and the votes of my colleagues would result in the adoption of this motion, I would disregard the limitation imposed by collective responsibility." His point was that voting for the opposition motion would not assure its passage and would merely result in violating the principle of collective responsibility, which would inevitably force Mafdal to leave the government. But it was not reasonable to do this for the sake of a demonstration, that is, for a futile vote in support of the Agudah motion. Far more could be done for religion and religious interests by remaining within the government than by withdrawing from it.

Mafdal found itself in similar straits on December 18, 1961, when Agudat Israel moved that all El-Al* flights cease on the Sabbath, not merely inside but also outside Israel, and further, that Sabbath flights to Israel by non-Israeli airlines also be ended. The Minister of Transport explained that such restrictions on El-Al planes would put the Israeli airline at a serious disadvantage, and that its schedule would be seriously disrupted. Regarding foreign airlines using Lod airport on the Sabbath, the Minister pointed out that Israel was bound by international treaty to keep its airport open every single day of the year and to maintain the required services. If Israel was to maintain its own aviation and shipping, complete Sabbath observance was impossible in a world of keen international competition.

Again the Agudah motion was defeated, with Mafdal abstaining. This time Jacob Greenberg explained the abstention on behalf of Mafdal: "It was with pain that we abstained from voting on Rabbi Porush's motion dealing with Sabbath violation by El-Al. It was not because we underrate the gravity of these violations, or ignore their importance. The contrary is true. We regard this as a grave desecration of the Sabbath, which is one of the sublime and holy symbols of our entire nation. If we had known that by voting for the motion, we would assure its passage, we would not have hesitated to raise our hands and would have been prepared in that case to jeopardize our participation in the government. Unfortunately, voting for the motion would have been an empty demonstration and, to the best of our judgment, the loss would have exceeded the gain. Our record in the struggle for religious interests is well known; our achievements in this sphere are considerable. We shall continue our struggle for a complete and comprehensive Sabbath throughout Israel, and we do not despair of success."[19]

Such parliamentary debates have been a frequent occurrence in each Knesset session, and the initiative of the Agudah has succeeded, in no small degree, in creating the impression that Mafdal is prepared to compromise on important religious issues for the sake of remaining in the government and safeguarding its vested interests.

---

* El-Al is Israel's national airline.

Thus a pattern has evolved: Neturei Karta inveighs against the Agudah's participation in the Knesset, and Agudah counteracts by attacking Mafdal's participation in the Cabinet. Neturei Karta starts an agitation on a religious issue such as Sabbath observance or Kashrut. Once this agitation has assumed larger proportions or even resulted in violence, the matter is taken up in the Knesset by the Agudah, with Mafdal the first victim of the parliamentary debate. Mafdal, on its part, when sensing a rising alarm, would bring pressure to bear on the government; if unsuccessful, it would resort to the only alternative left short of withdrawing from the government: abstaining from voting, with some embarrassment and loss of face.

Agudat Israel has rarely failed to criticize the Ministry of Religious Affairs for its alleged discriminatory policies and practices. From the platform of the Knesset, Agudah has accused Mafdal of using the Ministry for the promotion of its party interests. In many places, they claim, rabbis are not appointed because no suitable Mafdal candidate has presented himself. The Minister for Religious Affairs has been accused of using the instrumentality of his office to attain objectives that his party failed to achieve "by mere party influence."[20] The religious councils "have become Mafdal party cells, which are run as if they were party branches. . . . There are towns and villages with a majority of religious people who belong to another religious party, and there the Ministry, by resorting to all kinds of stratagems, arranges for a Mafdal majority, so that the latter might be enabled to dominate the religious councils. No rabbi, except a Mafdal rabbi, can secure any kind of appointment in the religious establishment. All this is being done in order to overcome another religious party."[21] Again and again, Agudah representatives have complained of such discrimination.[22] On ideological grounds they are assailed by Neturei Karta, while in day-to-day activity they feel frustrated by the machinery of the religious establishment dominated by Mafdal.

Both parties have thus been locked in an intense struggle to secure domination of the religious establishment. Since there is no essential theological difference between these two factions, the fight between them has appeared as a competition for positions of influence and power with the religious public. On several occasions Agudah spokesmen in the Knesset have threatened to set up their own rabbinate and shehitah arrangements.[23] These threats have not been carried out. A separate rabbinate would not be recognized, but separate shehitah could indeed be set up similar to Neturei Karta's slaughtering-house.

In 1960, Poalei Agudat Israel parted company with the parent organization, and joined the government coalition with their two Knesset deputies; one of the deputies was appointed Deputy Minister of Education and Culture. For some time it was even thought that Pagi, as Poalei Agudat Israel are popularly known, would merge with Mafdal. The differences, however, in their respective backgrounds were considerable. Thus, though Pagi has been ideologically far closer to the Agudah than to Mafdal, it was on the receiving end of the parliamentary attacks made by its parent body on the government.

D. MAFDAL (NATIONAL RELIGIOUS PARTY)

Of the religious parties, the largest and most influential is the National Religious Party, which was formed in 1956 through a merger of the Mizrahi and the HaPoel HaMizrahi. Mafdal is also part of the World Mizrahi Organization, which in turn is part of the World Zionist Organization and actively participates in the administration of its affairs. Mafdal is by far the most influential constituent of Mizrahi throughout the world, not only because of its position in Israel, but also because the numerous Mizrahi constituencies, including the Mizrahists of North America, consider it a primary duty to lend moral and material support to their Israeli colleagues.

The strength and at the same time the weakness of Mafdal lies in its unqualified acceptance of the State of Israel as the beginning of the Messianic fulfillment. It lends Mafdal strength, in that its acceptance of the state as an aspect of Redemption enables the party to share unhesitatingly in the political life of the Jewish commonwealth and to participate in its manifold activities. Unlike Agudat Israel and Poalei Agudat Israel, whose attitude to the state is ambivalent and rent by internal contradictions, Mafdal wholeheartedly takes its stand on affirming the Jewish state as part of the Divine scheme. At the same time it is also a source of weakness, for the rival religious parties have sought to demonstrate that the new state is secular and resists the acceptance of Halakhic norms; and further, that the inevitable process of compromise with the non-Orthodox undermines the religious way of life. Thus Mafdal finds itself situated between two poles, each exerting its own pressures.

Mafdal regards the Halakhah as capable of regulating not only man's duties vis-à-vis God and vis-à-vis his fellow man, but also the rights and duties of the individual vis-à-vis society and the political state. Since the party participates in the running of the central and the local governments, it has, however, been unavoidably confronted with situations where the application of Halakhic rules has proved inadequate to meet changing needs. Where Mafdal has yielded, it has been forced to face the bitter criticism of the religious parties to its right, that it has more interest in political power than in adherence to Halakhah.

Yet, mindful of the attitude of the great majority of Orthodox Jews, Mafdal has continued to espouse the principle that the State of Israel, despite the imperfections arising from its failure to live up to Halakhic standards, is the Third Jewish Commonwealth, the legitimate continuation of earlier Jewish sovereignty. Some of the leaders of Mafdal have gone even further. Rabbi Judah Leib Maimon held that the commencement of the Redemption dated from the beginning of the Return to Zion.[24] "Now that we have lived to see the renewal of the state, and that we possess a territory as great as that of King Solomon's time, I think and believe that this is not merely a beginning of the Redemption, but an important part thereof."[25] Even more emphatic was Rabbi Meir Berlin who, taking note of the criticism of the Agudists, stated that "one can go to great lengths in quarreling with the government, but the State of Israel is not the government of Israel. The State of Israel is something celestial, it is the divine world, our eternal destiny."[26]

Mafdal is one of the better-organized political parties in Israel. No details of the financial resources at its disposal have been published, but the staff employed at its national headquaters in Tel Aviv and at the branches throughout the land is far greater than that of parties with a much greater popular following. In addition, Mafdal owns and controls a network of banks, economic enterprises, cooperatives, housing estates, publishing houses, and other properties. In addition to the state-supported religious schools, the party maintains and sponsors its own educational institutions at secondary and higher levels. It has promoted agricultural settlements, both kibbutzim and moshavim (smallholders' settlements). Its youth movement, Bnei Akiva, is regarded as one of the finest, if not the finest, in Israel. Last but not least, Mafdal has derived considerable strength both from the civil service patronage wielded by ministries headed by Mafdal cabinet members and from the large rabbinical establishment. In many cases, synagogues serve as nuclei of Mafdal membership and as its organizational units.

In the electoral contests Mafdal has shown great stability, and although it has tended to lose ground in the old established communities, it has made up for this by greater support in the newly established towns and villages. Thus far, the overwhelming population changes that have taken place since the establishment of the state have not affected the position of Mafdal in the totality of the electorate. In 1951 it obtained 8.3 percent of the total vote; in 1969 it was 9.6 percent. The number of seats held by Mafdal in the Knesset has varied consistently between eleven and twelve.[27] An analysis of the voting pattern shows that Mafdal derives its strength primarily from the immigrant element, from Oriental Jews, and from the poorer sections of the community generally. In the new cities, where the Oriental communities predominate and where there are pockets of poverty, 12.1 percent of the vote went to Mafdal, whereas in the older towns, where the bulk of the total electorate reside, Mafdal's share was 7.8 percent. A similar pattern is reflected in the urban vote, which shows that Mafdal has gained in the poorer quarters and lost in the more prosperous ones,[28] which suggests that a rising standard of living in the immigrant and Oriental communities may bring about an erosion in the strength of Mafdal. Unlike Agudat Israel and the Poalei Agudah, who derive their support primarily from the Orthodox quarters of Jerusalem and from the predominantly Orthodox town of Bnei Brak, the followers of Mafdal are evenly scattered over the land. In this respect Mafdal is a fully national party, and its representatives are to be found in every municipality and local council.[29] The proportional system of elections assures Mafdal of stability, while the introduction of a constituency system, as in the English-speaking countries, would be a disaster for the party, since it is not based on any territorial concentration of followers.

Mafdal has been in the government from the beginning of the state, except for a brief interval in 1958 when it left the government on the issue "Who is a Jew?"* and rejoined it at the end of 1959. Mafdal's demands have been confined to matters of religious policy. These demands have been incorporated in the government's Program of Policy, which the Prime Minister Designate customarily lays before the Knesset for approval. Thus the Program of Policy presented to the newly elected Knesset in 1965 contained the following statement: "The forging of unity within the nation requires mutual tolerance, and freedom of conscience and religion. The government will prevent religious or anti-religious coercion of any sort; it will assure freedom of conscience and religion of all non-Jewish communities, and provide for their religious needs at the expense of the State; and will provide religious education to the children of those parents who may demand it." The concluding clause was the most important: "The government will observe the status quo in matters of religion."[30] The general statement of policy has often been accompanied by special arrangements between Mapai and Mafdal, whereby the former has undertaken to support specific legislation, such as the Laws of the Sabbath or Kashrut.

Mafdal has from the beginning held at least two cabinet posts, and since 1959 it has consistently held three: Religious Affairs, Interior, and Social Welfare. All three departments are of special importance to Mafdal. The Minister for the Interior is in charge of local governments; thus, by determining the amount of the grant-in-aid given by the central government to a local authority, the Minister is in a position to assure the allocation of a suitable amount for the support of the local religious

---

* See chap. 9, below.

council. Furthermore, through its administration of the Population Registry Law,[31] the Ministry has seen to it that a person Halakhically not a Jew would be registered as a non-Jew.* The Ministry for Religious Affairs is in control of the rabbinate and of appointments to the religious councils, and is thus able to assure positions to its own followers, to the disadvantage of Orthodox Jews who are members of Agudat Israel or who are not affiliated with any party. The Ministry of Social Welfare, being in charge of tens of thousands of the underprivileged, has been of great political assistance to the party, which has derived considerable support from the poorer elements of the community. The control of these three ministries has placed Mafdal in a position where it could both safeguard religious interests as such, and in addition dispense social benefits to a significant section of the Israeli electorate. The policy of recruiting the civil servants of those ministries from among its own followers has not, of course, differed from the practice among other parties in the coalition governments. All have used their power to strengthen their positions.

The greater the dependence of the dominant Labor Party on its coalition partners, the greater have become the demands of Mafdal. A case in point were the negotiations that led to the formation of the coalition government in November–December 1969. Following the elections to the Seventh Knesset held on October 28, 1969, the Labor Party sustained a loss of over ten percent. Thereupon, in addition to the customary proviso for the maintenance of the status quo in religious matters and the appointment of three cabinet ministers, Mafdal managed to achieve several of its other demands, such as the appointment of a Deputy Minister of Education and Culture, and an agreement on the part of the government to prohibit television on the Sabbath.[32]

A similar pattern was reenacted in the municipalities, where the Labor Party suffered an even greater setback than in the Knesset. A classical example was Tel Aviv. There, the Labor Party obtained in 1969 thirteen seats of the thirty-one on the municipal council, as against twelve of Gahal, the Herut-Liberal bloc. The three votes of Mafdal and the one vote of the Agudah had the power to decide whether Labor or Gahal would form the city government. The Orthodox proceeded to negotiate with both sides, and when both expressed their willingness to meet the conditions of the religious groups, Mapai and Gahal each offered ever more attractive propositions. By the time a Labor mayor was elected, the price was heavy beyond all precedent.

The Orthodox gained these points: strict enforcement of the prohibition of public transport on the Sabbath; prohibition of all public entertainment on Friday evening; the closing of the municipal plane-

---

* See below, discussion of the Shalit case.

tarium on the Sabbath; a ban on any posters on municipal bulletin boards announcing anything that might entail a Sabbath violation; a ban on issuing licenses to butchers' shops without a Kashrut certificate issued by the rabbinate; construction of additional ritual baths; the building of a new Yeshivah; increased allocations for the budget of the religious council; and the erection of additional synagogues. Of the eight deputy mayors who would constitute the executive arm of the City Council, three were to be Orthodox: those in charge of the Board of Education, the Department of Municipal Properties, and the Department of Religious Affairs. Thus the Orthodox secured close to forty percent representation in the executive organs of the city government, while the election results had only given them twelve percent of total votes cast.[33] This arrangement aroused a good deal of resentment and was criticized in the independent press. The Labor Party itself was not held at fault, for a similar price would have been paid by Gahal. Rather, the system of elections by proportional representation was condemned and voices were heard in favor of an electoral reform.

The Tel Aviv pattern was repeated in other municipalities, where either Labor or Gahal had to satisfy Orthodox demands in order to achieve a coalition in the municipal councils. Critics of the system pointed out that such situations arising out of political stalemates were unlikely to enhance the image of democracy in Israel or, for that matter, to make religious parties more popular.[34]

E. MAFDAL AND THE DOCTRINE OF COERCION

From the religious point of view, Israel is an imperfect state and will continue as such as long as those whom the Orthodox term "Hiloniim" (secularists) constitute the majority of the population. It is therefore necessary to convert the Hiloniim to Orthodoxy, so that eventually there will be a majority that can make Halakhah the law of the land. The ideal way to achieve this objective is, of course, through education. Indeed, Mizrahi from its very inception has stressed the importance of religious public schools, and succeeded in establishing a network of such schools in the Jewish National Home. Mizrahi and, later, Mafdal also sponsored the religious public school system as part of the public school system of the State of Israel. This program was followed by the promotion of religious high schools, Yeshivot and other educational institutions, and by the establishment of a religious youth movement. Mafdal has remained faithful to the principle of its founders that the cornerstone of its practical work must be education.

Significant as this program is, its results are inevitably slow to come; it will manifestly be a matter of generations before the whole people can be expected to return to a Torah-true way of life. Meanwhile, the Orthodox have deemed it essential to ensure that the Jewish state be not irrevocably committed to a secular interpretation of Jewish exisence. The way to achieve this goal lies in active participation in party politics and political pressure. Such pressure can be exerted in many ways, through the administrative branches of the government as well as through legislative activity at the parliamentary level. The latter may be of either a negative or a positive character. On the negative side, the objectives of Mafdal's parliamentary activity have been to prevent the enactment of legislation that might be prejudicial to religious interests, such as the introduction of civil marriage, or the separation of religion from state, or legislation that might conflict with Halakhah, whether in the field of criminal or civil law. Continued opposition to the adoption of a written constitution is perhaps the principal objective of Mafdal's preventive action. On the positive side, Mafdal's parliamentary strength, which is derived from its strategic position in coalition politics, has been employed to secure the enactment by the Knesset of "religious laws." These are aimed not only at safeguarding the legal position of Orthodoxy, as the sole recognized form of Jewish religion in Israel, and of its state-supported institutions, such as the official rabbinate, but also at enacting laws that would force people to live in accordance with certain precepts of the Halakhah, such as Sabbath and Kashrut observance, banning of pig-breeding, and the regulation of matters of marriage and divorce and personal status in general, in strict accordance with the traditional law.

In their pursuit of "religious" legislation, Mafdal has constantly been confronted by critics from without, and at times from within also. The critics have contended that to impose the performance of a religious precept, a Mitzvah, by the operation of law is tantamount to religious coercion. They further maintain that it is neither the duty nor the function of a state to enforce religious observance or to prevent its citizens from observing Mitzvot. In fact, it is the duty of a democratic state to desist from legislating in matters of faith and belief, and to leave these matters to the exclusive province of the individual. The sole function of the state is to safeguard freedom of religion and conscience.

These arguments have been raised whenever a new item of religious legislation has come up for consideration before the Knesset or a municipal council. Yeshayahu Bernstein, one of the more articulate exponents of religious legislation, has explained that the Hiloniim are mistaken in rejecting such laws as contrary to democracy and to freedom of conscience.[35] In his opinion, no element of conscience is involved. One who eats non-kasher food or travels on Shabbat is not motivated by conscience, but by an evil impulse, and it is proper for the legislator to curb such impulses. Those who choose to eat pork are "transgressors," for it is not conscience that impels them to partake of pork. Jews know that it is a transgression, "but they cannot resist the evil impulse. Depriving them of a convenience and thus curbing their evil impulse, is not an infringement of freedom of conscience."[36] A line must be drawn, he said, between transgression and conscience. "Transgression is not conscience. One may be a transgressor all his lifetime . . . because of spiritual weakness and other circumstances, he is enslaved by passions and instincts, and although his conscience tells him he is a sinner, he cannot extricate himelf. . . . The people who violate the income tax laws do so because it is more convenient. . . . There are transgressors of the income tax laws, but there is no element of conscience in income tax law-breaking."[37]

But what is the authority for the proposition that the Mitzvot are binding on all Jews, whether they are believers or not? Yeshayahu Bernstein replies, that the laws of the Torah are fundamental laws, and are not subject to decisions by a majority or a minority, "even as the prohibition of theft or murder is not a matter of a decision to be democratically arrived at."[38] But what about those Jews who do not believe in the sanctity or the binding character of the Mitzvot? The reply is: "The law of Moses and of Israel is binding upon the totality of Israel . . . even upon those who have sinned. . . . No one is at liberty to divest himself of it, even if he so desires. We are commanded to coerce. This is the pure truth according to the Torah. There can be no doubt as to the duty to coerce in order to enforce compliance with the Mitzvot of the Torah, provided you have the power. This power can be exercised by a court of law, by royal edict or by the laws enacted by the competent authorities of the state. . . . This point of view is not contrary to the principles of democracy. Loyalty to the Mitzvot does not necessitate the relinquishment of democratic principles, for these principles are beyond the reach of a decision democratically arrived at. From the point of view of the believer, the Torah is the constitution, and as such has priority over any democratic structure, even as the principles of morality are prior to any democracy."[39]

Bernstein did not consider the principles he expounded to be theocratic; in his opinion they are not in opposition to democracy, for there can be only one Israeli democracy, one that is based on the Torah. To those who contend that the right of Parliament to enact laws enforcing religious observances also implies its right to enact anti-religious laws, Bernstein opposes the view that the two camps are not on an equal level. For to enact a law interfering with a religious observance is tantamount to a violation of the freedom of conscience, and is therefore a matter that cannot be imposed by a democratic majority, whereas to enact a law imposing observance is by no means such an infringement, for it is merely the restraint of an evil impulse. Therefore, whenever possible, it is necessary to enact laws imposing religious observances, at least the "minimum of what can be obtained under present circumstances." Even the bestowing of the Torah on Mount Sinai can be considered an act of coercion, rather than of free choice. "The very long rod of education and persuasion that leads to voluntary acceptance is by far the best. But its blessing could not take place without prior coercion. So long as a generation is not fit, laws must be imposed from above. After many generations, they will accept willingly what has been previously forced upon them."[40]

In their polemics with opponents of "religious legislation," the Orthodox have continually introduced a wealth of rabbinic authority in support of coercion by law. The matter was dealt with by Rabbi Moshe Zvi Neriah, leader of the Bnei Akiva movement and its spiritual guide. He quoted Maimonides to the effect that coercion as a term can only be applied in instances when one is forced to do something that he is not obligated to do by the Torah. "But if one is moved by an evil impulse to violate a Mitzvah or to commit a transgression, and is beaten until he does that which he is bound to do, or until he refrains from transgressing, that is not coercion, for he was coerced by the evil impulse . . . so he was beaten until the evil impulse subsided. . . . This is to be considered as his own will." In these circumstances the performance of an act under duress is to be regarded as an act voluntarily performed.[41]

Rabbi Neriah sees in all this no more coercion than in a parent forcing his child to behave correctly. He also advances a moral and nationalist justification for his views. "If you ask any Jew in this land whether it is his desire to be a Jew, he will answer in the affirmative. This warrants forcing him to abide by all those laws by virtue of which one is a Jew. You violate Mitzvot not out of a refusal to be a Jew, but because you find it more convenient not to be observant. Even as the state has the right to compel the citizen to observe the laws required for its existence, so Judaism has the right to do with its laws."[42]

Thus, while Mafdal accepts the existing Jewish state in spite of its Halakhic imperfections as the commencement of Redemption, it is at one with Agudat Israel in conceiving the future of the Jewish state as requiring that the laws of the Halakhah be identical with the law of the land. From this it follows that resort to legislation with the aim of enforcing Halakhic observances is to be regarded as a legitimate means of attaining the grand objective.

There are Mafdal leaders who realize that their official attitude on coercion by legislation estranges many who might otherwise be inclined to sympathize with traditional Judaism. Dr. P. Rosenblueth, a leading Orthodox educator, regards the Torah as having been accepted by the Jewish people of their own free will, rather than having been imposed upon them. Only by the exercise of free will was it that a Covenant was entered into between the Almighty and the Chosen People. Rosenblueth respects Rabbi Neriah's contention that coercion is sanctified by the Halakhah, but asserts that this applies only to those who accept it in principle. In support he cites Maimonides' premise, which speaks of a Jew who "wishes to be of Israel, to observe all the Mitzvot and to stay away from transgression, were it not for the urging of the evil impulse." The implication clearly is that coercion cannot be applied to instances where the individual does not wish "to observe all the Mitzvot." Dr. Rosenblueth further repudiates the contention that a democracy may impose religious laws by a majority of the numbers of the legislature, in the same manner as it imposes other laws, for the former are based on faith, while the latter are not. He likewise rejects the argument that Halakhah has preserved Judaism, as "this is not a religious argument," and, "in accordance with the views of many, there are other ways to preserve the nation."[43]

This statement reflects the uneasiness felt by many of the Orthodox intellectuals, who realize that the very debate on this subject—and the debate, indeed, has often become acrimonious—is harmful to the cause of religion. Many Orthodox youth, too, realize that the obvious incompatibility of coercion with democracy as generally understood has created an impenetrable barrier between them and the majority of their contemporaries. Among the leaders of the Kibbutz Dati and of the Bnei Akiva youth movement, voices have been raised in favor of dropping further religious legislation, and in support of increased educational activity.

The party as such remains committed, however, to the policy of religious legislation and the strengthening of the rabbinate and its authority. In the conflicts that have arisen between the government and the rabbinate, as for instance with matters of Kashrut or the exemption of Yeshivah students from army service, Mafdal has acted as intermediary between the two and has attempted to resolve such conflicts before they arouse public agitation. However, even the modern Yeshivot established by Bnei Akiva have tended to move in the direction of ultra-Orthodoxy, which has caused an observer to fear that "this movement, too, educates its best sons to a program that is becoming increasingly alienated from its origins."[44] Likewise, the gap between Mafdal and its own intelligentsia has continued to grow, the latter openly expressing their resentment that the party has supported the demands of the rabbinate and of the traditional Yeshivot for the total exemption of their students from army duty and of religious girls from any form of public service. Since rabbis are recruited from the traditional Yeshivot, there has been decreasing communication between them and that part of the Orthodox population who have had a university education.[45] All suggestions for setting up a modern Orthodox Rabbinical seminary have been set aside under the pressure of the rabbinate.

The hoped-for revival of Torah veAvodah ideals that had been expected to emerge from the religious Kibbutz movement has remained quite limited, although here is found the largest concentration of Orthodox intellectuals. The founders of Kibbutz TiratTzvi, which was established in 1937 in the Bet Sh'an valley, aimed at a combination of cooperative living, dedication to Zionism, socialism, and, at the same time, to a strict observance of Halakhah. Many of their adherents were the flower of German Jewish Orthodoxy. Kibbutz Dati, the Orthodox federation of cooperative settlements, now counts some four thousand souls. They have had to resolve some Halakhic difficulties arising out of the need to maintain vital services on Shabbat and on festivals. In their monthly publication, *Amudim,* they have suggested novel approaches to Halakhic problems.

Moshe Unna, their outstanding leader and for many years their sole representative in the Knesset, openly proposed that the civil courts be authorized to register—if but for civil purposes—marriages between a cohen and a divorcée* or of a childless widow whose brother-in-law might refuse to perform the rite of Halitzah.** Unna was reprimanded by the rabbis in extreme terms for these "free-thinking" suggestions.[46] Unna has also repudiated the doctrine of coercion. In his view, the possible gains therefrom will be vitiated because of the inevitable "antagonism between the religious and non-religious public, which is increasing and is bound to grow more acute."[47] The restoration of the Halakhic way of life will not come about through political activity but by the spread of the ideas, that is to say, by education in the broadest sense.[48]

The Kibbutz Dati has been the only group within Mafdal that has not hesitated to criticize the rabbinate.[49] Its members supported the drafting of Yeshivah students and religious girls, and indeed, its own young people serve in the army on a regular basis. They regard such exemption as immoral, seeing that many other settlers have made sacrifices to the point of exhaustion, and that men in their fifties have had to perform para-military duties. They have been especially critical of Yeshivah students who have refused to volunteer for the army chaplaincy, which from the religious point of view is an essential service.[50] However,

---

* Such a marriage is proscribed by Halakhah.
** Stating that he will not exercise the biblically imposed duty to marry the childless widow of his brother. Without such ritual renunciation, the widow cannot remarry.

though the Kibbutz Dati has in many ways been in the vanguard of progressive Orthodoxy, it has failed to make a real impact on Mafdal, let alone on wider Orthodox circles. This has in no small measure been due to the general predicament of the whole Kibbutz movement, which since the 1950s has been exercising an ever-diminishing influence on Israeli society.

Still, no other political party can boast of a more dedicated youth movement than Mafdal, whose youth are affiliated in Bnei Akiva. The movement originated in Poland and was affiliated with the world organization of Torah veAvodah. Its declared aim was to bring up "a generation of Jews loyal to their Torah, their people and their land, and to live from toil in the spirit of the Torah." Its first branch in Palestine was opened in Jerusalem in 1929, and the members were urged to join a religious kibbutz on reaching maturity. Its members joined the Haganah in the days of the mandate, and later the Defense Army of Israel. They have regularly been among the volunteers in establishing new settlements in the wilderness, and their response to patriotic duty has elicited wide admiration. In the 1960s Bnei Akiva had over one hundred branches throughout the country, with an educational system in which Yeshivah training has been combined with the study of secular subjects. Some of the best students have, however, moved into the traditional Yeshivot for further training, and thus have become alienated from the Bnei Akiva philosophy.

The growing gap between Mafdal and the religious intelligentsia has caused some outstanding adherents to leave the party. Prominent among these have been several professors at the Hebrew University of Jerusalem who were among the founders and leaders of HaTenuah LeYahadut shel Torah (Movement for Torah Judaism), a nonpolitical group that seeks to promote Orthodoxy through education, and eschews religion as the raison d'être of a political party. Small as it has been so far, there is a definite ferment within Mafdal. This may be seen as a part of the struggle typical of all political parties in Israel today, where the younger generation has been challenging the veterans. It is also a reflection of a growing conviction that coercion leads into a dead end and must in the long run be self-defeating.

6

Law, Legislation, and Religion

A. SOURCES OF THE LAW

The law of Israel consists of two distinct and chronologically separate parts, that is to say, the law in force in Palestine prior to May 15, 1948, and the law enacted by the Israeli legislature since that date. These two systems of law have continued to coexist during the third decade of Israel's sovereignty.

The laws of Mandatory Palestine, far from being homogeneous, were themselves of complex composition and origin. The basis of the law of Palestine was the Ottoman Law, as obtaining on November 1, 1914, Palestine having been a Turkish province on the date when the Ottoman Empire joined the Central Powers during the First World War. The Ottoman Law, however, was in its turn far from being a uniform structure; its bottom layer was the Moslem Religious Law, on which were superimposed parts of the Napoleonic Code (the French Law that had been borrowed during the nineteenth century), and the family or personal laws of the Christian and Jewish communities. The Moslem Law, deriving its authority from the Koran, was concerned primarily with civil transactions, and was subsequently systematized into a civil code known as the Mejelleh; some parts of it still survive in present-day Israel. Matters of personal status of Moslems, that is to say, the laws regarding marriage, divorce, wills, and other family matters, were also dealt with in accordance with Moslem religious tradition. However, as the need to modernize the Empire grew acute, the Sultans borrowed the commercial, maritime, and civil procedure and the criminal code of the French. Indeed, French influence was so profound that the Ottoman jurists consulted French legal texts, and at times based their decisions

174

on precedents set up by French courts of law, a practice that was followed by the courts of Palestine during the British Mandate.

This complicated body of law was overlaid by laws enacted or applied by the Mandatory legislature of Palestine, and was generally patterned on English common law and the principles of equity. During the thirty years of British rule, substantial sections of the Turkish laws, primarily in the fields of public law, civil and criminal procedure, and criminal and commercial law were repealed and new laws were enacted, based on English law and interpreted in accordance with British judicial decisions. This law flowed into the legal system of Palestine both through specific legislative enactments and through Article 46 of the Palestine Order-in-Council of 1922,[1] which provided that the substance of the English Common Law and the doctrines of equity in force in England would apply wherever there was a lacuna in the laws of Palestine. Through this aperture the English judges officiating in Palestine channeled more and more English law into what they regarded as lacunae in the local laws. The Supreme Court of Palestine, which also sat as a High Court of Justice with authority to issue original writs of habeas corpus, mandamus, and prohibition, became the protector of basic freedoms. The majority of the judges of the Supreme Court and all the presiding judges of the district courts were British, and they had brought with them their distinctive procedures and their flexible remedies and their individual opinions and dissents, which constituted a system that functioned through an independent judiciary. In a short time, the impact of English law and practice in Palestine under British rule became pervasive and far-reaching.[2]

There was, however, one field of Ottoman law that the Mandatory Power scrupulously preserved: the personal law and the system of religious community courts. Originally the establishment of non-Moslem religious courts in the Ottoman Empire was regarded as an act of tolerance and goodwill toward the religious minorities, and was indeed welcomed by them. Both Jews and Christians enjoyed autonomy in matters of personal status, and favored the existence of their own religious courts. Thus there was no uniform Ottoman civil code dealing with domestic relations; there were, instead, the several codes of the religious communities, and one's personal status was determined by the law of his religion and his rights thereunder were adjudicated by the ecclesiastical court of the religious community to which he belonged. These courts were also welcomed by the European powers that had assumed the role of protectors of the Christian religion in the Ottoman Empire in general, and in the Holy Land in particular. Such protection was at times extended to those Jews in Palestine who were nationals of the various European powers.

The British confirmed this situation in the mandated territory and defined the scope of the jurisdiction of the communities already existing in Palestine, without enlarging their number. Consequently, some small communities such as the Maronites (an Oriental offshoot of the Catholic Church) were confirmed in their status, while the Protestants, whose membership was larger than that of the Maronites, were not accorded the status of a community with its own religious court, for the simple reason that within the Ottoman Empire their number had been insignificant.[3]

Such was the maze of laws when the independence of Israel was proclaimed. War preceded and followed the Declaration of Independence; there was no alternative but to adopt the law as it existed in Palestine on the eve of independence. This was given effect in the first enactment by the Provisional Council of State, the Law and Administration Ordinance 5708–1948, which was passed with retroactive effect from May 15, 1948, the first day of Israel's independent existence.[4] The circumstances in which the Jews of Palestine attained their sovereignty were such as to preclude any possibility of a serious consideration of what legal system to establish for the new state.

As a result of these provisions, the Law of Palestine became the law of the newly born state, with some exceptions bearing on matters of political import, such as the abolition of restrictions on Jewish immigration and land purchase, and on the abolition of the privileged status of English as an official language. Since that time a considerable part of the law had been changed by the Israeli legislature, but parts of the old law were still in force in the third decade of the state's existence, most prominently the provisions dealing with the religious courts. Thus the link between religion and state that originated and developed in the peculiar circumstances of the Ottoman Empire, and was consolidated by the British rulers of Palestine, fell to the State of Israel as an inheritance.

B. FREEDOM OF CONSCIENCE

Article 83 of the Palestine Order-in-Council of 1922, which is still valid law in Israel, provides that "all persons in Palestine shall enjoy full liberty of conscience and full exercise of their forms of religion, subject only to the maintenance of public order and morals."[5] This principle was reiterated in the Declaration of Independence of Israel: "The State of Israel will be based on freedom, justice and peace as envisaged by the Prophets of Israel; will uphold the full social and political equality of all its citizens, without distinction of religion, race or sex; will guarantee freedom of religion, conscience, education and culture. . . ."[6]

Although the Supreme Court of Israel pronounced that "the Declaration of Independence gives expression to the vision of the people and its faith, but contains no element of constitutional law which determines the validity of various ordinances and laws,"[7] it has proved itself to be a consistent and staunch defender of freedom of conscience and of civil rights. In 1953, the Minister of the Interior, acting in pursuance of a Mandatory statute that authorized the High Commissioner to suspend the publication of any periodical that was likely to endanger peace, ordered the suspension for a period of 14 days of two communist papers that had sharply criticized the foreign policy of Israel. In setting aside the Minister's order, the Supreme Court stated: "The principle of free expression is a principle closely connected with the processes of democratic government. Every individual may, therefore, criticize the political action of the elected representatives at any time, whether with a view to having it amended, or in order to cause the immediate resignation of such representatives or their replacement at election time." The Court concluded its judgment by quoting a passage from Justice Louis D. Brandeis in the case of *Whitney* v. *The People of the State of California*: "Those who won our independence believed that freedom to think as you will, and to speak as you think, are means indispensable to the discovery and spread of political truth: that without free speech and assembly, discussion would be futile."[8]

Another case involved a teacher. The Ministry of Education and Culture insisted that its consent must be obtained when a teacher was to be engaged, and in this case withheld consent, alleging that the person concerned was suspected of being a member of a terrorist organization and was known to have published inflammatory articles against the government. The Supreme Court found neither legal sanction for the Ministry's insistence on its prior approval, nor justification for the withholding of such approval on security grounds. The Court, in ordering the Minister of Education to desist from interfering in this matter, observed: "Our state is based on the rule of law and not upon the rule of individuals. . . . The authorities will take such action against the Petitioner as the law allows, and he will then, at least, enjoy the right given to every citizen in the state, the basic right of a man to defend himself before the courts. If the opinions of a citizen are rejected, that is not to say that his life is at the free disposal of anyone; ways of earning a living are not closed to him, nor should his life be embittered by administrative action."[9]

The principle of religious freedom received similar attention from the Supreme Court in the case of *Israel Peretz and others* v. *The Local Council of the Township of Kfar Shmaryahu*, in a judgment delivered on November 2, 1962.[10] The petitioners, residents of Kfar Shmaryahu, applied for the use of the Town Hall in order to conduct a religious service there, "in accordance with the custom and style of Progressive

Judaism." The petitioners obtained the use of the hall for their New Year and Yom Kippur services, but were refused its use when they applied for the holding of Sukkot services.* Four arguments were advanced by the local council for its refusal: There was already a synagogue in the town that was able to satisfy the needs of religious people; certain groups in that town strongly objected to the use of the council hall for the purposes of the petitioners and regarded it as a grave affront to their feelings; the Local Council aspired to maintain public unity and, by letting the petitioners use the hall, dissension would be created, and the court had no power to coerce the local council into letting the hall, which was the property of the council, contrary to its owner's will.

The Supreme Court, in ordering the Local Council to permit the petitioners the use of the public hall, dealt with all the objections raised. Justice Chaim Cohen stated that religion and ritual are not only matters of Halakhah but are also matters of faith. The fact is that the petitioners feel a religious need that cannot be satisfied by the existing synagogue, and this is the overriding criterion. In a matter relating to publicly owned property, the Local Council may not be guided by the interests of any one religious group; the petitioners in turn should be at liberty to be guided by their own considerations. If this is seen as an affront to their opponents, a denial of the hall would be equally an affront to the feelings of the petitioners, and neither side is entitled to claim preference or superiority. The Local Council may be right in aspiring to prevent dissension, but this worthy desire is limited by the freedom of religion and ritual, which is one of the basic liberties guaranteed by every enlightened democratic regime. The preservation of liberty makes it indeed possible for various splinter religious trends and movements to appear, but this possibility cannot be allowed to detract in any way from the principle itself. The Court also affirmed its competence to interfere in the Local Council's handling of its own property, because a matter of public interest was involved.[11]

The Supreme Court further refused to allow the use of administrative power or of municipal by-laws for promoting particular religious policies, unless expressly authorized to do so by an act of the national legislature. In the case of *Aksel* v. *the Mayor of Natanya* in 1954,[12] the Supreme Court dealt with a nonkosher butcher to whom the municipality refused to issue a license for a shop unless he undertook to sell kosher meat only. The ruling of the Court was that a municipality may use its powers neither to attain religious objectives nor to enforce religious observances. The Court held that the action constituted a restriction of the freedom of the individual and indicated that, in the ab-

---

* These always come five days after Yom Kippur.

sence of a written constitution, such a restriction of freedom could be effected only by an act of the Knesset.

Similarly, when the Food Controller tried, in virtue of his statutory powers, to ban the raising of pigs in certain parts of the country, the Supreme Court in *Lazarovich* v. *the Food Controller* in 1956 invalidated his action. The Court found that the action of the Controller was motivated by "a desire to satisfy, by direction of the government, the demands of certain groups to which the raising of pigs in our country is abhorrent for purely religious reasons deeply rooted in our national tradition." Consequently the Court denied the right of the Controller to exercise his powers for the attainment of a religious aim, pointing out that only a legislative act of the Knesset might authorize him to do so. In 1966, the Supreme Court set aside a Bat Yam municipal business tax that was higher for nonkosher than for kosher butchers.[13]

In another case, brought in 1963 by an importer against the Minister of Trade and Industry for the refusal by the latter to authorize the importation of foodstuffs unless they were certified as kosher by the Chief Rabbinate, the Supreme Court ruled that the Chief Rabbinate had no standing in this matter, and that "matters of Kashrut are not the concern of the Ministry of Trade and Industry."[14]

The Supreme Court thus consistently upheld the view that, in the absence of an express legislative enactment by the national legislature, neither the organs of local government nor any administrative bodies might legislate or act in order to enforce a religious injunction.[15] For this reason, the religious parties have directed their energies toward the enactment of laws by the Knesset, which would provide the legal framework for the enforcement of religious norms.

C. LAWS OF MARRIAGE AND DIVORCE

Background

The most important objective of the religious parties has been to extend the scope of the jurisdiction of the rabbinical courts, so that resort to such courts would be obligatory for all Jews residing in Israel, whether nationals or not. Under the British Mandate, Jews who were not Palestinian citizens had not been subjected to the jurisdiction of the rabbinical courts. In 1953, the relevant provisions of the British "Palestine Order-in-Council" were replaced by the Rabbinical Courts Jurisdiction (Marriage and Divorce) Law. Because of its far-reaching significance for the relationship of religion and state, it is quoted in full:[16]

1. Matters of marriage and divorce of Jews in Israel, being nationals or residents of the state, shall be under the exclusive jurisdiction of rabbinical courts.
2. Marriages and divorces of Jews shall be performed in Israel in accordance with Jewish religious law.
3. Where a suit for divorce between Jews has been filed in a rabbinical court, whether by the wife or by the husband, a rabbinical court shall have exclusive jurisdiction in any matter connected with such suit, including maintenance for the wife and for the children of the couple.
4. Where a Jewish wife sues her Jewish husband or his estate for maintenance in a rabbinical court, otherwise than in connection with divorce, the plea of the defendant that a rabbinical court has no jurisdiction in the matter shall not be heard.
5. Where a woman sues her deceased husband's brother for Halitzah* in a rabbinical court, the rabbinical court shall have exclusive jurisdiction in the matter, also as regards maintenance for the woman until the day on which Halitzah is given.
6. Where a rabbinical court, by final judgement, has ordered that a husband be compelled to grant his wife a letter of divorce or that a wife be compelled to accept a letter of divorce from her husband, a district court may, upon expiration of six months from the day of the making of the order, on the application of the Attorney General, compel compliance with the order by imprisonment.
7. Where a rabbinical court, by final judgement, has ordered that a man be compelled to give his brother's widow Halitzah, a district court may, upon expiration of three months from the day of the making of the order, on application of the Attorney General, compel compliance with the order by imprisonment.

While Article 2 did not specify what that "Jewish religious law" was to be, it was obvious that it meant the Halakhah as interpreted by the Orthodox. This understanding was never challenged, especially since the official rabbinate consisted of Orthodox rabbis only. Thus the civil law left the interpretation and application of Halakhah to the rabbinical courts, headed by the Rabbinical Court of Appeal as the chief Halakhic authority. In this way the Israeli legislature not only divested itself of its sovereign right to provide the substantive law in matters of family relations, and to amend and alter such law, but by delegating this right to the Orthodox rabbinate, created a situation where the law applicable to these matters could only be interpreted, and neither amended nor altered, for the Halakhah, understood as divinely ordained, cannot admit of legislative change. This immutability of the ancient law is at the root

---

* Release from levirate obligation.

of a good deal of the tension between a large segment of the Jewish population of Israel and the civil as well as religious authorities.

Only a narrow field of family relations is not within the exclusive jurisdiction of the rabbinical courts. When a suit for maintenance is brought other than in connection with divorce proceedings, the civil and religious courts have concurrent jurisdiction. But even civil courts, when dealing with a matter of family law, or where personal status is incidental to a litigation, are bound to apply the religious law of the person concerned. This means for a Jewish person that Halakhah is to be applied. In such cases the civil courts deviate from the Halakhah in only two instances: when principles of private international law are involved, in which case these principles take precedence over Halakhah, and in matters of procedure and of the rules of evidence, when the courts have ignored the principles of Halakhah.

Marriages Abroad

A possibility for the application of the principles of private international law in family relations arose because Article 2 of the Law provided that "marriages and divorces of Jews shall be *performed in Israel* in accordance with Jewish religious law [Halakhah]." When the rabbinical courts attempted to apply the Halakhah also in instances where such acts had been performed abroad, the Supreme Court of Israel rejected this extension.

Even before the Rabbinical Courts Jurisdiction Law had been enacted in 1953, such a case had been adjudicated. A wife sued a husband for maintenance; the couple had been married in Poland in 1948 in a civil marriage. Some time after their arrival in Israel in 1950, the husband abandoned his wife, who then applied to the district court for maintenance. The husband pleaded that he owed nothing inasmuch as the civil marriage he had contracted in Poland was void; since both he and his bride were Jewish, he claimed that they should have been married by a rabbi. The matter reached the Supreme Court, which laid down the proposition that the personal status acquired by an individual is determined in reference to the law applicable to that individual at the time he had acquired his status. In such cases, the rules of private international law apply.[17] The Supreme Court rejected the contention of the rabbis that, so far as Jews are concerned, the Halakhah should be considered to have universal application, regardless of the country in which they may be domiciled. The principle was thus established that a marriage that was valid in accordance with the laws of the country in which it was celebrated, would be considered valid also in Israel, in conformity with principles well established in private international law.[18]

Another case involved a Belgian national, a Christian girl, who in 1961 married an Israeli Jew. Since the parties were unable to be married in Israel by the rabbinical authorities, they married in Cyprus in accordance with the local civil law, and were duly registered in the ministry of the interior in Cyprus, and an entry to the effect that she was wedded and had assumed the husband's name was made in the woman's passport by the Belgian Consul in Nicosia. After the couple arrived in Israel, the wife, in accordance with the provisions of the Registration of Inhabitants Ordinance of 1949,[19] applied for an identity card and requested to be registered as a married woman bearing the name of her husband. The registration office refused to issue the identity card as requested, on the ground that the marriage was not valid in accordance with the Halakhah. She applied to the High Court, which ordered the registration office to issue the identity card as requested, on the ground that that office is not a judicial body but merely an administrative office, whose duy it is to register a person as married upon the production of a prima facie document of marriage—in this case, the marriage certificate issued by the Cypriot ministry of the interior. From the practical point of view, this was tantamount to recognition of the marriage, inasmuch as regisration in the Office of the Registry of Inhabitants is prima facie evidence of personal status, until and unless changed by order of the court.[20]

Justice Moshe Silberg, in his minority opinion, contended that it was inadmissible for a state to allow its citizens to proceed to a foreign country in order to enter there into a contract that would be null and void. He further contended that recognition of such marriages would enable Israeli citizens to ignore the Halakhic prohibition of mixed marriages by contracting them in a neighboring country.[21] In the majority judgment Justice J. Sussman pointed out that "a country desirous of living within the family of nations must be prepared to renounce the implementation of some of its own laws, when a foreign element is injected into a legal action . . . when we demand recognition of the law of Israel from other nations, we cannot invalidate an act of a foreign law merely because it differs from our own law. . . . There are exceptional cases, where recognition of a foreign law and of an act performed thereunder would adversely affect the public order in accordance with which we live, and only where a foreign law would be repugnant to the feeling of justice and morality of the people of Israel would we invalidate it." He then proceeded to inquire whether a civil marriage contracted abroad would be repugnant to the moral principles of the people. In Israel, an immigrant country, there were tens of thousands of people who had contracted civil marriages abroad, and to disrupt such marriages on Halakhic grounds would raise grave problems. "Neither British nor American law invalidates marriages contracted by persons who went abroad to get married because they were not able to marry in their own country."[22]

While in common law jurisdictions such marriages are generally recognized, there are West European jurisdictions in which they are not. The Supreme Court majority took the more liberal attitude, in view of the heterogeneous condition of the population of Israel on the one hand, and of the immutability of the Halakhah on the other.

The Cohen

In addition to prohibiting marriages between Jews and non-Jews, and between certain categories of family relationships, the Halakhah also prohibits marriages between a cohen and a divorcée or a convert to Judaism; or when one of the parties is a mamzer within the specific meaning of this term in the Halakhah; nor may a childless widow remarry until the Halitzah ritual has been duly performed. Some of these prohibitions have created serious difficulties, and have called forth a good deal of public discussion and, not infrequently, indignation.[23]

> The most numerous of these categories involve persons presumed to be of Cohanitic or priestly origin whose numbers run into many thousands. Persons whose names are Cohen, Katz, Kaplan and certain other names are presumed to be of priestly descent, and may not marry a divorcée or a lady converted to Judaism. In many instances, this difficulty is overcome by such couples proceeding abroad, particularly to the near-by island of Cyprus to be married there. In the contemplation of the Halakhah a marriage between two such persons, once contracted, constitutes a valid marital relationship, which although contracted as a result of a transgression, cannot be dissolved, except by way of a duly executed bill of divorcement (*get*). In accordance with the Halakhah it is the duty of such a couple to be divorced, but until they perform this duty their status is one of married persons.[24]

On November 11, 1970, the Supreme Court rendered a judgment in a matter that had aroused considerable public interest.[25] In 1945, Eliezer Cahane, a cohen, married a divorcée, and a son was born to them. In 1959 he abandoned his wife, and was ordered to pay alimony. In 1967 he applied for a decree of divorce on the ground of his being a cohen, and the wife, a previous divorcée. The rabbinical court accepted this fact as a valid ground for divorce, ordered the payment of alimony to be discontinued, but directed the husband to pay to his wife the trifling sum of IL.100. The Supreme Court rejected the plea of the wife for the payment of alimony on the ground that such a decision is in accordance with the rabbinical law. Said Justice Sussman: "The result is that a woman who has been married for twenty-five years and has borne a son . . . now has to leave with the mere sum of a hundred pounds. Such are the laws of personal status in Israel, and no remedy can be afforded."[26] Commenting on this judgment Professor Amnon Rubinstein, Dean of the Law Faculty of Tel Aviv University, bitterly observed:

> There is something ironic in the fact that in a country where a woman is head of the government, it has been determined that a woman is a second-class citizen, and that in many cases she is not only discriminated against, but is also deprived of all rights. The responsibility for this situation, which makes a mockery of the principle of woman's equality, is that of the legislature and of the government, who have delivered the citizens of Israel into the hands of the rabbinical establishment, which treats women as objects to be cast away once they have been made use of.[27]

Another Halakhic restriction on marriage, of serious consequence to young widows, results from the institution of levirate marriage.[28] In order to cope with the problem in Israel, the Rabbinical Courts Jurisdiction (Marriage and Divorce) Law, in the above-quoted section 7 of 1953,[29] had provided that the recalcitrant brother-in-law may be compelled to give Halitzah, but frequently widows will hesitate to have the Attorney-General apply to the civil court for an order of imprisonment. The widow is in an even more difficult position if her husband is survived by a brother who is a minor, for she has to wait until that child reaches the age of legal maturity; similar difficulties arise if the brother-in-law is domiciled abroad, and no pressure can be brought upon him to submit to the Halitzah ritual.

A much-discussed attempt to help a widow and yet comply with the Halakhah occurred in 1967. A deaf-and-dumb man, a resident of Ashdod, who was himself married, was willing to participate in the Halitzah ritual, but it was impossible for him to do so, since he was physically incapable of reciting the prescribed formula: "I do not wish to take her."[30] The Chief Rabbis circumvented the difficulty by means of a rabbinically approved marriage, even though the groom already had a wife. They were then taken to a hotel where a room had been reserved for them by the rabbinate. The next morning the couple, having performed Mitzvat HaHityahdut (the act of union), were taken to the rabbinical court, where the husband proceeded to divorce his bride of one day. Before the marriage ceremony the bride had obtained an undertaking from the brother-in-law that he would pay her a substantial amount for as long as he remained married to her; this was in order to ensure that he would not go back on his pledged word and refuse to divorce her.[31] This incident aroused a highly negative reaction among the public, especially since it was clear that the Chief Rabbis had aided and abetted an offense against the penal code that makes bigamy a crime. Professor Ernest Simon of the Hebrew University, himself an observant Jew, expressed this sense of widespread indignation at this humiliating performance, which, he commented, revealed how far observance of archaic rituals is removed from ethical principles and humanitarian considerations.

Instances of other hardships caused by the application of Halakhic rules in matters of family law have frequently been reported in the press, and at times became the subject of highly charged public debate. On August 10, 1965, a lengthy account appeared in *Davar* of an effort by the rabbis to dissolve an existing relationship when they discovered that a cohen had married a divorcée. In 1964, a blackmail attempt relating to the law of Halitzah was publicized, involving a young childless widow whose 15-year-old brother-in-law was demanding IL.8,000 for consenting to perform the prescribed ritual. The young widow could not raise the money, and although the rabbis tried to persuade the youth to accept a small sum, they were unsuccessful.[32]

That this situation was likely to lead to incessant tension between the rabbinate and the majority of the population was realized by some of the traditionalist leaders themselves, who tried to design forms of escape from the hardships caused by the strict application of Halakhic rules in the field of family law. A leading Orthodox scholar, noting that 8% of all men applying for marriage in Israel were cohanim, expressed a doubt as to the necessity for the rabbinate to investigate whether a prospective groom was in fact a cohen. It was sufficient, he argued, for the rabbi to mention before the ceremony that the Torah law forbids a cohen to marry a divorcée, thus leaving the responsibility for observing this law to the parties. This procedure, however, could not be followed where the bridegroom's name immediately indicated that he was a cohen. In such cases he proposed to establish a ceremony based not on the law of Kiddushin (the Halakhic marriage ritual that creates the binding relationship between husband and wife), but on the law of Pilagshut (concubinage). This was an established institution in the biblical and Talmudic periods, when the children of the concubine had equal rights with those of the legitimate wife. In such ceremony the officiating rabbi would instruct the groom to say to the bride "you are hereby set aside for me," instead of the customary formula "you are hereby sanctified unto me," and would dispense with the ring and the Ketubah, the document containing the obligations that a bridegroom undertakes toward his bride as prescribed in a Halakhic marriage. Under a Pilagshut arrangement, the woman would be considered the man's wife in all re-

spects in the contemplation of civil law, while in the eyes of the Halakhah she would be his concubine. In both cases, the children would be
legitimate.[33]

As the non-Orthodox received this proposal with sentiments ranging
from indignation to ridicule, a suggestion was made by Knesset member
Moshe Unna, a leading member of Mafdal, who was one of the first
among the Orthodox to address himself to this problem. In an article
published in 1964 in the official monthly periodical of the Kibbutz Dati,[34]
he warned that unless a solution was found to the hardships created by
Halakhah, an intolerable situation would develop that might eventually
lead to the official introduction of civil marriage. He therefore proposed
that limited civil marriage facilities be provided in cases of cohen-and-
divorcée, or a Halitzah-bound widow. His solution, he stated, would
not pose Halakhic problems, for the civil marriage of such couples
could not be dissolved Halakhically, except by a duly executed bill of
divorcement, even though the union had been contracted in contravention of a Halakhic prohibition. Unna made it quite clear that his
object was to alleviate the lot of persons falling in these two categories,
and to ease the tension arising out of the state and religion relationship.
His proposal, however, was rejected by a group of influential rabbis,
who branded the whole idea as "contrary to Torah and Halakhah,"
and voiced their indignation that a person purporting to be a leader of
the Orthodox should dare to make such a proposal, and that a periodical issued by an Orthodox group should publish such a statement.[35]
Subsequently, no further initiative was taken by either Unna or by his
own party. Only the Liberal Party adopted a resolution welcoming Unna's proposal, but they similarly did not pursue the matter further.
There was no likelihood that the coalition government would support
it.

Divorce

While the Halakhic rules of divorce are, in general, liberal, and in
many ways progressive when compared with those prevalent in many
other countries, certain of the rules, both of substantive law and of
procedure, create severe hardships for women. Under biblical law the
husband could divorce his wife at his pleasure by giving her a *get*, a
bill of divorcement (as is the rule in Islam today). In the course of
the centuries, restrictions were placed on the arbitrary right of the husband to divorce his wife.* Since the time of Rabbenu Gershon in the
eleventh century, a wife could not be divorced against her will, so that
the normal and common procedure for a divorce was through the mu-

---

* The term employed is *legaresh*, to drive away, expel.

tual consent of the parties. Once this had been obtained, the formality consisted of a ceremony in which the husband delivered to his wife a *get* in the presence of a rabbinical court. In theory, the court itself does not dissolve the marriage; it merely supervises a procedure resulting from the free decision of the husband to deliver a *get* to his wife, and from her readiness to accept it. For even as marriage is a contractual act of the willing parties, so is a Halakhic divorce. Where a divorce is warranted but one of the parties witholds consent, a rabbinical court may try to induce the unwilling spouse to grant it. The recognized grounds for divorce are wide, ranging from ill-treatment, moral turpitude, and grossly insulting behavior, to impotence. But even when the court decrees that the husband is to deliver the *get,* or the wife to receive it, as the case may be, that decree is of no effect until and unless the defendant in the proceedings agrees to comply with it.

Where a deadlock ensues, the sanction against a recalcitrant wife consists of giving permission to the husband to remarry without the dissolution of his previous marriage, since a Jewish religious marriage may be polygamous. In that event the husband is relieved of all his obligations to the first wife, although in theory she is still his wife. In order to render the second marriage immune to the penalty imposed by the state's criminal law on polygamous marriage, the Penal Law Amendment (Bigamy) Law of 1959 provided in Section 5 that: "Where the law applicable to the new marriage is a Jewish religious law, a person shall not be convicted of an offense under Section 2, if the new marriage was contracted after permission to marry had been granted by a final judgment of the rabbinical court, and the judgment had been approved by the two Chief Rabbis of Israel." The same procedure is applied by the rabbinical court where the wife cannot accept a *get* by reason of insanity or by her disappearance, or the lack of decisive evidence establishing her death.

Altogether different is the reverse situation, that is, when the husband disobeys the decree of the rabbinical court and refuses to deliver the *get* to the wife. Her recourse is limited. She may apply to the Attorney-General to institute proceedings in the civil court for the imprisonment of the husband until such time as he complies with the order.[36] But not many wives are willing to resort to this drastic measure, and even when it is invoked, it may not always be effective. In 1968, the case of Yehya Abraham came before the Supreme Court. He refused to comply with the decree of the rabbinical court that he deliver the *get* to his wife; upon the application of the Attorney-General, he was jailed by order of the court. After he had spent five years in jail, the Attorney-General applied to the court to order his release, on the ground that imprisonment had failed to make the reluctant husband comply with the decree. The Supreme Court refused to order the release, and in a reasoned judgment Justice Silberg suggested to the rabbis how, on the basis of Talmudic and rabbinic sources, a solution to the impasse could be devised. Justice Landau added that he could not reconcile himself to the thought that Israeli justice could force a woman to remain single because "her fate is in the hands of a husband who persists in his refusal to grant the *get* to which she has been pronounced entitled."[37] The remarks of the justices were not taken up by the rabbinate, who severely condemned them for their criticism of a Halakhic tradition.

In 1969, a similar incident caught the attention of the public. Adrian Schwartz was found guilty of six indecent assaults and three acts of rape, and was sentenced to 14 years' imprisonment. Upon the wife's application, the rabbinical court ordered the convict to deliver a *get* to her. The husband refused, and there was no further pressure that could be brought upon him, since he was in any case serving a lengthy jail sentence. The Minister of Justice, who was questioned regarding possible relief for his wife, admitted that nothing could legally be done to release the woman from her conjugal status.[38] Throughout this controversy the rabbinical authorities made no attempt to devise a Halakhic solution to the plight of this wife or other wives in similar circumstances.

A man's refusal to deliver the *get* or to undergo Halitzah are not the only instances where technical noncompliance with Halakhah condemns women to perpetual celibacy. There are especially those women whose husbands have deserted them and whose whereabouts are unknown. Unlike the civil codes of many countries, the Halakhah does not create a presumption of death when a person disappears and nothing is heard of him for a period of years; only death proved by two witnesses is recognized by the Halakhah. The great upheavals of this century and particularly the shattering events of World War II and the Holocaust, as well as the three wars that Israel fought, produced a number of women whose husbands had vanished but whose death could not be proved. These women, referred to as Agunot (Heb. "chained") are shackled to an, in fact, nonexistent marriage and they may not remarry. In Israel, where the majority of Jews are immigrants, the number of Agunot is further increased by instances of divorce having been decreed abroad in accordance with civil law only. Finally, there are those women whose husbands are stricken with insanity, and for that reason cannot deliver a *get*. The number of unfortunate women in these categories cannot be precisely established, but it is undoubtedly considerable. In all such situations men would be entitled to remarry, and likewise the Halitzah law imposes no burden on the man. In short, discrimination against married women is legally sanctioned, and all attempts on the part of women's organizations to remove it have met with no success.[39]

Bastards

Equally in need of equitable treatment are children who are illegitimate in the view of the Halakhah; they are known as Mamzerim, that is, offspring of the union of a married woman and a man other than her husband. The status of the mamzer is regulated in accordance with the rule that "a mamzer shall not enter into the congregation of the Lord; even to his tenth generation shall he not enter into the congregation of the Lord" (Deuteronomy 23:2). When a mother has not been divorced in strict accordance with the Halakhah, the offspring of her subsequent marriage is also treated as a mamzer. The mamzer may marry another mamzer or a proselyte, but is Halakhically forbidden to marry any Jew. Since the *get* of the Karaite Jews was not considered to be in accordance with Halakhah, the entire Karaite community is tainted, and consequently may not marry a Jew.

In the spring of 1971, the issue made headlines in Israel, when Moshe Dayan, Minister of Defense, brought to the attention of the government the case of Chanoch and Miriam Langer, a brother and a sister, both then serving in the army, who were unable to make arrangements to marry the partners of their choice. The rabbinical court, upon the application of the prospective bride and bridegroom for marriage licenses, came to the conclusion that their mother had not been properly divorced from her first husband, and therefore her subsequent marriage to their father was invalid and the two were mamzerim. It was reported that the Minister of Defense was demanding the introduction of civil marriage unless both were declared eligible to marry.[40] Dayan's call aroused a public storm and found widespread support in the press. When questioned on the subject, Chief Rabbi Unterman stated that "the feeling of compassion must not permit the citadel of Judaism to be shaken."[41] Regarding the hardship caused to the two young soldiers, the Chief Rabbi said: "I do not consider it as a tragedy. One cannot say that these people are prevented from marrying. They can marry male or female proselytes. We do not lack proselytes; indeed there is quite a selection of them."[42]

This controversy was resolved when Rabbi Shlomo Goren, on becoming Chief Rabbi in 1972, reconsidered the case and adjudicated that the brother and sister were not mamzerim. He arrived at this decision after finding that their father's conversion to Judaism was not in accordance with the Halakhah. Having invalidated the conversion of the father, it followed that his marriage to the mother of the brother and sister, who was a Jewess, was void in the view of the Halakhah. They were consequently never married, hence their offspring were not mamzerim. The real casualty of this controversy was their father, who unexpectedly was adjudicated a non-Jew. His indignation at this action was shared by many of the ultra-Orthodox rabbis, who considered the judgment illegal, arbitrary, and as having been made in pursuance of Rabbi Goren's promise to government to remove the stigma of mamzerut upon his being elected Chief Rabbi.

Redress of Hardships

It is not surprising that the number of persons who have contracted de facto marriages in contravention of the Halakhah is considerable. They have been instrumental in persuading the Knesset to accord them, for certain limited and specified purposes, the legal benefits of a lawful spouse. A number of laws were enacted primarily for the purpose of protecting the interests of the "reputed wife." Thus Article 1 (a) of the Invalids (Pensions and Rehabilitation) Law of 1949–5709[43] defines *wife* as including "a woman living with an invalid, and commonly reputed to be his wife." This enabled wives of persons killed or disabled while serving in the Defense Army of Israel or the Police Force to be granted benefits as a so-called reputed spouse. Likewise, Article 1 of the Tenants Protection Law 1955–5715, which extended the benefits of the law to the widow of a protected tenant, defines *spouse* as including a person commonly reputed to be a spouse.[44] Similarly, the Names Law 1956–5716 provides: "A child born while his mother is not married to the father shall receive at birth the surname of his mother, unless the mother wishes him to receive the surname of the father, and the father has consented thereto, or unless the woman is generally known as the father's wife."[45] For purposes of exemption from Estate Duty, the Estate Duty (Amendment No. 3) Law of 1969–5724 treats a reputed wife as a wife.[46] Finally, the Law of Inheritance provides in Section 55: "Where a man and woman, though not being married to one another, have lived together as husband and wife in a common household, then, upon the death of one of them, neither being married to another person, the deceased is deemed, subject to any contrary direction expressed or implicit in the will of the deceased, to have bequeathed to the survivor what the survivor would have inherited on intestacy, if they had been married to one another."[47] Although in this particular instance the term "reputed spouse" excluded persons who were Halakhically married, the law nevertheless was a step forward in granting recognition to de facto marriages in so important a realm as that of inheritance.

The legislative enactments of the Knesset, made for the protection of the reputed wife, represent one attempt on the part of the civil authorities to redress the hardships inflicted by Halakhah in the sphere of family relations. These laws, are, in effect, the result of the confrontation between the values of the majority of the Israeli electorate and the values of strict adherents of tradition. Thus the gap between the two approaches is not bridged by the formal introduction of civil marriage, but is mitigated through a series of laws that bestow upon persons living as husband and wife outside the framework of the Halakhah, certain rights that are otherwise the privilege of Halakhically married persons.

The judges of the civil courts were invariably confronted with the argument that the laws conferring rights on a reputed spouse are contrary to another law, which recognizes only one form of family relationship, that is, the Halakhic form. They approached the dilemma from a moral point of view. Said Justice Chaim Cohen in the case of *Fassler* v. *The State of Israel*: "Wy should a woman who has given her labor and love, who has been devoted to a man in his suffering and kept up his spirits when in distress, be deprived of certain benefits merely because she does not possess a marriage certificate? The state bestowed rights upon widows, not because they were lawfully married to their husbands, but because they had lost their supporters . . . and because they had earned those rights through their devotion to and toil for their supporters, and the state recognizes and safeguards those rights. The rights bestowed by these laws do not depend upon the observance of a certain law, or of a certain form of registration; they are based on the fact that that woman lived with that man over a lengthy period, and on evidence of such long existence. It is sufficient that the public knew that they were living as husband and wife."[48]

An attempt to assist a helpless woman beyond the scope of the specific laws enacted for the benefit of the reputed spouse was made in the case of *Yager* v. *Palevich*. A woman living abroad was abandoned by her husband in 1946. Taking her child with her, she immigrated to Israel. Some time later she established a household with one Zeev Palevich, where the daughter born to her abroad grew up along with the son of Palevich from his first marriage and the son who was born to her and to Palevich. To all intents and purposes, they lived as husband and wife. Later on, however, Palevich wished to sever his connection with the woman, to whom he believed he was married, and applied to the rabbinical court for a divorce. The court ruled that they had never been married, because the death of her first husband had not been proved, although all trace of him had been lost for 17 years; therefore the rabbinical court refused to grant alimony requested by the reputed wife from Palevich. Justice Zvi Berenson admitted that while none of the laws dealing with a reputed spouse would grant alimony in such a case, there was an implied contract between the parties, whereby it was agreed that Palevich would bestow on her all the rights of a duly married wife. This included the right to be supported by him, in consideration of her agreeing to bring up his son of a previous marriage. It was upon the theory of implied contract that he based his judgment, which differed from that of the rabbinical court. He rejected the view that there was something immoral about this arrangement. "The Knesset protected the reputed wife in a series of laws, and granted her various monetary and material benefits. Is it conceivable that the legislators were ignoring public morals and the public good? The legislators had deemed it right to grant the reputed wife—although she may be actually married to another person at the time—various benefits. Are we entitled to place ourselves above the legislators, and to decide that the basis for the grant of these rights—the agreement to live as husband and wife—is unstable and precarious? Can there be two views of morality and the public good, one in legislation and the other in judicial decisions?" By a majority opinion the Supreme Court ruled that in this instance the reputed wife, although Halakhically neither divorced nor a widow, was entitled to alimony from her reputed husband.[49]

This particular Agunah was saved by the fact that she had brought up the son of her reputed husband, which afforded the court the possibility of deducing an implied contract for her maintenance. But this very judgment, informed as it was by a human approach, also brought into sharp focus the limits imposed by law on a well-intentioned judiciary anxious to break out of the tight grasp of the Halakhah.

D. THE PUBLIC DEBATE

More than any other law enacted by the Knesset, the passage of the Rabbinical Court Jurisdiction (Marriage and Divorce) Law of 1953 has caused a permanent public debate, involving not only matters arising out of this law, but those touching on the place of religion in modern society in general, and the relationship between state and religion in particular. The public debate preceded the enactment of the law; it accompanied the discussion of the bill in the Knesset, and has remained on the public agenda ever since.

The parliamentary debate that took place in the Knesset when the bill was introduced in 1953 afforded the first opportunity for a comprehensive airing of the problem in its broadest aspects.

Dr. Zerah Warhaftig, then Deputy Minister for Religious Affairs, stated that the importance of the bill lay in the fact that it would assure the unity of the Jewish people, which was of special significance in the period of the ingathering of the exiles, and of the fusion of the heterogeneous immigrant groups into one national entity. "Were civil marriage to be introduced," he observed, "it would lead us to the creation of two separate nations." The result would be that the Orthodox would withdraw from the totality of the community, and thus become spiritually alienated from the Jewish state.[50]

He further dwelt on the danger of intermarriage, which, he said, would result from the introduction of civil marriage. "Imagine a situation in Israel where intermarriage is permitted under the civil law—this would certainly weaken the restraints on intermarriage in many lands. If it is permitted in Israel, why should inhabitants of the Diaspora refrain? It is impossible to maintain the unity of the people in the Diaspora, if it is not maintained in the State of Israel."[51]

Dr. Warhaftig admitted that imposing a religious marriage ritual on nonbelievers would amount to a coercion of conscience. But, he said, "there is no state which does not coerce. State laws amount to coercion. . . . In the same way as a state may appoint government officials to register marriages, so it may authorize rabbis to be persons having exclusive power to adjudicate in matters of divorce. The state may vest this power in the rabbinical courts, and the latter, deriving their power from the Knesset, become in fact state courts."[52] He made it clear that once the Knesset had enacted this bill and vested in the rabbinical courts the exclusive authority to adjudicate in matters of family relations, it thereby abdicated its right to influence by legislation the kind of law that these courts would apply. "When we discuss the laws of marriage, we must take them as they are, since it is impossible for the Knesset to amend or alter them."[53]

Dr. Warhaftig further adumbrated this aspect of the law in a speech he delivered in the Knesset in 1954. In extolling the Halakhah, he said: "We have a legal system that has always sustained the people. It may contain within it some thorn that pricks a certain individual, but here we are not concerned with this or that individual, but with the totality of the people." To those of his critics in the Knesset who urged him to introduce reforms so as to eliminate the sufferings caused by those "thorns," he replied: "When human beings create a religion, it is idolatry. He who repudiates the proposition that religion can be created by man thereby asserts his belief in the Creator of the Universe, and in the divine origins of religion. . . . When people reform religion, it is a human act. An idol may be made of wood, or of silver, or a human action; and that constitutes idolatry, not religion."[54]

Here was a classical exposition of Halakhic fundamentalism. The Halakhah was divine and therefore immutable. Reforming it would be an act of idolatry. The Halakhah cannot be accepted except in its entirety. The Knesset may decide to revoke the power delegated to the rabbinic courts to administer the Halakhah, but it may not amend it.

Moshe Unna, of Mafdal, sought to minimize the gravity of the charge that the proposed law was an infringement on freedom of conscience. Every legal system, he said, possesses a code regulating family relations. The State of Israel was called upon to adopt such a code, and in adopting one that is identical with the Halakhic code it would prejudice no basic right. The fact that a particular code happens to possess divine authority in the eyes of a religious person does not, of itself, interfere with the freedom of conscience of the nonbeliever.[55]

The reluctant supporters of the bill from the non-Orthodox parties, particularly the spokesmen for Mapai, were aware of the hardships inflicted by the Halakhic family code, particularly on women, and expressed the hope that the rabbinate would find ways of alleviating their plight. They dwelt on Halitzah and Agunah, on the fate of women bound to insane husbands or exposed to the malice of husbands who refuse to deliver the *get*, in defiance of rabbinical decrees. Instances of tragedies were cited, of injustices left unredressed, of women humiliated, of prospects of happier life frustrated. Yet, the critics of the Halakhah joined with the Orthodox in believing that unity of the Jewish people would be torn asunder unless the Halakhic family code were established by law. Said Israel Yeshayahu, a leading Mapai member: "If Israeli marriages and divorces are not in accordance with the traditional laws, intermarriage will spread, and the national identity will be obliterated."[56] He voted for the bill, as did most of the non-Orthodox, fearing that if civil marriage were introduced, a separate register would be kept of those marrying Halakhically and those marrying civilly, with the offspring of the latter being precluded from marriage with the offspring of the former. All were haunted by the specter of a split in the House of Israel; for the sake of avoiding what seemed to them the danger of creating two nations within Israel, the secularist majority was prepared to yield to the minority and to subject themselves to a legal code, the sanctity of which they did not acknowledge and the application of which they frequently had occasion to criticize.

Only the parties of the extreme Left voted against the bill. Dr. Moshe Sneh, appearing in that debate on behalf of the "Left List," affirmed that Orthodox Jews were entitled to live in accordance with the tenets of the Written and Oral Law, and that the state was bound to safeguard that right. He criticized those supporters of the bill who were urging the rabbis to introduce reforms into the Halakhah; they had no right to do this, he contended. "We do not wish to interfere in the way of life of the Orthodox. On the contrary, we support freedom of religious ritual, and claim that religious needs must be provided for." However, he said that the principle of freedom of conscience or freedom of religion also includes the freedom of being nonreligious. "The law that is being prepared now, imposes on the non-religious, laws and customs in the sphere of family relations that are alien to them. We agree to the jurisdiction of the rabbis over the Orthodox, but demand civil jurisdiction over the secularists."[57]

Mr. Eliezer Peri, on behalf of Mapam, the United Worker's Party, drew the attention of the Knesset to the fact that the bill was being enacted in order to satisfy the religious parties, who had obtained only

12% of the total vote in the previous election. This law, then, was contrary to the expressed will of the people, but was being imposed on the nation because of the need of the coalition government to have the religious in their ranks, thus assuring government stability. Mr. Peri, who declared himself a nonbeliever, demanded the right to lead the life of a nonbeliever, and repudiated anyone's right to impose religious norms on the nonreligious. This would not lead to national unity, he said. Turning to the Orthodox, he said: "If you really wish to inculcate faith in, and respect for religion, your present methods will yield the opposite result. Will you, by coercion, lead to faith? True faith and coercion are mutually exclusive. You are only arousing indignation against yourselves; each single nonbeliever can tell you how indignant and humiliated he is when he presents himself to the rabbi at his wedding. I can respect a rabbi as a human being, but I have no respect for him when he appears as the representative of a superior authority. I do not acknowledge his moral or superior authority, and this is the feeling of most people . . . . If you coerce us to submit to this authority, you are not cultivating faith but hypocrisy; you are encouraging disrespect for rabbis; . . . you are humiliating religion itself."[58] His proposal was to have two sets of courts, rabbinical and civil, both having jurisdiction in matters of personal status, with each person being at liberty to choose his form of marriage.

The bill passed its first reading, and was referred to committee. In the course of the second reading of the bill, the debate was as heated and at times as acrimonious as at the first reading. On August 26, 1953, the bill was enacted into law.[59]

Although Article 2 of the Rabbinical Courts Jurisdiction (Marriage and Divorce) Law, which provided that marriages and divorces of Jews shall be performed "in accordance with Jewish religious law," did not specify that "Jewish religious law" meant the Halakhah as interpreted by the Orthodox, it was clear to all concerned that this was the intention. First, only the Orthodox interpretation was recognized under the British Mandate, and the entire rabbinic establishment was Orthodox. There were no organized groups of Conservative or Reform Jews to demand for their rabbis the right to perform marriages, or otherwise to be represented in the official rabbinate. During the long parliamentary debate on the bill, not a single speaker alluded to the fact that in the Diaspora the Conservative and Reform movements were regarded as legitimate expressions of Judaism, and in fact constituted the majority of the Jewish people outside Israel. Even those members of the Knesset who were fully aware of the weight of non-Orthodox groups in the Diaspora desisted from pressing this point, for during the earlier years of the State of Israel the public still accepted as axiomatic the notion propagated by the Orthodox that Conservative and Reform Judaism were synonymous with de-Judaization and assimilation. In Israel, Judaism thus continued to be equated with Orthodoxy.

The law providing for the appointment of Dayanim, judges of the rabbinical courts, ensured that no non-Orthodox rabbi would be appointed. The Dayanim law of 1955–5715 provided that the Dayanim "shall be appointed by the President of the State upon the recommendation of the Appointments Committee." The latter was to consist of 10 members: the two Chief Rabbis, two Dayanim elected by the body of Dayanim, the Minister of Religious Affairs, another member of the government, two members of the Knesset elected by secret ballot, and two members of the Bar Association.[60] Thus five of the ten places on the Committee were reserved from the outset for the Orthodox; in addition, one of the Knesset members was always representative of Mafdal, by prearrangement with Mapai and as part of the coalition agreement.

In the contemplation of Israel law, Judaism is a monolithic religion that admits of no pluralism. Is then the denial to a Reform or Conservative Jew of the right to have his marriage celebrated by a rabbi of his choice tantamount to the denial of religious freedom in a country where no marriage can be celebrated except by a religious authority? This question has not yet been adjudicated by the Supreme Court. Professor Rubinstein of the Law Faculty of the University of Tel Aviv considers that this situation does not accord with the accepted principles of religious freedom.[61] Regarding people who are not religious, Professor Rubinstein observes: "Here the individual is subjected to norms whose essential source is religious, and whose binding force is drawn from their adoption by the legislature. The operation of this law is not governed by the ordinary rules applicable to statutory enactments, neither from the point of view of its amendment nor from that of inquiry into its mode of operation. To subject persons to religious law and religious judges in matters of marriage and divorce is equivalent to forcing them to participate in religious rites."[62] Yet, in his opinion, there is no established "church" in Israel as in England or Sweden. Jewish Orthodoxy is an established "church" only within Judaism. Religious freedom is guaranteed to non-Jewish religious denominations only. Thus the problem of religion in Israel is, in effect, a Jewish problem, arising out of an attempt to force, by law, a pluralistic society into a monolithic mold.[63]

Professor Isaiah Leibowitz of the Hebrew University, an Orthodox Jew, supported civil marriage and divorce for those who want it. "The contention that the recognition by the state of civil marriage will split the Jews into two peoples is false. . . . It is equally false that the institution of civil marriage will wipe out *kiddushin* [Halakhic marriage]. One who raises this argument is ignoring the reality of hundreds of thousands of Jews in the Western world who lead Torah-true lives under laws which provide for civil marriage and divorce. Torah-true Jews will continue to marry by means of *Huppah veKiddushin,* and if, God forbid, they should divorce, it would be in accordance with Jewish law. Those who rebel against religion will be satisfied to have their 'marriages and divorces' recorded in a government office, in accordance with civil law. The terms 'marriages and divorces' are placed in quotation marks, because in the view of Jewish law, no marriage has taken place under such circumstances, but merely cohabitation with an unmarried woman, and consequently the question of *get* does not arise. Where there is no *kiddushin,* there is no bastardy, for a child born out of wedlock to an unmarried woman is Halakhically not illegitimate; the term is reserved for the offspring of a married woman and a man who is not her husband. So far the Halakhic authorities have not given serious consideration to the consequences of civil marriages from the Halakhic point of view. . . . Such a situation [civil marriage], which reduces the risk of bastardy to a minimum, would be a great improvement as compared with the existing law of marriage and divorce, which in fact causes bastardy to multiply. . . . We must not, however, expect the rabbinic authorities to consider the matter objectively, for they have a vested interest in it."[64]

As an Orthodox Jew, Professor Leibowitz considers those who would resort to civil marriages as Jews "who rebel against religion," but he would not coerce them into a religious ceremony. Thus civil marriage in itself should pose no difficulty to the Orthodox Jew, nor should it lead to a schism within the nation. A view of civil marriage as non-marriage would in fact prevent a split between Israeli Jewry and the Diaspora.[65]

It was Professor Leibowitz who was the first Orthodox scholar in Israel to come out in favor of separation of religion and state: "The demand for separation stems from the vital need of preventing religion from becoming the handmaid of political or social interests, from turning into a government department of a secular authority, a function of an administrative bureaucracy. . . . From a religious point of view, there can be no greater abomination than a secular state which recognizes religious institutions as state institutions, maintains them, and imposes on the general public not religion, but certain religious functions, by an arbitrary selection determined by party-politics—and all this, while claiming that this is not a Halakhic state, but one where civil law prevails. And what about a rabbinate whose appointment, jurisdiction and salary are determined by the secular authority, whose status is thus comparable to that of the police force, the sanitary department, the post-office? . . . There can be no greater humiliation for a religion, nothing that detracts so much from its influence, than the establishment and maintenance of religious institutions by a secular state." His conclusion is: "All this is a falsification of social and religious truth, and a source of spiritual and intellectual corruption."[66]

Other Orthodox scholars also took up the cudgels for separation. Rabbi Menahem Cohen predicted: "Separation of religion from the state will pave the way for a confrontation between the two in a struggle to win the hearts of the people. This will be achieved by the exercise of moral and spiritual influence. . . . If religion is free and emancipated, it will be able to confront the secular reality, and in this struggle, its spiritual, educational and social prestige will be enhanced."[67]

E. OTHER LEGISLATIVE ENACTMENTS

Days of Rest

Some three weeks after the establishment of the state, the Provisional Council of State enacted the Days of Rest Ordinance, 1948. It provides: "The Sabbath and the Jewish festivals, namely, the two days of New Year, the Day of Atonement, the First Day of the Feast of Tabernacles and the Eighth Day of Solemn Assembly, the First and Seventh Days of Passover, and the Feast of Pentecost shall be prescribed days of rest in the State of Israel. Non-Jews shall have the right to observe their own Sabbaths and festivals as days of rest."[68]

Local authorities were empowered "to regulate the opening and closing of shops, workshops, restuarants, coffee and tea shops, drinking places, canteens, cinemas, theatres and other places of public entertainment, and to control their opening and closing on any particular day."[69] The municipalities took advantage of this provision in accordance with their own needs. In Bnei Brak there is a complete ban on private as well as public transport during the Sabbath and no form of entertainment; in Haifa, all forms of transport are permitted, restaurants are open, and a variety of entertainments is offered. The degree of Sabbath restriction is the subject of perennial bargaining following the election of new municipal councils.

In 1951 the Knesset enacted the Hours of Work and Rest Law, Section 7 of which provided: "An employee's weekly rest shall be not less than 36 consecutive hours in the week. The weekly rest shall include, in the case of a Jew, the Sabbath day, and in the case of a person other than a Jew, the Sabbath day, or Sunday or Friday, whichever is ordinarily observed by him as his weekly day of rest." An exception to this rule was provided in Section 12 of this law. "The Minister of Labor may permit an employee to be employed during all or any of the hours of weekly rest, if he is satisfied that interruption of work for all or part of the weekly rest is likely to prejudice the defense of the state, or the security of persons or property, or seriously to prejudice the economy, or some process of work, or some supply of services which, in the opinion of the Minister of Labor, may be essential to the public or part thereof. A general permit shall be given only upon the decision of a committee of Ministers consisting of the Prime Minister, the Minister of Religion and the Minister of Labor."[70]

This committee of Ministers meets frequently to deal with the implementation of the law, especially since conflicts between the Minister of Religion and his colleagues are bound to occur. Some general rules have been laid down: Israeli ships may not enter or leave a port on the Sabbath; El-Al planes neither take off nor land in Lod Airport on the Sabbath (except under exceptional circumstances); telegrams are not delivered on the Sabbath; and all railways are at a standstill.[71]

Dietary Laws

In 1962 the Pig-Raising Prohibition Law was enacted, which provided that "a person shall not raise, keep or slaughter pigs." Detailed provisions empowered the police to enforce the law. The law applied to Jews and Moslems who are also forbidden by their religion to raise pigs, but exempted Christian communities and specified "permitted areas," localities in which Christians form a majority.[72] Although some Jews who had been engaged in pig-raising moved to these areas, pig-breeding on the whole was reduced in most parts of the country.

The overriding problem in the relationship of state and religion and a subject of incessant disputes between the public and the rabbinate, has been Kashrut, the observance of dietary laws in accordance with rabbinic tradition. Since the maintenance and supervision of Kashrut touches every area of public life, it has developed into a substantial civil service, with hundreds of supervisors operating on a full-time basis in hotels, hospitals, army camps, passenger ships, supermarkets, restaurants and factory canteens, prisons and slaughter houses. Fees collected from the places supervised provide the salaries of the supervisors. Supervision has extended beyond the country, for Israel imports considerable quantities of meat from the Argentine, Rumania, and other countries, and Israeli supervisors are dispatched there even to those countries where the local Orthodox rabbinate is capable of handling Kashrut. While the official Israeli rabbinate is the dominant element in this field, it does not have a monopoly; rabbis affiliated with Agudat Israel carry out their own supervision, primarily in places owned by their members. Neturei Karta repudiate the Kashrut certificate of the official rabbinate, and in Jerusalem they undertake their own Kashrut supervision. They likewise repudiate the shehitah (ritual slaughter) certification of the official rabbinate and at a considerable cost to themselves operate a slaughterhouse of their own. But these exceptions aside, the food that Israelis eat is controlled by the official rabbinate. It is a large, influential operation with powerful leverage in many areas.

In 1963, under Mafdal pressure, the government submitted a bill entitled: "A bill for the observances of Kashrut of businesses, slaughter-houses and merchandise" (Bill No. 546). Zerah Warhaftig, the Minister of Religions, explained that the object of the bill was to prevent the cheating of customers by unscrupulous individuals who represent non-kasher food as kasher. The Minister pointed out that in the State of New York a similar statute has been enacted.

A closer study of the subject revealed that the New York statute and the proposed bill were poles apart. Whereas the former made the sale of nonkasher food as kasher a punishable offense, the latter made the use of the word *kasher* when applied to a business a punishable offense where the user has not obtained the license of the rabbinate to such use. The critics of the bill pointed out that the selling of kasher food without a license would be a criminal offense, while the selling of nonkasher food by a person who had obtained the license would not be an offense under this law—a patent absurdity. They contended that the object of the bill was to vest in the rabbinate the exclusive authority to issue Kashrut licenses, an authority that would enable it to determine the fate of many businesses, large and small, as well as to impose on the applicants conditions unrelated to the Kashrut of foodstuffs.

The Kashrut bill passed its first reading in the Knesset, but did not emerge from the Committee on Law and Legislation. In 1966 the government, at the instance of Mafdal, introduced a new bill entitled "Law for the Prevention of Fraud in Kashrut."[73] It was drawn up along the lines of the earlier bill, but a proviso was added that, when issuing licenses, the rabbinate should not be guided by extraneous considerations, such as imposing the duty of Sabbath observance on the applicant. The bill has not reached the stage of first reading because of the vehement opposition of the rabbinate to the proviso intended to deprive them of the power to apply extraneous considerations. They preferred the existing state of affairs where, through the absence of a law, they were in a de facto position to impose in many instances conditions they deemed feasible. In 1974 a new bill dealing with Kashrut was presented to the Knesset by the government, but neither Mafdal nor the other parties displayed any interest in proceeding with it.

This controversy brought another important development to the fore. It demonstrated the growing gap between Mafdal and the rabbinate. The latter, being largely the creation of the former, was no longer prepared to be guided by its political sponsor. In terms of legal coercive power, vested in it, it felt it could afford to break loose from Mafdal and venture forth on an independent policy, ignoring the sensitiveness of Mafdal to the pressure of public opinion.

However, in the absence of a law, Kashrut became a source of end-less conflict and agitation. The lack of uniformity in the rules that were applied and discrimination between various places of business led to protest and public controversy. Thus, the Chief Rabbinate ruled that in Class A hotels, which usually have a considerable number of non-Jew-ish guests, supervision should be confined to the kitchen and dining-rooms. All other hotels, however, which generally attract a small per-centage of non-Jewish guests, are subjected both to a Kashrut and to Sabbath supervision, which involves nonadmission of guests on the Sab-bath and a prohibition of writing in the public rooms.[74] The second-class hotels protested but could get no relief. However, the ruling was not uniformly applied everywhere.[75]

The Marbek Case

The most notable conflict in the field of Kashrut broke out in 1964. The kibbutzim and moshavim in the Negev formed a company, Marbek, for the construction of a large and modern slaughterhouse and a meat-packing plant, which would serve these settlements, the major part of whose activities was cattle-raising. The company was intended to mar-ket the output of the new slaughterhouse throughout the country, and it was estimated that it would be able to supply about one-third of the national consumption. In order to forestall possible difficulties with the rabbinate in matters of Kashrut, it was decided to invite the kib-butzim and moshavim affiliated with Mafdal and Agudat Israel to join the company. The offer was accepted, and in 1964 the construction of the plant was completed. The company agreed with its religious part-ners that a regional Kashrut authority be set up, consisting of the rab-bis of the Mafdal and Agudah Israel settlements in the Negev. The company, being primarily interested in the most promising market, ap-plied to the rabbinate of Tel Aviv, who refused to issue a Kashrut cer-tificate, contending that they could not be responsible for the Kashrut of products manufactured a considerable distance away from Tel Aviv. They cited Halakhic precedents against the importation of food slaugh-tered outside the immediate vicinity (shehitat hutz).

The company in turn contended that in times of old it had been difficult to communicate with distant places and to supervise transpor-tation. These considerations did not apply in modern times, they con-tended, and pointed out that the rabbinate did not object to the impor-tation of meat products from the Argentine and other distant places. The matter developed into a major scandal, for it became obvious that not religious but economic reasons were at stake. Some members of the religious establishment who were employed in local plants might find themselves out of work, and the religious council of Tel Aviv would lose revenue.

The Mafdal and Agudah kibbutzim and moshavim criticized the rabbinate on the ground that the principle of *shehitat hutz* was out of place in a modern society.[76] The Tel Aviv rabbinate reacted by reiterating its position in a statement published in its official organ,[77] a ruling that was confirmed at a sitting of the Chief Rabbinical Council in Jerusalem in the summer of 1964. The company appealed to the High Court of Justice, alleging that the refusal to issue the Kashrut certificate was based on extraneous considerations, not on Halakhic principles. The court issued an order nisi against the Chief Rabbinical Council to show cause why it should not give instructions to inspect the Kashrut of the petitioners' plant.[78] The Council made no reply to the order, as it was bound to do by law, but through its secretary resorted to the unusual procedure of addressing a letter to the court in which it denied the jurisdiction of the High Court to interfere in the Halakhic considerations that guide the Chief Rabbinical Council. The latter, it said, "is subject to the Torah and cannot receive instructions from others how to adjudicate. The rabbinate determines on the basis of Halakhah when and how a Kashrut certificate is issued, and it cannot depart from this principle."

The High Court rejected the contention of the Chief Rabbinate, holding that it claimed for itself "immunity from the overriding power of the courts of this country." The court confirmed that it would not interfere in the Halakhic question, but would grant relief if it were proved that the Council had indeed exceeded its authority by having regard to considerations that bore no connection with the Halakhah concerning the grant of a Kashrut certificate for meat slaughtered in the plant of the petitioners.[79]

The court thus rejected the contention of the Chief Rabbinate, and it now remained to be seen whether the Chief Rabbis would comply with the order of the court and "show cause" why the Kashrut certificate should not be issued. If they refused to comply with the order, they might be guilty of contempt of court; if they attempted to show cause, it would become patent that they were not guided by Halakhic considerations alone. The Chief Rabbis escaped from the predicament by effecting a compromise with the company, and arranged for the issuance of a Kashrut certificate that was applicable only to a part of the country.

The Marbek controversy marked an important shift, if not a turning point, in the average Israeli's attitude toward the rabbinate. On this occasion the rabbinate failed to obtain the support of even the religious parties in the Knesset. In addition, the religious kibbutzim took the unprecedented step of disagreeing with the Chief Rabbinate, which had lost important ground in its struggle to maintain absolute religious authority. In the years that followed, the criticism became more insistent and now came from quarters that in the past had always supported the rabbinate.

Thus, the late Minister of the Interior, Moshe Chaim Shapiro said: "The Chief Rabbinate fails to realize that we are no longer living in some East European village."[80] Dr. Warhaftig stated that the rabbinate could no longer act as it did two hundred years ago; in solving problems, it would have to show some audacity. "We must lend our support to the rabbinate," said the Minister, "but that does not mean that we must blindly follow its lead." But the rabbinate was unyielding, although there were some exceptions. Rabbi Shlomo Goren, as Chief Chaplain of the Defense Army of Israel and later as Chief Rabbi of Tel Aviv, exerted himself to relieve some of the acutest instances of Halakhic hardships. Sefardic Chief Rabbi Isaac Nissim also appeared to exhibit occasional concern at the rising tide of public indignation, and supported the request for the establishment of a special court to accelerate conversions.[81] The general policy of the rabbinate, however, both in the regional courts and in the Chief Rabbinate, was to adhere to the strictest interpretation of the Halakhah and take full advantage of the authority vested in them under the Rabbinical Courts Jurisdiction (Marriages and Divorce) Law.

With the closing of the sixties, the end of the road had been reached as far as new legislation on religion was concerned. It became clear to all concerned that further pressure would yield no results. Even among committed Orthodox elements, the realization grew that the cause of religion was not always served by legislation and the coercion resulting therefrom. The rigidity of the rabbinate, as exemplified in the Marbek slaughterhouse controversy, was at times repugnant even to the Orthodox, let alone the majority of the people. There appeared to be no attempt on the part of the rabbinate to explain its position to the people with a view to gaining its approval. Between the rabbinate and Mafdal a growing gap was to be discerned, for the latter, being close to grass roots and dependent on the support of the electorate, could not ignore public sentiment, and were thus constrained on occasion to dissociate themselves from some of the actions of the rabbinate.

7

Halakhah in a Jewish State

A. HALAKHIC RULES AND ESSENTIAL PUBLIC SERVICES

Problems of Sabbath Observance

For the first time in nineteen centuries, the Jewish people has assumed the responsibility for the functioning of a sovereign state. No longer a minority group geared to securing for itself conditions that would assure its survival, the Jews in 1948 had assumed the burden of responsibility for the safety and well-being of a political entity and for its normal and orderly functioning. Sovereignty implied the imposition of duties that the Jews as a collectivity had not been concerned with since the days of Bar Kokhba. With the emergence of the State of Israel, Orthodox Jews were faced with the need to shoulder civic duties, on the one hand, and with reconciling those duties with Halakhic precepts, on the other hand. It was recognized that the maintenance of certain public services and the performance of certain functions every day of the year was essential for the public good. To the Orthodox Jew, however, this novel situation posed the question whether it was incumbent on him, as a citizen of a Jewish state and as an observant Jew, to perform those essential functions when they were at variance with the Halakhah.

Thus for the Orthodox Jew the new state posed serious problems, and the problem of Sabbath observance was the immediate one. It was admitted by all that on the Sabbath the police force could not be dispensed with, nor the army, nor the security and diplomatic services and activities, all of which must function twenty-four hours a day every day in the year. It was also recognized that water and electricity supplies and hospitals had to be maintained without interruption. The Halakhic justification for the maintenance of all these services was the

204

principle of *pikuah nefesh*, the preservation of human life. Thus, an Orthodox Jew is permitted to use water and electricity supplied from a central system operated on the Sabbath, as well as to summon a doctor from a first-aid station. Whether an observant Jew could himself be engaged on the Sabbath in operating any of the essential services without violating Halakhah was still another question.

Shortly after the establishment of the state, young Orthodox Jews approached the rabbinate with an inquiry as to whether they could join the police force and go on duty on the Sabbath if required. For several years no clear answer was forthcoming, except discreet advice to keep away from the force, or to ask for exemption from service on the Sabbath.[1] Chief Rabbi Isaac Halevi Herzog eventually defined certain rules of conduct for the Sabbath which, if adopted by the police force, would enable an observant Jew to serve in it:[2]

(a) It is permitted to use a vehicle in order to reach a place where a quarrel has broken out, and there is a possibility for homicide to occur. It is also permitted to use a vehicle in order to frustrate a robbery, where information has been received that unknown persons have been found in suspicious circumstances.

(b) This permission is valid only for the purpose of reaching the place of the criminal act; thereafter it is not permitted to return from that place by car until the end of the Sabbath.

(c) Mobile police units are forbidden. If it is known that the presence of the police can prevent an outbreak of disorder, they may use bicycles, but not motor-cycles.

(d) If a thief is caught a considerable distance from the police station, he must be kept on the spot, and may not be transported by vehicle to the place of detention until the end of the Sabbath.

(e) The telephone may be used only when it is warranted by the principle of *pikuah nefesh*.

(f) The writing of important matters, such as the drawing up of a report of a murder, or even of a robbery, is permitted if done by the left hand (for one who is right handed, and vice versa) and in non-Hebraic script, or by a manner of writing which is perishable, or by use of invisible ink, which can be developed later. In all other instances, writing is absolutely forbidden.*

---

* A similar ruling was issued later, by Chief Rabbi Isser Isaac Unterman, with regard to records kept by hospital nurses. For those unacquainted with the nature of Halakhah these requirements will seem incomprehensible. However, they derive their meaning from a system with certain premises and traditional safeguards that Orthodox persons, committed to these principles will find acceptable and logical. For instance, the writing on the Sabbath with one's other hand was to remind the writer that he was engaged in an exceptional act, which was ordinarily prohibited.

The police authorities could not accept these rulings as practicable or adequate for the maintenance of public order and safety on the Sabbath. The result was that an arrangement instituted under British mandatory rule that allowed Jews serving in the police force to stay away on the Sabbath was used as a model. During that period this problem presented no difficulty, since Jews constituted a minority within the police, and their places on that day could be taken by Arab or British constables. In the State of Israel, however, the overwhelming majority of the police consists of Jews, who carry out all normal duties. The compromise provided that their Orthodox colleagues would be permitted to stay away on the Sabbath. This solution was possible only because Orthodox Jews were a minority in the police force.

A conflict of principles and personal hardships in time became unavoidable. For instance, an Orthodox young man was employed in the Ministry of Foreign Affairs. The branch in which he worked was concerned with receiving code messages and necessitated the use of radio and recording equipment. The official inquired from the rabbinate whether he might perform his duties on the Sabbath. An eminent rabbinical authority who dealt with this inquiry ruled that permission would be given if some of the following conditions were observed: the equipment was to be used with the left hand, and the writing was to be done in non-Hebraic script. The head of the department, however, replied in turn that he was responsible to the people of Israel for the peace and security of the state. He would entrust this particular work only to someone who could perform it with total efficiency and was not hindered in his labor.[3] In time, such inquiries became rarer, and the problem lost its acuteness as Sabbath exemption for Orthodox Jews employed in the essential services became a general and hardly challenged practice. Similar arrangements were introduced into factories and installations that from a technical point of view had to be operated on a 24-hour basis all year round; this applied to glass and cement factories, power stations, iron foundries, paper mills, and so on. After the Israeli shipping industry accepted a rabbinical ruling that no ship was permitted to leave or enter port on the Sabbath, no prohibition was placed on Orthodox young men serving in the merchant marine, though in actual fact there are very few Orthodox sailors. This type of exemption from Sabbath service has been generally accepted by both Orthodox and non-Orthodox Jews, and thus it has come about that in the Jewish state the non-Orthodox are expected by the Orthodox to perform the services that in the Diaspora were within the province of the "Shabbes Goy."*

---

* *Shabbes Goy* was the term applied to the Gentile who used to come into a Jewish home on the Sabbath or Holydays to perform duties forbidden to Jews but not to Gentiles. He would, for instance, come to make a fire to heat the house.

An open conflict broke out between the government and the rabbinate when the National Service Bill was introduced in the Knesset in 1953.[4] The Army Service Law had exempted from military service girls who swore an affidavit that they were Orthodox, and the government now introduced a bill providing for girls exempted on religious grounds from military service to be recruited for "national service," which was meant to include work with new immigrants, teaching their children, assisting with medical services, and the like. It was the period of mass immigration from the concentration camps and from the Islamic countries, and the various agencies concerned with the absorption of immigrants were desperately short of help. The implementation of the National Service Bill would, it was hoped, relieve a good deal of human suffering and at the same time afford those girls who had opted out of the army on religious grounds an opportunity to perform a valuable social service. The National Religious Party (Mafdal) was in favour of the bill, but met with vehement protests by the rabbinate.[5] The bill was nonetheless duly enacted into law, but was not enforced.[6]

One reason for the recurrence of such conflicts between the needs of a modern state and the demands of traditional Judaism was that at no time was there a comprehensive and organized attempt on the part of the Orthodox to deal with the matter. There had been annual conferences of Halakhic scholars, but they usually dealt with limited problems. Thus the 1966 meeting dealt with the problem of the Sabbath and electricity—the use of refrigerators, microphones, and loudspeakers, and battery-powered devices for the hard of hearing.[7] A previous attempt in that direction had been made directly after the establishment of the state in 1948. The Chief Rabbinate had appointed a committee of Halakhic scholars to consider the problem, who unanimously resolved to try to establish the Sabbath as a national institution by drawing up a positive Sabbath constitution. "First we shall determine those works and services which, in accordance with our religious convictions and our understanding of the Halakhah, must be maintained on the Sabbath, and which we shall maintain once we attain control of the government; then we shall be able to demand most firmly the prohibition of all other works and services." A minority in the commission, however, stipulated that the recommendation should include a proviso that exemption be granted to any persons employed in essential services "if their conscience forbids them to work on the Sabbath." The majority rejected the proposal. They regarded such a proviso as a fundamental admission that the Torah was unable to cope with the needs of running the state, and that Sabbath observance was not compatible with the requirements of political independence. They realized further that the exemption implied the management of the state by Sabbath violators, while the Sabbath proper would be the concern of a sectlike minority rather than of the whole people. The proceedings and recommendations of the commission were referred to the Chief Rabbinical Council for their decision. The rabbinate, however, decided not to pursue the matter and to discourage its public discussion.[8]

Proposals

Professor Isaiah Leibowitz, one of the few among the Orthodox who has devoted much attention to this problem, concluded that the Halakhah, as presently interpreted, is a way of life for the individual, but one that does not include his functions and duties as a citizen of a state. "It is a way of life suited to a community which does not have to shoulder the burden of the external and internal security of the state, of its foreign policy, of the maintenance of an army and police force, of economic production, and so on. Moreover, the Halakhah is deliberately based on a way of life for a people which does not and need not assume responsibility for any national functions. But, as neither a people nor an individual can exist without social and governmental services being performed . . . the net result is that foreign rule becomes a precondition and basis for a Jewish way of life in accordance with Halakhah . . . .[9] The Halakhah as presently crystallized posits the existence of a Galut among Gentiles, or the existence of foreign rule in our own land as an essential fact: it makes the absence of national independence and the avoidance of civic duties a sine qua non for the very possibility of the existence of the Halakhah in its present form."[10]

He proceeded to demonstrate why and how Halakhah had evolved its indifference to the problems of a Jewish sovereign state. "There is something sublime in the opening lines of the Shulhan Arukh . . . 'to gird oneself as a lion to rise in the morning to worship the Creator.' But one will not be able to rise in the morning to worship the Creator, nor to sleep in the night, unless certain conditions are fulfilled which make it possible to sleep and to rise. These are not conditions created by nature, but the result of planned, ramified and complex interaction. A large apparatus of social order is required . . . in order to afford the individual and the community the minimum security for activity and for those most vital needs which make existence itself possible. Consequently, the Torah way of life cannot in fact commence with the morning prayer, but must begin with a plan for such a civic order as would provide for the needs of society and for the maintenance of public services in accordance with the Torah. This, of course, was well appreciated by Joseph Karo."* He, Karo, could, however, rely upon another factor that would provide the framework and basis for his ex-

---

* The author of the Shulhan Arukh, who lived in Safed in the sixteenth century.

istence, without resorting to the Torah and the provisions of the Shulhan Arukh. This factor was the Turkish pasha who was stationed in Acre, and under whose jurisdiction the city of Safed lay. It was he who was responsible for public order and security. "It was owing to this fact that Joseph Karo was enabled to devote his attention to the matters dealt with in the Shulhan Arukh. . . . Thus the Shulhan Arukh was the product of a relationship between Karo and the Turkish pasha, for without it Karo would have been constrained to direct his attention to those matters for which the Turkish pasha made himself responsible, and so make provision for them in the Shulhan Arukh, perhaps even giving them precedence before the other matters. In that case the Shulhan Arukh would have presented an entirely different image from that which it actually has."[11]

Halakhah as codified in the Shulhan Arukh was thus shown to be a product of the Diaspora, laying down a way of life for a minority group that is not expected to assume responsibility for meeting the needs of organized society. It is a way of life that is concerned only with certain aspects of human existence, namely, one's relationship to the Creator and one's relationship to his fellow man. The third dimension, one's relationship to organized society, is missing. The Halakhah is thus seen not only as a product of the Diaspora, but as a way of life possible only in the Diaspora and not in a sovereign Jewish state. It is therefore not surprising that in the long catalogue of 613 Halakhic precepts, the precept to uphold organized society is conspicuous by its absence. It would appear that the Halakhah substantiates the assertion advanced by Neturei Karta that the traditional Jewish way of life is not possible in a Jewish state except upon the arrival of the Messiah, when the totality of existence will be so transformed as to become compatible with the overall application of the Halakhah.

Professor Leibowitz noted that this unresolved situation has had a demoralizing effect on the people, and on the youth in particular. It has given Orthodoxy the aspect of a parasitic sect who live on the services of non-Orthodox Jews. "Orthodoxy has knowingly given up the idea of a Sabbath for the state and the people, in favour of a Sabbath for a sect of Sabbath observers within a society of Sabbath violators who, by their work, provide for the needs of the sect. Orthodox Jews do not deprive themselves of water and electricity on the Sabbath, provided they are not called upon to operate these services, that is, provided other Jews do operate them on the Sabbath. Orthodoxy is interested in the operation of a police force on the Sabbath, provided it is other Jews who perform police duties. It is also interested in the existence of an Israeli merchant marine, provided other Jews serve as sailors. Orthodoxy has become reconciled to girls serving in the army, so long as religious girls are exempted from that service. The Orthodox in the Knesset vote in favour of a law granting women equality so far as giving evidence in court and the right to inheritance are concerned, provided that the law is not made applicable to rabbinical courts.* They obtained exemption from army service for Yeshivah students, knowing that the army will be well manned by boys who do not study Torah to the exclusion of all other activity. Orthodoxy extols the holiness of the land, and at the same time 'conveys' it to a Gentile, in order to preserve the fiction of the Shemittah year.** And after all this, religious Judaism is surprised that its prestige is at a low ebb, and many, religious youth in particular, become alienated from Torah."[12] It was, he asserted, "no longer a conflict on the political plane between religion and the state, concerning the regulation of their mutual relations, but a crisis inherent in the religion of Israel."[13]

What then of solutions? Professor Leibowitz called for a comprehensive Torah program for state and society, but insisted that this process had to be initiated by Orthodoxy. Such a program would be based on new Halakhic rules in all those areas of social activity which are not dealt with in the Halakhah. It would necessitate considerable departures from a religious way of life that had evolved in the absence of political independence and civic responsibility. "The decisive religious problems of our generation can no longer be *adjudicated* in accordance with the Halakhah; a Halakhah needs to be *legislated*."[14] This then was the innovation advocated by Professor Leibowitz: to legislate a Halakhic law, rather than to interpret it, since the latter method was no longer adequate. Professor Leibowitz thus implied that a supreme rabbinic authority be instituted that would assume legislative authority, and therefore be able to lay down a new Halakhah which, going beyond the traditional one, would cover the realm of one's duties toward organized society.

A similar view was expressed by Dr. Louis Rabinowitz, former Orthodox Chief Rabbi of Johannesburg, South Africa. He, too, held that for nearly two thousand years the Halakhah had had to legislate for the individual or, at most, for the limited community. Now it had to legislate for a national entity. "What was needed was a new section in the Shulhan Arukh to deal with the application of the Halakhah to the reality of our independent, sovereign state."[15] Rabbi Rabinowitz turned for solutions to the principle of *pikuah nefesh,* the Halakhic regard for the preservation of human life. Before the state's existence, this principle could be applied only in the case of individuals. The establishment of Israel, however, has added a new dimension, which may be termed the *pikuah nefesh* of a state. Put in simple terms, it can be expressed in the question: What are the vital services upon which the existence

---

* In Halakhah, women's legal rights are circumscribed.

** In the 1880s this particular problem was in fact cause for the first confrontation between Halakhah and the needs of the community.

and security of the state depend? Once these are defined, the law of *pikuah nefesh* would apply to them, making it Halakhically obligatory upon observant Jews to operate them. The Chief Rabbinate, however, never considered this possibility, and adheres to the traditional view that "what is forbidden or permitted to the Jew as an individual is forbidden or permitted to all Jews." The end result of this policy was that, whereas in the Diaspora essential services were performed on the Sabbath by the Shabbes Goy, in Israel they were being performed by the "Shabbes Jew."

A rather novel approach to this problem was advanced by Dov Rosen in his book *Etz HaDat* (Tree of Religion), which received an award from Heikhal Shlomo, the seat of the Chief Rabbinate.[16] In the attempt to find Halakhic solutions, Rosen considered that technology would eventually resolve all difficulties. Observant Jews, he said, were in even greater need of scientific progress than others. They needed it in order to prove to those loyal to the Torah, as well as to its opponents, that even in the State of Israel Halakhic precepts could be observed. It was not proper that Sabbath observers should benefit from services performed by violators of the Sabbath. "We are therefore bound to encourage science and make technology the instrument of the Halakhah, so that science can come to replace the Shabbes Goy."[17]

Rosen, however, offered no immediate substitute for the institution of the Shabbes Jew, and, in fact, he justified the status quo by a theory of give and take. "The religious enjoy the services performed on the Sabbath—medical aid, police, and so on; the secular have occasion to resort to synagogues, rabbis, circumcisers, ritual slaughterers, and cemeteries. A tacit agreement exists, as it were, between the secularists and the Orthodox, an agreement to desist from criticizing one another. The one does not say: 'Because of me you dwell in peace, fear neither violence nor thievery, and benefit from medical aid,' nor does the other say: 'Because of me your son celebrates his Bar Mitzvah in the synagogue, where you also find solace on memorial days; through me rabbis are made available to you for the performance of marriages, as are circumcisers and other servants of religion.'"[18]

An intermediate position was taken by Rabbi Moshe Zvi Neriah, mentor of Bnei Akiva, the Mafdal youth movement.[19] He maintained that the Halakhah as presently codified and interpreted was indeed adequate for sovereign Jewish existence. His key to the solution of the problem was the extension of the principle of *pikuah nefesh*. In order to implement an arrangement based on the extension of this principle, it would be necessary to establish most scrupulously what services were vital to the security of state and society from without and within. Rabbi Neriah was of the opinion that the rabbinical authorities could theoretically define and enumerate the services that must be performed on the Sabbath and Jewish Holydays. But they would be entitled to decree that observant Jews should in fact perform certain duties on the Sabbath only if Israel were a Halakhah-bound society.

Taking the case of the Orthodox young man also cited by Professor Leibowitz, whose work at the Ministry of Foreign Affairs put him in charge of code messages reaching the office on the Sabbath, Rabbi Neriah agreed that such work could be of a vital character and had to be performed even on the Sabbath—but not under present circumstances. "If the Minister for Foreign Affairs were an observant Jew, he would issue a strict direction to all his offices abroad that no messages be communicated on the Sabbath, except such messages as actually constitute the *pikuah nefesh* of the state. . . . This, however, is not the case. The Foreign Affairs Ministry is headed by a person who is not an observant Jew."[20] That being the case, routine as well as very important messages were being sent on the Sabbath, and under those circumstances the principle of *pikuah nefesh* could not operate. The same applied to the operation on the Sabbath of electric power stations, a vital service in all respects. As the managers of the electric corporation, however, were nonobservant Jews and were not prepared to perform their duties in accordance with the directions of the rabbinate, there was always the danger that nonessential work would also be carried out on the Sabbath. It was therefore advisable for the observant Jew not to work in the power station on the Sabbath.[21] Rabbi Neriah concluded that the Halakhah was adequate for meeting the needs of a modern state, provided the state was governed and administered by Halakhah-committed Jews.

Rabbi Neriah's argument was, in fact, a justification of the practice of the Shabbes Goy. The State of Israel was not, nor was it likely in the foreseeable future, to be administered by Halakhah-committed Jews. To maintain the view that, in the Jewish state as presently constituted, essential services had to be performed on the Sabbath by nonobservant Jews only, was tantamount to admitting that the function of a nonobservant Jew in the Jewish state in relation to an observant Jew was similar to that of the Shabbes Goy in the Diaspora. There was, however one difference; in the Diaspora an observant Jew would never wittingly avail himself of the services of another Jew, observant or not. In Israel, Rabbi Neriah and other rabbis attempt to confer legitimacy on the employment of Jews on the Sabbath.

In the course of the first quarter of Israel's independence there has evolved a tacit agreement as regards a division of functions between the Orthodox and the non-Orthodox in relation to the maintenance of essential services on the Sabbath and Jewish Holydays. This modus vivendi is widely regarded as a practical solution to an insoluble problem and is in consonance with the policy of compromise and accommodation often displayed by the two groups. During this period the Orthodox have made hardly any progress toward making the Halakhah compatible with the needs of a modern state. The situation in this respect is very much as it was in 1948.

B. CONFLICTS WITH THE ORTHODOX

Despite a number of practical accomodations, areas of tension have continued to exist, especially in that undefined no-man's-land of what constitutes an essential public service for an Orthodox Jew committed to Sabbath observance. The way in which these conflicts have been resolved has been a function of the political power at the disposal of the groups engaged in the controversy.

Transportation has been an ever-recurring topic on the public agenda. In accordance with the terms of the religious status quo, all public transportation in Israel is banned on the Sabbath, except in Haifa where the urban bus service functions as it did in the years of British rule in Palestine. Railways and interurban bus services come to a standstill, as do the ports, where ships may neither enter nor leave on that day.

In a country where a six-day work week prevails—there being no tradition of a two- or two-and-a-half-day weekend—such restrictions create serious problems. Depriving a whole population of all means of public transportation on their only day of rest imposes burdensome restrictions: people cannot visit friends and relations beyond walking distance nor visit the sick who are in hospitals; they cannot get to the beach in the long and hot Israeli summer, nor can they ever enjoy an outing. Such and similar hardships do not affect people who own cars, but this amenity is confined to a minority who may also have the means of hiring expensive taxicabs. The Sherut system is a significant and fairly novel institution. Privately owned taxicabs offer urban and interurban transportation by selling individual seats in their vehicles. In comparison with the public transportation services, the Sherut is costly, and has the additional disadvantage of operating only in certain districts of the larger towns. Thus the system is limited to a small section of the country and a large proportion of the population find themselves observing the Sabbath in or near their homes, whether they wish to or not.[22]

Attempts have been made by private entrepreneurs to organize other and cheaper forms of transportation on the Sabbath, primarily to enable people to get to the sea or to swimming pools. Such attempts have frequently been met with political pressures on the local or national level, and have at times even led to violence. A typical incident occurred in Herzliah, some miles north of Tel Aviv, in the summer of 1970. A partnership named Galei Yam ("Sea Waves") hired five buses from Egged, the public bus cooperative, and established a regular service on the Sabbath going from the town's outlying quarters to the sea. Its fares were far below taxi rates. The municipal authorities prescribed the bus route in order to prevent their passing streets where synagogues were situated. Despite this precaution, the Herzliah rabbinate warned the municipal authorities against granting the permit and, when the Sabbath arrived, hundreds of demonstrators forcibly attempted to prevent the buses from moving. A strong police detachment confronted the demonstrators, and force had to be used to clear the road. Along other streets the buses were stoned and windows were broken.[23] The incident was debated in the City Council of Herzliah, the majority standing firm and appealing to the Orthodox to be tolerant. The latter, however, continued to agitate against Sabbath transportation to the sea. They took the matter to the Minister for Religious Affairs, in the hope that he might persuade the Minister for Transport to take action against Sabbath violations in Herzliah.[24]

Since wide powers of enactment of regulation are bestowed by law on local authorities, these have often become the political battlefield between the Orthodox and their opponents. Because of the balance of power held by the religious parties in most of the local councils, extensive restrictions have been imposed on public services on the Sabbath. Thus, with some exceptions, museums, public libraries, and art galleries are closed to the public on that day, and since December 1969 the Tel Aviv Planetarium has been subject to the same fate. In most cities theaters and cinemas and public youth clubs are closed on Friday nights.* Thus the majority of the population is deprived of access to cultural treasures on the one day when they have leisure. The religious parties have also exerted pressure to prevent trade unions from organizing entertainment on the Sabbath for the benefit of their members.[25] An equally onerous fate has befallen the playing of music in hotels; not only may no live orchestra be employed on the Sabbath, but recorded music may not be heard either. While this prohibition has not been enforced by law, it has been enforced by the rabbinate, which makes the observance of this prohibition a condition precedent to the issuance of a certificate of Kashrut.[26]

The Orthodox have never attempted to secure legislation aimed at banning private cars on the Sabbath, nor have they raised it as an issue. Dr. Zerah Warhaftig, when confronted with the challenge that in the view of the Halakhah driving a car on the Sabbath is as much a transgression as driving or riding a public vehicle, replied: "Orthodox Judaism does not wish to interfere in the private domain of the individual. The Almighty will deal with him. . . . We fight for the public domain,

---
* The Sabbath begins at dusk on Friday evening and lasts until sunset the next day.

the street . . . we seek to prevent Sabbath violation of a public character, involving buses, railways, airplanes, and so on."[27]

Similarly, Yeshayahu Bernstein, leading Mafdal publicist, regarded the observance of the Sabbath in the public domain as a basic precondition for coexistence of the Orthodox and the non-Orthodox. In his opinion, the Orthodox have a valid moral claim to be respected by the non-Orthodox as far as the public observance of the Sabbath is concerned. It is the moral duty of the non-Orthodox to avoid offending the Orthodox. Even as the nonobservant Jew feels it his duty, when visiting an Orthodox friend on the Sabbath, to refrain from smoking in his house, so must he feel it his duty to refrain from violating the Sabbath in the street.[28]

Bernstein did not regard this policy as coercion of the non-Orthodox to behave in a manner conflicting with the dictates of their own conscience. In his opinion the two groups were arguing from two unequal starting points: the one is commanded to observe the Sabbath and all the other Halakhic injunctions, while the other, though in terms of his own beliefs not commanded to observe, is also not commanded to violate such injunctions. By eating kasher food or by refraining from driving on the Sabbath, the non-Orthodox are not doing any violence to their conscience, for there is nothing that obligates them to eat forbidden food or to drive on the Sabbath. Thus, by refraining from violating Halakhic injunctions, the non-Orthodox not only does no violence to his conscience, but he actually acts in a moral way—in terms of secular morality—for he acquires merit by failing to offend the deep feelings of the Orthodox.[29] The imposition by law of religious norms of behavior on the non-Orthodox does not impinge on the freedom of conscience of the latter. Said Abraham Shaag of the Religious Bloc in a Knesset debate on Oct. 17, 1950: "If I observe the Sabbath in the street, it does not hurt you, but if you violate the Sabbath in my presence, you wound my soul."[30]

Rabbi Shlomo Goren, however, admitted that coercion was involved: "The act of the Giving of the Law on Mount Sinai was an act of imposition and an infringement, as it were, on one's freedom of choice. . . . When it comes to shaping the image of our national life we are commanded by the Torah and by the ethics of the prophets to employ the coercive power of the state."[31]

The non-Orthodox have rejected the argument of the Orthodox in support of their demand to impose upon "the street" the outward appearance of an observant community. The outward image, they contend must reflect the authentic spiritual content of the community, and if the public imprint of Orthodoxy is imposed against the sentiments of the majority of the people, an artificial and therefore intolerable situation is created that must eventually redound to the disadvantage of the

Orthodox. To coerce people to behave in "the street" in accordance with religious norms that they repudiate is itself immoral.

One of the critics of the Orthodox view has been historian Professor Jacob Talmon of the Hebrew University of Jerusalem. He draws a line between the right to believe and the right to coerce others on religious grounds. While the line cannot be clearly drawn in all cases, there are certain areas where it definitely can be done. "I do not detract in the least from the social potential and do not hurt the wellbeing and happiness of the public, if I, being a cohen, marry a divorcée. I am then told: 'You offend the feelings of the faithful, cause them sorrow and agitation, and bring distress and disunity to the nation.' But who can assess the sorrow of the faithful as compared with the sorrow occasioned to a man whose beloved is denied to him because of his priestly status, while he neither believes in nor desires this status, and regards the biological determinism inherent in the priestly privileges as a relic of the caste system, which he rejects *ab initio*? The very posing of the question of offense to the feelings of the religious implies the notion that the latter possess sublime, pure and refined feelings to a greater degree than do the secularists. The time has arrived to reject this notion in its *a priori*, dogmatic form, which covers up a large measure of self-assumed superiority and conceit. From the moment that the religious sentiments of the Orthodox serve as a justification for imposing acts of commission or omission on nonbelievers, they objectively become an expression of an urge to coerce, derived from a sense of superiority. Is it necessary to be reminded, two centuries after Immanuel Kant, that no man may regard another as a means, but only as an aim unto himself?"[32]

Professor Talmon rejects the sincerity of persons who deny to others the right of enjoying the Sabbath in their own way, such as resorting to transportation, or visiting an art gallery. "Here subjective sincerity is irrelevant. Sincerity ceases to be authentic when it arrogates to itself rights which it denies to others."[33] Even as the non-Orthodox are expected to respect the religious feelings of the Orthodox, so should the latter respect the moral and aesthetic feelings of the former. The Orthodox complain that they are offended by the behavior of the nonreligious on the Sabbath, but it is an even greater offense to deny access on that day to art galleries and libraries to people who are seeking aesthetic enjoyment. The individual Orthodox Jew is in no way expected to alter his own way of life and conduct to please the nonobservant; the latter, however, are expected to conform to certain religious norms that are unacceptable to them. Thus, the secularists place no demands on the Orthodox; it is from the latter that all demands emanate.[34]

Confrontations with the Orthodox on the issue of Sabbath and other Halakhic observances have appeared in a variety of unexpected instances and have been settled on an *ad hoc* basis. The conflict with the Jerusalem rabbinate over its refusal to grant a Kashrut certificate to a hotel on the grounds that its swimming pool was open to mixed bathing* was followed years later by a conflict at the Hebrew University of Jerusalem, which had decided to keep its newly opened swimming pool open on Saturdays as well. The protest of the Orthodox and the threat of a considerable number of professors to resign their posts unless the pool was closed on the Sabbath proved of no avail. The University took an unyielding stand.[35]

In January 1968 a sudden snowstorm swept Jerusalem. The supply of water and electricity was interrupted in many places; schools closed down and transport came to a standstill. Army vehicles were summoned to secure regular supplies. The shortage of electricity not only prevented many homes from being heated, but seriously affected the hospitals. The Minister of Development, in charge of the Electric Corporation, applied to the Minister of Labor for the issuance of a license authorizing the repair work to be done on the Sabbath. The license was issued, and some 200 people, some of whom lived outside Jerusalem, were summoned to their posts in order to restore electric power. The Minister for Religious Affairs attempted to interfere, with the object of preventing what he considered to be a Sabbath desecration. In turn, the Minister of Development justified the continuance of the work on the grounds of *pikuah nefesh*.[36] The matter did not assume the proportions of a major crisis, since the work had already been completed before any further action could be taken by the Orthodox.

C. ECONOMIC ASPECTS OF HALAKHIC RESTRICTIONS

The application of Halakhah has not only given rise to difficulties for those Orthodox individuals who have sought employment in areas affected by Halakhic controversies, but has at times also imposed financial burdens on the national economy, especially when competition in foreign markets has been concerned. While the Orthodox would agree that certain violations of the Halakhah may be excused when the defense of the country or the maintenance of internal order are involved, they vigorously object to the extension of this principle to the economic welfare of the state. No matter how high the price in terms of economic welfare, it should be paid, they hold, in order to uphold the religious law.

A case in point was the launching of the Israeli ocean ship S.S. *Shalom* in December 1963. It was intended to compete in the

---

* Joint swimming by the two sexes is considered forbidden by the Orthodox.

luxury liner class, and in order to be profitable, it had to attract a non-Jewish as well as Jewish clientele. With this in view, it was arranged that the vessel would provide for separate kasher and nonkasher cuisines, and that the former would be under the supervision of the rabbinate. Furthermore, the nonkasher kitchen would not serve pork or other items of food forbidden by the Halakhah. The Orthodox, however, registered their opposition to the scheme, insisting that the ship should have a kasher kitchen only. The ensuing controversy threatened to bring about a government crisis. The Orthodox threatened to boycott the liner, so that the profits from non-Jewish passengers would be counterbalanced by the losses arising from a Jewish boycott. The spokesmen for the government pointed out that the proposed arrangement would parallel that of many foreign ships, which install a kasher kitchen in addition to the usual nonkasher one. The Orthodox retorted that what was natural on a non-Israeli vessel could not be tolerated on an Israeli ship, which was not only Israeli territory but government-owned property on which, by law, kasher food only must be served. The matter was debated in the Knesset,[37] and in order to avoid a cabinet crisis the government gave in on the issue. A kasher kitchen only was installed.

In 1965 a further question arose. It was decided to run the S.S. *Shalom* on Carribbean cruises in the winter season, and it became clear that a single kasher kitchen could not attract an adequate number of holiday-takers. The rabbinate agreed that for these cruises there could be a nonkasher kitchen, but that no kasher kitchen would be certified during the cruises. The cost later of converting the kitchen back from nonkasher to kasher for the full Atlantic crossings was $10,000.[38]

Substantial losses are incurred because Israeli ships may neither enter nor leave any port, whether in Israel or abroad, on the Sabbath, and must stay an extra day at sea if the timetable does not permit them to reach port before sunset on Friday.[39] Non-Israeli ships, too, may not enter an Israeli port on the Sabbath, a practice unknown elsewhere. That these losses are considerable is admitted by the Orthodox, who contend that economic considerations may not be taken into account when it is a question of observing a religious commandment, for "its price is above rubies."[40]

In 1964, an Israeli shipping company launched the S.S. *Bilu,* the first steamer intended for popular cruises along the Mediterranean. It provided for an exclusively kasher kitchen, and included a self-service restaurant. The Chief Rabbinate refused a Kashrut certificate unless a promise were given that on the Sabbath no music would be played, smoking would be prohibited in the public rooms, and no money would be taken in the cafeteria. The shipping line contended that these restrictions would make most non-Jews as well as many Israeli and other Jews prefer a non-Israeli cruiser.[41]

Similar restrictions were imposed on Israeli hotels. In order to obtain a Kashrut license, hotels in Jerusalem had to undertake not to register guests arriving on the Sabbath, not to permit writing by hotel employees, not to serve meals to guests in their private rooms unless ordered a day before, and to prohibit smoking and music on that day. Certain hotels were required, in addition, not to sell wine manufactured by non-Jews. The hotel industry argued that these regulations would seriously impair their business, and expose them to the competition of hotels that had never applied for a Kashrut license, or that were owned by non-Jews. In many cases these conditions were, however, complied with, especially by hotels for which weddings and Bar-Mitzvah celebrations were an important source of revenue.[42]

In 1969 a dispute arose between the Chief Rabbinate and the inhabitants of a village in the vicinity of Jerusalem. The latter, finding it difficult to derive a livelihood from farming the mountainous terrain, developed the specialized industry of fattening geese for the local market, and also exporting the goose liver. They built a modern, largely mechanized operation, with the feeding done electrically. They applied for a Kashrut certificate and in time the application reached the Chief Rabbinate, which ruled that the geese were trefah (nonkasher) because the electric feeding-machine operated on the Sabbath. The farmers, who had been waiting for nearly a year for their certificate, were now in danger of losing the whole of their investment, amounting to a quarter of a million pounds.[43] The government intervened and eventually a formula was found by which the slaughterhouse was permitted to function as kasher.

Another incident took place in May 1971, in connection with railway tracks near Haifa, where many accidents had occurred at the level crossing. It was decided to construct a pedestrian tunnel, and the railway authorities indicated that the work would be done on the Sabbath, because no trains were running on that day, and because on any other day railway traffic over a wide area would have to be paralyzed. The Orthodox promptly staged demonstrations; the matter was raised in the Knesset and was discussed in the light of the economic losses that would follow a railway stoppage on a weekday.[44]

It was in the course of this controversy that the spokesman for the religious parties pressed the point that work opportunities were being denied to observant Jews in enterprises and in services that operate on the Sabbath. A case in point occurred in 1964, when it was brought to the attention of the Minister of Labor that four persons who had applied for employment in the chemicals and fertilizers plant in Haifa had been requested to work on the Sabbath. The Minister replied in the Knesset: "The uninterrupted process of production in chemicals and fertilizers requires work to continue throughout the week, including

Saturday. This enterprise has received a special permit to operate on the Sabbath, and in such unavoidable circumstances it was the duty of the enterprise to enquire whether those particular people would agree to work on the Sabbath. There is nothing in it that can be interpreted as discrimination against persons loyal to their religion. The nonreligious workingmen too would prefer to rest on the Sabbath, but understanding as they do the circumstances of the enterprise, they are prepared to work on that day too. By releasing a number of workers from Sabbath duty, an additional and unjustified burden would be imposed on those willing to take their turn on the Sabbath. The enterprise employs a considerable number of observant Jews, but they perform administrative functions and are not engaged in the production process." The Minister concluded by saying that the Labor Exchange had found other employment for the four applicants.[45]

This reply constituted an admission that in certain areas of employment observant Jews were not being employed and that, as a consequence, Orthodox Jews were tending to concentrate in those areas where no Sabbath work was required. The authorities concerned have argued that to admit a large number of Orthodox Jews to processes of production that require a seven-day operation would place an intolerable burden on other employees, who would have to take more frequent turns at Sabbath work. The inevitable result has been that in certain industries Orthodox Jews are found in the administrative and clerical departments, rather than in production. Shelomo Zalman Shragai of the National Religious Party inveighed against this development which, he said, would push the Orthodox into an economic ghetto, a process that would further accentuate the gap between them and the majority of the people.[46] Indeed, two rightful but opposing claims have been advanced: the Orthodox claim exemption from Sabbath work, while the nonobservant claim that they should not be unduly burdened with additional Sabbath duties. The problem has not so far assumed serious proportions, because labor permits to operate on the Sabbath have been issued to but a small fraction of the entire labor force, for in the majority of occupations no necessity to work on Shabbat exists.

Another problem, which eventually reached the Supreme Court, involved the Broadcasting Authority, which was requested to discontinue its television programs on Friday evenings. Television came to Israel rather late, and after prolonged debates. Finally, preparations for the installation of a television service were approved and reached an advanced stage in 1969. When the government decided to provide a program for every evening of the week, all Orthodox parties objected, since they regarded the provision of programs on Friday evenings as a desecration of the Sabbath, and the matter came up in the Knesset for a full-dress debate.[47] The government defended the plan as an extension of the practice of radio broadcasts on Friday nights and Saturdays, which had been instituted by the British in the days of the mandate, and which the Orthodox had come to take for granted, though individuals would not avail themselves of the programs. The government further pointed out that Friday evening was usually the only evening when the family were together and that since no public entertainment was available on Friday nights, young people generally had come to wander aimlessly about the streets. Now they would have an incentive to stay home. The Orthodox countered that through the introduction of a Friday evening TV program, they would before long find themselves excluded from employment in yet another area.

The Knesset approved the decision to operate the TV on Friday nights, whereupon several individuals representing the labor organizations affiliated to Mafdal and Poalei Agudat Israel filed a lawsuit against the Broadcasting Authority, the Minister of Labor and the Chief Inspector of Labor. In their petition to the Supreme Court sitting as a High Court of Justice, the complainants sought an order directing the Minister of Labor to cancel the permit issued by him under Section 12 (a) of the Hours of Work and Rest Law 5711–1951,[48] which authorized the employment of labor on the Sabbath in the operation of the television service. The complainants quoted the case of a government department that had rejected a certain applicant because of his unwillingness to work on the Sabbath. The complainant had based himself on Section 703 (1) of Title VII of the American Civil Rights Act of 1964, which provided that "it shall be an unlawful employment practice for an employer to fail or refuse to hire, or to discharge, any individual . . . because of such individual's race, color, religion, sex or national origin." While the Supreme Court had dismissed the action on formal grounds, a strong and well-reasoned minority opinion by Justice Kister had upheld the complaint on the grounds urged by the complainants.[49]

This question was also raised in a parliamentary debate held on January 26, 1972. Dr. Yehuda Ben-Meir, appearing for Mafdal, protested against the practice that had been introduced into a number of places of employment, by which applicants for employment were requested to agree to take turns in working on the Sabbath. He regarded such a practice as a flagrant discrimination against observant Jews, and as bound to lead not only to their exclusion from many branches of the economy, but even to their reduction to second-rate citizens of the state. Speaking as he did for the younger generation of the Orthodox, "who have served in the army and fought its battles, and are fully involved in the life of the state," Dr. Ben-Meir exclaimed: "We shall not tolerate a situation where there exist areas of employment that are 'Judenrein', that is, from which observant Jews are excluded. . . . . . the Orthodox will not agree to be discriminated against."[50]

Replying for the government, Mr. Almogi, the Labor Minister, dwelt both on the extent of the problems, and on the principle involved. He pointed out that out of a total of 740,000 employees in the various branches of the economy, 7,557 jobs are necessary on a permanent footing, and 1,095 on a temporary footing, in order to assure the maintenance of essential services and works on the Sabbath; that is, just over 1% of the total number of employees are involved. He not only admitted that in a number of enterprises applicants are requested to agree to take their turn in work on the Sabbath, but offered justification for this. He pointed out that in many instances the work involved is of a specialized character, and the number of employees qualified to perform it is limited. These people were willing to take their turn, out of a sense of responsibility, on the Sabbath, but would resent it if some of their colleagues were exempted from such duties, for this would impose additional burdens on themselves. "The State of Israel as a Jewish state must be operated by Jews," said the Minister of Labor, "and not by Shabbes Goyim," as suggested by one Agudat Israel deputy. As was to be expected, the motion of Dr. Ben-Meir to place this subject on the agenda for a full-dress debate was defeated.[51]

It was obvious from studying this and similar cases that, with the best will in the world, observant Jews would not be welcome in certain fields of employment, and while these opportunities were few compared to the total labor market, they were often highly specialized and attractive pursuits. This was true not only in television, which might or might not be regarded as a vital service, but also in the wider areas of employment that even in the opinion of the Orthodox were in fact vital services, such as electric power, water, and police. The view of Rabbi Neriah, that even in vital services Orthodox Jews could not work on the Sabbath until such time as the management was manned by Orthodox Jews only—did not help to solve the problem.

Thus the situation has remained unsatisfactory, for Orthodox Jews are through their convictions confined to routine jobs in certain limited fields of employment. Everyone admits that there exists goodwill on the part of the nonobservant to accommodate the observant as far as is possible, but it is obvious that, without some bold initiatives in the realm of the Halakhah, the present tendency of Orthodox concentration in certain areas of employment and their restriction in, and even exclusion from, others will continue.

The tensions arising out of the need to maintain essential public services and installations on the Sabbath had their origin in the total unpreparedness of the Orthodox to confront the realities of a sovereign Jewish state. In generations past, rabbis and Halakhic scholars failed to apply themselves to solving problems that would confront an observant Jew when called upon to perform civic and other essential functions in a Jewish state. When, shortly after the establishment of the State of Israel, Rabbi J. L. Maimon faced the critical issue: can Torah-loyal Jews assume responsibility for the functioning of a modern state, he urged the summoning of a Sanhedrin that would, in fact, legislate a new Halakhah. This unique opportunity of enriching the Halakhah by making it three-dimensional, that is, adding to the rules governing man's duties toward his Creator and man's duties toward his fellow man, also man's duties toward organized society, was missed. Nor did they take full advantage of the possibility of extending the doctrine of *Pikuah Nefesh,* the preservation of human life, from the individual to organized society. These tensions erupted at times and assumed the proportions of a public controversy. These were often settled to the satisfaction of the Orthodox, on other occasions to the satisfaction of the non-Orthodox, the settlement often being a function of the relative political strength of the parties involved. From the solutions adopted in these controversies, no principle could be deduced for future guidance.

Although groups of Orthodox scientists have been exploring ways and means of obviating Sabbath desecrations by technological innovations, their labors so far have failed to advance viable solutions. Thus, Torah-loyal Jews are put on the defensive, for they must reconcile themselves to a situation where nonobservant Jews are expected to perform essential works on the Sabbath, from which they, the observant, also benefit. At the same time they resent instances of their being denied employment opportunities by reason of their refusal to work on the Sabbath.

It is indeed painful for an Orthodox Jew to see the Sabbath desecrated in public, either by driving, by public entertainment, or even by keeping a museum or zoological garden open on the day of rest. His appeal to his brethren not to offend his feelings and abstain from certain activities is genuine and is understood as such by many nonobservant Jews. Holders of high public office will, as a rule, avoid in their behavior any act that might offend the Orthodox. In the field of legislation, both the central government and the municipal governments have gone a long way toward meeting the sensibilities of the Orthodox.

The controversies occasionally arising out of Sabbath violations were settled on an ad hoc basis, without thereby creating any precedents for future guidance. This basis, however, had the merit of being motivated by a spirit of compromise and mutual accommodation.

8

The Climate of Orthodoxy

A. RELIGIOUS EDUCATION

The System

The network of primary schools of the Religious Trend, sanctioned by the World Zionist Conference in 1920, developed during the next 28 years into one integral and generally accepted part of the autonomous Jewish public school system in Palestine. These schools, where boys and girls were brought up in the spirit of Orthodoxy and of Jewish nationalism, were, in many respects, the crowning achievement of the Mizrahi. Agudat Israel and other ultra-Orthodox groups maintained schools of their own; these consisted of the traditional Talmud Torahs for younger boys, and Yeshivot for adolescents and adults, while only a few educational institutions were provided for girls.

As preparations for the establishment of the Jewish state were being initiated in 1947, the Orthodox were naturally concerned not only with the future status of religion in general, but also with the status of religious education in particular. The Executives of the World Zionist Organization and of the Jewish Agency, as well as the Va'ad Leumi (as the representative of Palestine Jewry) were on their part anxious to secure the maximum degree of national unity in order to meet the grave events that were anticipated. They were especially eager to ensure the adherence of Agudat Israel to the coming state. "The full autonomy of every trend in education will be guaranteed," Agudat Israel was assured by the Agency. "There will be no interference on the part of the government with the religious convictions and the religious conscience of any section in Israel. The state will naturally determine minimal compulsory studies, in the Hebrew language, history, the sciences, etc., and will supervise the fulfillment of this minimum; it will, however, give full freedom to every trend to conduct education according to its own convictions, and will refrain from any interference with religious conscience."[1] This undertaking paved the way for an Agudat Israel school system within the educational framework of the new state.

One of the first laws enacted by the Knesset was the Compulsory Education Law of 1949,[2] which provided compulsory and free education for all children aged 5 to 13 inclusive, one year in Kindergarten, and 8 years of primary school.* This law left intact the three recognized school "Trends," the General, the Labor, and the Religious. Since these Trends (except for the General) were controlled by political parties, strife and competition developed between them, particularly over the children of newly arrived immigrants. The period preceding the opening of each academic year was one of an "ideological civil war organized by the state," to use the expression of Professor B. Z. Dinur, the then Minister of Education and Culture.[3] To better gain its political ends, Mapai went to the extent of initiating, through the Histadrut, a religious Trend of its own. Interparty conflict over the school system led to a government crisis, and to the dissolution of the first Knesset in the spring of 1951.

In the newly elected Knesset, those who opposed the system of school Trends controlled by political parties gained the upper hand. The General Zionists, long advocates of the abolition of the political control of schools, entered the government and, due to their pressure and the full support they obtained from Prime Minister David Ben-Gurion, the control of schools was taken out of the hands of the political parties and replaced by the establishment of state-controlled schools, with two autonomous orientations, general and religious. Political parties, at least de jure, were to be excluded from the control of the schools. In August 1953, the Knesset enacted the State Education Law,[4] which abolished the three recognized Trends, and placed "state education" under the control of the Ministry of Education and Culture, and teachers were henceforth prohibited from engaging in party politics. "State education" was to be based on the "values of Jewish culture, and the achievements of science, on love of the homeland and loyalty to the state and to the Jewish people; on practice in agricultural work and handicrafts, on pioneer training and on striving for a society built upon freedom, equality, tolerance and love of mankind."[5]

This formulation enabled both the Orthodox element and the secular nationalists to interpret "values of Jewish culture" as they saw fit. A prescribed curriculum obligatory for all schools was to be created. It

---

* Subsequently, the period of compulsory education was extended to fourteen years.

did not, however, make for a uniform school system, for although the law emancipated the schools from the control of political parties, it provided for a two-tier system: schools were either "state-educational institutions," or "religious state-educational institutions." In addition to the basic studies demanded by the curriculum, the religious state schools had a supplementary program, defined as "comprising the study of the Written and Oral Law, and aimed at a religious way of life, including religious observance and a religious atmosphere within the institution." Thus the state provided two types of schools on a footing of equality, and the parents had the right to choose for their children the type of school they preferred. In the academic year 1972/73, 68.5% of all elementary school pupils were enrolled in state schools, 25.1% were enrolled in religious state schools, and the remainder in other religious schools.[6]

In addition to state education, the law also made provision for "non-official recognized educational institutions." Section II of the Law provided that the Minister for Education and Culture may "prescribe procedures and conditions for the declaration of nonofficial institutions as recognized educational institutions, the introduction therein of the basic program, the management and supervision thereof, and the assistance of the state towards their budgets, if and to the extent that the Minister decides on such assistance." Those who took advantage of this provision were a number of Christian institutions and Agudat Israel. The school network of Agudat Israel, known as Atzmai (Independent Education, that is, independent of state religious education), had in 1972/73 an enrollment of 6.4% of all elementary school pupils. Thus, within the total system of Jewish primary education, the religious state schools and the Agudat Israel Schools together accounted for nearly a third of the total enrollment.[7] Agudat Israel provided part of the budget for its own schools; by far the greater part, 85%, was derived from the government.

The religious state schools enjoy a wide measure of autonomy. Before taking any decision regarding the supplementary program and other matters affecting the religious schools, the Minister of Education and Culture has to consult and obtain the approval of the Council for Religious Education set up in accordance with Article 12 of the Law, and consisting of persons the majority of whom are to be appointed by the Ministry of Religious Affairs, the Union of Religious Teachers, and "religious members" of the Knesset Committee of Education. This Council may, "on religious grounds, disqualify a person from appointment or further service as a principal, inspector or teacher at a religious educational institution." To assure an ample supply of teachers, the government maintains teacher training colleges for the religious state schools. While secondary education is not compulsory, most pupils go on to secondary education, either in academic or trade and vocational schools which are largely financed from government or municipal funds. The enrollment in the religious secondary schools, including those of the Hinukh Atzmai system, was 26.7% of the total number of secondary school pupils, a rather lower percentage than on the elementary level.

Curricula

In the general schools, both on the primary and the secondary level, Bible, Hebrew language and literature, as well as Jewish history are taught extensively; in the religious state schools the stress is on Talmud, liturgy, and on the rules of religious observance. As to Bible, the stress in the religious schools is on the Pentateuch and the laws contained therein, and a fundamentalist approach is used; in the general schools, the emphasis is on the whole Bible as the basis of national culture, as well as on the moral and social values adumbrated by the Prophets. More time is allotted to the natural sciences and mathematics in the general schools than in the religious schools. Still less time is allocated to these subjects in the Agudat Israel schools, where the supplementary programs amount to about 60% of all instruction, thus exceeding by far the projected 25% limit laid down by law.[8] The only condition the government was able to impose on Agudat Israel was that the language of instruction in all subjects be Hebrew; an exception had to be made for Talmud, which continues to be taught in Yiddish.

The Council for Religious Education has promulgated strict rules to assure the Orthodoxy of the teachers employed in the religious state schools. Thus a teacher may not continue to hold his position if he is married to a person who is not Orthodox, unless he has satisfied the Council that a religious way of life is maintained in his household. A teacher is also disqualified if he sends his own children to a school that is not religious.[9] In consequence of a dismissal, a lawsuit was instituted by a teacher who had been discharged because she had allegedly prepared coffee on the Sabbath; she was reinstated when the charge against her was not proved.[10]

While the law details the autonomy of the religious state schools, there prevails a basic and unsolved disagreement about the extent of that autonomy. The Ministry of Education and Culture, reflecting the view of the majority, sees the autonomy of the religious state schools in the area of the supplementary program, with its special subjects, particularly Talmud, and the Orthodox way of life. The Ministry has held that the other subjects studied should be of a neutral character, and the textbooks prescribed for these subjects in the general schools should be used in the religious schools as well. While the Orthodox agree on "the values of Jewish culture" formulated in Article 2 of the State Education Law, as being the basis of the state educational system, they disagree with the majority on the meaning to be attached to those values. In their view religious education is more than a mere addition of subjects to the curriculum. Rather, a religious spirit is expected to inform all the subjects taught. The interpretation of Jewish history or of Hebrew literature by the non-Orthodox does at times differ from an Orthodox interpretation, and consequently textbooks prescribed for these subjects in the general state schools would be unfit for religious schools. In this view, even textbooks for the teaching of the English language and of the sciences should be permeated by a religious spirit.[11]

This view, however, has been challenged on the ground that in practice it creates two totally separate school systems, rather than one unified system founded on a basic secular curriculum, with a supplementary religious program not exceeding 25% of all subjects of instruction. The proponents of religious state education have also been criticized for treating their schools as instruments for the promotion of the interests of the National Religious Party. This charge is vehemently denied,[12] although it is admitted that it is in the very nature of the situation that the party has a vital interest in the existence of religious education, and that many, if not most, of the teachers are its members or sympathizers. Few indeed would choose a career in teaching in the religious school system unless they were committed to its objectives, and naturally in sympathy with the party that rightly regards itself as the founder, promoter, and guardian of the system.

Notwithstanding occasional tensions, a working coexistence has emerged from the two parallel types of school that constitute the major educational network in Israel. The religious state schools, claiming to raise boys and girls in the spirit of Orthodox Judaism, and at the same time as good and useful citizens, can point to one of the best youth movements in Israel, the Bnei Akiva, whose membership is drawn from these schools. Graduates are to be found in the pioneer settlements along the frontiers of the country; girls as well as boys serve in the army. Many other graduates of these schools have reached positions of prominence in the professions and in academic life. On the other hand, while the percentage of pupils is about 28% of the total school population, a rather constant figure despite the varying waves of immigration, the percentage of votes cast at national elections for the National Religious Party has never exceeded 10% of the total electorate. The proponents of religious state education point to this very circumstance as conclusive proof of their contention that there is no party propaganda nor indoctrination in their schools, and that the teaching personnel do not take advantage of their position to promote the interests of the party to which most of them adhere. This may indeed be a contributing reason for the discrepancy between the percentage of the religious school population and the percentage of the electorate that supports Mafdal, but as in many other countries, voters do not always take their religious proclivities into the election booth. They will choose parties that offer political, economic, and social platforms corresponding to their own individual outlook. Such Jews may be observant, but feel free to support the political party of their choice so long as the state does not interfere in any way with their personal way of life. There is also a natural degree of erosion in the adherence of the graduates of these schools to Orthodoxy and, not unexpectedly, a number of them will not resist the temptations of the open society.

In order to meet certain circumstances unique to Israel, the Compulsory Education Law of 1949 made provision for exempting children from attendance at state schools or state-recognized schools. It was enacted in order not to antagonize the interests of a number of French Catholic and Italian Catholic missionary institutions, and to avoid a frontal confrontation with the ultra-Orthodox, who would not allow the education of their children to be directed or supervised by the state. While some of the missionary schools applied for, and were granted, recognition by the Ministry of Education and Culture, the ultra-Orthodox retained their traditional Hedarim (houses of study for children), and kept them altogether beyond any control by the government. In these schools, few if any secular subjects are taught; neither the Hebrew language nor Jewish history is on the curriculum, nor, for that matter, is the Bible, except for the Pentateuch. The principal subject of tuition is the Talmud, through the medium of Yiddish.[13] About 5,000 pupils attend these houses of study.

Yeshivot

In the field of postprimary education, there exists a wide network of Yeshivot. In 1973/74, 4,152 boys between the ages of 14 and 18 were enrolled in 28 secondary Yeshivot, where a full program of general education on a secondary school level is offered, in addition to intensive Talmud training, and where the language of instruction is Hebrew. These institutions enable the student to take examinations leading to university entrance. Many, if not most, of these Yeshivot were established by the Bnei Akiva movement. In these Yeshivot, many of the talented graduates of the religious state elementary schools continue their studies.

The ultra-Orthodox will generally be found in three types of Yeshivot. A total of 3,523 boys between the ages of 14 and 17 were enrolled in 1972/73 in 64 "junior" Yeshivot, *Yeshivot Ktanot*, while older students may attend "senior" Yeshivot, *Yeshivot Gdolot,* which

are for young men between the ages of 17 and 25.* In 1973/74 there
were 80 such institutions with 7,940 students.

Third, there are the Kolelim, which afford advanced students, among
them married men, the opportunity to carry on their talmudic studies
within an institutional framework. In 1973/74 there were 5,400 such
married students, the great majority of them ultra-Orthodox. The language of instruction in the Kolelim is Yiddish, and no general subjects are
taught. Here, religious isolation reaches its peak; army service is avoided
and alienation from the Jewish state is growing. The numbers both of
institutions and of students of this type has been steadily growing. The
increase in the Yeshivot Gdolot was from 4,305 students in 1968 to
7,940 in 1973/74, and in the Kolelim from 2,662 to 5,400 in the same
period.[15] Many of the graduates of these Yeshivot possess no trade or
skill; some are without financial means and find it difficult to obtain
employment. A practice was prevalent in Eastern Europe before World
War I, whereby a wife would work in order to enable her husband to
devote his entire time to the study of the Torah; this custom, which
had practically disappeared, has recently made its reappearance in Israel. Most of these ultra-Orthodox institutions are situated in Jerusalem and in Bnei Brak. The latter is the seat of the Ponivezh Yeshivot,
founded after World War II, and now the largest of its kind in the
country. A considerable number of students in these Yeshivot come
from abroad.

B. EXTREMISM AND VIOLENCE

Patterns of Confrontation

The essential patterns of Orthodoxy, which evolved in the Old Yishuv in the second half of the nineteenth century, have hardly been affected by the great upheavals of the twentieth century. Neither the 30-
year Western-style rule of the British nor the tragedy of the Holocaust,
nor even the restoration of Israel to statehood, made a significant impact on the core of Orthodoxy. Its theology, general outlook, and approach to problems posed by a radically transformed world—none of
these has experienced real modification. To be sure, in some Orthodox
quarters there is a groping toward a new approach, even toward a kind
of neo-Orthodoxy, but Orthodox fundamentalism generally characterizes
both the rabbinate and the Yeshivah world (*Olam HaYeshivot*). Mafdal, which remains a significant and influential factor in Israel's political

---

* There are 15 other institutions for boys between the ages of 14 and 18, known as
  Yeshivot for Torah and Vocational Training; some of these are sponsored by the
  Poalei Agudat Israel, and receive state aid.[14] They had an enrollment of 2,793 boys.

and social life, representing as it does the great majority of traditionally minded Jews, has not of its own initiative attempted to evolve a new approach to Orthodox Judaism. In matters of religion it recognizes the authority of the rabbinate, and its rulings in Halakhic controversies have been accepted, albeit grudgingly in certain cases.

This has meant that, while in matters of politics and economics Mafdal determines its own policies, once a matter of religious import arises the party follows the ruling of the Chief Rabbinate, even though this may be at times contrary to its previously declared position. Thus, after Mafdal had prevailed on the government to introduce into the Knesset a bill safeguarding Kashrut and appointing the Chief Rabbinate as the sole authority for issuing Kashrut licenses, it was forced by the latter to abandon the project, on the ground that the bill contained a proviso subjecting the actions of the rabbinate to judicial review by the Supreme Court.[16]

In consequence of this development, the confrontation between the Orthodox and the non-Orthodox is in fact one between the latter and the official rabbinate. In the Diaspora, too, religion is on occasion a divisive force, in the sense that distinctions are made between Jews who are religious and those who are not, and also between Jews who are Orthodox, Conservative, and Reform. These differentiations, however, lead to confrontation only in a limited sense, for there is also dialogue and at times a measure of cooperation. In Israel, on the other hand, differences of opinion between Orthodox and others lead at times to conflicts, because the state as such is called upon, by operation of law or by administrative action, to settle those differences. Consequently, confrontations between the non-Orthodox majority and Orthodoxy became a matter of political action. In such cases, Mafdal will usually attempt to mediate between the position taken by the Chief Rabbinate and that of the non-Orthodox, to relieve tensions and to effect compromises. The party as such, however, does not offer solutions in cases of conflict, for it has gradually abdicated its position as spokesman for Orthodox Jewry in favor of the rabbinate, and thus has maneuvered itself into the unenviable position of intermediary between the majority of the population and the Chief Rabbinate.

While Neturei Karta is a numerically insignificant group, as it was when the state was established, and is regarded by the other Orthodox as extremist and irresponsible, its influence on the rabbinate has grown stronger. A quarter of a century of coexisting in the midst of the Jewish state has in no way attenuated the group's opposition to it, nor have the rigidity of its fundamentalism and its readiness to translate zeal into violence abated. Its members have not brought about any organizational changes among themselves; they remain essentially nonorganized, and have neither a registered membership, nor office, nor executive committee. They cherish no political ambition within a state that they do not recognize. They are not known to possess any treasury, nor have they at any time appealed for funds. They regard themselves, and themselves only, as the remnant of Israel. Says one of their spokesmen: "We are in 'Golus'* for our sins. We have been exiled by Divine Providence, and we must lovingly accept our sentence. Our sages have told us that three oaths were taken by the Jews when they went into exile: one, that they should not hasten the end (i.e., the coming of the Messiah) ; two, that they should not enter Eretz Israel in a body before the predestined time; and three, that they should not rebel against the inhabitants of the world. . . . For believing Jews the words of the Sages constitute a reality which no amount of Zionist propaganda can alter. . . . In their eyes, the Zionist salvation has brought with it the almost complete destruction of the Torah. Believing Jews have stood firm against all kinds of attempts to defile them, and they will survive this last, powerful Zionist campaign of defilement."[17]

These admonitions against defilement are reserved not only for the non-Orthodox, or the Zionists, but also for Agudat Israel, a political party that has always been outside the framework of the Zionist Organization, and which, except for a brief interval, has consistently been an opposition party in the Knesset. In the eyes of Neturei Karta, it has, however, become part of the Zionist machine. "The Agudah was founded with one main aim in view, namely, as a defense against the Zionist heresy. Today it has become the most dangerous adversary of religious Jewry, a kind of centre for the distribution of bacteria in places where they can do the most harm."[18] Neturei Karta regard the Agudah as encroaching on their "Lebensraum," "aimed only at that remnant of religious Jewry which, by reason of its being but a remnant, must be most jealously guarded, and every demoralizing penetration into that last citadel is progressively more painful."[19] This "last citadel," besieged, as it considered itself to be by the overwhelming forces of the heretics and their supporters, not only has allies within the Orthodox establishment, but exerts in general a considerable influence over it. While there has been no movement toward an overt identification with Neturei Karta on the part of *Olam HaYeshivot*, the "Yeshivah world," nevertheless has gradually altered its basic approach to the Jewish state. It now tends to believe that the state has no religious significance and that consequently, in terms of the Jewish religion, an Orthodox Jew is not commanded to identify himself with it. In short, although physically dwelling in the Holy Land, these Jews feel themselves spiritually to be in Exile. Owing no spiritual allegiance to the political entity known as the State of Israel, they regard the secularist majority in some ways more

---

* Exile.

negatively than the Jewish minority in the Diaspora views the non-Jews.

Resort to physical violence on the part of the Orthodox extremists, a phenomenon hardly known during the thirty years of British rule, has become a frequent occurrence since the establishment of the state. Such acts of violence were in most cases initiated, planned, and executed by Neturei Karta in Jerusalem, but before they were quelled, they usually attracted other extremist elements, notably the Yeshivah students. Most of the incidents occurred in the Meah Shearim area in Jerusalem and in Bnei Brak. The perpetrators of these deeds, like their ancestors in the ghettoes of Central and Eastern Europe, would not have resorted to violence in the lands of the Galut in order to enforce religious observances. Such violence in the Galut would have constituted a criminal offence punishable by the law of the sovereign state, as well as a violation of the Halakhic doctrine of "Dina deMalkhuta Dina," which enjoins a Jew to respect the laws of the country in which he happens to dwell.[20] The State of Israel, on the other hand, claiming to be a Jewish state, is illegitimate in terms of fundamentalist Orthodoxy. Consequently, observance of the laws of such a state is not warranted by religious doctrine, and lawlessness committed in pursuance of religious objectives has generally enjoyed religious acquiescence, if not sanction. The perpetrators rely on the police not to deal with them harshly, on the courts to mete out lenient sentences, and on the rabbinical authorities to refrain from condemnation.

Sabbath Violence

On Saturday, October 26, 1963, acts of violence occurred in the northeast section of the Meah Shearim quarter in Jerusalem, where a group of Neturei Karta demonstrated against the passage of vehicles along the neighboring Shivtei Yisrael street leading from the Mandelbaum Gate to the city center.* Stones, bottles, and pieces of furniture were thrown at the police, who quelled the disturbance by directing hoses at the demonstrators. Policemen and passengers in some of the passing vehicles were injured; on that same evening the nearby office of the Ministry of Education was broken into and ransacked. This riot was the climax of a series of Sabbath disturbances in the vicinity, where

---

* The Mandelbaum Gate was the only crossing-point between Jordan and Israel before the Six Day War. Through this gate tens of thousands of Christian pilgrims visiting their holy places in East Jerusalem, then under Jordanian control, could reach Israel. The great majority of the pilgrims were clergy, who were wont to cross the frontier on a Saturday in order to celebrate the Mass at the Church of the Annunciation in Nazareth on Sunday. It was against these pilgrims, when their vehicles had to pass through Meah Shearim, that the stone-throwing of the ultra-Orthodox was directed.

the main road from the then Jordanian frontier led through the stronghold of the extremists.[21] The outbreaks kept up with varying degrees of intensity until the frontier itself disappeared in the wake of the Six Day War.

The attacks were the subject of heated debates in the Knesset[22]. The majority of the members condemned the acts as hooliganism, criticized the police for its leniency, and urged stronger measures to protect public order. Representatives of Agudat Israel and some of the members of Mafdal accused the police of brutality, and insisted that traffic be stopped on the Sabbath. The removal of the Mandelbaum Gate after 1967 did not, however, lead to a return to calm. Indulgence in violence had become a powerful precedent for further acts of violence. Now they were directed at Jews who drove their cars in the direction of Tel Aviv, even though they did not pass through the Orthodox quarters. The zealots now massed in order to seek out Sabbath violators. The Egged Bus Company became a favorite target, because of its long-established practice of resuming bus traffic a short while before the actual sunset on Saturdays. Noteworthy in all this violence was the silence of the rabbinical authorities, who never condemned the perpetrators, a reticence all the more glaring since stone-throwing on the Sabbath was in itself a highly dubious activity, if not an outright desecration of the Sabbath.

In 1961, a bus transporting staff on Sabbath duty from the newly opened Hadassah Hospital in Ein Karem to the city of Jerusalem, a distance of some seven miles, was stoned, and a number of persons were injured. The bus was carrying a large sign "For Hospital Personnel Only," and a Red Shield of David. The attackers contended that a bus was not an ambulance, which they might have let pass on the Sabbath, albeit grudgingly. Appeals to the rabbinical authorities to condemn the violence were of no avail. Under the circumstances, the directors of the Hadassah Hospital negotiated a settlement with the Chief Rabbinate, which ruled that "Sabbath transport would be authorized only in an ambulance driven by a non-Jew. This vehicle was to be used by special duty staff who were not able to remain in the Medical Centre over the weekend." The rabbinate thus took advantage of the turbulence and procured a stricter observance of the letter of the religious law, thus implicitly offering protection against a repetition of the violence. The *Jerusalem Post* castigated Hadassah Hospital for the compromise: "To some it may seem equally distressing that the Hadassah negotiations and agreement are clearly concerned with fictions. The public is held up to ransom by the rabbinate, and must pay with legal fictions, and major and minor inconveniences and deprivations, not that the Sabbath may be preserved—which is important to many—but that the Rabbinical Council may save face and claim a victory."[23]

The Abduction of Yossele Schuhmacher

Few episodes agitated public opinion as did the case of Yossele Schuhmacher. The Schuhmachers arrived from Russia in 1957, with their children, Yossele and Zina. Until the couple found housing and work, they placed their children in the care of Mrs. Schumacher's parents, Nahman Shtarkes and his wife, who lived in Meah Shearim. Schuhmacher eventually found work in Holon, near Tel Aviv, and requested the return of the children in time for the beginning of the 1959 school year. The grandfather returned the girl, but not the boy. The parents applied to the High Court of Justice for the custody of their own son, and the court ordered Shtarkes to deliver Yossele to his parents. The grandfather did not obey the directive, and when the police arrived at Shtarkes's home to enforce the order, the boy was no longer there. Shtarkes justified his refusal to return Yossele by displaying the written authority to that effect that he had received from Rabbi Zvi Frank, a member of the Chief Rabbinical Council, who justified his action by alleging that it was the intention of Yossele's parents to return to Russia with their children. The Schuhmacher couple denied any intention of returning to Russia, whereupon the court ordered the grandfather to be imprisoned until he complied with the court order, or until he disclosed the whereabouts of the boy.[24] The grandfather remained in jail, refusing to cooperate with the authorities.

It later turned out that the boy had been placed in the care of a family in an Orthodox village; police investigations were intensified, whereupon the boy was clandestinely removed to Europe, and later on to New York; there he was placed with a family of the followers of the Satmarer Rebbe, leader of a Hasidic sect and known for his unyielding opposition to Israel.

Public opinion in Israel and abroad was outraged, especially in view of the fact that the Chief Rabbinate refused to issue an appeal to the kidnappers to return the boy to his parents, who, incidentally, had intended to register him in the local state religious school. In the Knesset debate,[25] Emma Talmi, speaking for Mapam, alleged that Chief Rabbi Isser Unterman had been requested to issue an appeal for the return of the boy, but had refused to do so, instead offering himself as "arbitrator" between the parties. The search for the boy yielded no results, and a further debate was held in the Knesset, at which the spokesman for the religious parties hinted that the return of the boy could be facilitated by the government promising to take no action against the kidnappers.[26]

The uncle of Yossele, who was suspected of aiding and abetting the abduction of the boy, and whose extradition from England was requested by the Israel government, pleaded in a London court that extradition should be refused on the grounds that Jerusalem—his domicile—was not part of Israel. Eventually, in 1962, Israeli agents caught up with the boy, and he was brought back to his parents in Holon. The boy's recovery was entirely the work of these agents; no cooperation was obtained either from the many who were implicated in the abduction, or from the even greater number of persons who had some knowledge of the facts.

Other Incidents

During 1961, the Youth Aliyah Department of the Jewish Agency succeeded in bringing some 500 Jewish youngsters to Israel. On arrival they were placed in a classification center to await their eventual placement in either religious or secular institutions. Such enrollment was to be determined by the wishes of the parents. The Orthodox alleged that certain children had been placed in non-Orthodox institutions contrary to their parents' expressed desire. Youth Aliyah denied this, but to no avail. Demonstrations and rallies were held in Bnei Brak and Jerusalem. In the synagogues of Meah Shearim the shofar was blown and the "uprooters" of Israel were denounced. Later, members of the Mahaneh HaTorati (Torah Camp) attacked the classification center and wrought considerable havoc, all in the presence of the bewildered and terrified children.[27]

Another type of spontaneous militancy occurred in Bnei Brak on March 12, 1962. A man dropped dead while talking in the street. The police arrived on the scene and, acting in accordance with law, attempted to remove the body for a postmortem examination. A crowd of several hundred Yeshivah students vehemently objected—since they considered such an autopsy to contravene religious law[28]—and attacked the police. The battle raged for hours and there were many casualties. The police eventually succeeded in removing the body. The crowd retaliated by proceeding to the office where the local municipal council was in session, and wrecked the place.[29]

These incidents formed a pattern of violence that has been repeated many times. What has been significant in this series of continuous resort to such violent means against both persons and property has been the general silence of the rabbinic authorities in general, and of the Chief Rabbinate in particular. A major reason for this reticence has been the unwillingness of the rabbis to incur the wrath of the extremists. In this way, a minority within a minority has often foisted its will on the majority. Thus, a small group of extremists, whose religious legitimacy in the eyes of the Orthodox was unimpeachable, could terrorize the rabbinic authorities, while the latter, unsure of their own ground and branded by the extremists as collaborators with the secularists, would not dare to challenge them.

C. ORTHODOXY AND THE STATE

The Religious Establishment

The Ministry for Religious Affairs is in charge of all recognized religious communities, Jews, Moslems, Druze, and Christians. It not only maintains the ecclesiastical courts of these communities, but also affords financial assistance for the construction and maintenance of synagogues, mosques, and churches, and for a variety of other religious activities and functions. Since Jews form the majority of the population, the Ministry is principally concerned with the institutions of Jewish religion, both financially and otherwise. Except for a brief interval, its office has always been filled by a leading member of the Mafdal, which thereby controlled (in 1973/74) a budget of over IL. 33 million, employed nearly 400 officials and, indirectly, has wielded considerable influence in the appointment of local religious officials,[30] including 409 local rabbis and hundreds of officials employed by the religious councils, as well as large numbers of Kashrut supervisors and others.

The Ministry's Department for Jewish Religious Affairs is responsible for all administrative and financial matters involved in the maintenance of the rabbinical courts, id est, the Bet-Din HaRabbani HaGadol (Supreme Rabbinical Court) in Jerusalem, and the district rabbinical courts established in the nine principal cities of the country. These employed (in 1971) 185 officials, of whom 66 were Dayanim (judges of the rabbinical courts).[31] The Ministry maintains a division dealing with Kashrut, which supervises dietary arrangements in governmental institutions and hospitals and controls the importation of foodstuffs from abroad, particularly of meat, for which purpose it dispatches supervisors stationed in the countries supplying the meat. It likewise makes sure that the Orlah (the forbidden fruit of young trees during their first three years of production; see Lev. 19:23–25) is not passed off as kasher; this is particularly important in the case of wines, and therefore supervisors are provided in all wine cellars. The Ministry further supervises some 400 rabbis who are licensed to register marriages.[32] In the immigrant towns and villages, it maintains full-time and part-time rabbis, and many other officials who perform ritual functions. It also constructs and maintains Mikvaot (ritual baths), and sets up the Eruv by which cities and villages are surrounded by wires or poles in order to legalize the carrying of objects on the Sabbath in the public domain.[33] Other functions of the Ministry are to certify the ritual fitness of religious objects, and to provide financial assistance to Yeshivot.

The religious establishment includes the local religious councils, which exist wherever organs of local government function. While the Ministry for Religious Affairs supervises all religious functions, religious councils execute them on the local level: the maintenance of the local rabbinic institutions, Kashrut arrangements, the upkeep of synagogues and ritual baths, and the Eruv. In the fiscal year 1971/72, these budgets amounted to IL. 42,136,000, and paid 2,512 officials, half of whom were employed on a full-time basis.[34]

The councils are set up by the Minister for Religious Affairs in virtue of the powers vested in him by the Jewish Religious Services Budget Law, which provides that one-third of the cost of religious services be covered by the government, and the remainder by the organs of local government.[35] In 1966 an amendment to the law provided that 45 of the members of the religious councils were to be appointed by the Minister of Religious Affairs, another 45% by the municipality, and the remainder by the local rabbinate.[36] Because the Minister of Religious Affairs has generally been a member of Mafdal, it was certain that his party virtually controlled the local religious councils, a situation that Agudat Israel, non-party-affiliated Orthodox groups, and the non-Orthodox in general have not been able to alter.

Thus the Ministry for Religious Affairs, the Chief Rabbinate, and the local religious councils constitute the basic political-religious establishment in Israel. Yet, significantly, they determine neither the image nor the fundamental policy of Orthodoxy. These are shaped by the official rabbinate, particularly the Chief Rabbinate, and the heads of the Yeshivot. The interaction between the two, while neither formalized nor coordinated, largely determines policy. Theoretically, the rabbinate is the creation of the religious-political structure, that is, Mafdal, but the latter has long ago ceased to exercise any important influence on the former. The rabbinate itself is heavily influenced by the inflexible, fundamentalist views of the Yeshivot.[37]

Olam HaYeshivot: The Seat of Influence

Of the several types of Yeshivot, those of Torah uMelakhah (Torah and Work) pursued religious instruction along with vocational training and the acquisition of manual skills. In 1971, there were 2,218 students enrolled in such schools, and of a total of 1,143 yearly hours of instruction, 508 hours were devoted to secular studies; 127 hours were set aside for the study of the Bible, and all the rest for Talmud study.[38] These Yeshivot are for the 14- to 18-year-olds, and nearly all of the boys join the army, where they are often able to make use of the skills they have acquired. Another type of Yeshivot are the Yeshivot Tikhoniot (High School Yeshivot), also for the 14-18 age group, which combine a regular high school program with Talmudic instruction. In 1971 their enrollment stood at 3,657 boys. Of a total of 2,046 hours of instruction, 558 hours, all in the afternoons or the evenings, were set aside for secular studies, while the rest was reserved principally for the study of the Talmud.[39] Some of the graduates of the Yeshivot Tikhoniot go on to study at the Yeshivot Gdolot (advanced Yeshivot), but the great majority join the army and some continue their studies in the universities. Only a few prepare themselves for the rabbinate.

The three other groups of Yeshivot exert the greatest influence on the Orthodox establishment. The first of these are the Yeshivot Ktanot (Junior Yeshivot) for boys aged 14–17, with an enrollment of 3,299 in 1971. These are, in fact, the preparatory schools for the ultra-Orthodox Yeshivot, where the language of instruction is frequently Yiddish. Of the 2,250 yearly hours of instruction, only 225 hours are set aside for secular studies, with the same for the study of the Bible, and all the rest for Talmud study only. With only one-tenth of the time devoted to general studies, the graduates of these schools are exposed to but a minimal secondary education, and are not qualified for university entrance. Many of the graduates of these Yeshivot proceed to the Yeshivot Gdolot, which enroll the 17–25 age group; in 1971 these had an enrollment of 6,028 students. Of the 2,815 hours of instruction, none is set aside for either general studies or the study of the Bible; the entire time is devoted to the Talmud, with the exception of 175 hours set aside for pietist readings. The same applies to the Kolelim for married men, whose number was 3,817 in 1971, where the entire instruction is centered on the Talmud. Of the 6,028 students in the Yeshivot Gdolot who were liable for military service, about 5,000 opted out of serving.

The Yeshivot Gdolot and the Kolelim exercise the strongest influence on the rabbinate. The great majority of the students do not intend to join the rabbinate; they devote themselves to the study of the Talmud for its own sake, to the exclusion of all other subjects, and are consequently not concerned with making their study relevant to the problems of the society in which they live. Not only are secular subjects omitted from their curriculum, but also the Hebrew language and literature, as well as Jewish history. From these Yeshivot come the majority of rabbis and Dayanim, and it is they who create the intellectual climate of the rabbinate.

The intellectual climate prevailing in these Yeshivot has been described by Rabbi Rafael Katzenellenbogen, one of the leading Talmudic scholars in Israel. Writing in *Emunah, Dat uMada* (Faith, Religion and Science), a collection of essays published in Jerusalem in 1966 by the Ministry of Education, the Rabbi expounded the reason for the avoidance of Bible study in the Yeshivot. He referred to the Mishnaic provision enjoining the reading of the Ten Commandments before the *Shema* prayer, a provision later annulled in the Gemara because of *Minim* (heretics), for the untutored might think that the Torah was confined to the Written Law (i.e., the Bible).

In consequence, Rabbi Eliezer the Great issued the dictum: "Keep your sons away from logic,"[40] which was interpreted by Rashi to mean, "Do not get them too accustomed to the Written Law." According to Rabbi Katzenellenbogen, Rabbi Eliezer's rule is just as valid today as it was in his time. "The Testament of Rabbi Eliezer the Great was a ruling for generations to come. So it was in the period of the perversion called Haskalah in Western Europe, when the spirit of assimilation penetrated into the fortress of Israel, and extolled *Juedische Wissenschaft,* which proclaimed war against the Hałakhah, and especially against the sanctity of the Oral Law. . . . Their first act of cunning was a widespread agitation, especially among the youth, encouraging the study of and research into the Hebrew language, its grammar, history and origin, and most particularly research into the Book of Books, the Bible, on the basis of inquiry without regard to tradition." The study of Jewish history was similarly indicted if it was carried on by scholars who were not prepared to admit the sacred character of that history. Orthodox Jewry, the author added, eschews the study of the natural sciences, not because of any objection in principle, "but because many of the university professors in our land are not only far removed from pure Judaism, but are also full of hatred for the Torah and the faith of our people."

Thus Rabbi Katzenellenbogen explains clearly the underlying principle of Yeshivah education, and why it has turned its back on general culture, the sciences, and the humanities, the study of Jewish culture as expressed in the Bible, the rich non-Halakhic literature, and the annals of Jewish history, let alone the study of modern Jewish literature and thought. His is a spirited defense of the philosophy of deliberate isolation from all currents of thought, and from any contact with any intellectual discipline, apart from the Talmud and its traditional commentaries, and even the Talmud itself may not be studied in its historical setting and evolution. Instead of confronting the problems posed by the contemporary world, the Yeshivot detach themselves from immediate contact with the society in which they dwell. In the Yeshivot they have created a universe of their own, the so-called *Olam HaYeshivot* (Yeshivah world), detached from the rest of society in which they exist physically but not spiritually.

Some of the moderate Orthodox educators express their fear of the consequences of this development. One of the leading educators wrote: "Olam HaYeshivot breeds an air of self-assurance and of arrogance, which all leads to extremism and fanaticism. Extremists have come to the fore. . . . Alienation from the secular state has turned into hostility towards the state; these feelings of hostility find their expression in repeated acts of violence—throwing stones and breaking windows of cars driven on the Sabbath, injuring doctors and nurses driven in those cars, attacking the police who seek to protect the attacked, organizing attacks on Christian missionary schools . . . all these are alarming symptoms which testify to the methods adopted by the militant Orthodox to bring the Kingdom of Heaven nearer. These are the products of hatred and self-isolation."[41]

Religious fanaticism has a way of spreading. Some of the graduates of *Olam HaYeshivot* have taken teaching positions in the Bnei Akiva sponsored Yeshivot, which aim at cultivating a positive attitude toward the upbuilding of the Jewish homeland. It is feared that the result would be for these Yeshivot to become uprooted from their Zionist background, "turning into satellites of the classical Yeshivot."[42] *Olam HaYeshivot* has consistently rejected suggestions made by Mafdal leaders for the setting up of a rabbinic seminary resembling Orthodox theological seminaries in America and Europe, where in addition to talmudic studies, the study of Jewish history, literature, and the Bible is prescribed rather than proscribed.

The tenor of religious life in Israel is ultimately determined by the *Olam HaYeshivot,* for it supplies the core cadres of the rabbinic establishment. There are very few among the rabbis who hold a university degree, or even a secondary school certificate. Hardly any of them are familiar with Western culture, or with any European language, nor are they acquainted with the trends of contemporary thought. Many of them, although technically civil servants, have but little regard for, or affinity with, the state that employs them, and have little knowledge of the social and moral problems of the people they are called upon to serve.

Attitude toward the State

The attitude of the rabbinate toward the State of Israel constitutes the background for the religious-secularist confrontation. Were the Chief Rabbinate to possess legally coercive powers within the framework of a non-Jewish state, no such confrontation would take place, for it would unhesitatingly accept the validity of the civil law within which it functioned, in accordance with the Halakhic principle of *Dina de Malkhuta Dina.* Since, however, the State of Israel is a Jewish state, the attitude of the rabbinate to it is ambivalent and equivocal; it neither rejects the state, nor does it accept it without qualification. At best it is a conditional acceptance, contingent on the "good behavior" of the state. This became clearly apparent in proceedings leading to the enactment of the Dayanim Law of 1955.[43]

This law provided the framework for the appointment of Dayanim (judges of the rabbinical courts), for the term of their office, their remuneration, and other provisions, all of which resembled the provisions governing the civil courts. In the course of the enactment of this law, the Knesset also discussed the oath of office to be taken by a Dayan upon his appointment. The Judges Law of 1953 had formulated the declaration of allegiance to be made by judges on their assuming office as follows: "I pledge myself to bear allegiance to the State of Israel and its laws, to dispense justice fairly, not to pervert the law, and to show no favor."[44] A similar provision was suggested for Dayanim. The rabbinate, while agreeing to pledge "allegiance to the State of Israel," insisted on the omission of the words "and its laws." This reflected the basic attitude of the rabbis to the Jewish state: a Jewish state must in all respects be based on the Halakhah, and as long as it is based on civil law, the rabbis may recognize the state but not swear allegiance to its laws. In so doing the rabbis meant to reserve the right not to obey the law of the land when performing their official public functions.

Moshe Unna, of Mafdal, strove to justify the omission of the contended words. In the Knesset debate he said: "The declaration of allegiance provides that the Dayan must pledge allegiance to the State of Israel. In this is encompassed all that the state provides, including its laws, and it is immaterial whether or not the words "its laws" are included. . . . The importance of this omission is that if we impose on the Dayanim the duty of taking a declaration of allegiance in which reference is made to allegiance to the laws of the state, we thereby imply that when there is a contradiction between the law of the land and the religious law, it is their duty to resolve the conflict in favor of the law of the land. . . . I do not know what might happen if one day a law is enacted that explicitly contradicts the laws of the Torah. Such a possibility exists."[45] Others in the debate pointed out that it is the duty of a judge to administer a law, even if such law runs counter to his conscience, and if he cannot resolve an inner conflict, he ought to resign his office. The fact that so moderate a leader of Mafdal as Moshe Unna failed to support unequivocally the proposition that allegiance to the laws of the State of Israel must be binding on all citizens of Israel and, in particular, on all holders of public office, whether rabbis or not, indicated to what extent the acceptance of the Jewish state by the Orthodox establishment has been conditional.*

An example of this attitude was the case of a man who had sued his employer for wages and had obtained a judgment. The defendant failed to pay the judgment debt and the plaintiff proceeded to have it enforced. It so happened that both parties to the litigation were Orthodox Jews. To his surprise, the plaintiff received a summons issued at the instance of the defendant from the regional rabbinical court in Petah Tikvah, requesting him to appear before the court to adjudicate his claim against his employer, and also ordering him to refrain from en-

---

* The rabbinate prevailed, and the oath of allegiance in Article 10 of the Dayanim Law now reads: "I pledge myself to bear allegiance to the State of Israel, to dispense justice fairly, not to pervert the law and to show no favor."

forcing the judgment issued in his favor by the civil court. The plaintiff replied that his claim had already been adjudicated: "In accordance with the law of the land, which I and my employer must accept, the rabbinical court has no jurisdiction to deal with this matter." The rabbinical court thereupon issued a "Decision": "Every Jew who is summoned by a fellow-Jew to adjudicate a dispute before a rabbinical court is bound in accordance with the law of the Torah to appear, plead before it, and abide by the judgment that is issued by it, even in cases where he has brought action in a secular court and succeeded there in his action. If he refuses to appear, or to abide by the judgment, he is to be treated as is provided in Tractate Baba Kama 112–113, by Rambam, Hilkhot Sanhedrin 25 and 26, and by the Shulhan Arukh, Hoshen Mishpat, articles 11 and 26."*

The incident aroused a great deal of public interest because it appeared to reflect the attitude of at least some of the rabbis toward the Jewish state. By treating the civil courts as tribunals of idolaters, the rabbinate implied that the state that had set up those very courts was one of idol worshipers. The rabbinate regarded itself and its adherents as authentic Jews, treating the majority of the Jewish population in the same way that the Jews in Eastern European ghettoes used to regard the non-Jewish majority, and where they were generally enjoined to refrain from resorting to the civil courts in litigations between Jews.[46]

In spite of rising protests, the Chief Rabbinate remained silent. In the Knesset, the Minister of Justice was urged to take action against the regional rabbinical court in Petah Tikvah. Replying to questions, the Minister confirmed that the rabbinical court had no jurisdiction to interfere in this matter, that the plaintiff had no duty to heed the demands of that court, and that he had in fact ignored its ruling. However, since it was not a widespread practice of the rabbinical courts to interfere with the actions of the civil courts, he preferred to ignore the matter.[47] By way of buttressing his argument, he pointed out that the Chief Rabbinate had assured him of its opposition to lower rabbinical courts exceeding their jurisdiction.

Nevertheless, the Chief Rabbinate itself has attempted on several occasions to interfere with the executive branch of the government. In 1970 the Chief Rabbinate ordered the three cabinet ministers of Mafdal to resign from the government, in view of the enactment of the much-debated amendment to the Law of Return, which admitted as a Jew

---

* The rabbinical court thus relied on the Talmud, on Maimonides (Rambam), and on the code of Joseph Caro. Article 26 of the Hoshen Mishpat provides: "It is forbidden to appear before judges who are idolaters and their tribunals . . . and he who appears before them is an evildoer who has vilified, insulted and raised his hand against the Torah of Moses, and the court is entitled to cast him out and excommunicate him."

one converted to Judaism, without stipulating that the conversion must be Halakhically valid. The ministers ignored the ruling of the Chief Rabbinate. In the same year, the Chief Rabbinate issued an edict ordering Moshe Shapiro, the then Minister of the Interior, who was the leader of Mafdal, as well as the officials of his ministry, to refrain from registering as a Jew a person who had been converted to Judaism by a non-Orthodox rabbi, although an order to effect such a registration had been issued by the High Court of Justice. The Chief Rabbinate thus ordered a cabinet minister and his officials to violate the law of the land. Although this involved the minister in serious personal embarrassment, he carried out the registration as ordered by the High Court of Justice.

Another case that caused considerable controversy arose out of the National Service Law, which provides that girls who opt out of military service on religious grounds are liable to perform civilian duties, such as social service or aid in hospitals. The Chief Rabbinate and the leaders of the Yeshivot opposed not only military service for girls, but also compulsory civilian service. A ministerial committee was set up to explore ways and means of solving this problem by way of promoting volunteer service. It was a time when not only the Army but essential social services were suffering from an acute shortage of manpower. Michael Hazani, Minister of Social Welfare and one of the leaders of Mafdal, was appointed a member of the committee. Thereupon a rabbi residing in Jerusalem petitioned the regional rabbinical court for an order to be issued directing the minister to withdraw from the committee, on the grounds that compliance with the National Service Law, even by way of volunteer service, was one of those grave transgressions which a Jew is commanded to avoid even at the peril of death. The regional court did not act on the petition, presumably because of lack of jurisdiction. The petitioner then applied to the Supreme Rabbinical Court, which in composition is largely identical with the Chief Rabbinate. The Court issued an order directing Hazani to appear before it and reply to the petition. The minister applied to the Attorney General for a legal opinion and was advised that he had no obligation to reply to the summons issued by the Supreme Rabbinical Court. The latter took no further action.[48]

Independence Day

The ambivalent attitude of some of the Orthodox toward the Jewish state has also been reflected in its treatment of Israel Independence Day.* To Neturei Karta it is a day of mourning, at times accompanied by the burning of the national flag. Many of the Yeshivot ignore the

---

* Yom HaAtzma'ut, which is celebrated on the 5th of Iyar (usually falling in May) On that day in 1948, Israel's independence was proclaimed.

day; they carry on their studies as usual and do not participate in the festivities. In the summer of 1968, a written question was put to the Minister for Religious Affairs concerning a number of Yeshivot (all recipients of grants from the Ministry), whose students had been warned against participating in the celebrations and even against viewing the parade. In his reply the minister observed that it was customary in some Yeshivot to study even on Sabbaths and Holydays, and that the request "not to run round the streets on Independence Day" was motivated by educational considerations, "so as to avoid loss of study time." The explanation was patently evasive.[49]

The attitude of the Chief Rabbinate toward Independence Day has been one of equivocation and contradiction. The late Rabbi Judah L. Maimon was from the very outset of the opinion that Orthodox Jewry should regard this day as a religious holiday. He proposed that although it happens to fall in the Sefirah period,[50] when festivities and celebrations are banned, it should be treated like Lag B'Omer, the 33rd day of the Sefirah, when marriages and other festive occasions are allowed.[51] He pointed out that the reestablishment of national sovereignty certainly exceeded Lag B'Omer in significance. He therefore proposed that on Independence Day a proper festive service be conducted in the synagogues, including the recitation of the Hallel psalms.* Rabbi Maimon wrote: "We have achieved with Divine aid more than the Hasmoneans did in their time, and if the days of Hanukkah were then appointed as a holiday of thanksgiving . . . we too are enjoined to appoint the Day of Independence as a day of thanksgiving and Hallel. There is only one restriction: Hallel is not recited on the occasion of a miracle which occurred abroad. Miracles, however, which occurred in the Land of Israel, especially the kind of miracle we have witnessed in our lifetime, not only entitle but actually obligate us to offer up thanksgiving and Hallel."[52]

Rabbi Maimon anticipated the argument advanced by many rabbis that the Hasmoneans had been observant Jews, but that the leaders of the government of the State of Israel today were nonobservant. "This government is better than that of Ahab who did evil in the sight of the Lord above all that were before him (1 Kings 16:30); nevertheless, the hand of the Lord was upon Elijah, and he girded up his loins and ran before Ahab (18:46), which the Talmud interprets as Elijah paying respect to royalty. Likewise, rabbinic scholars were commanded to respect Herod, who, although a despot, was the King of a Jewish state. How much more are we enjoined to respect the government with all its shortcomings, and to remember that Independence Day symbolizes our deliverance from death, and our emergence from oppression to Re-

---

* Psalms 113–18.

demption. . . . Now that the Land of Israel has again become the State of Israel, I consider it a sin and a transgression not to offer Hallel and thanksgiving for the Divine grace."[53]

In the early days of the state, the late Chief Rabbi Isaac Halevy Herzog had defined the reestablishment of Jewish sovereignty as "the beginning of the growth of our redemption." Chief Rabbi Isaac Nissim had expressed an opinion that Independence Day should be assimilated to Lag B'Omer as far as celebrating marriages and having one's hair cut, and the like.[54] However, when it came to the order of prayers, the Chief Rabbinate, with a view to placating the extremists, effected a compromise. It ruled that the service should consist of prayers from the Friday evening service, a Psalm customarily recited on Friday afternoon, and passages from other prayers including the Hallel, but without a special benediction. Many Orthodox Jews objected, among them army chaplains and members of Mafdal and the Kibbutz HaDati. The latter published a booklet setting out an Independence Day service that included the complete Hallel. A group of synagogues published an "Order of Prayers" for the occasion, and the Director-General of the Chief Rabbinate assisted in its distribution, but the Chief Rabbinate subsequently ordered this "Order of Prayers" to be eliminated from those synagogues—a telling example of ambivalence.[55]

Jerusalem Day

The Six Day War of 1967 afforded the Chief Rabbinate another opportunity of proclaiming a new Holyday. The 25th day of the month of Iyar was declared a Festival to commemorate the fall of the Old City of Jerusalem (East Jerusalem), held by Jordan since 1948, to the Israel Army on the third day of that brief war. Unlike the order of prayers for Independence Day, the full Hallel was to be recited, and since it happened that this day, too, fell within the Sefirah period, the rabbinate lifted the usual prohibitions for "Jerusalem Day," as the new holiday was named. Thus it was invested with a far greater religious significance than the restoration of Jewish statehood as symbolized by Independence Day. Many of the moderates among the Orthodox raised their voices in protest against this demotion of Independence Day, and pointed out that it was erroneous to regard independence as a secular occurrence, but the capture of the Old City as an act of Divine grace. One of the leaders of the Kibbutz HaDati pointed out that there could have been no Six Day War victory without previous independence.[56]

Chief Rabbi Unterman said the upgrading of Jerusalem Day was justified because it was "an outstanding miracle"; hence Hallel must be recited. "A tiny people like us routing the Arab nations on all fronts," he added, "is not something to be explained in purely naturalistic terms

. . . . Thus it is clear that the victory in the Six Day War—with all due respect and honour to our valiant soldiers . . . was a victory miraculous in every sense of the word. . . . We cannot allow this miracle wrought by God to be unmarked by recitation of the full Hallel with the Blessing. . . . And, of course, there is no need to dwell on the great spiritual, practical and eternal value of the reunification of Jerusalem." He called Independence Day "also a great thing worthy of public celebration. But this was more in the way of being a great achievement that stemmed from our own inner strength and unshakable belief in the justice of our cause. . . . In the case of Independence Day, we certainly had cause to rejoice and celebrate, but this does not obligate the recitation of the full Hallel with the Blessing, or suspension of the Sefirah restrictions, as in the case of Jerusalem Day, when we palpably saw a miracle occur."[57]

The attitude of the Chief Rabbinate reflected both the pressure exerted by *Olam HaYeshivot* and its own ambivalence toward the Halakhic legitimacy of the Jewish state. The fact that the state was the achievement of Zionism, essentially a secular movement, embarrassed the rabbinate, and confronted it with a dilemma essentially insoluble in terms of Halakhah as currently interpreted.

Tisha B'Av

Similarly revealing was the attitude of the Chief Rabbinate toward Tisha B'Av, the 9th day of the month of Av. This is traditionally a day of mourning and fasting in commemoration of the destruction of the First Temple, in 586 B.C.E. and of the Second Temple, in 70 C.E.* The distinctive liturgy is the recitation of the biblical Book of Lamentations and of dirges (*Kinot*). In many synagogues these are read by dim candlelight, with the worshipers sitting on low stools or on the floor. After the establishment of the State of Israel, a number of Orthodox rabbis and scholars asked that the liturgy for the day of mourning be modified. Rabbi Menahem Emanuel Hartom favored abolishing the mourning on Tisha B'Av altogether, citing talmudic and rabbinical authorities in support of the proposition that now that the Land of Israel was free from the yoke of alien rule, the laws of mourning for the loss of sovereignty should be repealed.

After the Six Day War, there was greater insistence on the abolition of the day of mourning, or at least on some modification of its liturgy, since the Old City with the Temple site had been liberated. Talmudist Shraga Kedari appealed to the rabbinate to cancel the day of mourning entirely.[58] Professor Efraim Elimelekh Urbach, another eminent Ortho-

---

* Other calamities also occurred on Tisha B'Av: the fall of Betar in the war against Hadrian (135 C.E.), and the expulsion from Spain (1492 C.E.).

dox scholar, while favoring the retention of Tisha B'Av as a day of fasting, urged that the liturgy be changed through the omission of references that describe the Jews as existing in a state of misery and humiliation. It was unthinkable to him that at a time when Jerusalem was a united and thriving city, full of vitality and creativeness, a major center of Jewish learning and scholarship, the liturgy should retain the passage in the Minhah service of Tisha B'Av: "Comfort, O Lord our God, the mourners of Zion, the mourners of Jerusalem, and the city that is in mourning and in ruins, despised and desolate: she is mourning, for she is without her children; her dwellings are in ruins; she is despised for the loss of her glory; she is desolate, having no inhabitants; she sits with her head covered like a barren woman who has not given birth; legions devoured her, worshippers of strange gods possessed her, they threw the people of Israel to the sword." This awesome description of the final destruction of Jerusalem at the hands of Hadrian in the second century was the very antithesis of Jerusalem rebuilt, the rejuvenated capital of the Jewish state. Rabbi Louis I. Rabinowitz and other Orthodox scholars also urged the omission of this and similar passages from the liturgy.[59] The Chief Rabbinate, however, at the instance of Chief Rabbi Unterman, ruled out any changes either in the liturgy or in the mode of observance of the day.[60]

Army Service

A further illustration of the attitude of the Chief Rabbinate to the Jewish state and to its vital needs was the renewed controversy concerning the drafting of Yeshivah students, and of the implementation of the National Service Law regarding girls who opted out of military service on religious grounds.

In the wake of the Six Day War, the problem of the exemption of thousands of Yeshivah students from army service, which had been lying dormant for some years, came up again for public discussion. In January 1968 the initial 30-month period of military service for men was extended to three years. The government reached this drastic decision only after very serious consideration, for it affected the entire able-bodied youth of Israel. There was only one exception, the Yeshivah students, exempt from military service as long as they were registered on the rolls of a Yeshivah. This practice had originated in 1948 as the result of an agreement between Ben-Gurion and Chief Rabbi Herzog. It provided that the then relatively few Yeshivah students were to be exempted during their period of study. The agreement now came under severe and widespread criticism.[61]

Not all Yeshivah students took advantage of this privilege. The youth movements of Bnei Akivah and Ezra, affiliated respectively with Mafdal and Poalei Agudat Israel, joined the Nahal* shortly after the establishment of the state. Since time for the study of Talmud within the Nahal framework was necessarily limited, the heads of some Yeshivot founded a Yeshivah Nahal. By arrangement with the army, the student would remain for five years in the Yeshivah, during which time he would complete his basic and advanced commando training in two five-month periods, and otherwise remain on call for emergencies. This assured a fairly regular study of the Talmud, and at the same time prepared the young men for military duties on a level comparable to the rest of the army.

However, the core of *Olam HaYeshivot* insisted upon the continuation of unconditional and unlimited exemption from military service. In the meantime their student bodies had grown from a few hundreds to a few thousands. Replying to a question in the Knesset, Minister of Defense Moshe Dayan put the number of those who had been exempted at 4,500 in 1966 and at 5,000 in 1967.[62] Many felt that while theological students might rightly claim deferment from military service for the period of their studies, it was intolerable that their deferment was unlimited in time and therefore constituted in effect a total exemption from regular service as well as from service with the reserves. Exemption could duly be claimed for an officiating rabbi; the Yeshivot, however, claimed exemption regardless of whether their students became officiating rabbis—which few of them actually did. Leading Orthodox scholars even appealed to the students themselves: "We believe that your conscience is not at ease when you are exempted from military service, when your friends, among them Talmud scholars like yourselves, are risking their lives for their people and for their country, and in so doing sanctify the Lord every day and enhance the Torah in the eyes of those who stand with them. Remember: your blood is not redder than that of others.** Those who speak on your behalf and claim to act for your good are in actual fact desecrating the Torah. Emancipate yourselves from their patronage, and sanctify the Name of the Lord."[63]

An editorial in *HaAretz* put it more strongly: "The problem is one of principle: by what consideration are Yeshivah students exempted? Why should others defend them? . . . . Yeshivah students cannot even excuse themselves as conscientious objectors to violence. It is an established fact that those Yeshivah students who shirk their duty are in the forefront of all acts of violence directed at the secular public—that is, the arm that refuses to hold a weapon against our enemies is raised

---

* Abbreviation for *Noar Halutzi Lohem* (Fighting Pioneer Youth). These units of mixed military-agricultural formations were formed to establish strategic points of settlement in border areas.
** A talmudic phrase meaning that one's own life is not more sacred than another's (Pes. 25b, Sanh. 74a).

in violence when it is a matter of a "holy" war against the nonreligious public."[64]

The youth movement of Mafdal, as well as the Kibbutz Dati, induced Mafdal to send a delegation, which included cabinet ministers, to the Chief Rabbinate, with a view to obtaining a change in the existing practice. They pointed out that popular indignation was not confined to the secularists, but was shared by many if not most traditional Jews, and that the operations of the Arab terrorist organization necessitated that every citizen be able to bear arms in his own defense. The delegation achieved no result. The rabbinate refused to agree to any change whatsoever, and declared that it was in fact the duty of the cabinet ministers of the Mafdal to prevail upon the government to abide by this decision.[65]

In the climate of opinion prevailing after the Six Day War, when hundreds of families were bereaved and some thousands were directly and indirectly affected by casualties, the silence of the rabbinate in the face of public clamor and the pleas of so many of the Orthodox themselves, caused considerable embarrassment to the majority of observant Jews. Prominent rabbinic scholars asserted that the drafting of Yeshivah students was permitted by the Halakhah. Rabbi Eliezer Waldenberg of the Jerusalem regional rabbinical court summed up the Halakhic position as follows: "Maimonides lays down explicitly that it is the duty of every Jew who can physically do so, to bear arms in the defense of his brethren besieged by the enemy. This ruling implies that in a war of self-defense, where Israel is threatened with extermination, even the great scholars of Israel, if they only can bear arms, must do so. They cannot relegate the duty to others less pious or learned."[66] Extensive Halakhic documentation in support of the proposition that Yeshivah students were enjoined to serve in the army was prepared by Rabbi Menahem Hartom and by Eliezer Steinberg, one of the leaders of the Kibbutz Dati.[67] The latter expressed grave concern over the adverse impact of this development on the religious and spiritual image of Israel: "The question of drafting Yeshivah students does not, in fact, worry the secularists. In their view, these students belong in the category of parasitic elements, or of those disloyal to the state, and their exemption does not seriously affect the military set-up. This, however, is likely to mold the attitude of the secularists to religion and to its official exponents. The secularists may even have an interest in the present situation, which enables them to stress the negative image of the Orthodox. It is natural to make generalizations, so that the face of the entire Orthodox community is blackened. This phenomenon, together with other episodes in the religious life of the country, are far from creating a positive image, and it is indeed to be wondered that we fail to realize that we are walking into a trap."[68]

Kibbutz Dati, in defiance of the Chief Rabbinate, appealed to Mafdal to take steps that would lead to the drafting of Yeshivah students: "Many border settlements are burdened with the overwhelming task of keeping watch; even persons over the age of 50 are often called upon at night to patrol their settlement. In addition to military service, Orthodox Jewry has a special interest in the strengthening of the chaplaincy, and of the personnel charged with religious activities in the army. Recently, the chaplaincy appealed to young people to perform religious services in the army. Suitable candidates for this can easily be found in the Yeshivot."[69] In effect, the great majority of Orthodox Jews found itself in confrontation with a minority consisting of Neturei Karta and *Olam HaYeshivot* and their adherents; still, the majority did not carry the day and the Chief Rabbinate, as so frequently, deferred to the ultra-traditional position.

A similar fate awaited the initiative undertaken by Mafdal, in response to public clamor, to promote volunteering by religious girls for National Service, that is, service in hospitals, social welfare agencies, and educational institutions. This initiative was approved as a compromise between the demand of the government for the enforcement of the National Service Act for religious girls who opted out of military service, and that of the Orthodox establishment for total nonenforcement of the law. To facilitate matters, the government had arranged that girls who volunteered would perform their service in the towns where they resided, so that they would not have to spend nights away from their families. A special committee to promote such volunteering was set up by Mafdal, which was headed by the wife of Knesset member Rabbi Z. M. Neriah. But before this committee could proceed with its program, *Olam HaYeshivot,* officiating rabbis, and Agudat Israel alike protested vehemently against the idea of any service, however voluntary, under the National Service Law. Even Poalei Agudat Israel, which in 1952 had agreed to some form of service for religious girls, came out in opposition to the scheme, and justified its altered position by the allegation that secularism had been growing stronger since 1952. The Council of Sages issued an edict against the volunteering project. Mrs. Neriah, who had received personal threatening letters, resigned from the chairmanship of the committee.[70]

In an interview with the daily *Maariv,* Rabbi Shlomo Kroll, of Kfar Hassidim near Haifa, opposed the National Service Law altogether, whether obligatory or optional. When it was pointed out that many girls who opted out of military service took up employment in shops, offices, and factories, the rabbi replied that it was certainly not an ideal situation that demanded that they should always remain under direct parental control. When pressed to reply to the suggestion that opposition to volunteering was a result of nonidentification with the State of Israel, the rabbi said: "I identify myself with the state in everything which does not contradict the Halakhah. If the Knesset adopts laws contrary to the Halakhah, I will consider myself bound by the Halakhah only. I shall not submit to laws because they are enacted by 120 Knesset members. The National Service Law is in no shape or form binding, since it is superseded by the Halakhic edict of great scholars." He called the National Religious Party and its ministers in the Cabinet, who supported the National Service Law in contravention of the Halakhic edict, a collection of hypocrites.[71] The controversy within Orthodoxy engendered by the National Service Law was well expressed by Professor Murray Roston of Bar Ilan University, himself an Orthodox Jew, who stated that he was educating his daughters in the expectation that they would serve in due course in the army. He held that the opposition of the ultra-Orthodox arose out of their fundamental nonidentification with the Jewish state.[72]

The Role of the Rabbinate

In no other single instance was the failure of Mafdal to make headway against the *Olam HaYeshivot* and the rabbinate so evident as' in the case of Yeshivah students and religious girls exempted from army and national service. It was a case of chain reaction, initiated by Neturei Karta, seized upon by the *Olam HaYeshivot,* and finally involving the Chief Rabbinate. Mafdal, fearing that its religious credentials would be questioned by the rabbinate and *Olam HaYeshivot,* was not prepared to challenge its opponents on their own grounds, that is to say, on the grounds of Halakhah, even though an impressive array of Halakhic precedents and authorities was available. Mafdal realized that the controversy was not truly concerned with the interpretation of a Halakhic principle, but moved rather to the more sensitive plane of identification or nonidentification with the Jewish state. Mafdal leaders, however, were not prepared to challenge the rabbinic authorities who claimed unqualified adherence to the Halakhah.

These and similar differences and even conflicts between the rabbinate and Mafdal have not reflected any basic doctrinal divergence, but have primarily been a function of the different roles each is called upon to play. The rabbinate, secure in its legal status and recognized by public law, considers itself free to determine matters of religious import in accordance with the Halakhah, to which it generally gives the strictest interpretation, reflecting Orthodox fundamentalism. Feeling secure, it tends to ignore popular outcry and indignation at its rulings rather than incur the displeasure of *Olam HaYeshivot* and Neturei Karta. Mafdal, on the other hand, which as a political party is close to the grass roots of public opinion, cannot escape paying heed to the needs of its electorate. Besides, it actively participates in the running of the state, both on the local and the national level. Feeling the pressure from below, and bearing the brunt of the criticism leveled at the rabbinate, Mafdal has maneuvered itself into a position of playing the role of intermediary between the rabbinate and the government and, wishing to appease public resentment against the former, it has taken up a position that neither enhances its own prestige, nor narrows the gap between the rabbinate and the great majority of the nation.

On various occasions, Mafdal has attempted to soften the attitude of the rabbinate on crucial issues and to have it adopt a more liberal interpretation of the religious law and, in so doing, avoid painful confrontations with the state. All requests made by Mafdal to the rabbinate, or to *Olam HaYeshivot* to urge their students to do military service, or to appeal to religious girls to volunteer for service, were rejected with finality. Nor did the rabbinate act upon, nor even give serious consideration to, the pleas of Mafdal for a more liberal construction of Halakhah in matters of marriage, divorce, and conversion. After successfully securing legislation for the observance of Halakhic rules and for vesting the rabbinate with exclusive legal authority in matters of personal status, Mafdal finds itself in a position where it exercises little, if any, influence on the rabbinate. It was with a sense of bitterness that the late Moshe Haim Shapiro, in his time Minister of the Interior and undisputed leader of Mafdal, exclaimed: "The Chief Rabbinate fails to understand that we no longer live in a small European 'stetl.' We have a state, and we have problems. The rabbinate is subjected to influences that fetter its hands. During the long centuries we knew how to introduce reforms and to alleviate hardships. Here, however, anyone who is bent on aggravating our difficulties, does so."[73]

Rabbi Emanuel Rackman, of the Yeshivah University in New York, went even farther. He accused the Chief Rabbinate of extremism, and of promoting dissension and schism in the midst of the nation: "The religious leaders and rabbis of today have failed to promote unity. Instead they have promoted antagonism and hatred. . . . Today the love of Israel flows from the State of Israel . . . which is therefore part of my religious experience. The state has succeeded where the Halakhah has failed." He accused the rabbinate of betraying the great heritage bequeathed by Rabbis Kook, Herzog, and Maimon, and of stirring up controversy and estrangement instead of concentrating on making the Halakhah acceptable. "Our Sages in days gone by did not dare to compile lists of mamzerim, whereas the rabbis of today do so out of fear of the extremists. This exercises a destructive influence on youth in the Diaspora." He held that the Halakhah was capable of solving contemporary problems, but that mere talmudic erudition was not sufficient for such a task, which also required spiritual and moral greatness of the rabbis. Turning to the leaders of Mafdal, he urged them to stay on in the government and to work for the unity of the Jewish people.[74]

Similarly, Professor Nathan Rottenstreich of the Hebrew University, criticized the increasing rigidity of the rabbinate: "Slowly but surely rabbinical institutions and a rabbinical hierarchy are solidifying into a structure as imposing as the Catholic Church. . . . Today we are witnessing the arrogation to itself by the rabbinate of ecclesiastical status . . . . The process is perceptible in the replacement of rabbis by a rabbinate; the replacement of great scholars by Assemblies; the replacement of individual decisions by hierarchically structured institutions, by courts and courts of appeal and by Chief Rabbis. . . . This organization of religious activity is modelled after the pattern of the secular state."[75] According to Dr. S. N. Eisenstadt, Professor of Sociology at the Hebrew University, "influence of the extremist religious groups is felt most strongly here because it is they who enjoy full religious legitimation. . . . In the debate between tradition and modernization, therefore, tradition is in general becoming increasingly militant and intolerant."[76]

The Absence of Dialogue

The situation has been rendered even more difficult by the policy of the rabbinate of avoiding any discussion of the justification for its decisions, and particularly by its avoidance of the evocation of ethical grounds for its pronouncements. Consequently, any serious dialogue between the rabbinate and the majority of the people has been impossible. In fact, most of the religious debate traditionally carried on in Israel is not really religious in the sense of discussing values and conceptions. Throughout the whole discussion, no serious contribution has been made toward a deeper and more meaningful understanding of religion in modern life. Zvi Yaron, a leading Orthodox intellectual, once observed: "Religion has been debated as a set of external behavioral actions relating religious persons to non-religious persons. . . . Both observant Israelis and their opponents have conducted their discussions on the assumption that religion is something that cannot be talked about in intellectually meaningful terms."[77]

The public is accustomed to unilateral rabbinic pronouncements against infringements of the rules of Kashrut, against interurban transport before the end of the Sabbath, against engaging in sports on that day, or against operating a swimming pool for the use of both sexes. People have become accustomed to widely publicized appeals to have one's hair cut early on Friday, so as to avoid the desecration of the Sabbath by barbers who close their shops late; or warnings against the admixture of milk in pastry that is advertised as being *Parveh* (suitable for consumption with either dairy or meat products); or precise instructions as regards *kapparot;** or intricate instructions regarding the disposition of unleavened matter on the eve of Passover. While the rabbinate has displayed diligence and zeal in proclaiming its position on these ritual aspects, "the duties of man toward God," it has rarely addressed itself to issues of moral import, "the duties of man toward his fellow man." It has been observed that if all Jews were vegetarians, preferred not to travel on the Sabbath, and avoided matrimonial complications, the voice of religion as represented by the rabbinate would never be heard at all. Thus, the term *dati*** is identified in the public mind with a person who punctiliously carries out the ritual observance of Orthodox Judaism, while ethical behavior is not considered to be implied in the word. The rabbinate has never been known to take the initiative in focusing attention on social or economic evils. In the eyes of the rabbinate such issues do not present "religious" problems at all, and none of the religious parties in the Knesset has of itself raised any problems involving ethical principles for debate.

The Growing Estrangement

There is no gainsaying the fact that a rift has developed between the Orthodox establishment, that is, the rabbinate, and *Olam HaYeshivot* and the bulk of the nation. The nonobservant majority are not hostile to religion and do not repudiate the Halakhah, but they subject its rules to close scrutiny in the light of ethical criteria, while the rabbis, regarding the Halakhah as divinely ordained, will not deviate from it in order to reconcile its rules with moral principles. While the average Israeli does not object to being married by the rabbinical authorities, he does question the moral justification for the rule that prohibits a cohen from marrying a divorcée, or the rule that prevents a young childless widow from remarrying without the consent of her late husband's brother.*** The average Israeli may be quite content to have his divorce case adjudicated by Halakhah; his sense of justice is, however, offended when a husband can continue to defy a rabbinical decree and refuse to deliver the *get* to his wife.

Another issue that arouses indignation is the unfortunate position of the mamzer, whom the Halakhah allows to marry only another mamzer, or a convert from another faith; such a prohibition will descend

* "Expiations," name of a ceremony performed on the morning preceding the Day of Atonement, consisting of taking a fowl in the right hand and reciting specified verses from the Psalms and the Book of Job.

** Literally, "observant of the law." The word is often translated as "religious," but does not have the same connotation as in English.

*** By the ceremony of Halitzah, which may involve her in waiting until a young brother-in-law attains his religious majority, before which he is not competent to give the reqnired consent.

ineluctably from generation to generation. The average Israeli Jew is satisfied to buy kasher food, but cannot easily come to terms with the proposition that he may not drink wine that has been prepared by non-Jews, since the touch of a Gentile on wine renders it Halakhically impure.[78] He cannot accept the Halakhic denigration of women's evidence in court, and he considers the question of army exemption on religious grounds a matter of fundamental morality, and one involving the question of loyalty to the state. Thus, while the rabbinate tends to regard the so-called secularists as a generation of transgressors in open revolt against the ordinances of the Torah, the latter see the controversy as a confrontation between a Halakhah that seems to be indifferent to moral values, which they, the non-Orthodox regard as the essence of Judaism.

The growing estrangement arising out of the different approaches to ethical issues was in 1966 highlighted by a widely discussed incident that turned on the question: Was the Halakhic principle of *Pikuah Nefesh Doheh Shabbat** applicable only to save the life of a Jew? Although the precise circumstances of the incident were never quite cleared up, the issue revolved around the point whether it was permissible to use the telephone on the Sabbath to summon medical aid to a non-Jew in distress. The local rabbinical authorities were embarrassed and their utterances were confused. The matter reached the Chief Rabbinate, and Chief Rabbi Unterman issued a pronouncement, supported by Halakhic authorities, which concluded; "It must be understood that the approach to the performance of any work on the Sabbath must be strict. The rationale for the principle that *Pikuah Nefesh* overrides the Sabbath lies in the idea that the Sabbath may be violated for the sake of a person so that he may later be able to observe many Sabbaths. . . . This applies to those who were commanded to observe the Sabbath, but it does not apply to Gentiles. However . . . in our days the refusal to extend medical aid to an alien may give rise to that enmity which jeopardizes existence."[79] Stripped of its archaic verbiage, the Chief Rabbi thereby permitted Sabbath violation for the purpose of saving the life of a non-Jew, not on moral grounds but out of fear that resentment at nonaction might lead to the shedding of Jewish blood. With his argument, Rabbi Unterman succeeded in offending both the ultra-Orthodox and the vast majority of Israelis, in whose scale of justice and humanity the Rabbi's reasoning was plainly immoral.

The ethical objections raised to certain Halakhic rules are met by the rabbinate with exhortations to obey the Divine law because it is Divine. Thus, Rabbi Mordekhai Lopez argued: "We, the faithful, have

---

* *Pikuah Nefesh*—regard for human life; the term is applied to the rabbinic doctrine that the duty to save human lives supersedes almost all other considerations. It is elaborated in the Talmud and codes, especially with regard to Sabbath observance.

never presumed to say either to ourselves or to the world in general that we are able to comprehend rationally all the laws of the Torah. We know that there are laws and commandments which we are unable to understand. Our greatness consists in our knowledge that obedience to the law is not dependent on our comprehension of them. The sublimity which the Children of Israel attained was their willingness to declare 'We shall do and we shall listen,' implying that observance and obedience preceded understanding."[80] Similarly, Professor Yeshayahu Leibowitz wrote: " 'Ethics of Judaism' is a meaningless concept. . . . In Judaism, a person is not a value in himself but an image of God. Man has no significance beyond what arises from this fact. Therefore . . . the Torah does not recognize 'that which is good and right,' but 'that which is good and right in the sight of the Lord thy God' (Deut. 12:28) . . . . Judaism as a defined and specific entity possessing an uninterrupted continuity of three thousand years has been embodied neither in philosophy nor in literature, nor in art, nor in anything at all, but in a life in accordance with the Mitzvot, that is, in an entirely Halakhic way of life."[81]

While Yeshayahu Leibowitz justifies Halakhic fundamentalism in intellectually meaningful terms, the official rabbinate, being self-isolated and deriving its authority from the law of the land, feels relieved of that confrontation with modern reality which Orthodox circles in the Diaspora cannot escape if they wish to carry influence in the communities they serve. The latter are consequently driven to confront the problems of applying the Halakhah in contemporary situations. This was formulated by Professor Eliezer Berkowitz of the Hebrew Theological College of Skokie, Illinois, who conceives of the Halakhah not as a fixed code, but as a process capable of evolving to meet ever-changing conditions. "Halakhah is the technique of Torah application to a concrete contemporary situation. But while the Torah is eternal, the concrete historic situation is forever changing. Halakhah, therefore, as the application of Torah to a given situation, will forever uncover new levels of Torah depth and Torah meaning, and thus make new facets of Judaism visible. . . . It is the spiritual tragedy of Orthodox Judaism that our inadequacy lost us the creative power of the Halakhah. . . . The fault lies not with the Halakhah, but with the Halakhists."[82]

In the view of the Orthodox, that which at any given time is considered to be ethical cannot warrant a restriction or modification of Halakhic rules. The rule prohibiting a cohen from marrying a divorcée, or a young childless woman from remarrying without Halitzah, may constitute a hardship, but the acceptance of that hardship is an act of obedience to the Divine Law and, in that sense only, an ethical act. In the view of the secularists, however, individual freedom cannot be denied or restricted except for reasons that pass the test of moral criteria. By asserting the right to subject the rules of the Halakhah to scrutiny on ethical grounds, that is to say, by reserving the right to repudiate those Halakhic rules which are repugnant to ethical principles, an apparently insurmountable barrier has been created between the two schools of thought.[83] Some attempts to narrow the gaps between the two schools of thought were made in the sixties by Orthodox groups acting independently of the rabbinate and of Mafdal.

D. FERMENT WITHIN ORTHODOXY

The first dissenting voices against the religious establishment were raised within the ranks of Mafdal, but when the party proved inhospitable to new ideas and regarded such dissent as inimical to its interests, a few of the more independent spirits left the party. They shared the apprehension that continued resentment against the Orthodox establishment would totally alienate large masses of Jews from the Jewish religion, and also that on the Orthodox side, the tendency toward self-isolation pursued by the rabbinate and the ultra-Orthodox might harden into animosity toward the Jewish state.

In the early sixties the Orthodox dissenters formed the "Amana Circle," consisting primarily of educators. It was formed to clarify the problems involved in the renewal of religious life, and appealed to persons who, in pursuance of this objective, would endeavor to embody their principles in their own way of life. Their deliberations, however, while constituting a clarification of issues and a reasoned critique of the Orthodox establishment, offered no blueprint for a course of action.

Joseph Bentwich, author and educator, denounced the stress on the ritual aspects of Orthodoxy, such as Kashrut and Sabbath travel, and the rabbinate's failure to castigate those guilty of unethical practices. "Such a religion is not Judaism," he stated plainly. He saw the source of the religious predicament in the attempt to reestablish on the soil of the sovereign Jewish state a type of Galut Judaism. Diaspora Judaism, though it aspired to a society built upon social justice, "was constrained to render unto Caesar that which was Caesar's, and sought its comfort in a Messianic future. This is the kind of Judaism we have inherited, with a Shulhan Arukh which never alludes to a Jewish state and posits a Galut existence. . . . To this day this is the conception of Meah Shearim which regards itself as a 'Jewish' enclave within a secular alien state." What was needed was a complete Jewish way of life that would retain the essentials of the old, and yet strike a balance between all the Mitzvot: those pertaining to ritual and those obligating man to his fellow man and society.[84]

Another well-known Orthodox educator, Dr. Benjamin Oppenheimer, inveighed against Mafdal for its policy of religious legislation aimed at the enforcement of religious norms by legal coercion, an effort that, in his opinion, was self-defeating. He deplored the adverse impact of *Olam HaYeshivot* on the Yeshivot established by Bnei Akiva and the fundamentalist approach prevailing in the religious state schools, where freedom of enquiry was suppressed and crucial questions raised by pupils were left unanswered. "Pupils may not raise 'heretical' questions relating to the connection between the Torah and the Prophets, on the one hand, and the Halakhah on the other." Dr. Oppenheimer condemned Mafdal for what it considered its significant achievement, namely, maintaining a coexistence between the nonreligious and the Orthodox, as if these were two nations between whom a balance of power had to be struck. But, he said, even that shaky status quo had been upset by the creeping extremism that had overtaken the Orthodox establishment.[85]

The only formation within Mafdal that has been actively concerned with the growing estrangement between the Orthodox and the non-Orthodox majority is the Kibbutz Dati. It has endeavored to maintain a dialogue with the non-Orthodox, with a view to bringing about a *kiruv levavot* (meeting of hearts). They consider that further estrangement will accelerate the trend on the part of the Orthodox toward self-isolation and completely alienate them from the Jewish state. In the dialogue with the non-Orthodox, Kibbutz Dati has unhesitatingly exposed the shortcomings of Orthodoxy, and at times has even questioned some generally accepted attitudes. Rabbi Adin Steinsaltz, well-known Talmudist, goes so far as to repudiate the very classification of Orthodox and secularist. The latter cannot be regarded as "transgressors," for even if transgression were the criterion, hardly any of the Orthodox observe all the 613 Mitzvot enumerated by tradition. The secularists should therefore be regarded as good Jews who comply with some of the Mitzvot, though not with all. Such an attitude could pave the way to a real approach to the so-called secularists.[86] Others point out that while the term *transgressors* has traditionally referred to persons who sought to escape Judaism, the secularists of Israel affirm their Jewishness with great intensity, and in fact regard themselves as good Jews in active pursuit of Jewish values. The dialogue with them must therefore be pursued on a footing of equality, each side treating the other as good Jews and each pursuing its own ideal of Jewishness. Professor Haim Hillel Ben Sasson of the Hebrew University goes as far as to suggest that Judaism has traditionally been pluralistic, citing the division between Sadducees and Pharisees, Hassidim and Mitnagdim, and others that preceded the present division into Orthodox, Conservative, Reform, and unaffiliated.[87]

Moshe Unna, leader of the Kibbutz Dati, elaborated a program for the consideration of the Orthodox and the non-Orthodox. Though rejecting all suggestions that religious parties were inimical to the interests of religion, he repudiated coercion by legislative or administrative action, not because of its being contrary to the Halakhah, but because pragmatically coercion could achieve only negative results. A new approach was required, one stemming not out of a religious claim, but out of the need to achieve national unity.

According to Unna, the need for national unity will be understood and accepted by the non-Orthodox, for they too are committed to such unity. On behalf of this principle, the Orthodox should advance only one claim: that conditions be created that would enable them to share fully the burden of building the nation and the state, a claim that the non-Orthodox will readily acknowledge. The essence of the claim is not the imposition of religious norms on those who reject them, but the creation of conditions that would enable the Orthodox to lead their own way of life, and thus make it possible for them, together with the non-Orthodox, to achieve national unity by participating fully in the life of the nation. In practical terms, such an accommodation must be based on four essential conditions, all of which the non-Orthodox would find acceptable. The first, which is accepted in practice and has never been challenged, is the observance of Kashrut in the army, thus enabling Orthodox boys to share the burden of the defense of the country. The second, which has also been accepted, is to enable the children of Orthodox parents to receive a religious education. The third is the maintenance of the rabbinical courts for the purpose of adjudicating matters of family law, with the proviso that civil courts be empowered to arrange for civil marriage in all instances of persons who are prohibited from marriage on Halakhic grounds. Last, the assurance that the right of an Orthodox Jew to earn his living shall not be prejudiced by reason of his refusal to violate the Sabbath. Once such conditions are created, the Orthodox will have secured all that is necessary for their full participation in the life of the nation.

Unna also spoke up against various types of religious legislation, such as the prohibition of public transportation on the Sabbath, or the ban on pig breeding. Such inculcation of religious principles should be left to persuasion, example, and education.[88] The program was duly repudiated by Mafdal, and the rabbis associated with Mafdal castigated Unna "for having expressed an opinion which is not compatible with the views of those who are loyal to the Law of Moses."[89]

The most important contribution to the discussion was made by Rabbi Efraim Urbach, Professor of Talmud at the Hebrew University, who offered a radical program for the solution of the religious conflict. A former leading member of Mafdal, Urbach first made his views known in 1964: "It is a sad reflection: the ideal of the Yeshivah remains what it always was: the husband studies, the wife supports him. . . . How many rabbis with a cultural standard do we possess in Israel who can offer guidance to the people? . . . Many of them dissociate themselves in public from the doings of Neturei Karta, but in their heart of hearts they are with them." He repudiated legislation in matters of religion. "Any form of coercion in matters of religion and faith is contrary to the concept of Judaism, and carries with it no Halakhic authority."[90]

Two years later a new Orthodox movement was launched by Urbach and other Orthodox intellectuals, many of whom had at one time been prominent members of Mafdal. At a conference held in Jerusalem, a "Movement for Torah Judaism" was inaugurated. Its sponsors proclaimed that it would not become a political party, but rather remain a strictly nonpolitical body dedicated to the inculcation of Torah by persuasion. It declared its devotion to the State of Israel as the fulfillment of a centuries-old aspiration, as well as a "framework for realization of the Torah and its laws." It went on: "This great event opens up an opportunity for the revival of the Torah. The establishment of the state, however, has brought into clear focus the crisis of the Halakhah which occurred because the last generations have been ignored by those responsible for Halakhah. This has resulted in a situation where many people, though they have not entirely lost their affinity to the Torah are experiencing a crisis of confidence . . . doubt whether the Halakhah can be regarded as authoritative in private and public life." Realizing that this reference to the Halakhah may expose the new movement to criticism on the part of the Orthodox establishment, they hastened to assure their audience that they had nothing in common with Reform. At the same time they were at pains to assure the general public that "the spread of the Torah . . . is possible in an atmosphere of mutual respect and by means of persuasion, education and setting a personal example, all without resorting to pressure or coercion."

The movement laid stress on ethical principles, and on the duties of man toward his fellow man, and it urged its members to set a personal example. Implicit in the statement was a criticism of the Chief Rabbinate, because it concerned itself with ritual and ignored moral issues. The program called for "the revival of the Halakhah," and appealed to the religious authorities to concern themselves with the reality of Israel and with its modern industrial society. Religious Jewry should not accept state aid for the establishing of synagogues but support them and their rabbis entirely by their own contributions. The rabbinate was castigated for its rigidity, and *Olam HaYeshivot* for its self-isolation and alienation from the Jewish state.[91]

This frontal attack on the Orthodox establishment and on Mafdal by a group of Orthodox scholars, scientists, and intellectuals, with its call for separation of religion from politics, was tantamount to a denial of the very raison d'être of Mafdal. If persuasion and education were to be the means of inculcating religious values, the state had already provided the instrumentality for a religious educational program by its network of state religious schools; furthermore, the state did enable Orthodox boys to participate in the army by assuring its Kashrut, and no further legislation was needed on these points. In the publications of Professor Urbach's group, suggestions were made for changes in the prayer book in order to make the synagogue service more meaningful, and there were also discussions of such delicate points as the attitude of the Halakhah to non-Jews and proselytes.[92]

As was to be expected, the program of the new movement was favorably received in the general press. *Maariv* wrote: "It was high time for someone to arise and attempt to elevate the prestige of religion, which has sunk so low, even in the eyes of those whose hearts still beat with sympathy for religious values and traditions. Someone had to come to emancipate religion from the present mixture of pure religion with none-too-pure politics, a mixture which grants concessions in the sphere of principles, in exchange for all kinds of religious and sometimes of economic 'attainments.' "[93]

HaAretz expressed willingness to listen to the new message: "It does not mean that all are interested in religious inspiration, but we are all the poorer because religion appears in the guise of an authority—rabbinic, parliamentary and administrative—while Judaism is presented in the form of edicts on what is forbidden or permitted. The spiritual life of the Jewish people will be enhanced if Orthodox Judaism endeavors to confront contemporary problems."[94]

The students of Bar Ilan University also expressed sympathy and interest in the new movement.[95] Kibbutz Dati, although part of Mafdal, devoted considerable space in its official organ to the deliberations of the new movement, and concluded: "The Kibbutz will initiate a dialogue with organized religious groups which are based on the observance of the Torah and are interested in propagating religion by persuasion, with a view to mitigating the antagonism between the religious and the non-religious. . . . The aim of this dialogue should be the advancement of the cause of Judaism."[96]

The reaction of Mafdal itself was negative. Its official organ, realizing that the Movement for Torah Judaism was attempting to undermine the basic premise for the existence of the party, equated the leaders with those secularists who were advocating the separation of religion from the state. "It is to be regretted that men of Torah and learning, some indeed of our leading members, have left the party . . . and have organized a movement to work against the very party in which they had been active for very many years."[97] The anti-coercion attitude of the movement came in for special criticism. Rabbi Moshe Zvi Neriah stated: "Religious coercion among Jews is legitimate. . . . We do not rejoice at the idea of coercion, for it is better to achieve what is desired by the free exercise of will. As a way of teaching the masses, however, the employment of force has proved its efficacy. In order to preserve that which is precious—and for us the historical process of three thousand years of Torah and Mitzvot is most precious—coercion is needed . . . . There is no warrant for the thesis of the Movement for Torah Judaism; its aim is merely secular practice. . . . It has sought for a compromise between its European outlook and Judaism itself, and that has led to a collision. Calls for a renovation of the Halakhah do not come from those who were educated in the world of Halakhah, but from those who derive their views from another world."[98] Rabbi Neriah was alluding to the university education that the leaders of the new movement possessed, as an explanation for their deviation from the "correct" position.

The new movement, having sprung from the very midst of Mafdal, presented it with a powerful challenge. The Orthodoxy and personal integrity of the leaders, formerly eminent Mafdal men, could not be impeached. While the traditionalist daily *Hatsofeh* refused to publish an advertisement announcing the forthcoming conference of the new movement, it could not resist public pressure altogether and printed letters from some of its readers who referred to the movement with approval. Agudat Israel, on its part, cast doubt upon the Orthodox loyalty of the leaders of the Movement for Torah Judaism. An editorial in *HaModia* stated: "It is an exact copy of the beginning of the Reform movement in Germany, of the Haskalah movement in Russia and Galicia, and of the destructive actions of Reform in Hungary." It called its founders "idolators," "ignorant of Judaism," "petrified limbs, who in their boorishness and conceit seek to introduce rottenness into the vineyard of Israel."[99]

The movement, which has a core of several hundred members, has found itself faced with an uphill struggle, since it does not enjoy the support of the government, or of any political party, or of the religious establishment. It is surrounded by suspicions that it is in league with Reform. It has set itself the task of promoting an independent Orthodox movement, something for which there has been no precedent in the quarter-century history of the State of Israel. In its periodical publications it deals critically with the policies of the Chief Rabbinate and of Mafdal, and advances innovative approaches to Halakhic problems. Its influence, however, is confined to academic and intellectual circles within Orthodoxy; and while the movement has been growing, its impact on either the general public or on the Orthodox authorities has not been significant.

E. THE ARMY CHAPLAINCY

A rather unique position in the Orthodox establishment is held by the military chaplaincy, officially designated as the Army rabbinate. This body, numerically rather small, has been called upon to deal with important and intricate Halakhic problems that could be neither evaded nor indefinitely postponed. While the tensions arising out of attempts to impose Halakhic norms on the realities of contemporary life have not seriously affected the course of normal existence, in spite of occasional high feelings and vigorous debates, such tensions within the army would have raised far more serious difficulties. Thousands of Orthodox boys serve in the military, and it was essential that they be spared the need to violate their religious duties in order to fulfill their military duties. It was, therefore, imperative that conditions be created that would, on the one hand, enable Orthodox soldiers to feel at ease with their nonobservant colleagues, with whom they have to share close quarters for some three years at a time, and on the other, to avoid any interference with army requirements.

The circumstances of Israel's existence have always necessitated the maintenance of a strong and well-integrated people's army. Many soldiers, as well as their parents, came from a variety of countries and cultures and, when in Israel, continued to live in homogeneous communities with limited opportunities of active intercourse with other groups. Even those soldiers who had their schooling in Israel, came to the army from a religious state school or from a general state school. The army, Israel's most potent melting pot, afforded the first opportunity for Orthodox boys to meet non-Orthodox boys, and to share grave dangers in a spirit of comradeship and solidarity.

The need to mold the Army into a closely knit unit posed from the very beginning a challenge to the Army command, and to the Army rabbinate as well. It was all but unavoidable to call upon the nonobservant, id est, upon the majority of soldiers, to make concessions to the Orthodox minority in the name of national unity. With this aim in mind, and in order to obviate the danger to national unity inherent in the idea of setting up separate units for Orthodox soldiers, the Kasher Food for Soldiers Ordinance was enacted in the early days of Israel's independence, in order to provide kasher food in all branches of the military establishment.[100] The situation imposed a particular responsibility on the Army rabbinate, which attempted to apply the Halakhah to the needs of a modern army. In doing so, the Army rabbinate achieved what the civilian rabbinate had failed to do. An imaginative Halakhic approach of the Army rabbinate was evolved through the initiative and efforts of the first Army Chief Rabbi, Brigadier General Shlomo Goren, an acknowledged talmudic scholar and Halakhic authority, which made it possible to avoid a gulf between the Halakhah and the needs of the army. Rabbi Goren served in the Defense Army of Israel from its inception in 1948 until 1971, when he retired from active service to become Chief Rabbi of Tel Aviv, and, a year later, Chief Rabbi of Israel. His term of office established a pattern that became firmly entrenched in the life of the army.

The Halakhah has interpreted the doctrine of *Pikuah Nefesh*[101] as applying to the individual only, that is, that it is permissible to violate the Sabbath in order to save a human life. The rabbinate has consistently refused to apply this doctrine to the community at large, and to declare it permissible to violate the Sabbath in order to safeguard the peace and vital needs of the public. Rabbi Goren took a broader view of this doctrine. "The army is necessary for the saving of many lives, for without defense by the army the whole nation is in danger," and it is on the basis of this principle that the religious code for the army was evolved.[102] The principle was: "What is prohibited to a religious soldier is also prohibited to the nonreligious soldier, and what is permissible to him is similarly permissible to all. If a task is essential for defense, then there is no desecration of the Sabbath, and the religious soldier should perform that task himself, and not attempt to find a non-religious soldier who does not mind working on the Sabbath." Thus, by extending the doctrine of *Pikuah Nefesh* beyond its original confines and by attaching to the preservation of organized society the same importance that the Halakhah attaches to the preservation of the individual, a way was found to apply the Halakhah to the needs of the army.

The provisions dealing with matters of religion in relation to the army were incorporated in a code of "Orders and Instructions in Religious Matters," which after approval by the Army Chief of Staff became an integral part of the Army Code.[103] This code deals with matters applying to the army in its entirety, as well as with matters affecting the individual soldier bent on observing the precepts of religion while within a military framework. The basic provisions binding on the entire army are set out in Article 8 of this code:

a) Sabbaths, Holydays and official state holidays as determined by the Knesset shall be complete days of rest for all ranks, and in all installations and institutions of the Defense Army of Israel.

b) On these days all operations shall be discontinued, except such as are most essential for the security of the state, of the army and of its installations, i.e.,

    1) works which constitute a military operation or any part thereof or are auxiliary thereto.

2) works which are urgently required for the defence and security
of the state, which, if not done, would endanger the security of
the state and the essential functions of the army and its installations, or would harm the war effort, the army or its installations.

To remove any doubt as to the duties of a soldier who is Orthodox,
the code further provides that "work essential for the war effort and
which suffers no delay shall be performed on the Sabbath and the Holydays."[104] These provisions, in fact, represented a restatement of *Pikuah
Nefesh* as applied to the needs of organized society and consequently
obligatory upon the observant Jew. Unlike in the police force and in
other essential civilian services, where civil servants are released from
duty on the Sabbath, Halakhah as interpreted by the military chaplaincy
precludes the employment of the "Shabbat Goy," or even the "Shabbat
(secular) Jew," in the army.

While, however, the Army rabbinate made it obligatory for Orthodox soldiers to perform essential duties on the Sabbath and religious
Holydays, it also imposed religious norms upon the entire army. Thus,
not only must all food served by the army be kasher, but no food may
be cooked on the Sabbath; it may merely be kept warm, provided the
warming process began before the Sabbath set in.[105] Elaborate procedures have been set out for cleaning all kitchens, as well as all cutlery
and food containers before the Passover festival, when not only bread
but many other categories of food must be eliminated. Food parcels
sent to soldiers on the eve of Passover may not be distributed until
after the holiday is over, lest they contain food unfit for Passover consumption.[106] Smoking on the Sabbath is forbidden in dining-rooms, nor
may music be played, either recorded or by radio, in dining-rooms or
other meeting halls. When asked in the Knesset whether it was true that
soldiers in the army camps were not allowed on the Sabbath to turn on
the radio, to hear recorded music, nor to dance to the accompaniment
of music, the Prime Minister and Minister of Defense Levi Eshkol replied on February 17, 1964, that this was indeed the case, and that the
Army High Command had sanctioned it.[107]

The Army Code on religion also deals with matters that are applicable to observant soldiers only. In order to achieve unity among the
observant, the Army rabbinate introduced a uniform prayer book, as
well as a uniform service for Sabbaths and Holydays; thus soldiers,
whether Ashkenazic or Sefardic or Yemenite or of other communities
with differing prayer patterns, may worship together in accordance with
a standard model, unusual for the religious life of Israel.[108] Provisions
are likewise made for such matters as haircutting and shaving, so that

they may be performed in accordance with Halakhic precepts.*[109] For emergency situations there are special provisions for abridged services, or for the performance of religious duties by individual soldiers when on the battlefield or in other extremities. For instance, soldiers in exposed positions are exempt from the duty of blowing the shofar during the Rosh Hashanah service.[110] During the Yom Kippur fast, a soldier in battle, in order to preserve his fighting ability, "must eat in order not to jeopardize the result of the battle."[111] Thus, the entire code is permeated with a far-ranging approach to the doctrine of *Pikuah Nefesh*.

Unlike the civilian Chief Rabbinate, whose attitude to Independence Day has remained ambivalent, the Army rabbinate has invested the day with full religious significance, and the order of worship includes the full Hallel prayer, as befits a Holyday.[112] A suitable prayer for the well-being of the state was specially composed and included in this service. Special prayers were also composed for soldiers on the eve of battle, for pilots, paratroopers, and submarine personnel.[113] It may thus be seen that, in contrast to the official rabbinate, the Army rabbinate unqualifiedly identifies itself with the state and with the interest of the nation as a whole. By so doing, it has been successful in its appeal to the entire army to forgo certain conveniences and practices and to acquiesce in a series of arrangements designed to make their Orthodox comrades feel at ease in a mixed religious milieu. Consequently, the avoidance of nonkasher food or of music on the Sabbath is regarded by the majority of uniformed young men and women not as an odious imposition but rather as a necessity justified by the national interest.

The activities of the Army rabbinate have expanded beyond the immediate military sphere, and in certain areas have encroached on the rabbinical courts. Thus, the Army Code empowers chaplains to celebrate marriages of soldiers who are duly registered as eligible for marriage by the civil rabbinate.[114] A rather unusual ruling was introduced into the Army Code that makes it obligatory for every married soldier to execute a power of attorney to deliver a bill of divorcement (*get*) to his wife in case he disappears without trace and his death cannot be established in accordance with the Halakhic rules of evidence. In this way a potential widow is released from the danger of becoming an Agunah.[115] The disaster that befell the submarine *Dakar* on January 25, 1968, led to considerable public agitation for fear that a large number of Agunot had been created by it. The ship was on its maiden voyage from England to Israel and disappeared under circumstances that to this day have not been accounted for. The entire crew of 69 was and is

---

* Traditional law prohibits the use of razors for such purposes, to conform to the biblical command not to cut the corners of the beard (Lev. 19:27; 21:5).

missing. Since there were no survivors, nor any witnesses to the tragedy, nor could the sunken submarine itself be located, there was no direct evidence to establish the deaths of the members of the crew as required by the rules of the Halakhah. In this, as well as in other instances, Rabbi Goren was able to evolve a Halakhic solution, which saved the unfortunate widows an added cause of distress.

Clearly the Army rabbinate is committed to the stance of "Bet Hillel" (House of Hillel) with its more lenient interpretation of the Halakhah, rather than to that of "Bet Shammal" (House of Shammal) with its stricter interpretation.* The divergence between the civilian religious establishment, which generally follows the latter mood, and the Army rabbinate with its leaning toward the former, is in no small measure due to the fact that the civilian rabbis have remained isolated from the people and their problems, and too often have simply relied on the coercive power vested in them by the law of the land; while the Army chaplains live and function among the soldiers, and are thus intimately aware of their problems and, in order to deserve their respect, have to rely on persuasion and personal example.

The Army rabbinate is headed by a chief rabbi holding the rank of brigadier general, who is appointed by the Minister of Defense. Ordained rabbis, with preference given to university graduates, are attached to regiments, while "officers of religion," not necessarily ordained rabbis, are attached to battalions. "Sergeants of religion" are attached to smaller units. In addition, Kashrut supervisors and cantors are appointed as part of the military establishment. All Army rabbis and officers of religion are required to complete the military training provided by the officers' training corps, and in this way they become an integral part of their units, performing military duties when the need arises, and participating in operations alongside the other officers.

The total indentification of the Army rabbinate with the army as a whole is largely the result of the personal example set by Rabbi Goren. He himself completed training as a parachutist, followed the army during fighting, and during the war of attrition that terminated in a cease-fire in August 1970, spent many days in the exposed bunkers along the Suez Canal, and helped to sustain the morale of soldiers during the massive and prolonged shelling. He would appear in the most dangerous spots at critical moments, in total disregard of his personal safety.[116] Rabbi Goren tried to emphasize that he was in no way a Halakhic innovator, nor did he incline toward religious reforms. On the crucial issue of employing the authority of the state in order to coerce people in matters of religious observance, he was on the side of the civilian rab-

---

* The academies of Hillel and Shammal represented two differing approaches to Jewish law at the beginning of the Current Era.

binate. "We are commanded," he wrote, "by the Halakhah and by the rules of logic to employ the instrumentalities of the state in order to ensure the observance by the people of the Torah, its values and its precepts. . . . The Torah and the ethical teachings of the prophets sanction coercion by the state."[117] Nevertheless, by adopting a new approach to the doctrine of *Pikuah Nefesh,* and by adhering to the School of Hillel, Rabbi Goren has broken fresh ground—though lately (after he left the army) not without bitter and even violent opposition.[118]

The Army rabbinate has had the further advantage of being totally independent of the civilian Chief Rabbinate, since it derives its authority from the Army Code. "The Army Chief Rabbi is the competent authority to pass judgment in matters of Halakhah and the laws of the Jewish religion in the Defense Army of Israel," is the opening clause of the Code.[119] Thus, his decisions in matters of Halakhah are not subject to judicial review by the Chief Rabbinate. The Army religious establishment is outside party politics and independent of the religious parties, and this fact has given it enhanced prestige.

Judging by most standards, the Army rabbinate may be regarded as a success, and no serious objection has been raised either to its position and practices or to the restrictions imposed at its instance on the great majority of soldiers who are nonobservant. The religious establishment in the Army, far from turning soldiers against religion, has frequently succeeded in inculcating in many secular soldiers a positive attitude toward tradition. Successful as the Army rabbinate has been in this respect, its impact on the official rabbinate has been negligible.

9

Who Is a Jew?

A. THE SCOPE OF THE PROBLEM

Of the many controversies periodically agitating public opinion in Israel, none is more acute and more fraught with emotion than the legal, religious, and historical definition of a Jew. No other issue has engendered so much dissension and public debate as this one. While the Jews in the Diaspora ever since the Emancipation have been increasingly concerned with the problem of Jewish identity in relation to the modern world and to an open secular society, in Israel the problem has been focused not on the nature of this identity but on the legal definition of *who* a Jew is. In the sovereign Jewish state the problem of *what* a Jew is arouses little public debate. The Jews in Israel, with their differing attitudes toward religion, proceed on the assumption that they know what being a Jew means; they feel that they are in the process of evolving out of the heterogeneous Jewish communities a Jewish nation, possessing a broad although not always readily identifiable common denominator. Secularists and Orthodox Jews regard each other as full-fledged Jews, rightful members of the "kingdom of priests and a holy people," who together form one indissoluble community. But while the discussion of "What is a Jew?" is conducted on a theoretical or philosophical plane, the question "Who is a Jew?" has sought a definitive answer and has generated a gamut of responses ranging from scholarly contemplation to acrimonious debate and political crisis.

To many outsiders, the very existence of this problem is puzzling. Here is a people with a history of over three thousand years, who have survived many adversities because of their very determination to remain Jews, and who have recently achieved statehood—yet they are concerned with defining who they are! Gentiles seem to know who a Jew is, and anti-Semites have considered themselves experts in this field. Adolf Hitler in Nazi Germany and Benito Mussolini in Fascist Italy determined the question in their respective legislative enactments without asking the Jews. In the Diaspora the question has been considered as a spiritual problem and of little practical import, but in Israel it has become a serious legal and political issue.

Historical Notes

The question of what or who a Jew is did not arise until the end of the eighteenth century, when the advent of Emancipation led to a revaluation of the nature and essence of Judaism. While in the history of the Diaspora there had been organized attempts to modify the Halakhah, or even to depart from it, as in the case of the Karaites, the Jewish religion remained on the whole monolithic, and Halakhah was universally accepted as normative Judaism. The foundation of Judaism was the Covenant between God and His people; it was a faith granted to or accepted by a defined group. Thus, the practice of Judaism became the exclusive possession of one people only. Consequently, one could not be a member of the Jewish people without professing the Jewish religion, while by the profession of this religion one became a Jew. According to the Halakhah, a person could not opt out of his Jewish affiliation, even if he opted out of his religion. Thus, in the view of the Halakhah, a Jew who converted to another religion was still a Jew, though a sinner. "Israel who has sinned is still Israel" was an established Halakhic maxim; thus a Jew who had converted to Christianity but was desirous of returning to the fold did not need to be reconverted, merely to repent. One could join the Jewish people only by adopting the Jewish faith; in other words, admission to the Jewish people was possible only through the Jewish religion. One was a Jew by birth if both parents were Jewish. A child, one of whose parents was not a Jew, took his status from the mother. The Halakhic definition therefore was: a Jew is a person born to a Jewish mother, or one who has been converted to Judaism. The indissolubility of the religious and national components of Jewish existence was the underlying and unquestioned principle of Jewish identity.

Two hundred years ago, the phenomenon of a secular Jew was unthinkable. To be a Jew was not merely to have a passive membership in a community, carried over by inheritance from one's mother, but to be evidenced by the active observance of the commandments as set out in the Halakhah and codified in the Shulhan Arukh. Failure to observe was discouraged by the possibility that a *herem* might be imposed, the Jewish form of excommunication, which involved the culprit in the choice between two alternatives: to return to observing the divinely ordained Mitzvot, or to be ostracized. To be nonobservant and yet remain a Jew in the community was, in fact, an impossibility. One's Jewish identity was demonstrated by the observance of the rules laid down by one's religion. The very notion of a secular Jew constituted a contradiction in terms. Thus, he who abandoned religious observance was almost inevitably one who had the intention of leaving the Jewish fold, for there was no category of Jews who were Jewish and yet nonobservant. Consequently, even the nonobservant created no Halakhic issue, for by leaving the Jewish fold they removed the problem itself.

In pre-exilic days Jews had constituted a nation, with all that implies—the observant and nonobservant, the religious and nonreligious—but in the course of time they had evolved into a community that was predominantly religion-oriented, while the national element was downgraded. Both fusion and the eventual fission of religion and nation paralleled the earlier development in the wider European society, where the process of secularization transformed religious entities into nations. This development, which gained momentum with the disruption of the monolithic Catholic Church early in the sixteenth century, made its appearance among the Jewish people late in the eighteenth.

From the nineteenth century on, the traditional answer to "What is a Jew?" no longer obtained. With the rise of Reform Judaism early in the nineteenth century the monolithic structure of Judaism was shattered. The adherents of strict Halakhah became known as Orthodox,* as distinct from their rivals, who also claimed to be giving legitimate expression to Torah Judaism. It thus came about that abandonment of some or many of the Halakhically ordained Mitzvot no longer constituted a move toward leaving the Jewish fold, but created a novel phenomenon in the history of the Jewish religion in the Diaspora, the advent of religious pluralism, as distinguished from regional and cultural variations, which carried with it a plurality of interpretations of Jewish identity. During the struggle to achieve legal and political emancipation, there were Jews, as there were Gentiles, who separated Judaism as a religion from its national character. These Jews were mostly adherents of Reform, but there were Orthodox Jews also who adopted this point of view. In addition, the state authorities generally preferred to deal with Jews as individuals professing faith rather than treat them as a nation within a nation. Consequently, at the end of the nineteenth century the definition of a Jew acquired religious emphasis—though often for somewhat different reasons than in the past.

---

* Originally they were known as "Conservatives"; the term *Orthodox* was a later cognomen. The Reformers in turn developed a radical ("classical") and a conservative wing; the latter separated into a distinct "Conservative" movement at the beginning of the twentieth century. In Israel, an Orthodox Jew is known as *dati* (literally, "law-abiding"), plural *datiim*.

But there were significant exceptions among the Jews themselves; those who considered themselves to be nationalist Jews, although they had abandoned all, or the majority of, religious observances, or had declared themselves to be agnostics or even atheists. This new type of secular Jew became the most dynamic force in modern Jewish history. By accepting the prevalent nineteenth-century ideal of liberal nationalism, secular Judaism secured a theoretical foundation. Whether organized as Folkists, who advocated a Jewish national existence in the Diaspora within a framework of national minority rights, or in the Bund, which attempted to organize Jews within a socialist context, or in the Zionist movement, which preached a Jewish national renaissance in the ancient homeland—all were expressions of secular Judaism. Although religious, cultural, and ethnic elements remained inextricably intertwined in these new expressions of Jewish life, the national element emerged as dominant.

Thus, a number of new options became available to the Jew. He could practice Orthodoxy as his forefathers did; if he wished to retain a definite religious affiliation without Orthodoxy, he could identify himself with either Conservative or Reform Judaism. Or he could remain a Jew without religious affiliation and yet pursue a variety of Jewish interests and activities. One could now be a committed Jew, although uncommitted in terms of religion. This latter type, the secular Jew, became increasingly conspicuous following the establishment of the State of Israel. To a great many Jews of the Diaspora, work for and on behalf of Israel afforded a new content for Jewish commitment, while to the Jew in Israel, the upbuilding of the homeland was in itself a Jewish way of life. If the question "Who is a Jew?" were to be answered in terms of the Jewish commitments of particular individuals, the variety of criteria would call forth correspondingly different responses, and the Halakhic definition would be only one of several. Furthermore, while in the Diaspora one is usually a Jew only on a part-time basis, in Israel one is a Jew on a full-time basis, for living and working in a society that is Jewish and is dedicated to promotion of Jewish interests is in itself a Jewish commitment.

While in the last two centuries, and in particular since the Holocaust, the Jewish landscape has changed beyond recognition, the Halakhic conception of the Jew has remained unaltered. In the Diaspora this has not generally led to great difficulties. In North America, Conservative, Reform, and occasionally Orthodox synagogues admit proselytes; the process of admission is through conversion to the Jewish faith, with each of the three major religious groups providing its own standards and procedures of admission. While the Reform and the Conservatives generally treat a non-Jew converted to Judaism by any of the three groups as a full-fledged Jew, the Orthodox usually recognize their own conversions only. In some instances such limited recognition may create difficulties for those immediately involved, but no communal crises of any extent have developed as a result of it. The absence of any serious controversy in the Diaspora communities over this problem is due to the fact that the law of the land is not called upon to resolve it. No legislative enactment is called for or is even possible, and the state authorities are indifferent to it, leaving the matter entirely to individuals concerned and their voluntary associations to deal with it in accordance with their own lights.

Not so in Israel. There, the problem has become acute because it is expected to find its solution by legislative enactment, rather than by groupings of individual citizens organized in voluntary religious or secular associations. In a way, the problem was already built into Israel's Declaration of Independence, which proclaimed "the establishment of a *Jewish* state in Eretz Israel, to be known as the State of Israel," and charged with the mission of the ingathering of the exiles from the four corners of the earth. The process of ingathering, to be effective, had to be followed by a process of fusion. The exiles who came from a variety of cultures, backgrounds, and historic experiences, and speaking many different languages, had to be fused into a national entity. *Kibbutz galuyot* ("ingathering of the exiles") had to be followed by *mizug galuyot* ("fusion of exiles"). It soon transpired that both of these historic processes required an acceptable definition of the term *Jew*. Disappointment was in store for those who believed that, in a sovereign state, where the Jews constituted the majority group and where the danger of assimilation into an alien society was nonexistent, this problem would easily lend itself to a flexible solution. It was in the Jewish state that the question proved intractable, and this in turn caused repercussions in the Diaspora, too.

The young state found itself faced with the need to determine whether a particular individual was a Jew in the contemplation of the law. Once the Law of Return was enacted, the question was bound to arise. Being a civil and not a religious law, it had to be administered by the civil authorities; in the eyes of the Orthodox, however, it involved a religious problem that had to be governed by the rules of the Halakhah. In the application of the laws of marriage and divorce, administered by the rabbinical courts, problems were also bound to emerge, since the Halakhic definition of "Who is a Jew" determined eligibility for marriage. In none of the laws in which the word *Jew* is mentioned, is the term defined. The legislature deliberately avoided a definition, preferring ad hoc settlements and a variety of adjustments to a decision on the applicability of the Orthodox definition.

While to the Orthodox the definition of the term Jew is a religious problem, to the others it poses considerations of national interest. The

Israeli leadership is understandably anxious to remove technical and legal obstacles to the admission of persons who regard themselves as bona fide Jews, and who by opting to settle in Israel have expressed a commitment to assume the burdens of citizenship in a Jewish state. The government has been equally eager to see to it that a person, once admitted, suffer no disability by reason of a Halakhic defect in his ancestry, and that no hindrance be placed in his way to establish a family.

The Orthodox position, taking its stand solely on the Halakhic definition, takes no cognizance of possible adverse effects on immigration, on *kibbutz galuyot,* and on *mizug galuyot.* They demand the enactment of legislation incorporating the Halakhic definition of Jew. Such legislation would be of unique character, for it would apply not only to persons residing within the jurisdiction of the State of Israel, but also to Jews the world over. By enacting such a law, the State of Israel would, inter alia, deny the Jewishness of persons who regard themselves as Jews and are regarded as such by the vast majority of Jews both in the Diaspora and in Israel. Such legislation would affect adherents of Reform and Conservative Judaism and deny them legitimacy, and thus antagonize these two major religious groups that afford significant assistance to the upbuilding of the Jewish state.

Because of unusual historical circumstances in which some of the dispersed Jewish communities found themselves, certain Halakhic provisions were either neglected or deliberately set aside. However, the communities remained Jewish in their own eyes and were regarded as Jews by the non-Jews in whose midst they dwelt. Among these, the Bene Israel and the Karaites were the first to test the definition of "Who is a Jew?"

B. THE BENE ISRAEL

Little is known of the origin of the Bene Israel (literally, "Children of Israel"), the oldest Jewish community in India. Legend has it that they are descendants of Jews who arrived in India in the second century B.C., fleeing the persecutions of Antiochus Epiphanes in Palestine. They concentrated in the Bombay area and were called by their neighbors "Shanwar Telis," words that suggest that oil-pressing was their main occupation, and that the Sabbath was their special day of sanctity. In their mode of living, language, and custom they assimilated to the ways of the Hindus, but always considered themselves to be observant Jews. Of the Hebrew language they had preserved only the words of the *Shema* prayer, but they circumcised their children, kept most of the Jewish festivals, the laws of the Sabbath, and some of the dietary laws. In the days of British rule in India, many army recruits were Bene Israel, a considerable number reaching officer rank; they were also prominent in the Indian Civil Service.

The arrival in India of a number of Jews from Baghdad in the first half of the nineteenth century brought the Bene Israel for the first time into contact with other coreligionists. With the aid of rabbis and educators from Baghdad, and the schools opened by them, the Bene Israel were brought closer to Jewish tradition and learning, and in the closing years of that century they published their own prayer books and periodicals. In 1897, Theodore Herzl included them in those invited to send representatives to the First Zionist Congress held in Basel. They declined the invitation, for they were awaiting the restoration of the Jewish kingdom by Divine hand, and did not feel that they could recognize a human agency that aspired to that end.[1] They changed their attitude in time and in 1919 established a Zionist association and contributed funds for Zionist activity in Palestine. In 1881, they numbered about 7,000 souls, but by the middle of the twentieth century their number had increased to 24,000.[2]

While the Jewish origin of the Bene Israel was not questioned, some of their practices raised doubts as to their eligibility to marry Jews of other communities. The rabbis who first arrived in India from Baghdad observed that divorces were not carried out in strict accordance with Halakhic provisions, and that the rite of Halitzah was not observed at all. These deviations from the Halakhah raised the question of possible *mamzerut*. In 1944, a member of the Bene Israel wanted to marry a Jew of another community; the matter was referred to the then two Chief Rabbis of Palestine, Isaac Halevy Herzog and Ben-Zion Meir Hai Uziel, who ruled that marriage was permissible.

Since the establishment of the state, and until the end of the 1960s, about 12,000 Bene Israel, nearly half of the entire community, emigrated to Israel. They concentrated mainly in Beersheba, Ashdod, and Eilat. Although their communal attachment still remained strong and the process of their absorption was at first slow, the younger generation tended to integrate into Israeli society. However, in 1954 the right of the Bene Israel to marry other Jews in Israel was questioned again. The dispute aroused the indignation of Bene Israel, developed into a major public issue in Israel, and was debated in India as well.[3]

In the initial stages of the controversy, Chief Rabbi Isaac Nissim appointed a commission to investigate the problem. The Supreme Rabbinical Council, after studying the report of the commission, issued the following ruling in 1961: "There are no doubts concerning the Judaism of Bene Israel. From the earliest period they have been closely bound to, and maintained relations with, the seed of Israel. Because, however, they were cut off for a long period from the centers of Torah, Halakhic concern has arisen over the procedures and the laws of marriage and

divorce practices which prevailed among them."[4] The representatives of
Bene Israel rejoiced at this decision, especially at the confirmation of
their Jewishness, but before long the refusal of a number of rabbis in
some cities to celebrate "mixed" marriages led to serious controversy,
and the Chief Rabbinate was urged to issue clear directives to the local
authorities.[5]

In February 1962, the Chief Rabbinate finally issued directives:

"When a request is made to register a marriage between a member
of the Bene Israel community and a person not belonging to that community, it is incumbent upon the registering rabbi:

a) to search and investigate whether the mother and grandmother of
a Bene Israel applicant, and as far back as possible, was a Jewess or
of families which had married with non-Jews or proselytes, and
b)   to ascertain if the parents of the applicant, and their parents, as
far back as possible, had married after divorce, or any among them had
married kin forbidden by Jewish law.
c) Should the registrar rabbi find that none of the above doubts exists,
he will then marry the applicants. Should such doubts arise, the registrar
rabbi will direct the applicants to the district rabbinical court, which
will consider the question and decide whether the marriage is permissible or not, and, if permissible, whether there is a need for conversion
or immersion."[6]

The Bene Israel community was up in arms. Mass meetings were
held, and their community in India was alerted. In the Indian press
articles appeared accusing Israel of racism. The Bene Israel Actions
Committee condemned the directives as discriminatory, and stated that
no Jew would agree to an investigation of his lineage. In the meantime,
reports from various localities indicated that the registering rabbis were
refusing to celebrate "mixed" marriages of Bene Israel, while in other
places, the registering rabbis raised no objection and did register such
"mixed" marriages.[7] In the face of rising emotions, Dr. Zerah Wahrhaftig, Minister of Religions, suggested that regional registrars be appointed to celebrate "mixed" marriages, that is, registering rabbis known
for their more liberal attitude toward the problem should be authorized
to celebrate marriages even of persons residing outside their jurisdiction.
In the course of a parliamentary debate held on July 9, 1962, the original decision of Chief Rabbi Nissim was said to have been intended to
qualify all Bene Israel for marriage with persons outside the community,
and that the directives of February 1962 had been issued as a result of
pressure by extremists within the rabbinate itself.[8] It appeared that the
controversy reflected a struggle for power within the Chief Rabbinate.
The *Jerusalem Post*[9] reported Mafdal to be "seriously embarrassed by
the Bene Israel dispute, especially so because of the split it has en-

gendered between members of the Chief Rabbinical Council," who were now "hardly on speaking terms." The refusal of the rabbis of Eilat, Yokneam, and Herzliah to register "mixed" marriages was regarded as an attempt to embarrass Chief Rabbi Nissim.

In another editorial the *Jerusalem Post* dealt with the wider issues involved, and their impact on future developments. "In a sense it is good that the matter has come to a head. One day we may have to face the problem in a quantitatively much greater dimension—when Russian Jews, whose Jewish religious-legal family status is also in question, and American Jews, many of whom will be children of Conservative or Reform marriages, which the Israel rabbinate does not recognize, start coming in larger numbers. Meanwhile, perhaps, our national character will have crystallized a little more—the Bene Israel problem will have been solved, and we shall again have acquired a religious leadership of sufficient stature as to feel able to make a decision that will be recognized and followed."[10]

Meanwhile, the Actions Committee of Bene Israel took to demonstrations in the streets and finally requested the Jewish Agency to return their people to India, where they would suffer no discrimination. There were rumors that the Bene Israel were about to apply to the United Nations and to claim the rights due to them under the Charter of Human Rights.[11] The problem was raised again in the Knesset.[12] Agitation continued, and during the morning of July 21, 1964, representatives of Bene Israel arrived in Jerusalem from many localities in Israel, encamped in the courtyard of the Jewish Agency compound, and declared a hunger strike. They demanded the annulment of the directives issued by the Chief Rabbinate that provided for investigations into their ancestry; they claimed that such investigation was discriminatory inasmuch as it was not required of Jews belonging to other communities. Under pressure of public opinion, an extraordinary session of the Knesset was summoned during the parliamentary recess and took place on August 17, 1964. A national conference of rabbis, held the previous night, warned the Knesset to keep its hands off the controversy. The debate in the Knesset was opened by Prime Minister Levi Eshkol, who stated that the Cabinet had adopted a series of resolutions on the issue, among them the following:

a) The government of Israel declares that it regards the Bene Israel of India as Jews in all respects without exception, who are equal to all other Jews in respect of all matters, including matters of personal status.

b) The government declares that it is vital that the rabbinate should pay regard to public opinion, and remove the causes that have given rise to a feeling of injustice and discrimination.

This resolution of the Cabinet, submitted to the Knesset for approval, was in many respects a far-reaching innovation. The government thereby assumed the authority to declare that a certain group of persons were Jews, an authority that the rabbinate had and always considered to be within its exclusive competence. Furthermore, in declaring such persons to be Jews in all respects, "including matters of personal status," the government, speaking on behalf of the nation, was declaring "who is a Jew." In his speech Eshkol pointed out that the ingathering of the exiles was the major task of this generation. Turning to the rabbinate he stated: "We expect, we are entitled to expect, a solution in the spirit of love of Israel, a solution that will enable us to gather in the scattered tribes without let or hindrance. Out of consideration for *Klal Yisrael,* our law has entrusted matters of personal status to the hands of the rabbis; but this deed of trust carries with it an obligation: the rabbinate is in duty bound to observe the greatest Mitzvah of our age, to enable our people to lead their own lives and to reassemble the dispersed."

It was the first instance in the annals of the state that the leader of government had told the rabbinate that they had to concern themselves as much with the national interest as with the Halakhah. "It is up to the rabbis to assume the burden of this Mitzvah, to foresee the future, and to avoid dangerous conflicts between the Halakhah and the needs of a nation in the process of revival, a conflict that is liable to shatter its exclusive power and authority."

It was one of the tensest debates in the history of the Knesset. Obviously more was at stake than the Bene Israel problem. If the ancestry of each Jew was to be investigated in accordance with the rabbinic decree, the consequences could be incalculable. In the debate Yisrael Yeshayahu summed it up: "These directives make one shudder. This may mean that from now on, such investigation will be imposed upon Conservative and Reform Jews from America and Europe; they will be followed by Jews from Russia, of whom it will be said, as has already been said about Bene Israel, that there are doubts as to whether their marriages and divorces were in accordance with the Halakhah," and he concluded by saying to the rabbis: "If there is no alternative, we shall summon the power of the legislature to put each matter and each institution in its right place."

Only the deputies of Agudat Israel and Poalei Aguda lent their unqualified support to the rabbinate. Agudat Israel recommended that the Knesset consider the rabbis and the rabbinical courts to be subject "to the eternal Halakhah only, that they accept no authority that may be imposed upon them by the secular power, and that any pressure that may be brought upon them be condemned." Poalei Agudat Israel moved that the Knesset dissociate itself "from any attempt to undermine the exclusive authority of the rabbis in matters of religion and religious law." Both motions were defeated by an overwhelming majority.[13] Mafdal, being part of the coalition, voted for the government-sponsored motion, however embarrassing this was to its traditional ideas, and the Knesset approved the government's proposal.[14]

The debate clearly gave expression to the pent-up indignation of the nation over the policies of the Supreme Rabbinical Council. The latter, highly critical of the tenor and outcome of the decision, heeded the warning. While there was no official cancellation of the directives issued by the Chief Rabbinate, no instance was henceforth brought to public attention of a member of Bene Israel being subjected to an investigation of his ancestry or denied the possibility of marriage with whomever he wished. It was the first time that the representatives of the people, expressing the national interest as they saw it, assumed authority in an area that the rabbis had heretofore regarded as their exclusive privilege, thereby implying that where the Halakhah and the national interest clash, the latter will prevail.

C. THE KARAITES

In the ninth century A.D. existing schismatic elements within the Jewish community of Babylonia were given cohesion and leadership by Anan ben David.[15] He founded a movement that rejected the Oral Law evolved in Mishnah and Talmud and interpreted by the rabbis over the generations, and called for a return to the Scriptures as sole authority. The first members of the sect were known as Ananites but, as their doctrines were more fully developed, they came to be called Karaites, that is, "readers of the Scriptures,"* while the adherents of the Talmud were referred to by them as Rabbanites.

In trying to return to the Bible, the Karaites abolished such hallmarks as *tefillin* (phylacteries worn in the course of the morning service on weekdays by males over the age of 13) and *Mezuzot* (small parchments containing the first two paragraphs of the *Shema* prayer to be affixed to doorposts). They adopted a more rigid interpretation of biblical laws relating to Sabbath observance, ritual cleanliness, and degrees of propinquity in marriage. No light or fire was permitted on the Sabbath, and no work was permitted to be done by a non-Jew for a Karaite. Their liturgy featured biblical selections. Simple Hebrew formulas were employed for the marriage ceremony and for divorce proceedings instead of the lengthy and involved formulas in Aramaic used by the

---

* Another interpretation is "callers" or "propagandists."

rabbis. Individual but literal interpretation was the rule for scriptural reading, a prescription repeated 700 years later by the Protestant reformers in the Christian context.

During the early centuries of its existence, Karaism spread widely among the Jews, and claimed many converts in Babylonia, Egypt, Palestine, Syria, and Persia. The unrestricted study of the Bible as the only source of religion was attractive not only to members of earlier anti-rabbinic sects, but also to the more liberal elements within traditional Judaism who were dissatisfied with what they considered the increasing stagnation in the Babylonian academies. Before long the movement spread into Byzantium with its large Jewish community, and after the twelfth century to the Crimea and to Eastern Europe. By the end of the twelfth century, however, Karaism began to wane; its literary output declined, and its rigid adherence to biblical injunctions caused a state of stagnation. At the time of the Second World War there were about 12,000 Karaites in the world.

Relations between the Karaites and rabbinic Jews varied over the centuries. Instances of intermarriage were not unknown, particularly in Egypt, and there were Karaite scholars known to study under Rabbanites. Over the years, however, as the two groups drew further apart, both instituted a ban on marriage with the other. The Karaites in Russia sought and received exemption from some of the Czarist restrictions imposed on Jews, and they were generally saved from the Holocaust because the Germans believed that Karaites were not Jews. The establishment of the State of Israel aroused hostility toward them in Arab countries and in turn encouraged Karaites to aspire to reunification with the Jewish people, thus healing the thousand-year-old schism. Prominent Karaites in Egypt performed valuable services on behalf of the Jewish state, and sometimes did so at the risk and sacrifice of their lives. By the end of the 1950s almost the entire Karaite community of Egypt, numbering some 7,000 souls, had emigrated to Israel, which thus became the center of the remnant of a once-influential community. About half of them live in the Ramleh District, the others in Ashdod, Ofakim, Beersheba, and Acre.

The Karaite elders, with the active aid of the Ministry of Religious Affairs, established a religious court in Ramleh to deal with matters of personal status. Although this court was not created by law like other recognized religious courts, the Ministry and the local religious councils at the request of the Ministry, allocated public funds for its maintenance. In spite of its lack of legal authority, the court has adjudicated matters of personal status where both parties to the proceedings were Karaites.[16]

The rabbinical courts interpret the Halakhah to prohibit the marriage between Karaite and non-Karaite.[17] A tug-of-war within the Karaite community has been in progress ever since its arrival in Israel: the older generation insist on an ecclesiastical establishment of its own, while the younger element urge total integration within the Jewish community and an obliteration of past differences. A number of them have even succeeded in marrying into the general community by concealing their origin. These problems have from time to time become the subject of public discussion, and were raised in the Knesset on several occasions.[18]

In 1964 the Karaite court issued a decree of divorce against the wishes of the husband. The latter then applied to the High Court of Justice for an order *nisi,* calling on the three members of the Karaite Court to show cause why the decree of divorce should not be set aside, on the grounds that the three Karaites who purported to constitute the court were in fact members of an institution that had never been recognized by the law of the land as possessing jurisdiction. The representative of the Attorney-General who appeared at the hearing declared that "the documents purporting to be a 'decree of divorce' and a 'certificate of divorce' had no legal validity, and that the Ministry of Religious Affairs never intended nor purported to grant validity" to such decrees. As a result of the nonrecognition of the judicial status of the Karaite court, this decree, as well as decrees and decisions issued by it on all previous occasions, became of no legal force or effect. Thus the entire Karaite community found itself in a position where its members were denied the judicial authority that could legally adjudicate matters of personal status.

Subsequently, the Ministry of Religious Affairs appointed a public commission, headed by deputy Chief Justice Moshe Silberg, to examine the legal position of marriages and divorces among the Karaites and recommend the legal and administrative steps to be taken in order to "solve problems concerned with matters of marriage and divorce among Karaites, for the benefit of that community." It was thus obvious that the terms of reference of the commission excluded any authority to find ways and means that would enable the Karaites to marry non-Karaite Jews and place them on an equal footing with the entire Jewish community in Israel. While the authority of the commission was thus confined, its members nevertheless raised and considered the question of their integration into the totality of Israel.

In its report, the commission established the Halakhic principle guiding the question of marriages between Karaite Jews and others. While the Halakhah recognizes the Karaites as Jews, it prohibits marriages between Karaites and Rabbanites. This prohibition is grounded in the slight difference between the rabbinic and the Karaite *get.** The latter is in-

---

* Divorce document.

valid in the eyes of the Halakhah, and consequently a woman divorced through a Karaite *get* remains in Halakhic consideration a married woman, and any children born to her from a second marriage are *mamzerim*,* a status adhering to their descendants also. Even if a Karaite can prove that there have been no instances of divorce in his ancestry, he will not be allowed to marry a non-Karaite Jew, for the *safek mamzer* (suspicion of illicit birth) is considered to apply to the whole Karaite community, and the *safek mamzer* himself is treated like a *mamzer*.[19]

The two Chief Rabbis appeared before the commission and were asked whether the breach with the Karaites could be healed by lifting the ban on marriage. Said Chief Rabbi Nissim: "I once said to the Minister for Religious Affairs that he should summon the elders of the Karaites and ask them whether they were prepared to give up their beliefs and join the full Divine Heritage. . . . There is no point in raising this question until they have been summoned and expressed their opinion." When asked about the position of an individual Karaite, Rabbi Nissim replied: "We will not admit an individual. There is no remedy for him. His position is worse than that of a Christian who desires to be converted, because of the suspicion of *mamzerut*.** When asked whether he could promise that the ban on marriages would be lifted once the Karaites abjure their beliefs and join the full Divine Heritage, Rabbi Nissim asserted that no such promise could be made.[20]

Chief Rabbi Unterman was equally emphatic: "Can the breach be healed by lifting the ban on marriage? To me this is the same as if one asked whether the distance between Moscow and St. Petersburg could be obliterated by removing the road signs between the two cities. Such action would not bring the two nearer. Our position was established in the course of generations, and the ancients imposed a curse on those who would lift the marriage ban. Thus lifting the ban is an impossibility."[21]

The spokesman for the Karaites, who represented the clergy and elders, pleaded that his community be granted the status of a separate religious group like the Druze, in which case it would enjoy the privileges of a special Karaite religious court that would exercise jurisdiction in matters of personal status affecting Karaites. Another spokesman, however, who represented the younger generation of Karaites, advocated a merger with other Jews and a lifting of the marriage ban. His people had come to live in the homeland, he said, and to live in dignity. "If

---

* Offspring of illicit marriages, e.g., adulterous or incestuous unions. To be distinguished from illegitimate children (born of unmarried women), to whom no such disabilities apply.

** The implication was that Karaites were Jews and therefore could not be converted to Judaism.

a separate Karaite community is established, this will mean a schism, which makes no sense at all. I do not want to be a member of a separate community and of a minority group. . . . I have a daughter of 12 and a son of 10, and they do not know that they are Karaites. . . . If we are to be members of a minority group, there is no reason for me to be here. In that case our Aliyah was made in vain." Here was the *cri-de-coeur* of a Jew who had come to his homeland by virtue of the Law of Return, yet found himself once again relegated to minority status. Another Karaite stated: "I belong to a generation that transcends the bounds of a narrow religious sectarianism. I therefore view the entire matter from a broad nationalist point of view, rather than from a religious one. Our community has arrived in the State of Israel, and it is the function of the state to heal the schism."[22]

The majority of the commission members recommended a compromise. They suggested the enactment of a law that would establish a Karaite religious court (but not a separate Karaite community) that would adjudicate matters of personal status where both parties to the proceedings were Karaite Jews, but that they could, if both parties agreed, refer the matter to the rabbinical courts. Thus, while the ban on marriages between the two Jewish groups would not be lifted, the Karaites were at least given the option of access to the rabbinical courts, thus bringing them closer to the larger community. The most significant recommendation was that this law would remain in force for a period of four years only, in the hope that a solution would evolve in the meantime for the healing of the centuries-old schism.

It took some years before the government laid before the Knesset a bill entitled: "Jurisdiction of Karaite-Jewish Courts (Marriages and Divorces) Law,"[23] which provided for the setting up of separate courts for the Karaite Jews; the option of resort to the rabbinical courts was virtually withdrawn, and so was the four years' limitation suggested by the commission. The first reading of the Bill took place on February 2, 1971, and on June 6, 1971, it passed the first reading and was referred to committee. While the voting reflected the discipline imposed by the coalition government, the great majority of the participants in the debate, including supporters of the government, urged the lifting of the ban on marriage and the healing of the breach between the two Jewish groups. The contrary would be achieved by the passage of the proposed law. But a strong appeal for creating unity and accelerating the process of *mizug galuyot* encountered the resistance of the religious parties, which insisted on branding all Karaites as incurably tainted with bastardy and therefore inadmissible to the congregation of Israel.*[24]

---

* At the time of this writing, the bill had not yet reached its final reading.

D. THE CASE OF BROTHER DANIEL

The Law of Return, enacted in 1950, provides that every Jew has the right to come to Israel as an *Oleh* (Hebrew, one who ascends) .[25] Every Jew who expresses his desire to settle in Israel is granted an immigration visa as of right, unless the Minister of the Interior has reason to believe that the applicant is acting against the Jewish people, or is likely to endanger public health or the security of the state. The law was intended to give legal expression to the raison d'être of the Jewish state, which is the Ingathering of the Exiles and was based on the principle that a Jew, wherever he might be, was a potential citizen of the Jewish state. By expressing a desire to settle in Israel, he would acquire the legal right to obtain the visa of an Oleh. A Jew who is already in Israel on a visitor's visa, and subsequently expresses his desire to settle in the country, is entitled to change his status to that of an Oleh.

The status of an Oleh is a privileged one, for Section 4 of the Law of Return provides that "every Jew who immigrated into this country before the coming into force of this law, and every Jew who was born in this country, whether before or after the coming into force of the law, shall be deemed to be a person who has come into the country as an Oleh under the law." Thus, unlike the practice of most other countries, it is not the immigrant whose status is raised to that of the native-born, but rather the natives of the land whose status is raised to that of the Oleh. Implicit in this provision is the view that all Jews in Israel, regardless of their period of stay in the country, are deemed to have come under the Law of Return.

The latter provision is of practical significance in connection with the Nationality Law of 1952, which bestowed Israeli citizenship on every Oleh under the Law of Return.[26] Thus citizenship is acquired automatically upon arrival, unless the Oleh, within a prescribed period of time, chooses to opt out. This automatic acquisition of citizenship is a privilege conferred on Jews; other persons may become Israeli nationals through naturalization.[27]

One further act of legislation bears directly on Jewish status. The Registration of Inhabitance Ordinance, promulgated on February 4, 1949, created a national register of all inhabitants and enjoined all persons who had attained the age of 16 to provide the officials of the Ministry of the Interior with certain particulars concerning themselves.[28] The government then issued such persons their identity cards. Among the particulars to be noted by each inhabitant were his national or ethnic group (Leom), his religion, and his citizenship.[29] The significance of this law is that any person admitted under the Law of Return not only automatically acquires Israeli nationality, but is also registered as a

Jew on his identity card, and is thus eligible to be married to another Jewish person. The application of the Law of Return, of the Nationality Law, and of the Population Registry Law in relation to the definition of the term *Jew* has given rise to some of the most intense and often acrimonious public debates and political confrontations in the history of the state.

In 1962 Brother Daniel, a member of the Order of Carmelites, applied to the Supreme Court for an order *nisi* directing the Minister of the Interior to show cause why he should not issue to him a *Te'udat Oleh* (Oleh's certificate), in accordance with the Law of Return. The Minister of the Interior had ruled that Brother Daniel, having been converted from Judaism to Christianity, could no longer be considered a Jew, and therefore was not entitled to the status of an Oleh under the terms of the Law of Return.

Although the circumstances of the case were extraordinary, the issue involved therein was unmistakably clear. Brother Daniel was born a Jew with the name Oswald Rufeisen, and was brought up as a Jew in Poland by his parents who were Jews. In his youth he was active in the Zionist movement, and after completing his secondary school education he underwent training for pioneering work in Palestine. With the outbreak of the German-Russian war in June 1941, he was imprisoned by the Gestapo but managed to escape; he succeeded in obtaining a certificate to the effect that he was a German Christian, and as such he became secretary and interpreter at a German police station in the district of Mir, Poland. While there, he established contact with the Jews of the town, and would inform them of German designs against them. When he learned that the Germans were about to exterminate the local ghetto, he reported this to the Jews and supplied them with arms, so that many of them were enabled to join the partisans. Some of them survived and eventually settled in Israel. His true identity was later discovered by the Gestapo, but he again escaped and hid for some time in a convent. Before long he joined the partisans, and was finally awarded a Russian decoration for his services with the fighting underground.

In 1942, while in the convent, Oswald Rufeisen embraced Christianity, and at the end of the war became a monk, entering the Order of the Carmelites. He chose this Order deliberately because he knew that it had a chapter in Palestine, which in due course he hoped to join. During the War of Independence and several times thereafter, he sought the permission of his superiors to emigrate to Israel. In 1958 he obtained that permission.

After the Israeli Consulate in Warsaw informed him that he would be granted an entry visa into Israel, he applied to the Polish authorities for a passport in the following terms: "I, the undersigned, the Rev.

Oswald Rufeisen, known in the monastic order as Brother Daniel, hereby respectfully apply for permission to travel to Israel for permanent residence, and also for a passport. I base this application on the ground of my belonging to the Jewish people, to which I continue to belong, although I embraced the Catholic faith in 1942, and joined a monastic order in 1945. . . . I chose an Order which has a Chapter in Israel in consideration of the fact that I would receive leave from my superiors to travel to the land for which I have yearned ever since my childhood, when I was a member of the Zionist youth organization. My national allegiance is known to the Church."

The Polish authorities agreed to comply with his request, after he waived his Polish citizenship. On his arrival in Israel, he applied for an Oleh status and for registration as a Jew on his identity card. This application was refused on the basis of the government's decision of July 20, 1958, which provided that "anyone declaring in good faith that he is a Jew, and does not profess any other religion, shall be registered as a Jew."[30]

The attorney for Brother Daniel took the position that the term *Jew* in the Law of Return should be given its Halakhic interpretation, and proceeded to cite talmudic and rabbinic authorities in support of the dictum: "A Jew, even if he has sinned, remains a Jew."[31] Consequently Brother Daniel, although viewed as a sinner because of his adoption of Christianity, was to be regarded as a Jew, and was entitled to all the privileges flowing from the Law of Return. The State Attorney, in opposing this position, submitted other rabbinic authorities in support of the view that a Jew converted to another religion may not be considered a Jew, or should be considered at most a partial Jew, that is, one who is not entitled to all the rights accorded to full Jews under the Halakhah. Thus the attorneys on both sides of the case took their stand on an interpretation of the term *Jew* in the Law of Return in accordance with the Halakhah, though each drew different conclusions from it.

The majority opinion of the Supreme Court was delivered by Justice Moshe Silberg. In a scholarly statement sparkling with an array of rabbinic quotations, he overruled the contention that under the Halakhah one who has been converted to another religion has ceased to be a Jew. He agreed with the attorney of the petitioner that Brother Daniel was in fact, in the view of the Halakhah, a Jew. Justice Silberg concluded this part of his opinion by stating that, were he to agree that the term *Jew* in the Law of Return was identical with the Halakhic definition, he would grant Brother Daniel's petition.

But, he went on, while the term *Jew* in the Rabbinical Courts Jurisdiction (Marriage and Divorce) Law was to be interpreted Halakhically, in the Law of Return that term "has a secular meaning, that is, as it is usually understood by the man in the street—I emphasize, as it is understood by the ordinary plain and simple Jew." Because the Law of Return was an Israeli statute, it stood to reason that the term *Jew* in that statute was to be interpreted as understood by Jews, for they were the nearest to the subject matter of the law, and who better than they could know the significance and the meaning of the word *Jew*? This being the criterion, the answer of Justice Silberg was: "A Jew who has become a Christian is not called a Jew."

He added: "There is one thing shared by all Jews who live in Israel, and that is that we do not detach ourselves from our historic past, and that we do not deny our heritage. . . . Whatever national attributes may be possessed by a Jew living in Israel, whether he is religious, non-religious or anti-religious, he is bound by an umbilical cord to historical Judaism, from which he draws his longings, and from which he derives his idiom, whose festivals are his own to celebrate and whose great thinkers and spiritual heroes—not least of whom are martyrs who perished at the stake in Spain—nourish his national pride. Would a Jew who has become a Christian be able to feel at home with all this? What can all this national sentiment mean to him? Would he not see through different eyes, would he not regard in a different light our draining to the dregs the bitter cups from which we drank so deeply in those dark Middle Ages? I have not the least doubt that Brother Daniel will love Israel. This he has proved. But the love of this Brother will come from without—the love of a brother far distant. He will not be a true part of the Jewish world. His living in Israel in the midst of the Jewish community, and his sincere affection for it cannot take the place of identification that can come only from within, and which here is absent."

Justice Silberg's decision was a significant departure from an established norm. He differentiated between the Halakhic definition, which is essentially familial in that it confines itself to one's family origin, and takes no account of one's Jewish convictions or life-style, and the nationalist view of a Jew which, though not ignoring one's ancestral link, lays stress on his spiritual stance. Thus, the Halakhah would ignore Oswald Rufeisen's conversion to Christianity and regard him as a Jew, whereas the nationalist attitude as expessed by the court held that he could not be regarded as a Jew because as a Catholic he could not identify himself completely with the Jewish people. It was, in the words of Justice Silberg, "the healthy instinct of the Jewish people, and its thirst for survival that are responsible for this general axiomatic belief."[32]

Justice Moshe Landau also rejected the Halakhic interpretation and emphasized the national approach. In his view, Brother Daniel by his conversion had "rejected his national past, and can no longer be integrated into the organized body of the Jewish community. By changing his religion, he has erected a barrier between himself and his fellow Jews. . . . That is the fact of the matter, and that is still the feeling of the overwhelming majority of the Jews of today, both inside and outside the state, a feeling that springs from positive national sentiments, and not from any desire to repay the Catholic Church for its treatment of Jews in days gone by."[33]

Justice Zvi Berenson joined the majority, albeit with a good deal of hesitation. He observed that if Brother Daniel had fallen into the hands of the Nazis after his conversion to Catholicism, he would certainly have been destroyed by them as a Jew. "And now that the petitioner comes knocking at the gates of Israel can it refuse to recognize him as a Jew?" He proceeded: "A Jew who does not believe in religion, any religion, who even fights religion and all that is considered holy, is still a Jew. Can it be that the petitioner, who has embraced another creed, but has remained attached to the Jewish people, is not a Jew? Had he declared that he believed in the Buddhist faith, which does not require a change of religion . . . he would apparently have been recognized as a Jew. Thus, as a Buddhist monk he would be acceptable, but as a Christian monk not?"[34] Still, Justice Berenson sided with the majority. "It is not for nothing that a Jew who has changed his religion is called in Hebrew a *meshummad* (literally, "one who has been destroyed") , because from the national point of view he has destroyed himself and become lost to the nation, both he himself and his descendants. Simple people could never conceive of anyone being a Jew and a Christian at one and the same time, and certainly not a Jew who was a Catholic priest—to them that could only be a contradiction in terms." He nevertheless expressed the hope that, with a fresh wind blowing even in the world of religious creeds, such views might be altered, but "it will take a long time, apparently, until convictions change, and the sense of grievance so deeply felt by the Jews for all the wrong that Christianity has done to their people disappears. Until that day dawns, it is not possible to recognize the petitioner as a Jew for the purposes of the Law of Return."

The judgment of the court was that Brother Daniel, having waived his Polish citizenship, was a man without a nationality, and that part of his identity card which is reserved for Leom (nation) would have to be blank. Consequently, Brother Daniel could not claim automatic citizenship as an Oleh, but was entitled to obtain citizenship by naturalization.

The operative part of the judgment was favorably received by the overwhelming majority of public opinion. To the great majority of the people, a dynamic nationalist definition of "Who is a Jew?", which called for a man's identification with the Jewish people, was a welcome development. The Orthodox, too, were pleased that the Law of Return would not be used as a medium for the admission of *meshummadim* to the Jewish state; they were, however, fully alive to the explosive nature of the decision, which replaced Halakhic criteria by national considerations.[35]

E. IDENTITY CARDS

The Cabinet Crisis of 1958

The question "Who is a Jew?" had also been dealt with by the government in connection with the implementation of the Registration of Inhabitants Law, which requires every applicant for an identity card to furnish particulars about his and his children's Leom and religion. In March 1958, Israel Bar-Yehudah, the Minister of the Interior, issued a directive according to which "any person declaring in good faith that he is a Jew, shall be registered as a Jew," and as regards children, "if both parents declare that the child is Jewish, the declaration shall be regarded as though it were the legal declaration of the child itself." Bar-Yehudah felt justified in formulating the instructions as he did, because it was consistent with the instructions of the Minister who had preceded him in office. However, rabbis officiating at marriages were instructed by the Chief Rabbinate not to rely on the entries in the identity cards, but to investigate the status of the applicants in accordance with the Halakhah.[36]

At the instance of the cabinet ministers of Mafdal, the question was reconsidered by the entire cabinet, which appointed a Ministerial Committee consisting of the Minister of the Interior, who is a member of Ahdut HaAvodah; the Minister of Religious Affairs, Moshe Shapiro of Mafdal; and the Minister of Justice, Pinhas Rosen of the Progressive Party. Some three months later, the cabinet, on the basis of the report of this Ministerial Committee, adopted the ruling that a person who declares in good faith to the registration official that "he is a Jew and professes no other religion" shall be registered as a Jew, and, as regards a child one of whose parents is not a Jew, he shall be registered as a Jew if both his parents declare in good faith that he is a Jew and not a member of another religion. The Mafdal ministers felt they could not accept this directive, and on June 22, 1958, announced their resignation from the government.[37]

The resignation was a grave move for a party that has always formed part of the government coalition. Mafdal now joined the opposition, and instead, Rabbi Moshe Toledano, then Sephardic Chief Rabbi of Tel Aviv and a nonpolitical figure, was coopted into the government as

Minister of Religious Affairs. Explaining the position of his party—despite the fact that the entry "Jew" on the identity card did not make a person's recognition as a Jew binding on the rabbinical courts—Zvi Bernstein pointed to the policy that until then had guided Mafdal in relation to its participation in the government. While it could never force the latter to govern in accordance with the Halakhah, the party was pledged to withdraw from that government if it adopted a decision that was in violation of the Halakhah. Since the government's criterion for registering the offspring of a mixed marriage as a Jew was the mutual consent of the parents, rather than the status of the mother as provided by the Halakhah, Mafdal had felt itself compelled to leave the coalition.

Such registration, Mafdal averred, although not binding on the rabbinate, would create serious practical difficulties. The offspring of such marriages would study like all Jewish boys in a Jewish school, he would then do his army service, and would in all respects behave as a good Jewish patriot. When applying for marriage, however, an enquiry into his parentage would reveal that his mother was non-Jewish, and that consequently, in regarding himself as a Jew, he had erred all his life. The shock that this revelation would occasion him might have serious repercussions, and should be avoided by a proper registration at the very beginning. It was also easy to imagine what pressure would be brought to bear on the rabbis to allow certain marriages to take place and, with that pressure failing, an added impetus would be given to the introduction of civil marriage.[38]

The cabinet crisis was followed by intense agitation on the part of the Orthodox, both in Israel and in the Diaspora. To counteract this rising pressure and, no doubt, to gain time, the government announced its decision to appoint Prime Minister David Ben-Gurion, as well as Bar-Yehudah and Rosen as a committee to lay down directives for the registration of the children of mixed marriages. The committee was to solicit the opinions of Jewish scholars in Israel and in the Diaspora, and would formulate directives in consonance with "the accepted traditions in all circles of Jewry, including all religious trends both Orthodox and non-Orthodox," and having regard to the special conditions prevailing in Israel as a sovereign Jewish state and as the center for *kibbutz galuyot*. As a further conciliatory move, the government announced a few days later that, until further notice, no entries should be made on identity cards if children of mixed marriages were involved.[39]

This procedure was in many respects highly unusual for the government. It was bypassing the Chief Rabbinate in a matter of distinct Halakhic import, and was soliciting opinions not only from the Orthodox, but from the non-Orthodox as well. It was the first time that the government took official cognizance of non-Orthodox religious trends. It was also significant that the government stressed the importance of the problem in relation to *kibbutz galuyot,* and to the special conditions prevailing in a Jewish state. Not only were the opinions of rabbis solicited, but also those of other Jewish scholars and writers, both religious and nonreligious.[40] It was a summons to reevaluate the question of Jewish identity in relation to the specific character of Jewish life in a Jewish state, as well as in relation to a major objective of Israeli national policy, the facilitation of the process of *kibbutz* and *mizug galuyot.*

The Scholars' Responses

The great majority of Jewish scholars were of the opinion that Jewish nationalism and religion were so intimately linked that they could not possibly be separated.[41] Just as one could leave the Jewish people only as a result of conversion to another religion, so one's admission into the Jewish fold could be gained only as a result of a religious act, namely, conversion to Judaism. The majority agreed that the subjective criterion of such a person was irrelevant, and that no matter how intensely he considered himself to be a Jew, he could not be so regarded by others if his mother was non-Jewish; by the same criterion, a person who had severed all links with the Jewish people and even acted contrary to its vital interests, was a Jew if his mother was Jewish. In the view of Solomon Freehof, a leading Reform rabbi and scholar, the religious status of the mother continued to determine the status of the offspring.[42] This was also the view of most of those who urged that the process of conversion be rendered less burdensome. Rabbi Shlomo Goren, then Chief Chaplain of the Israel Defense Army, while adhering to the strict Halakhic position, made the suggestion that the rabbinical court might, with the consent of both parties, convert a child, even if his mother refused to be converted to Judaism, provided that the child, upon attaining majority, did not repudiate Judaism (in which case the conversion would be void *ab initio*).[43]

Even those who advocated a secular rather than a Halakhic definition of a Jew, feared that it was premature to adopt it and that a confrontation should be avoided "until with the passage of time, and the psychological adjustments of the Jewish people to the new situation created by the emergence of the State of Israel, a situation less unfavourable to a peaceful solution is created". Sir Leon Simon proposed a form of provisional registration of half-Jews whose mother was non-Jewish.[44] A similar interim solution was expressed by Sir Isaiah Berlin. He suggested the creation of a category of persons who would be registered as Jews by nationality, but not by religion.

Rabbi Mordecai Kaplan, formerly professor at the (Conservative) Jewish Theological Seminary in New York, and founder of the Reconstructionist movement, made a more radical suggestion. He rejected Ben-

Gurion's suggestion that it was possible to find a common denominator acceptable to all Jewish religious trends and to nonreligious Jews as well. "The very emergence of the state came about in disregard of the traditional position that we have to await the Messiah." He also rejected the view that freedom of conscience and religion were assured in Israel. Such a view, he said, was incompatible with the imposition by the rabbinate of religious laws in matters of personal status. He concluded that the Jewish state was in matters of Leom and religion utterly different from the old states of biblical and immediately postbiblical times, but that it had not yet evolved either a pattern of life or a status for its people. Indeed, he averred, no pattern of Jewish life before the French Revolution had true relevance for contemporary Jewry, whether in Israel or in the Diaspora. His solution of the problem of Jewish identity was for the Knesset to define in the Law of Return "Who is a Jew" in consonance with the national interest. "Therefore, if in the view of the government the recognition of a child born to a non-Jewish mother, where both parents wish to register him as a Jew, will enlarge and strengthen the Jewish majority in Israel, it is entitled to recognize him."[45] The view that not only the Halakhah but the Jewish people in the State of Israel themselves have the authority to determine who a Jew is, is probably shared by the majority of Jews in Israel.

Attorney-General Haim Cohen, a jurist as well as a rabbinic scholar, also submitted an opinion. He maintained that for the civil authorities of the state there was no solution more reasonable than that of allowing the child of mixed marriage to be registered in accordance with the declaration of both parents. The Laws of Return and of Population Registry were secular laws, he said, and were administered by secular authorities, and consequently the interpretation of the term *Jew,* or any other term in these laws, was not subject to Halakhic interpretation.[46] With two concurrent judicial systems, it was unavoidable that a person might be a Jew or a divorcée in civil law, whereas that same person might be neither Halakhically. The registry official was neither a judge nor an investigating officer, and his sole duty was to register such data as a resident was required by law to furnish, even as it was his duty to register that person's address without investigating it or requiring evidence therefor.

Such a policy would in no way prejudice the application of the Rabbinical Courts Jurisdiction (Marriages and Divorces) Law, for the entry on the identity card regarding religion was not binding for the rabbinical court. Cohen pointed out that even among the rabbis in the Talmudic period there was no unanimity as to the status of a child born to a Jew and a non-Jewish mother, and that there was a general presumption that a person was a Jew if he alleged that he was so. In this respect, however, there was a difference between the Diaspora and the

Jewish state. The overwhelming body of rabbinic opinion was that in Israel, where the majority of the people were Jews, one who declared himself to be a Jew was presumed to be such, until and unless this presumption was rebutted by two qualified witnesses. In the Diaspora such a declaration was insufficient to create a presumption, and supporting evidence was called for. Consequently, it appeared that according to the Halakhah a declaration of Jewishness made by a person living in Israel created a presumption of Jewishness. In fact, it was expected of one who had knowledge of a defect in the Jewish ancestry of some particular person not to reveal it, in order not to destroy that presumption. Thus, instead of applying the Halakhic differentiation between the different rules applicable to the determination of Jewishness in Israel and in the Diaspora, the Israel rabbinate has been ignoring it and has adopted the more rigid norms applicable to the Diaspora situation only.

Cohen turned to the special cases of "aliens." In the biblical days of Ezra and Nehemiah, foreign wives were seeking to turn their husbands away from the Jewish faith and toward the worship of idols; but most of the non-Jewish wives who arrived from Europe after the Holocaust willingly followed their husbands to Israel with the intention of living there with and as Jews. Many of them had been persecuted and even tortured; others had tried to save Jews from death at the hands of the Nazis. These women, with their husbands and children, went to Israel in the firm belief that their children were Jews. And now, "in the name of the Torah we are requested to separate ourselves from them, not to recognize them as Jews, nor to love them as converts, unless and until they have satisfied the rabbinate that they were duly converted." "It seems to me," said the Attorney-General, "that in the name of the Torah we should call for the very opposite." This, to him, would be the spirit of true Israeli tradition. "God does not reject any creature; He accepts everybody. The gates are open at all times and anyone wishing to do so may enter."[47]

Finally, the argument put forward by Professor Gad Tedeschi, law professor at the Hebrew University in Jerusalem, is worth noting. He took the position that any attempt on the part of the government or the legislature to define a Jew, or a Moslem, or a member of any other faith, would of necessity be granting to one religion a privileged or preferred position. By adopting a criterion acceptable to one religion but not to another, the law would give that religion a privileged status. Thus, in Islamic religious law the offspring of a Moslem father and a Jewish mother (there are several hundred such instances in Israel) would be a Moslem, while under the Halakhah he would be a Jew. The same would apply to a Jew converted to Christianity, or to a Christian converted to Judaism: both Halakhah and Christianity would claim these converts as their own. "It is in the very nature of a religious law that it does not concern itself with its compatibility with the law of another religion. . . . The mere fact that the state will accord recognition to one religious law, or accord it a privilege over other religions, will be sufficient to make the legislature suspected of bias. If, on the other hand, the status of all religions is equal, Gordian knots will be created that only the legislature will be able to untie. Since in Israel no religion is granted a privileged position . . . we must adopt a criterion that is general and free of bias." Therefore the civil law should take account of a person's own decision in the matter, rather than impose upon him an unwanted religious status. To be sure, such a solution might create cases of incompatibility between the civil and the religious law, but that would be preferable to a situation where the state would be called upon to legislate in favor of one, and against another, religion.[48]

Compromise

From a perusal of the scholars' opinions, it became obvious to the government that it was premature to introduce a definition of the term *Jew* that was at odds with the Halakhah. The interim arrangements proposed by some did not appear practicable, and in the meantime other issues arose to divert the public mind. The directives issued a year earlier to the local registrars were replaced by new directives compatible with Halakhic rules. Mafdal rejoined the cabinet, and the government crisis was resolved. Nevertheless, the issue itself was not at rest, and new *causes célèbres* occurred that once more caused serious religious and political controversy. Since the new directives dated January 1, 1960, were not legislative acts but administrative orders, they were subject to judicial review, and when their legality came up for consideration before the Supreme Court, a new crisis flared up that called for legislative action.

F. LEGISLATIVE ATTEMPTS TO SOLVE THE PROBLEM

The Eitani Case

Although the government crisis was solved and the traditional Labor-Mafdal coalition restored, new cases caused the entire issue to be reopened for further discussion. The first instance concerned Mrs. Rina Eitani, a resident of Upper Nazareth, and a member of its city council, where she represented the Labor Party. The city council of Upper Nazareth was run by a coalition of the Labor Party and Mafdal in a rather uneasy partnership, and Mrs. Eitani in particular had incurred the displeasure of Mafdal. It appeared that a neighbor had informed the official in charge of the local population registry office that Mrs. Eitani's mother was not Jewish. The official initiated an enquiry from the Records Office in Germany concerning Mrs. Eitani's mother and her ancestry, and obtained the information that she was indeed a non-Jewish woman who had married a Jew. The Nazareth official thereupon requested Mrs. Eitani to return her Israeli passport for cancellation, on the ground that it had been obtained by false representation, having alleged that she was an Olah and as such entitled to Israeli citizenship under the Law of Return. The Ministry of the Interior, in order to forestall an altercation, announced that Mrs. Eitani, if she so wished, could obtain Israeli citizenship by naturalization.[49]

The local Mafdal leaders praised the action of the Upper Nazareth registrar and indicated that there would be further disclosures of the origin of other persons. This in turn occasioned a public outcry, which gathered momentum when all the facts of Rina Eitani's case were revealed. She and her parents had lived in Germany, and had gone through the horrors of the Nazi regime. During that ordeal, her non-Jewish mother did not seek to save herself by asserting her Aryan origin and her Christian faith, but rather identified herself with her Jewish husband and children. Rina, too, had suffered at the hands of the Nazis, and when the war was over she had smuggled herself into Palestine in defiance of the British ban on immigration. She served in the Israel Defense Army during the War of Independence and subsequently married; the marriage was solemnized by the rabbinical authorities and her children were brought up as Jews. She took an active part in municipal affairs and won election to Council.

A number of jurists held the action of the registry officers to be contrary to law. The Supreme Court, in the Brother Daniel case, had laid down the principle that since the Law of Return was a secular or civil law, the term *Jew* appearing therein had to be interpreted in its commonly accepted meaning, rather than Halakhically. The authority to annul Israeli citizenship could not be exercised by a registry officer, but only by the Minister of the Interior; and the latter could exercise that authority only when citizenship had been obtained by knowingly false representation. A representation made in good faith, even if mistaken, was no ground for cancellation. Mrs. Eitani, having represented herself as Jewish in good faith was therefore Jewish in terms of the civil law.[50]

What added fuel to the fire was the fact that a Jew, an official of the government of Israel, had made use of records on Aryan and non-Aryan ancestry collated by the Nazis in furtherance of their policy of exterminating the Jewish people. So the issue was once again aired with considerable intensity whether the identity of an offspring of mixed mar-

riages was to be determined by the Halakhic emphasis on the physical
tie to the mother's origin, or by a person's own inner commitment.
Wrote Professor Jacob Talmon of the Hebrew University: "If the non-
Jewish blood of the mother was indeed an insuperable barrier, surely
there was here a case of biological racialism overriding spiritual content
and freedom of choice. And the panacea of religious conversion, even
if granted by the rabbis, smacked too much of coercive pressure." The
controversy touched on "those basic dilemmas which go to make up
the human condition. Ancient exclusive loyalties, one may almost say
desperate convictions, are pitted against the overwhelming forces of
change and sweeping innovations. A battle is fought between the urge
for free individual self-expression, and the grantedness of a concrete,
most sharply contained historic totality." Thus the basic issue was: "What
are the legitimate limits which the heritage of all the ages may set upon
the sovereign right of the generation here and now to fashion its life?"
It was an issue that was almost sure to resist solution.[51]

As so often in public discussions of religion, each side restated its
position without making the slightest impression on the other. To the
bulk of Israeli opinion, Rina Eitani was Jewish, because she not only
regarded herself as Jewish, but led in all respects the life of an average
Jewish woman in Israel, maintaining the same degree of observance or
nonobservance of the Mitzvot as she thought fit. The fact that her Jewish ethnic origin was related to her father rather than to her mother
could not, to the man in the street, be an overriding consideration. To
the Orthodox, on the other hand, it was self-evident that she was not
Jewish until she underwent a formal conversion; and, similarly, the Minister of Religious Affairs held that the lot of persons like herself lay in
a choice of either being converted or leaving the country.[52] While Mrs.
Eitani's passport and Israeli citizenship were not seriously contested, it
was reported months later that she had been formally converted to
Judaism, presumably with her children.

The question of identity tended to arise in a variety of cases. There
had been instances of Jewish husbands who had sought to escape their
obligations to their non-Jewish wives to whom they were lawfully married in their countries of origin, by asserting in the rabbinical courts
that they were unmarried in terms of the Halakhah. A husband who
had deserted his wife pleaded before the rabbinical court in Rehovot
that he was not liable to pay alimony because the plaintiff, being non-
Jewish, was not legally his wife. The latter asserted that she was Jewish, but was unable to produce evidence to that effect. At the instance
of the court, a search was made in the racial records compiled by the
Fascist regime in Italy, which left doubts about the authenticity of her
Jewishness. The rabbinical court decreed thereupon that the husband
must deliver a bill of divorcement—*get*—to his wife, but relieved him

of the payment of alimony. The Supreme Court annulled this decision on the ground that the rabbinical court had no jurisdiction in this matter.[53]

The Shalit Case

The directives issued by the Minister of the Interior to the registry officers on January 1, 1960, which followed on the cabinet crisis of 1958, laid down that only a person born of a Jewish mother could be registered as a Jew, both under the heading of "Religion" and that of "Nation, ethnic group" (Leom). These directives were uncontested for about eight years, when their legal validity was challenged by Benjamin Shalit, a career officer in the Israeli Navy.[54] Lieutenant Commander Shalit, a native of Palestine, had attended the University of Edinburgh in Scotland, and there, in 1958, he married Anne Geddes, daughter of a distinguished architect. Her father, Sir Patrick Geddes was one of the early non-Jewish supporters of the Zionist cause in England, and had assisted Chaim Weizmann in drawing up the first plans for the Hebrew University on Mount Scopus. After settling in Israel, Anne became a naturalized Israeli and had herself registered as British under "Leom," and as professing no faith under "Religion." Benjamin Shalit, when submitting particulars concerning his own status, described himself as Jewish in terms of national affinity. Both regarded themselves as atheists.

A son and a daughter were born to them: the boy was circumcised, but without the traditional religious ceremony, and both children were brought up like all Israeli Jewish children. There ensued a lengthy correspondence between the father and the registry officer regarding the mode of the children's registration. Shalit insisted that they be registered as persons professing no religion, and as Jewish in terms of Leom. The registry officer, acting in pursuance of the directives issued in 1960, entered under the heading of "Religion" the words "No registration," and under the heading "Leom" the words "Jewish father and non-Jewish mother." Finally, Shalit petitioned the Supreme Court, sitting as a High Court of Justice, for an order *nisi* directing the Minister of the Interior and the registry officer to show cause why they should not register the children as Jews in terms of national affinity, and as persons without a religion. The petition proved to be a time bomb, in view of the explosive controversy which followed.

From Shalit's point of view, his fight was of little practical significance for his children. Both parents and children enjoyed Israeli citizenship, were entitled to all its rights and privileges, and were subject to all its obligations. Even had Shalit succeeded in registering his children as Jews in terms of Leom and as professing no religion, he would still not have been able to remove the religious restrictions that would be placed on his children in the future; for if they, being non-Jewish, should wish to marry Jewish partners, the rabbinical courts could not marry them. Being an atheist, Anne Shalit would not consider conversion to Judaism; her husband, a Jew in terms of the Halakhah, stated in his declaration to the High Court that it was their intention to raise their children loyal to the Jewish people and homeland, but without any religious attachment. Shalit's fight was waged not in order to secure for himself, his wife, and his children any legal rights, but as a test case to establish the proposition that there existed a new category of Jew who, while not professing the Jewish religion, yet was a Jew in terms of national affinity (Leom).

The Supreme Court was mindful of the seriousness of the case and its disturbing political implications, and hearings were, at the order of the Chief Justice, held before the full court of nine. The proceedings began in October 17, 1968, with the entire country's attention focused on the case. It was announced by the Orthodox that if the Supreme Court invalidated the government directives of 1960, whereby only one who was a Jew in the Halakhic sense could be registered as a Jew in terms of Leom, the Mafdal members of the government would resign and thereby disrupt the Government of National Unity that was then in office. The war of attrition was then in progress along the Suez Canal, and casualties were being reported almost daily. The Orthodox launched a massive campaign, and Orthodox rabbis from abroad warned the government of Israel of the consequences that would follow if the pro-Halakhic directives were invalidated as the result of a court decision. The two Chief Rabbis went so far as to warn the Supreme Court officially and in writing of the consequences of a deviation from the existing practice. At no time in history did the Supreme Court find itself under such pressure. It was obvious that its decision might be the cause of a serious political crisis.

The government instructed the Attorney General to defend the directives of 1960, which he did in a scholarly brief, basing his case not only on a wealth of legal arguments but also on the writings and utterances of leading Jewish scholars, authors, rabbis, and leaders. His comprehensive argument led to the proposition that, religion and Leom being inseparable, one could not be a Jew in terms of Leom without being one in terms of religion. His contention was that a person's subjective feelings about his national or religious affiliation were irrelevant, since there were objective criteria that determined one's status as a Jew. A person, if he was born a Jew, was a Jew regardless of his belief; admission of a non-Jew to the Jewish fold, however, could be achieved only through admission to the Jewish religion, that is, by conversion. Likewise, one could leave the Jewish fold only by abandoning the Jewish religion through conversion to another faith. In brief, it was the religious criterion that regulated one's entry into and one's exit from the Jewish people.

Benjamin Shalit argued his case in person. Appearing in the uniform of a naval officer, and in the company of his wife, unassisted by lawyers, he pleaded the cause of a secular conception of the term *Jew*. In a sovereign Jewish state, the equation of nationhood and religion was inadmissible. One's identity was a matter for one's own determination, and could not be imposed contrary to conviction; he contended that a new Jewish identity was evolving in the present Jewish society of Israel. He reached the climax of his argument when he mentioned Kamal Nimri, an Arab terrorist, who had been tried and sentenced by an Israeli court, and whose mother happened to be a Jewess married to an Arab. Turning to the court, he posed a dramatic question: "Kamal Nimri, an Al-Fatah member . . . is entitled to call himself a Jew; and I, a native of country, and my wife who regards herself a Jewess in all respects, may not register our children as Jews?" Equally disturbing was his concluding observation: "What will happen when the day comes and Jews start arriving from Russia? Are we not longing for them? Many of them are the offspring of mixed marriages, yet regard themselves as Jews. In Russia, one's national identity is registered in accordance with one's own choice. Are you going to tell such a person he is not a Jew?"[55]*

While the court contemplated its decision, the nine Justices made an unprecedented appeal to the government to delete the item Leom from the list of particulars required for registration. This would relieve them from the necessity of making a decision. The proposal was discussed by the cabinet and was rejected.

The Supreme Court was in addition faced with a political situation that made its task all the more onerous. The year 1969 was an election year, and any decision reached by the court would inevitably become the subject of political agitation and be employed as an electoral weapon for or against the religious parties. A decision against Mafdal would immediately result in a cabinet crisis, unless the Labor Party were prepared to reverse the decision by amending the law. The court therefore deemed it advisable to postpone its decision until after the elections, and it was only on January 23, 1970, that the Supreme Court Justices read their respective decisions, in a judgment covering over two hundred closely printed pages.[56]

There were three groups of opinions. Justices M. Silberg and J. Kister were in favor of dismissing Shalit's petition, thus validating the di-

---

* Shalit was referring to the Soviet law that provides that the offspring of parents who belong to different national groups are entitled, at a certain age, to determine their national identity.

rectives of January 1, 1960. Justice Silberg held that professing the
Jewish faith was a prerequisite of being a Jew and being part of the
Jewish people. The concept of secular Jewish-Israeli nationhood was
illusory, and ran counter to the experience of Jewish history. He was
in favor of the traditional Halakhic definition.[57]

Justice Kister came out against the proposition that the registry officer was bound to register the particulars furnished by the person whose
duty it was to furnish them under the Population Registration Law. On
the contrary, it was the duty of the registry officer to make an entry in
accordance with the evidence presented, that is, if the parents of a
child were not of the same Leom, the entry should so indicate. Being
a citizen of a Jewish state did not make one a Jew; to be a Jew, one
must be affiliated with an ethnic group, with the Halakhic criterion as
the sole test. The court could not bring into the Jewish fold persons
who up till that point had not been recognized as Jews.[58]

Chief Justice S. Agranat and Justice M. Landau took the position
that, since the controversy was of a distinct ideological character, it
did not readily lend itself to judicial treatment; it was for the legislature
to resolve the conflict. The court was not bound to decide an ideological issue when there was no general consensus on the subject. The court,
therefore, must exercise self-restraint, and not be guided by the personal
opinions of each of its members, especially since it was lawful for the
court to exercise its discretionary powers and desist from interfering
in this matter.[59]

As against the opinions of four members of the court, five Justices
held that the directives issued in 1960 were not valid; that they were
neither legislative enactments nor administrative orders based on any
law, and were therefore unenforceable. There was, said Justice Cohen,
not one single answer to the question "Who is a Jew?", but many answers, for the question ought to be formulated: "Who is a Jew within
the meaning of a specific law?" While it was clear that the rabbinical
courts, exercising power under the Rabbinical Courts Jurisdiction (Marriages and Divorces) Law, were entitled and bound to resolve the question in accordance with the Halakhah—because that law enjoined them
to apply the Halakhah—in all the other laws enacted by the Knesset
in which the word *Jew* appears, no such duty was imposed. Thus, the
Supreme Court in the Brother Daniel case ruled that the Law of Return,
being a civil law, was not necessarily to be interpreted in accordance
with the Halakhah. The registering official, acting in pursuance of the
Population Registry Law,[60] was an administrative and not a judicial officer, who had no authority to reject the data furnished to him and to
replace them by what he thought should have been the right answer.
The entry in the Population Registry was therefore not evidence of its
correctness, but merely evidence of data supplied by the applicant. Only

when these data were not given in good faith could the registering offi-cial refuse to make the requested entry. In this particular case, no one had alleged that Shalit, when he represented his children as Jews, had done so in bad faith.

The opinion of Justice Cohen was generally followed by the other four, who together with him made up the majority of the court. Justice J. Sussman added that by applying the Halakhic criterion to the imple-mentation of the Law of Population Registry, an absurd situation would be created. A Jew converted to Christianity would not be admitted un-der the Law of Return, but one such settled in Israel as a tourist who had become a permanent resident would be registered as a Jew if the Halakhic test were applied.* The same anomaly could arise out of the enforcement of the Hours of Work and Rest Law[61] in that the deter-mination of a man's identity might affect his official Day of Rest. Jews were thereby enjoined to rest on the Sabbath and on Jewish festivals, and a Jew converted to Christianity might be prosecuted if he refused to abide by the Jewish Days of Rest. To avoid conflicts between the laws of the various religions, it was essential to apply the subjective test in determining the question.[62]

Justice Witkon expressed regret that the government had failed to adopt the suggestion made by the court, either to initiate legislation in the Knesset regulating the matter, or else to strike out the item Leom from the particulars of registration. The government not having found it possible so to act, it was within the competence of the court to ad-judicate the matter. The term Leom had to be interpreted within the context of the Population Registry Law in the generally accepted mean-ing of this term, rather than Halakhically. He then proceeded to argue the proposition that one's identification with Leom was a matter of a person's subjective choice and could not be imposed upon him. He re-inforced Justice Sussman's argument in support of the proposition that even in the Population Registry Law one's subjective determination was respected. It might happen, for instance, that two brothers could arrive from Britain as tourists, and later be granted the status of permanent residents. They then would apply for registration according to the law. Both would register as Jews in terms of their religion and British in terms of citizenship, but whereas one would declare himself to be of the Jewish Leom, the other would declare himself as British under this item, and both would be registered accordingly. The difference between the two arises from subjective factors, for one wished to identify him-self so completely with the Jewish people that he chose to register him-self as belonging to the Jewish national or ethnic group, whereas the other confined his affiliation to the Jewish religion only.

_____

* The state would reject him, in accordance with the Brother Daniel precedent, but the Halakhah would consider him a Jew.

Regarding the contention that the adoption of the subjective criterion would bring about a split in the nation, Justice Witkon argued that differences of opinion on this issue would not cause a rift. "The real conflict that may lead to a rift is between those who seek to impose their views on others, and those who cherish the freedom of the individual and reject conformism. I belong to the latter. In this case, the court cannot be neutral. Since the establishment of the state, we have always dealt in a spirit of tolerance with the views of others, and more than once have we invalidated administrative acts that were aimed at levering non-conformists into conformity." He cited decisions where the court had always adhered to the principles of human rights and the liberal tradition, which were "the essence of our unwritten constitution." Acting in this spirit, one could not possibly confront the petitioner with the alternative of "either give up your desire to have your children registered as belonging to a people in whose spirit they are being brought up, or force them, against your will, to undergo the religious ritual of conversion."[63]

Thus, by a five-to-four decision, the court invalidated the directives of 1960, and ordered the registry officer to register the children as belonging to no religion, and as belonging to the Jewish Leom.[64]

Orthodox Reaction and Government Response

Although the decision of the Supreme Court did not purport to establish a definition of "Who is a Jew?" except for the limited purpose of the implementation of an administrative law, the various Orthodox groups and institutions rose up in arms. Even before the full text of the judgment was published, the Supreme Court was attacked in an unprecedented manner. Mafdal announced that it would have its ministers resign from the government unless a law were enacted to give a Halakhic definition to the term *Jew* that would be retroactive, thereby annulling the court's judgment. Orthodox groups abroad lodged vigorous protests with the prime minister, stressing the danger of a split between the Jews of Israel and those of the Diaspora. The Chief Rabbinate instructed Moshe Haim Shapiro, the Minister of the Interior, to disobey the decision of the court, and not to effect the registration as required by that decision, and he intimated that he would follow the rabbinic injunction. At a time when the war of attrition waged by Egypt against Israel was reaching its climax on the Suez Canal battlefield, the country was swept by an acerbic debate.

It was primarily the threat of Mafdal to leave the Cabinet and thus to disrupt the Government of National Unity that prompted Prime Minister Golda Meir and the Labor Party to work out a compromise with the Orthodox. The warnings issued by the Orthodox, particularly in the Diaspora, that the imminent crisis would lead to a rift with Diaspora Jewry and encourage intermarriage there, had their impact on public opinion. The Prime Minister, Mrs. Meir, would agree to a Halakhic definition of the term *Jew* provided that it did not hinder Aliyah nor lead to a rift with the non-Orthodox religious trends in the Diaspora.

The bill finally introduced into the Knesset seemed to reconcile both the Halakhah and the interests of Aliyah. Thus Section 4 (b) of the Law of Return (Amendment No. 2) as finally enacted on March 10, 1970, provided:

"For the purpose of this law, 'Jew' means a person born to a Jewish mother, or who has become converted to Judaism, and who is not a member of another religion."[65]

The Orthodox had insisted on adding the words "in accordance with the Halakhah," after the words "converted to Judaism," in order to disqualify conversion to Judaism performed under the auspices of Conservative or Reform rabbis in the Diaspora. Mrs. Meir, however, refused to yield on this point, on the ground that the Knesset could legislate with respect to conversion in Israel, but was not entitled to determine the kind of conversions that might be carried out in the Diaspora. Implicit in this definition was the recognition by the Knesset that, though in Israel Orthodoxy enjoyed a monopoly of religion by operation of the law, in the Diaspora Judaism was pluralistic and its pluralism was to be respected. Thus, a person converted to Judaism by Conservative or Reform rabbis abroad would come within the definition of *Jew* for the purposes of the Law of Return.

By way of further concession to the Orthodox, The Population Registry Law of 1965 was amended to bring it in line with the new definition. Thus no person could now be registered as a Jew, either in terms of religion or of Leom, unless he satisfied the registering official that he was indeed a Jew, as defined in the Law of Return. The bill so formulated was presented for first reading in the Knesset by Minister of Justice Yaakov Shimshon Shapiro on February 9, 1970.*

Parliamentary Debate

The debate that ensued was one of the most momentous in the history of the Knesset. It ranged far beyond the scope of the bill, and en-

---

* Section 4 (a) of the new law extended the rights under the Law of Return, i.e., the right of Aliyah, the acquisition of Israel citizenship on arrival, as well as rights extended under other laws. Among these were economic benefits accorded to Olim, as well as to "the children and grandchildren of a Jew, to his spouse, as well as the spouse of his child or grandchild, excluding a person who was a Jew and who of his own free will has embraced another religion." Thus non-Jewish spouses of Jews, as well as their offspring, regardless of whether they were Jews in terms of the Halakhic definition, would be admitted to Israel and entitled to all the benefits accorded to such persons.

compassed the entire complex of the problems of religion in their relationship to the Jewish people. For the three Orthodox parties in the Knesset, there was no difficulty in arguing their case; as for the deputies of the Labor Party, many of whom were in open revolt against the bill for which they were expected to vote, their position was highly embarrassing. Before long it became clear that the controversy revolved round a basic issue:

Should, or should not, the children of a mixed marriage be regarded as Jews if their mother is non-Jewish and both parents want them to be Jews (just as the offspring of a mixed marriage is considered Jewish if the father is a non-Jew)? Is it not sufficient for one parent to be a Jew, to enable the offspring, if of age (or his parents, if he is a minor), to determine his religious and national affiliation? Should not the subjective-spiritual element be the determining factor, rather than the biological connection with the mother, even where such connection is devoid of any spiritual content?

The original issue, which had loomed so large in the Shalit case, that is, whether one could belong to the Jewish Leom without being a Jew by religious profession, now receded into the background. It was accepted as axiomatic by the majority of the non-Orthodox deputies that in the case of Jews, religion and peoplehood are so intimately interwoven as to be inseparable. But many found it difficult to reconcile themselves to giving preponderance to the biological over the spiritual factor when determining the religious and national status of the offspring of mixed marriages.

The spokesman for the Orthodox argued that to adopt the subjective criterion in determining the status of the offspring, that is, to register the child of a non-Jewish mother as a Jew, or to register someone converted to Judaism under non-Orthodox auspices, would in the long run be an embarrassment to such a person. When applying for marriage, he would be informed by the rabbinate that he was not a Jew within the meaning of the Jurisdiction of Rabbinic Courts (Marriages and Divorces) Law, and thus could not be married. It would not only be an injustice to register such a person wrongly and then expose him to a cruel disappointment, but it would also turn him against the Jewish religion. Furthermore, he would be supported by many sympathizers, and thus strengthen the cause of those clamoring for civil marriage. The ultimate result would be the end of rabbinic authority in this vital and sensitive area.

In the opinion of the Orthodox, such a result would bring about a schism in the unity of the Jewish people. To be sure, religious pluralism in the Diaspora had caused no such rift in the Jewish community; on the contrary, the major religious trends abroad had on the whole cooperated with one another, and even frequently recognized the conversions performed by each of them as being valid.* But many members of the Knesset were impressed by the argument that under the conditions prevailing in Israel, Orthodox Jews would be unwilling to marry with "dubious" Jews and would therefore be compelled to withdraw into a "ghetto" to prevent such Jews from entering their society. This point was eloquently presented for Mafdal by Rabbi Moshe Zvi Neriah; he stressed that while the Jews in Israel shared a variety of conflicting opinions, they were nevertheless one family. "The bridges are open. All are allowed to mix with all others; all meet together, whether on joyous or on sorrowful occasions, as did the united tribes of Israel. A boy from Kfar HaRoeh, an Orthodox village, may marry a girl from Givat Haim, a non-Orthodox kibbutz, and one from Tirat Tzvi [another Orthodox kibbutz] may marry one from Ein Shemer, a notably secularist kibbutz. The importance of marital links for the unity of the Jewish people cannot be overrated."[66] If a non-Halakhic definition of a Jew were adopted, the Orthodox might be compelled "to set up barriers" and even avoid social contact with other Jews, for fear of meeting "non-Jews" possibly registered as Jews. "We shall be constrained to grow apart, to destroy the existing bridges and social contacts, and to erect fences." And turning to the non-Orthodox, he asked them to regard his insistence on the Halakhic definition as motivated by a genuine craving for unity. "We come to you with our protests, demands and appeals, because you are our sons and our brethren, because we do not want to give you up. . . . Do not hasten to give us up."[67]

The case for the opposite opinion was presented by Yaakov Hazan, one of the leaders of the left-wing Mapam party. His was a spirited defense of secularism; he vehemently rejected the generally prevailing opinion that the confrontation was between believers and nonbelievers. "Both sides of the barricades are manned by believers. One man believes that God is in heaven—another that God dwells within himself. What is common to both is the conviction that one must live in accordance with faith. What separates them is the fact that, whereas the secularist respects the faith of the religious person, and will not impose his views on him, the religious person on the other hand strives to impose his norms on the secularist, even by means of a law that is in itself secular." In Hazan's view, secularism was not a negation of, or a break with, Jewish historical continuity; in fact, it represented that very continuity and its renewal.[68]

Because the secularists, said Hazan, regarded Jewish survival as the sole criterion for national action, certain Halakhic principles appear to

---

* In the United States and Canada, for instance, Reform and Conservative Jews generally accept each other's conversions, and except for some recent hardening of standards, Orthodox rabbis have usually not insisted on renewed conversions.

them as a hindrance to the Ingathering of the Exiles. "Aliyah* to Israel is a Mitzvah-precept which outweighs other precepts. Aliyah is the supreme Mitzvah of our renewed national life. It is the supreme act of identification, although of a secular character, an identification that recognizes no limits with the destiny of the Jewish people. If you wish, Aliyah is the most profound act of conversion for everyone who wishes to join the Jewish people and become attached to it. To reject these people, rather than welcome them as good Jews in our midst, is the very opposite of the supreme national imperative."[69]

Hazan thus presented the case for secular Judaism as a legitimate expression of Judaism for this age, with the act of Aliyah raised to the level of a precept. He buttressed his case by a call to sentiment when he quoted a letter addressed to Golda Meir written by a member of kibbutz Revadim. This young man from Holland, son of a Gentile mother and a Jewish father who had worn the yellow badge during the Nazi occupation but managed to survive the ordeal of the period, had lost both his legs while serving in the Israeli army. Now he had heard of the proposed law, and asked Mrs. Meir the following question:

a) "What should the offspring of mixed marriages in Europe do, where it is the father who is the Jew? In Europe we are regarded as Jews, and here we are considered non-Jews.

b) "Do you think I was right in coming here? Do you think that there is a place for me here as a "non-Jew"?

c) "Was I right in doing what other Jews do, that is, to join the army? Did I lose my legs fighting for a country that is truly my homeland? Regarding myself as a Jew, I arrived here as an Oleh and served in the army. Evidently this was not enough. What shall I, as a Jew, do? Shall I remain here and feel ashamed because my mother was not Jewish, or shall I return to Holland, and feel ashamed because my father is a Jew?"[70]

To many it seemed that the young man from Holland could solve his dilemma by conversion to Judaism by Halakhic formula. But as a secularist he felt that he could not in all sincerity contemplate such a solution. In his own eyes he was a committed Jew, albeit an atheist, for not only was his father Jewish, but he himself had performed the supreme act of conversion, namely, Aliyah. Hazan went on to advance a similar argument on behalf of many Olim from the Soviet Union who claim to have been "converted" twice: once, when attaining legal majority in Russia, they had officially opted for "Nationality: Jewish," although their mothers were non-Jewish; and second, when they braved the risk of renouncing Soviet citizenship and applied for an exit permit to go to Israel. They regarded both these acts, in the context of

---

* Immigration to and settlement in Israel by Jews who are, literally, "going up" to their homeland.

Soviet society, as evidence of a far-reaching commitment to, and association with, the Jewish people which, they averred, entitled them to be regarded as Jews in all respects, without undergoing a Halakhic conversion, which calls for the profession of a religious faith.*

The debate was in many ways philosophical and theological rather than political, an almost unique phenomenon in the annals of parliaments. While it was generally felt that the great majority of Israelis would unhesitatingly regard the offspring of a mixed marriage who had opted to settle in Israel as a Jew, a parliamentary vote in accordance with the majority view would serve no purpose. Were the majority view incorporated into law, the Orthodox would indeed withdraw into their own shell, as Rabbi Neriah had claimed, and would avoid social contacts with the majority of the community for fear of marriage with "doubtful" Jews. In brief, this was not a problem that could be definitively solved by legislative action, which could at best provide a technical but not a substantive solution.

For this reason the spokesman for the Liberal Party urged the Knesset to desist from any kind of legislation on this subject. Ever since Emancipation the Jewish people had veered away from the Halakhah, he said, with the result that for much of contemporary Jewry the Halakhah and its norms no longer represented an acceptable way of life. In spite of all the ravages of assimilation, however, the abandonment of the Halakhic way of life had not necessarily been an evil. Some of the most remarkable developments in Jewish life had taken place since the emergence of secular Judaism. The Hebrew language had been revived; Hebrew culture had undergone a renaissance; untold thousands formerly alienated from Halakhic Judaism had found meaningful self-expression in Jewish nationalism; and a Jewish sovereign state had arisen, which had been regarded as an impossibility only two generations before. While the majority had forsaken the Halakhic way of life, the search for a new Halakhah and a new Jewish identity consonant with contemporary life had not yet been completed. Consequently, the Gordian knot could not be untied by the expedient of law; it must untie itself, and for this both time and patience were required. With all the difficulties involved, it behooved the Knesset to heed the advice of the Supreme Court by eliminating the item Leom from the particulars of registration, and to leave the decision of "Who is a Jew?" to future generations.[71]

While the two-day debate was still in progress, demonstrations and counterdemonstrations were taking place outside the Knesset. Inside,

---

* Since the Knesset debate in 1970, a dramatic rise of Soviet Jewish immigration has taken place. Many of the Olim, born and bred in the atheist climate of a communist society, are not religion-oriented. Their affinity with the Jewish people is of a nationalistic or ethnic character.

Golda Meir had to enforce strict party discipline on her own party in order to secure passage of the bill. The Labor Party, Mafdal, and Herut voted solidly for it, assuring its adoption. Agudat Israel voted against it. Rabbi Menahem Porush, speaking for the Agudah, scandalized the Knesset by throwing a Reform prayerbook on the floor, in order to express his indignation at the possibility that conversions performed by Reform rabbis abroad might be recognized in Israel.* With some exceptions, the members of the Liberal Party, of the Independent Liberals, and of Mapam voted against the bill; after the second and third readings the bill was enacted into law.

In effect, the new law represented a compromise hammered out between Mafdal and the Labor party. Mafdal won out on the definition of a Jew, for the Halakhic criterion was incorporated into the law of the land. Yet, the way was left open for the recognition of non-Orthodox conversions carried out in the Diaspora by the fact that no proviso was included in the law that conversions must be carried out "in conformance with the Halakhah." The non-Orthodox secured a significant gain in that the Law of Return had been liberalized so as to admit non-Jewish spouses and their offspring. Finally, the Labor Party refused to make the law retroactive, so that the Supreme Court decision in the Shalit case was not invalidated, and the children of the Shalits were recognized as Jewish in terms of Leom. The public debate subsided, and the controversy was settled. Before long, however, a new problem made its appearance.

G. WHO IS A CONVERT TO JUDAISM?

Background

The problem of "Who is Ger?" (a convert to Judaism) is closely connected with the answer to the question of "Who is a Jew?" For unless an act of conversion is recognized as valid, the person claiming to have been converted cannot be considered a Jew. This is no longer a marginal problem, because the number of converts to Judaism has been on the increase both in Israel and in the Diaspora. It has been estimated that by the end of the 1970s every fourth or fifth Jewish child born in the United States will be raised by parents, one of whom is a convert.[72] No exact data as to the number of converts are available, but that they are to be counted in the thousands per annum seems certain.[73] In numerous Reform and Conservative congregations, regular classes for teaching Judaism to prospective converts are held, such courses sometimes lasting a year and having various requirements.

---

* At the request of the Speaker of the House, Rabbi Porush had to apologize.

The great majority of conversions among Americans are performed by Conservative and Reform rabbis, both because these religious trends represent the great majority of synagogue-affiliated Jews, and because they generally extend a welcome to converts, while the Orthodox do not readily facilitate their acceptance, especially when the motivation is marriage to a Jew.* The growing number of converts admitted to Judaism under the auspices of non-Orthodox rabbis is now posing a serious problem for Israel. The rabbinate does not recognize the validity of conversions performed abroad under non-Orthodox auspices, and if its views should receive the imprimatur of the laws of Israel, many thousands of Jews and their offspring in the Diaspora would be regarded as non-Jews, although they are generally regarded as an integral part of the Jewish community abroad and have usually been absorbed into it. Has the State of Israel the right to deny the Jewishness of all these persons, many of whom are devoted to Israel and deeply involved in a variety of activities on its behalf? Would not Israel then be held responsible for creating a schism within Diaspora Jewry, where such a schism does in fact not now exist? The problem becomes all the more serious when these persons seek to immigrate to Israel and, as Olim, intend to join those whom they consider their people in their homeland.

The prerequisites for conversion appear to have become fixed about the second century C.E. Previously, a male candidate for conversion was expected to be circumcised, to be immersed in a ritual bath, and to offer a sacrifice. With the destruction of the Temple, the sacrifice was dispensed with. Converts were readily accepted until the beginning of the second century, but during the Hadrianic persecutions a number of converts were known to have infiltrated the Jewish ranks as Roman spies, and in consequence conversion was made more difficult. When, however, a convert was finally admitted to the community, he was highly respected and considered as a Jew in all respects, with the exception of the provision that a woman convert would not marry a cohen.

The procedure for conversion was carried out in the presence of a rabbinic court. The applicant was always warned of the disadvantages of being a Jew, and of the burden involved in observing the precepts of the religious law. The candidate was asked: "What induces you to join us? Do you not know that in these days the Israelites are in trouble, oppressed, despised and subjected to endless suffering?"[74] If he replied in the affirmative, he was reminded of the penalties that would be inflicted on him if he failed to observe the Sabbath or the dietary laws, or commtted other such trespasses. If the applicant still remained firm in his resolve, he was circumcised, and underwent ritual immersion in

---

* The tradition requires "pure" motives for entering Judaism: a love of God and His Torah, rather than the "ulterior" motive of love for another human being, for the purpose of marriage. See below.

the presence of three men as witnesses. Their presence was also required at the immersion of woman converts, although suitable precautions were taken not to affront their modesty. In all cases the rabbinical court had to be convinced that the candidate was sincere in his belief in Judaism. He would be disqualified if his interest was merely worldly, such as the desire to marry a Jew.

It is worthy of note that, while in the Jewish community of Babylon the rules for conversion were stringent, they were far more liberal in Palestine. In the talmudic tractate Gerim ("Converts"), the sages declared: "Behold, the Land of Israel validates converts. He who says in the Land of Israel 'I am a convert,' he is received immediately; outside of Israel, however, he is not received unless he has witnesses with him."[75] The fact that in Israel there was no danger of assimilation, nor a great need for a long period of integration into the Jewish community, was the basis of these different approaches to conversion. In the course of centuries, the Diaspora approach prevailed, mirroring the Jew's continual fear of assimilation so long as he was not in his own land. The dictum, "Converts are as burdensome to Israel as leprosy,"[76] and the opinion that converts impeded the arrival of the Messiah,[77] expressed the general negative attitude in the Diaspora toward the admission of converts. Non-Jews were converted only when they had satisfied the rabbis that they were impelled by a sincere religious motivation, and that they intended to adopt the Halakhic way of life in its entirety—in other words, that they intended to integrate completely into the Halakhah-bound Jewish community as it then existed.*

This conversion policy remained unchanged as long as the Halakhah was universally accepted by the Jews. Following the Emancipation, however, the rise of Reform Judaism led to the emergence of a pluralistic Judaism in the Diaspora, and the approach to conversion began to change, especially as mixed marriage tended to increase. The pressure to accept non-Jews as converts has become ever stronger within the Reform and Conservative movements, and particularly so in the United States, where about one-half of Diaspora Jews now dwell. To refuse or impede conversion when non-Jews wish to marry Jews would be tantamount to the loss of numerous Jews, who would drift away from the community altogether. Consequently, changes in conversion procedures have gradually evolved. Reform rabbis no longer require immersion in a ritual bath; circumcision is insisted on, though in some circumstances it might be dispensed with.** They do not require the observance of

---

* This is the generally accepted view of the development. Some scholars have shown, however, that certain Jewish communities continued to pursue an aggressive conversionist policy well into the Middle Ages.

** There are lately, however, growing numbers of Reform rabbis who have returned to Halakhic requirements.

the dietary laws, but do teach candidates the principles of the Jewish religion with stress on ethical values, explain and encourage the celebration of the festivals, and impart a knowledge of Jewish history. In the eyes of the Orthodox, the omission of the ritual bath in itself nullifies a Reform conversion. This circumstance, however, has not led to serious crises in the life of the Jewish community in America, because conversions by one religious trend are in most cases recognized by the others, and instances of non-Orthodox conversion are generally treated by the Orthodox on an ad hoc basis.

In Israel, the law of 1970 defined a Jew as a person born of a Jewish mother, or of one "who has been converted," but did not specify whether conversion had to be in accordance with the Halakhah. In order to clarify this point, the spokesman for the Liberal Party, in the course of the Knesset debate of February 10, 1970, posed the following questions to the Minister of Justice: "Will a visa be given to one who has been converted in the United States according to the custom of the Reform movement, and seeks to immigrate to Israel according to the Law of Return, or will it be said that Reform conversion disqualifies him? . . . How will the registration official deal with a person who appears before him to register in pursuance of the Population Registry Law, and declares that he is a Jew, and as evidence thereof produces a certificate which attests to conversion in accordance with the custom of the Reform movement? Will that official register him as a Jew by Leom and by religion, or as an American by Leom and Christian by Religion?"[78]

In his response, the Minister of Justice referred to the instruction of the Minister of the Interior in 1960, where the reference to conversion was followed by the proviso "according to the Halakhah," whereas in the new law the words "according to the Halakhah" were omitted. "It is completely clear," said the minister, "and the intention is extremely simple. . . . Whoever comes with a conversion certificate of any Jewish community, and as long as he does not profess another religion, will be accepted as a Jew. What is the meaning of accepting him as a Jew? He will enjoy all the rights of the Law of Return, he will be registered in his identity card as a Jew." This was consonant with the principle that the Knesset could legislate only for the people of Israel, and not for those dwelling beyond its confines. The State of Israel would therefore not impose the definition of the term *Jew* or stipulate "Who is a convert?" for the Diaspora; there, and for purposes of Aliyah, it would accept the definition prevalent in the Diaspora. When, however, the question arose in connection with the definition of a Jew for purposes of marriage under the laws of Israel, the situation would be different: "When he wishes to marry, I am not the master of the house. There is a law of marriage and divorce."[79] Since the rabbinical courts have exclusive jurisdiction to celebrate marriages of Jews in Israel, they would certainly apply the Halakhic definition of a Jew and of a convert in respect to all candidates for marriage.

Reform Conversion in Israel

Conversions performed in Israel are recognized only in cases where they have been performed in accordance with the Halakhah by a duly constituted rabbinical court. This matter is regulated by an old Mandatory law of 1927, which provides: "A person who has changed his religious community, and desires legal effect to be given to such change, shall obtain a certificate from the head of the religious community which he has entered, to the effect that he has been received into that community, and shall certify the fact to the District Commissioners of the District in which he resides."[80] This ordinance is still part of the law of Israel and is interpreted to mean that "the head of the religious community" that the convert has entered, in the case of Jews, is the official rabbinate. Consequently, under the law of the land, no conversion in Israel is recognized in civil law, unless certified by the rabbinate as valid.

While the law of 1970 left the term *convert* undefined and took no further position on the recognition of non-Orthodox conversions, it did, by implication, accord recognition to non-Orthodox conversions in the Diaspora. This in turn was tantamount to giving recognition to the existence of religious trends in Judaism outside Orthodoxy. These implications were not lost on the leaders of Orthodoxy in Israel and Ameriica, who inveighed against the law as offering an opening to Reform and to Conservative Judaism,[81] and carried on a vigorous campaign to have the words "according to the Halakhah" reentered in the law. A "Committee for Jewish Survival" has been created for this purpose, with its headquarters in New York. The rabbis in Israel, as well as leading Orthodox rabbis in the Diaspora, have demanded that Mafdal ministers should resign from the government unless the latter supported this amendment.* Mafdal was seriously embarrassed by this criticism and especially by the Helen Zeidman case, which threatened to bring about another government crisis shortly after the passage of the law of 1970.

In 1964 Helen Zeidman arrived from America as a tourist; she was not Jewish, but long before her arrival had displayed an active in-

---

* The matter came up again in 1972, when Agudat Israel presented a bill to have this amendment added to the law of 1970. After an emotional and often acerbic debate in the Knesset, the motion was defeated 57 to 19 on July 12, with Mafdal abstaining. Golda Meir sharply criticized the rabbinate, saying it was "impossible to continue under the strictures of ancient customs. Our rabbis must find a way to ease the nation's burdens."

terest in Judaism. She became a permanent resident, and eventually a member of kibbutz Nachal Oz. In 1967 she married a member of the kibbutz and, since she was a Unitarian, the marriage was contracted in accordance with the law of Mexico, which permits civil marriage by proxy. A few months later, she applied to Rabbi Moshe Zemer of Congregation Kedem (Progressive) in Tel Aviv, and after six months of instruction became a convert to Judaism. She did not apply for conversion to the rabbinic authorities, because she understood that they would deny any such request, inasmuch as she was a member of a nonreligious kibbutz and was in no position to keep the dietary laws, a prerequisite for Halakhic conversion. Following the judgment in the Shalit case, which recognized a person's bona fide declaration as sufficient ground for registering him as a Jew (and before the enactment of the law of 1970, which amended that law), Helen applied to the High Court of Justice for an order directing the registration office to show cause why she should not be registered as a Jew. The enactment of the law of 1970 did not actually alter her situation, for this law was not made retroactive, and her case would thus be adjudicated on the basis of the principle of the Shalit case.

The Mafdal cabinet ministers insisted that the Attorney-General be instructed to appear in the High Court of Justice to resist the petition and, in case of an adverse decision, that the government introduce a bill in the Knesset with a view to amending the Law of Return and the Population Registry Law by the addition of the words *in accordance with the Halakhah* following the word *converted*. The government rejected the demands of Mafdal. A crisis seemed unavoidable following the decree issued by the Chief Rabbis "ordering" the leader of Mafdal, in his capacity as Minister of the Interior, not to register Helen Zeidman as a Jewess, even if ordered to do so by the High Court. As the day of the court hearing drew near, leading Israeli personalities, as well as some members of the kibbutz, approached Helen with the request that she agree to an Orthodox conversion, with the object of saving the country a government crisis at a time of serious external difficulties. The hearing was fixed for June 15, 1970. On June 14, Helen appeared before a rabbinical board consisting of Rabbi Shlomo Goren, then Chief Chaplain to the armed forces, and two other army chaplains, and underwent conversion that same day. She thereupon signed an application to the court for leave to withdraw her petition. In this manner the dreaded government crisis was averted.[82]

While the public heaved a sigh of relief, the conversion seemed to many to have been a farcical performance, a blow to the prestige of religion in general and the rabbinate in particular. Here was a conversion performed in a matter of hours, when in most cases it would take months, if not years, with many applications rejected altogether. Here was the case of a person who was converted by Orthodox rabbis, even though she could and would not agree to lead an Orthodox life, for she would return to her kibbutz where dietary laws were not observed. To compound these irregularities, Helen had been a divorcée when she married Benjamin Zeidman, who as a cohen was prohibited from wedding a divorced woman and was thereby guilty of transgressing a Halakhic injunction. Rabbi Zemer was in all respects right when he wrote that Rabbi Goren had in fact performed a Reform conversion, in that he had ignored well-established Halakhic rules.[83]

A number of Orthodox supporters were very unhappy about the "happy ending" of the Zeidman case. Mafdal had exerted itself to bring about a conversion in order to avoid a cabinet crisis; it had acted independently of the Chief Rabbinate, for the conversion itself was carried out not by the official rabbinate but by the Army chaplaincy, in violation of Halakhic rules and rabbinic practice.[84]

Reform Conversions in the Diaspora

Prior to the enactment of the Amendment to the Law of Return in 1970, difficulties were experienced by prospective immigrants, when one member of the couple had been converted to Judaism under non-Orthodox auspices. Not all cases were reported in the press, but a few did come to the attention of the public. In the summer of 1964, a young British Jew, a member of a Liberal congregation, applied for an entry permit into Israel under the Law of Return. He made his application for himself and for his wife, who had been converted to Judaism in a Liberal synagogue in England. He was told that he could certainly obtain such an entry permit. His wife, however, not being Jewish, could not qualify under the Law of Return, but could be admitted either as a temporary resident or as a non-Jewish immigrant. The spokesman for the Jewish Agency Immigration Department in London was quoted as saying: "Israel government rules apply—and the Israel government does not consider a Reform convert a Jew." In response, Liberal Rabbi Bernard Hooker wrote: "At a time when Liberal and Reform Congregations in this country—exhorted by various Zionist bodies—are showing an increasing interest in the State of Israel, it is tragic that they should be told by the Jewish Agency that many of their members are not to be considered as Jews."[85] No official comment was forthcoming from Israel.

The Executive of the Jewish Agency could no longer ignore this problem, which had turned into a public issue. The then chairman of the Executive of the Jewish Agency, Moshe Sharett, who was very much concerned with the repercussions of the matter on Israel-Diaspora relations, wrote to the (Reform) Union of American Hebrew Congregations: "The Executive of the Jewish Agency has taken note of the information furnished to it at its plenary session by the Immigration Department, to the effect that its facilities and assistance are extended to all immigrants to Israel without any exception or discrimination whatsoever, including those converted to Judaism by Reform or Liberal rabbis." Sharett concluded by expressing the hope that "this authoritative statement, which fully accords with the facts of the situation, will allay all doubts entertained or expressed on this subject by the Union of American Hebrew Congregations in the United States or by similar organizations in other countries."[86]

These doubts, however, were not allayed. Following the decision adopted by the Executive of the Jewish Agency, S. Z. Shragai, head of the Immigration Department and a prominent leader of Mafdal, averred: "Every mixed-marriage couple is permitted to immigrate, but the law of Return applies only to the Jewish partner. My department is not competent to authorize it, but once the government sanctions the immigration of a non-Jew, we give him all the help extended to every immigrant." Shragai was thus referring to the marriage of a Jew with a person converted under Reform Judaism as a "mixed-marriage couple." This is evident from a further passage in his statement: "According to the law of the land, a Jew is one who was born of a Jewish mother, or was converted according to Halakhah."[87]

A most striking case involving a non-Orthodox conversion occurred in 1968, when 22-year-old Galia Ben-Gurion applied to the Haifa rabbinate to register for her forthcoming marriage. Galia was the granddaughter of former Prime Minister David Ben-Gurion. During the Second World War her father, Amos Ben-Gurion, was serving in England in the Jewish Brigade and wished to marry a non-Jewess. The latter was willing to be converted in accordance with the Halakhic ritual, but the Orthodox rabbinate in London asked her to wait a year, as is often the custom. The couple, however, were anxious to leave for Palestine, and therefore resorted to a Reform rabbi who converted her to Judaism. In the judgment of the Halakhah, therefore, Mrs. Amos Ben-Gurion had never been converted, which made her daughter Galia, born in Israel, also non-Jewish. Having no alternative, Galia had to consent to be converted before she could marry.[88]

The rules of conversion practiced by the rabbinate in Israel are in general more lenient and less exacting than those of most Orthodox rabbis in the Diaspora, and largely depend on the attitudes of the individual rabbi. Thus, in many cases a year's period of waiting is strictly enforced, while in others the period may be considerably shorter. In the year 1966/67, 319 applications for conversion were filed with the rabbinical courts in Israel, of which 283 were adjudicated, while 649 remained pending from previous years.[89] In 1967/68, 348 persons applied, 422 were adjudicated, while 575 were pending,[90] whereas in 1970/ 71, there were 641 applications with 587 cases adjudicated, and 633 still pending.[91] An increase in applicants for conversion occasioned an increase in the number of adjudicated cases, but there was also an even heavier backlog of pending cases.

When women are candidates for conversion, special stress is laid on instruction in the dietary laws and the rules of family purity, the assumption being that the proselyte will follow the Halakhic way of life after the conversion has taken place. Although the Halakhah generally regards an applicant for conversion who is motivated by desire to marry a Jew as unacceptable, the rabbis in Israel do not as a rule disqualify an applicant on that ground alone. In many cases they do raise objections, insist on the year's waiting period and occasion other delays, in the expectation that the applicant may abandon his plan. Conversion proceedings seldom come to public notice, for the applicants invariably avoid publicity. From time to time instances of particular hardship have, however, been reported, particularly in cases of residents of kibbutzim, because the majority of the members are nonobservant. The dietary laws are usually not observed except in the Orthodox kibbutzim, and therefore applicants for conversion are usually asked to leave the kibbutz as a prerequisite to conversion procedures. In the Knesset a spokesman for the kibbutz movement commented bitterly: "This is an affront . . . to those self-respecting Jews who have created a society in which all take pride. Their contribution to the upbuilding of this country, to the setting up of this state and the molding of our society is most considerable. The members of the kibbutzim along the frontiers, holding the plough in one hand, the rifle in the other, constitute a tight ring of security that is one of the country's finest defenses. . . . It would better behoove the rabbis, instead of denying the Jewishness of the kibbutz, to see to it that Yeshivah students, who come under their direct influence, fulfill their duty towards the defense of the state, and thus relieve the burden imposed upon the members of the kibbutzim whom they presume to defame."[92] The difficulties in the way of conversions within kibbutzim assumed such proportions that Prime Minister Golda Meir was forced to make strong representations to the Minister of Religious Affairs, and requested his urgent intervention.[93]

Leaders of Mafdal, too, were critical of those rabbis who deliberately withheld the possibility of conversion from those settled in kibbutzim. Since no fixed standards for granting conversions existed and requirements depended on the character of the local rabbinate, Sefardic Chief Rabbi Yizchak Nissim suggested the setting up of a central rabbinic court to deal with all applications. The suggestion was accepted by the Chief Rabbinate, but was not implemented because of internal opposition.[95]

Russian Jews

With the appearance of many Olim from the Soviet Union, the number of intermarried couples has increased considerably. In their case, it has not been an instance of conversion from Christianity to Judaism, for the non-Jewish partner is rarely a Christian who has undergone the rite of baptism. Thus the process has not involved giving up one religion in favor of another. In order to facilitate the Ingathering, the office of the Immigration Department of the Jewish Agency, which handles the arrivals from Eastern Europe, saw to it that an Orthodox rabbinical court was set up in Vienna to deal with all persons seeking conversion on their way to Israel. It was felt desirable to arrange for their conversion while en route, so that they should be regarded as full Jews on their arrival in the Jewish state.

This measure was strongly supported by leaders of Mafdal, for it was bound to eliminate difficulties and embarrassments, and the Minister of Religious Affairs asserted that it was justified on religious grounds.[95] Even Chief Rabbi Unterman supported the arrangement; in his view it was desirable that conversion take place before Aliyah, because otherwise some of the people involved might, after arrival in Israel and on seeing the wide measure of nonobservance of Halakhic rules prevailing there, decide against conversion.[96] Nevertheless, owing to the pressure of the ultra-Orthodox, the Chief Rabbinate adopted a ruling which, while it did not actually invalidate the Vienna conversions, nonetheless made them subject to review by the Israeli rabbinate. In justifying this reversal of policy, Rabbi Unterman belittled its importance: "Suppose that the immersion in the ritual bath were performed in the presence of two, instead of three, qualified witnesses, because one of the potential witnesses was late in arriving, then the person will undergo the rite again. Where is the problem? What is all the noise about?"[97] It was he, also, who invalidated conversions performed in Copenhagen by Rabbi Benjamin Melchior, Chief Rabbi of Denmark, who, though Orthodox, was considered to have shown a sympathetic attitude to the Conservative trend.[98]

H. SUMMARY

In the logical course of events, the question of arriving at a generally accepted definition of "Who is a Jew?" should have awaited the culmination of the evolutionary process related to the problem of "What is a Jew?", that is, what is the content of Jewish life in modern society? The Orthodox political and religious leadership forced a consideration of the issue in the hope of safeguarding Halakhic principles by enacting them into the statute books.

This controversy, emotion-laden as it was, helped to clarify a number of basic points of agreement and disagreement. It was generally realized that the religious and ethnic-national components of Judaism are so intimately interwoven as to be indissoluble. A person of Jewish origin who is an agnostic or an atheist is still a Jew; if, however, he opts out of the Jewish faith through conversion to another religion, he also opts out of the ethnic-national group into which he was born. Even as exit from the Jewish fold can be effected in only one way—abandonment of the Jewish faith by conversion to another, so can admission into the Jewish ethnic-national group be achieved only by the adoption of the Jewish faith.

This was and is the general consensus. Sharp differences appeared in the application of these principles, and these reflected the full extent of the gap separating the adherents of the Halakhah as interpreted by the Orthodox and the adherents of other religious trends in Judaism, as well as the secularists. By taking their stand on the Halakhic rule that a Jew was one born of a Jewish mother, or one converted to Judaism in accordance with the Halakhah, the Orthodox reasserted their position that the Halakhah transcends history, rather than being shaped by history. Consequently it is the Halakhah that should mold the Jewish people, rather than the Jewish people who should mold the Halakhah. Halakhah is the raison d'être of the Jewish people rather than the means for its survival, and consequently the Halakhah stands eternally immutable even in the presence of a totally novel and unforeseen reality. Judaism is to be viewed not so much as what it is, but rather as what it should be. Pluralistic Judaism in contemporary life may be an undeniable fact, but in determining norms for the Jewish way of life, it should be ignored.

Against this conception is pitted the historical school of thought, which conceives of the Jewish religion as a component (in the past, to be sure, the most important component) of Judaism, which includes the totality of Jewish culture and experience. Judaism, like all historical phenomena, is the result of an evolutionary development, in which the weight and nature of the religious component have varied at different times. This view, which was first elaborated by Simon Dubnow, received a distinct nationalist emphasis at the hands of Ahad HaAm, for whom the religious component was a means of assuring the survival of the nation.[99] Judaism is conceived of as a dynamic development reflecting the characteristics of the age, and therefore the problem of "Who is a Jew?" cannot be answered by dogmatic and immutable definitions.

This historical approach was summarized by Gershom Scholem:

> I define Zionism as a utopian return of the Jews into their own history. With the realization of Zionism, the fountains of the great deep of our historical being have welled up, releasing new forces within us. Our acceptance of our history as a realm whence our roots grow is

permeated with the conviction that the Jews, after the shattering catastrophe of our times, are entitled to define themselves according to
their own needs and impulses; and that Jewish identity is not a fixed
and static thing, but one dynamic and even dialectical, because it involves in its spiritual, no less than its social and political aspects, a
living and creative body of people who call themselves Jews.[100]

The attempt to remove the problem from the historical plane to the
legal-political plane by inscribing the definition of *Jew* in the statute
books of the Jewish state, reflects the irreconcilability of two distinct
schools of thought. At the moment the gulf appears unbridgeable. Both
sides are devoted to what they consider the Jewish ideal to be. The
Orthodox views the problem of "Who is a Jew?" in terms of perpetuat-
ing a Halakhic principle; the undoubted majority of the people call for
a solution best conducive to the survival of the Jewish people in an age
of diversity and pluralism. In terms of Israeli realities, the prerequisites
of survival call for inclusion rather than exclusion; for the fostering of
Aliyah, and the fusion of the diverse communities, rather than the per-
petuation of schisms and of ancestral stigmata. The task of this generation, therefore, is to welcome and assimilate all who in good faith seek
to join the Jewish people and to share its burdens and perils. The di-
vergencies between these schools of thought cannot be reconciled by political action or by legislation. It is to be assumed that the traditional
policy of avoiding confrontation by resort to compromise and ad hoc
arrangements will pave the way for the eventual emergence of a consensus on this crucial issue.

10

The Crisis of Secularism

A. SECULARISM AND SECULARISTS

A religious person is referred to in Israel as "Dati." The word *religion* in the Western sense has no equivalent in the Hebrew language. The term *Dati* is derived from the biblical word *Dat,* which is translated as "law." The term *Dati* is applied to a person who observes the law, that is, the precepts of the Halakhah, particularly those precepts relating to one's behavior and actions.[1] In contrast, a person may be pious in his own way, believe in God, and lead a righteous life, or he may be a devoted follower of a non-Orthodox religious trend—yet, in the eyes of the Orthodox, he is a *Hiloni,* a secularist. This term, less derogatory than *Epikoros,* current in the early years of this century, began to be applied by the Orthodox to describe not only assimilated Jews, but also all nonobservant Jewish nationalists, including, to be sure, the militantly anti-religious elements who were then vocal among Jewish socialists in Eastern Europe as well as among the Labor Zionists in Palestine. Thus, all who were not Orthodox were lumped into one category, *secularists.* It has been one of the more notable achievements of Orthodoxy that it has succeeded in attaching to all shades of non-Orthodox opinion the label of secularist, thus implying that there is no Jewish religion other than the Orthodox. From this it logically followed that secularism was the only ideological alternative to Orthodoxy, there being no religious alternative. The Orthodox have thus been relieved of the need to justify their position in dialogue with non-Orthodox religious trends or to engage in a meaningful discussion with the secularists, for they had no common ground with either. Orthodoxy has thus been recognized as the only legitimate expression of Judaism, and, therefore, entitled to exclusive control of all religious offices. Thus a clear line of demarcation was drawn between the secularists and the Orthodox, with the latter secure in their enjoyment of an ideological and institutional monopoly of religion.

To be sure, secularism has been firmly grounded in Zionist theory and practice. Even those who maintain that the century-old Jewish renaissance—which encompassed the revival of the Hebrew language and literature, the return to the cultivation of the ancient soil, and the ingathering of the exiles within a reconstituted commonwealth—could not have been brought about without a messianic impulse, admit that Zionism was essentially a form of secular nationalism. It was the nationalist movements in Italy and in central Europe in the second half of the nineteenth century, movements that were liberal and secular, that stimulated the early stirrings of Zionism. To Herzl and his associates in the creation of political Zionism, as well as to Ahad Ha'Am, exponent of cultural Zionism, the new and essentially secular nationalism was an expression of the imperishable Jewish urge to survive, in a period when the cohesion of the Jewish people as a monolithic religious community had begun to give way. Zionism was in open revolt against the heretofore unchallenged traditional view that *Geulah,* the redemption of the Jewish people, culminating in a return to Zion, would come about in God's own time, and that any attempt to force the Divine Hand by bringing it about through a human agency was an act of sacrilege. Even the false messiahs of the past, including the very conspicuous Messianic movements led by Shabbetai Zvi in the seventeenth century and Jacob Frank in the eighteenth, claimed divine authority for their pretensions. The founders of Zionism advanced no such claim.

Zionism, on the other hand, did not purport to act in pursuance of a religious authority or to achieve a religious goal. To Herzl and his associates, Zionism meant the end of the homelessness of the Jewish people. To Ahad Ha'Am, a Jewish state was a means of assuring the survival of Jewish culture, which he conceived in terms of the ethical teachings of the prophets of old rather than in terms of traditional Judaism. While the Zionist movement freely borrowed religious and traditional symbols in its educational and propagandist activities, and also incorporated certain religious rituals into its system of national festivals, it remained essentially secular. Even the revival of the Hebrew language and the consequent return to the Bible and the sources of Jewish culture in their original tongue did not alter the basically secular character of Jewish nationalism.

Some of the men of letters among the nationalists went far beyond Ahad Ha'Am. For the latter, the objective of a Jewish renaissance was the preservation of Judaism as a national rather than a religious culture, while for his principal opponent, Micah Joseph Berdichevsky, the essence of the Jewish revival was the emancipation of the Jew from the bonds of normative Judaism. He viewed the course of Jewish history in the Diaspora as an unwholesome phenomenon, characterized by the subjection of the individual to the rigid discipline of the Halakhah. This emancipation could be achieved through a return to a terrestial Jerusalem rather than to a celestial Zion. He preached a "transvaluation of values," a far-reaching revolution in the Jew's view of himself. "We are children and grandchildren of the generations that preceded us, but we are not buried in them. It is up to us either to be the last Jews, or the first of a new people."[2]*

A far more radical philosophy was advanced by Jacob Klatzkin, a Hebrew writer, Zionist publicist, and the leading exponent of the "negation of the Diaspora" theory. He regarded the Jews as "neither a denomination nor a school of thought." Thus, to deny Jewish spiritual teaching "does not place one outside the community, and to accept it does not make one a Jew. In short, to be part of the nation one need not believe in the Jewish religion as the Jewish spiritual culture." As against the "subjective" definition of a Jew, that is, according to one's choice of a creed, Klatzkin advances the "national" definition, whereby being a Jew is an objective fact. Jewish nationalism does not deny Jewish spiritual values; "it only refuses to raise them to the level of the criterion by which the nation is defined. It refuses to define being a Jew as something subjective, as a faith, but prefers to base it on something objective, on land and language." This, to him is the uniqueness of Zionism, in contradistinction to Judaism as a faith, or to Judaism as expressed in Diaspora nationalism. "What is new in Zionism is its territorial-political definition of Jewish nationalism."[3] In brief, Judaism as a religious creed cannot sustain the Jewish people in the Diaspora. Therefore a secular definition of a Jew was called for to assure the survival of the Jewish people.[4]

Early Zionists

In their own outlook and way of life the leaders of Zionism personified secularism. Theodore Herzl, Max Nordau, Chaim Weizmann, Otto Warburg, and many others were nonobservant Jews. This held true for many of the movement's early leaders in the United States as well. Louis D. Brandeis, the most outstanding leader in the history of American Zionism, was a freethinker who conceived of Zionism as an ideal that would replace the Jewish religion.[5] Jewish nationalism "seemed to Brandeis an attractive substitute for the Jewish religion. It promised to give

---

* He thus anticipated by half a century the total rejection of Diaspora Judaism by the Canaanite movement.

meaning and substance to Jewishness without imposing the religious aspects of Judaism."[6]

The extent to which Brandeis was determined to assure the secular character of the Zionist movement was demonstrated in 1917, a crucial year for Zionism. Weizmann and his associates in London were bending every effort to obtain from the British War Cabinet what later became known as the Balfour Declaration. The achievement of unity within the American community on behalf of a Jewish Palestine was essential. With that aim in mind, Brandeis, Felix Frankfurter, Judge Julian Mack, and other Zionist leaders carried on complex negotiations with Jacob Schiff and his associates of the American Jewish Committee, involving matters of ideological import. The negotiations seemed to be reaching their conclusion, and Jacob Schiff appeared ready to join the Zionist Organization. At a most crucial period, so prominent a non-Zionist as Jacob Schiff, generally regarded as a principal leader of American Jewry, would through his membership have given Zionism a great impetus and wide acceptance. When the agreement was sent to Schiff for signature, he signed it, but added a clause that stated: "Jews are those who accept the Jewish concept of the Deity." This injection of religious dogma led to a breakdown of the negotiations. In a letter to Schiff, Judge Mack stated: "Just as a Jew remains a Jew, notwithstanding that the weakness of the flesh may lead him even to commit murder, so the Jew remains a Jew, a part of our people, even though he personally rejects the Biblical conception of the Deity. . . . I personally should want to cast out the former, not the latter; you doubtless want to reject both; but I believe both of us are impotent to do so."[7]

The main factor for creating the secularist climate of the Yishuv in Palestine was the revolutionary mood that engulfed the masses of Russian Jewry in the early years of this century. The First Aliyah had still been generally traditional, reflecting the state of mind of Russian Jewry at the end of the nineteenth century. However, the Second Aliyah, which exerted the most far-reaching influence on the shaping of the modern Yishuv, was a product of the revolutionary changes that occurred in the Russian Empire in the years 1903–1906. The impact of those changes on Jewish youth in Russia was equally revolutionary: it radicalized and thereby secularized the young Jewish generation.

In a long letter addressed to Theodore Herzl on May 6, 1903, Weizmann describes the upheaval:

Young Jews have turned revolutionaries, thousands of them are in prison or exiled to Siberia. Almost all students belong to the revolutionary camp. . . . Children are in open revolt against their parents. The elders are confined within tradition and Orthodox inflexibility. The young make their first step a search for freedom from everything Jewish. In one small town near Pinsk, youngsters tore the Torah scroll to shreds. This speaks volumes.

Weizmann criticized Herzl's policy of encouraging the Mizrahi, with a view to attracting the Orthodox to the Zionist fold: "This will lead straight to catastrophe. If there is anything in Judaism that has become intolerable and incomprehensible to the best of Jewish youth, it is the pressure to equate its essence with the religious formalism of the Orthodox. Jewish youth, he added, could be saved through Zionism and a return to Jewish culture, but the latter should no longer be confused with Jewish religious worship.[8]

Second and Third Aliyot

The radically minded young Jews of the stormy years of the first Russian revolution who flocked to the banner of the Second Aliyah were militantly anti-religious, but it was not only they who were thoroughly secular. The liberal-minded Jewish intelligentsia were also rejecting the religious practices of their fathers. Vladimir Jabotinsky, one of the most brilliant figures on the Zionist horizon, was the idol of Russian Jewry, personifying as he did some of the finest traditions of West-European secular liberalism. His biographer writes of him that "in his spiritual budget there was simply no place for God. . . . A child of the rationalist and secular-minded later nineteenth century, Jabotinsky well remembered Laplace's remark to Napoleon that, whilst writing his *Mécanique Celeste,* he found no need to assume the existence of God." In spite of his traditional background, Jabotinsky made no effort to observe the Sabbath or the Jewish dietary laws.[9] Even in 1926, when he had become leader of the Revisionist party within the Zionist movement and well knew the importance of support from the Orthodox, Jabotinsky in his writings referred to Orthodoxy in derogatory terms, deplored its negative attitude to free inquiry and the low legal status accorded to women.[10] Years later, when he established the New Zionist Organization and found it advisable to solicit the favor of the Orthodox, he hastened to reassure his atheist son that "I am now, as ever, for the freedom of thought. . . . I myself see no holiness in the Jewish ritual."[11]

Secularism was the spirit of the age; in fact, it was the hallmark of any progressive movement.[12] As a liberation movement, Zionism, born and nurtured in the liberal-nationalist climate of pre-World War I days in Europe, was infused with a secular impulse. Following the outbreak of the Communist Revolution in 1917, the radicalization of Jewish youth assumed ever-wider proportions, and it was from this element that by far the larger part of the Third Aliyah was drawn. The Second and the Third Aliyah molded the image of the Yishuv and its social, economic, and political life, consequently creating a secular climate. Their impact on the Yishuv was overwhelming and enduring, and was not altered substantially by the mass immigration of Jews from Moslem countries, who were predominantly traditional. Zionism, like all nationalist movements in Europe, was secularist.[13]

Statistics

No accurate percentages of the Orthodox and of the secularists are available. It is doubtful, indeed, if exact data could be obtained, because there is no clear-cut division between the two groups. There are degrees of nonobservance among the Orthodox, and there are degrees of some observance on the part of the secularists. It can, however, be safely assumed that those voting for the religious parties are Orthodox; their percentage in the seven election campaigns held since 1949 has been fairly constant and has never exceeded 15%. The percentage of Orthodox practitioners is no doubt higher, for not all who are Orthodox vote for the religious parties.[14] A poll conducted in June 1965 by the Central Bureau of Statistics showed that on the Sabbath 29% of regular listeners do not turn on the radio. Another criterion for ascertaining the percentage of the two groups is school enrollment; the percentage of children attending state-religious and other religious schools is one-third of the total enrollment, but it is known that there are nonobservant parents who choose a religious education for their children.

In 1963, a study initiated by the Israel Institute of Applied Social Research was published. Some 30% of the respondents declared themselves as observing most religious commandments, while 24% declared themselves to be "not at all observant, completely secular." Some 4% failed to reply, while 46% stated that they observed tradition "to some extent." An analysis of the latter group, which comprises nearly half of the total, indicates that it is far from homogeneous and only its outer fringes are totally secular. In reply to the question, "Should the government see to it that public life is conducted in accordance with Jewish religious tradition?", some 23% replied definitely in the affirmative, an additional 20% replied "probably yes," while 53% replied in the negative. Again 4% failed to answer.[15]

The mass Aliyah from Islamic countries, the great majority of whose members are traditional Jews, made them the majority in the state-religious schools. However, their traditionalism, intellectually and emotionally, is different from the Orthodoxy of the Ashkenazic communities. They have not associated themselves with Neturei Karta, they have not been involved in acts of assault for religious reasons, nor have they otherwise been identified with excesses in the name of religion. They are on the whole far more tolerant of differences than Orthodox Jews of European origin and also reveal a higher proportion of change from observance to nonobservance. This change is part of the general disintegration of their patriarchal way of life, which characterized the Oriental communities in their lands of origin.

This tendency was highlighted in a survey of maternity cases conducted in 1959–60. Of the new Oriental Olim, 68.9% were observant, while the percentage of the observant among veteran settlers of the same category was less than half, only 31.8%. In a study of social change in Israel, Dr. Judah Matras observed that intergenerational change in religious observance was more frequent among Oriental women, whether Israeli-born or Olim, than among women of European origin. The degree of change showed an accelerated pace, which corresponded to the duration of their stay in Israel, to their schooling, and also to the extent of their acceptance of employment. "Although the European-born observant sector appears to be relatively stable . . . the religious sector of Israeli-born and Oriental immigrant population groups are experiencing large scale 'defections' to the partially observant and nonobservant camp."[16] This trend was also confirmed by Professor Simon H. Herman of the Hebrew University, who in 1964–65 conducted a survey among 3,679 eleventh-graders in 117 high schools, as well as among a subsample of parents and pupils. When asked to classify themselves as religious, traditional, or nonreligious, the respective percentages were 25%, 32%, and 42%, with 19% within the latter category describing themselves as anti-religious; among the parents the percentages were 33% and 37%, with only 27% nonreligious. The trend toward nonobservance was more pronounced among pupils of Oriental origin. Whereas 85% of the Ashkenazic pupils who classified themselves as religious and 14% as traditionalists described their parents as religious, only 62% of the Orientals described their parents as religious and 33% called their parents traditionalists.[17]

Thus, while no definite figures are available—indeed, the nature of the subject does not lend itself to statistical accuracy—it can be estimated that close to 30% of the total Jewish population may be classified as Orthodox, about 20% as nonreligious, and about half neither Orthodox nor nonreligious, but rather favorably disposed to some degree of traditional observance. Together with the nonreligious, this large group is categorized by the Orthodox as secularists, though its general attitude to traditional observance is not at all negative. A person may be incensed at the imposition of some of the Halakhic rules that run counter to his moral feelings, yet he may participate in varying degrees of ritual observance, whether it be occasional visits to the synagogue or adherence to the dietary laws. The mood of this significant segment is summed up by a well-known student of Israel's religious landscape: "They are not willing to commit themselves to a religious way of life, but they want to retain a good deal of the religious tradition. They prefer to be inconsistent, rather than to break completely with Judaism. This attitude represents a synthesis of opposition to a total commitment to religion, together with an equally strong attachment to the religious traditions of Judaism."[18]

The urge to retain a degree of attachment to Judaism as a religion is facilitated by the fact that many religious observances, and especially Holydays, readily lend themselves to a nationalist interpretation. Both the Orthodox and non-Orthodox may cherish the same traditional symbol, the one because of its religious content, the other because of its national. Thus, both groups do, in a manner of speaking, complement each other, and in fact have a common ground for potential dialogue.

B. THE CRISIS OF SECULARISM

Nationalization of Religion

While Israel is regarded as a secular state, and its society—at least as the Orthodox view it—is predominantly secular, yet it is a Jewish state and a Jewish society, not only because it consists of Jews, but because of its Jewish character. Israel is a product of Jewish history and is an integral part of Jewish continuity, hence separation of religion from the body politic is an impossibility, even for committed secularists. A total separation would entail a separation from Jewish culture. Thus, the secularists regard the observance of the Sabbath and the Jewish religious festivals as their national days of rest and their national holidays. Hardly anywhere in the Christian world is Sunday as strikingly observed as is the Sabbath in the most secular of Israeli cities. One has to witness the total public observance of the Day of Atonement (Yom Kippur) in order to experience an overwhelming demonstration of a nation's solidarity, exemplified not only by crowded synagogues and other ad hoc worship halls, but also by a total abstention from any public activity that could be regarded as giving the slightest offense to an observant Jew.

The act of circumcision is universally observed as a religious rite and a festive celebration. The same generally applies to the celebration of Bar Mitzvah, the traditional ceremony incumbent upon a boy when he attains the age of thirteen, considered to be the age of moral maturity, and therefore entailing the obligation to perform religious precepts. The blowing of the shofar, the traditional ram's horn, on the occasion of the inauguration of a newly elected President of the State, is regarded as befitting the solemnity of the occasion. The practice of attaching Mezuzot to the doorposts of both private and public buildings in Israel meets with hardly any objection.[19] Equally acceptable is the funeral service, conducted always in accordance with the minutiae of the religious law. All these features of traditional Judaism, so generally accepted, are regarded by the secularists not so much as "religious" but rather as significant aspects of the national culture.

Israel is conspicuously Jewish also because of its national language. The use of Hebrew is far more than the adoption of a common tongue by immigrant groups arriving from all corners of the globe, each bringing its own linguistic tradition; Hebrew has the quality of imparting idioms and symbols that are charged with Jewish content. The teaching of the Bible in its original tongue in every school from the age of 6 through 18 as a central feature of the curriculum leaves an enduring impact on the younger generation. While the Orthodox teach the Bible as an act or aspect of Divine revelation, the secularists teach it as the expression of the Jewish genius revealed in the ethical teachings of the Prophets. Thus the Bible remains the basic cultural heritage, the national common denominator. Israel is more than a realization of Herzl's *Judenstaat,* a state populated by Jews, but a *Jüdischer Staat,* a Jewish state, in the sense that it is Jewish not only ethnically but, first and foremost, spiritually and culturally.

In fact, the term *secularists* was never a fair description of the non-Orthodox, even in the days of the militant anti-religious of the Second and Third Aliyot. The upbuilding of the Jewish homeland since the modern "Shivat Zion"* in 1881, especially during the years preceding the establishment of the state, called for a degree of dedication, self-denial, and complete immersion in the ideal, such as has rarely been encountered in the experience of self-emancipating nations. Zionist aspirations were not confined to the attainment of political objectives, nor to the betterment of suffering peoples, but rather demanded the achievement of spiritual and ethical ideals. Zionism found its tangible expression in the attachment to the tilling of inhospitable soil, both as a means of employment and livelihood and as a sublimation for a nation so long alienated from nature. When employing the traditional concept of Redemption (*Geulah*), the secularists were possessed by a quasi-Messianic fervor, setting themselves the goal of the Good Society. It was, to be sure, a secular Messianism, but it was pursued with a religious intensity that richly sustained two generations of young Jews.

With the creation of the independent Jewish state in 1948, a crisis within secularism emerged. The establishment of a sovereign state represented the achievement of the goal for which the Zionists had been striving. The Basle Program as formulated in 1897 had called for the establishment "for the Jewish people of a publicly and legally assured home in Palestine." This had been attained, and a new platform, the "Jerusalem Program," was adopted by the Zionist Congress in 1951, which called for the solidarity of the Jewish people with the Jewish state, for the promotion of the ingathering of the exiles, and for the spread of Jewish culture in the lands of the Diaspora. Before long it became obvious that there were few specific Zionist ingredients in the

---

* "Those that return to Zion," a term taken from Psalm 126:1.

program, for its aims and activities had become the common possession
of the predominant majority of all Jews, Zionist and non-Zionist. Organized Zionists in the Diaspora found themselves "underemployed," or
even "unemployed," inasmuch as the major fund-raising activities, pro-
Israel propaganda, and political activities were taken over by institutions, organizations, and agencies, all functioning outside the Zionist
framework. The establishment of a truly "Zionist" qualification for membership in the World Zionist Organization, that is, the duty of a member
to go on Aliyah to Israel, was resisted by Zionist Congresses, and only
at the 1971 Congress was a rather diluted version of the "Duty of Aliyah" adopted.

Both in Israel and the Diaspora, the very *raison d'être* of the World
Zionist Organization was challenged. No less a personage than David
Ben-Gurion declared that the organization no longer had a real Zionist
objective, and that, in consequence, its functions in Israel, in the fields
of immigration, absorption, land settlements, and housing, should be
taken over by the appropriate departments of the government of Israel.
Contact between Israel and the Diaspora could be direct, that is, with
the various Jewish institutions and organizations in the Diaspora, rather
than through the medium of the Zionist Organization. Said Ben-Gurion:
"It is a frequent phenomenon in history that concepts and causes are
stubbornly retained long after they have lost their meaning. It is like a
wine bottle that has been drained and refilled with water, but owing to
inertia no one has bothered to remove the label. This is what has happened to the term 'Zionist' in our generation."[20]

Not only was the Zionist movement in a crisis following the establishment of the state, but the Yishuv, too, was confronted with the
need to reevaluate ideological concepts. Halutziut (Pioneering), which
was the most elevated expression of secular nationalism, had lost a
good deal of its motivation, and was deprived of much of its traditional
scope. To be sure, in the sphere of land settlement, pioneers were working on a scale larger than ever before, for vast opportunities were now
being offered; yet a good deal of the original voluntary aspect was lost.
Activities previously carried on on a voluntary basis were now largely
taken over by the state. Volunteer service in the Haganah was replaced
by service in the Defense Army of Israel. Huge projects of land reclamation and settlement were now the task of institutional bodies fit to
cope with mass immigration. Not only was the miraculous emergence
of the state exalted, but the state itself was cherished as a precious possession, and its preservation was regarded as being of supreme value.
Thus, Halutziut was gradually transformed into patriotism, which was
best expressed in the spirit animating the Defense Army of Israel, which
has succeeded in retaining its character as a people's army. Before long,
however, a large bureaucracy began to replace the functions of volun-

tary effort in extensive areas. With all its highly gratifying elements, the emergence of an Israeli patriotism could not bridge over the void created by the decline of Zionist ideology. Accepted ideas and values came under scrutiny and the relationship of an Israeli Jew in his sovereign state to a fellow-Jew in the Diaspora raised once more the question of Jewish identity, particularly for the younger generation.

In this groping for reorientation, religion was of little interest in the early years of the state. There was now an abatement, if not a total disappearance, of the militant anti-religious sentiments that had characterized certain left-wing elements in the Yishuv. Religion was accepted as an institution. Both the left-wing Mapam and the Communist Party supported the appropriation of public funds for the maintenance of the rabbinate. The attitude to religion as a spiritual force, however, was one of indifference. To the bulk of the secularists, religion, which to them meant Orthodoxy, appeared to be concerned with the technicalities of a ritual, but not with what they considered the pressing issues of existence. Wrote an Orthodox intellectual: "This is reflected in the almost wholly practical character of the Israeli Rabbinate, which is concerned solely with 'conspicuous' religion, particularly the public observance of Kashrut and the Sabbath, and with marriage and divorce. It is almost completely silent on matters of belief and thought, and rarely speaks out on social problems."[21]

Had it not been for the violence of Orthodox extremists and publicity given to the application of certain Halakhic rules in matters of marriage and divorce, the rabbinic attitude toward Bnei Israel, the Karaites, and certain groups of converts to Judaism, coexistence between the Orthodox and the secularists—based on their mutual indifference to each other—would have been quite smooth. But the price of such indifference was the inhibition of a healthy evolution of a meaningful spiritual life.

Canaanites

Of the various attempts to reevaluate generally accepted concepts, that undertaken by the Canaanites was the most novel and extreme. This small literary-artistic group, led by one of the most talented contemporary Israeli poets, Yonatan Ratosh, made its appearance in the nineteen forties and reached its climax in the early fifties. In their view, Jewish history was interrupted in the first century by the severance of the Jewish people from its territorial base following the abortive revolt of Bar Kokhba, and by its evolution from a nation into a religious community. Throughout the centuries of Galut, the Jewish people had no history of their own. In the newly established state the process was reversed and a new nation was emerging. To make the reversal com-

plete, it ought to emancipate itself from Diaspora Judaism, detach itself from the Galut, and establish a direct continuity with the authentic
Canaanites and the pre-Israelite myths, which were the origin of the
Israelite culture. Only that which could be traced directly to the ancient territory of Israel, and to the Middle East in general, was worthy
of being perpetuated.

The new Canaanites thus rejected the entire Jewish experience in
the millennia of dispersion, and sought to create a new nation, identified
by, and deriving its spiritual sustenance from, its territorial base, which
would now resume the course of history interrupted by the Emperor
Hadrian's expulsion of the Jews from Palestine. The new national-ter-
ritorial entity, the emerging Hebrew nation, would be open to any person, irrespective of race or religion.[22] This new Hebrew nation would
include all who would dwell within the confines of its national territory,
regardless of their religious origin, and who, by detaching themselves
from the Diaspora heritage, would evolve a new Hebrew culture inspired by its Canaanite-territorial past. Some of the members of the
group formed a political circle called "Semitic Action." While its activities subsided eventually, and "Semitic Action" vanished, a residual
impression was left that manifested itself particularly in greater interest
in the Palestinian past.[23]

Ben-Gurion

Cognizant of the spiritual crisis, David Ben-Gurion sought in a variety of ways to promote a non-Orthodox, essentially secular, conception of Judaism that was in some respects an intermediate position between the Canaanite ideology and traditional Judaism. While he did not
seek to eliminate the Diaspora heritage, he downgraded it. He did not
preach a return to the Canaanite, but to the biblical past.

> The Jewish faith is not only monotheistic. Intrinsic is the national
> and the territorial motif, which led to the profound spiritual allegiance
> of the Jews to their ancient land, even when they lived in Exile. In-
> trinsic to it is the body of moral principles which proclaim the su-
> preme values of righteousness, mercy and love. And equally intrinsic
> to it is the idea of redemption, both of the Jewish people and of
> all the peoples of the world.[24]

By redemption Ben-Gurion meant "the fulfillment of the aspirations
of our prophets and teachers for the restoration of Jewish national life
on its own soil, and for the establishment there of a model society
which will become a light unto the nations." He tried to inculcate the
idea that a return to the ancient soil must be accompanied by a return
to the source of the cultural heritage, the Bible; the pursuit of the ethical

teachings of the prophets was to provide the spiritual content that would shape a model society.

Much to the chagrin of the Orthodox, he bypassed the post-biblical Talmud and its Halakhah. He deliberately chose as a model for the reconstituted Israel that period of Jewish history when the Jews were a nation rather than a religious community.

> Until the first destruction of our independence I doubt whether there was Halakhah generally. . . . The Bible was written by Jews at a time when there was no Halakhah. The great prophets asked of the Jews only two things: to believe in one single God . . . and to lead a moral life. Not a single prophet . . . asked the Jews to eat only kasher food; not a single word was said that a girl who is going to be married must go to the Mikveh.[25]

Ben-Gurion not only expressed a prevailing mood, but also promoted a climate of opinion that negated the only form of Jewish religion known to the Israelis. He thus became the exponent of a secular Judaism, anchored, to be sure, in the Bible and in Jewish ethical teaching, as well as in the soil of the ancient homeland. Ben-Gurion constantly sought to promote interest in the Bible, in word and in deed. For many years during his premiership, Saturday afternoons were devoted to sessions of a Bible class in his home. It was he who initiated the national and international annual Bible contests, which tens of thousands of young people followed with keen interest. The annual sessions of the Bible society were attended by thousands of people, and became national events, widely reported in the press. The keen interest in the study of the Bible and of archaeology manifested not a mere intellectual curiosity, but rather "a search for new links with the historic past."[26]

Ben-Gurion's stress on ethical principles as constituting the essence of Judaism added a significant weapon to the arsenal of the secularists. Over against the precepts of the Halakhah, the secularists posed the principles of morality. To deny to mamzerim the right to marry, for no fault of their own, appeared as a violation of a moral principle; the same applied to the case of a soman who, being a childless widow, was prevented from remarrying because of the obstinate refusal of her brother-in-law to agree to the Halitzah ceremony, or who, having been declared by the rabbinical court to be entitled to a divorce, could not in fact be divorced because of the refusal of the husband to deliver the get. While the secularists claimed that morality was on their side, the Orthodox invoked the sanctity of the Halakhah as transcending morality; the observance of the Halakhah, being a sacred duty, bound a Jew to obey its precepts even at the cost of considerable sacrifice to himself.[27] Each side restated and reenforced its own position; neither side moved toward a dialogue.

Israelis and Jews

There now appeared alarming signs of estrangement on the part of Jews in Israel toward Diaspora Jewry. Many of the younger generation, alienated from any contact with institutionalized religion, tended to regard themselves primarily as Israelis, and only secondarily as Jews. This was particularly apparent in the behavior of Israeli students abroad, who often felt themselves ill at ease in the Jewish communities in the Diaspora, although they were made warmly welcome there. Their lack of familiarity with the rudiments of ritual practices embarrassed them when in the homes of their hosts, who were themselves often disconcerted or distressed. There was often a total lack of even a minimal religious link to create an immediate affinity between host and guest. The Israelis abroad rejected the synagogues of the Orthodox as they would in Israel, while the places of worship of Conservative and Reform Jews were completely alien to them.

This tendency toward estrangement was studied by Professor Simon Herman. His authoritative study, *Israelis and Jews,* concluded that, while the great majority of the high school pupils demonstrated a sense of Jewish identity, the religious pupils scored highest on every scale of Jewish identity, followed by the traditionalists, and last of all by the secularists. When asked if they would choose to be born again as Jews, 94% of the religious, 76% of the traditionalists, and 54% of the secularists answered in the affirmative. Asked whether they would choose to be born as Jews if they lived outside Israel, 84% of the religious, 75% of the traditionalists, and only 37% of the secularists replied in the affirmative.[28] Finally, when asked to reply to the question: "When I feel more Israeli, do I also feel more Jewish?" 89% of the religious, 72% of the traditionalists, and 54% of the secularists said they did. It also appeared that the remaining 46% of the secularists reported that when they felt more Israeli, they felt either less Jewish (5%) or felt no relationship to their Jewishness.[29]

The author's conclusion was that Jewish identity showed signs of weakening because of the decline in the percentage of the religious, particularly among the Oriental communities, and because of a parallel weakening of Jewishness among the nonreligious. While in "the case of many of the nonreligious parents from Eastern Europe the defection from religion did not always seriously impair the sense of Jewish identity" in the case of the youth growing up in Israel, a greater void was created by the absence of the religious factor.[30] While the sense of Jewishness of the youth of Israel was still strong, the indications of a dangerous trend should be closely watched. "Religion and ethnicity are so closely interwoven into Jewish identity that any tendency towards their separation raises serious problems."[31]

Government Policy

Long before the publication of Herman's study, however, Israeli leaders expressed concern at the adverse impact of secularism on the attitude of Israeli youth toward the Diaspora. Zionism had revolted against the Galut, viewing it as an abnormal existence for the Jewish people. In Israel, religion was being equated with Halakhah, and Halakhah, as codified in the *Shulhan Arukh,* was being regarded as a product of the Galut—hence religion was by many equated with what was abnormal in Jewish life. Nevertheless, before long it was realized that, as the religious bond weakened, the link with the Diaspora was also bound to weaken. In 1955, the Ministry of Education and Culture announced a school program "to deepen the Jewish consciousness" of the younger generation of Israel. The government's policy, presented to the Knesset in 1955, stated that "in primary and secondary schools, and in higher education, the government will endeavor to deepen the Jewish consciousness of Israel's youth, to root it in the past and in the historical heritage of the Jewish people, and to strengthen its moral ties with world Jewry, founded upon recognition of the community of fate, and of the historical continuity which unites the Jews throughout the world in all countries and all generations." It was not until 1959 that this proposal was crystallized in a directive published by the Ministry of Education and Culture; this provided that the curriculum of the nonreligious state schools should stress the teaching of Jewish Diaspora history, with emphasis on national survival, and should familiarize the pupils with the liturgy, rites, customs, folklore, and religious symbols of Israel. Larger portions of the Talmud and some of the masterpieces of rabbinic literature were also to be added to the curriculum.[32]

The leftist parties voiced opposition to this program on the ground that it represented an attempt to introduce the teaching of religion in nonreligious schools. The Orthodox, on the other hand, opposed it on other grounds. To teach Jewish religious rites and symbols without imparting belief in their Divine validity, they said, would have no educational value, for it would not evoke an emotional response on the part of the pupils. Furthermore, the teaching of religious values would have no chance of success unless those teaching this subject were themselves imbued with a sincere religious belief. Therefore, since the great majority of such teachers were nonobservant, they would be unqualified to impart to their pupils a consciousness of Jewishness that they themselves did not possess. The program was, however, introduced, but because of the comparatively short period during which it has been instituted, its impact on the pupils cannot be properly assessed.

These attempts of the nonreligious—to evolve a new content by promoting a return to the Bible and to the universalist teaching of the prophets, by intensive study of the ancient past and preoccupation with archaeology, and finally by the attempt to inculcate Jewish conscious-ness in the school system—meritorious as they are in themselves, lead one to the inescapable conclusion that secularism is a spent force. Its limitations have become obvious and its inadequacy apparent. "Secu-larism has stopped making conquests," remarked one of the leading Israeli thinkers. "The primary limitation of secularism lies in its failure to furnish a global, all-embracing world outlook which would not fall short of the religious world picture in breadth, depth and insight. . . . In the very triumph of secularism lies its weakness. And this weakness of secularism in its turn fortifies the position of religion."[33]

Israeli secularism has exhausted its élan. Its advocates are no longer sure of their position.

C. SOUL-SEARCHING AMONG SECULARISTS

New Stimuli

One of the reasons that secularism is waning is the inadequacy of the traditional Zionist ideology in the face of an existing state. By cul-tivating a return to biblical Judaism, to a period of a "normal" national life, the link between the younger Israeli generation and Diaspora Jewry was visibly weakened. Secular Zionism, essentially a revolt against Dias-pora existence, was leading to an estrangement from the Diaspora that continued to be at the same time the essential reservoir of Jewish man-power, talent, and economic as well as political strength. This estrange-ment appeared on the school level when high school pupils expressed reluctance to study postbiblical Jewish history because of its overwhelm-ingly religious content. Israeli youth in army uniform could not compre-hend the apparent passive submission of millions of Jews to the dreadful fate that awaited them in the Nazi slaughterhouses. Such passivity was regarded as the product of a mentality nurtured in the centuries of "abnormal" Diaspora existence. Finally, the lack of readiness on the part of masses of Jews living in the free world to return to a homeland anxiously awaiting them, was further proof that there was a serious and organic lacuna in the make-up of Diaspora Jewry.

Yet, the apparent weakness of the link with the Diaspora proved to be an actual stimulus to reexamination of generally accepted attitudes. In the first instance, the day-to-day contact between Israel and the Dias-pora, particularly the Jewry of North America, was intimate and active, and the support of the Diaspora was essential for the survival of the young state. There were, moreover, certain developments that led Israeli youth to reconsider their attitude to the Diaspora, and in so doing, to reconsider their attitude to the religious problem. The first inkling of a reorientation occurred in the early sixties, when a group of Israeli sportsmen and youth leaders visited the Soviet Union. The deep emotions they experienced in the Moscow synagogue, where they found themselves surrounded by Jewish brethren whose emotion-laden silence spoke volumes, were told and retold in the Israeli press. These young Israelis were moved to tears by living through the rare experience of Jewish solidarity, and by the speechless affection lavished on them by fellow Jews who had been regarded as a withered limb of the body of the people. In the presence of these brothers, they seemed to have rediscovered their own identity and the source of their own faith.

The trial in Jerusalem of Adolf Eichmann, principal executor of the Nazi "final solution," unfolded in concrete and vivid terms the vast and horrifying panorama of the Holocaust, and left an indelible impression on Israeli-born youth. The sense of humiliation with which that youth had contemplated the fate of millions of Jews was superseded by the realization that they, the younger generation of Israel, were, directly or indirectly, the survivors of the Holocaust, and as such must bear the responsibility for the continued existence of the Jewish people. They realized that in the regard of the Gentile world they, like their brethren in the Diaspora, were Jews and nothing but Jews, and that consequently they constituted, whether as Jews or as Israelis, a single and indivisible community of fate.

The Six Day War

Of even greater impact was the Six Day War. The weeks of tension preceding the war, and the threats of extermination uttered by Arab leaders, resurrected thoughts of a Holocaust, and brought forth an unprecedented degree of internal cohesion and solidarity. This was further intensified by the material support of Diaspora Jewry, and by the flow of volunteers to Israel. Both Israel and the Diaspora were fused into one entity, which experienced the presentiment of a Holocaust. The impact was far-reaching and stimulated the urge toward soul-searching and a reexamination of Israeli and Jewish selfhood.

There is no more revealing document of the emotional upheaval occasioned by the Six Day War than a collection of recorded conversations with 140 soldiers drawn from 27 kibbutzim. These conversations were published in a volume entitled *Siach Lohamim*,[34] which achieved mass circulation in Israel. The utterances of the soldiers were most revealing, for they represented an elite community. Although they represented only 4% of the total population, members of kibbutzim accounted for over 25% of all the war casualties.

The war experience, the volume revealed, made the kibbutzniks realize that, although Israeli, they were first and foremost Jews. "They felt they had been re-united with the Jewish people." They discovered that the phraseology that had been suspect for them when uttered by their fathers had now a new meaning for themselves. Said a young soldier:

> Few are able to understand how the Jews of Europe could be slaughtered without a fight. Most feel more kinship with their ancestors of the biblical period . . . than with their more recent forebears in Europe and the Middle East. Suddenly threatened with annihilation, they identified themselves with the Jews in the Hitler era. In those days before the war, one came closest to that Jewish fate from which we have run like haunted beings all these years.[35]

Another soldier said:

> The first experience was Jerusalem. In my unit we heard the news on a transistor radio. When we heard of the conquest of Jerusalem, there was not a single soldier who did not weep, including me. Then for the first time I felt, not the 'Israeliness,' but the Jewishness of the nation.[36]

Not only the discovery of "Jewishness" however, was brought about by the experience of the war, but also an anxious search for the meaning and the purpose of life. The discovery of Jewishness led to the discovery of the religious ingredient inherent in Jewishness, or rather of the indivisibility of the ethnic and the religious, of the secular and the sacred.

Undoubtedly, the conquest of the Old City of Jerusalem and the liberation of the Western Wall, from which Jews had been excluded by the rulers of Jordan from 1948 till 1967, were powerful factors in the engendering of an enduring emotion. To quote some sayings by kibbutz members, born and bred in the secularist tradition:

> For me what symbolizes this war is the paratrooper who stood facing the Western Wall, and could find no other outlet for his emotion than tears; he was facing two thousand years of exile, the whole history of the Jewish people.[37]

Another said:

> And at this point I felt it. I became one with the House of David, the Kingdom of Solomon and the Temple. This is my inheritance. I feel as if a curtain had suddenly been lifted, and the very letters of the Eternal Book had sprung to life, familiar and immediate. I am no longer a stranger; suddenly I am a son of my people, stronger and with deeper roots.[38]

With their sharpened sensitiveness to spiritual problems, the kibbutz-born generation rediscovered their authentic identity; they were first and foremost Jews, an integral part of the world fellowship of Jews, united by a common fate. They were in quest of a new direction, and religion often became the subject of their conversation; it was now referred to approvingly, especially when it was related to Jerusalem. Theirs is a humanism that leaves room for religion, not so much as an ideal in itself, but as a significant element in Jewish survival.

Kibbutz and Religion

In the kibbutz society, more than in any other sector of Israeli society, the inadequacy of secularism is both felt and discussed. In many respects, the kibbutzim—except, of course, the Kibbutz Dati—have always represented the most deliberate and articulate secularism; this applied not only to the Marxist kibbutzim affiliated with the HaShomer HaTzair movement, where all traces of religious observance were obliterated, but to other kibbutz movements as well. Originally, the kibbutz was a Jewish community without a synagogue; synagogues were instituted at a later stage for the benefit of the elderly parents of kibbutz members. The members, constituting an enlarged family, were thrown upon their own resources, and developed into a closely knit ideological group; their commitment to values and ideals was characterized by an intensity that closely resembled religious fervor. Many universal problems were discussed, and the problem of religion eventually appeared in discussion and in publications.

It thus became inevitable for the kibbutzim to initiate discussions on Judaism, for they, more than any other secularist group, cherished their secularist ideals with religious fervor. Not surprisingly, they were the first to feel that treating the Sabbath merely as a period of work avoidance was tantamount to depriving it of any positive content. The literature of the various kibbutz movements is replete with discussions of the place of the Sabbath within the life of the kibbutz. It proved somewhat easier to confront the problem posed by Passover, for the tale of emancipation from Egyptian bondage was highly conducive to a nationalist interpretation. Freedom and the celebration of spring become the leitmotifs of the kibbutz Passover, and soon kibbutzim vied with one another in composing special Haggadot* for the occasion. Similarly, it was possible to employ a national and agricultural emphasis for the Shavuot (Pentecost) festival. It was far more difficult to impart a meaningful content into Rosh HaShanah and Yom Kippur (which are festivals not based on historical or agricultural precedent), without ex-

---

* Haggadah (plural, Haggadot), literally "tale," is the name for the traditional book that is read on Passover, at the Seder.

tensive borrowings from the traditional ritual.[39] To ignore these Holy-days was found impossible; to make them meaningful was, in secular terms, embarrassing.

The longing for a religious framework became increasingly pro-nounced in the second generation of the kibbutzim, that is, among those born in Israel and brought up in the kibbutz. The synagogues built at first for the benefit of elderly parents are now also frequented by the young. Some kibbutzim have even applied to the Ministry of Religions for grants to help in the construction of synagogues for their members. "We have seen how the children in our settlements delight in putting up tabernacles during Sukkot (Tabernacles). They sense the lack of ceremonial symbolism far more than we do; so acutely do they feel this void that they seek a means of filling it."[40] The writings of the young people give wide expression to the quest for a deeper Jewish content. Rachel Rubinov of kibbutz Na'an writes:

> We have dethroned God without replacing Him. We have brought Him down from his elevated seat. Man has now become master. . . . Religion was in the past a haven of security. It was from faith that strength was derived to assure survival in the Galut. . . . Symbols became crystallized and tradition developed . . . and what are we now left with? We are in need of a tradition.[41]

From kibbutz Givat Brenner, Amos Redner writes:

> I want to refer to the subject of rootlessness. . . . I feel that one of the things that makes it difficult for us to find ourselves is our arbi-trary detachment from our own origins. Our people dwelt in the Galut for a longer time than in their land. I therefore regard our educational work where "sources" are confined to an agricultural tradition, as a cruel amputation which causes our roots to atrophy.

Yohai Gilead of Kibbutz Bet HaShittah comments:

> I am left with an uneasy feeling. I have completed ten years of edu-cation, beginning with kindergarten. . . . When I ask myself what I am left with as a Jew, I am bound to say: very little. A person is not born a Jew—there is no bacillus Judaicus. . . . I do not mean to say that we are all Goyim, but the fact is that we are not able to cast our eyes beyond the Bible. . . . I ask myself why life in a kibbutz is not saturated with Jewish content?[42]

The search for a new content to Jewishness assumed greater inten-sity following the Six Day War, when secularism was subjected to criti-cism in kibbutzim of all shades of opinion. In the summer 1967 issue of *Shdemot,* published by the Youth Department of the Kibbutz Fed-eration affiliated with the Labor Party (Ihud HaKvuzot ve HaKibbutzim) , the kibbutz-born generation sought to crystallize its views on religion.

Full scope was given to the question of rejecting the dogmatic secularism that was preached and practiced by their parents. The writers realized that in ignoring the history and culture of two millennia of Diaspora history and in trying to recreate a biblical Judaism, a void was created, which was bound to lead to nihilism. The impact of postbiblical Judaism on Jewish culture and tradition was so far-reaching that its excision was tantamount to an act of willful amputation.

These discussions continued for months, in each kibbutz separately, as well as in interkibbutz gatherings, and quite an extensive literature was published about these deliberations.[43] Whether they belonged to the moderate socialist or to the more dogmatic Marxist trends, all participants in the discussions had been brought up in a socialist climate and were imbued with a secular humanism. Their self-examination in the light of a new reality was highly revealing, coming as it did from young people in the course of free discussions. Said Avishai:

> I believe faith is a supreme human need. A man is happy only if he believes in something, whether in an ideology or in a Supreme Being. Our faith in the past—Socialism, Zionism . . . has evaporated, and we are returning to Jewish tradition. You may say it is reactionary, it is bad, it is medieval, but it is a fact. Recently, on Sabbath Eve in the communal dining-hall, Hannah hesitated whether or not to light Sabbath candles, and wondered how it would be received. . . . She lit the candles, and everything went off peacefully.[44]

Avishai attempted to draw a conclusion:

> There is no escape from a return to religion. I do not think we can return to religion in the style of Neturei Karta . . . , but I do think that our deliberate break-off that stemmed from some notion of creating an original culture, a labor culture failed. . . . We have reached a stage where we have to turn in the direction of Jewish knowledge, towards the Jewish people and all that is associated therewith.[45]

What recurs in most conversations of these groups is the feeling of a spiritual void experienced by sensitive young people brought up in the climate of a secular faith. It is far easier to point to a void, or even express a longing for a religious attachment, than to define the nature of the religious experience for which many of the kibbutz members crave. Not surprisingly, with such groping for a new vision of religion comes a good deal of confusion and embarrassment. Uri, of kibbutz Ein Shemer, seeks to differentiate between tradition and faith. He is not concerned with faith, for that is a matter for each individual.

> Tradition, on the other hand, is compounded of a certain mode of behavior and certain customs, partially based on faith and partially on concrete reality. . . . I believe that some of us have absorbed elements of faith in the course of the war. This matter of blind fate, of bullets . . . of luck; surely somebody is responsible for the luck?

The fault of the parents was their having severed the link with tradition.

> I believe they failed to create a substitute. They developed a new form of life indeed, but failed to provide it with content. I can state categorically that our life is arid; it is one long weekday. . . . We live through 365 grey days each year.

An attempt should be made to reintroduce tradition, without, for the time being, dwelling on the element of faith. He suggests the introduction of Kabbalat Shabbat (the traditional family Sabbath ceremony), with lighting of candles.[46]

> Would it do any harm [asks another participant] if we set aside one day in order to take stock of ourselves, of our place among our fellows, and of our ideals? Why should this stock-taking not take place on a definite day, and why should we not revive Yom Kippur, not necessarily as a religious occasion? On that day the religious person has the inner strength to ask for forgiveness; I wish we had the inner strength to ask for forgiveness, as well as to forgive others.[47]

Apparently this young man is seeking to revive a religious experience within a purely secular setting.[48]

Nowhere has the sense of a void been more keenly felt than among the younger generation of the kibbutzim of the HaShomer HaTzair movement.[49] Their intensive Marxist upbringing was intended to render them immune to any unorthodox social philosophy. Precisely to this committed Marxist youth the Six Day War administered a shattering blow, and brought them at times into open conflict with their elders. For in that war Israel was pitted not only against the armed forces of the surrounding Arab states, but also pitted against the Soviet Union—where Marxism was state policy—the land that many of the older HaShomer HaTzair members regarded as their second homeland. But those who fell on the field of battle were after all the victims of Soviet shells and bullets, and of the Soviet rulers who had encouraged Arab aggression. The young Israelis who had been brought up in the belief that they were creating a new Jewish culture, rooted in rationalism and in Marxism and dedicated to the pursuit of universal values, now faced a serious dilemma. In a seminar held in the summer of 1969 at Givat Havivah—the cultural center of HaShomer HaTzair—full scope was given to "heretical" views, which were summed up in the movement's periodical, *Hedim*. The *cri-de-coeur* of one of the young leaders was most significant: "We believed with a religious faith that the revolution would take place. We studied *Das Kapital* or the *Short Course* as one studies the Talmud. For example, when Stalin died, many kibbutzim cancelled the feast of Purim, and the members had no doubts that this was justified. . . . Now, this faith which was to a large extent a religious faith, has been destroyed and no longer exists. The result of this destruction is that HaShomer HaTzair, which used to be a 'religious' movement, has lost its god."[50]

Indeed, the secularists of the socialist faith, more than any other group, had lost their god and were experiencing spiritual discomfort in their godless lives. It was only natural that in their search for a new faith they should seek to reestablish a link with that Jewish tradition from which they had been deliberately alienated by their parents. These young people, however, realized that while it was possible to revive traditions and observe precepts, it was far more difficult to revive the faith of which the traditions and precepts were the symbols. Religious behavior and religious faith, unless both are part of one spiritual whole, cannot possibly fill the void painfully experienced by people whose "God has failed," and who are in search of a new ideal.

It is at this point that the numerous dialogues and seminars on the problem of religion have generally come to an abrupt end. Not only is religious behavior shown to be inadequate unless it is steeped in faith, but religious precepts cannot even be accepted unless they are compatible with ethical principles.

There was little in the deeds and words of the Orthodox to ease these young people out of their impasse. The Ministry of Religious Affairs, to be sure, was useful in setting up synagogues in kibbutzim, and the rabbinate was always ready to distribute prayer books and objects of religious ritual. Most helpful was the Kibbutz Dati, whose members were anxious to bring about Kiruv Levavot (a meeting of hearts), and would meet fellow kibbutzniks of secular trends to discuss problems of religion, or would invite them to spend a Sabbath in a religious kibbutz, so that they might be exposed to a religious atmosphere and way of life. Many of the young people so exposed were impressed by the faith and inner harmony prevailing within the Kibbutz Dati. Yet, official Orthodoxy offered no real opportunities to this sincere quest for attachment to a religious ideal. The rabbis confined themselves to exhortations to observe the Mitzvot because of their divine origin, without making any attempt to discuss religion on an intellectual level. When confronted with the critical question of the indispensability of faith as a precondition for observng the Mitzvot, the invariable reply was that deeds would eventually lead to faith. This was not a summons to religious belief, but to religious behavior; to the young people in quest of a faith, religious behavior without faith was incomprehensible and, therefore, unacceptable. The dictum that the observance of precepts would eventually lead to faith may have been an effective educational device for inculcating religious values from early childhood on; it could not be applied to intellectually inclined young persons who had not had the benefit of a religious upbringing. Nor could they accept the proposition that the Halakhah, being divine, was binding, especially since some of its rules were creating morally embarrassing situations. Nor could they be reconciled to the view that religion, as embodied in the Halakhah, and religion as embodied in ethical principles, were on two separate planes, with the former taking precedence over the latter; to them, religion, if it was to possess any meaning at all, implied the supremacy of ethical principles.

Nor did the political religious parties help to resolve the impasse for the faith-seekers among the secularists. Mafdal, being closer to daily life than the rabbinate, and even more so its members in Kibbutz Dati, were fully aware of the gravity of the problem. Being a political party, however, they were exposed to the inevitable and irreconcilable conflict between political expediency and moral principles, with the latter often subordinated to the former. Mafdal had little alternative but to uphold the official rabbinate, and to support it even in instances when it ran counter to their and popular convictions.

Thus, neither the rabbinate nor Mafdal offered a guiding hand to the perplexed secularists. Commenting on this tragic predicament, the poet Yizchak Lamdan gave vent to a widely felt frustration:

> It is not a paradox to say that if there are enemies of religious revival in Israel, enemies of faith and of the lofty values of the Torah, those enemies are none other than the official leaders of our religion, and they it is who more than any others drive away the younger generation through their limited vision and striving for power—a striving that troubles itself not at all about the means thereof.[51]

In sum, the quest for a religious faith on the part of many of the young secularists has failed to advance beyond an awareness of the inadequacy of secularism. The urge to revive a religious tradition has so far been stifled by the lack of religious faith. Orthodoxy, except for Kibbutz Dati, has not been a source of encouragement. By insisting on the "conspicuous" observance of Mitzvot, that is, on outward manifestations of religion, rather than by stressing the inner element of faith, Orthodoxy was denying the faith-seekers the very substance they were seeking. The quest for religious faith was further aggravated by a prevailing belief that the only alternative to Orthodoxy was secularism, which meant that there was no religious alternative to religion as they knew it to be.[52] The ferment within secularism was thus an admission of its inadequacy as a sustaining spiritual force as well as a realization of the inadequacy of the traditional observances, unless they could be nurtured by faith.

This groping seems presently to have reached an impasse, though the continued yearning for religious experience is undeniable. It still lacks depth and is replete with frustration, yet it can be said that this situation in Israel is more fertile than almost anywhere else in the world. In Israel we are witnessing a new stage in the evolution of the Jewish religion.[53]

11

Beginnings of Religious Pluralism

A. MONOLITHIC STRUCTURE OF JEWISH RELIGION IN ISRAEL

Immigration Patterns

In many respects the State of Israel represents one of the most vigorously pluralistic societies in the world. Not only is Israel at the crossroads between East and West, and between the Christian and the Moslem worlds, but it is also the meeting-place of the three monotheistic faiths, each of which is represented there by its adherents and institutions. In addition, the state itself is the dwelling-place of Arabs as well as of Jews. Linguistically, too, it is a pluralistic society, for people hailing from nearly all countries of the world continue to converse in their original tongues as well as in Hebrew. It is likewise pluralistic in terms of the rich variety of customs, traditions, and ways of life; it is a whole world in miniature, one that encompasses both the ways of the nomadic Bedouins and the most sophisticated life-styles of the present day. Last but not least, the Jewish community in Israel is the most pluralistic of all Jewish communities in the world, culturally, linguistically, socially, and politically—except in one respect. It lacks religious pluralism.

While Israeli Jews may be classified as religious or as secularists, almost all consider Orthodoxy as the only legitimate expression of the Jewish religion and since there is no religious alternative to Orthodoxy, only one option is open to the non-Orthodox Jew: to be a secularist.

Most of the eight-and-a-half million Jews who live outside Israel and the Soviet bloc are familiar with religious pluralism. By far the largest Jewish population of the free world Diaspora is to be found in North America, with about 5,870,000 in the United States, and some 300,000 in Canada.[1] In these countries religious pluralism is the prevailing religious pattern, and Jews, too, reflect this phenomenon. The oldest religious trend was Orthodox. The Reform movement made its first appearance in the twenties of the nineteenth century, and Conservatives evolved their specific characteristics in the first decade of the twentieth century. Nowadays the Reform and the Conservative movements represent by far the predominant majority of synagogue-affiliated Jews in the United States, and there is much cooperation among the three religious trends, especially in communal matters. In issues bearing on religion, however, some of the more extreme Orthodox groups refuse to have any traffic with the others. In Australia, South Africa, and Latin America, the majority of synagogue-affiliated Jews are still associated with Orthodoxy; still, religious pluralism is an established feature of their Jewish institutional and communal life. Each of the three principal religious trends maintains centers of learning, rabbinical seminaries, schools, youth activities, and rabbinical and lay organizations, and also sponsors a variety of publications. Only in the Jewish state is Orthodoxy still regarded as the one and only form of Jewish religion.

There have been a variety of reasons for this development. The first of these was the unfamiliarity of the Yishuv with non-Orthodox religious trends. The Jewish community in Palestine, which in 1918 numbered some 65,000, grew during the thirty-years period of British rule to about 650,000 in May 1948. This steep increase was due primarily to immigration. Of the 453,000 immigrants during that period, the predominant majority were Jews from Central and Eastern Europe.[2] A breakdown shows that 56% arrived from Eastern Europe, 20.4% from Central Europe, 9.5% from Asian countries, 8.3% from the Soviet Union, 4.1% from the Balkan countries, 1.9% from Western Europe, and a mere 1.8% from the entire American continent.[3] In nearly all these countries, religious pluralism was nonexistent.

In the quarter century following the establishment of the state, the Jewish population has more than quadrupled, reaching about 2,900,000 souls in 1974, the increase being again chiefly due to immigration. Unlike in the pre-state period, however, Asia and Africa provided a very large share of these immigrants.

The number of Olim from the American continent, Western Europe, and South Africa was in absolute figures larger than in the pre-state period, but this percentage remained about what it had been prior to 1948. Thus the great waves of immigration during the period of British rule and ever since, arrived from countries where religious pluralism was nearly nonexistent, and where Orthodox Judaism was the only recognized form of the Jewish religion. The few Reform Jews who settled in Palestine, among them Rabbi Judah L. Magnes, for many years

President of the Hebrew University in Jerusalem, made no attempt to form a congregation. Nor did the Conservatives make any move in that direction. The latter, however, did acquire before World War II a valuable plot of land in Jerusalem, but the building erected on it became an Orthodox Synagogue known as the Yeshurun Synagogue.

Reform Judaism

Of the non-Orthodox religious trends in Judaism, Reform is the oldest. It made its first appearance in Germany in the eighteen-twenties and started as an attempt to modernize the synagogue service. In time it evolved a new theological approach to Judaism that was at complete variance with Orthodoxy; it repudiated many ritual elements of the Halakhah and emphasized the ethical teachings of the prophets as the central theme of Judaism. As an organized religious movement, it achieved significant support in Germany and modest support in England and in France. In the United States, however, the Reform Movement developed into a significant factor in the religious and communal life of the Jewish community beginning with the middle of the nineteenth century.

To the Orthodox rabbis the theology of Reform Judaism was nothing less than heresy. "Classical Reform"* denied, in fact, the sanctity of the Halakhah and its immutable validity. The doctrines of Classical Reform, as formulated in the Pittsburgh Platform of 1885 by a conference of 15 Reform rabbis in the United States, were a total repudiation of Halakhic Judaism. The laws of Moses were not intended for eternity, the platform said, but were a legal system suitable for the Jewish people "during its national life in Palestine; and today we accept as binding only the moral law, and maintain only such ceremonies as elevate and sanctify our lives, but reject all such as are not adapted to the views and habits of modern civilization." Thus, all Halakhic rules, "such as regulate diet, priestly purity and dress," were abrogated as being "foreign to our present mental and spiritual state."

In the spirit of confidence in uninterrupted human progress that prevailed in the second half of the nineteenth century, the exponents of Classical Reform regarded Judaism to be an instrumentality for the spread of universal ideas. The Pittsburgh Platform proclaims: "We acknowledge that the spirit of broad humanity of our age is an ally in the fulfillment of our mission, and therefore we extend the hand of fellowship to all who cooperate with us in the establishment of the reign of truth and righteousness among men."[4]

Equally repugnant to the Orthodox was the proposition that the

---

* The second phase of the movement is generally known by this name, but it should more properly be called "Radical Reform."

fall of the Second Commonwealth was not a punishment for the "sinfulness of Israel, but a sequence of Divine intent . . . to send the members of the Jewish nation to all parts of the earth, so that they may fulfill the high priestly task of leading the nations to the true knowledge and worship of God."[5]

Thus Classical Reform constituted a repudiation of the basic tenets of rabbinic Judaism as they had been understood for two millennia of Jewish history. The Orthodox regarded Reform not only as a negation of Judaism, but as an ill-disguised attempt to bring about the assimilation of the Jewish people and the obliteration of their religious and, eventually, also of their ethnic identity. Reform Judaism was viewed as an arch enemy also by the emergent Jewish nationalists in the closing years of the nineteenth century, and particularly by the founders of Zionism. They, to be sure, were not defenders of the Halakhah, nor did they reject the view that the ethical teachings of the prophets, rather than the ritual, comprised the central theme of Judaism. In fact, it was Ahad Ha'Am, the exponent of cultural Zionism, who outraged the Orthodox by insisting on prophetic Judaism as the unique feature of Jewish culture. On this important question, Reform and Zionism were not at variance. It was rather over the Pittsburgh Platform, which negated Jewish nationhood and a return to Palestine, that Reform and Zionism found themselves in opposing camps.[6]

Thus not only the Orthodox but also the secularists brought up in the classical Zionist tradition took a dim view of Reform Judaism. The writings of the founders of Zionism, and particularly those of Ahad Ha'Am, are taught in today's Israeli high schools, and they portray Reform in negative terms. Not even the devoted and valuable services rendered to the cause of Zionism by such leaders as Judah L. Magnes, Stephen S. Wise, and Abba Hillel Silver, all of whom came from the ranks of the Reform rabbinate in the United States, succeeded in altering this impression. The fact that in the last forty years Reform Judaism underwent its own "reform" received little attention in Palestine and, later, in Israel. Until the early nineteen-fifties, Reform leaders hardly attempted to enlighten public opinion in Israel on the changes that had taken place in their ranks, especially in their attitude to Jewish nationalism and the Jewish state; the image of Classical Reform shaped by the writings of the founders of Zionism hardened into an anti-Reform prejudice.

Conservatism

The Israeli public was equally unfamiliar with, and indifferent to Conservative Judaism, the other major non-Orthodox religious trend in the United States. Intellectually the latter was an offshoot of the historical school of Judaism in Germany led by Zacharias Frankel, and thus was in fact a conservative wing of Reform. While stressing the importance of the application of the scientific approach to the study of Judaism, Conservatism reaffirmed, in contradistinction to Reform Judaism, the importance of Jewish nationhood, the land of Israel, and the Hebrew language, and, led by the Jewish Theological Seminary in New York, it had by the middle of this century become the largest Jewish religious trend on the North American continent.[7] It developed a distinct Zionist orientation, and was influenced by the teachings of Ahad Ha'Am, who hoped for the creation of a spiritual center in Palestine that would revitalize Jewish life throughout the Diaspora. While adhering to the Halakhah, Conservatism believes in strengthening it through change from within, with particular emphasis on ethical principles. Conservative Judaism thus possesses important elements that could appeal to many Israelis as a religious alternative, but this movement, too, made next to no impression on the Israeli public. Oriented as they were to the Eastern and Central European cultural tradition, the Israelis remained unfamiliar with developments in Conservatism; the limited numbers of Conservative Jews from America and Canada who settled in Israel at first took no initiative in establishing congregations. Nor were they encouraged by the Conservative movement in the United States, where the leadership of the Jewish Theological Seminary, with its strong pro-Orthodox orientation, fought shy of every move that might be resented by the Israeli rabbinate or by Mafdal. And since Israelis were largely unaware of either the evolution or the achievements of Reform and Conservatism in the Diaspora, they were not motivated to explore these movements as religious alternatives.

The other circumstance that contributed to this situation was the failure of the non-Orthodox religious trends to appear as an organized force in the Zionist movement. The Orthodox, in the early days of Herzl, joined the Zionist movement as individuals, but it did not take long until they grouped themselves into a party, the Mizrahi; as such they fought the battle of Orthodoxy first in Palestine and then in Israel with notable success. The Conservative movement in the United States, which provided the Zionist Organization of America with a most important part of its membership, failed to organize itself as a distinct entity within the Zionist movement. The same applied to the Reform Jews, from whose ranks came some of the greatest leaders of American Zionism. The reluctance of both Reform and Conservatism in America to engage in Zionist politics was in part due to the American tradition of keeping religion and politics apart.*

---

* Lately, however, attempts to rectify this earlier failure have been made, only to be met with a not-unexpected opposition from Mizrahi.

B. EMERGENCE OF
NON-ORTHODOX CONGREGATIONS

*Progressives and Conservatives**

Among the arrivals in Palestine from Germany in the nineteen-thirties were a number of outstanding Orthodox rabbis, men of learning and piety who also possessed a general Western culture and held doctoral degrees from leading German universities. None of these was admitted into the local rabbinical offices, although some did become officiating rabbis in Orthodox congregations formed by German Jews in Tel Aviv, Haifa, and Jerusalem. Their innovation was the sermon, which for a number of years was delivered in the German language.

There were also Liberal rabbis among the Olim. In 1935 Rabbi Max Elk founded Beth Israel in Haifa, where he preached in German; four years later he founded the Leo Baeck Elementary School, which evolved in 1947 into a secondary school and became affiliated with the World Union of Progressive Judaism. In 1937, Rabbi Kurt David Wilhelm, a liberal rabbi from Germany,** founded the Emet veEmunah Congregation in Jerusalem, which started as a non-Orthodox synagogue and developed into a Conservative congregation. Such local beginnings in the direction of non-Orthodox religious services were very small indeed.

It took about a decade following the establishment of the state until new non-Orthodox congregations made their appearance in various parts of Israel. The initiative for these establishments was local, largely reflecting the population in each place. In most places it came from old-time settlers in Palestine; the membership included the young as well as the old, and also new immigrants. It was largely an indigenous growth, experiencing the difficulties of trial and error, and making an attempt to evolve a congregational pattern of religious, educational, and social activity that had hardly a precedent in Israel.

Since then, nine congregations have been founded, affiliated with the World Union of Progressive Judaism; ten congregations, affiliated with the Conservative movement in the United States; and one synagogue in Jerusalem, led by an adherent of the Reconstructionist movement. Har El in Jerusalem is the oldest of those affiliated with the World Union of Progressive Judaism; it was founded in 1958 by old-established residents of the city, many of them members of the liberal

---

* *Mitkadem* (Progressive) is the term generally adopted by the Reform type of movement in Israel. This word is included in the title of the roof organization of the Reform movements: "The World Union of Progressive Judaism." The terms *Reform* and *Progressive* are interchangeable.

** He later became Chief Rabbi of Sweden, where he died in 1965.

professions, university teachers, and civil servants. In 1962 they moved into their own building, a small structure, formerly a private dwelling, containing a synagogue hall and facilities for offices. A cantor officiates, and an organ is used. In 1962 they published a prayer book, which is now used by the congregations affiliated with the World Union, as is the Machzor for the High Holydays, which they published in 1964. Har El is served by a full-time rabbi. It was followed by a congregation founded in 1961 in Upper Nazareth, a new city established in the late fifties and inhabited predominantly by an immigrant population. The initiator of the congregation was a blind organist, a recent arrival from Hungary, a member of the Neologues there, and the cantor was a native Israeli. The membership has reflected the heterogeneous character of the community. The synagogue, named after Herzl, holds services in a rented hall; it has not had the continued services of a permanent rabbi.

In 1962 Emet veShalom was formed in Nahariya; its founders were mostly arrivals from Germany. It has a part-time rabbi who is a retired high school principal, a graduate of the Rabbinical Seminary in Breslau. Services are held in a hall rented on a weekly basis. The same year, Emet veEmunah was formed in Ramat Gan. In 1964 Rabbi Reuben Samuels, a graduate of Hebrew Union College-Jewish Institute of Religion in the United States, and assistant principal of the Leo Baeck School founded Or Hadash congregation in Haifa. The Mayor of Haifa granted the congregation the use of an elementary school hall for holding services. He likewise arranged for the city to allocate to the congregation a building plot for the future construction of a synagogue. The membership has reflected the middle-class, largely Western, community of the Central Carmel.

In 1966, Rabbi Moshe Zemer, a Reform rabbi from the United States and now a citizen of Israel, formed Kedem congregation in Tel Aviv. After trying in vain for a long time to procure a place for holding services, he finally succeeded in renting a small basement hall. In 1972 the City Council of Tel Aviv approved the grant of a plot of ground for the construction of a synagogue.

In 1969 a Progressive congregation was set up in Natanya, and in 1971 congregations were established in Ashkelon and Beersheba. These nine congregations are affiliated with World Union for Progressive Judaism, but so far only four of them—Jerusalem, Tel Aviv, Haifa, and Ramat Gan—are served by rabbis, all of whom were originally trained as Reform rabbis.

The religious services held in the congregations affiliated with the World Union for Progressive Judaism differ from the Reform services in the United States in that all prayers and the sermon are exclusively in the Hebrew language. The men cover their heads and wear a Tallit (prayer shawl) on Saturday and Holyday morning services. These differ from the Orthodox services in that men and women worship together and stress is laid on order and decorum. The rabbi's sermon is an integral part of the service, and the order of prayer is shortened by the elimination of repetitions, and by the omission of all references to sacrifices. Women are encouraged to participate in the service, and may be summoned to the reading of the Torah. Bat Mitzvah* is celebrated in the synagogue. The connection between the land of Israel and the Holydays is emphasized by the introduction of appropriate ceremonies; the prayer book is enriched by the addition of selections from medieval and modern Hebrew poetry. In some of the synagogues the organ is played.

The rabbis who officiate in these congregations have constituted themselves a Council of Progressive Rabbis in Israel (Maram). One of their present tasks is the composition of a new prayer book.

The largest of the Progressive synagogues, Kedem, holds its services in a rented hall in Tel Aviv, with a seating capacity of 300; on Friday Eve and on Saturday morning the hall is full, while on the Holydays more than 700 worship there. Young people, including soldiers on leave, are very much in evidence, and the majority of worshipers are long-settled Israelis. The synagogue has a mixed choir composed of members of the congregation; it has evolved a program of adult education, and a youth club serving four youth groups; it has also organized a sisterhood. The congregation engages in social work, and assists in the absorption of immigrants by including them in its own celebration of festivals.

The Haifa congregation, Or Hadash, has developed an active youth program, in close cooperation with the like-minded Leo Baeck High School; one of its projects is extending home hospitality to students at the school who come from abroad. The congregation numbers some 250 dues-paying families, and about 100 youths who hold separate membership. Har El congregation in Jerusalem, in addition to its synagogal program, has adult education courses, and has developed a social project aimed at the underprivileged children of parents hailing from Arabic-speaking countries. Ramat Gan has a well-established congregation with a membership of 120 families. The other five congregations are smaller and, in the absence of permanent rabbis, depend on the initiative of their lay leaders. It is estimated that about one thousand families altogether are affiliated with the Progressive congregations.[8]

Conservative Judaism has also established a foothold in Israel. It has constituted itself as the United Synagogue of Israel and is the Israeli affiliate of the World Council of Synagogues. It now numbers some ten

---

* The female counterpart of the Bar Mitzvah ceremony.

congregations with a dues-paying membership of about a thousand families. The oldest of these, established in the mid-fifties in Haifa, consists of old-time residents as well as of Olim, the latter including a number from English-speaking countries. Services are held in a public hall, and as in all Conservative synagogues, men and women worship together.

In the middle and late sixties congregations were established in Ashkelon, Rehovot, Nathanja and Tel Aviv, all with permanent rabbis. In the seventies, congregations were established in Beersheba and Ashdod. There are several Conservative Synagogues in Jerusalem, the oldest being Emet veEmunah; the Center for Conservative Judaism as well as Neve Schechter congregations have a membership of some 180 families. More recently Conservative congregations were established in the Ramat Eshkol quarter in Jerusalem as well as in the smallholders agricultural settlement (Moshav Ovdim) of Sde Nitzan in the Negev, both congregations functioning without a permanent rabbi. Nearly all Conservative rabbis are Americans, graduates of the Jewish Theological Seminary who settled in Israel.

Neve Schechter, named after Solomon Schechter, one of the founders of Conservative Judaism and its mentor, is an institution of higher Jewish learning established in Jerusalem. It is an integral part of the Jewish Theological Seminary in New York, and students of the New York School spend a year in Jerusalem taking credit courses for their degree.

In terms of numbers, there are indeed a few non-Orthodox congregations, with a relatively small membership. The outlay for the upkeep of a synagogue, including the pursuit of a variety of activities and the employment of a full-time rabbi, is considerable, and quite beyond the means of the average Israeli congregation. The membership fees, even if doubled or tripled, still would not cover the expenses involved. While Orthodox synagogues are situated in permanent buildings erected in a great majority of the cases by the government, by municipal council, or by the publicly financed religious councils, Progressives or Conservatives have not received any aid from public funds for the erection of synagogues, or for the maintenance of rabbis. Orthodox rabbis are paid largely from public funds, whereas Progressive or Conservative rabbis are dependent on contributions from their members supplemented by allocations made by their respective movements abroad. Thus, the non-Orthodox congregations are constrained to function within a very narrow scope, the most serious handicap being the lack of synagogue buildings, but even the few congregations that have buildings of their own can hardly meet the financial needs of an active congregation.

Restrictive as the financial aspect is, it did not constitute the sole handicap; there was also a shortage of qualified rabbis. While there are Reform rabbis in the United States who consider settling in Israel with a view to taking up rabbinical appointments, there is a shortage of Israeli-born and educated young men who would be prepared to study for the non-Orthodox rabbinate. So far, there is only one such qualified Israeli, and there are very few candidates among Israeli-educated youth for such a career; for the time being they have to seek their training abroad.

Finally, rabbis who serve non-Orthodox congregations are not only deprived of support by the authorities, but they are not considered as rabbis in the judgment of Israeli law. Having been qualified through the Reform or Conservative seminaries, they are not recognized as rabbis by the official rabbinate. They cannot be members of rabbinical courts, nor can they adjudicate matters of marriage and divorce, nor deal with applications for conversions. They may not even celebrate marriages of members of their own congregations. A marriage in Israel may be celebrated only by a rabbi recognized as such and for this purpose by the official rabbinate, that is to say, by one who is an Orthodox rabbi. Likewise, a non-Orthodox rabbi may not officiate at a funeral ceremony. In other words, Reform or Conservative rabbis may not perform in Israel the functions generally regarded as appertaining to their office.

Although the non-Orthodox synagogues are small, inconspicuous, and of very modest dimensions, they have created a totally novel phenomenon in the religious life of Israel. The pattern of their services has created an experience differing in feeling and temperament from that of the traditional synagogue. The first impression of this difference experienced by a secularist was described by a veteran Israeli who happened to attend a Sukkot service with a Progressive group, of which he was not a member.

> At Sukkot time, after an interruption of many years, I went to the synagogue. I prayed, and my prayer was in the Reform mode. . . . The prayers were few—they were selected, in simple Hebrew, and everyone could bring to them his own yearning and his own spirit— and not the perfunctory, required routine. Many, like me, who occasionally seek solitude for its own sake, must have felt for the first time the essence and the worth of public prayer in a public place. . . . I felt the grandeur of the modern prayer, "Rock of Israel, cause Thy spirit to dwell in the midst of all the inhabitants of our land." I immersed my soul in this call to the creator of the universe. . . . There are thousands among us who believe with perfect faith in the God of Israel, who are nevertheless unable to accommodate their lives to the bounds of the ancient tradition, neither to the traditional mode of prayer nor to the traditional synagogue. . . . These people seek religious renewal—not a *new* religion, not a *different* Judaism, but a modified mode of worship and a modified Shulhan Arukh. They look into their inner world, at the dying members of grandfather's house, they look at the broken world of their children, empty of all tradition and uprooted from Judaism. And they are shaken by the

very idea that their houses are being destroyed by the torpor forcibly imposed upon them by the powerful agents of the "authorised tradition."[9]

This eloquent rendering of a spiritual experience is indicative of a potential reawakening, although the actual impact of the Progressive and Conservative congregations after the first decade of their activity has been rather marginal. The quest for a new mode of religious expression has not advanced far enough to arouse intense or widespread interest in a new spiritual movement. The very existence of these congregations is known to but a limited number of people. They have generally come to public attention only on occasions when the Orthodox have sought to interfere with their activities.

One Progressive congregation did come into prominence in October 1966, as a result of an incident that took place in the synagogue at Kiryat Gat. On October 8, 1966, a Bar Mitzvah ceremony was to be held there; the boy's father, a practicing physician, had recently immigrated from the Argentine. As the ceremony was about to begin and the boy waited to recite the Haftarah, the local rabbi ordered the boy and his father to leave the synagogue, on the grounds that some members of the family and their friends had driven to the synagogue in cars.[10] The cancellation of the Bar Mitzvah ceremony, and the punishment inflicted on the boy for the acts of others, aroused considerable controversy in Kiryat Gat and in the whole national press. The Latin-American Immigrants' Association lodged a protest with the municipal council, which contributed to the budget of the synagogue. The president of the synagogue resigned, and it was rumored that the rabbi would apologize. In an open letter published in *Maariv* on October 19, 1966, the rabbi stated, however: "I hereby declare that I do not repent of my deed, and I am still of the opinion that what I did was just and necessary." The immediate problem of the boy was solved on October 15, 1966, when his Bar Mitzvah ceremony was duly celebrated in the presence of an overflow audience in the hall of the Progressive Synagogue in Tel Aviv. The proceedings at this service, the sermon delivered, and the active participation of the boy's mother were widely reported in the press.[11]

Developments in Reform Judaism

In the four decades that have elapsed since the rise of Nazism, Reform Judaism in North America has undergone considerable transformation. Jews of East European origin have increased in wealth and in education, and have joined Reform congregations, gradually weakening the hold of the original German element, the exponents of "Classical Reform." Although the movement is numerically second to the

Conservatives, it has had a full share in the general growth; the number of congregations affiliated with the Union of American Hebrew Congregations grew from 330 in 1946 to over 650 in 1964. Before long, the rise of the East European element, among both the laity and the rabbinate, as well as the climate engendered by a militant and brutal anti-Semitism, combined to move Reform Judaism away from its classical and radical background toward the sources of traditional Judaism.

The impact of the Holocaust and the emergence of an independent Jewish state called for a reappraisal of the Classical Reform position. As early as 1937 the Pittsburgh Platform had been replaced by the Columbus Platform, which repudiated the former negative attitude to Zionist endeavor in Palestine. It declared that "in the rehabilitation of Palestine, the land hallowed by memories and hopes, we behold the promise of renewed life for many of our brethren. We affirm the obligation of all Jewry to aid in its upbuilding as a Jewish homeland by endeavouring to make it not only a haven of refuge for the oppressed, but also a centre of Jewish culture and spiritual life."[12] While this was not a Zionist position, its positive attitude toward Palestine as a "Jewish homeland" and "a centre of Jewish culture and spiritual life" embodied the principal elements of Ahad Ha'Am's Zionist philosophy. The Reform movement was thus moved to increasingly greater involvement and participation in the religious and spiritual developments in Israel. A significant move in this direction was the amalgamation of the Hebrew Union College of Cincinnati, whose background was Classical Reform and anti-Zionist, with the Jewish Institute of Religion in New York, founded in the nineteen-twenties by Rabbi Stephen S. Wise, whose stress was on Hebrew and on a pro-Zionist orientation. Under the presidency of Professor Nelson Glueck, the renowned archaeologist of Palestine, a branch of the College was established in Jerusalem. The Reform rabbinate began to assume a new complexion, away from the radicalism of its founders and toward a greater appreciation of the role of Mitzvot. Some Reform rabbis felt that Israel had restored balance and perspective to Reform Judaism, and had reinforced its ties with the totality of the Jewish people. Still others felt that the so-called secularist climate prevailing in the Jewish state offered an unrivaled opportunity for the revitalization of religious life through the planting of the seeds of prophetic Judaism on the soil of the Jewish homeland. Their thought was that while the downgrading of Halakhah-bound Judaism and the upgrading of prophetic Judaism was at times fraught with danger to Jewish survival in the Diaspora, no such danger existed in the Jewish state itself.

In 1963, the Jerusalem School of the Hebrew Union College-Jewish Institute of Religion* was opened in Jerusalem. The School actively

---

* The other campuses are in Cincinnati, New York, and Los Angeles.

engages in archaeological field work and is a center for postgraduate research, offering scholars and graduate fellows intensive advanced studies in Bible, Archaeology, and Palestinography. Over fifty American and Canadian universities and colleges are affiliated with the School in an archaeological consortium.

The Jerusalem School had from its beginning served also as a study center for rabbinic students from the United States. They either took courses in Jewish studies at the Hebrew University or pursued the study of the Hebrew language. Later, the College-Institute made it mandatory for all its entering rabbinical students to spend their first year of studies at the Jerusalem School.[13]

In 1972, the government of Israel leased to the Hebrew Union College a valuable tract of land in Jerusalem for the erection of a World Educational Center to serve all the major institutions of Reform Judaism. It is intended to be the site of the headquarters of the World Union for Progressive Judaism, which resolved at its international conference held in Geneva in 1972 to move its central office from New York to Jerusalem. Thus, while the Progressive constituency in Israel is in its incipient stages, and is numerically minute in relation to the world movement, Jerusalem is becoming a world center of Progressive Judaism.

The World Union for Progressive Judaism has assisted in the maintenance and growth of the Leo Baeck School in Haifa, a high school where the curriculum is oriented toward a Progressive view of Judaism. Teenagers from the United States attend summer programs offered by the school. A full-time rabbi from the U.S.A. serves the Progressive youth movement, and another rabbi is engaged at Ben Shemen, a youth village, where the Reform sisterhoods have erected a synagogue cum cultural center. In 1971, Rabbi David Polish, then President of the Central Conference of American Rabbis, initiated a program of activities with the kibbutz movements in Israel. For the first time in its history, the World Union for Progressive Judaism held its biennial conference in Jerusalem, in June 1968, and the Central Conference of American Rabbis held its national convention in Jerusalem in March 1970. Spending a sabbatical year in Israel has become a frequent practice for Reform rabbis and their families.[14]

While not all shades of opinion within the Reform movement accept the centrality of Israel, yet the impact of the Jewish state on the Diaspora has been so pervasive as to engulf, as it were, the whole movement. Through the curricula of the religious schools, Holyday observances, and a variety of other activities, modern Israel has made a significant impact on the movement. Some of the younger rabbis feel that Reform Judaism holds out for Israel the prospect of a religious alternative to Orthodoxy. Reform shares with tradition-seeking Israelis the same humanistic orientation, the primacy of prophetic Judaism over the Halakhah, and both welcome innovations that are rooted in tradition yet relevant to the demands of the present. Thus Israel, rather than the Diaspora, may, in the opinion of some of its leaders, provide the ultimate testing ground for Reform Judaism.[15]

While the rabbinate and the religious parties in Israel have denounced attempts by either the Conservative or the Progressive movements to establish footholds in Israel, its principal thrust was against the Progressive; the latter appeared bold and determined, the former hesitant and inhibited. The Reformers, however, were also more vulnerable, for it was possible to employ against them the arguments used by the founders of Zionism against the Classical Reform of the nineteenth century.

C. ATTITUDE OF THE ORTHODOX TO NON-ORTHODOX RELIGIOUS MOVEMENTS

The Chapel Controversy

The rabbinate, as well as the religious parties, viewed the modest beginnings of non-Orthodox religious activity with apprehension and animosity. In the first instance, such a development threatened to involve them in an intellectual confrontation with believing Jews, and thus terminate the comfortable situation that had prevailed till then, when the estrangement between Orthodox and secularists relieved the former of any ideological arguments with the latter. The modern Orthodox groups in Western Europe, and in particular in the United States, were used to varying degrees of communal cooperation with the Conservatives and Progressives and even engaged from time to time in theological dialogues with them; in Israel, on the other hand, the Orthodox establishment has not been intellectually equipped for such confrontation.

Vis-à-vis the secularists, the Orthodox have explained their deviations from the Halakhah way of life as motivated by an urge toward ease and comfort, and have expressed the hope that before long they would return to the fold. But non-Orthodox groups who try to deviate from the Halakhah in the name of Torah Judaism represent a totally novel and highly disturbing phenomenon. The controversy that developed around the construction in Jerusalem of an institution of higher learning sponsored by the Reform movement in America afforded the Orthodox their first opportunity to take an official stand.

The Hebrew Union College School of Archaeology in Jerusalem was inaugurated in 1963, but a controversy had swirled around it for about a decade before. The government of Israel had allocated to it a plot of land in one of the central parts of Jerusalem so that the College could construct a building to house its School of Archaeology, as well as a chapel where services could be held for the students of the College and for others. In accordance with law, the building plan was submitted to the municipality for approval, but the issuance of a permit was held up for a long period because of the opposition of the Agudat Israel and Mafdal members on the municipal council. It appeared that the Orthodox found it intolerable that a Reform house of prayer be established in the Holy City. There were pressures and counterpressures, and eventually, following government intervention, the permit was issued.

The question reached the Knesset in 1955. Eliahu Genichovsky of Agudat Israel expanded on the subject:

> In accordance with an agreement entered into between the government of Israel and the Reform, a School of Archaeology will be built in Jerusalem on land allocated by the government . . . and in it there will be a Reform synagogue for some 400 worshippers—the first of its kind in Israel. On top of the plague of missionary activity, conversion to Christianity and Sabbath violation, we have to have here in Jerusalem, not far removed from the Western Wall, a huge "image,"* which has symbolized over the last century and a half alienation and betrayal of Jewish values. And I indignantly ask: Is it possible that the government of Israel is ready to betray Jewish history?[16]

Mr. Moshe Sharett, then Prime Minister, replied in the Knesset:

> Mr. Genichovsky . . . uttered a warning which I cannot ignore. Professor Nelson Glueck, an eminent archaeologist, perhaps the greatest living authority on the archaeology of the Negev and the Jordan Valley, is the head of two American institutions, the Hebrew Union College and the Jewish Institute of Religion. . . . Both these institutions wish to strike root in the land, so that their students may come here and spend shorter or longer periods. . . . There have already been instances of scientific, rabbinic and educational institutions in America establishing a foothold here, and it seems to me that we ought to regard this process as beneficial, as it strengthens the ties and intensifies the affinities between the culture of Israel and the Jewish culture of America.
>
> Now Mr. Genichovsky has made a declaration that if the intention is to construct a Reform synagogue, it shall not come to pass. Let us suppose that among the Olim who come to settle here there are people who have previously adopted a certain mode of prayer, as well as a certain conception of Judaism, and these people express the wish to worship God in their own way, what then is the significance of that "it shall not come to pass?" They will not go to the Dead Sea Scrolls, but they will go to the Scroll of Independence, and they will point a finger on the provision that there shall prevail in Israel freedom of religion and freedom of conscience. They will further say: This is our religion, for we ourselves determine what

* The Hebrew word used was *tselem,* usually denoting an idol.

our religion is, and this is our form of prayer which satisfies our spiritual needs. By what legal or moral right can we deny them this right, or interfere with its exercise? From this platform speech should not easily issue which is not compatible with our democratic way of life, and with the cultural and spiritual climate that we hope to see developing in this land.[17]

The controversy about the proposed Reform chapel continued for some time. It elicited a closely reasoned statement from Chief Rabbi Isaac Nissim. He objected neither to the establishment of a School of Archaeology, nor to the coming of Reform rabbis as students, but, he claimed, "the presence of these students in the School does not justify the setting up of a Reform Synagogue. Prior to, as well as after the establishment of the state, many Reform Rabbis and students visited Israel, and there never appeared a need to set up a synagogue for them in accordance with their customs. . . . If they pray in Hebrew and have their heads covered, surely they can worship in the synagogues already existing in Israel." Rabbi Nissim went on to argue that a chapel such as was proposed might attract not only Hebrew Union College students, but also the public at large.

> Even assuming that it is intended to confine attendance to the small circle of students, we are bound firmly to reject it. . . . I am far from regarding the penetration of Reform a matter of freedom of religion and of conscience. Freedom of religion is intended for members of all religions, including the minorities, to enable them to pursue their own faith; this freedom of religion, however, is not intended to achieve an opposite objective, with the result that the dominant religion in the state, i.e., the Jewish religion, be jeopardized and torn asunder . . . . Reform is not a religion. Religion is divine and eternal, and is not man-made. The authors of Reform and its leaders adjust religion to conform to their views, and adapt it to the pattern of life which they have chosen for themselves. . . . Reformers have erected the bridge and paved the way through which men may pass from Judaism to Christianity.

To those who pointed to the greater stress on tradition and to the greater interest in Zionism and Israel that has lately been apparent in the Reform movement, the Chief Rabbi replied:

> This is not to be regarded as a return to Judaism. It is within this movement, [Zionism], that these people are active on behalf of the State of Israel. Nor is this a return to Judaism. Even in their ritual they imitate Christianity, so that it is not impossible that some among them seek to resemble leaders of the Christian clergy, among whom also are to be found supporters of the idea of Israel's revival. The motives which operate in Christianity as regards its attitude toward the Land of the Bible could operate among the Reformers also.

Regarding the new synagogue under construction, the rabbi said:

> From that little Reform synagogue which it is intended to set up,
> there will no doubt emerge those who will undermine the vineyard
> of Israel. Even assuming that it is not the intention to admit to it
> those who are not students, who will restrain them? Not only each
> generation will soon be demanding reforms, but also every new situ-
> ation will demand it; we must not condone developments that may
> constitute a menace to the nation and the state.[18]

Rabbi Nissim's pronouncements represented a comprehensive statement of the attitude of the rabbinate toward non-Orthodox Judaism.
The principle of religious freedom was to be upheld toward all other
religions, but not for "the dominant religion in the state, i.e., the Jewish religion." The rabbinate did not object to any Christian denomination, however small its following in Israel, nor, for instance, to the
small Druze community organized for religious worship. But, there being only one Jewish religion, Reform and Conservative Judaism were
not Judaism, and consequently their adherents needed no religious freedom and must not be accorded it. Judaism was conceived as a mono-
lith, and the official rabbinate as its legally recognized custodian.[19]

The view expressed by the Chief Rabbi was echoed by other rabbis
as well as by leaders of the religious political parties. Whether Mafdal,[20]
Poalei Agudat Israel,[21] or Agudat Israel,[22] all referred to the Reform
movement as a factor making for the liquidation of Judaism. Some, indeed, did not see in it a danger to Orthodoxy as such; the late Mafdal
leader and Minister of the Interior, Moshe Haim Shapiro, was quoted
as saying that "Jews will know how to distinguish between real Judaism
and a caricature of it."[23] To the great majority, however, it represented
a serious danger to Orthodoxy. The official organ of Agudat Israel declared:

> The number of anti-religious and non-believers is not large; the
> largest group are the doubters, those who do not tolerate heresy as such,
> but are rather led into avoiding the performance of Mitzvot by their
> pursuit of comfort. Because of their very ignorance, many of them
> are likely to fall prey to the new Moloch. These hundreds of thousands
> of doubters, who attend synagogue only on Holydays, who send their
> boys for two or three years to a state religious school . . . all these
> may yet flock to Reform temples.

The writer called for a united front to eliminate this danger:

> One could agree with those who believe that Reform does not con-
> stitute a danger, if a united front were formed against them, that is,
> if the Orthodox, on the one hand, and the secularists on the other,
> were to tell them to go home to the United States, where they are

wanted, there to pursue their work of fraud and fabrication, and that they are not wanted here, neither by the Orthodox for their own reasons, nor by the secularists for their own reasons.[24]

The writer went on to express his regret at the unwillingness of the secularists to cooperate in the elimination of the Reform.

Aliyah and Recognition

Spokesmen of the Orthodox criticized Mr. Eshkol, the late Prime Minister, who had welcomed Aliyah on the part of Conservative and Reform Jews. Speaking in the Knesset in the course of the debate on the budget of the Prime Minister's Office, Jacob Katz, of Poalei Agudat Israel, stated:

> The Prime Minister cabled to the Conservative and Reform Rabbis that the land is open before them, and that they can work here. . . . Many of them hate the State of Israel, their eyes are not turned towards Zion, and the education they give their children attaches them neither to Judaism in America nor in Israel. All they can do in Israel is to create dissent and hostility. There does exist a religious way of life in Israel; religion is the true Jewish religion only when it is integral and faithful to its origin; the danger arises when people come to castrate it, falsify it and turn it into a caricature. *It is easier to co-exist with a secularist than with a person who falsifies the religion of Israel.*[25]

Speaking in his capacity as Minister of Religious Affairs, Zerah Warhaftig rejected any suggestion of recognizing non-Orthodox religious trends, and, as a consequence, authorizing them to solemnize marriages.

> The state can recognize only one Halakhah, and not splinters therefrom, as this would make no sense. . . . He who invokes trends or sects is actually affording assistance to the undermining of religious marriage, with the object of introducing civil marriage. Let it not be said that this is a controversy which concerns the recognition of this or of that trend. The state cannot recognize several Jewish religions. There is but one Halakhah.[26]

The Minister of Religious Affairs did not deny the right of freedom of worship to Conservative and Reform Jews. He assured the House in the course of the debate that freedom of worship existed, and that it was absolute.[27] This freedom of worship, however, was not to be equated with recognition by the state of Reform or of Conservative Judaism as Jewish religion. There was one Jewish religion and one law of marriage and divorce, namely, that prescribed by Halakhah. Consequently, neither Conservatives nor Reformers could claim the right to celebrate marriages.

Soul Searching

Among some of the Orthodox intellectuals, the appearance of religious pluralism did give rise to an examination of their attitude to the matter. Were not Reform and Conservative Judaism, unwelcome as they might be, to be preferred to secularism? Would it not be more desirable for young people to attend a synagogue that was not Orthodox rather than be severed from any contact with institutional religion? Would not a dialogue between religious trends stimulate ferment among the secularists? Opinions were divided.

Professor Ephraim Urbach, leader of the movement for Torah Judaism, adopted a benevolent attitude. While reemphasizing his own unqualified adherence to Orthodoxy, he added: "I am for enabling the Reformers to hold their services in their own way. I wish they would come to our country and open synagogues of their own. I want the same in respect of the Conservative Jews. . . . American Jews who wish to settle here, who are Reform and feel the need of the place of worship for themselves should be enabled to achieve this."[28]

One of the leading Orthodox educators, Dr. Pinchas Rosenblueth, reacted in a similar way when referring to a Reform service he had attended in Haifa. He said: "I wish more people attended the Sabbath service, instead of spending their time in the streets or in places of amusement."[29]

A more cautious attitude was adopted by Rabbi B. Rabbinowitz of Holon. Addressing an academic audience in Jerusalem, he referred "to the existence of a void among youth, as well as a yearning for religious values. Youth poses questions and seeks solutions in religion. Since the religious themselves are torn by conflict, no guidance is afforded to youth." He therefore appealed for unity in the Orthdox camp, since without such unity there was serious danger of Reform penetration into Israel.[30]

Professor André de Vries of the University of Tel Aviv, suggested a working compromise. As an Orthodox Jew, he was opposed to the recognition of Reform rabbis on the grounds, *inter alia,* that the knowledge of the Halakhah imparted in Reform seminaries was altogether inadequate. He would recognize the Reform rabbis as "Pastors" (Ro'ei Tzon). Inasmuch as the Halakhah does not require the presence of a rabbi at a marriage ceremony, a Reform rabbi—though not a rabbi within the "legal" meaning of the term—could officiate at a marriage, provided that such a marriage had been previously approved by the official rabbinate.[31]

The problem was discussed within the Kibbutz Dati, where conflicting views were expressed. Moshe Unna came out strongly against religious pluralism and viewed such a development as fraught with grave danger to Judaism. Admitting that in Israel the most Orthodox type of Judaism was now confronted with the most extreme type of secularism, he nevertheless reversed his previous view that some religious affinity was preferable to outright heresy. The growth of religious pluralism, he said, would lead to a situation where recognition of marriages and conversions performed by Reform or Conservative rabbis would eventually become inevitable, with the result that the position of Halakhah as the uniform law regulating matters of personal status would be undermined. While it was relatively easy to reach a political accommodation with the secularists, any accommodation between Orthodoxy and other religious trends was quite inconceivable. A spiritual conflict with the secularists was not necessarily a lost battle, for the secularists might yet repent. A battle between two religious trends, however, would lead to two irreconcilable religions, and to a perpetual conflict between them. "Between authentic Judaism . . . and a Protestant Judaism," which regarded Mitzvot as man-made, and as a product of historic developments, there was an unbridgeable gulf. Finally, the secularists, who could not challenge Orthodoxy on the spiritual plane, would gladly support the non-Orthodox religious trends in order to undermine the authority of the Halakhah.[32]

Thus, not only do the Orthodox rabbis and the religious parties view the rise of religious pluralism as a grave menace to Orthodox Judaism, but also most of the intellectuals among the Orthodox share this view. Neither the Orthodox nor the secularists have had any experience with religious pluralism, nor has religion in Israel been discussed in any meaningful intellectual terms. The steps toward rapprochement, however slight and slow, and the cooperation between the three religious trends in North America are generally unknown to the Israelis, and therefore the prospect of a religious schism resulting from pluralism is a deterrent even to the moderate and intellectually inclined Orthodox. They are inclined to believe that a denial of recognition to non-Orthodox rabbis on the one hand, and the apparent indifference of the secularists to religion on the other, will prevent the emergence of true religious pluralism.

D. OPPOSITION TO NON-ORTHODOX CONGREGATIONS

Freedom of worship and of free exercise of religion being guaranteed by law, the non-Orthodox religious trends are at liberty to establish congregations and to hold services of their own. The influence of the religious parties was, in numerous instances, strong enough to create difficulties in certain localities for the non-Orthodox congregations.

The non-Orthodox congregations were particularly vulnerable because, with the exception of the Progressive Congregation in Jerusalem, which had a building of its own, all had to make temporary arrangements to secure a place for holding services. In 1962, Sharon Progressive Congregation in Kfar Shmaryahu rented the hall of a local hotel for the holding of High Holydays services. Shortly before Rosh HaShanah, the hotel manager informed the congregation that he was being threatened by the local religious council with the withdrawal of the hotel's Kashrut certificate. This would mean such a loss of potential income that he had no alternative but to cancel the lease. The congregation then applied to the mayor of Kfar Shmaryahu for the lease of the Maccabi Sport gymnasium, owned by the municipal council. Rosh HaShanah and Yom Kippur services were actually held in the gymnasium, but the mayor yielded to the pressure of the local rabbinate, and refused the use of the hall for the Sukkot service. It was only as a result of an action lodged in the High Court of Justice, directing the mayor to show cause why the hall should not be placed at the disposal of the congregation, that the use of the hall was secured. Since, however, the order of the court was issued at the very last moment, there was no time to prepare the hall, and the Sukkot service was held in an open space in the center of the town. A Sukkah was improvised, and a record crowd turned out, including many from Tel Aviv and elsewhere. The event was widely reported in the press.[33] The press quoted the dialogue that had taken place during the course of the High Court proceedings between one of the judges and the attorney for the municipal council of Kfar Shmaryahu. The judge asked: "Would it be better for them not to pray at all?" And the reply of the attorney for the council was: "In my opinion, it would certainly be better for them not to pray at all than to pray in the Reform manner."[34]

In December 1963, the new Progressive congregation of Ramat Gan, Emet veAnavah, held its first service in the home of an employee of the municipal council of that city. The matter came to the knowledge of the religious council of Ramat Gan, which requested the municipal employee to discontinue holding services in his house. The employee refused, and services continued to be held. In January 1964, a delegation of members of the municipal council who belonged to the religious parties, called on the mayor, and requested his intervention with a view to putting an end to the services. A few days later, the mayor summoned the employee and talked to him on the subject. Services continued to be held in his home. On March 13, 1964, the Orthodox weekly, *Panim El Panim,* reported prominently that the mayor had "promised to expel Reform from the town." A few days later, the municipal employee was again summoned by the mayor; he subsequently requested the congregation to discontinue the holding of services in his house.

The congregation was thus left without facilities, and services were suspended.[35]

For some weeks a public storm raged. The entire press, with the exception of the Orthodox periodicals, condemned the action of the mayor and of the religious councillors who had exerted pressure on him. Professor Jacob Talmon of the Hebrew University canceled a scheduled lecture he was to have given under the auspices of the Ramat Gan municipality.[36] The matter drew so much attention that the rabbi of the Progressive congregation was interviewed on the radio. After the broadcast M. H. Shapiro, the Minister of the Interior and leader of Mafdal, criticized the Broadcasting Authority for having allowed "some sort of a Reform rabbi" to make unfriendly references to Orthodoxy.[37] Rabbi Max Nussbaum of Los Angeles, then in Israel, issued a statement condemning intolerance:

> One could understand it, if the influence of the Orthodox came as a result of conviction . . . but they operate by virtue of the power derived from the attachment of religion to politics. Religion is represented by Rabbis who belong to political parties with representation in the government. The fact that the Mayor of Ramat Gan persuaded the municipal official to deny his home to the Reform is directly due to that Mayor's dependence on a municipal coalition which hinges on Councillors of the religious parties.

Under the impact of public pressure, the matter came up for consideration by the Cabinet, which decided to instruct the Civil Service Commissioner to notify the municipal authorities that civil servants and public officials may not be summoned by their superiors for discussion of matters that are personal to the individual.[38]

For some time services in Ramat Gan were held in private homes, until a permanent lease was acquired. Attempts were made, however, to prevent by force the holding of these services. On October 17, 1964, a group of neighbors attempted to hinder a service, and police had to be summoned to restore public order.[39]

In September 1965, the newly organized Progressive Congregation in Tel Aviv applied to the management of the Zionist Organization of America House for the lease of their hall for High Holyday services. The House, a leading cultural and social center in Tel Aviv, also has a restaurant, and provides accommodation for the celebration of weddings and Bar Mitzvah parties. At first the management of the House gave consent to the lease, but later refused use of the hall on the ground that withdrawal of the Kashrut license was likely should the hall be leased as requested, which would seriously harm the institution. A similar refusal, on similar grounds, was given by the Farmers' Union in Tel Aviv, when asked for the lease of their basement hall.[40]

At the end of 1965, Rabbi Moshe Zemer of the Tel Aviv Progressive Congregation ("Kedem") obtained the lease of a hall in the recently completed building of the Order of Bnai Brith, which had been erected largely through funds provided by the Order in the United States. Two days before the services were to be held, the manager of the building approached the rabbi with a view to canceling the lease. He pointed out that Chief Rabbi Unterman, himself a member of the Order, objected to the lease. Further, the management of the building was just then negotiating for a reduction of municipal rates, and the power of the religious parties on the municipal council was strong enough to influence the decision of the council. It was finally agreed that the Congregation would hold one service only; this took place on January 21, 1966, when the worshipers were informed that no further services would be held in the hall, even though Orthodox services had been held in the building on a number of occasions. The incident aroused much indignation in Israel and abroad. The Secretary-General of Bnai Brith in Israel declared: "Bnai Brith has not adopted and does not adopt a stand with regard to Reform Judaism. Reform Rabbis and their circles find an honourable place amongst the ranks of Bnai Brith. However, as the President of Bnai Brith pointed out, we will continue to refrain from any act which leads to difference of opinion amongst our members and, therefore, without taking any position on the matter of Reform services, we will not allow any activity that will hurt any member of our brotherhood."[41] This action elicited vehement condemnation on the part of many of the leaders of Bnai Brith. Similar difficulties were reported from Ashkelon where an attempt was made to force a Conservative congregation to discontinue its activities.[42] *Yediot Ahronot* reported on February 4, 1966, from Ashkelon that two public school teachers employed in the state religious school, who were reported to have attended the Conservative services in Ashkelon, were officially told that they would be dismissed if they continued to attend those services.[43] At a later date, however, WIZO allowed the Conservative congregation the use of its premises. The pressure of public opinion had had an effect.

The Influence of Public Opinion

During the early sixties, the attempt to interfere with the activities of non-Orthodox religious groups agitated public opinion and caused much criticism of the Orthodox. The latter, on their part, realizing the dangers inherent in this development, mobilized support in Israel as well as abroad. Speaking to Orthodox rabbis in the United States, Chief Rabbi Unterman inveighed against Reform rabbis who come to Israel, allegedly "to convert Israelis to Judaism. This will not be allowed." The President of the Rabbinical Council of America, Rabbi Israel Miller, warned that Reform Judaism "is attempting to undermine the religious unity of Israel." He called on both the Reform and the Conservative movements "to desist from further efforts to bring elements of strife and disunity into the religious life of Israel." The problem of "religious diversity and conflict has been plaguing the American Jewish community for several years," he said. "There is no justification for permitting such divisions and tensions to be imported into the Israeli body politic."[44] Thus, the burden of the argument of the Orthodox was not only the need to assure religious unity in Israel, with the object of preventing a Kulturkampf. They also asserted that it was to the advantage of both Orthodox and secularists not to allow small groups of non-Orthodox to stir up trouble.

Israeli public opinion, however, was tiring of acts of interference with Reform and Conservative congregations; the government, on its part, was also under pressure from Conservative and Reform leaders in the United States. The statement made by Rabbi Israel Goldstein, formerly a leading Conservative Rabbi in New York and later head of the Keren HaYesod in Jerusalem, to the effect that the treatment meted out in Israel to the Conservative and Reform congregations was discrediting Israel "in the eyes of the world and particularly in the eyes of world Jewry," did not pass unnoticed.[45] The government of Israel could not remain indifferent and, following the Bnai Brith Hall controversy and other incidents, issued a statement reaffirming "the existence of freedom of religion in Israel. Every person in Israel is entitled to pray wherever he wishes, and in the form he wishes."[46]

Even the Ministry for Religious Affairs declared that Reform and other non-Orthodox congregations requiring financial help to build places of worship or acquire religious appurtenances might obtain such help. "It is understood that the Ministry is prepared to extend the same assistance to these congregations as it extends to Orthodox congregations. Leaders of the Reform movement in the United States have been informed of the Ministry's instructions."[47]

In pursuance of this policy, the Har El Progressive Congregation did receive from the Ministry for Religious Affairs a one-time subvention of 500 Israeli pounds, and the Progressive congregation in Haifa was given a Sefer Torah. Small as these contributions were, they nevertheless constituted a departure from the previous policy of completely ignoring the very existence of non-Orthodox congregations.

The Ministry of Religious Affairs was clearly on the defensive. A statement in the *Jerusalem Post* on Feb. 1, 1966, avowed: "The Ministry often complains that actions of the Chief Rabbis and of the local rabbinates and the religious councils are wrongly attributed to it. The Ministry protests that, whereas it might wish to adopt a more liberal position on some particular issue, it has no control over these other elements, and cannot prevent a local rabbinate from threatening to withdraw Kashrut certification for weddings from a public hall that may be considering renting its premises to a Reform congregation." The fact that the Ministry of Religious Affairs found it necessary to justify its position was an indication of the government's sensitiveness to public opinion, and particularly to public opinion in the Diaspora.

In a subsequent debate in the Knesset, the Minister of Religious Affairs, Dr. Warhaftig, while reiterating the government's position on the principle of equality of treatment for non-Orthodox congregations, gave voice to his party's view of the problem in its broader aspect. He declared that "to the extent that the people in Israel are religious, they are Orthodox only. . . . If there were a large immigration of Reform Jews . . . it would create a serious problem. At least if they came in large numbers, that would be a separate problem—but as it is, they arrive in a trickle, and surely we do not have to bestow the rights that are held by the religious on a mere hundred or so. That's hardly a practical policy."[48] He reiterated the official position that

the state can recognize only one Halakhah. . . . All those who speak of trends [in Judaism] are affording active help to those who oppose religious marriage and divorce, and seek to introduce civil ceremonies in their place. Let them not tell me that their intention is to secure recognition of another trend in Judaism. It is clear that the intention is to bring about a secularization of these institutions [i.e., marriage and divorce].

Regarding any proposed separation of religion and the state, he declared: "Separation today is impossible."[49]

The firm stand taken by the government in response to pressure from within and from without in fact put an end to the attempts to prevent non-Orthodox groups from establishing synagogues; such pressure, however, was not strong enough to induce the government to make any concessions that might in the slightest degree jeopardize the legal monopoly of the Orthodox. Thus, on May 25, 1967, the rabbi of the Tel Aviv Progressive Congregation inquired from the Ministry of Religious Affairs whether it was possible to acquire a burial plot for an American Jewish couple, whose will provided that their remains be brought to Israel for burial in accordance with the Reform ritual. The Ministry replied that there could be no burial service in accordance with the ritual of Progressive Judaism.[50]

The rabbi of the Progressive congregation Emet veAnavah in Ramat Gan, Tuvia Ben Horin, applied to the military authorities to be attached to the Army Chaplaincy. He had studied at the Hebrew University, was ordained as a rabbi by the Hebrew Union College, and had been for several years the spiritual leader of the Progressive congregation.

In reply to the application, dated October 24, 1965, the army authorities rejected the request, on the grounds that his services as an officer in the Tank Corps were essential. A further application was made, whereupon the army authorities requested the production of a certificate from the Ministry of Religious Affairs that the applicant was in fact a rabbi. Application was duly made for this purpose to the Ministry of Religious Affairs; the latter replied that the Ministry did not issue rabbinical certificates, since this was within the competence of the Chief Rabbinate alone. Further action was useless, for rabbinical certificates were being issued to none but Orthodox rabbis.[51] Thus, while freedom of worship for the non-Orthodox was assured, the exclusive legal status of Orthodoxy also remained unimpaired.

World Union Conference

In 1968, a dramatic confrontation took place between the Orthodox and the World Union for Progressive Judaism, involving the government of Israel as well as public opinion. The World Union resolved to hold its fifteenth international conference in Jerusalem. It was the first time in its history that the Union was meeting in Israel. This was regarded by many as a unique event, a further manifestation of Jewish unity brought about in the wake of the Six Day War, a "turning-point in the movement's history, making amends for the 1885 Pittsburgh decision to eliminate Zion from the liturgy, which was only partly corrected by the 1937 revision."[52] The government of Israel facilitated the arrangements in every way, and the Hebrew University of Jerusalem placed its halls at the disposal of the conference. Some 500 delegates, from 25 countries, and from all the continents, including some 200 leaders of Reform Judaism in the United States, converged on Jerusalem and were warmly welcomed by public opinion.

The proceedings opened in Jerusalem on July 3, 1968. Rabbi Jacob Shankman, President of the World Union, proclaimed in his opening address: "The Six Day War generated a mood, and released emotions which were overpowering. . . . We Jews are inseparable, now and forever."[53] He also utilized the occasion to voice the demand of non-Orthodox religious trends to be recognized in Israel, and of their rabbis to be enabled to perform their normal rabbinical functions, including the celebration of marriages among members of their congregations.

Prime Minister Levi Eshkol came in person to deliver the greetings of the government. He addressed the convention as "a Jew talking to fellow-Jews," and could not contain his pleasure that "the very fact of holding this conference in our holy and united capital . . . spells out triumph for the Jewish national trend in your movement." He made a direct appeal for Aliyah: "Nothing short of direct involvement, of a physical bond between people and country will suffice. A constant flow of members of your congregations to this country is bound to influence the depth of Jewish commitment of those Jewish congregations."[54] Anticipating the argument that an appeal to the Reformers for Aliyah must be accompanied by the assurance that Reform would be recognized in Israel as a legitimate expression of Torah Judaism, Eshkol added: "I know that you hold views concerning religious life in this country. This, however, is not the occasion to deal with the matter. One thing is certain nevertheless; the life-style here will be molded by those who live here, and your influence will increase in proportion to the number of your adherents here."[55] The Prime Minister's speech not only contained an appeal for Aliyah, but referred to the rights of the non-Orthodox religious trends: their small numbers at present did not warrant a change of policy; nevertheless, with their numerical growth, the natural course of events would bring about a change, so it was implied.

The warm welcome extended by the government of Israel was echoed in the press, which prominently reported the proceedings of the conference. The resolution appealing to members of the movement to "ascend" to Israel was seen as particularly gratifying. Realizing the legal limitations placed on the government, and unwilling to upset the legal status quo, the conference formulated and presented to the Prime Minister three demands that it felt could be met without altering the law. These were: that Progressive rabbis in Israel be authorized to perform the marriage of those members of their congregations whom the Orthodox rabbinate certified as eligible for marriage; that Progressive congregations enjoy equality with Orthodox congregations in the support they receive from the Ministry of Religious Affairs and from local religious councils; and that persons converted to Judaism by Progressive rabbis be recognized as Jews under the Law of Return. The last demand was met when, in 1970, the Knesset amended the Law of Return; the second demand was partially met; while the first—though in no way repugnant to the Halakhah—has been ignored.

The program for the conference had called for a religious service at the Western Wall (formerly known as the Wailing Wall), the only remnant of the Second Temple. After the liberation of the Old City of Jerusalem on the third day of the Six Day War, the Western Wall became the object of pilgrimages for Jews from all over the world; the more recent structures that had cluttered the Wall area were removed in order to enlarge the approach to the site, and to accommodate the thousands of visitors. The decision to hold a service there was regarded by the organizers as an appropriate way of demonstrating Jewish solidarity. For not only did pilgrims gather at the site, but regular services were being held there three times a day every day in the year. A formal application was made to hold a service for the delegates. On June 13, 1968, the Ministry of Religious Affairs informed the representatives of the World Union for Progressive Judaism that the regulations of the Chief Rabbinate did not permit the holding of services where men and women would worship together, the section directly in front of the Western Wall being considered as a synagogue.

This announcement caused a public uproar, and the controversy between the Orthodox and the proponents of pluralistic Judaism, as well as the secularists, flared up and reached the proportions of a national debate. The Orthodox denounced Reform as a betrayal of Judaism; some urged that the Reform rabbis be driven out, "for they seek to uproot the people, not only from its Torah but also from its Land."[56] Agudat Israel warned that a conflict with Reform would be fought out as a war for survival. Equally vehement was the organ of Mafdal, which denied the religiousness of Reform, and cited an array of Halakhic authorities to prove that it was a sacrilege for men and women to worship together.[57] Within a matter of days the issue was the cause of a stormy debate in the Knesset, which was held on June 19, 1968.

The Minister of Religious Affairs, speaking for the government, rejected the request. The Chief Rabbinate was recognized as the official spokesman for the Jewish religion, and was therefore the sole authority to regulate religious services at the Western Wall. He denied the moral right of the Reformers to hold a service in Jerusalem, since in their Pittsburgh Program they had expunged all references to the restoration of Zion. The Minister conveniently omitted any references to the evolution of the Reform movement since 1885.[58] Epithets such as "enemies of Zion" were hurled at Reform by spokesmen of the Orthodox.

The agitation did not subside and the government was in a quandary. The question came before the cabinet, and when no consensus was reached, a ministerial subcommittee was appointed to seek a solution. The subcommittee, too, failed to reach an agreement, and the matter was referred back to the cabinet. In the meantime, the Orthodox took matters into their own hands, and the day set for the holding of the service, July 4, threatened to become a day of battle. Thousands of Yeshivah students and adherents of Neturei Karta were directed to converge on the Western Wall, with a view to preventing the delegates to the conference from holding a service, and to do so by force, if necessary.

It was an embarrassing dilemma for the government. The decision lay between refusing a legitimate demand made on behalf of a large section of the Jewish people in the Diaspora, and risking a major riot in a sacred area, in the full view of the world press and of public opinion. Equally perplexed were the leaders of the conference themselves. Some of them sought to force the issue. Others advocated caution, and pointed out two dangers: that of being accused by friendly Israelis of providing the Orthodox with a pretext to create a public scandal, and, what seemed even more significant, that of creating a situation where Israel would be seen as unable to protect even the religious rights of Jews, and therefore not fit to be trusted with the protection of the religious rights of non-Jews. Under the guidance of Rabbi Maurice Eisendrath, then President of the Union of American Hebrew Congregations, the Progressives decided to cancel the service, much to the relief of the government.

Levi Eshkol was among the first to express the government's appreciation of the decision of the conference. He stated, in fact, that in the event of a riot breaking out between the Orthodox and the Progressives, the Security Council of the United Nations might have been called into session, and the problem of the Holy Places and the internationalization of Jerusalem would have been raised once more. He again stressed the importance of Aliyah as the surest way of promoting Progressive Judaism, and said: "Some of us in the government will be ready to assist you."[59]

The decision of the leaders of the conference to cancel the scheduled service was well received by the entire press, and so was the explanation offered for that decision. Rabbi Eisendrath declared: "We have not been intimidated by threats of stone-throwing or bloodshed. Our decision not to hold an afternoon prayer service at the Western Wall was determined solely by the fear of physical violence to others, and, even more, of the possibility of political repercussions reflecting on Israel's rights in the Holy Places."[60]

The attitude of the Israelis was summed up by the *Jerusalem Post* of July 7, 1968: "The Reform group, by definition liberal and tolerant, found itself at a hopeless disadvantage in this struggle for its right to pray as it wishes, against a section of the community that glories in its illiberalism, intolerance and fanaticism. They could not solemnly march out to battle, and capture the Wall. . . . But still we have reason to be grateful for their good sense in withdrawing in time from a painful conflict, and saving Jerusalem the likelihood of shame and disgrace. They showed more respect and regard for the Wall than many others have done."

Since then there has indeed been only one significant instance of interference by the Orthodox. At the instance of the official rabbinate of Tel Aviv, the Progressive Congregation of Tel Aviv, Kedem, was prevented from holding a Passover Seder for new Olim. Following a successful Purim Ball held by this congregation at the Immigrants' Absorption Centre in Jaffa, and designed to advance the integration of the newcomers, Kedem was asked to arrange a Passover Seder. The Board of the Synagogue responded affirmatively, and ordered food from a caterer whose Kashrut was certified by the Tel Aviv rabbinate; they also purchased new crockery, cutlery, and utensils. Two weeks before the Seder, the Director of the Immigration Department of the Jewish Agency instructed the Absorption Centre to cancel the Seder, on the ground that all religious activities in immigration centers were under the control of the official rabbinate. All attempts to have this order rescinded failed, for the authorities of the Jewish Agency wished to avoid a conflict with the rabbinate. The latter subsequently sent an Orthodox rabbi to conduct the Seder; however, the Seder at the Absorption Centre was very sparsely attended, because the majority of the Olim accepted the invitation of the Kedem Synagogue to join their members in the Seder that they had arranged in their own hall.[61]

E. OTHER ASPECTS
OF RELIGIOUS PLURALISM

Diaspora Reactions

The Western Wall episode further illustrated how sensitive world Jewry was to religious developments in Israel. By legislating on matters of marriage and divorce, and on the question "Who is a Jew?", the Israeli parliament has in fact been legislating for the whole of the Jewish people. The Jewish communities in the Diaspora, anxious to safeguard their position as a minority in a Gentile world, have upheld principles in which they believe and that they would therefore wish to be maintained in the Jewish state as well. Understandably, they have felt entitled to express their views and make representations to the government of Israel.[62]

Various Orthodox groups in the Diaspora, and particularly in the United States, were the first to make representations to the government of Israel in protest against actions that seemed prejudicial to Orthodoxy. While the major bodies of Orthodox organizations confined their activities to protests or to propaganda campaigns, some of the extreme elements resorted to more spectacular action. In the fall of 1963, Orthodox youths picketed the Israeli Consulate in New York and painted swastikas on its walls, to protest the action of the Israeli authorities against Neturei Karta riots in Jerusalem. The Committee for the Unity of the Jewish People, set up by the Hassidim of the Lubavitch group with headquarters in Brooklyn, carried on a persistent campaign against the Law of Return of 1970, which recognized persons converted to Judaism by non-Orthodox rabbis as eligible for Aliyah like other Jews. Orthodox leaders in America demanded that marriages and divorces effected by non-Orthodox rabbis be invalidated in Israel. They mounted their campaign for the alleged sake of the unity of the Jewish people, for, they contended, only by preserving the supremacy of Orthodoxy in Israel and the rigorous application of Halakhic rules would that unity be preserved. In their view, the Conservative movement constituted a serious threat to Israeli Jewry.[63]

But non-Orthodox groups, too, as well as leading Jewish civic organizations in the Diaspora, began to be heard from. They regarded the harassment of Conservative and Progressive congregations in Israel as a violation of religious freedom. Some Jewish leaders found it embarrassing that the principle of separation of religion and state, which they considered to be the cornerstone of religious freedom in America, was not applied in Israel, with the result that the Progressive and Conservative movements there were legally discriminated against, while Orthodoxy had been raised to the level of the established religion.

In March 1964, seven major Jewish organizations, including the American Jewish Committee, the American Jewish Congress, Bnai Brith, and the rabbinical and the lay organizations of the Conservative and Reform movements, addressed a cable to Prime Minister Levi Eshkol, urging him to stand firm against the demands of the Orthodox in Israel and in America to place restrictions on religious freedom. They stated that they represented the overwhelming majority of American Jews who rejected the attempt of the extremist religious elements to polarize the American Jewish community into two opposing groups—religious and secularist—and their claims that they and they alone represented the Jewish religious community. "We abhor," they declared, "any attempt by Government authority . . . to interfere with the expression of religion in all its aspects. . . . The truth is that in the American Jewish community there are several recognized and acknowledged Jewish religious constituencies. The overwhelming majority of Jews, whatever their religious commitment, support the basic Jewish position of separation of 'Church' and State, and of freedom of religious belief, practice and instruction for all."[64]

The reaction to this unprecedented step was immediate, both in the United States and in Israel. American Jewish Orthodox leaders accused the signatories to the cable addressed to Eshkol of "communal irresponsibility," and declared that "the Government of Israel must be considered duty-bound to adhere to policies conformable with respect for Jewish religious law and traditional heritage in the public life of the Jewish state." The Rabbinical Council of America denounced the cable as a "scurrilous attack and a complete fabrication," and demanded a retraction. The Religious Zionists of America (Mizrahi and HaPoel Ha-Mizrahi) withdrew from the American Jewish Congress.[65] Rabbi Joachim Prinz, President of the American Jewish Congress, justified the action of his organization: "What we think is right and just in our own country must be right and just in Israel. What we find wanting in America—the imperfections of democracy that we recognize and seek to correct—must also be considered faulty and in need of correction in Israel."[66] This was an unequivocal statement of the position that the Jews in the Diaspora have the right not only to point out "the imperfections of democracy" in the Jewish state, but also to demand that they be corrected.

In Israel, too, the publication of the cable aroused controversy. For the first time the voice of the Conservative and Reform movements was heard in the land, and Israeli public opinion was made to realize that the signatories to the cable had expressed views shared by the predominant majority of the Jews in the United States. The Orthodox felt cornered, and spokesmen for Mafdal denied the right of the Americans who had signed the cable to interfere in an internal Israeli matter. They were reminded, however, that they themselves had always urged their own counterparts in the United States into pressuring the Israeli government to adopt certain types of religious legislation.[67] The non-Orthodox, on the other hand, welcomed the action of the American leaders, and approvingly noted their concern with religious life in Israel. The Liberal daily *HaBoker* defined the action as a "beneficent precedent," and welcomed any future "interventions" of the kind.[68] What was most important in this controversy was that Prime Minister Eshkol in fact also welcomed the action, and did not regard it as intervention in the internal affairs of Israel. In his reply to the signatories to the cable, he interpreted their action "as not an interference by an alien body, but an indication that the Jewish world lives Israel's problems . . . what affects Israel, affects them. I see nothing wrong in the expression of opinion on these matters."[69]

Another instance of Reform-Conservative cooperation vis-à-vis the government in Israel occurred in 1972. Shlomo Lorincz submitted a private bill to the Knesset on behalf of Agudat Israel, designed to amend the Law of Return as enacted in 1970, which defined a Jew, for the purposes of that law, as a person born to a Jewish mother, or as one converted to Judaism. Lorincz's amendment called for the addition of the words "in accordance with the Halakhah," following the words "converted to Judaism." The amendment, if adopted, would deny the visa of an Oleh to persons converted to Judaism under the auspices of Reform or Conservative rabbis. The debate on this bill, which took place in the Knesset on July 12, 1972, and ended in a defeat for the proposed amendment,[70] was preceded by a vigorous campaign in both Israel and the Diaspora. The Progressive and Conservative movements made a joint representation to the government of Israel to the effect that they would not "tolerate a paradox, where persons who consider themselves Jews in every respect should discover that in fulfilling the Mitzvah of Aliyah to Israel, they are thereby disqualified from membership in the

Jewish people." To the contention of the Orthodox that strict adherence to the Halakhah was "essential to assure the unity of the Jewish people," the Reformers and the Conservatives replied that the consequence of adopting the Orthodox position "would be to divide the Jewish people at the very time when solidarity is so essential. . . . A prime task of our generation is to gather in the exiles, to broaden the dimensions of Jewish life . . . to include, not exclude." They also appealed for the recognition of diversity in religion in the Diaspora, and warned against its being "subverted in the Jewish State by a small minority of Jews" who desire that the "State of Israel should be used as a tool to impose the authoritarian will of that small minority on the majority of Jews outside its borders."[71]

Interaction

The very emergence of non-Orthodox religious groups in Israel, representing extensions of the Conservative and Reform movements in the Diaspora, brought into bold relief one of the most sensitive areas of the Israel-Diaspora relationship. It appeared that religious pluralism, which was an accepted feature of religious life in the Diaspora, engendered internal tensions in Israel and, in addition, created friction between the Diaspora and Israel. It further demonstrated the direct influence of religious developments in Israel on the Jewish communities in the Diaspora.

From the point of view of the Orthodox, the appearance in Israel of Reform and Conservative congregations is fraught with grave danger to Judaism, and also to the unity of the Jewish people. The existing tension between the Orthodox and the secularists is not regarded by them as a threat, since the latter neither pose a religious alternative nor aim at challenging Orthodoxy. The non-Orthodox religious trends, on the other hand, claiming as they do to be also legitimate expressions of the Jewish religion, pose religious alternatives to Orthodoxy, and thus undermine its position as Judaism's sole legitimate exponent.

The unity of the Jewish people, in the opinion of the Orthodox, will be jeopardized once the Conservatives and the Reform grow in number, when their pressure will surely induce the legislature of Israel to accord recognition to their marriages, divorces, and conversions. They fear that instead of a uniform Halakhah there will be two or more Halakhot. The day may come when there will be a large number of Jews in Israel whose marriages, and particularly whose divorces and conversions, will be regarded by the Orthodox as invalid. Such Jews will, in some cases, be tainted with Mamzerut, while others will not be regarded by the Orthodox as Jews at all; and in both cases they will be members of a section of the people with whom the Orthodox will not marry. Thus, there will arise a category of Jews who will be suspect in the eyes of the Orthodox, a new Bene Israel community, as it were, or, what may be worse, a category of Jews disqualified like the Karaites.

The Orthodox have viewed the emergence of non-Orthodox religious trends as an alien importation, a kind of missionary activity, carried out in Israel at the instance of the non-Orthodox in the Diaspora,[72] and have continually appealed to the secularists in the name of Jewish unity to join forces with them in order to resist the rise of disruptive elements. Only the strict application of Halakhic rules in matters of family law and of conversions will assure unity, they say; consequently, this policy should be supported by the secularists on nationalist grounds, just as it should be defended by the Orthodox on religious grounds. The Orthodox have endeavored with no small measure of success to establish common ground with wide sectors of the secularists, who are sensitive to appeals to their sense of national unity.

So long as this problem was a purely internal Israeli affair, the attitude of the secularist majority to non-Orthodox trends was an amalgam of indifference and some sympathy. From the point of view of civil rights, the secularists found it intolerable that non-Orthodox religious activity be interfered with, restricted, or discriminated against. They always insisted that no obstacles be placed in the way of the development of non-Orthodox congregational activities, and welcomed whatever facilities the government placed at their disposal. As the secularists' knowledge of either Conservative or Progressive Judaism was either very limited or prejudiced by the image of the Classical Reform, interest on their part in non-Orthodox Judaism has remained quite marginal, and particularly so since many of them regarded any kind of ritual as a product of Galut, and therefore alien to the spirit of a modern Jewish state.

The attitude of the government of Israel has been guided by practical considerations. While it has protected religious freedom and encouraged the development of non-Orthodox institutions and seats of learning, it has not been prepared, in view of the small numbers of the adherents of the non-Orthodox religious trends, to upset the religious status quo. It has not considered it politic to introduce legislation that might either create a rabbinic establishment parallel to the Orthodox, or bring about a separation of religion and state—and all for the sake of a few thousand souls. Such a development, it was felt, would inevitably lead to a Kulturkampf, an eventuality the secularists have consistently sought to avoid for as long as possible.

The Politics of Compromise

Thus, the government of Israel, supported by public opinion, is prepared to accept the Orthodox position that the cause of social unity requires that in Israel domestic relations and conversions be regulated by the Halakhah. Guided as they are by considerations of national unity, they cannot, however, accept the rules of Halakhah as the basis for the unity of Israeli and Diaspora Jewries. The imposition of Halakhic norms on Diaspora Jewry, where religious pluralism prevails, would be disruptive of Israel-Diaspora harmony.

If the Knesset were to legislate that marriages performed by non-Orthodox rabbis in the Diaspora were to be held as invalid, or that persons regarded in the Diaspora as Jews would be regarded as non-Jews in the view of the law of Israel, Israel-Diaspora unity would sustain a serious blow. The Progressive and Conservative movements in the Diaspora, outnumbering the Orthodox there, would certainly not tolerate a denial of the legitimacy of their Judaism by the law of Israel. In such a situation, Israel would forfeit its moral claim to call on fellow Jews affiliated with these movements to settle in Israel and help in its upbuilding, nor could it summon them to lend it moral and material support. Thus, while the unity of Jewish society within Israel can, in the foreseeable future, be maintained on the basis of Halakhah, no Israel-Diaspora unity can be maintained except on the basis of the recognition of Jewish religious pluralism in the Diaspora.

It is clear that this double standard, the Halakhah for Israel and religious pluralism for the Diaspora, is bound to create friction; from the point of view of the national interest of Israel, however, the acceptance of such conflicting norms is less dangerous for the unity of the Jewish people and for Israel-Diaspora harmony, than the adoption of either one of these norms as the sole basis for worldwide Jewish unity.

Short of a complete separation of religion and state in Israel—not a likely occurrence in the near future—the pragmatic solution evolved by its government and supported by the bulk of its public opinion is, in fact, the only one feasible under the circumstances. The critics of this policy assert that it is no solution but merely a delaying action. No doubt it is, to a significant degree. For that matter, the whole policy of Israel regarding religion can be regarded as one long delaying action. It began in 1949, when David Ben-Gurion successfully resisted any attempt to adopt a written constitution; its most recent manifestation was the rejection by the Knesset in 1972 of the above-mentioned bill to amend the Law of Return. While this policy has all the faults of inconsistency, it nevertheless has had the supreme merit of affording the religion-state complex an opportunity of resolving the problem by an evolutionary process rather than by a direct and painful confrontation.

12

Evaluations and Perspectives

A. ORTHODOX VERSUS NON-ORTHODOX

The century that has elapsed since the first modern attempt at Jewish resettlement in its ancient land has witnessed most momentous changes in the condition of the Jewish people. Formerly a predominantly Central and Eastern European people, its center of gravity has shifted to North America and to Israel. Yiddish, the spoken language of the majority of the Jewish people and the vehicle for its literary expression, has given way to English and to Hebrew. An even more far-reaching transformation has occurred in its spiritual life, one that has affected its very identity. From a community of faith characterized by its adherence to Judaism as traditionally interpreted, the Jews have been transformed into a highly pluralistic society, where traditional Judaism is no longer the dominant spiritual force, and varieties of Judaism, religious as well as secular, compete for influence and acceptance. It would seem that in this century of upheaval, the Jewish people has rediscovered the full range of its attributes, some of which lay dormant during the many centuries when tradition reigned supreme, but have now erupted forcefully and creatively, assuming a variety of patterns, both religious and secular. Within this period, the Jews were largely transformed from a religious community to a group possessing the characteristics of a national entity; it was their delayed response to the challenge of secularism and of nationalism that has been agitating the peoples of Europe ever since the French Revolution.

Over the centuries, traditional Judaism has had experience with Jews who, having abandoned the observances of religious precepts, drifted away from the community and, before long, severed all links with the

Jewish people. These lost Jews, painful as their loss was, posed no problem for the faithful; there was no need to confront them or to engage in a dialogue with them. In the course of the last century, however, Orthodoxy was confronted with a totally novel predicament. A growing number of Jews abandoned the observance of religious precepts, but the great majority, unlike in generations past, did not drift away from the Jewish people. On the contrary, whether rejecting the ritual aspects of Halakhah as the Reformers did, or whether downgrading religion, as the secular-nationalists did, they all proclaimed their commitment to the Jewish people; they all presumed that they had discovered the true essence of Judaism and its authentic values. It is the unprecedented confrontation with Jews who rejected traditional Judaism and yet proclaimed their commitment to the Jewish people that has created a crisis for Orthodoxy. The latter were found, emotionally as well as intellectually, unequipped to cope with this novel challenge and, choosing the path of least resistance, they tended to withdraw into their own milieu, devoting their energies to the creation of strongholds of Torah-Judaism, both in the Diaspora and in the Holy Land. On the eve of World War I, the Old Yishuv in Palestine had evolved into one of the most powerful and self-contained citadels of Orthodox Judaism.

The flowering of pluralism, religious and secular, created tensions, engendered conflicts, occasioned ideological debates, and occasionally led to cooperation in important fields of communal activity, but its overall impact has been a lasting and positive one. It has broadened and enriched Jewish life, has enabled it to respond to external challenges and absorb new ideas, and has thereby retained within the Jewish fold many of its talented people who would otherwise have drifted away. Although the ideological gaps separating the Orthodox from the innovators, religious and secular, have hardly narrowed, this diversity has not weakened the sense of Klal-Israel, nor has it impeded the attainment of some of the truly historic goals achieved in the twentieth century by the united effort of the Jewish people. Earlier animosities and conflicts gradually gave way to dialogue and fructifying debate, and to a large measure of tolerance and cooperation. Orthodoxy became reconciled to a degree to religious pluralism. Such was the impact of pluralism in the Jewish communities in the Diaspora.

This, however, was not the case in Palestine, nor later in contemporary Israel. There the relationship between the Orthodox and the non-Orthodox groups was characterized by tensions that occasionally developed into serious conflicts; there was little of the intellectual intercourse and tolerance that generally characterized this relationship in the Diaspora. While in the Diaspora religious problems have occasionally arisen, in Israel a religious problem has emerged that is constantly on the agenda of public opinion.

This problem first arose in the eighties of the last century, when the New Yishuv, by its very existence, constituted a challenge to that unique community which later became known as the Old Yishuv. A dialogue between the two was ruled out by the latter, for the exposure of the Old Yishuv to the ideals and aims of the New Yishuv would have undermined the spiritual foundations of the former. The new settlers regarded themselves as the vanguard of a future modern Jewish commonwealth; the Old Yishuv was dedicated to the meticulous observance of the divinely ordained precepts, and to the patient expectation of the advent of Redemption in God's own time. The new settlers, on the other hand, did not make the attainment of their goal conditional on the observance of the Divine Law; in fact they were even ready to violate the Law of Shemittah, and other laws as well, in order to assure their material well-being. They also extolled the virtue of being self-supporting, a policy that tended to undermine the system of the Halukhah, and with it the very structure of that Orthodox community. Thus, the Old Yishuv regarded the founders of the agricultural settlements not only as transgressors of the Divine Law, but also as a danger to their continued existence as a self-contained and unexposed Orthodox community. It was in the confrontation between these two irreconcilable groups that the religious problem was first made manifest.

Parallel to developments in pre-World War I Palestine, the religious problem also arose within the framework of the World Zionist Organization. Initiated and promoted largely by young Westernized and non-observant Jews, they before long realized that in order to become a movement of the masses, they had to draw into their fold that Eastern European Jewry which was then predominantly traditional. Herzl regarded the Zionist movement as embracing—at least in miniature—the entire Jewish people, and the World Zionist Organization as "Medina baDerech" (the state in becoming), and the presence in both of the Orthodox was therefore essential. Writing to one of the leaders of the Hasidic movement in Poland as early as May 1896, Herzl stated that "the cooperation of the Orthodox Jews would be highly welcome."[1] In fact, he spared no effort in drawing them into the ranks of organized Zionism and retaining them there, and he encouraged the formation of the Mizrahi movement.

The religious problem first emerged at the Fifth Zionist Congress, held in Basle in 1901, when Chaim Weizmann and Martin Buber moved that the World Zionist Organization adopt a program of educational and cultural activity. The Orthodox delegates, rightly suspecting that the intention was to promote nationalist-secular education, threatened to bolt the Congress, and warned against a Kulturkampf. A similar crisis threatened the unity of the Zionist movement at the Tenth Congress in

1911, when the Zionist Organization decided to engage in educational work. Since the means at its disposal were modest, the scope of its educational program was limited, and so were the conflicts with the Orthodox-Zionists.

Until the end of World War I, there in fact existed two Jewish peoples in Palestine, the Old and the New Yishuv, having little in common. One of the first acts of Chaim Weizmann, on his arrival in Palestine in 1918, was to try to heal the breach between the two, so as to create a united Yishuv able to face the grave difficulties, both internal and external, inherent in the upbuilding of a National Home. His efforts were largely futile, for the religious issue proved to be an insurmountable barrier. The Old Yishuv remained hostile to the Jewish National Home and obstructed the development of Jewish self-government in Palestine; when the latter had been achieved, they withdrew from the organized Yishuv.

B. THE RELIGIOUS PROBLEM AS VIEWED BY THE ORTHODOX

It was with the establishment of the state that religion became a national problem; in fact, the rise of the state made the emergence of this problem unavoidable. The new state was not a mere territorial sovereignty in which Jews dwelt but, unlike all other states in the world, was a Jewish state, a home not only for its inhabitants but for Jews everywhere. It did not deserve to be called a Jewish state unless it was endowed with a Jewish character and identity. Voluntary initiative would not be sufficient to endow the state with these qualities, let alone to define the criteria for its identity, and the state, as a political entity, was called upon to do its duty in this realm. Objective circumstances and the need to resolve immediate problems made it impossible for the state to remain neutral.

For the Orthodox, particularly for their Zionist wing, Mafdal, the new state represented "the beginning of Redemption," the first stage in the unfolding of a divine scheme. To meet their requirements for religious legitimation, the state had to incorporate in its legal and administrative system certain minimal features without which it could lay no claim to being Jewish. The Orthodox fully realised that their slogan of "the land of Israel for the People of Israel in accordance with the Torah of Israel" was a remote ideal, and that the Halakhah as traditionally interpreted could not conceivably meet the needs of a modern state. But while the ideal was not immediately attainable, certain minimal requirements had to be met, without which, they could not identify themselves with the state and would have to regard themselves as dwelling in the Galut. They asked that these requirements be fulfilled, not only for themselves, but for the whole nation, which would endow the state with its minimal Jewish qualities. Thus, they were acting not only as religious Jews, but as nationalists, concerned with the spiritual life of the entire people—very much unlike the ultra-Orthodox, who were only concerned with securing for themselves certain religious interests. They, Mafdal, contended that they were in no need of legislation to make them and their adherents observe the dietary rules, marriage norms, and the Sabbath rest as prescribed by the Halakhah. Such legislation was required for others, for the nonobservant; the imposition of minimal Halakhic norms by the operation of law was therefore an urgent national need indispensable for the achievement of national unity and cohesion.

To achieve these objectives in a democratic society, political action through the instrumentality of a political party was called for. To the argument that religion was not a proper raison d'être for a political party, Mafdal replied that there was nothing undemocratic about a party dedicated to the pursuit of religious objectives. There was likewise nothing undemocratic about Mafdal's taking advantage of political opportunities to derive advantages on behalf of its cause. Nor was there anything undemocratic in employing the coercive power of the state in order to impose religious norms. All laws were coercive, but so long as they were adopted in accordance with democratic procedures, they were legally and morally binding.

To the protagonists of separation of religion and state, Mafdal replied that it was ruled out by the very nature of the Jewish people, which is a unique amalgam of religion and people, in which the national and the religious elements in the concept of their identity are inextricably interwoven. For the Jew, faith is not a mere profession of spiritual truths or of dogmatic principles detached from the historical evolution of the Jewish people as a nation; it is a profession of national and religious unity. Religion is built into the very structure of the Jewish state by virtue of a unique historic experience that has enriched Jewish nationalism with a theological dimension. Consequently, the truly unique and authentic character of Jewish identity militates against the separation of the two basic components. Religion is as much a part of the state as it is a part of the people.

The Orthodox likewise reject the charge that they have, in fact, succeeded in creating a theocratic state. It is true that the State of Israel takes legal cognizance of the individual's religious affiliation, and has established formal links with the institutions of the several religious denominations. However, the state does not presume to derive its legitimacy from a religious source, but from the will of the people democratically expressed, and organized religion is not a partner in the government of the state. To the extent that religious institutions exercise coercive powers, these are derived from legislation enacted by a democratically elected parliament.

The adoption of the minimal religious program as crystallized in the "religious status quo" has made it possible for the Orthodox, particularly for Mafdal, to participate in the political life of the state. To their opponents in the ultra-Orthodox groups, who contend that it is illegitimate for Torah-loyal Jews to participate actively in a Jewish state that deviates from their standard of Jewish statehood, the leaders of Mafdal have two answers. First, by such participation, recognition by the state of minimal religious norms can be secured. Second, while such participation will not assure the commitment of the state to traditional Judaism, it will at least prevent its commitment to secularism. They cited their successful campaign against the adoption of a constitution as a case in point. A constitution making no reference to the religious basis of Jewish nationalism would officially sanction the purely secular character of the state, that is, the adoption of a constitution with no religious commitment would virtually imply acceptance of the secular principle, thus, rendering the state illegitimate in the judgment of Orthodoxy. So long as no constitution was adopted, the Orthodox could in good conscience participate in the public life of the state.[2] They would respect the laws of the Knesset but would regard them as provisional, to be eventually superseded by Halakhah-based laws.

In their attempt to persuade the nation of the importance of observing the precepts of religion, the rabbinate resorted to exhortations stressing the divine and therefore binding character of the precepts. The efficacy of these exhortations has been marginal. Mafdal, on the other hand, approached the problem of religion from a different angle altogether, one that is compatible with their Zionist outlook. They do not necessarily view the non-Orthodox as transgressors, possessing no spiritual values. While the latter are committed primarily to the preservation of the Jewish state and people, the Orthodox are committed to the preservation of Judaism. Yet there is a very effective common denominator linking the two groups—their mutual concern for the Jewish state and the Jewish people.

It is on behalf of Jewish unity, which is indispensable for the existence of the Jewish state, that Mafdal based their appeal for the maintenance of the religious status quo. The religious status quo is projected as a national, rather than a religious asset, for without it, minimal national unity will not be achieved. Unless the laws of marriage and divorce are Halakhic, binding on all the Jews in Israel, there will before long arise a situation where, because of suspicion of Mamzerut as well as on other Halakhic grounds, Orthodox Jews will not marry other Jews; in fact the Orthodox would have to maintain a separate register of the faithful to safeguard against instances of prohibited marriages. The nonobservance of Kashrut in state and public institutions would make it impossible for the Orthodox to attend public functions, nor could Orthodox boys serve with non-Orthodox in the same army units. Active coexistence and cooperation between the two groups would be ruled out, and the Orthodox, being in a minority, would grow alienated from the state and would retreat from active participation in its affairs. Consequently, the adoption of the religious status quo, irksome as it may be for many Jews, is the minimum that the Orthodox would accept in consideration for their according religious legitimation to the state. The strict observance of the status quo is therefore justified on purely nationalist grounds. It is equally necessary for worldwide Jewish unity, since religion is the traditional link between the Jews of Israel and those of the Diaspora.[3]

After a quarter-century of vigorous activity, Mafdal has succeeded in anchoring the religious status quo to the political, administrative, and educational texture of Israeli public life. While the status quo is subjected from time to time to severe criticism by the non-Orthodox, its position is firmly secured for the forseeable future. Yet, a feeling of uneasiness pervades the Orthodox in general, and Mafdal in particular. This feeling is grounded in the growing realization that the status quo represents a dead end from the point of view of the future of traditional Judaism.

The Orthodox have not succeeded in advancing the cause of traditional Judaism, nor have they made any inroads into the world of the secularists. They are in a minority that has made no numerical progress. In fact, there have been disturbing signs of retreat. In the parliamentary elections held on December 31, 1973, the religious parties lost one-sixth of their Knesset representation, the number of their deputies dropping from 18 to 15, an unprecedented low in their political career. Even more disturbing are the returns of school registration. From 1968 to 1974, the percentage of pupils attending religious state schools declined from 29% to 24.7%, from 110,887 pupils to 99,288, while the state schools gained numerically as well as proportionally. A similar decline was observed in the school system of Agudat Israel.[4] This trend is expected to continue, for the immigration from Islamic countries has come to an end, and with the break-up of the patriarchal authority in Oriental families, which were generally traditionalist, a growing trend away from religion has set in.

Nor can Mafdal derive great satisfaction from the rabbinate in general, the Chief Rabbinate in particular. It has not developed into a supreme Halakhic tribunal that would radiate moral and spiritual influence; the Chief Rabbinate has remained aloof from the people and its problems. It has been irked by the feeling that its judicial powers are derived from a civil law enacted by the non-Orthodox majority in the Knesset, and that some of its decisions may be subjected to judicial review by the Supreme Court, thus demonstrating the supremacy of the civil over the religious law. Its members resent pressure by the non-Orthodox, who clamor for a less rigid application of Halakhic rules; they would feel justified in adopting a more liberal interpretation of the Halakhah had the people lovingly accepted the burden of the Divine Law. But they have not, and are therefore not deserving of leniency. The lack of harmony within the Chief Rabbinical Council, the dissensions and bickering between the two Chief Rabbis, and their occasional sorties into politics, have lowered the prestige of their office and correspondingly enhanced the standing of the ultra-Orthodox *Olam HaYeshivot*. Nor has the Chief Rabbinate had the firmness, much to the chagrin of Mafdal, to adopt a clear and unambivalent attitude on such cardinal issues as the religious legitimacy of the Jewish state or the religious significance to be attached to Independence Day.

The vision of the early leaders of religious Zionism of a prestigious rabbinate affording spiritual guidance to the people, and of a religious party operating on the political level, with the one complementing the other, has largely come to naught. The rabbinate has neither exerted spiritual influence nor gained the people's respect; the political party, lacking a comprehensive religious program and preoccupied with the technicalities of the status quo, has lost its élan, and has drawn upon itself a good deal of the criticism leveled against all political parties in Israel. As a party, Mafdal finds itself in a far more difficult position than other parties. The non-Orthodox public, inclined as it is to equate religion and morality, is more outraged by some of the less-than-ethical tactics adopted by Mafdal than they would be by similar tactics practiced by any of the secular parties. Thus, a moral stigma attaching to a religious party casts a negative reflection, not only on the party, but on religion as well.

Mafdal faces a crisis that afflicts all movements that have attained their objective. They have succeeded in consolidating and extending the scope of the religious status quo, and in firmly riveting it to the political and administrative structure of the state. Lacking any program for the advancement of religion as a spiritual force, content with the safeguarding of the status quo and of the vested interests, material and others, associated with it, Mafdal has become ideologically and in leadership quite impoverished. Most of its intelligentsia and academically trained people have left it; it is ridden with internal strife and personal antagonisms, and its standing among the Orthodox is at a low ebb. Its moral and intellectual stature is too feeble to resist the inroads of the ultra-Orthodox and of *Olam HaYeshivot*.

The policy of Mafdal has inevitably led to a situation where the confrontations between the Orthodox and the non-Orthodox occur on the political, rather than on the spiritual-ideological plane. The role of religion as a significant element in the spiritual life of the nation has not been projected in terms intelligible to the contemporary world. Mafdal has succeeded in persuading the non-Orthodox of one proposition only, namely, that the imposition of certain Halakhic norms within the framework of a religion-state relationship, was essential for forging the unity of the nation. Some of the more sensitive among the Orthodox are painfully aware of the irony implicit in appealing to nationalist sentiments in order to advance the cause of religion.

In the circumstances attending the establishment of the state and the critical developments following it, national unity in general, and the identification of the Orthodox with the state, in particular, were essential. The religious parties, and Mafdal especially, by their active participation in the political life of Israel, made a significant contribution to national cohesion. They obtained, to be sure by political action, the imposition of important Halakhic norms on the entire Jewish community. In achieving this objective, however, "they harnessed religion to the State,"[5] and by developing a significant vested interest through the religion-state relationship, they limited the range of their initiative and lowered their targets. In brief, neither the securing of statutory powers for the rabbinate, nor the political gains scored by the religious parties, succeeded in advancing the cause of traditional Judaism as a creative force in the life of the nation.

C. THE PROBLEM AS VIEWED BY THE NON-ORTHODOX

In the nearly eight decades since the First Zionist Congress in 1897, there were numerous occasions for the outbreak of a Kulturkampf, first within the Zionist movement, and later in Palestine and in Israel. The great upheavals that characterized these decades have given rise to a wide range of ideological controversies, some of which were resolved by their participants, others by the irresistible course of events; these have largely become matters of historical interest. There remains, however, one constant item on the agenda of the Jewish people, and particularly of the Jewish state, namely, the problem of religion.

The potential for a Kulturkampf, with all its perils, was inherent in the unbridgeable gulf separating the non-Orthodox, who were primarily concerned with the Jewish people, and the Orthodox, who were primarily concerned with Judaism as a faith and a way of life for the individual. Leon Pinsker in his *Autoemancipation* and Herzl in his *Judenstaat* were so oblivious to considerations of history and tradition that, in advocating a territorial solution, they even failed to suggest Palestine as the territorial base. Nor did Ahad Ha'Am, concerned as he was with the problem of Judaism, succeed in healing the rift, for his interpretation of Judaism as a national culture expressed in ethical values afforded little comfort to the Orthodox. Yet, despite the ideological gap and the conflicts that it has generated, a certain coexistence, however uneasy, has evolved and endured. This notable achievement was largely due to the non-Orthodox, by far the majority group, who accorded top priority to preserving the unity of the people, and were ready for its sake to make concessions to the Orthodox. This policy of compromise was initiated by Herzl, pursued by his successors in the Zionist movement, and later followed by the leadership of the Jewish state.

In his all-too-brief career, Herzl succeeded in keeping the religious issue outside the orbit of Zionist activity. To avoid a controversy, he endeavored to sidetrack the proposals for an educational program to be undertaken by the Zionist Organization. He employed delaying tactics to gain time for the consolidation of the movement. At the Conference of Russian Zionists in 1902, held in Minsk, Ahad Ha'Am urged the adoption of a program of educational activity. As was to be expected, the leaders of Mizrahi vehemently protested. The imminent conflict was resolved, and at this conference the seed of a far-reaching compromise was sown: it was decided to appoint two commissions, one for a "nationalist-traditionalist" and another for a "nationalist-progressive" education program, the term *progressive* implying non-Orthodox.[6] This compromise, which was subsequently confirmed at the World Zionist Conference held in London in 1920, introduced the principle of a dual school system in Palestine, a "general" trend and a religious trend. This decision represented the first in a series of major compromises agreed to by the non-Orthodox majority in order to keep the Orthodox within the ranks of the Zionist movement and, later, within the framework of the institutions of Jewish self-government in Palestine.

The thirty years of British rule witnessed a series of compromises arrived at with a view to avoiding religious conflicts. In creating the institutions of self-government, the non-Orthodox agreed that the Chief Rabbinate should rank as the highest organ in the institutional hierarchy, and bear its costs, as well as the cost involved in the maintenance of local rabbinic offices and other religious services. Leasehold contracts granted by the Jewish National Fund contained a clause obligating those who settled on the land to observe the Sabbath and Jewish festivals.

How urgent the need was for Jewish unity on the eve of the establishment of the state, was manifested by the decision of the Executive of the Jewish Agency, to obtain the support of Agudat Israel for the state project and for its participation in the public life of the state when established. For that purpose the Executive of the Jewish Agency, in an official communication to Agudat Israel dated June 19, 1947, undertook to maintain the religious status quo in the future state.[7] This communication, which secured the adherence of Agudat Israel to the Provisional Government set up on May 14, 1948, laid the foundation for the religious status quo in the state of Israel and for its subsequent extension and incorporation into the law of the land.

The leadership of the new state has fully implemented the undertakings contained in the communication of June 19, 1947, and within a few years, legislative enactments and administrative arrangements were safeguarding Sabbath observance, observance of dietary laws in public institutions, the Halakhic family law, and the right of the Orthodox to have their children educated in religious state schools. The Orthodox succeeded in obtaining further concessions. The jurisdiction of the rabbinical courts in matrimonial matters was enlarged, the term *Jew* in the Law of Return was defined in accordance with the Halakhah, and in 1962 the Pig Raising Prohibition Law was enacted. In deference to the opposition of the Orthodox, a constitution had not been adopted.

Thus, the religious status quo, as incorporated in the political system of the state, was the price paid for the avoidance of a Kulturkampf. In assessing the impact of the status quo on the non-Orthodox, each of its components has to be separately dealt with. Of the four principal ones, that providing for the right of parents to choose for their children a religion-oriented school maintained by the state, was regarded as fully justified, and as being in consonance with liberal principles. On identical grounds, state support for the religion-oriented Bar-Ilan University, equally with other universities, is also regarded as fully justified. Over the years Israeli public opinion has been generally favorable to a substantial degree of pluralism in the educational system. Occasionally there would be resentment at manifestations of separatism appearing in the religious state schools, but those did not lead to serious controversies nor was the principle of pluralism in education challenged.

The provisions for the observance of dietary laws were viewed with understanding, although their application has at times given rise to resentment and indignation. The non-Orthodox readily agree that Kashrut observance in army units is essential for national unity. It is further agreed that to enable the Orthodox to participate in state and public functions, kasher food is to be provided and the same would apply to factories and other installations where restaurants are set up for employees. Resentment is aroused where Kashrut develops into a vested interest, or where it is employed in order to impose the observance of Halakhic precepts other than Kashrut. Thus, the denial of a Kashrut certificate by the rabbinate to a hotel or public hall where music is played on the Sabbath, or to a hall where a microphone is used on that day, or which offers facilities for holding a Reform religious service, have aroused strong feelings. The controversy over the Kashrut on S.S. *Shalom,* the protests of the Orthodox in the United States against the government of Israel, and the statement made by Rabbi Joseph D. Soloveitchik, one of the most eminent Orthodox rabbis in America, that he would be prepared to call for a boycott of Israeli passenger ships unless an exclusively kosher kitchen were installed, were long remembered. Public resentment was so strong that some of the leaders of Mafdal felt that their success in the S.S. *Shalom* controversy was in the nature of a Pyrrhic victory. Some of the practices involved in supervising the manufacturing of foods and their processing, aimed at protecting vested interests, called forth much criticism. While the problem of Kashrut has rarely developed into a major public controversy, its application has not enhanced the prestige of religion or the standing of the rabbinate.

The problem of Sabbath observance has occasioned numerous conflicts. While the non-Orthodox readily accepted the Sabbath and Jewish holidays as days of rest, the application of the principle has given rise to conflicts. While private motor cars were free to circulate on the Sabbath, public transport, urban and interurban, was prohibited. This indeed has occasioned many hardships, and some regard it as a social injustice, in that transportation available to persons who could afford to own cars was denied to those who had to resort to public transport. The closing by the municipal authorities of libraries, museums, and observatories on the Sabbath was resented. Exemption from working in essential services on the Sabbath, as granted to the Orthodox, would at times be burdensome to their nonobservant colleagues, who had to give up their day of rest more often than their due share. The strict observance of the Sabbath has at times led to economic losses. as well. The not infrequent resort to violence by the ultra-Orthodox against Sabbath violation has always aroused resentment.

The most difficult aspect, from the point of view of the non-Orthodox, and one that has aroused the most acrimonious controversies, was the one concerned with the enforcement of the Halakhic family law, and the problem closely associated with it, that concerned with Jewish identity. It was in this realm that the religion-state tension was most conspicuous and ubiquitous. It was in the sensitive sphere of family law that the state ceded its prerogative of enacting a civil code and delegated its powers to an ecclesiastical court, which was to apply a law of its own, one that the legislature could neither change nor amend. It was a deliberate abdication of state powers in favor of a religious authority. The application of the Halakhic family law inevitably led to a reexamination of the entire religion-state relationship.

It is indeed most remarkable that the political parties in Israel—

even the communists—do not agitate in favor of the abrogation of the religion-state relationship. If the principle of separation of religion and state is to be understood as it is in the United States, the non-Orthodox in Israel do not advocate separation. None of the parties in Israel object to the state's affording financial support to religious institutions. None advocate the introduction of civil marriage for all; it is only the more radical parties that urge that, along with the ecclesiastical courts, but without in any way derogating from their powers, civil courts should administer a civil marriage law, meaning that each person should be free to choose the family law that will be applicable to him. Under this system, the ecclesiastical courts of all religious denominations, Jewish, Moslem, and Christian, would be state-maintained courts, exercising jurisdiction over persons who choose that jurisdiction. It is not the abolition of these religious courts that the more radical elements among the non-Orthodox demand, but the abolition of their exclusive jurisdiction and its replacement by the concurrent jurisdiction of two judiciaries, religious and civil. The great majority of the non-Orthodox, however, are not in favor of the introduction of civil marriage, nor of the abolition of the religion-state relationship. They fully realize that the introduction of a civil code of family law, wheher one having exclusive jurisdicion or even concurrent jurisdiction, would result in "the division of the House of Israel into two parts," and in the estrangement of wide sections of the population from the state. The most that the non-Orthodox advocate is the institution of a limited form of civil marriage intended only for such persons as, on Halakhic grounds such as Halitzah, Mamzerut, cohen-divorcée or cohen-proselyte, are disqualified from marriage. Such a form of civil marriage is also advocated by some Orthodox, who realize that by the solution of these painful problems, the rabbinical courts would be spared the harsh criticism leveled against them. But even the introduction of a limited form of civil marriage confined to those Halakhically disqualified persons would not resolve all instances of personal hardships. The position of the Agunah, the "chained woman," would hardly be altered. One whose husband is insane or has refused to obey a rabbinical decree to deliver a *get*, would not be able to remarry.

Few subjects have agitated the public so intensely as some of the gruesome instances of suffering occasioned, particularly to women, by the inflexible application of Halakhic rules. Press reports and parliamentary debates abound in descriptions of misery inflicted on women; these debates are of a standard pattern: the advocates of ethical values are pitted in an inconclusive battle against the advocates of the supremacy of the Halakhah, and the arguments proceed along parallel lines that never meet. Great as the indignation may at times grow, the non-Orthodox as a whole do not even consider the introduction of civil marriage. This was best illustrated in the course of a startling statement made in 1964 by the late leader of Mafdal and then Minister of the Interior. In addressing his colleagues at a cabinet meeting at which criticism was leveled against the rabbinate, Mr. Shapiro said: "If the negative attitude to religion continues . . . I cannot escape the distressing idea that besets me against my will, the idea of separating religion and state. We desist from uttering it aloud, for this may bring about a schism. But should this tragedy occur, the Torah-loyal Jews will continue with their way of life. . . . Separation of religion from the state is contrary to our religious-national outlook, but we are not prepared to tolerate the contempt poured on religious values." Mr. Shapiro assured his colleagues that Orthodoxy will not be the loser in the event of separation, and he firmly expressed the conviction that the unity of the people and the existence of the state depended on the preservation of tradition.[8] He in fact challenged his colleagues to proceed with separation, but no one dared to take up his suggestion. It was an authentic reflection of the state of mind of the non-Orthodox that to tamper with Halakhic marriage was to court the danger of some kind of a schism within the people. They had no doubt felt that Mr. Shapiro was sincere in implying that the cause of religion would not be prejudiced by separation, and that, in bearing the brunt of criticism leveled against the Halakhah and the rabbinate and by not insisting on separation, he was loyally serving the cause of Jewish unity.

The retention of the Halakhic marriage law is, therefore, the result of a profound conviction that it serves a vital national interest, rather than being the result of an inner political situation that necessitates the cooption of Mafdal into the government. Even in the event of Mafdal being in opposition to a government enjoying a stable majority in the Knesset, the non-Orthodox majority would desist from curtailing the jurisdiction of the rabbinical courts in matters of personal status, and would at most introduce a form of civil marriage restricted to the category of persons who are Halakhically disqualified from marrying.

There are two further considerations that have precluded any serious considerations of civil marriage. One is of a purely political-electoral character. A departure from the status quo on so serious a matter would strengthen the position of the religious parties at elections.[9] Second, civil marriage would result in the introduction of mixed marriages in Israel, which would encourage mixed marriages in the Diaspora. The non-Orthodox have uncritically accepted the latter proposition. The attitude of the non-Orthodox to this issue more than any other reflects their own hesitations and uncertainties arising out of the tension between two conflicting urges—one of change, and the other of preserving venerated traditions.

The developments of the first quarter-century of Israeli history also show the limits that the non-Orthodox are prepared to set to the demands of the Orthodox, limits that are also related to consideration of national unity. When there appeared a danger of the stigma of Mamzerut attaching to the Bene Israel community of India, there was a public outcry, and the Knesset, by an overwhelming majority, adopted a resolution declaring the Bene Israel as Jews equal in all respects with other Jews. In the face of such massive popular clamor, the rabbinate yielded. When the question of "Who is a Jew," or rather, "Who is a convert" came up for consideration, it was resolved in a dual fashion. One solution was adopted for Israel, where, to preserve unity, only conversions Halakhically performed were recognized. The other, aimed at preserving the unity of Israel and of the Diaspora, recognized the existence of religious pluralism in the Diaspora, and therefore provided for "conversion" without stipulating that it be in accordance with the Halakhah. Despite pressure by the Orthodox in Israel and Diaspora to amend the Law of Return with a view to recognizing Halakhic conversions only, the government would not yield. Following the elections of December 31, 1973, when the government of Premier Rabin led a rather precarious existence, depending as it did on a Knesset majority of one only, it refused to broaden its parliamentary base by the cooption of Mafdal, which insisted on a change in the conversion clause.

In pursuing the policy of national unity in Israel, the non-Orthodox had to follow a similar policy for the avoidance of a rift with the Diaspora, and particularly with the important Jewish community in the United States. In formulating its policy on religion, the government had to be sensitive to its impact on the Diaspora. The argument that civil marriage in Israel would encourage mixed marriages in the Diaspora was seriously taken into account, and Premier Golda Meir often stressed this point. Reaction from abroad had to be taken into account. Orthodox groups never hesitated in pressuring the government of Israel by appeals, by demonstrations, and even by appeals to non-Jewish authorities, as was done in 1954 by Mr. Harry Goodman, Agudat Israel leader in London, when he filed a complaint against Israel to the United Nations Commission on the Status of Women on the occasion of the enactment of the National Service Law, which would obligate Orthodox girls who opted out of army service to engage in social and educational work in civilian institutions.[10] It was only later that the leaders of Conservative and Reform Judaism, particularly the latter, made official representations on matters affecting their position in Israel. Their belated entry into this controversy made the people of Israel realize that Orthodoxy was not the only religious group in the United States, and that they were, in fact, a minority in the totality of religion-affiliated Jewry. The reactions and representations of Conservative and Reform groups were far more restrained and responsible than those of the Orthodox. By asserting their position, the non-Orthodox religious trends succeeded, in some measure, in making the government of Israel and its public opinion adopt a more balanced assessment of its responsibility to Diaspora Jewry.

Mafdal, on its part too, made a contribution to national unity and to the avoidance of a Kulturkampf. Unlike the ultra-Orthodox and *Olam HaYeshivot,* who have always manifested isolationist tendencies and varying degrees of disassociation from the Jewish state, Mafdal, with its commitment to the Zionist philosophy, is totally identified with the State of Israel. For the various ultra-Orthodox groups, a Kulturkampf would merely facilitate their total withdrawal into a world of their own, whereas for Mafdal it would spell veritable disaster, an admission that its Zionist philosophy was false; its opponents who had repudiated Zionism as essentially secular and irreligious would be proved to be right. In fact, a Kulturkampf would undermine its position as a political party and as an influential element in Orthodoxy. These considerations were, no doubt, present in the minds of Mafdal leaders and have moved them to exercise a restraining influence both on the Chief Rabbinate and on Orthodox militants in general.

In the exceptionally adverse circumstances in which the Yishuv had developed and the Jewish state has emerged, maximum national unity was essential for survival. This being the supreme national objective, the non-Orthodox felt justified in making concessions to the Orthodox. Bent on preventing a Kulturkampf, they have avoided any measures that would lead to the estrangement of the Orthodox from the state. The policy of compromise, therefore, was warranted by circumstances and, judging by the results it sought to achieve, was a success. The great majority of the Orthodox became integrated in the life of the state and identified with its objectives. A crisis was averted and a national consensus has emerged, so that attention can be focused on urgent problems. From the strictly party point of view, the policy of compromise has not strengthened the religious parties nor enhanced the stature of Orthodoxy in general. Viewed by the Orthodox and in particular by Mafdal, the policy of compromise was a notable victory for religion. Thus, each side could regard its policy as a success. The one and only victim of the status quo and of the religion-state relationship was religion itself, which failed to develop as a creative force in the spiritual life of the Jewish state.

D. PERSPECTIVES

The ferment within Orthodoxy, and the search for ways and means for its renewal, has been largely confined to academic circles. The Movement for Torah Judaism was its only organized expression, and although it counted leading intellectuals within its ranks, its impact was limited. Surrounded as they were by suspicion on the part of the rabbinate—suspicion of their being reformers, and by fear on the part of Mafdal—fear of having its position as a political party undermined, their progress has been minimal. The hope for a renewal of Orthodox Judaism from within has not been realized.

A study of religious confrontations has led some observers to conclude that it was the religion-state relationship that accounted for the failure of Orthodoxy to wield spiritual and moral influence. They contended that the exercise of coercive powers by the rabbinate and the imposition of religious norms by law were responsible for the low image of religion and have led to insensitiveness to ethical values on the part of the acknowledged representatives of religion. Therefore, the dissolution of the religion-state relationship was a precondition for the enhancement of the image of Orthodox Judaism.

This was the attitude of the movement for Torah Judaism, and the attitude of other Orthodox intellectuals. There can be no doubt that the elimination of religion from party politics and the abstention from resorting to the exercise of state powers for the enforcement of Halakhic rules would have improved the stature of religion. The cause and effect were reversed. It was the immobilism that characterized Orthodoxy, in Palestine and later in Israel, the inadequacy of the Halakhah to meet the problems of a modern society, and the haunting fear of innovation that have driven the leaders of Orthodoxy to seek a religion-state arrangement. The estrangement from religion of a very large part of the people was caused by the image of religion as projected by the Orthodox, that is, religion as a ritual rather than as faith, as a form of behavior rather than adherence to a moral way of life. The keen resentment against the enforcement by the state of Halakhic rules, which were regarded as divorced from moral considerations, was an aggravating factor, rather than the root cause.

Other Orthodox thinkers advocated the retention of the religion-state relationship, but urged a rather bold measure aimed at removing some of the grounds that occasioned resentment. Such a measure would, in their view, meet the criticism leveled against the rabbinate, and would thus buttress its position. Mr. Moshe Unna was the first to advocate the introduction of civil marriage for persons Halakhically disqualified from marrying. One of the leaders of Orthodox Judaism, Dr. Immanuel Jakobovits, Chief Rabbi of Britain, known for his strict application of Halakhic rules, did support this proposal. Speaking from his own experience, he expressed the view that it would be advisable to allow "some form of civil marriage in hardship cases which rabbinic law cannot take care of." The rabbi stated that he was able to maintain "strict religious controls over communities under his jurisdiction" because people can opt out and could be married by a Reform rabbi or in a civil registry office. He frankly admitted: "If I had a situation in which there were no exit doors nor safety valves . . . I would not be able to maintain the standards of Halakhic integrity I can maintain today. Hence I am not sure whether the Halakhah would not be better off and under less pressure if we contemplated some system whereby those whose conscience is outraged by religious law, or who cannot comply with rabbinic requirements could solve their problems."[11]

This statement of Rabbi Jakobovits represents a very lucid formulation of the dilemma facing Orthodoxy. He readily admits that Halakhic rules create hardship cases, in consequence of which there are persons "whose conscience is outraged by religious law." Rather, however, than reinterpret the Halakhah so as to solve the problems of hardship cases and avoid a situation where one's sense of morality is offended, the rabbi suggests an extra-Halakhic solution, that is, civil marriage. In Jewish tradition marriage is a religious act; but rather than create conditions that would facilitate the celebration of marriage by a religious ritual, spiritual leaders of Orthodoxy would prefer a form of civil marriage for some in order to safeguard the application of inflexible Halakhic rules for others. Implicit in Rabbi Jakobovits's candid statement was the admission that in the confrontation between Halakhah and moral principles, the former would prevail, and that nothing could be devised within the framework of the Halakhah to avoid such a confrontation.

Thus, contrary to the view of the leaders of the Movement for Torah Judaism, who stress the evils of the religion-state relationship, its dissolution will of itself not advance the cause of Orthodox Judaism. Its renewal can come about only through a reinterpretation of the Halakhah in the light of moral criteria. Such an approach would have to be based on the recognition of the profound and indissoluble link between religion and ethics. Those Orthodox thinkers who lay stress on the religion-state relationship rather than on the Halakhah-ethics link, confuse cause and effect.

A far more perceptive approach is exhibited by Mr. Zvi Yaron, an observant Jew and a leading authority on the philosophy of Rabbi A. H. Kook. He sees in the "moral torpidity on issues affecting live human beings" the cause for "the amazing ossification of the religiosity of the established rabbinate . . . which practises and preaches a religion which is deliberately shorn of theological confrontation with the present." This is the kind of religiosity that expresses itself "in a coarse piety which is keen on finding in traditional literature the precise rule for action or abstention . . . and avoids new questions by entrenching its piety in religious behaviorism." In this state of affairs the religion-state relationship is not of the greatest significance. "The tragic situation is rooted in Orthodoxy's adamant rigidity, and its unthinking fear of the new. It has no ideology that has meaning for contemporary questions."[12] What is so eloquently implicit in these trenchant sentences is that a reinterpretation of the Halakhah in the light of moral criteria is essential for a renewal of Orthodox Judaism.

A revival of Orthodoxy from within appears quite unlikely. One fails to discern there elements of authority and daring that would attempt to reinterpret the Halakhah and enrich it by the addition of a code defining the rules that would guide a religious person in his relation to organized society. Such a reinterpretation was implicit in Rabbi Maimon's abortive attempt to summon a Sanhedrin shortly after the establishment of the state. A policy of renewal, on however modest a scale, cannot be initiated except through a united Orthodoxy, headed by a universally respected rabbinic authority. Such an authority is nonexistent, and the fragmentation of Orthodoxy and the rampant factionalism within its ranks rule out the emergence of such in the foreseeable future. Fear of the more extreme elements on the one hand, and suspicion of anything suggestive of innovation on the other, seem to preclude any prospect of a breach in its immobilism.

These circumstances would suggest that the time was ripe for the development of a religious alternative to Orthodoxy. Surely the Jewish state is so suffused with religious symbols and abounds in so much traditional content that the differentiation between the religious and those referred to by the latter as secularists is in many respects artificial; the area of overlapping of the religious and the nationalist is extensive, and the degree of observance on the part of the non-Orthodox is far from negligible, as has been brought out in recent surveys.[13] Likewise, the groping for new patterns of religious expression on the part of the non-Orthodox is discernible in more than one quarter.

The very slow progress toward religious pluralism is inevitable and may be attributed to two principal factors, one of which is the general unfamiliarity with the idea. The predominant majority, whether native or foreign-born, have not had any opportunity of encountering non-Orthodox religious trends. The existence of religious pluralism in the Diaspora has as yet hardly made an impact on the awareness of the people in Israel. While in the Diaspora, Jews are conscious of the wide range of pluralism prevailing in the Christian world and are alive to the intellectual activity in its midst. Jews in Israel have not been exposed to such external stimuli.

The other cause for this development is rooted in the adverse circumstances with which the New Yishuv, and the state of Israel in particular, had to struggle in order to achieve their objectives. The conditions for the realization of the vision of a national revival in the ancient homeland were always difficult in the extreme. Zionism had to combat assimilation, inertia, indifference, and active antagonism on the part of Jews, not to mention the external world. Its material resources were limited and its principal assets were the devotion and singlemindedness of a small but determined minority. It was only the rise of Nazism and the impact of the Holocaust that led the great majority of the Jews to support Jewish statehood. Being a latecomer among national movements, "Zionism from the very beginning was a movement in a hurry, forever racing against time."[14] Even the establishment of the state has not eased the strains and stresses of "ingathering exiles" and of coping with the pressing needs of a quadrupled population—all in the course of a quarter of a century. The new state had no respite from massive external pressures, which have exacted a heavy and painful toll. Human energies were in the first instance applied to the attainment of urgent goals, and intellectual endeavor and ingenuity were focused on forging instruments for survival. The constant sense of urgency that permeated all levels of national activity placed, no doubt, a strain on the spiritual resources of the people, diverting them from concentration on other significant aspects of its cultural life, religion being one of them.

The existence of some twenty small congregations and synagogues sponsored or aided by the Union for Progressive Judaism (Reform) and the World Council of Synagogues (Conservative) has established a non-Orthodox religious presence in Israel. Limited as the influence of this development is, it represents, potentially at least, a significant contribution by the Diaspora to the spiritual life of the Jewish state, and to the forging of a religious link between the two great Jewish centers. So far, this link appears to have had an enriching effect on the Reform and Conservative movements in the lands of their origin more than on religious life in Israel.

The Reform and the Conservatives are further handicapped by functioning separately. One attending their services or listening to their sermons will not perceive a difference. The historical circumstances that have led to their separate existences are irrelevant when applied to the Israeli scene. The climate of Israel, saturated as it is with religious symbols and traditions, has had a leveling effect on the two movements. A unified program of action jointly pursued by the Reform and the Conservatives would be of advantage to the development of a religious alternative in Israel.

It is not likely that in the near future non-Orthodox rabbis will be granted legal status on a par with the Orthodox. Both the late Levi Eshkol and Golda Meir have stated that the relatively small number of non-Orthodox congregations hardly warrants a radical change in the religion-state structure; only a large increase in their numbers would warrant it. Their approach is generally supported by public opinion as being in consonance with the general policy of avoiding a direct confrontation with Orthodoxy. The Orthodox have expressed the view that a major departure from this policy would lead to a schism within the people and to the termination of the religion-state relationship.[15] It is conceivable that in the forseeable future non-Orthodox rabbis may be authorized to celebrate weddings of persons Halakhically qualified for marriage. Lack of legal recognition, however, is marginal to the fundamental problem of a religious revival. Exclusion of the non-Orthodox from the status quo may in the long run be a benefit rather than a drawback; reliance on their own resources, rather than on the state itself, may in the long run prove to be a boon to spiritual development.

The Orthodox regard Reform and Conservative Judaism as a "foreign importation." This charge is true only in the sense that most of the non-Orthodox rabbis are not Israelis, nor are some of the congregants. It is indeed an interesting reflection that with all its impressive contributions in the field of Jewish scholarship, in the realm of Hebrew language and literature, biblical research, talmudic studies, and archaeology, whatever innovation the Jewish people in Israel has initiated in religion has been in the form of an "importation." This development appears to have been unavoidable, since Diaspora Jewry, exposed as it is to external spiritual challenges, sensitive to new intellectual currents, and called upon to define its identity, has been free to express religious thought in meaningful terms. It will be the rise of an indigenous spiritual leadership that will be the test of the viability of a religious alternative. The ground for it is ready; its progress will depend on a variety of factors, among them the prospects of peace in the Middle East.

After three millennia of uninterrupted development, the Jewish people today, as in generations past, is concerned with distilling from its rich and varied experience the meaning and purpose of its existence. With the destruction of the First Temple, the Jews went into Babylonian exile as a nation, but returned as a religious community. In the relatively short period of its existence, the Second Commonwealth witnessed tense confrontations between its national and religious components. During the exile that began following the suppression of the revolt of Bar Kokhba, the Jewish people shed many of its national elements and fashioned itself into a community of faith.

In the long period of Dispersion, the Jews became the object, rather than the subject of history; no longer involved in political decision-making, their energies were turned inward, toward molding a distinct way of life that would set them apart from other nations, and thus preserve their individuality. As a community of faith, it was exposed to religious controversies and to the danger of schisms. The Karaite heresy, which repudiated the Oral Law (the Halakhah), led to a schism and to the emergence of two Jewish peoples. The Messianic movements of the seventeenth and eighteenth centuries, which rocked the Jewish world, also culminated in schisms. The rise of Hasidism in the middle of the eighteenth century ignited a conflagration that threatened Jewish unity. On this occasion a schism was averted, and the adherents of the two opposing camps learned to coexist. Hasidism may in a sense be regarded as the forerunner of religious pluralism in Judaism.

It was only in the following one hundred and fifty years that the full range of pluralism unfolded on a scale hitherto unknown. Conservative and particularly Reform Judaism rejected a varying number of the rules of the Halakhah. The most novel phenomenon of all, however, was the dynamic rise of a secular Judaism, which developed its own momentum, encompassed a wide range of interests, and was motivated by a commitment to the Jewish people and its survival.

The challenges to traditional Judaism posed by the non-Orthodox religious trends would in centuries past have led to a schism. This, however, was not to be. Controversies abounded, to be sure; conflicts ensued; and each school of thought, whether religious or secular, advanced its own interpretation of Judaism, representing it as a revival of authentic Judaism. The spectrum of those controversies ranged from fundamentalist Orthodox to secularists. An abyss separated the two, yet the unity of the people was not impaired. The Jews entered an era when their religion, no longer a united and unifying force, became a divided and divisive element; religion ceased being the people's common denominator. It was superseded by a new ideal, commitment to the people and its survival, in the instinctive belief that this people, with all its conflicting ideologies, would preserve an individuality that would be Jewish. Indeed, the ideal of Jewish peoplehood manifested itself in the twentieth century in a worldwide solidarity, in an active concern for the fate of the less fortunate and in a heightened sense of mutual responsibility, on a scale and with an intensity hitherto unknown in Jewish experience. This worldwide solidarity was achieved in spite of, and possibly because of, the remarkable pluralism prevailing in contemporary Jewry.

This remarkable diversity in religious and secular activity in the communities of the Diaspora was carried on in voluntary associations, and expressed itself in debates, controversies, and in organizational rivalries. The reenactment of these controversies on the soil of a state that proclaimed itself to be Jewish was bound to assume a more intense character. Differences of opinion were transformed into confrontation, and organizational rivalries into party strife. It was not only a difference in the intensity of the conflict, but also in its scope.

This was unavoidable, for the issue at stake was that which was held precious by all schools of thought, that is, in what shape and form the Jewish character of the new state would express itself. Conflicting solutions to this crucial question have inevitably led to confrontations. This development was inherent in the special circumstances of a Jewish state which, as a state, could not remain neutral on this issue. When dealing with this issue in the Diaspora, associations of Jews expressed themselves in the language of resolutions or manifestos; a state, on the other hand, expresses its consensus in the language of law and, the legislative process being a political one, the involvement of religion in politics becomes unavoidable.

The confrontations arising out of the conflicting views on the nature of the Jewish image of the state assumed at times serious proportions, resulting in violence and political strife. Few issues have aroused so much tension and animosity as that of religion. Indeed, it possesses the ingredients for a schism, in the sense that important sections of Israel's citizenry may dissociate from the state, regarding themselves as dwelling in a Galut located in their Holy Land. To a limited extent, such a schism already occurred when several thousands of Neturei Karta repudiated the Jewish state and proclaimed themselves as being under alien rule.

Throughout the quarter of a century of its existence, the danger of alienation of large numbers of Jews from their state had to be reckoned with. To preserve unity, the Founding Fathers had no alternative but to initiate a policy of compromise. They have yielded ground to the Orthodox, but the latter have not gained ground thereby, nor have they made any inroads among the nonobservant. This policy was in the nature of a delaying action, and the time gained enabled the new state to consolidate itself and strengthen its social cohesion. It has also afforded an opportunity for the development of a Jewish culture within a climate of a broad national consensus.

The tensions between tradition and change, between preservation and innovation, have always loomed large on the unfolding panorama of Jewish history. In the State of Israel, where hallowed traditions had to be applied to the new and unfamiliar reality of Jewish sovereignty, these tensions escalated. Even when guns roared and armies fought, conflicts bearing on the meaning of Jewish identity were never silenced. Confrontation between tradition and change will continue to agitate the people as long as they, in the best traditions of their past, pursue the quest for identity and the meaning of their existence.

Notes

Notes to Chapter 1

1. Haim Hillel Ben Sasson, Toldot Yisrael byYmei Ha Benayim (Tel Aviv: Dvir, 1969), p. 89.
2. Yitzhak Ben Zvi, in Louis Finkelstein, ed., *The Jews, their History, Culture and Religion*, 3rd ed., (New York: Harper Brothers Publishers, 1960), 1:606.
3. *Ibid.*, p. 603.
4. *Entsiklopedia Ivrit* (Jerusalem: Massada, 1957), 6:490.
5. Ben Zvi, p. 640.
6. *Ibid.*, p. 647.
7. A. M. Hyamson, *Palestine* (London: Methuen & Co., 1917), pp. 57, 59.
8. Raphael Mahler, *A History of Modern Jewry* (New York: Schocken Books, 1971), p. 606.
9. Arthur Ruppin, *Soziologie der Juden* (Berlin, 1930), 1:146.
10. Ben Zvi, *Eretz Israel veYishuvah biYmei HaShilton HaOttomani* (Jerusalem: Mosad Bialik, 1955), p. 388.
11. *Ibid.*, p. 397.
12. James Parkes, *A History of Palestine from 135* A.D. *to Modern Times* (London, 1949), p. 263.
13. Ben Zvi, p. 365.
14. Jacob R. Marcus, *Early American Jewry* (Philadelphia: Jewish Publication Society, 1951), 1:1964.
15. Mordecai Eliav, *Ahavat Zion veAnshei Hod* (Tel Aviv University 1970), pp. 14–16.
16. *Ibid.*, pp. 18–19.
17. Frank E. Manuel, *The Realities of American-Palestine Relations* (Washington: Public Affairs Press, 1949), pp. 34–35.
18. Ben-Zion Gat, *HaYishuv HaYehudi beEretz Yisrael 1840–1881* (Jerusalem: Friends of the Hebrew University, 1963), pp. 37, 95.
19. *Ibid.*, p. 40.
20. *Ibid.*, p. 105.
21. *Ibid.*, p. 104.
22. Joseph Ulitzky, *MiPezurah laMedinah* (Jerusalem: Ahiassaf, 1959), p. 21.
23. Gat, p. 47.
24. Mordecai Eliav, ed., *Perakim beToledot haYishuv beYerushalayim* (Jerusalem: Yad Ben-Zvi, 1973), p. 52.
25. F. E. Manuel, p. 21.
26. Arthur Ruppin, *Reshit Avodati baAretz 1907–1920* (Tel Aviv: Am Oved, 1968), p. 30.

27. Ben Zvi, p. 414.
28. Mordecai Eliav, *Ahavat Zion veAnshei Hod,* p. 19.
29. Gat, p. 76.
30. Eliav, *Ahavat Zion veAnshei Hod,* p. 17.
31. Gat, p. 79.
32. *Ibid.*
33. A. R. Malakhi, *Perakim BeToldot Ha Yishuv Ha-Yashan* (Tel Aviv: Tel Aviv University, 1971), p. 375; see also Yehuda Ben-Porat and others, ed. *Perakim beToldot Ha Yishuv HaYehudi be Yerushalayim* (Jerusalem: Yad Ben Zvi, 1973), p. 302–3.
34. Gat, p. 223.
35. Eliav, *Ahavat Zion veAnshei Hod,* p. 328.
36. *Ibid.,* p. 329.
37. Eliav, *Perakim,* p. 58.
38. Zvi (Heinrich) Graetz, *Jewish History,* Hebrew ed. (Jerusalem: Mosad Bialik, 1959), pp. 271–85.
39. Getzel Kressel, *Rabbi Yehiel Mikhel Pines* (Tel Aviv: Sifriat Shorashim, 1946), pp. 20–22.
40. Eliahu Young, ed., *Noterei Moreshet* (Jerusalem: Mosad HaRav Kook, 1968), p. 208.
41. Mordecai Ben-Hillel HaCohen, *Olami* (Jerusalem: Mizpah, 1927), Pt. 1, p. 118.
42. Young, n31.
43. *Ibid.,* p. 316.
44. *Ibid.,* p. 219.
45. Joseph Klausner, *Eliezer Ben Yehuda* (Tel Aviv: Omanuth Publishing Co., 1939), p. 35.
46. Malakhi, *Perakim,* p. 371.
47. *Ibid.,* pp. 372–74.
48. Eliav, *Ahavat Zion,* p. 304.
49. Klausner, *Eliezer Ben Yehuda,* p. 42.
50. Arthur Ruppin, *Milhemet HaYehudim leKiyumam* (Tel Aviv: Mosad Bialik, 1940), p. 30.
51. For a fuller discussion of Haskalah in Russia, see Jacob S. Raisin, *The Haskalah Movement in Russia* (Philadelphia: Jewish Publication Society, 1913), and Raphael Mahler, *A History of Modern Jewry,* pp. 536–601.
52. Simon M. Dubnow, *History of the Jews in Russia and Poland* (Philadelphia: Jewish Publication Society, 1918), 2:247–58.
53. *Ibid.,* p. 417.
54. Yisrael Klausner, *BeHit'orer Am* (Jerusalem: HaSifriah HaTzionit, 1962), pp. 164–68.
55. Robert Shershevsky, Avshalom Katz, Yisrael Kolatt, Chaim Barkai, *Yemei HaShilton HaOttomani* (Tel Aviv: Sifriat Maariv, 1968), p. 88.
56. *Ibid.,* p. 162.
57. *Ibid.,* p. 142.
58. Walter Laqueur, *A History of Zionism* (London: Weidenfeld and Nicholson, 1972), p. 76.
59. Abraham Salomon, *Petah-Tikva* (Tel Aviv: Omanuth Publishing Co., 1939), p. 35.
60. *Ibid.,* p. 37.
61. S. Ben-Zion, *Yesud Gedera* (Tel Aviv: Omanuth Publishing Co., 1930), p. 72.
62. *Ibid.,* p. 73.

63. Leviticus 25:2.
64. Deuteronomy 15:2.
65. Mishnah Yadayim 4:3.
66. Ben-Zion, p. 79.
67. Yisrael Klausner, *Me Katowitz ad Basel* (Jerusalem: Ha Sifriat HaTzionit, 1965), 2:325.
68. *Ibid.*, p. 326.
69. *Ibid.*, p. 335.
70. *Ibid.*, pp. 330–32.
71. *Ibid.*, pp. 326, 330.
72. *Ibid.*, p. 336.
73. *Ibid.*, pp. 332–35.
74. Yechiel M. Pines, *Binyan HaAretz* (Tel Aviv, 1937), 2 (Bk. 1) :57.
75. Leviticus 19:19; Deuteronomy 22:9–11.
76. Pines, p. 57.
77. Shmuel Yavnielli, ed., *Sefer HaTzionut* (Tel Aviv: Mosad Bialik, 1942), 2 (Bk. 1) :243–49.
78. *Ibid.*
79. *Ibid.*, p. 26. This document was drawn up on Dec. 19, 1881.
80. *Ibid.*, p. 262.
81. *Ibid.*, p. 263.
82. Moshe Smilansky, *Rehovot* (Tel Aviv: Omanuth Publishing Co., 1935), pp. 12f.
83. *Ibid.*, p. 35.
84. *Ibid.*, p. 36.
85. Moshe Burstein, *Self-Government of the Jews in Palestine* (Tel Aviv: Published by the Author, 1934), p. 70.
86. *Ibid.*, p. 69.

Notes to Chapter 2

1. See W. Gunther Plaut, *The Rise of Reform Judaism* (New York: World Union for Progressive Judaism, 1963), pp. 133ff., 200.
2. The classical statement of Dubnow's view on Diaspora nationalism is contained in his *Essays on Old and New Judaism* (Cleveland: World Publishing Co., 1958), p. 43: "When a people loses not only its political independence, but also its land, when the storms of history uproot it and it becomes dispersed and scattered in alien lands, and, in addition, it also loses its unifying language; if, despite the fact that its external national ties have been destroyed, this nation still maintains itself for many years. . . . reveals its stubborn determination to carry on its autonomous development; such a people has reached its highest stage of cultural-historical individuality, and may be said to be indestructible, if it but clings forcefully to its national will. We have many examples in history of nations that have disappeared from the scene after they lost their land and became dispersed among the nations. We find only one instance, however, of a people that has survived. . . .despite dispersion and loss of homeland—this unique people is the people of Israel." (Dubnow's major work on the world history of the Jewish people has so far appeared only in Hebrew and German.)
3. *Ibid.*, p. 46.
4. For a further discussion of the Bund, see Lucy Davidowitz, *The Golden Heritage* (New York: Holt, Rinehart & Winston, 1967), pp. 58–63.

5. Theodor Herzl, *The Jewish State,* trans. from the German by Sylvie D'Avigdor (London: Central Office of the Zionist Organization, 1934), p. 15.

6. *Ibid.,* p. 15.

7. *Ibid.,* p. 28.

8. *Ibid.,* p. 27.

9. *Basic Writings of Ahad Ha'Am,* ed. Hans Kohn (New York: Herzl Press, 1962), p. 127.

10. *Ibid.,* p. 148.

11. *Ibid.*

12. *The Complete Diaries of Theodor Herzl,* ed. Raphael Patai (New York and London: Herzl Press, 1960), 2:581.

13. Joseph Adler, *Religion and Herzl* (New York: Herzl Press, 1962), pp. 271–308.

14. *Jewish State,* p. 71.

15. *Ibid.*

16. Ben Halpern, *The Idea of a Jewish State* (Cambridge, Mass.: Harvard University Press, 1961), p. 144; W. Gunther Plaut, *The Growth of Reform Judaism* (New York: World Union for Progressive Judaism, 1965), pp. 153f.

17. Alex Bein, *Theodor Herzl: A Biography* (Philadelphia: Jewish Publication Society, 1943), pp. 220–21.

18. Marvin Feinstein, *American Zionism* (New York: Herzl Press, 1965), p. 99.

19. *Ibid.,* p. 219.

20. *Ibid.,* p. 127–28.

21. W. Gunther Plaut, *The Growth of Reform Judaism,* p. 150, quotes Felsenthal as saying: "We do not charge all the opponents of Zionism with consciously aiming at and working for the disappearance of Israel from the world. But this disappearance will become a sad fact, in case the Zionist movement should, God forbid, turn out a failure. What is the gospel preached by the anti-Zionist leaders of the masses? Assimilation. But assimilation leads to amalgamation, and amalgamation leading to becoming absorbed, and becoming absorbed leads to becoming extinct, to total annihilation of Israel. We do not quarrel with individuals who honestly think that mankind would best be served by Israel committing a national suicide. But there are still millions who differ; there are still millions who are not ready or willing to assimilate."

22. Feinstein, p. 134.

23. Julien Weill, *Zadoc Kahn* (Paris: Librairie Felix Alcan, 1912), pp. 192–93.

24. It should be pointed out that those of Herzl's followers who were not Orthodox were referred to as "secularists," not in the sense of persons who had rejected religion, but rather as those for whom the strict observance of the minutiae of the ritual as prescribed by religious law was not the most important expression of the Jewish spirit. In this respect the secular nationalists agreed with Dubnow's dictum: "by separating the national idea from religion, we aim only at negating the supremacy of religion but not at eliminating it from the storehouse of cultural treasures." It should also be borne in mind that the term *religion* as then employed referred to its traditional form, and particularly to the observance of its ritual commandments as expounded by the Orthodox Rabbis. Dubnow, p. 157.

25. *Ibid.,* p. 46.

26. Nahum Sokolow, *History of Zionism* (New York: Longmans, Green & Co., 1919), pp. 262–63.

27. *Verhandlungen des II Zionisten-Congress 23* (Vienna: Verlag des Vereines Erez Israel, 1898) , p. 222.

28. *The Letters and Papers of Chaim Weizmann,* Series A, vol. 1 (Oxford: Oxford University Press, 1968) , p. 24; Adler, p. 298.

29. *Ibid.,* p. 382.

30. Mordecai Nurok, *Ve'idat Zionei Russia beMinsk* (Jerusalem: Hasifriah HaTzionit, 1963) , p. 17

31. R. Meir Berlin, *MiVolozhyn ad Yerushalayim* (Tel Aviv: Yalkut, 1940) ; R. Moshe Ostrowski, *Toldot HaMizrahi beEretz Yisrael* (Jerusalem, 1943); R. Judah L. Fishman (Maimon), *HaTzionut.*

32. Fishman, pp. 288–90.

33. J. L. Maimon, *LaShaah ve-laDor* (Jerusalem: Mosad HaRav Kook, 1965) , p. 33.

34. Nurok, p. 43.

35. Weizmann, *Letters,* p. 395.

36. *Ibid.*

37. *Entsiklopedia shel HaTzionut HaDatit* (Jerusalem: Mosad HaRav Kook, 1965) , 3:346.

38. *Ibid.*

39. J. L. Fishman, *HaTzionut HaDatit veHitpathutah* (Jerusalem: Zionist Organization, 1937) , p. 272.

40. *Ibid.,* p. 346.

41. *Entsiklopedia shel HaTzionut HaDatit,* 3:347.

42. Rabbi J. L. Maimon, ed., *Yovel HaMizrahi* (Jerusalem: Mosad HaRav Kook, 1952) , p. 33.

43. Fishman, p. 379.

44. *Entsiklopedia shel HaTzionut HaDatit,* 3:435–36.

45. *Yovel HaMizrahi,* p. 27

46. *Ibid.,* p. 27.

47. Fishman, p. 99.

48. *Entsiklopedia shel HaZionut HaDatit,* 3:436.

49. *Ibid.,* p. 437.

50. *Ibid.*

51. Yaakov Rosenheim, *Ketavim* (Jerusalem: Histadrut Olamit Agudat Yisrael, 1970), pp. 93–107.

52. Maimon, p. 202.

53. *Ibid.,* p. 204.

54. *Ibid.*

55. Moshe Rinot, *Hevrat HaEzrah leYehudei Germaniah* (Jerusalem: Hebrew University, 1972).

56. *Kol Kitvei Ahad Ha'am,* 2d ed. (Tel Aviv: Dvir Publishing Co., 1949) , p. 409.

57. Arthur Hertzberg, ed., *The Zionist Idea, A Historical Analysis and Reader* (New York: Meridian Books, 1964), p. 373.

Notes to Chapter 3

1. Israel Cohen, *The Zionist Movement* (London: Frederick Muller, Ltd., 1945) , p. 104.

2. For a full treatment of German intervention on behalf of the Yishuv during World War I, see chapter 29 of Eliezer Livneh, Joseph Nedava, Yoram Efrati, *Nili: Toldotehah Shel Heazah Medinit* (Tel Aviv: Schocken Pub-

lishing House, 1961); also Richard Lichtheim, *Shear Yashuv* (Tel Aviv: Neumann Publishing House, 1953), Part III, and Egmont Zechlin, *Die Deutsche Politik und die Juden im Ersten Weltkrieg* (Gottingen: Vandenhoech & Ruprecht, 1969), pp. 285–413.

3. Israel Cohen, p. 117.
4. Leonard Stein, *The Balfour Declaration* (New York: Simon and Schuster, 1961), pp. 101f.
5. Plaut, *The Growth of Reform Judaism,* p. 154.
6. Israel Cohen, p. 114.
7. *Ibid.,* p. 116.
8. Menahem Friedman, *HaTzionut* (Tel Aviv University, 1971), 2:105–10.
9. Moshe Attias, ed., *Sefer HaTeudot shel HaVaad HaLeumi* (Jerusalem, 1963), p. x.
10. *Ibid.,* p. xi.
11. *Ibid.*
12. Sergio Minerbi, *Angelo Levi Bianchini a la sua opera nel Levante* (Milan: Fondazione Sally Mayer, 1967), p. 31. On Nov. 14, 1918, Antonio Meli Lupi di Soragna, the Italian agent in Jerusalem suggested that the Ministry of Foreign Affairs rely on "those local elements favourable to internationalization, and asked whether he should also encourage those opposed to a Jewish state and to Jewish immigration." On Nov. 22, 1918, Baron Sidney Sonnino, the Foreign Minister, cabled his agent in Jerusalem that he was at liberty "to let the anti-Zionists act." Evidently Soragna proceeded to carry on propaganda in favor of internationalization. Reporting from Jerusalem to his Foreign Minister on Jan. 5, 1919, Soragna stated: "The conviction that England has sold Palestine to the Zionists for her own ends is the principal reason that the Moslems, the Christians and the Orthodox Jews are on the point of uniting in order to demand internationalization."
13. *Sefer HaTeudot,* p. xiii.
14. *Ibid.*
15. Moshe Burstein, *Self Government of the Jews in Palestine Since 1900* (Tel Aviv, 1931), p. 100.
16. *Ibid.,* p. 101.
17. *Sefer HaTeudot,* p. 34.
18. *Ibid.,* p. 35.
19. *Ibid.*
20. Israel Cohen, p. 143.
21. The text of the Palestine Mandate is set out in full in *Palestine Royal Commission Report* (London: H. M. Stationary Office, 1937), pp. 34–37.
22. Palestine Order-in-Council, Article 17, *Laws of Palestine,* rev. ed. (London, 1934), 3:2591.
23. M. Friedman, pp. 110–18.
24. Burstein, p. 175.
25. *Sefer HaTeudot,* pp. 42–43.
26. Burstein, p. 175.
27. *Official Gazette,* published by the Government of Palestine, April 1, 1921.
28. *Laws of Palestine,* 3:2581.
29. *Ibid.,* p. 2134: Section 10 (d) of Jewish Community Rules of January 1, 1926.
30. Menahem Elon, *Hamishpat Haivri* (Jerusalem: Magnes Press, 1973), 1:74–88.
31. Menahem Elon, "The Sources and Nature of Jewish Law and its application in the State of Israel," *Israel Law Review* 2 (no. 4) : 551–2.

32. Arthur Hertzberg, *The French Enlightenment and The Jews* (New York: Columbia University Press, 1968), p. 8.

33. Elon, *Israel Law Review* 3 (no. 1):123, 125.

34. Menahem Elon, *Hamishpat HaIvri*, 1:71–72.

35. Menahem Elon, *Israel Law Review*, 3 (no. 3):425–26.

36. Zvi Yaron, *Mishnato shel HaRav Kook* (Jerusalem: Education Department, World Zionist Organization, 1974), pp. 13–21.

37. Hertzberg, *The Zionist Idea*, pp. 425ff.

38. *Ibid.*, p. 426.

39. *Ibid.*, p. 430.

40. *Ibid.*

41. M. Lipson, ed., *MiDor Dor* (Tel Aviv: Ahiasaf, 1968), 1:9.

42. *Ibid.*, 2:14–15.

43. Richard Lichtheim, *Toldot HaTzionut beGermania* (Jerusalem: HaSifriah HaTzionit, 1951), p. 171.

44. Israel Cohen, *The Zionist Movement* (London: Frederick Muller Ltd., 1945), p. 155–56.

45. Jack J. Cohen, *The Case for Religious Naturalism* (New York: Reconstructionist Press, 1958), p. 207.

46. Attorney-General C. A. Altschuler, (18/28), Palestine Law Reports, 1:283.

47. *Sefer HaTeudot*, p. 78.

48. Burstein, p. 168.

49. *Ibid.*, p. 160.

50. *Sefer HaTeudot*, p. 80.

51. *Ibid.*, p. 120.

52. Burstein, p. 109.

53. *Sefer HaTeudot*, p. xix.

54. *Laws of Palestine*, 2:1292.

55. *Ibid.*, 3:2581, as amended in 1939.

56. *Official Gazette of the Government of Palestine*, no. 202, pp. 10–19; also *Laws of Palestine*, 3:2132–44.

57. *Official Gazette of the Government of Palestine*, no. 254, pp. 142–45.

58. Burstein, p. 285.

59. Burstein, pp. 170–71.

60. *Sefer HaTeudot*, p. 148.

61. *Encyclopedia Ivrit*, 6:991.

62. *Ibid.*, p. 992.

63. *Sefer HaTeudot*, p. 192.

64. *Ibid.*, pp. 62–64 of the Introduction.

65. Yitzchak Ben Zvi, *Eretz Yisrael veYishuvah* (Jerusalem: Mossad Bialik, 1955), p. 394.

66. Isaiah Press, "Eretz Yisrael" in *Encyclopedia Topographit Mikrait*, 2:423.

67. Leonard Stein, *Zionism* (London: Kegan Paul, 1932), p. 127.

68. *Encyclopedia shel HaTzionut HaDatit*, 3:442.

69. *Ibid.*, 3:235.

70. *Sefer Toldot HaHaganah*, Yehudah Slutsky, ed. (Jerusalem: HaSifriah HaTzionit, 1959), p. 252.

71. Walter Laqueur, *A History of Zionism* (London: Weidenfeld and Nicholson, 1972), p. 410.

72. *Palestine Royal Commission Report*, p. vi.

73. *Ibid.*, p. 381.

74. *Ibid.*, p. 395.

75. *Torah uMeluchah,* Simon Federbusch, ed. (Jerusalem: Mosad HaRav Kook, 1961), p. 231.

76. *Ibid.*, p. 239. See also Laqueur, *A History of Zionism,* pp. 411–12.

77. Menahem Elon, *HaMishpat HaIvri,* 1:87.

Notes to Chapter 4

1. E. Marmorstein, *Heaven at Bay* (London: Oxford University Press, 1969), p. 117.

2. Federbusch, p. 241.

3. David Ben-Gurion, *Israel: A Personal History* (New York: Herzl Press, 1971), p. 77.

4. Menahem Elon, *HaMishpat HaIvri* (Jerusalem: Magnes Press, Hebrew University, 1973), pp. 93–94.

5. Hilkhot Melakhim 1:4.

6. *Dat Yisrael uMedinat Yisrael* (New York: World Zionist Organization, 1961), pp. 13–19.

7. *Ibid.*, p. 16.

8. *Ibid.*, p. 17.

9. *Mitzpeh, Shnaton HaTzofeh* (Jerusalem: Mizrahi World Center, 1953), pp. 129–31.

10. *Entsiklopedia Datit,* 3:477.

11. *Ibid.*, p. 478.

12. *Dat Yisrael uMedinat Yisrael,* p. 40.

13. *Ibid.*, p. 38.

14. *Ibid.*, p. 49.

15. *Entsiklopedia Datit,* 3:480.

16. *Dat Yisrael uMedinat Yisrael,* p. 44.

17. *Ibid.*, p. 51.

18. *HaPraklit* 5 (May–June 1948) :102.

19. *Laws of the State of Israel,* authorized translation from the Hebrew, 1:6.

20. *Ibid.*, pp. 7–12.

21. *Ibid.*, p. 18.

22. *Ibid.*, p. 15.

23. *Ibid.*, 2:24.

24. Asher Zidon, *The Parliament of Israel* (New York: Herzl Press, 1967), p. 16.

25. *Laws of the State of Israel,* 2:81.

26. *Ibid.*, 3:3.

27. *Proceedings of Provisional State Council,* Ninth Session, July 1949, p. 13.

28. *Knesset Record,* 4:715.

29. *Ibid.*, p. 145.

30. *Ibid.*, p. 734.

31. *Ibid.*, p. 820.

32. Asher Zidon, p. 285.

33. *Knesset Record,* 4:728–33.

34. *Ibid.*, p. 733.

35. *Ibid.*, p. 732.

36. *Ibid.*, p. 744.

37. *Ibid.*, p. 810.

38. *Ibid.*, p. 812.

39. *Ibid.*
40. *Ibid.*, p. 811.
41. *Ibid.*, p. 814.
42. *Ibid.*
43. *Ibid.*, p. 815.
44. *Ibid.*, 5:1742.
45. *Ibid.*, p. 1743.
46. *Laws of the State of Israel,* 12:85.
47. *Ibid.*, 14:48, 111.
48. *Ibid.*, 18:111 and 22:247.
49. *Ibid.*, 1:17.
50. *Ibid.*, 3:7.
51. *Dat Yisrael uMedinat Yisrael,* p. 180.
52. *Ibid.*, p. 187.

Notes to Chapter 5

1. Asher Zidon, *The Knesset* (New York: Herzl Press, 1967), p. 323.
2. *Ibid.*, pp. 317–22.
3. In his work *The Foreign Policy of Israel* (London: Oxford University Press, 1972), p. 179, Michael Breecher observes that "neither the NRP (i.e., Mafdal) nor the Agudah groups has ever displayed much interest in foreign policy. Their raison d'être is Torah and their aim, the recreation of a theocratic society. At the global level, they followed Mapai's lead."
4. The budget of the Ministry of Religious Affairs in the year 1972 amounted to IL. 31,000,000 and that of the local religious councils to nearly IL. 34,000,000 (Jerusalem: Government Yearbook, 1971/72), Hebrew ed., p.99.
5. In Tel Aviv, the largest city of Israel, where the religious parties at the 1969 election secured only 9% of the total votes, there were two deputy mayors with extensive powers, because here Mapai was relatively weak and had to make maximum concessions to secure the support of its partners. It is interesting to note that in Tel Aviv in 1965 the opponents of Mapai presented a list headed by an Orthodox Jew who was a member of the Liberal Party. Still, the Mafdal and Agudat Israel councillors voted for a non-Orthodox candidate for the mayoralty (a member of Mapai) rather than an Orthodox Jew who was not a member of one of the religious parties. See also Alan Arian, ed., *The Elections in Israel* (Jerusalem: Academic Press, 1972), passim.
6. Peter Y. Medding, *Mapai in Israel* (Cambridge: Cambridge University Press, 1972), pp. 78–79.
7. An Aramaic term stemming from the Talmud; see Jerus. Talmud, Hagiga I, 76c.
8. Neturei Karta, *LeHasir HaMasveh* (Jerusalem: Neturei Karta Edah Haredit, 5710), p. 14.
9. *Yediot Aharonot,* April 22, 1969.
10. *Knesset Record,* 40:2041.
11. *Jerusalem Post,* April 8, 1969.
12. Neturei Karta, *LeHasir HaMasveh,* p. 51.
13. S. N. Eisenstadt, *Israeli Society* (New York: Basic Books, 1967), p. 137.

14. *Laws of Israel* (1949) , 3:112–18.
15. *Knesset Record,* 2:1446.
16. *Laws of Israel* (1953) , 7:137 (National Service Law) .
17. *Ibid.,* 5:125 (Hours of Work and Rest Law) .
18. *Knesset Record,* 28:598.
19. *Ibid.,* 32:687–89, 598.
20. *Ibid.,* 52 (June 10, 1968) :2170.
21. *Ibid.,* 54 (May 13, 1969) : 2486-87.
22. *Ibid.,* p. 2488.
23. *Ibid.,* p. 2489.
24. From the beginning of the Jewish resettlement of Palestine by the Hovevei Zion in the early 1880s.
25. *Mipi Rishonim,* ed. J. Bernstein (Jerusalem: Centre of World Mizrahi and Hapoel HaMizrahi, 1969) , p. 132.
26. *Ibid.,* p. 133.
27. Hanoch Smith, *HaKol Al HaBehirot beYisrael* (Tel Aviv: Adi Publishing House, 1969) , p. 30.
28. *Ibid.,* pp. 75–76.
29. *Ibid.,* p. 77.
30. *Knesset Record,* 44:404.
31. Population Registry Law, *Laws of the State of Israel* (1965) , 19:288–97.
32. Prior to the formation of the government, Golda Meir, to placate Mafdal, issued an order prohibiting television on Friday night. The Supreme Court later invalidated the order.
33. *Maariv,* Nov. 17, 1969.
34. Shevah Weiss, *Ha Shilton HaMekomi beYisrael* (Tel Aviv: Am Oved, 1972) , pp. 149–55.
35. *HaDat veHaMedinah,* ed. Matityahu Rotenberg (Jerusalem: Mafdal, 1964) , pp. 147–49.
36. *Ibid.,* p. 146.
37. *Ibid.*
38. *Ibid.,* p. 148.
39. *Ibid.,* p. 149.
40. *Ibid.,* p. 154.
41. *HaAretz,* Sept. 12, 1699; interview with Rabbi Neriya.
42. *Ibid.*
43. *HaAretz,* Sept. 25, 1965.
44. Mahalachim, published by HaTnuah LeYahadut shel Torah, Jerusalem, no. 1, March 1969, p. 44.
45. *Ibid.*
46. *Amudim,* no. 224 (Dec. 1964) , p. 86.
47. *Amudim,* no. 229 (May 1964) , p. 251.
48. *Ibid.,* p. 255.
49. Marbek Slaughterhouse controversy (see chap. 6) .
50. *Amudim,* no 263 (Jan. 1968) , p. 119.

Notes to Chapter 6

1. *Laws of Palestine,* 3:1580.
2. Henry E. Baker, *Legal System of Israel* (Jerusalem: Israel Universities Press, 1968) , pp. 61f.

3. *Laws of Palestine,* rev. ed. by Robert H. Drayton (London, 1934), 2:1391. The following were the non-Moslem communities that the British administration recognized as official communities for the purpose of the maintenance of religious courts: the Eastern Greek (Orthodox), Latin (Catholic), Armenian (Gregorian), Armenian (Catholic), Syrian (Catholic), Chaldaean (Uniate), Greek Catholic, Melkite, Maronite, Syrian Orthodox, and Jewish. All these courts were on a footing of equality, in terms of the scope of their jurisdiction, while the Moslem religious courts, as in the Ottoman Empire (where Islam was the state religion), obtained much wider jurisdiction. Under this system, as in the Ottoman Empire, there was no civil law regulating family relationships; there was consequently neither civil marriage nor divorce. While the bulk of the law of Palestine under British rule was civil law, one branch of it, family law, was regulated by a number of varying religious codes, and administered by a number of religious courts, with every inhabitant being subject to that court to which he was deemed to be affiliated in terms of his religion, regardless of whether or not he actually practiced that religion. Under this system, Palestinians who belonged to none of the recognized religious communities, such as members of the various Protestant denominations, Bahais, or Buddhists, could neither be married nor divorced, nor could adherents of different religious groups intermarry, since the religious courts were authorized to celebrate marriages only when both parties were members of the same religious community.

The British administration in Palestine was fully aware of the hardships created by this system. In order to afford a measure of relief, it amended the Order-in-Council in 1939 by adding thereto Clause 65A, as follows: "Provision may be made by Ordinance for the celebration, dissolution or annulment of marriages of persons, neither of whom is a Moslem, or a member of another religious community, and for the granting by the Courts of orders or decrees in connection with the marriages of such persons, or their dissolution or annulment." (*Palestine Official Gazette,* no. 496, p. 197.) This provision was intended to vest the High Commissioner with authority to enact legislation to regulate family relationships of persons belonging to none of the recognized religious communities. This was a first step toward the introduction of a unified civil code of family law to be administered by the Civil Courts. However, during the closing years of the British administration, the High Commissioner failed to take advantage of this enabling act, with the result that no legislation was actually enacted that would have removed the disabilities of persons belonging to none of the recognized religious communities.

4. Article 11 of that Ordinance is as follows:

11. The law which existed in Palestine on the 5th Iyar, 5708 (14th May, 1948), shall remain in force, insofar as there is nothing therein repugnant to this Ordinance, or to the other laws which may be enacted by or on behalf of the Provisional Council of State, and subject to such modifications as may result from the establishment of the State and its authorities.

It was followed by Article 14:

14. (a) Any power vested under the law in the King of England or in any of his Secretaries of State, and any power vested under the law in the High Commissioner in Council, or the Government of Palestine, shall henceforth vest in the Provisional Council of State by any of its Ordinances.

(b) Any power vested under the law in British Consuls, British consular officers or British passport control officers, shall henceforth vest in consuls and officers to be appointed for that purpose by the Provisional Government.

Article 15 (a) provided:

"Palestine," wherever appearing in the law, shall henceforth be read as "Israel." (*Laws of the State of Israel*), pp. 8–10.

5. *Laws of Palestine*, 3:2588.

6. *Laws of the State of Israel*, 1:3.

7. Zeev *vs.* District Commissioner and others, *Supreme Court Judgements* (1948), 1:72.

8. Kol Ha'Am *vs.* Minister of Interior, *Supreme Court Judgements* (1953), 7 (Pt. 1), 90ff.

9. Shaib *vs.* Minister of Defence, *Supreme Court Judgements* (1951), 5:399.

10. *Supreme Court Judgements*, 16:2101ff.

11. *Ibid.* (1954), 6:1524.

12. *Ibid.*, 20 (Pt. 2):327.

13. *Ibid.*, 21: (Pt. 2):325, 329.

14. *Ibid.*, p. 140.

15. Amnon Rubenstein, *HaMishpat HaKonstitutzioni shel Medinat Yisrael* (Tel Aviv: Schocken, 1969), pp. 66–68.

16. *Laws of the State of Israel*, 7:139.

17. Skornik *vs.* Skornik, *Supreme Court Judgements* (1951), 8:155–56.

18. Edoardo Vitta, *Conflict of Laws in Matters of Personal Status in Palestine* (Tel Aviv: S. Bursi, 1947), pp. 50–59.

19. *Laws of the State of Israel*, 2:103.

20. Funk, Schlesinger, *vs.* Minister of the Interior (*Supreme Court Judgements*), 17:225ff.

21. *Ibid.*, p. 234.

22. *Ibid.*, p. 258.

23. *Jewish Encyclopedia*, 4:144; and Zeev Falk, *Deot* (*Bitaon HaAkademayim HaDatiim*), no. 27, (1965), pp. 35–40.

24. A different manner of evading rabbinic authority was tried out by arranging a Halakhic marriage in Israel without the benefit of the official rabbinate. In the case of Haklai and Gurfinkel, application was made to the Haifa rabbinical office to celebrate a marriage. Permission was refused because it was established that Mr. Haklai was a cohen, while his prospective wife was a divorcée. The parties thereupon celebrated a marriage in private, i.e., they arranged for a ceremony of Kiddushin, which in itself is that which creates the binding relationship between husband and wife. Of the three original forms of acquiring a wife by Kiddushin—"by money, by a written deed, or by cohabitation"—the only one actually practiced today is that of "money," that is, any article of value, commonly a gold ring. In the presence of witnesses, the bridegroom hands a ring to the bride, and says: "Behold, you are consecrated unto me by this ring according to the law of Moses and Israel." The presence of a rabbi is not required by Halakhah. In the case of the Haklais, the ceremony was duly performed in the presence of witnesses, and the couple applied to the Registry of Inhabitants Office of the Ministry of the Interior to be registered as married. The official in charge refused to make this entry in the Register, on the ground that no "official certificate of marriage" was produced. They applied to the rabbinate for an official certificate, claiming that their marriage had been celebrated in accordance with

Halakhah. When the rabbinate refused to issue such a certificate, the parties applied to the High Court of Justice for an Order Nisi directing the Rabbinical Court to show cause why such a certificate should not be issued, on the ground that the marriage was Halakhically valid. The High Court, while admitting that a marriage relationship had been established by a Halakhically valid ceremony, considered that it was not in the interest of good public order to celebrate marriages in a private manner, and that such an act must be performed officially. Consequently, the application was dismissed, and the parties were referred to the Rabbinical Court. It is worthy of note that in the majority judgment Justice M. Landau considered it proper to state that he found nothing improper in the conduct of the couple, "who do not observe the religious commandments, and in accordance with the laws of the land, they are free not to do so. . . . They are confronted by a prohibition which is purely religious-ritualist . . . the imposition of such a prohibition on a non-believer cannot be reconciled with freedom of conscience and the freedom of action resulting therefrom." (Gurfinkel *vs.* Haklai, *Supreme Court Judgements,* 17:2069.)

The parties then applied to the rabbinical court for a judgment, declaring that they were in fact married. The rabbinical court refused to issue such a declaratory judgment because it did not want to "assist transgressors," for by issuing such a judgment it would not merely acknowledge that a state of marriage existed, but would lead men to think that such a marriage might persist. "They cannot be regarded as duly married . . . nor can they be regarded as unmarried, for so long as they are not duly divorced, they may not remarry" (*Rabbinical Courts Judgements,* 5:219ff.) . The official in charge of the Register of Inhabitants, however, registered the couple as married, presumably on the grounds that, because being Halakhically subject to the requirements of divorce, the couple can therefore not be considered unmarried.

25. Leah Kahane *vs.* Eliezer Kahane, 571/69, *Supreme Court Judgements,* 24 (Pt. 2) :549ff.
26. *Ibid.,* p. 557.
27. *HaAretz,* Jan. 29, 1971.
28. See above. At stake is the biblical injunction that a man must marry the widow of his brother who has died childless. The biblical authority for this is found in Deuteronomy 25:5: "If brethren dwell together, and one of them did die, and leave a child, the wife of the dead shall not marry without unto a stranger: her husband's brother shall go in unto her, and take her to him to wife, and perform the duty of a husband's brother unto her."

The inheritance of the deceased brother passed to the brother who married the widow. This law is considered to have originated in the need to keep family property intact upon the death of one of the brethren "who dwell together," and who is childless. Where the brother refused to fulfill the obligation, or when the widow refused to marry her brother-in-law, the rite of Halitzah had to be observed. It was performed in the presence of judges, and consisted of the taking off of the brother-in-law's shoe by the childless widow, and this ceremony released the man from his obligation to marry the widow, and left her free to marry whom she pleased. In the talmudic period the ancient institution of levirate marriage fell into disuse, and Halitzah became the general rule. This, however, placed the brother-in-law in a position where he could extract money from the childless widow of his brother for obtaining his consent to perform the ceremony of Halitzah. Various devices were instituted to alleviate such abuse. For instance, at the wedding of a young couple all the brothers of a bridegroom signed a "shtar halitzah," pledging themselves not to claim remuneration in the case of their brother dying childless. This device, however, is not generally followed, and the problem continues to plague childless widows.

29. *Laws of the State of Israel,* 7:139.

30. *London Jewish Chronicle,* March 10, 1967.

31. *Ibid.*

32. *Maariv,* Jan. 3, 1964.

33. *Deot,* no. 27 (1965), pp. 35ff.

34. *Amudim,* May 1964.

35. *Amudim,* Dec. 1964.

36. *Laws of the State of Israel,* 7:139.

37. *Supreme Court Judgements,* 22 (Pt. 1):52.

38. *HaAretz,* Feb. 2, 1969.

39. *Conservative Judaism,* 20, no. 1 (Fall 1965).

40. *Yediot Ahronot,* March 10, 1971.

41. *Maariv,* April 6, 1971.

42. *Maariv,* April 9, 1971.

43. *Laws of the State of Israel,* 3:119.

44. *Ibid.,* 9:172.

45. *Ibid.,* 10:95.

46. *Ibid.,* 18:179.

47. *Ibid.,* 19:66.

48. *Supreme Court Judgements,* 17:102.

49. *Ibid.,* 20 (Pt. 3):249ff.

50. *Knesset Record,* 14:1478.

51. *Ibid.,* pp. 1410f.

52. *Ibid.,* p. 1411.

53. *Ibid.,* p. 1477.

54. Speech in the Knesset on July 27, 1954; *Knesset Record,* 16:2220.

55. *Ibid.,* 14:1457.

56. *Ibid.,* p. 1465. To those advocating the introduction of civil marriage, Mr. Yeshayahu replied: "The secularist must realize that a religious Jew may marry a non-religious Jew, in the hope that the latter may undergo for the better, but he cannot marry a Jew issuing from a non-Halachic marriage. If we should permit such a form of (civil) marriage for part of our public, serious tragedies will inevitably follow. Just imagine a situation where two young persons decide on marriage, and then the parents suddenly explain to them that they cannot marry, owing to their own previous non-Halachic marriage. Who needs all this?"

57. *Ibid.,* p. 1464.

58. *Ibid.,* p. 1472.

59. *Ibid.,* pp. 2542–63.

60. *Laws of the State of Israel,* 9:74.

61. *Israel Law Review,* 2:403.

62. *Ibid.,* p. 408.

63. *Journal of Contemporary History* (Autumn 1967), pp. 107–21.

64. Quoted in *Ovnayim* (Spring 1966), p. 62.

65. This is also the view of Dr. Yaakov Levinger, another Orthodox scholar, who urges the rabbinical authorities to rule that civil marriages are not marriages in the contemplation of the Halakah, thus preventing a situation that would cause the disqualification of the offspring of women who remarry without a prior *get* for marriage with observant Jews. This would obviate a split with the great numbers of Jews in the Diaspora, in the West as well as in the Soviet Union, where family life is sanctioned by civil law only. *Ibid.*, pp. 65–72.

66. *Beterem,* Sept. 10, 1959, pp. 14–18.

67. *Ovnayim* (Spring 1966) , p. 84.

68. *Laws of the State of Israel,* 1:18.

69. *Dinei Medinat Yisrael* (new version) , no. 8.

70. *Laws of the State of Israel,* 5:125.

71. Even where the Committee of Ministers has given a general permit in accordance with Section 12, difficulties do arise. Thus, the Hadera Paper Mills obtained a general permit on the ground that, as the only paper mill in Israel, it rendered indispensable work. The Chief Rabbinate agreed but stipulated that paper manufactured in this plant could not be used to print Bibles. Finally, a compromise was reached whereby non-Jews were employed in those processes of production which had to be maintained on Shabbat. *Israel Weekly Digest,* 1, no. 17 (January 23, 1958) .

72. *Laws of the State of Israel,* 16:93.

73. Government Bill, No. 692, pp. 118–19, dated May 8, 1966.

74. *HaAretz,* Dec. 2, 1964.

75. In Haifa and Beershba the local Rabbis imposed on Class A hotels the additional restrictions elsewhere confined to B hotels. The Tourist Corporation pointed out that the new type of "popular tourist" brings to the country a class of tourists of rather limited means, who cannot resort to Class A hotels, and the imposition of extreme Sabbath observance would inevitably present serious difficulties. (*HaAretz,* Dec. 3, 1964.)

The imposition of these rules also depended on the ability of the applicant to resist them. The proprietor of a hotel in Herzliah was informed that his Kashrut license would be withdrawn if he allowed the use of his hall for the holding of services by a Reform congregation. The hotel proprietor yielded, and canceled the lease of the hall. The proprietor of a Jerusalem hotel was likewise threatened, unless he closed the swimming pool, where there was mixed bathing. This proprietor resisted, and through government intervention the swimming pool remained open. Equally successful was the Dan Carmel Hotel in Haifa, which rejected demands that there be neither writing nor registration on the Sabbath. Most hotels, however, yielded to the extent that no music is permitted on the Sabbath, nor are loudspeakers used, and smoking is forbidden in the public rooms. Equally onerous conditions were imposed successfully on the manufacturers of foodstuffs. It was the contention of the critics that the criterion of Kashrut should be solely the nature of the food manufactured or cooked, with no extraneous considerations. (*Knesset Record,* 37:2115–48, 2226–39.)

76. *Amudim* (March 1964) , pp. 142–43; (May 1964) , p. 256.

77. *Halikhot,* Nissan 1964.

78. *Supreme Court Judgements,* 18 (Pt. 2) :329.

79. *Ibid.,* p. 324.

80. *Yediot Aharonot,* January 30, 1970.
81. *HaTzofeh,* March 25, 1979. See also his meliorating efforts in a case of *Mamzerut, HaAretz,* March 14, 1971.

Notes to Chapter 7

1. Yeshayahu Leibovitz, *Torah uMitzvot baZman Hazeh* (Tel. Aviv: Massada Publishing House, 1954), p. 93. (A collection of essays beginning in 1943.)
2. *HaTorah veHaMedinah,* 5–6:32–33.
3. Leibovitz, p. 91.
4. *Laws of the State of Israel,* 7:137.
5. *HaAretz,* July 19, 1953.
6. *Knesset Record,* 53:1976.
7. *London Jewish Chronicle,* Aug. 26, 1966. The Halakhic problems arise out of the biblical law that forbids lighting a fire on the Sabbath (Exod. 35:3).
8. Leibovitz, p. 89.
9. *Ibid.,* pp. 112f.
10. *Ibid.,* p. 110.
11. *Ibid.,* p. 113.
12. *Ibid.,* p. 126.
13. *Ibid.,* p. 121.
14. *Ibid.,* p. 129.
15. *Conservative Judaism* 25, no. 2 (Winter 1971) : p. 30.
16. *Etz HaDaat,* (Jerusalem, 1963).
17. *Ibid.,* p. 198.
18. *Ibid.,* p. 184.
19. *BeTerem,* Feb. 15, 1952, pp. 22ff,
20. *Ibid.,* p. 26.
21. *Ibid.,* p. 28.
22. See *Al HaMishmar,* September 16, 1970.
23. *Maariv,* June 7, 1970.
24. *Ibid.,* June 29, 1970.
25. *Al HaMishmar,* July 16, 1970.
26. *HaAretz,* Jan. 21, 1970.
27. *HaDat veHaMedinah,* p. 73.
28. *Ibid.,* p. 152.
29. *Ibid.,* p. 151.
30. *Knesset Record,* 7:31.
31. *Ibid.,* p. 82. A talmudic tradition depicts Israel as being coerced, as it were, by God Himself to accept the yoke of Torah at Sinai (Babyl. Talmud, Sab. 88a).
32. Jacob Talmon, *Ahdut veYihud* (Tel Aviv: Shoken Publishing House, 1965), p. 186.
33. *Ibid.,* p. 86.
34. *Ibid.,* p. 188.
35. *Jerusalem Post,* Feb. 7, 1969.
36. *Knesset Record,* 50:920.
37. *Ibid.,* 38:640–42.
38. *Ibid.,* 42:1486.
39. *Ibid.,* 30:877–80.
40. *Ibid.,* 44:53f.

41. *HaAretz,* 19 March, 1964. The government eventually gave in, and one kitchen only was installed.

42. *HaAretz,* Jan. 21, 1970. Under pressure from the Ministry of Tourism, the rabbinate did waive some of its conditions for Class A hotels, on the ground that those hotels were attracting many non-Jews. The stipulations were retained in their entirety for Class B hotels and others. In many cases the issuance of a Kashrut certificate has depended on the ability of the hotel proprietor to withstand the demands of the rabbinate. Cf. also *HaAretz,* Dec. 2, 1964.

43. *Maariv,* Oct. 7, 1969.

44. *HaTzofeh,* May 27 and 31, 1970.

45. *Knesset Record,* 40:2539.

46. *BiYmei Metzukah uMevukhah,* Jerusalem, 1964, p. 21.

47. *Knesset Record,* 54:2546–57.

48. *Laws of Israel,* 5:128.

49. *Supreme Court Judgements,* 24 (P. II) :649–72.

50. *Knesset Record,* 62:1156–57.

51. *Ibid.,* p. 1158.

Notes to Chapter 8

1. *Beit Yaacov,* nos. 62/63 (1964) , Jerusalem.

2. *Laws of Israel,* 3:125.

3. *Knesset Record,* 4:1661.

4. *Laws of Israel,* 7:113–19.

5. *Ibid.,* article 2, p. 113.

6. *Statistical Abstract of Israel* (Jerusalem: Central Bureau of Statistics, 1973) , p. 635.

7. *Ibid.*

8. Aharon Kleinberger, *Society, Schools and Progress in Israel* (Oxford: Pergamon Press, 1969) , p. 170.

9. Ruth Stanner, *Dinei Hinukh* (Jerusalem, Published by the Author, 1966) , p. 116.

10. *Ibid.,* p. 117.

11. Dr. J. Goldschmidt, *Hatzofeh,* July 13, 1971; also *HaAretz,* July 11, 1971.

12. *HaAretz,* July 12, 1971; also July 11, 1971.

13. Kleinberger, p. 117.

14. *Report on the Activities of the Ministry for Religious Affairs,* submitted to the Knesset in 1974, p. 31.

15. *Ibid.*

16. *Jerusalem Post,* January 21, 1966.

17. I. Domb, *The Transformation* (London: n.p., 1958) , pp. 138–39.

18. *Ibid.,* pp. 62–63.

19. *Ibid.,* p. 67.

20. The principle of *Dina deMalkhuta Dina* ("the law of the state is also binding for us.") ; see *Jewish Encyclopedia,* 4:224, and the limitations of the principle.

21. *Jerusalem Post,* October 27, 1963.

22. *Knesset Record,* 38:14ff., 33ff., 43ff., 334ff.

23. *Jerusalem Post,* July 21, 1961.

24. *Ibid.*

25. March 7, 1962; *Knesset Record,* 33:1502–7.

26. *Ibid.,* 33:1758–74.

27. *Reconstructionist,* 28, no. 13 (Nov. 2, 1962).

28. On the Halakhah regarding autopsies, see *Encyclopedia Judaica,* 3, cols. 931–33.

29. *Jerusalem Post,* March 16, 1962.

30. *Budget for the Year 1971/72* (Jerusalem, 1971), pp. 175ff.

31. *Report of the Ministry for Religious Affairs,* submitted to the Knesset, May 1971, p. 12.

32. *Ibid.,* p. 30.

33. *Ibid.,* p. 44. In accordance with the Halakhic interpretation of Exodus 16:29, it is forbidden to carry objects on the Sabbath, even a book or a gift, from an enclosed space, which is *Reshut HaYehid* (private property or domain), to an open space, i.e., a street, which is in *Reshut HaRabim* (public domain). Likewise it is forbidden to carry objects a distance of more than four cubits within the public domain. To remove the inconvenience, the *Eruv* was established, which created the legal fiction of converting the public domain into a private domain. This was effected by placing rods and drawing wires around inhabited areas. See *Jewish Encyclopedia,* 5: 203f.

34. *Report,* pp. 35–36.

35. *Laws of the State of Israel,* 3:66.

36. *Ibid.*

37. *Report of the Ministry for Religious Affairs,* submitted to the Knesset, May 1971, p. 54.

38. *Budget for year 1971/72, Ministry for Religious Affairs,* p. 32.

39. *Ibid.*

40. *Babylonian Talmud,* Berachot 28b.

41. *Tmurot,* April 1964.

42. *Ibid.,* p. 40. See also Rabbi Alexander Carlebach, *Jerusalem Post,* June 28, 1970.

43. *Laws of the State of Israel,* 9:74.

44. *Ibid.,* 7:126 (§ 11).

45. *Knesset Record,* 18:1621ff.

46. *HaAretz,* Dec. 17, 1967.

47. *Knesset Record,* 50:438–40.

48. *HaAretz,* Nov. 11, 1971 ("The Rabbis are above the law"). See also *HaAretz* of June 16, 1970 ("The Rabbinate has not yet recognized the State of Israel").

49. *Knesset Record,* 52:2781–82.

50. Sefirah ("counting") or Omer, a period of semi-mourning that extends over a period of seven weeks, from the second day of Passover until Shavuot. The ceremony is observed at evening services and is followed by a prayer for the restoration of the Temple.

51. Lag B'Omer, a minor festival, is the 33rd day of the Omer period. On this day the semi-mourning is lifted, and weddings, celebrations, and haircuts are permitted. It is traditionally regarded as commemorating the end of the plague that had attacked thousands of Rabbi Akiba's disciples in the time of Bar Kokhba (second century).

52. *Torah uMelukhah,* ed. Simon Federbush (Jerusalem: Mosad Ha-Rav Kook, 1961), p. 116–18.

53. *Ibid.*, p. 53. Rabbi Maimon offers an additional interpretation, which may serve to solve the dilemma posed by those who deny the religious significance of Independence Day, on the ground that the new state is ruled by nonobservant Jews. In his view, "total repentance," i.e., return to the ways of the Torah, will come only after the completion of the process of the Ingathering of the Exiles. He refers to Deuteronomy 30:3 and 6: "Then the Lord your God will turn your captivity and take you back in love. He will bring you together again from all the nations where the Lord your God has scattered you. . . . Then the Lord your God will circumcise your heart and the heart of your offspring to love the Lord your God with all your heart and soul, in order that you may live." Consequently, so long as the ingathering of the exiles is not completed, a Jewish state, even one ruled by nonobservant Jews, has definite religious validity *(ibid.,* p. 152).

54. *Ibid.*, pp. 170–76.

55. *HaZofeh,* April 26, 1968. Chief Rabbi Isaac Nissim, whose attitude toward Independence Day was more in line with the national conception, was apparently not a party to this decision.

56. *Amudim,* March, 1969.

57. *Jerusalem Post,* May 22, 1969.

58. *Dapei Yeshurun,* ed. Zvi Korekh, July 1971.

59. *Yediot Aharonot,* Aug. 2, 1968; July 30, 1971; *Eretz Yisrael,* August 1971.

60. *Yediot Aharonot,* July 30, 1971.

61. See e.g., *Jerusalem Post,* Feb. 2, 1968.

62. Feb. 20, 1968, *Knesset Record,* 51:1111.

63. *HaAretz,* Feb. 14, 1968.

64. *HaAretz,* Jan. 22, 1968.

65. *HaAretz,* Feb. 4, 1968.

66. *Jerusalem Post,* Jan. 29, 1968.

67. *Amudim* (March 1968), pp. 159–68.

68. *Ibid.*, p. 168.

69. *Amudim* (Jan. 1968), p. 119.

70. *Jerusalem Post,* Nov. 25, 1971.

71. *Maariv,* Nov. 25, 1971.

72. *Ibid.*

73. *Yediot Aharonot,* Jan. 30, 1971.

74. *Yediot Aharonot,* July 20, 1971. The address was delivered at a memorial meeting honoring Moshe Chaim Shapiro.

75. *Judaism,* 15, no. 3, pp. 278–79.

76. S. N. Eisenstadt, *Israeli Society* (New York: Basic Books, 1967), p. 379.

77. Zvi Zinger, *Jerusalem Post* Supplement, April 26, 1968.

78. Such wine is called Nesekh. See *Jewish Encyclopedia,* 9:227.

79. *HaYom,* April 4, 1966.

80. *Alei Mishmeret, Bitaon HaDor HaTzair beMafdal,* nos. 6–7, Jan. 1971.

81. Yeshayahu Leibowitz, *Torah uMitzvot baZman Hazeh,* (Tel Aviv: Massada, 1954), pp. 11–12.

82. *Judaism,* 19, no. 1 (Winter 1970).

83. The unwillingness of the non-Orthodox to abide by the Halakhah unreservedly is not a case of rejection of religious values or traditions. Says Eliezer Goldman, one of the leaders of the Kibbutz Dati: "Instances of confrontation between Halakhic rules and principles which are regarded as ethical are growing. It would be a fatal mistake to regard it as a collision

between well-established Halakhic norms and the urge of human passions. It is the collision of two principles. . . . Contemporary cultural developments tend towards ethical conceptions, which may clash with the Halakhah. A realistic comprehension of our condition is possible only by understanding the nature of the conflict between ourselves and broad sections of the non-Orthodox." *Bitaon HaAkedemaim HaDatiim,* 33:169–73.)

84. *Amana,* (Jerusalem: Reuven Maas, 1964), pp. 78f.

85. *Ibid.,* p. 93.

86. *Kiruv Levavot* (Tel Aviv: Kibbutz Dati Publications, 1966), pp. 23–30.

87. *Ibid.,* pp. 55–64.

88. *Amudim* (May 1964), pp. 251–56.

89. *Amudim* (Dec. 1964), p. 86.

90. *Maariv,* March 13, 1964.

91. *Tenuah LeYahadut shel Torah,* Publication no. 1, (Jerusalem, 1966), pp. 24–26.

92. *Mahalakhim,* 1 (March 1969) :23ff.

93. *Maariv,* Jan. 28, 1966.

94. *HaAretz,* Jan. 25, 1966.

95. *Bat-Kol,* nos. 9–10, May 29, 1966 (pub. by the student body of Bar-Ilan University).

96. *Amudim* (August 1966), pp. 244–45.

97. *HaTzofeh,* January 25, 1966.

98. *Tenuah LeYahadut shel Torah,* p. 84.

99. *Hamodia,* April 17, 1966.

100. *Laws of the State of Israel,* 2:37, enacted November 25, 1948.

101. See Yoma 85 a-b; Sanh, 74a; *Shulhan Arukh,* Yore De'ah 116; Orah Hayim 278. Further details in *Encyclopaedia Judaica,* 13, col. 509.

102. Lecture delivered by Zvi Zinger Yaron over the Israel Radio, June 6, 1971.

103. *The Army Code on the Subject of Religion,* issued in Oct. 1968 by the Army Chief Rabbinate, on the authority of the General Staff of the Defense Army of Israel, Military Printing Office.

104. *Ibid.,* p. 23.

105. *Ibid.,* p. 12.

106. *Ibid.,* pp. 13–20.

107. *Knesset Record,* 39:1090.

108. *Army* Code, p. 35.

109. For details, see *Encyclopaedia Judaica,* 4, col. 356–58.

110. *Rosh Hashanah Prayer Book,* 1963.

111. Army *Yom Kippur Prayer Book.*

112. *Prayer Book for the Soldiers of the Israel Defense Army,* 1967.

113. *Ibid.,* pp. 72–76.

114. *Ibid.,* p. 49.

115. *Ibid.,* p. 50.

116. David Blokh in *Davar,* Oct. 20, 1972.

117. *HaDat veHaMedina,* pp. 81–82.

118. This opposition has come from the Agudah and other right-wing Orthodox leaders, chief among them the Lubavitcher Rebbe in New York. It broke into the open over Rabbi Goren's handling of the Langer case shortly after his assumption of the position of Ashkenazic Chief Rabbi of Israel.

A complete review of the "Mamzerim Affair" can be found in *Yediot Ahronot,* Nov. 20, 1972.

119. *Army Code,* p. 3.

Notes to Chapter 9

1. Prof. Charles S. Liebman, writing on American Jewry, is of the opinion that "Israel has a special appeal for the non-religious Jew, for the Jew who finds no outlet for his Jewish identification in a religious context. To him, Israel may be the carrier of a secular Jewish culture which virtually disappeared in the United States. Israel's role as the representative of secular Judaism helps account for the fact that the Jewish community center movement which was indifferent to Zionism prior to 1948, now makes it an important component of its programing" (*The Ambivalent American Jew* [Philadelphia: Jewish Publication Society of America, 1973], p. 101).

2. See *Encyclopedia Judaica,* 4, cols. 493ff.; Schifra Strizower, *The Children of Israel: The Bene Israel of Bombay* (Oxford: Basil Blackwell, 1971). See also Strizower, *Exotic Jewish Communities* (London: Thomas Yoseloff, 1962).

3. As early as 1952 an Indian minister had read this statement into the parliamentary record: "The government of India has received complaints from some Indian Jews who had returned from Israel that there was discrimination against them on account of their color. The government has not verified any of these complaints, and in any event, such individual complaints do not justify a general statement that there is a color bar in Israel." The young generation of Bene Israel has become integrated into Israel society and found its place in all fields of Israel life. Their communal attachment is still strong and finds particular expression at meetings on festivals (*Encycl. Jud.,* 4, col. 498).

4. *Reconstructionist* 30 (no. 5):19.

5. S. N. Eisenstadt, *Israeli Society* (New York: Basic Book, 1967), pp. 312–14.

6. *Jerusalem Post,* Feb. 23, 1962.

7. *Ibid.,* Feb. 15, 1962.

8. *Knesset Record,* 34:2622–45.

9. July 6, 1962.

10. July 1, 1962.

11. *Maariv,* April 30, 1964.

12. *Knesset Record,* 39 (May 13, 1964):1783–85.

13. *Ibid.,* 40: 2658–59.

14. *Ibid.,* pp. 2633–56.

15. See *Encyclopedia Judaica,* 10, cols. 761ff.

16. *Knesset Record,* 60:1425–35.

17. M. Corinaldi, "LeSh'elat Ma'amadam shel Karaim beYisrael," *Mehalkhim* (1969), 1:1–19, deals with the hardening attitude of the rabbinate toward Karaites. Prof. Menahem Elon, in *Hakikah Datit* (Tel Aviv: HaKibbutz HaDati, 1968), p. 180, cites an instance of a Karaite marriage with a rabbinic Jew being permitted by the Haifa rabbinical court as late as 1966.

18. *Knesset Record,* 18:1598, 2096; 19:932–34; 31:1833; 32:361.

19. The talmudic luminary Radbaz (Rabbi David Ibn-Zimra, born in Spain at the end of the fifteenth century (died in Safed in 1589) adopted a different interpretation, designed to bring about a rapprochement between the two Jewish groups. While agreeing that the Karaite formula for the *get* deviated from the rabbinic formula, he also held that the Karaite marriage procedure itself was not wholly in accordance with the Halakhah, and was therefore in its turn invalid. Such being the case, no legal marriage has taken place, and thus there is no need for a divorce; in such a situation neither *mamzerut* nor *safek mamzerut* can possibly exist. His interpretation was followed in some instances, but generally the Jewish authorities enforced the rule of nonintermarriage with Karaites.

20. *Report of the Public Commission of Inquiry on Matters of Personal Status of the Karaite Community in Israel,* dated Jerusalem, 22nd Tammus, 1967.

21. *Ibid.*

22. *Ibid.*

23. Bill no. 923, pp. 100–101, dated January 27, 1971.

24. *Knesset Record,* 60:1425–35; 61:2623–34.

25. *Laws of Israel,* 4:114.

26. The Law of Return and the Nationality Law are not unique in contemporary legislation. A similar provision is inserted in the Constitution of the Federal Republic of Germany of May 3, 1949.

27. *Laws of Israel,* 6:50–53.

28. *Ibid.,* 2:104.

29. The identity card, which every resident of Israel is required to possess by law, contains the above-mentioned particulars. The Population Registry Law of 1965 enlarged and extended the previous law, and called on each resident to submit particulars concerning, inter alia, his name and previous name, if any, names of parents, particulars of personal status, citizenship, religion and *leom* in the sense of a distinct group with cultural, linguistic, and ethnic links. Section 5 of the Law imposed upon every inhabitant the duty of furnishing these particulars to the Registry Office within 30 days of his arrival in Israel, or from the date of his becoming a resident. It is followed by the issuance of the identity card, containing all the particulars, and any changes that may occur after the date of the issuance of the card. Marriage and divorce are also items noted on the identity card.

30. *Supreme Court Judgements,* 1962, 16:2428ff.

31. Babylonian Talmud, Sanhedrin 44a.

32. *Supreme Court Judgements,* 1962, 16:2428, 2437.

33. *Ibid.,* pp. 2444–48.

34. *Ibid.,* pp. 2448–55.

35. S. N. Eisenstadt, pp. 314–16.

36. *Knesset Record,* 24:2236ff.

37. *Ibid.,* p. 2314.

38. Zvi Bernstein, *Bemaarakhah leShlemut HaUmmah* (Tel Aviv); Avner Ch. Skaki, *Mihu Yehudi.*

39. *Knesset Record,* 25:432.

40. In addressing the Rabbis and scholars, Ben-Gurion set forth the genesis of this question as it had arisen out of the implementation of the laws enacted by the Knesset, particularly the Law of Return and the Registration of Inhabitants Law. While expressing no personal opinion on the merits of the controversy, he drew attention to the specific conditions prevailing in Israel. "The Jewish community in Israel is unlike that in the Diaspora,

for here we are not a minority subjected to the pressure of an alien culture, and fear no assimilation of Jews in the midst of non-Jews. . . . On the contrary, possibilities and tendencies exist here of non-Jews assimilating to Jews, particularly in the case of mixed couples who arrive in Israel. Whereas mixed couples abroad are one of the decisive factors making for total assimilation . . . in Israel, mixed couples arriving here, particularly from Eastern Europe, become in fact completely integrated with the Jewish people."

41. Collected in *Kuntrass Mihu Yehudi* (Jerusalem: Government Press Office, 1959). The responses have also appeared in English: *Jewish Identity*, ed. B. Litvin and S. H. Hoenig (New York: Feldheim, 1965).
42. *Ibid.*, pp. 22–25, (English edition pp. 122–27).
43. *Ibid.*, pp. 98–105 (English edition, pp. 32–51).
44. *Ibid.*, pp. 66–68 (English edition, pp. 216–20).
45. *Ibid.*, p. 76 (English edition, pp. 232–35).
46. *Ibid.*, p. 88.
47. *Ibid.*, pp. 88–93 (English edition, pp. 247–61). Cohen also cited the well-known fact that among the tens of thousands of Jews who arrived in Palestine after 1933, and among the survivors of the Holocaust who arrived after 1945, there were thousands of couples of mixed marriages; among them were many non-Jewish wives who concealed their non-Jewish origin, and were able thereby to have their children integrated into the Jewish milieu without leaving a trace of their non-Jewish ancestry.
48. *HaPraklit*, 19, no. 1 (Feb. 1963) :101–6.
49. *Davar*, Dec. 29, 1964.
50. An analysis of the legal aspects of the Eitani case by Prof. Amnon Rubinstein appeared in *HaAretz*, Jan. 3, 1965.
51. *Encounter* 24, no. 5 (May 1965) :28–36.
52. Quoted in Prof. Amnon Rubinstein's article in *HaAretz*, Dec. 25, 1964.
53. *Knesset Record* 36 (March 26, 1963) : 1649.
54. For a competent survey of this case and its ramifications, see Lawrence S. Nesis, "Who Is a Jew?" *Manitoba Law Journal* 4, no. 1 (1970) :53–88.
55. *Yediot Ahronoth*, Nov. 22, 1966.
56. *Supreme Court Judgements*, 23 (Part 2) :477–608.
57. *Ibid.*, pp. 492–503.
58. *Ibid.*, pp. 537–72.
59. *Ibid.*, pp. 517–31, 574–604.
60. *Population Registry Law, 1965 (Laws of the State of Israel,* 19) , pp. 288–97.
61. *Laws of the State of Israel,* 5: 125–32.
62. *Supreme Court Judgements,* 23 (Pt. 2) :504–16.
63. *Ibid.*, pp. 532–36.
64. Noteworthy is the case of Dr. George Raphael Tamarin, a Jew and a professed atheist, who applied to be registered as "Israeli" under the category of Leom. He contended that in Israel there had evolved an Israeli Leom to which he felt attached and which made him an Israeli not only in terms of citizenship but also in terms of Leom. The Supreme Court rejected his contention in a judgment delivered in 1970, as it would imply that since the establishment of the State of Israel a schism had taken place within Jewry, and a new Leom, distinct and separate from the Jewish Leom, had emerged. This was obviously not a fact, and the petitioner could not claim to belong to a nonexistent Leom. *Supreme Court Judgements,* 26 (Pt. 1) :197–226.

65. *Laws of the State of Israel*, 24:28.
66. *Knesset Record*, 56:735.
67. *Ibid.*, p. 736.
68. *Ibid.*, pp. 737–38.
69. *Ibid.*, pp. 738–39.
70. *Ibid.*, p. 739.
71. *Ibid.*, pp. 754–57.
72. *Reconstructionist*, 37, no. 2 (April 2, 1971) :11.
73. See the study by David Max Eichhorn, ed., *Conversion to Judaism* (New York: KTAV, 1965) .
74. Babylonian Talmud, Yevamot 47a.
75. 4:3.
76. Yev. 47b.
77. Nid. 13b. There were, however, many opinions recorded that appreciated proselytes. See *Encycl. Judaica*, 13, col. 1186; also Bernard J. Bamberger, *Proselytism in the Talmudic Period.* 2nd ed (New York: KTAV, 1968) .
78. *Knesset Record,* 56:757.
79. *Ibid.*, p. 781.
80. *Laws of Palestine,* rev. ed. (London) , 2:1294.
81. *Modiin* (house organ of Agudat Israel, Jerusalem) , no. 44 (1970) .
82. *Yediot Ahronot,* June 16, 1970.
83. *Petahim* (Sept. 1970) , pp. 39–41.
84. Pinhas Peli, *Panim El Panim,* no. 579, June 26, 1970.
85. *London Jewish Chronicle,* Aug. 28 and Sept. 11, 1964. A similar case occurred in 1965 with a young Jewish scientist of outstanding academic attainments, who had spent six months studying Hebrew in an Ulpan in Israel. While there, he accepted an appointment in a scientific institution affiliated with the Ministry of Defense. On returning home to England, he proceeded to the Immigration Department of the Jewish Agency to arrange for his settlement, and for that of his wife, in Israel. She was a Dutch-born Christian converted to Judaism under Reform auspices. The official of the Jewish Agency explained that it would be impossible for his wife to proceed to Israel under the Law of Return. The scientist, however, pressed the case and after many delays and referrals, the case was finally referred to an interministerial committee in Israel. But even though by now nearly a year had passed since the application was first made, no decision was announced. The prospective Oleh felt that it was the intention of the authorities to procrastinate and to tire out the applicant until he dropped the matter. In the meantime, the scientist, unable to take up the promised job in Israel, accepted a call to the University of Leyden in Holland. (*Maariv,* Sept. 20, 1969 and April 29, 1966; *LaMerchav,* Sept. 9, 1969; *Midstream,* Oct. 1966, pp. 12–13.)
86. This letter was placed at the disposal of the author by the Union of American Hebrew Congregations in New York.
87. *Jerusalem Post,* Nov. 20, 1964.
88. *London Jewish Chronicle,* March 1, 1968. Ben Gurion's own account of the episode appeared in the *Central Conference of American Rabbis Yearbook* 53 (1971) :149–50.
89. *Annual Report of the Ministry for Religious Affairs,* 1966/7, p. 23.
90. *Ibid.*, 1967/8, p. 23.
91. *Ibid.*, 1970/1, p. 16.
92. *Knesset Record,* 56:745.

93. *Yediot Ahronot,* March 12, 1972.
94. *Knesset Record,* 56:745. See also *Maariv,* March 14, 1972.
95. *Davar,* Oct. 21, 1971.
96. *Maariv,* April 20, 1971.
97. *Ibid.*
98. *Maariv,* Jan. 11, 1972.
99. Gershom Scholem, *Shabbetai Zvi* (Tel Aviv: Am Oved, 1957), 1:270.
100. *Central Conference of American Rabbis Yearbook* 53 (1971):139.

Notes to Chapter 10

1. The word *Dat* appears in the Bible only in the Book of Esther, where it is usually translated as "law" (1:13; 3:8; 4:11, 16).
2. M. J. Berdichevsky, *Baderekh* (Warsaw, 1922), 2:20.
3. *The Zionist Idea,* ed. Arthur Herzberg (Philadelphia: Meridian Books, 1960), pp. 317–19.
4. Yigael Eilam, *Mavoh leHistoria Tzionit Aheret* (Ramat-Gan: Levin-Epstein Publishers, 1972), pp. 12–15. Eilam, a young Israeli historian, advances the view that secularism was in fact a precondition to the rise and development of Zionism.
5. Jacob de Haas, *Louis D. Brandeis, a Biographical Sketch* (New York: Bloch Publishing Co., 1929), pp. 197–98.
6. Yonatan Shapiro, *Leadership of the American Zionist Organization, 1897–1930* (Urbana, Ill.: University of Illinois Press), p. 60.
7. *Ibid.,* pp. 114–16.
8. Chaim Weizmann, *Letters and Papers,* 2:301–22.
9. Joseph B. Schechtman, *Fighter and Prophet: the Jabotinsky Story* (New York: Thomas Yoseloff, 1969).
10. *Rassviet* 22, no. 39 (Sept. 26, 1926).
11. Schechtman, p. 289.
12. Some of the Zionist ideologists developed the theory that secularism was the distinctive and unique feature of Zionism; in fact, they regarded it as a precondition of Zionism. Within the context of Zionist ideology and achievement, secularism was an affirmation of Judaism rather than an escape from it. To support their proposition, some referred to Spinoza's statement that "unless the fundamentals of their religion bring upon them effeminacy of mind and character, I am inclined to believe that, since human affairs are notoriously changeable, and with the opportunity afforded, they may again recover their empire, and God elect them to Himself anew." *Tractatus Theologico-Politico,* 2d ed. (London: N. Trubner & Co., 1868), p. 87. The point is elaborated by Zeev Levi in his work *Spinoza veMussar HaYahadut* (Tel Aviv: Sifriat HaPoalim, 1972), pp. 25–29.
13. Zvi Zinger-Yaron, *Jerusalem Post,* Oct. 5, 1966.
14. Asher Arian, *HaAm HaBokher* (Ramat Gan: Massada Publishing, 1973), pp. 67–69. Dr. Arian is of the opinion that many Orthodox vote for non-religious parties because of identification with their economic and social policies. But should the religious "status quo" be threatened, they might vote for the religious parties. Thus, the latter possess a political potential beyond their present electoral strength.
15. S. A. Antonovsky, "Social and Political Attitudes in Israel," *Amot,* no. 6 (June–July 1963).

16. Judah Matras, *Social Change in Israel* (Chicago: Aldine Publishing Co., 1965) , p. 107.

17. Simon N. Herman, *Israelis and Jews,* (Philadelphia: Jewish Publication Society of America, 1971) , p. 123.

18. Zvi Zinger-Yaron.

19. Mezuzah (plural, Mezuzot) , literally "doorpost," is the name given to a small case containing a parchment on which the first two paragraphs of the "Shema" (Deut. 6:4–9, 11:13–21) are inscribed; it is affixed to doorposts in accordance with the precept in Deut. 6:9.

20. *Ben-Gurion Looks Back* (London: Weidenfeld and Nicholson, 1965), p. 238.

21. Zvi Zinger-Yaron, *Midstream* (March 1967) , p. 51.

22. *Aleph* (Tel Aviv) (June 1951) .

23. Baruch Kurzweil, one of the outstanding literary critics in Israel, traced the origins of the Canaanite ideology to the secularism that was implicit in the Haskalah movement (*HaAretz Annual,* 1953) , pp. 107–29. His pessimistic prognosis of the impact of this ideology, however, proved to be exaggerated.

24. *Ben-Gurion Looks Back,* pp. 226, 230.

25. *Yearbook,* 81st Annual Convention, Central Conference of American Rabbis, vol. 53 (New York, 1971) :151.

26. S. N. Eisenstadt, *Israeli Society* (New York: Basic Books Inc., 1967) , p. 378.

27. S. Z. Abramov, *HaAretz* (April 19, 1971) , and Gideon Hausner, *HaAaretz* (July 28, 1972) .

28. Simon N. Herman, *Israelis and Jews,* p. 52.

29. *Ibid.,* p. 54.

30. *Ibid.,* p. 198.

31. *Ibid.,* p. 199.

32. Aharon Kleinberger, *Society, Schools and Progress in Israel* (New York: Pergamon Press, 1969) , pp. 327–28.

33. Nathan Rottenstreich, *Judaism* 15, no. 3 (1966) .

34. *The Seventh Day: Soldiers' Talk about the Six Day War* (London: Penguin Books, 1970) .

35. *Ibid.,* p. 23.

36. *Ibid.,* p. 220.

37. *Ibid.,* p. 320.

38. *Ibid.,* p. 104.

39. For a fuller discussion of Holydays in the Kibbutz, see Jack J. Cohen, *The Case for Religious Naturalism,* pp. 209–18.

40. *Ibid.,* p. 35.

41. *Kiruv Levavot,* a collection of essays published by HaKibbutz HaDati (Tel Aviv, 1967) , p. 81.

42. *Ibid.,* p. 82.

43. The largest of these publications is *Bein Tzeirim* (i.e., Young People's Talk) (Tel Aviv: Am Oved, 1969) , edited by members of the Kibbutz movement.

44. *Ibid.,* p. 12.

45. *Ibid.*

46. *Ibid.,* p. 25.

47. *Ibid.,* p. 63.

48. *Ibid.,* p. 19.

49. *Ibid.,* p. 40. Interest in Christianity on the part of young Israelis was observed in the early fifties. Writing in *Commentary,* July 1955, pp. 38ff.,

Herbert Weiner noted that "interest in missionary activity is symptomatic of a profound spiritual problem in Israel, and not to be dismissed lightly. . . . A definite spiritual vacuum was felt by many young people since the establishment of the State: they were yearning for an intangible something to replace Zionism which had previously engaged their spiritual yearnings."

50. Quoted from Zvi Zinger-Yaron's translation in the *Jerusalem Post*, Sept. 12, 1969.
51. Quoted from Herbert Weiner's rendering, *Commentary*.
52. Jack J. Cohen, *Reconstructionist* 30, no. 5.
53. Jack J. Cohen, *The Case for Religious Naturalism*, p. 231.

Notes to Chapter 11

1. *American Jewish Yearbook*, 1971, pp. 11, 279. For detailed figures, see *Jewish Communities of the World*, 3rd rev. ed. (London: Andre Deutsch, 1971), pp. 119–21.
2. *Hebrew Encyclopedia*, 6:666.
3. *Ibid.*, p. 670.
4. W. Gunther Plaut, *The Growth of Reform Judaism* (New York: World Union for Progressive Judaism, 1965), p. 34.
5. *Ibid.*, p. 30.
6. *Ibid.*, p. 34.
7. Prof. Charles Liebman estimates that in the U.S.A. about 1½ million Jews are affiliated with Conservative congregations; about 1 million with Reform, and about ¾ million with the Orthodox. See his study in the *American Jewish Yearbook* of 1965.
8. These data are collated from the *Special Edition for the 17th International Conference of the World Union for Progressive Judaism in Geneva*, Haifa, 1972.
9. *HaAretz* (Oct. 22, 1962).
10. *Jerusalem Post* (Oct. 9, 1966).
11. *Maariv* (Oct. 16, 1966).
12. W. Gunther Plaut, *The Growth of Reform Judaism*, p. 97.
13. All first-year students, many of them married, come to live for a year in Jerusalem. Their program of studies is oriented toward the attainment of Hebrew-language skills, both conversational and academic. Students attend an intensive Ulpan program twenty-four hours a week for the entire scholastic year. The instructors begin with modern Hebrew, and by the end of the year have introduced biblical as well as classical rabbinic texts. The scope and intensity of this program are such that at the end of his stay the student has acquired a working familiarity with the full span of the Hebrew language and is better prepared to resume his rabbinical studies at the College-Institute in America. Additional courses in liturgy, archaeology, and current Reform Jewish thought are integrated into the program, making maximum use of the language and the land.

   Intimate contact with contemporary Israeli life is a major goal of the program. The School arranges for a work-study period on kibbutzim, a volunteer program that includes tutoring in the poorer sections of Jerusalem and at the Ben-Shemen Youth Village, and a regular lecture series given by leaders of Israeli society. A weekend sponsored jointly with the Jewish Agency becomes an intensive workshop on the problems in government and society. Filling out the rabbinical program are courses for more than twenty advanced students from American campuses, who come to perfect their language skills and to take advantage of educational oppor- tunities in Jerusalem. In addition to the courses offered at the Jerusalem School, the advanced students attend sessions at the Hebrew University. "This program," according to Aharon Yadlin, the Deputy Minister of Education and Culture in Israel, "is a part of the ongoing dialogue which brings future spiritual leaders of American Jewry into live contact with Israel's people and culture, and at the same time deepens our own knowl- edge of the institutions of higher learning of the great American Jewish community." The Jerusalem Rabbinical Program is guided by Prof. Ezra Spicehandler, who serves as Director of Jewish Studies. The faculty consists of visiting scholars from the College-Institute in the United States and professors from other American and Israeli institutions. In the 1971–72 academic year, approximately 85 students participated in the program. Dr. Alfred Gottschalk succeeded Dr. Glueck in 1971, on the latter's death.

14. All these manifold activities, including assistance to the Progressive Syna- gogue, are the financial responsibility of the Reform movement in America. While the Hebrew Union College-Jewish Institute of Religion maintains its Jerusalem affiliate through its own budget, the other activities are largely the responsibility of the Union of American Hebrew Congregations. To coordinate these activities, an Israel Committee has been established, and funds are raised by its member congregations.

15. Richard G. Hirsch, *Reform Judaism and Israel* (New York: Commission on Israel, 1972).

16. *Knesset Record,* 17 (March 1, 1955) : 963.

17. *Ibid.,* p. 999.

18. *HaAretz,* Aug. 6, 1956.

19. While the Orthodox extolled the pronouncement of Chief Rabbi Nissim, with some of them going as far as to declare that Reform is "a danger greater than that of the Arab states" *(Jerusalem Post,* August 13, 1956) , public opinion was on the side of Dr. Glueck. In its editorial of August 6, 1956, *HaAretz* pointed out that the rabbinate was reconciled to the grow- ing secularism, so long as it could claim a monopoly of the Jewish religion, and thus avoid an intellectual confrontation with other believing Jews. This controversy was reported in the world press as well *(Time Magazine,* August 23, 1956) and in the American Jewish press *(National Jewish Post,* August 26 and 31, 1956) .

20. *HaTzofeh,* July 1, 1966.

21. *Shearim,* May 29, 1966.

22. *HaModia,* Feb. 4, 1966.

23. *London Jewish Chronicle,* April 17, 1964.

24. *HaModia,* Feb. 4, 1966.

25. *Knesset Record,* 45 (May 23, 1966) ;1497.

26. *Ibid.,* 46 (June 29, 1966) :1966.

27. *Ibid.*

28. *HaAretz,* Jan. 24, 1966.

29. *Ibid.*

30. *HaAretz,* March 25, 1964.

31. *C.C.A.R. Journal* (Jan. 1965) , p. 8.

32. *Amudim* 19, no. 9 (Sivan 1971) :306–10.
33. *Jerusalem Post,* Oct. 11, 1962; *Maariv,* Oct. 14, 1962; and *HaBoker,* Oct. 19, 1962.
34. *HaAretz,* Oct. 10, 1962.
35. *Jerusalem Post,* March 23, 1964.
36. *Yediot Ahronot,* April 8, 1964.
37. *Maariv,* April 7, 1964.
38. *Yediot Ahronot,* April 6, 1964; *Maariv,* April 20, 1964.
39. *Maariv,* Oct. 19, 1964.
40. Data in the archives of the Kedem Progressive Congregation in Tel Aviv.
41. *Jerusalem Post,* Feb. 1, 1966. See also *HaAretz,* January 30, 1966. The President of the Order in Israel had explained the refusal to let the hall to the Progressive congregation on the ground that such an act would hurt the feelings of the Orthodox members of the Order.
42. *Ibid.,* Jan. 26, 1966.
43. *Ibid.,* Feb. 7, 1966.
44. *London Jewish Chronicle,* Nov. 27, 1964.
45. *HaYom,* Feb. 6, 1966.
46. *Jerusalem Post,* Feb. 7, 1966.
47. *Ibid.,* January 31, 1966.
48. *Knesset Record,* 46:1966–67 (June 29, 1966) .
49. *Ibid.,* p. 1968.
50. Archive of Rabbi Moshe Zemer, Tel Aviv.
51. Archive of Emet veAnava Congregations, Ramat Gan.
52. *London Jewish Chronicle,* June 12, 1968.
53. *Israel Digest,* July 12, 1968.
54. *Ibid.*
55. *Maariv,* July 4, 1968.
56. *HaModia,* June 14, 1968.
57. *HaZofeh,* June 25, 1968.
58. *Knesset Record,* 52:2353–60.
59. **Yediot Aharonot, July 5, 1968.**
60. *Jerusalem Post,* July 5, 1968.
61. *Davar,* March 29, 1972; *Maariv,* March 28, 1972.
62. Speaking for the Reform movement, Rabbi David Polish stated:
    "We are and must continue to be intimately identified with Israel and its fate and destiny. So far, we have manifested this identity not only financially but by bringing influence to bear on Israeli economic policies. We have no less a right and a claim to influencing for a time, its religious policies" (*New York Times,* August 24, 1968) .
63. *American Jewish Yearbook,* 65:79.
64. *Jerusalem Post,* March 8, 1964.
65. *American Jewish Yearbook,* 66:310.
66. *Ibid.*
67. *Jerusalem Post,* March 8, 1964.
68. *HaBoker,* March 13, 1964.
69. *American Jewish Yearbook* (1965) , pp. 310–11.
70. *Knesset Record,* July 12, 1972 (not yet in print) .
71. *Jerusalem Post,* June 13, 1972.
72. Dr. Z. Warhaftig, interviewed in *Jerusalem Post,* Sept. 25, 1962.

Notes to Chapter 12

1. *Herzl Yearbook,* 4:286.
2. Eliezer Goldman, *Religious Issues in Israel's Political Life* (Jerusalem: Mador Dati, World Zionist Organization, 1964) .
3. Moshe Unna, *Israel baUmmot* (Tel Aviv: Kibbutz Dati, 1971) , pp. 57–66.
4. Hayim Tuviahu, *HaTzofe,* August 19, 1974.
5. Shlomo Zalman Kahana, *Iyunim* (Jerusalem: Mizrahi and HaPoel Ha-Mizrahi, 1964) , p. 100.
6. Mordecai Nurok, *Veidat Tzionei Russia beMinsk* (Jerusalem: HaSifria HaTzionit, 1963) , p. 43.
7. Beit Yaakov (1964) , 5:62–63.
8. Iyunim, p. 148.
9. Asher Arian, *Ha'Am HaBoher* (Ramat Gan: Massada, 1973) , p. 69.
10. *Jewish Chronicle* (London) , February 12, 1954.
11. Rabbi Immanuel Jakobovits, *Jerusalem Post,* April 5, 1974.
12. Zvi Yaron, *Religion and Morality in Israel and in the Diaspora.* In *Dispersion and Unity,* nos. 17/18 (Jerusalem, 1972) , pp. 96–105.
13. *Ibid.,* pp. 58–70. A recent survey points out that the percentage of those who declared that they never attend synagogue services is 27%; of those who come to the synagogue on Yom Kippur only, 19%. Although 54% declared that they attended services with varying degrees of frequency, only 30% of those affiliated with Labour Alignment declared that they were altogether nonobservant, while the great majority indicated that they were observant in varying degrees.
14. Walter Laqueur, *A History of Zionism* (London: Weidenfeld and Nicolson, 1972) , p. 593.
15. Eliezer Don-Yehiya and Charles Liebman, *Molad* (Tel Aviv) , (August–September 1972) , p. 74. See also Moshe Unna in *HaTzofe,* March 8, 1974. In his opinion, the setting up of a non-Orthodox rabbinate vested with legal powers will split the nation into two. To avoid such a disastrous development, Unna urges the rabbinate to explore ways and means of reaching an understanding with non-Orthodox trends on a pragmatic basis, such as, for example, an agreement on minimal standards of conversion.

Glossary

Agudat Israel. World organization of Orthodox Jews, founded in Kattowitz in 1912, and one of the religious political parties in the State of Israel.

Ahdut HaAvodah. Zionist Socialist Labor Party in Palestine founded in 1919. In 1930 this movement merged with HaPoel HaTzair and formed Mapai, the Workers Party of Eretz Israel.

Aliyah. (1) Hebrew, "Ascent," coming to or immigrating in Eretz Israel, as contrasted with *Yerida,* Hebrew, "Descent," i.e., leaving Eretz Israel. (2) Being called up in the synagogue to participate in the public reading of the Torah.

Asefat HaNivharim. Representative assembly elected by Jews in Palestine during the period of the British Mandate (1920–1948).

Ashkenazi (pl. *Ashkenazim*). Jew of German or West-, Central-, or East-European origin.

Bar Mitzvah (Hebrew, "Son of the Commandment"). The initiation of a boy on attaining the age of 13 into the Jewish religious community and into the observance of the precepts of the Torah.

Bet Din. Rabbinic court of law.

Bnei Akiva. Religious Zionist pioneering youth movement affiliated with HaPoel HaMizrahi, founded in 1929.

Bund. Jewish socialist party founded in Vilna, Russia, in 1897, supporting Jewish national minority rights; Yiddishist, and anti-Zionist.

Cohen (Hebrew, "priest"). Denoting descent in the line from Aaron, the first High Priest; common Jewish surname.

Conservative Judaism. Trend in Judaism developed in the United States in the twentieth century which, while opposing extreme changes in

433

traditional observances, permits certain modifications of Halakhah in response to the changing needs of the Jewish people.

Dati (pl. *Dati'im*). Religiously observant.

Dayan. Member of rabbinic court.

Diaspora. Jews living in the "dispersion" outside Eretz Israel.

Galut. Exile; the condition of the Jewish people in dispersion.

Ger. Convert to Judaism.

Get. A bill of divorcement handed by the husband to his wife in the presence of a rabbinic court, thereby dissolving the marriage.

Goy (pl. *Goyim*; Hebrew, "nation"). A non-Jew, gentile.

Haftorah. A chapter from the Prophets read in the synagogue after the portion from the Pentateuch.

Hakham Bashi. Title of the Chief Rabbi in the Ottoman Empire, residing in Constantinople (Istanbul); also applied to chief rabbis in leading towns of the Empire.

Halakhah. Hebrew for road or path; custom or law; the legal part of talmudic and of later rabbinic literature, encompassing rules of ritual observances and ethical conduct as well as civil and criminal law.

Halitzah. Biblically prescribed ritual performed when one refuses to marry his brother's childless widow.

Halukkah. System of financing the maintenance of Jewish communities in the four Holy Cities of Eretz Israel by charitable collections made abroad, mainly in the pre-World War I period.

Halutz (pl. *Halutzim*; Hebrew). Pioneer, especially in the field of agricultural settlement in Eretz Israel.

Hanukkah. Festival of Lights commemorating the victory of the Maccabees.

HaPoel HaMizrahi. Religious pioneering and labor movement in Eretz Israel founded in 1922.

Haskalah. Enlightenment; movement for spreading modern European culture among Jews c. 1750–1880.

Heder. An elementary religious school.

Herem. (1) Excommunication imposed by rabbinical authorities for purpose of religious and communal discipline. (2) In biblical times, that which was separated from common use either because it was an abomination or because it was consecrated to God.

Hiloni (secular). A term applied by the Orthodox to a person who is nonobservant.

Histadrut (abbr. for Hebrew *HaHistadrut HaKelalit shel HaOvedim HaIvriyim beEretz Israel*). Eretz Israel Jewish Labor Federation, founded in 1920; subsequently renamed Histadrut haOvedim beEretz Israel.

Hovevei Zion. Lovers of Zion, early pre-Herzlian Zionist movement in Russia.

Karaite. Member of a Jewish sect that originated in the eighth century and that rejected rabbinic (Rabbinite) Judaism, accepting only Scripture as authoritative.

Kasher. Ritually permissible food.

Kibbutz (pl. *kibbutzim*). Large-size communal settlement based on agriculture and/or industry.

Knesset. Parliament of the State of Israel.

Kolel. (1) An Old Yishuv community in Eretz Israel of persons from a particular country or locality, often supported by their fellow countrymen in the Diaspora. (2) Institution for higher Torah study.

Mapai (initials of Hebrew *Mifleget Po'alei Eretz Israel*). Eretz Israel Labor Party, founded in 1930 by the union of Ahdut HaAvodah and Ha'Po'el HaTzair.

Mapam (initials of Hebrew *Mifleget HaPo'alim HaMe'uhedet; United Workers' Party*). A left-wing, labor-Zionist Israel Party, founded 1948, when HaShomer HaTzair Workers' Party merged with Ahdut HaAvodah Po'alei Zion. It later split by the withdrawal of the latter group.

Menorah. Candelabrum; seven-branched oil lamp used in the Tabernacle and Temple; also eight-branched candelabrum used on Hanukkah; also the State Emblem of the State of Israel.

Mikveh (Hebrew, "collection"). Collection of water; has become the term commonly used to designate a ritual bath for the immersion of persons or utensils that have contracted ritual impurity.

Mitzvah. (1) Biblical or rabbinic injunction or precept. (2) Good or charitable deed.

Mizrahi. Religious Zionist movement, founded in 1902 as a religious party within the World Zionist Organization. In the State of Israel it functions as the National Religious Party (N.R.P.).

Mizug HaGaluyoth (literally, "integration of the exiles"). Integration of Jews coming to Israel from various countries of the Diaspora.

Neturei Karta (Aramaic, "guardians of the city"). A group of ultra-religious extremists, mainly in Jerusalem, who regard the establishment of a Jewish state in Eretz Israel as a sacrilege, and therefore do not recognize the State of Israel.

Pikuah Nefesh. The sacred duty to save the life of a human being. This duty also takes precedence over the rules of Sabbath observance.

Purim. Feast celebrated in commemoration of the deliverance of the Jews from the plot of Haman, as recorded in the Book of Esther.

Reform Judaism. One of the three principal religious trends in Judaism, which originated early in the nineteenth century under the impact of European enlightenment and emancipation. To meet contemporary needs, it introduced modifications in traditional religious thought and practices, stressing the ethical teaching of the prophets as the central theme of Judaism.

Rosh HaShanah (Hebrew, "the beginning of the year"). The Jewish New Year.

Sanhedrin. The assembly of ordained scholars that functioned both as a supreme court and as a legislature before 70 c.e.

Seder. The ceremonial meal on the first night of Passover (first two nights outside of Israel).

Sephardi (pl. Sephardim). Jew of Spanish and Portuguese origin.

Shemittah. Sabbatical year, every seventh year "the land must keep Sabbath unto the Lord."

Shofar. Horn of the ram (or any other ritually clean animal except the cow) sounded on Rosh HaShanah and Yom Kippur services and also on other solemn occasions.

Shulhan Arukh. Joseph Caro's code of Jewish law, compiled in the middle of the sixteenth century.

Simhat Torah. The Festival of the Rejoicing of the Law (on completion of the reading each year of the Pentateuch).

Succot (singular Succa; Hebrew, "booth, tabernacle"). Festival of Tabernacles, autumn festival lasting seven days in commemoration of the protection afforded the Children of Israel during their journey from Egypt.

Talmud. Teaching; compendium of discussions on the Mishnah, by generations of scholars and jurists in many academies over a period of several centuries. The Jerusalem (or Palestinian) Talmud mainly contained the discussions of the Palestinian sages. The Babylonian

Talmud incorporates the parallel discussion in the Babylonian academies.

Tisha b'Av. Ninth day of the month of Av, commemorating the destruction of the Temple.

Torah. (1) Pentateuch or the pentateuchal scroll for reading in synagogues; (2) Entire body of traditional Jewish teaching.

Yeshivah. Jewish Orthodox academy devoted primarily to study of rabbinic literature.

Yishuv. Settlement; more specifically, the Jewish community of Eretz Israel in the pre-State period. The pre-Zionist community is generally designated the "Old Yishuv" and the community evolving from 1880, the "New Yishuv."

Yom Kippur (*Yom HaKippurim*). Day of Atonement, solemn fast day observed on the tenth of Tishrei.

Bibliography

A. OFFICIAL PUBLICATIONS

Annual Reports of the Ministry for Religious Affairs submitted to the Knesset (in Hebrew).

Government Yearbooks. Hebrew and English versions.

Judgments of the Supreme Court of Israel (Piskei Din Shel Beit HaMishpat HaElion) (in Hebrew). Jerusalem.

Knesset Record (Divrei HaKnesset) (in Hebrew). Jerusalem.

Kuntrasse, Mihu Yehudi (Who is a Jew) (in Hebrew). Jerusalem, 1959. A collection of opinions by Jewish scholars on the subject of "Who is a Jew," submitted to Prime Minister D. Ben-Gurion.

Laws of Palestine. Rev. ed. London, 1933.

Law Reports of Palestine. Edited by Sir Michael McDonnel. London, 1934.

Laws of the State of Israel. Authorized translation from the Hebrew. Jerusalem.

Official Gazette. Government of Palestine, Jerusalem.

Palestine Royal Commission Report. London, 1937.

Record of the Proceedings of Moetzet HaMedina HaZmanit (Provisional State Council) (in Hebrew). Jerusalem.

Report of the Public Commission of Inquiry on Matters of Personal Status of the Karaite Community in Israel (in Hebrew). Jerusalem, 1967.

Selected Judgments of the Supreme Court of Israel (in English). Jerusalem.

Statistical Abstract of Israel. Central Bureau of Statistics. Jerusalem, 1973.

B. PERIODICALS

1. *In Hebrew*

Dailies

Al HaMishmar, Tel Aviv. Official organ of Mapam.

HaAretz, Tel Aviv, nonparty.

HaBoker, Tel Aviv. Official organ of the Liberal Party. Ceased publication.

HaModia, Jerusalem. Official organ of Agudat Israel.

HaTzofe, Tel Aviv. Official organ of National Religious Party.

HaYom, Tel Aviv. Official organ of Gahal. Ceased publication.

Kol Ha'Am. Official organ of the Israel Communist Party. Ceased publication.

LaMerhav, Tel Aviv. Official organ of Ahdut HaAvoda. Ceased publication.

Maariv, Tel Aviv, nonparty.

Shearim, Tel Aviv. Official organ of Polalei Agudat Israel.

Yediot Aharonot, Tel Aviv. nonparty.

Periodicals

Alei Mishmeret, Tel Aviv. Published by the Youth group of the National Religious Party.

Aleph, Tel Aviv. Published by the Canaanite Movement. Ceased publication.

Amot, Tel Aviv. Bimonthly, sponsored by the American Jewish Committee. Ceased publication.

Amudim, Tel Aviv (monthly), Kibbutz Dati.

Beit Yaakov, Jerusalem (monthly), Agudat Israel.

Beterem, Jerusalem (monthly). Ceased publication.

Deot, Jerusalem. Religious Academic Youth.

Gvilin, Tel Aviv (quarterly). National Religious Party.

Halikhot, Tel Aviv. Monthly published by the Religious Council of Tel Aviv.

HaPraklit, Tel Aviv. Quarterly published by the Israel Bar Association.

MeHalakhim, Jerusalem. Published at irregular intervals by HaTenuah leYahadut HaTorah.

Molad, Jerusalem (quarterly). Nonparty.

Ovnaim, Tel Aviv. Annual published by Beit Berl. Ceased publication.

Panim el Panim, Jerusalem (weekly). Nonparty religious. Ceased publication.

Petahim, Jerusalem. Quarterly published by nonparty religious intellectuals.

Temurot, Tel Aviv. Monthly published by the Independent Liberal Party.

Turei Yeshurun, Jerusalem. Published under the auspices of the Yeshurun Synagogue.

2. *In Other Languages*

Central Conference of American Rabbis Journal (quarterly), New York.

Commentary (monthly), New York.

Conservative Judaism (quarterly), New York.

Encounter (monthly), London.

Israel Law Review, Faculty of Law Hebrew University (quarterly), Jerusalem.

Jerusalem Post (daily).

Jewish Chronicle (weekly), London.

Journal of Contemporary History (quarterly), London.

Manitoba Law Journal.

Midstream (monthly), New York.

New York Times (daily).

Rassviet (in Russian) (weekly), Paris. Ceased publication.

Reconstructionist (monthly), New York.

Tradition (quarterly), New York.

PUBLICATIONS IN HEBREW

Antonovsky, S. A. *Social and Political Attitudes in Israel. Amot* (June July), 1963.

Arian, Asher. *Ha'Am HaBoher.* Ramat Gan: Massada Publishing, 1973.

Attias Moshe, ed. *Sefer HaTeudot shel HaVaad HaLeumi.* Jerusalem: Published by the author, 1963.

Bein Tzeirim (i.e., Young People's Talk), ed. Muki Tzur et al. Tel Aviv: Am Oved, 1969.

Ben-Porat, Yehuda, et al. *Perakim beToldot HaYishuv HaYehudi be-Yerushalayim.* Jerusalem: Yad Ben Zvi, 1973.

Ben Sasson, Haim Hillel. *Toldot Yisrael biYmei HaBenayim.* Tel Aviv: Dvir, 1969.

Bentwich, Joseph, ed. *Hug Amana.* Jerusalem: Reuven Mass, 1964.

Ben Zion, S. *Yesud Gedera.* Tel Aviv: Omanuth Publishing Co., 1930.

Ben Zvi, Yitzhak. *Eretz Yisrael veYishuvah biYmei HaShilton HaOtto-mani.* Jerusalem: Mosad Bialik, 1955.

Berdichevsky, M. J. *Mica Yosef.* Warsaw: HaDerekh, 1922.

Berlin, R. Meir. *MiVolozhyn ad Yerushalayim.* Tel Aviv: Yalkut, 1940.

Bernstein, J., ed. *Mipi Rishonim.* Jerusalem: Center of World Mizrahi and HaPoel HaMizrachi, 1969.

Bernstein, Zvi. *BeMaarakhah leshlemut HaUmmah.* Tel Aviv, 1959; Tel Aviv: Avner Ch. Shaki, Mihu Yehudi, 1971.

Corinaldi, Michael. *LeSh'elat Ma'amadam shel Karaim BeYisrael.* Jerusalem: Mehalkhim, 1969.

Eilam, Yigael. *Mavoh leHistoria Tzionit Aheret.* Ramat Gan: Levin-Epstein publishers, 1972.

Eliav, Mordecai. *Ahavat Zion veAnshei Hod.* Tel Aviv: Tel Aviv University, 1970.

———, ed. *Perakim beToldot HaYishuv beYerushalayim.* Jerusalem: Yad Ben Zvi, 1973.

Elon, Menahem. *HaMishpat HaIvri.* Jerusalem: Magnes Press, 1973.

———. *HaKikah Datit.* Tel Aviv: HaKibbutz HaDati, 1968.

Entsiklopedia Eretz Yisrael, ed. Yeshayahu Press. Jerusalem: Reuven Mass, 1948.

Entsiklopedia shel HaTzionut HaDatit. Jerusalem: Mosad HaRav Kook, 1965.

Federbusch, Simon, ed. *Torah uMelukhah.* Jerusalem: Mosad HaRav Kook, 1961.

Fishman, J. L. *HaTzionut HaDatit veHitpathutah.* Jerusalem: Zionist Organization, 1937.

Friedman, Menahem. *HaMaavak al Dmut HaYeshivot veHaRabanut be-Yerushalayim-HaTzionut.* Tel Aviv: Tel Aviv University, 1971.

Gat, Ben-Zion. *HaYishuv HaYehudi beEretz Yisrael 1840–1881.* Jerusalem: Friends of the Hebrew University, 1963.

Graetz, Zvi (Heinrich). *Darkei HaHistoria HaYehudit* (Hebrew edition). Jerusalem: Mosad Bialik, 1959.

Greenberg, Hayim, ed. *Dat Yisrael uMedinat Yisrael.* New York: Published by World Zionist Organization, 1951.

Ha'Am, Ahad. *Kol Kitvei Ahad Ha'Am.* 2d ed. Tel Aviv: Dvir Publishing Co., 1949.

HaCohen, Mordecai Ben-Hillel. *Olami.* Jerusalem: Mizpah, 1927.

Kahana, Shlomo Zalman. *Iyunim.* Jerusalem: Mizrahi and HaPoel Ha-Mizrahi, 1964.

Kiruv Levavot. Collection of Discussions. Tel Aviv: Kibbutz Dati Publications, 1966.

Klausner, Joseph. *Eliezer Ben Yehuda.* Tel Aviv: Omanuth Publishing Co., 1939.

Klausner, Yisrael. *BeHit'orer Am.* Jerusalem: HaSifriah HaTzionit, 1965.

_____. *MeKattowitz ad Basel.* Jerusalem: HaSifriah HaTzionit, 1965.

Kressel, Getzel. *Rabbi Yehiel Mikhel Pines.* Tel Aviv: Sifriat Shorashim, 1946.

Leibowitz, Yeshayahu. *Torah uMitzvot baZman Hazeh.* Tel Aviv: Massada Publishing House, 1954.

Levi, Zeev. *Spinoza veMussar HaYahadut.* Tel Aviv: Sifriat HaPoalim, 1972.

Lichtheim, Richard. *Shear Yashuv.* Tel Aviv: Neumann Publishing House, 1953.

_____. *Toldot HaTzionut beGermaniah.* Jerusalem: HaSifriah Ha-Tzionit, 1951.

Lipson, M., ed. *MiDor Dor.* Tel Aviv: Ahiassaf, 1968.

Livneh, Eliezer; Nedava, Joseph; Efrati, Yoram. *Nili: Toldotehah shel Heazah Medinit.* Tel Aviv: Schoken Publishing House, 1961.

Maimon, Judah Leib. *LaShaah veLaDor.* Jerusalem: Mosad HaRav Kook, 1965.

_____, ed. *Yovel HaMizrahi.* Jerusalem: Mosad HaRav Kook, 1952.

Malakhi, A. R. *Perakim beToldot HaYishuv HaYashan.* Tel Aviv University, 1971.

Mitzpeh. *Shnaton HaTzofeh.* Jerusalem: Mizrahi World Center, 1953.

Neturei Karta. *LeHasir HaMasveh*. Jerusalem: Neturei Karta Edah Haredit, n.d.

Nurok, Mordecai. *Ve'idat Zionei Russia beMinsk*. Jerusalem: HaSifriah HaTzionit, 1963.

Ostrowski, R. Moshe. *Toldot HaMizrahi beEretz Yisrael*. Jerusalem, 1943.

Pines, Yehiel M. *Binyan HaAretz*. Tel Aviv 1937.

Rosen, Dov. *Etz HaDat*. Jerusalem 1963.

Rosenheim, Yaakov. *Ketavim*. Jerusalem: Histadrut Olamit Agudat Yisrael, 1970.

Rotenberg, Matityahu, ed. *HaDat veHaMedinah*. Tel Aviv: National Religious Party, 1964.

Rubinstein, Amnon. *HaMishpat HaKonstitutzioni shel Medinat Yisrael*. Tel Aviv: Schoken, 1969.

Ruppin, Arthur. *Reshit Avodati baAretz 1907–1920*. Tel Aviv: Am Oved, 1968.

_____. *Milhemet HaYehudim leKiyumam*. Tel Aviv: Mosad Bialik, 1940.

Salomon, Abraham. *Petah Tikvah*. Tel Aviv: Omanuth Publishing Co., 1939.

Scholem, Gerschon. *Shabbatai Zvi*. Tel Aviv: Am Oved, 1957.

Shaki, Avner Ch. *Mihu Yehudi*. Tel Aviv 1971.

Shershevsky, Robert; Katz, Avshalom; Kolatt, Yisrael; Barkai, Chaim. *Yemei HaShilton HaOttomani*. Tel Aviv: Sifriat Maariv, 1968.

Slutsky, Yehuda, ed. *Sefer Toldot HaHaganah*. Jerusalem: HaSifriah HaTzionit, 1959.

Smilansky, Moshe. *Rehovot*. Tel Aviv: Omanuth Publishing Co., 1935.

Smith, Hanoch. *HaKol Al HaBehirot beYisrael*. Tel Aviv: Adi Publishing House, 1969.

Stanner, Ruth. *Dinei Hinuch*. Jerusalem: Published by the Author, 1966.

Talmon, Jacob. *Ahdut veYihud*. Tel Aviv: Schoken Publishing House, 1965.

Ulitzky, Joseph. *MiPezurah laMedinah*. Jerusalem: Ahiassaf, 1959.

Unna, Moshe. *Israel baUmmot*. Tel Aviv: Kibbutz Dati, 1971.

Weiss, Shevah. *HaShilton HaMekomi beYisrael*. Tel Aviv: Am Oved, 1972.

Yavnielli, Shmuel, ed. *Sefer HaTzionut*. Tel Aviv: Mosad Bialik, 1942.

Young, Eliyahu, ed. *Noterei Moreshet*. Jerusalem: Mosad HaRav Kook, 1968.

BOOKS IN OTHER LANGUAGES

Adler, Joseph. *Religion and Herzl*. New York: Herzl Press, 1962.

Arian, Alan, ed. *The Elections in Israel*. Jerusalem: Academic Press, 1972.

Baker, Henry E. *Legal System of Israel.* Jerusalem: Israel Universities Press, 1968.

Bamberger, Bernard J. *Proselytism in the Talmudic Period.* New York: Ktav, 1968.

Bein, Alex. *Theodor Herzl: A Biography.* Philadelphia: Jewish Publication Society, 1943.

Ben-Gurion, D. *Israel, A Personal History.* New York: Herzl Press, 1972.

[D.] *Ben-Gurion Looks Back In Talks With Moshe Perlman.* London: Weidenfeld and Nicholson, 1965.

Brecher, Michael. *The Foreign Policy of Israel.* London: Oxford University Press, 1972.

Burstein, Moshe. *Self-Government of the Jews in Palestine.* Tel Aviv: Published by the Author, 1934.

Cohen, Israel. *The Zionist Movement.* London: Fredrick Muller, Ltd., 1945.

Cohen, Jack J. *The Case for Religious Naturalism.* New York: Reconstructionist Press, 1958.

Davidowitz, Lucy. *The Golden Heritage.* New York: Holt, Rinehart & Winston, 1967.

Deutsch, Andre. *Jewish Communities of the World.* 3d ed., rev. London 1971.

Domb, I. *The Transformation.* London: Published by the Author, 1958.

Dubnow, Simon M. *History of the Jews in Russia and Poland.* Philadelphia: Jewish Publication Society, 1920.

_____. *Nationalism and History, Essays on Old and New Judaism.* Philadelphia: Jewish Publication Society, 1958.

Eichhorn, David Max, ed. *Conversion to Judaism.* New York: Ktav, 1966.

Eisenstadt, S. N. *Israeli Society.* New York: Basic Books, 1967.

Feinstein, Marvin. *American Zionism.* New York: Herzl Press, 1965.

Finkelstein, Louis, ed. *The Jews, Their History, Culture, and Religion.* 3d ed. New York: Harper Brothers Publishers, 1960.

Ha'Am, Ahad. *Basic Writings.* Edited by Hans Kohn. New York: Herzl Press, 1962.

de Haas, Jacob. *Louis D. Brandeis, a Biographical Sketch.* New York: Bloch Publishing Co., 1929.

Halpern, Ben. *The Idea of a Jewish State.* Cambridge, Mass: Harvard University Press, 1961.

Herman, Simon N. *Israelis and Jews.* Philadelphia: Jewish Publication Society of America, 1971.

Hertzberg, Arthur. *The French Enlightenment and the Jews.* New York: Columbia University Press, 1968.

_____, ed. *The Zionist Idea, A Historical Analysis and Reader.* New York: Meridian Books, 1964.

Herzl, Theodor. *The Jewish State.* Translated by Sylvia D'Avigdor. London: Central Office of the Zionist Organization, 1934.

_____. *The Complete Diaries.* Edited by Raphael Patai. New York and London: Herzl Press, 1960.

Hirsch, Richard G. *Reform Judaism and Israel.* New York: Commission on Israel, 1972.

Hyamson, Albert M. *Palestine.* London: Methuen & Co., 1917.

Kleinberger, Aharon. *Society, Schools and Progress in Israel.* Oxford: Pergamon Press, 1969.

Laqueur, Walter. *A History of Zionism.* London: Weidenfeld and Nicholson, 1972.

Leibowitz, Yeshayahu. *State and Religion, Tradition.* New York, 1972.

Leslie, S. Clement. *The Rift in Israel.* London: Routledge & Kegan Paul, 1971.

Liebman, Charles S. *The Ambivalent American Jew.* Philadelphia: Jewish Publication Society of America, 1973.

Litvin, B., and Hoenig, S. H. *Jewish Identity.* New York: Feldheim, 1965.

Mahler, Raphael. *A History of Modern Jewry.* New York: Schocken Books, 1971.

Manuel, Frank E. *The Realities of American-Palestine Relations.* Washington, D.C.: Public Affairs Press, 1949.

Marcus, Jacob R. *Early American Jewry.* Philadelphia: Jewish Publication Society, 1951.

Marmorstein, Emile. *Heaven at Bay.* London: Oxford University Press, 1969.

Matras, Judah. *Social Change in Israel.* Chicago: Aldine Publishing Co., 1965.

Medding, Peter Y. *Mapai in Israel.* Cambridge: Cambridge University Press, 1972.

Minerbi, Sergio. *Angelo Levi-Bianchini e la sua opera nel Levante.* Milan: Fondazione Sally Mayer, 1967.

Nesis, Lawrence S. *Who is a Jew.* Manitoba Law Journal, 1970.

Parkes, James. *A History of Palestine from 135 A.D. to Modern Times.* London: Victor Gollancz Ltd., 1949.

Plaut, W. Gunther. *The Growth of Reform Judaism.* New York: World Union for Progressive Judaism, 1965.

_____. *The Rise of Reform Judaism.* New York: World Union for Progressive Judaism, 1963.

Raisin, Jacob S. *The Haskalah Movement in Russia.* Philadelphia: Jewish Publication Society, 1913.

Schechtman, Joseph B. *Fighter and Prophet: The Jabotinsky Story.* New York: Thomas Yoseloff, 1969.

The Seventh Day: Soldiers' Talk about the Six Day War. London: Penguin Books, 1970.

Shapiro, Yonatan. *Leadership of the American Zionist Organization 1897–1930.* Urbana: University of Illinois Press, 1971.

Sokolow, Nahum. *History of Zionism*. New York: Longmans, Green & Co., 1919.

Special Edition for the Seventeenth International Conference of the World Union for Progressive Judaism in Geneva. Haifa, 1972.

Spinoza, B. *Tractatus Theologico-Politicus*. 2d ed. London: N. Trubner & Co., 1868.

Stein, Leonard. *The Balfour Declaration*. New York: Simon and Schuster, 1961.

_____. *Zionism*. London: Kegan Paul, 1932.

Strizower, Schifra. *The Children of Israel*. Oxford: The Bene Israel of Bombay. Basil Blackwell, 1971.

_____. *Exotic Jewish Communities*. London: Thomas Yoseloff, 1962.

Verhandlungen des II Zionisten Congresses 23. Vienna: Verlag des Vereines Eretz Israel, 1898.

Vitta, Edoardo. *Conflict of Laws in Matters of Personal Status in Palestine*. Tel Aviv: S. Bursi, 1947.

Weill, Julien. *Zadoc Kahn*. Paris: Libraries Felix Alcan, 1912.

Weizmann, Chaim. *The Letters and Papers, Series A*. Oxford: Oxford University Press, 1968.

Zechlin, Egmont. *Die Deutsche Politik and die Juden im Ersten Weltkrieg*. Göttingen: Vandenhoeck O Rupprecht, 1969.

Zidon, Asher. *The Knesset: Parliament of Israel*. New York: Herzl Press, 1967.

Yearbooks

The American-Jewish Yearbooks. Philadelphia: Jewish Publication Society and the American Jewish Committee.

Herzl Yearbooks. New York: Herzl Press.

Central Conference of American Rabbis Yearbooks. New York.

Index